P9-DEO-883

Language Arts Activities
for the Classroom

Language Arts Activities for the Classroom

Second Edition

Sidney W. Tiedt

Iris M. Tiedt

SAN JOSE STATE UNIVERSITY

Allyn and Bacon, Inc.
Boston   London   Sydney   Toronto

Copyright © 1987, 1978 by Allyn and Bacon, Inc.
7 Wells Avenue, Newton, Massachusetts 02159

Series Editor: Susanne F. Canavan
Production Coordinator: Susan Freese
Editorial/Production Services: TKM Productions
Cover Administrator: Linda K. Dickinson
Cover Designer: Susan Hamant

Library of Congress Cataloging-in-Publication Data

Tiedt, Sidney W.
  Language arts activities for the classroom.

  Bibliography: p.
  Includes index.
  1. Language arts (Elementary) 2. Individualized instruction. I. Tiedt, Iris M. II. Title.
LB1576.T564   1987   372.6′044   86–22289
ISBN 0–205–10478–9

Printed in the United States of America

10 9 8 7 6 5 4 3 2 1   91 90 89 88 87

Contents

97419

Preface

As authors of *Language Arts Activities for the Classroom,* we are grateful for the marvelous reception granted the first edition, and we are honored to have the opportunity to present this new edition.

One of the major reasons we have prepared a new edition is to keep pace with the changing role of the classroom teacher. Today's teacher must accept much more responsibility, especially in the areas of language arts and reading. Teachers are expected to teach more actively, directly, and effectively. And they are held more accountable, as they are expected to teach students basic skills and demonstrate success through improved student test scores.

A second reason behind this new edition is to keep pace with the directional change of the elementary curriculum. Today's elementary curriculum emphasizes reading and writing, especially through interest in writing as a process, the reading/writing connection, reading defined as comprehension, and vocabulary development.

In response to these changes, we have revised *Language Arts Activities for the Classroom.* Every word has been reviewed, and more than half of the material is new. Information and resources have been updated, including recommendations on new technological advances in education, and the objectives have been made more current and explicit.

Plan for the Text

This second edition has been organized into a sequence that reflects how students learn language—from listening and speaking to reading and writing.

The book begins with an overview of the language arts and the teacher's role in planning instruction. Chapters 2 and 3, "Listening to Learn" and "Developing Oral

Language," initiate the language arts program because they begin at the students' level and give students strategies for becoming actively involved in their own learning.

Chapter 4, "Words and More Words," focuses on vocabulary development through direct instruction and contextual reinforcement. This chapter also serves as a bridge between students' growing awareness of language and the application of this knowledge to the reading task. The next chapter, "Reading, Literature, and Children," reflects the recent model of reading as a meaning-making process. In this chapter, we also show how the reading program can be enriched through effective use of children's literature.

Chapter 6, "Putting Words to Use," focuses on words again but from the perspective of preparing students for writing. Students learn to reflect on language and to become aware of patterns in spelling, grammar, and usage in order to become stronger, more effective writers. Finally, Chapter 7, "Children Can Write," presents the various stages of the writing process, with an emphasis on getting ready to write. Accompanying the writing chapter is Chapter 8, "Teaching Poetry." We believe that more teachers would incorporate poetry in the language arts program if they knew more about it and realized how much students enjoyed it.

In Chapter 9, we argue for implementing all the components of a language arts program—listening and speaking, reading and writing—throughout the curriculum. A strong language arts program will strengthen content area teaching, as well. The last chapter provides a selection of resources that would be invaluable to any teacher, including books and audiovisual materials.

We feel that this new edition maintains the strengths of the original book while meeting the needs of the contemporary elementary teacher. We know that teachers want a book filled with practical, adaptable, teacher-tested activities that can be put to use in any classroom immediately. We also know that teachers want a book that reflects the most effective instructional strategies, based on a sound theoretical foundation. This revision has been designed to meet both those needs.

Acknowledgments

Our heartfelt thanks go to all of our students, past and present, who have tried the ideas presented in this book and offered very helpful suggestions. We also wish to thank those individuals who reviewed our work at various stages, including Lois Exendine (Oklahoma Christian College), Barbara Townsend (Salisbury State College), and Anne Willekens (Antelope Valley College).

Finally, we want to thank Lucinda Surber, who contributed many fine ideas and artwork, and Marjorie Elmore, who was an excellent and very patient typist.

S. W. T.
I. M. T.

Language Arts Activities
for the Classroom

1 Effective Classroom Organization

Tell me,
I forget.
Show me,
I remember.
Involve me,
I understand.

ANCIENT CHINESE PROVERB

ROLE OF THE TEACHER

A teacher performs an enormous number of different roles throughout a typical school day, making countless spur-of-the-moment decisions and engaging in numerous types of interactions. In any one day, the average teacher will act as a manager, instructor, counselor, transmitter of information, listener, enabler, editor, facilitator, tutor, inspirer, and enforcer. Teachers need to recognize the many demands on them and develop strategies to cope with these demands. Good classroom organization and classroom management skills make it possible for teachers to carry out their diverse tasks. For example, classroom arrangements that allow the teacher to move around the room quickly, monitor student activities, and move students readily into different groups will enable teachers to function effectively in their many roles. Above all, the teacher's role is not only complex, but also challenging and rewarding.

Becoming a More Effective Teacher

Most teachers want to find ways of helping their students learn more and achieve more. Recent research such as the Beginning Teacher Evaluation Study (BTES) has

1

focused our attention on several factors that are fundamental to student learning. These factors are particularly significant because they represent areas where the teacher has some control and can affect student behavior and learning.

The following key recommendations are from the BTES for improving student learning:

1. *Allocate* more teaching time to the area in which students need to improve.
   The amount of time allocated to a subject (scheduled as teaching time) is directly related to how well students learn that subject. When a subject is scheduled for only a short time, students' opportunity to learn is limited.

2. Ensure that students are *actively engaged* in the learning activity.
   Students must have a chance to practice what they are supposed to learn. Of the time allocated for the teaching of a subject, students learn most when they are *doing* something related to the subject, such as reading, writing, interacting, speaking, or manipulating.

3. Organize instruction so that students experience a high *success rate*.
   When the task is too easy or too difficult for students, they learn less. Monitor students' skills and success rates so that you can assign tasks at an appropriately challenging level. Student inattention, boredom, or frequent questions may be signs that the task level is not appropriate.

4. Increase the amount and frequency of *feedback* given to students on their progress.
   Students benefit from working in small groups or one-on-one with the teacher, aide, or other tutor because they can get feedback while they work.

5. Provide concrete, positive *rewards* for student achievement.
   Teachers can chart student progress and hand out rewards (such as books) when students reach a goal, or they can pass out small, frequent rewards (such as stickers) for each step completed.

LANGUAGE ARTS

What are the "language arts"? In the schools, the following subjects usually comprise the language arts as defined traditionally and pragmatically. Each subject has separate texts or teaching materials, is assigned separate blocks of teaching time, and is listed separately on report cards.

- Reading
- Spelling
- Handwriting
- Language (usually grammar and usage)

The language arts, however, can also be defined in terms of the four major skill areas:

- Reading
- Writing
- Speaking
- Listening

From this perspective, spelling and handwriting are subskills that we teach in order to develop student writing. The four skill areas divide readily into expressive and receptive modes, as in the following diagram:

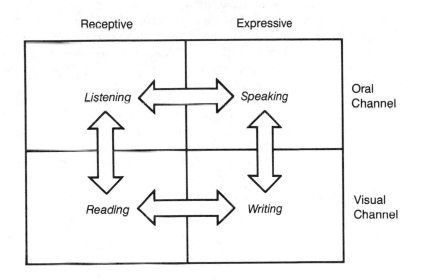

Language arts skills

Listening and reading are both ways we receive information (input) and speaking and writing are both ways we communicate information (output).

From this diagram, we can demonstrate the interrelationship of the four skills. For example, we talk about critical reading and we can apply similar strategies to critical listening. In reading, we study the structure of a prose text and we can use the same technique to analyze an oral presentation. Reading and writing are also very closely connected. The mapping that we use to analyze a story when we read can be used to construct a story when we write. As we look at the language arts in this fashion, we can see the dialogue between speaker and listener, reader and writer.

The theme that unites these skills is the fundamental nature of meaning. We define the four skills as follows:

- Listening: the process of gaining meaning from the spoken word.
- Speaking: the process of transmitting meaning through the spoken word.
- Reading: the process of gaining meaning from the printed word.
- Writing: the process of transmitting meaning through the printed word.

Therefore, we would define the language arts as the making of meaning.

A Model Language Arts Program

The preceding definitions help us outline a model language arts program. We want to integrate our knowledge of how children learn, what teachers can do to facilitate this learning, and the way in which the language arts are organized. The points listed below highlight the concepts that we think are the most important to consider when making short- and long-range plans.

In the model language arts program, teachers will:

1. *Read books themselves and talk about the books they have read.*
   When teachers show by their own behavior that they enjoy reading and that reading is an important part of their life, then they are modeling basic attitudes for the students. A liking for reading is often more readily "caught" than "taught," based on students' desire to please the teacher.

2. *Teach students to write by writing, and teach students to read by reading.*
   Both reading and writing are active processes and, therefore, are best learned through practice. Attention to the subskills involved in these processes has distracted us from the activity that integrates these skills. Teachers need to allocate more classroom time for the activity itself, through programs such as Sustained Silent Reading and Sustained Silent Writing.

3. *Teach vocabulary directly, instead of leaving it to chance.*
   Perhaps the most important gift teachers can leave with students is the development of a large working vocabulary. We know that there is a direct and positive relationship between student knowledge of vocabulary and reading comprehension, but vocabulary is central to all the language arts. The importance of vocabulary demands moving beyond looking up words in dictionaries and copying lists; it requires direct teaching that includes talking about words, collecting and using them, playing word games, and studying word structure, history, sound, and meaning.

4. *Keep a story going at all times in the classroom.*
   Listening to a story being read aloud is not only enjoyable for students but, at the same time, it serves as an introduction to the structures and patterns of written English. In fact, one of the best ways to improve a writing program is

to begin an extensive reading program. Reading aloud also gives teachers a chance to familiarize students with the classics of children's literature, extends student reading interests by introducing them to new areas, and teaches students a love of reading beyond the "how to."

5. *Teach reading comprehension rather than just assign it.*
Teaching reading comprehension includes topics such as focusing on prereading, working with students to develop their schema, setting a purpose for reading, and teaching students to predict. Teacher-directed activities in these areas will improve children's reading comprehension far more than workbook assignments will.

6. *Ask students higher-level questions, especially critical or inferential questions.*
When teachers ask literal questions, students learn literal comprehension. Now that teachers are more concerned about critical thinking skills, they will need to ask questions that require students to think, questions for which the answer is not explicitly stated in the text. In order to answer these questions, students must apply judgment, creativity, analysis, and synthesis, thereby practicing critical thinking. Also, these questions tend to be more interesting to both teachers and students, promoting a more dynamic and interactive classroom.

7. *Present language to students in all its diversity.*
When teachers recognize the richness and diversity of the English language— its dialects, variability, and history—students learn that a language is a system and an exciting area of study. Teachers can also promote the study of language in their classroom by talking about the other languages students bring to school, showing students how language changes, and analyzing the use of language in advertising and the media.

8. *Integrate the language arts throughout the curriculum.*
The language arts represent not only content areas of study but also a set of tools with which teachers can present information and students can learn other subjects. For example, a class studying Japan may read some Japanese haiku and write examples of this poetry form. Whenever students research a topic, write a report, present information in a panel discussion, or organize a debate, they are practicing important speaking and listening, reading and writing skills.

9. *Spend more classroom time teaching listening and speaking skills.*
We receive most of our information about the outside world by listening (to radio, TV). Others tend to judge us by the way we speak. All of these factors tell us the importance of listening and speaking, yet the classroom teaching time allocated to these skills does not reflect their crucial position.

10. *Explore the language arts connections.*
No language arts skill can be taught in isolation. Long before children enter school, they have constructed complex, sophisticated models of the way lan-

guage works. Students' subsequent learning of reading and writing is highly dependent on their oral language skills. Therefore, teaching the language arts in context and reinforcing the connections among them will support student learning. For example, students can learn about writing by reading good literature and, at the same time, they can learn about reading by writing their own stories and reading them aloud.

New Directions in the Teaching of the Language Arts

After discussing effective teaching and model language arts programs, it is appropriate to look ahead and speculate on what the next ten years hold for education, especially in the language arts. We have identified five major trends in the field, based on themes reflected in educational journals, professional conferences, and the popular media (newspapers, television, and radio). In these five trends we can examine the powerful impact of society on education and we can delimit the tasks facing us as teachers.

Trend 1.   There is a recognized need to improve education in all areas, but most specifically in developing reading and writing competency.

- SAT scores are declining; hence, we should raise standards and increase graduation requirements.
- Increased foreign competition has made us question the quality of our education and compare it to other countries.
- Concern about teacher quality has led to increased testing of teacher candidates.
- A comparatively high level of illiteracy for a developed country raises questions about our teaching of reading, as well as our definition of literacy.

Trend 2.   Technology is going to have an increasingly powerful influence on education.

- The computer's capability for word processing allows students to view writing as a process of prewriting, writing, and postwriting (editing).
- Observing students solving problems on computers will give teachers insight into how students structure knowledge and learn new information.
- The rapid pace of technological change, from invention to implementation, is putting pressure on the schools to play catch up.

Trend 3.   The more we know about the subjects we teach, the more we see the connections among them.

- Recent reading research validating the importance of students' prior knowledge in understanding a story has led us to modify the time allocated to different parts of the reading lesson.
- Concern for teaching science, math, and social studies concepts has heightened our awareness of the language arts as a tool for learning.
- Current technology such as interactive video, laser disks, speech synthesizers, and data bases allows us to conceptualize an integrated curriculum.

Trend 4. Schools are expected to develop students' critical thinking and other higher-level skills.

- As society relies more on complex information processing skills, teachers will need to teach reading and listening comprehension directly.
- Cognitive science will reinforce effective teaching practices such as clustering.
- Breaking away from the pathology model, we are asking good learners how they learn and we are gaining insight into which strategies are effective.

Trend 5. Classrooms are becoming more heterogeneous.

- Because students represent a variety of ethnic and cultural backgrounds, teachers must provide teaching materials and strategies that exemplify diversity in our society.
- As more students come to school from homes where other languages are spoken, teachers need to begin to recognize the patterns of second language learning and to be sensitive to the difficulty of learning another language.

Tips for Teachers

These ten maxims will enable you to improve instruction at any level.

1. Never do anything students can do.
2. Listen to children if you want to learn something.
3. Share yourself with your students.
4. Too much of anything, even an outstanding teaching idea, is good for nothing.
5. Displays of feelings, even anger, can be constructive.
6. Do something different every day.
7. Communicate directly with each student at least once a day.
8. Go easy on evaluation.
9. We learn more from our mistakes than our successes.
10. Enjoy, enjoy!

2 Listening to Learn

As the above quote indicates, listening is far and away the most frequently used of all the language arts. Recent research indicates that we can improve students' listening skills and comprehension by instruction. We as teachers need to make sure that our students learn how to be more effective listeners.

From the womb to the tomb, people learn through listening. Because this primary language skill will be fundamental throughout life, we must begin teaching listening early, spend more time on listening activities, and demonstrate the importance of listening in our classrooms. This chapter is organized into three sections. As a result of these activities:

- Students will develop auditory discrimination.
- Students will improve their listening comprehension.
- Students will respond to auditory input.

DEVELOPING AUDITORY DISCRIMINATION

Listening cannot be effective unless a minimum level of auditory discrimination exists. In listening for the presence or absence of a sound and similarities or differences between sounds, students are developing a base for more complex listening tasks. As a result of these activities:

- Students will identify specific sounds.
- Students will recognize similar and different sounds.

People Who Listen

Invite people who listen as a profession or hobby to your classroom. For example, a musician could demonstrate the importance of listening. A person whose avocation is bird watching could demonstrate the technique of listening to bird calls and determining the species from their call. Have a person who is blind or who works with blind people come in and discuss the importance of hearing for a blind person.

Simon Says

Playing Simon Says is a pleasant way to teach students the importance of listening carefully and to provide stimulating exercise. Explain to students how to play the game. The leader gives the students a series of commands: Stand up; Hop three times; Clap your hands; and so on. If the leader inserts "Simon says" before the command, the children are to obey. If the leader does not say "Simon says," they must not follow the directions. The directions are given as rapidly as possible to keep the class listening attentively. The last student standing can be the leader next time.

Vary this activity as follows: Let one person be the leader for five minutes to see how many persons he or she can make sit down. At the end of five minutes, record that person's score and choose a new leader. As you play the game periodically, others can challenge the best record.

Simon Says is a good indoor game for a rainy day when children cannot go outdoors. It combines fun, exercise, and a good listening activity, yet it does not require much space. It can also be played with large groups in a multipurpose room.

Sounds, Sounds, Sounds

Ask groups of students to record sounds commonly heard around school. They might tape sounds such as the secretary typing, the phone being answered, and so forth. They can also do this in the community or at home. Once the group has completed its tape, it can be played in the class and other youngsters can attempt to identify the sounds and where they came from. Have students check answers against an answer key prepared by the group.

Two books that are very practical for classroom listening activities are: *The City Noisy Book* (1939) and *The Summer Noisy Book* (1951) by Margaret Wise Brown (New York: Harper).

Active Games That Require Listening

Talk with students about how important listening is in some games. They can name some of the ones they play regularly, including:

- Steal the bacon!
- Dog, dog, your bone is gone!
- Who stole the cookies from the cookie jar?

Keep in Time

Teach students to hear different rhythms by clapping to the beat. Play songs with distinctive patterns, such as marchtime or ragtime, so that students learn to listen for the rhythm.

As a variation, have a student choose a certain pattern to clap. The class tries to reproduce the pattern. As students learn to hear these patterns, they can begin to match the beats to stressed syllables in words.

The Sounds of Silence

Is silence really silent? Have the students close their eyes and be absolutely quiet for three minutes so they can listen to silence. Then have them write down what they heard. The class can discuss what each student heard. Did the children notice more sounds with their eyes closed than they normally do? Why? Do they think that complete silence is possible? Where might one find complete silence?

As you talk about what the students have written, take the opportunity to introduce descriptive words for these sounds. What does breathing sound like? How does a bell sound? What kind of noise do the leaves on the trees make?

A Listening Walk

Take the students for a Listening Walk around the school. Ask them to be very quiet as they listen carefully to the sounds around them. When they return to the classroom, have them write (or tell) what they heard. The class can talk about what different sounds people heard. Did some people hear sounds that no one else heard? (As a variation, have students pair up. One wears a blindfold, the other acts as leader. Then reverse roles.)

Help the class write a group poem describing this experience. Write a beginning line on the board and have students volunteer lines until you have completed a poem. Print or type the poem to mount on the bulletin board for the class to see and to read.

> *I heard*
> *cars going by*
> *dogs barking*
> *boys talking*
> *the wind in the trees*
> *people walking.*

Repeat the Listening Walk with the class after a couple of weeks. Has the students' perception of sounds improved? What other sounds did they notice? Talk with the class about how this walk was different from the first walk. What do they think they gained from studying listening? This would be a good activity to begin and end a listening unit.

Listening Log

Ask your students to keep a log of how often they listen during a twenty-four-hour period. Divide their waking day into half-hour blocks of time and have them list several examples of what they listened to.

Who Is It?

Have your students talk into a tape recorder for about twenty seconds. They are not to identify themselves by name and they are not to change their voice. After everyone has had a chance to put his or her voice on the tape, play it for the class and see how many voices can be identified. How were students able to identify the voices? What helped in identifying the voices?

On another tape you might have your students try to change their voices. Play this tape and see how many voices can be identified.

Listening with Emotion

Play a tape with a series of sounds; for example, a dog barking, a siren, symphonic music, laughing, a door bell, the ocean surf, thunder, etc. While the tape is being played, ask students to write down how the sound makes them feel. What emotions do they connect with each sound?

Sound Language

Students sharpen their listening skills as they become aware of the rich vocabulary available to describe different sounds. What do you think of when you hear the words *chirp, hoot, jingle, screech?* Have the students list all the words for sounds that they can think of. They will be surprised at the number they can remember if they try.

There are different kinds of words for sounds. Some are words about people, some are words for animals, and some are for objects. What are other kinds of sound words?

Sound words can call up particular images. Make phrases for the students to complete with an image brought to mind by that sound.

As loud as . . .

- a motorcycle
- the wind when you are alone
-

As quiet as . . .

- an empty house
- smoke going out of a chimney
-

Sound Collage

This idea is a version of the art collage, where a number of different elements are combined on a sheet of paper to present an image and an idea. This can also be done by groups of students through the use of a tape recorder. The tape is, in effect, the blank sheet of paper, and sound images are imposed on this "paper" tape, just as they would be on a sheet of construction paper.

Youngsters can have fun and learn a great deal by experimenting with different sounds and putting them on a tape recorder to present an idea, a word, or a concept. For example, youngsters might take the word *fun* or the word *summer* and discuss what sounds are associated with these ideas. Then a group of youngsters might prepare a tape to be presented to the class to illustrate a selected concept. After they present it to the class, discuss what impressions, points, or ideas they succeeded in transmitting. This is an open-ended assignment and it is one that youngsters can really develop.

Sound tapes could be created that tell a story through the use of sound. After listening, students discuss what they think was happening, and then write a story.

Sounds Around Us

What are your favorite sounds? Ask students which sounds they like best and which sounds they like least. List their choices on the board. Students can discuss why they like certain sounds and why some people dislike sounds that others like. This is an excellent opportunity to introduce descriptive words for sounds, such as *cacophony, raucous, melodious,* and *screech.*

Identify and Remember

Have students put their heads down and listen as you make a series of five different sounds, identifying each by number. Then ask students to list what they think each sound was. This can be done orally or in writing. Sounds to make yourself include:

- striking a glass with a fork
- flipping pages of a book
- scratching a rock
- turning an eggbeater
- snapping a rubberband
- rubbing two pieces of sandpaper together

As students become more sophisticated, you can increase the number of sounds they must identify and remember or vary the difficulty by preparing a tape of unusual sounds. Some sounds to use on tape include:

- car starting
- door closing
- phone ringing
- child crying
- dog barking
- whistle blowing

Another exercise is to have students listen to familiar sounds but think of different explanations or sources. For instance, a creaking chair might really be a dragon shifting his scales, and a canned soda fizz could be a spaceship of tiny aliens taking off. With eyes closed and imagination open, anything goes.

I'm Going to . . .

Play the game I'm Going to Australia with students of any age to increase their listening and remembering capacities. One student starts off with "I'm going to Australia and I'm going to take my comb." The next student will say, "I'm going to Australia and I'm going to take my comb and a jumprope." The third student must remember what has been said before and add on another object for the trip. Students will probably need help remembering all the different objects that accumulate and the sequence in which they occur, but the game will stimulate them to listen closely and with enjoyment.

An easy modification is to have the objects in ABC order. For example, "I'm going to Australia and I'm taking an apple." The second youngster takes an apple and a banana, and so on.

How Well Do You Listen?

Tell students that they are to write the numbers 1 through 10 on a sheet of paper. Next, read them ten words associated with a topic you are studying, asking the students not to write down any word until the ten words are completed. Then the students write as many words as they can remember. After the activity is finished, discuss how well they were able to carry out this assignment and what approaches they used to help them remember the words.

A modification of this exercise is to give only five words the first time, then increase it to seven, and finally to ten words. With more mature students, it might be possible to enlarge the list even more. Since we are stressing the skill of listening in this activity, it is not imperative that students spell all the words correctly. Students find the task of remembering these words sufficiently challenging.

Discuss ways for students to remember what they have heard. If a tally was done of everyone's papers, most would remember the first, second, and the last words on the list. The closer words are to the middle of the list, the harder they are to remember. Prepare a class graph showing the results of trying to list ten words after hearing them once. Now read just five words and have students try to list them. Then read five more words and have students write them. Finally, graph the results. Point out that short lists are easier to remember. This can be applied to studying any type of list: spelling, math facts, and directions, for example.

Have the class try studying a spelling list by dividing it up into four smaller lists.

Personalized Stories

To make a story even more interesting as you read aloud to the students, change the names of the characters to those of children in the class. This is fairly easy if there is only one character, but you will have to concentrate if you try to change more. The children will soon be able to remind you, however, as they catch on to the game, which is an excellent listening activity.

This activity also serves as a stimulus to children to read aloud. They will have fun turning Cinderella into Janet and the prince into Robert as they literally create a modern fairy tale. Encourage them to make other adaptations to modernize the tale even further; for example, the chariot would become a Rolls Royce or a sleek airplane. Again, students who serve as the audience are motivated to listen attentively to hear all the humorous changes included.

Stump the Teacher

On a rotating basis, ask several class members to bring very difficult words to class and see if you, the teacher, can define them. If not, the students must define the words and use them in a sentence. During the day, you and the class try to use the new words. When the word is used, the student who originally brought the word to class must sit on the floor to indicate he or she has heard it!

Find the Secret Word

At the beginning of class, announce that you have a secret word for the day and that you will use this word once every half hour. Students are to listen carefully and try to guess the word. When students think they've got the word, ask them to share it with you secretly. If no one gets the word, tell the students what it was at the end of the day. Vary this listening exercise by having the first student to discover the secret word contribute the word for the next time.

Films

Listening
Churchill Films
Fourteen-minute film

Your Communication Skills
Coronet Films
Eleven-minute film

IMPROVING LISTENING COMPREHENSION

Listening for meaning may be the most important application of our listening skills. In this section we provide activities that show students how to increase their skills as critical and creative listeners and how to improve the accuracy of their listening. As a result of these activities:

- Students will remember significant details.
- Students will recognize sequences of events.
- Students will identify main ideas.

Does It Fit?

The primary purpose of this listening activity is to see how effectively youngsters can find out what does not fit. One strategy for doing this is to read a very short paragraph and ask them to discover what is wrong: What sentence is wrong? What word is wrong? What does not fit in the story? For example:

> Jim and Sharon were walking along a creek in California when all at once they saw a large whale. After a while they ran into a small group of penguins. They fed these tigers their peanut butter sandwiches which they had harvested from the bushes along the creek. Finally the moon came out and they knew it was time for lunch.

What Doesn't Belong?

Recite a list of five words with one word that doesn't belong. For example: apples, oranges, pears, airplane, grapes. Students are to listen to the list and select the word that doesn't belong.

Listen!

In math, is it correct to say "5 and 7 are 13" or "5 and 7 equal 13"?

Finding the Change

Read or tell a familiar story to your students, for example, *The Three Bears* or *Three Billy Goats Gruff,* and change one of the major details of the story. See if the students can locate where you have changed the story. For example, if you tell the story of *Little Red Riding Hood,* you might change the color of her hood and see if the students notice.

Listening in Sequence

It is important in listening activities to develop exercises that challenge students to put events in sequence. Read a brief story to a group and have the students relate the sequence of the events. The level of difficulty of this assignment can be varied by adjusting the length of the story.

Another activity is to prepare a topsy-turvy story with the sentences in scrambled order. After reading the story aloud, have the students rearrange the events so that they make sense. For example:

- We unpacked all of our groceries.
- We were lucky to find a parking place at the grocery store.
- We checked the cupboard for peanut butter before we made the shopping list.
- The checker was very courteous and helped take the bags out to the car.

This can also be done with a paragraph or a sentence. The following are examples of scrambled sentences that can be read aloud:

- Very start will school soon.
- Day a it's warm very fall for.
- Season Pam's autumn favorite is.

What Happened Next?

An exercise to involve the students in listening is to have them finish a story. Play a record or tape yourself reading a story. Stop it in the middle near an exciting part. Ask the students to write a suitable ending. They have to have listened carefully in order to understand what is going on and to make a contribution. After they have written their endings, ask them to supply a title for their stories. This is a good motivator for creative writing as well as practice in the organization of a story.

Now Hear This

Read several short speechs to your students. Have them list the main idea for each selection. Discuss in class whether they had any trouble locating the main idea. An analysis of the structure of a speech would help students locate the main idea. This speech might be on tape or on records. One example is the "I Have a Dream" speech by Martin Luther King.

> Remember: Don't ever assume that comprehension is taking place. Check it out in some form.

Headlines Summarize

An effective strategy for ascertaining students' levels of listening is to use articles from the newspaper. Students listen carefully while you read a short article and then help you write a suitable headline. Help them observe that the headline is a summarizer; it contains the main idea in the article. The articles that you select can come from different parts of the paper: sports pages, local news, national/international news, or travel.

A series of several articles can be recorded on tape so that students can work with this exercise independently at a Listening Center. Number the headlines mounted on a sheet of paper so students can check their work.

The reverse of this can also be used whereby you read the students the headline and they tell you what they think the story is about. They can then check their story against the one in the newspaper.

Listening for Ideas

Students enjoy listening to stories. You can encourage their active listening by reading a story to them and then asking them about it. Tell them before you read the story that they are expected to remember the story because you will ask them to perform a specific task related to it, for example:

- Ask them to write a summary of the story.
- Give them a list of the events in the story and have them put the events in order of occurrence.
- Act out the story.
- Draw a picture of the most important event.
- Tell why the events happened.

Humorous Language

Most jokes involve language in some form. A pun, often defined as "the lowest form of humor unless you think of it first," is an excellent example of the use of language for humor. The audience has to listen closely and understand that a crucial word in the joke can have two meanings. Students love jokes and enjoy telling the same ones over and over. Provide them with some new material and, at the same time, engage their interest in listening to the language used in jokes.

Joke books are a good source of humor in different forms. Remember, almost all jokes need to be read aloud to have an effect. Here are examples to try on the class:

- What did the ocean say when it left the shore?
  Nothing, it just waved.
- What did one wall say to the other wall?
  I'll meet you at the corner.
- What did the mayonnaise jar say to the refrigerator door?
  Close the door, I'm dressing.

Some suggested joke books include the following:

Sandra K. Ziegler, *Jokes and More Jokes* (Chicago: Children's Press, 1983). Illustrated by Diana L. Magnuson.

Giulio Maestro, *Riddle Romp* (New York: Clarion Books, 1983).

Joseph Rosenbloom, *Wacky Insults and Terrible Jokes* (New York: Sterling Publishers, 1983). Pictures by Sandy Hoffman.

Listening Cloze Procedure

The cloze procedure is a reading idea where every fifth word is left out of a selection. This activity can also be carried out as a listening comprehension idea. You can prepare material with every fifth word omitted and then read it to the students. The youngsters can suggest what word should be substituted for the blank.

A variation of this would be to first read the selection aloud to the class and then reread it, eliminating every fifth word. In all cases, there should always be a final reading of the selection so that students have an opportunity to see what word was actually used.

See Chapter 5 for more discussion of cloze techniques.

Critical Listening

By listening attentively, students can learn to distinguish between fact and opinion.

Students who watch television are already aware that words can be used to manipulate people. Talk about the power of words and how choice of words affects attitudes and emotions. Students can supply examples from their own experience. Introduce the word *propaganda* and explain what it means. Have students bring examples of propaganda from different sources to class and discuss them.

How do writers use words to influence people? Point out examples of slanted reporting, glittering generalities, name-calling, and loaded words. A common technique makes use of what is called the "halo" effect. The name of a person who is famous or valued for one thing is used to support or endorse another idea or product. When you have developed a list of the different kinds of propaganda, play a tape of a commercial and have students identify examples of each type.

Have students collect commercials on tape. A small group can listen to such tapes as they analyze the content. Some questions to address might be: What is the commercial selling? How does it try to "sell" the customer? Is a televised commercial still effective without the visual component?

Listening Comprehension Tests

Brown-Carlsen Listening Comprehension Test (World Book Co.)
Measures:
- recall of material
- following directions
- word meaning
- lecture comprehension

S.T.E.P. Test (Educational Testing Service)
Measures:
- comprehension of main ideas
- evaluating material
- applying material
- remembering details
- understanding implication

Listening to a Film

The object of this activity is to have students "listen to a film." Run a film with the picture off, but the sound on. Tell students the title of the film and darken the room just as it would be for a film. After students have listened to the film, ask them to write what they thought was going on as they listened to the sound track. When they have completed their stories, run the film again, with sound and picture. Students can compare their impressions from the sound track with what the film actually represents. A film that is effective for this purpose is *Leaf* (produced by Pyramid Film Co., Santa Monica, California, 1962).

Appreciative Listening

An important step in listening effectively is to be interested in what one is hearing. Play spoken records for the students. You can use records of plays, stories, or poetry. The students' enjoyment of "hearing" these records will involve them in "listening" with understanding.

Some excellent records for this purpose are available, including "Alice in Wonderland" (Riverside) and "Julie of the Wolves" (Miller-Brody).

The Mind's Eye (Box 6727, San Francisco, California 94101) has a fine collection of cassettes that include such classics as *Pinocchio, Cinderella,* and *Sleeping Beauty.*

Ten Tips to Improve Your Listening Skills

1. Determine your purpose for listening.
2. Listen with a pen in hand.
3. Try to visualize the speaker's plan or organization.
4. Think along the same lines as the speaker.
5. Try to predict what the speaker is going to say.
6. Ask yourself questions about the topic.
7. Talk about the speech as soon as possible.
8. Reward yourself for being a good listener.
9. Summarize several times during the speech.
10. Relate ideas and examples to your own life.

Listening to Poetry

Poetry is meant to be read aloud and to be listened to. The words of the poem create images in the minds of the listeners.

Teach students to appreciate the power of poetry to evoke images by reading poems to them. Ask them to listen for the picture words and words that appeal to the senses. After you read a poem, have them draw pictures of what they saw when listening to the poem. Talk about the words used in the poem to create pictures. Some words may be names of objects; others may only suggest particular images. Some poems create very different images for different people. Why is that?

Increase the number of poems students are exposed to and explore different styles of presentation by bringing records of people reading poetry to class. Students do not have to understand every word in a poem in order to appreciate the imagery used by the poet. Emphasize the creative listening necessary to understand the poet's intention.

Rhyming poems are easy to memorize. Studies have shown that children enjoy poems that rhyme. Play records of poetry for students and encourage them to memorize their favorite poems. They will have to listen carefully in order to memorize all the words.

RESPONDING TO AUDITORY INPUT

Effective listening is not a passive activity. Students' listening abilities improve when they must respond in some way to what they hear. In this final section, we ask students to put their listening skills to use and show their understanding by responding appropriately. As a result of these activities:

- Students will follow oral directions.
- Students will paraphrase an oral message.
- Students will answer questions based on oral material.
- Students will construct literal and inferential questions from oral material presented.

Giving and Following Directions

One concrete and practical way that we listen and speak is in giving and following directions. Give students practice in following directions for very simple paper folding. The Japanese art form of origami is an excellent technique because the students, by following directions closely, can make objects and animals that are pleasing to create. When these are completed, they make excellent room decorations hung from the ceiling as mobiles. Let students try giving directions to each other in pairs for other paper-folding activities.

Another way of sharpening a student's skill in listening is to make multiple copies of a map, or portions of a map, and have the students follow the directions on this map as they are given orally. Children can practice giving directions to their homes or to a particular building in the community: the post office, bank, or library. This activity can be carried out in the students' neighborhoods as they try to follow directions.

Direction Game

An interesting variation on the previous activity is to give each student a square piece of paper. As you give directions, students are to respond by drawing on their paper. For example, "Draw a line from the top left corner to the bottom right corner." Make a key on a large piece of white paper as you go along. When you have given three or four directions, students can then compare their papers with the answer key.

For more independent learners, students can work in pairs. One student acts as the teacher and prepares a list of directions and makes up a key. The other student listens carefully to the directions the first student gives and draws them on a piece of paper. The "teacher" then compares the answer key with the "student's" piece of paper. Student pairs then reverse roles.

Examples of directions: "Draw a line from the top to the bottom of the paper." "Put a tiny circle in the top right hand corner." "Draw a rectangle in the middle of the paper."

Communication Is an Art

To show that verbal communication is in some ways rather difficult, try this exercise. Ask for one volunteer to be "the sender." The rest of the students will be "receivers." Place a very simple drawing in front of the sender (similar to the one shown below). He or she is to then give directions to the receivers so that they may reproduce the drawing that the sender has in front of him or her. When he or she has finished giving the instructions, the sender can hold up the drawing or project it on the wall with an opaque projector, and students can see how accurate they were in reproducing the drawing. After completing this exercise it would be very valuable to have a discussion as to the characteristics of a good sender and a good receiver.

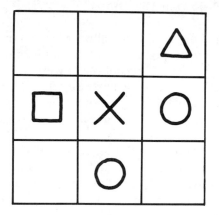

This exercise can also be done in pairs. Students may work independently to practice giving and receiving directions.

Selecting Relevant Information

Students need practice in following directions and in sorting out the important information from all that they hear. Provide examples of directions that include unnecessary or irrelevant details. Tell the students to listen closely and write down the irrelevant details. For example:

Study for a Test

1. Have the text or workbook.
2. Get out paper and pencil.
3. Sit down.
4. Find a quiet, well-lit spot.

Discuss why students selected certain directions as irrelevant.
A variation is to have students prepare directions and do this exercise with a partner.

Twenty Questions

Twenty Questions is a classic game that requires youngsters to listen very carefully to what has gone before. It is probably best for you to start the game. Mention the category—animal, vegetable, or mineral—and then the students can ask twenty questions to see if they can guess what the object is. With the leader of the game answering "yes" or "no," all questions must be phrased so that they can be answered positively or negatively. Youngsters quickly see that there are strategies in this game, but the most effective strategy is for them to be alert and to listen to what the responses have been to previous questions. This is a game that can be carried out with any grade level. It is also an excellent review for social studies or science.

Vocabulary Growth through Listening

When students are listening to a story or poem, they will frequently hear words they don't know. They don't find the strange vocabulary intimidating, however, because the meanings of the words are usually explained by the context. This is an excellent way to introduce new words. Discuss the new words when you have finished reading. Students will probably be able to suggest an approximation of the correct meaning. Talk about how they know what the author means when they can't understand all the words. Also talk about what clues they might use to gain the meaning of the words.

Add-a-line Stories

Telling a story provides both listening practice and oral language development. You or a student start a story by telling the title or a first line, such as, "I was on my way to . . . ." The next student adds a line or two to the story and passes it along by calling on someone else. Each person must pay careful attention to what the other students say in order to make an appropriate addition to the story.

Involve the students in reading their own work by taping the tale and typing it on a ditto so that the whole class can have a copy of the story they created together.

An interesting variation is to have several tales going at once in small groups. This allows greater participation and requires better listening skills.

Upside-down and Backwards

One morning, explain to the students that you got up on the wrong side of the bed and when you went to put on your clothes, you got them on inside out and backwards. Your coffee was white and your milk was black, the cat barked and the dog meowed, and everything was the opposite of the expected. In order to reverse your morning of opposites, the class is going to cooperate with you, and for the next hour, everyone in the class will say the opposite of what they mean.

This should make for a confusing class as some students forget to use opposites. But the object is to motivate the students to pay attention and to listen to each other.

Remembering Directions

Give students a series of directions, maybe five in number. They are not to begin following the instructions until you have finished giving all five directions. For example, you might say, "Stand on one foot. Clap your hands. Raise your arms. Shake your head. Sit down."

Active Listening

This exercise promotes listening comprehension skills. Students work in pairs. Each student takes a turn at being a "speaker" while the other is a "listener." The speaker tells the other person a true story about something that is important to him or her. For example:

- The most interesting thing I have ever done is . . .
- The craziest thing I ever did was . . .
- What I really think is important is . . .
- I laughed really hard when . . .
- My favorite place to . . . is . . .

The listener's role is to listen attentively and not interrupt, except to ask questions and encourage the speaker. After the speaker has finished, the listener repeats the story as accurately as possible. The first person corrects and adjusts the story as it goes along, to make sure that the listener really understands the speaker's story. Afterwards, students switch roles. This activity is especially valuable in conflict-resolution situations.

Questions

To encourage listening comprehension, read or tape a short article and then ask five questions pertaining to it. After the youngsters have had a chance to answer these five questions, reread the article so that they can make their own corrections. Make sure that at least two of the five questions are inferential. For example:

> *Story: Three Little Pigs*
> *Literal question:* What were the three houses made of? (The answer is explicit in the text.)
> *Inferential question:* Why do you think they made their houses of different materials? (The answer cannot be repeated from the text.)

Taking Notes

Students learn to listen productively when they have to take notes on content. Have the students listen to a tape of you reading a short passage from a textbook. As they listen, have them take notes on the passage. Collect what they have written and ditto excerpts from a few examples. Compare these with the class and discuss why some material was included and other information was not. How do students' notes differ? What was included that was most helpful in reconstructing the original material? What was not helpful?

The Listening Circle

This is an opportunity for youngsters to practice listening and speaking. Everyone sits in a circle and there is only one requirement: when one person talks, everyone listens to that person. This encourages those speaking; it also helps the class members to become more sensitive to each other. The listening circle is a great opportunity to deal with feelings. For instance, questions that might be asked include:

- What do you do for fun on rainy days?
- Why do you watch TV?
- What did somebody do that made you feel good or that made you feel bad?

The important thing is that everyone listens while someone else is speaking. A special time and place can be set aside for this listening circle. Both you and students should feel free to contribute other questions. There might be one question a day. This period should be kept short because listening to others for a long period of time is difficult.

Favorite Sounds

What sounds are the most pleasant and what are the worst? All students have their favorite sounds. Ask the students to describe their favorite sounds without telling the class what they are. Everyone else in the class has to listen to the description and think very hard to guess what the sound is. Every student gets a turn to describe his or her favorite sound. Some examples of favorite sounds might be:

- the bell ringing at the end of a class period
- the ice cream truck
- the splash of waves on the shore
- bacon sizzling in the pan

Before the students present their favorite sounds, talk about words that describe sounds in order to provide suggestions for descriptive words. Students will enjoy thinking up precise ways to describe their sounds without giving away what the sound is.

Silence Is . . .

Students can write a paragraph or a poem about silence. Beginning with "Silence is . . .," they could compose a list of the sounds they heard during one minute of silence in the classroom.

> *Silence is . . .*
> *outside noise*
> *breathing*
> *cars going by*
> *my brain working*
> *feet moving*

Noise Pollution

Noise pollution is a very real problem in our society. List local noise polluters and assign class members the job of writing letters of complaint to the responsible agencies.

Listening Guide to Oral Presentations

- What was the subject of the presentation?
- What was the major point? (Write it in one sentence.)
- What pattern did the speaker use? (Cause and effect, chronological order, comparison, or a combination)
- Did you agree with the speaker?
- What was your reaction to the presentation?

3 Developing Oral Language

> *Alone of all creatures on earth, man can say things that have never been said before—and still be understood. . . . Man has the capacity to create every time he speaks.*
>
> LINCOLN BARNETT

Next to listening, speaking is the most frequently practiced of the language arts. Not only do we speak more than we read or write, but our thoughts and ideas are judged by how well we express them. In order to become more effective speakers, students need opportunities to develop oral fluency, experiment with speaking for different purposes (such as describing or persuading), and talk to different audiences (such as small versus large groups).

This chapter is organized according to the developmental sequence of speaking skills. As a result of the activities in this chapter:

- Students will employ different modes of expression.
- Students will produce oral compositions.

STIMULATING TALK AND DISCUSSION

Fluency in oral language depends on providing the opportunity to talk. In this section, we present a variety of structured situations where students have a chance to develop confidence and express themselves orally. As a result of these activities:

- Students will produce speech clearly and coherently.
- Students will express ideas, opinions, and feelings.
- Students will contribute to group discussions and oral compositions.

Silence Is Golden

Proclaim a quarter hour of silence; for example: "There will be no oral communication between 10:45 and 11:00." The only way communication can take place is through writing or movement. This quarter hour will seem to go very slowly, for many people find it a real burden to be silent for fifteen minutes. But it might also be relaxing and peaceful. At the end of the quarter hour, discuss what the students thought and felt during this period of silence. What problems did they encounter? How did they overcome them? Use the discussion to open up the question of the importance of oral communication. Finally, ask the students if they would want a full hour of silence. This might provoke an interesting exchange of ideas.

Talking Words

Use creative dramatics to introduce different ways of talking. Ask the children to demonstrate how they would try to get a friend's attention without talking above a whisper. Have the class define the words *murmur, scold, shriek, chatter,* and *mumble.* Pairs of students can act out situations where they feel these word descriptions fit.

It's Not What You Say, It's the Way You Say It!

Give students the opportunity to experience different ways of saying the same word or a different way of saying the same sentence (intonation). For example, give a sentence to your class and have the students say it happily, sadly, or angrily. Let them experiment with the sentence: *What have you been doing?*

How many ways can the students think of to say "no"? Can they make "no" sound like "yes"? For example, ask different students to demonstrate how they would say "yes" if they meant:

- I would love to go to your party.
- I have finished my carrots.
- I am ready to go to the dentist.
- I would like some ice cream.
- The baby is asleep.

Looking at Our Dialects

Encourage students to talk about differences in pronunciation. As you help them develop speaking skills, draw these examples to their attention. Present the students with a list of words such as these so they can compare pronunciations:

pin/pen	cot/caught
car	greasy
merry/Mary/marry	roof
aunt/ant	vase

Can you find any patterns in the differences? Several students may pronounce a word differently from most of the other class members. Are these students from the same part of the country?

Recognition of these differences will lead to discussion of many questions. Why do these differences exist? When we move to a different part of the country, what happens to our language? How do we learn these differences? Do some dialects sound better to us and why? None of these questions are too advanced for your students because all students are fascinated by language.

People Talk

Ask each student to cut out a picture of someone from a magazine or newspaper. Instruct the children not to tell anyone the name of the person they choose. Have them think about this person. What is he or she like? What has he or she done? How would he or she talk? Ask the students to "become" the person in their picture, and put them in pairs to talk to each other.

Afterwards, discuss how different people talk. What can you tell about someone by the way he or she talks?

Pantomiming Animals

In pantomime, students can act out any kind of object or feeling they want to express, only without language. Although you may want to use pantomime in any number of different contexts, a special technique would be to use it in nonlanguage areas, for instance, when students are studying animals. Have students think of animals they would like to be. Each student pantomimes one animal's behavior for the other students to guess what animal she or he is pretending to be. This takes special creativity with smaller animals or insects. However, students can usually manage to suggest enough of the essential nature of the animal for the others to guess.

Discuss with students the problems and techniques of pantomiming after they have tried it. Pantomiming, of course, is a good lead-in for creative drama.

Techniques for Practicing Oral Patterns

These techniques can be used on an individual basis or in small groups with children. Each example can also be modified to suit the needs of the child.

Repetition: Listen and repeat exactly as heard:

Teacher: Here is a book.
Child: Here is a book.

Analogy: Repeat exactly with one change:

Teacher: The flowers are beautiful today.
Doris: The trees are beautiful today.
Ted: The bushes are beautiful today.
Mabel: The grass is beautiful today.

Inflection: Change the form of a word:

Teacher: A bird is in the nest.
Doris: The birds are in their nests.
Teacher: This class is going to play baseball.
Ted: These classes are going to play baseball.

Completion: Finish the statement:

Teacher: Bill will do exercises so that . . .
Mabel: . . . he will become stronger.
Teacher: Mary is hungry, but . . .
Doris: . . . John is hungrier.

Expansion: Expand the sentence:

Teacher: Greg is sleepy.
Ted: Greg is sleepy because he stayed up late last night.
Teacher: Joan is sad.
Mable: Joan is sad because her puppy is sick.

Transformation: Change the sentence to either a negative form or to a question form:

Teacher: Gail would like some ice cream.
Doris: Gail would not like some ice cream.
Ted: Would Gail like some ice cream?

Restoration: Make a sentence out of these words:

Teacher: broom, dirt, outside
Mabel: Let's use this broom to sweep the dirt outside.
Doris: Is there a broom outside to sweep this dirt?

Response: Make a comment or response to the statement:

Teacher: That dress is pretty.
Ted: Yes; it looks nice on her.
Doris: Don't you think that the colors clash?
Mabel: The dress looks comfortable, too.

The Interview

This is an excellent activity to use early in the year to help the class become better acquainted. Begin with a list of ten questions. Allow the students to compile a list of ten questions they would like to ask one another. Divide the class so that half of the students are interviewers and the other half are interviewees. After the interview is completed, students then switch roles. This gives each student a chance to interview and to be interviewed. For variety, allow the interviewer to ask a few questions in addition to the listed ones.

This activity can be done in front of the whole class. Have one student interview another before the class, and then switch the roles. This has the benefit of allowing everyone to hear the interview being carried out. You can also have the option of discussing the interview at its conclusion.

With the whole-class approach you might have only one student a day be interviewed. The total class can serve as an interviewer. One rule that should always be observed is that a student always has the right to *pass* on any question. Students enjoy this activity, both asking the questions and—even though they sometimes act a little shy about it—answering the questions.

A sample list of questions is:

- What is your favorite vegetable?
- If you could have any pet, what would you choose? Why?
- What is your favorite musical instrument?
- What is your favorite weekend activity?
- If you won a free vacation, where would you go? What would you do there?
- What is your job at home?
- What do you do best?
- What would you like to do better?
- What would you like to be doing twenty years from now?
- If you were in charge of the world for a day, what would you change?

Off to Timbuktu!

"I'm off to Timbuktu, and I'm going to take along a tiger. What will you take?"

Students take turns adding something that starts with *T* that they will take along to Timbuktu. The game can be changed by selecting a new location; for example: Zanzibar, Paris, London, or Borneo. If a student chooses a location with two names, the game becomes more difficult. "I'm off to South America" will require students to use an adjective with *S* before a noun beginning with *A*. For example:

- small apple
- slight ant
- sharp asp
- sunny ape
- smelly artichoke

Are You More Like the Mountains or the Ocean?

This exercise is designed to foster students' thinking about who they are and what matters most to them. Present your students with a list of paired items, some of which may be opposites. After discussing the list with the class to see that everyone knows what the words mean, ask students to circle the word in each pair that they think most describes who they are and what they like. Remind them that some of these objects will seem very strange applied to people but that they are supposed to stretch their imaginations and figure out which one is most appropriate. Here are some examples of possible questions:

Are you—

- More like thunder or lightning?
- More like the sun or the moon?
- More like cotton or wool?
- More like a butterfly or a caterpillar?
- More like fish or a bird?
- More like red or blue?
- More like dawn or sunset?
- More like breakfast or dinner?
- More like the mountains or the ocean?
- More like fall or spring?

After students have made their selections, begin a class discussion. Ask students to tell the class what they thought were some of the differences between the paired items and why they chose the one they did. Encourage students to appreciate choices different from their own and to be interested in learning why people might have made different choices.

If some students don't want to answer certain items, they can discuss instead what types of differences they see between the items in a pair and how they feel about them. The items in each pair can be varied for any grade level. You might include favorite characters from a book.

After the class members have discussed the exercise and each student has had a chance to talk about choices made, have the students write an unsigned list of the items they circled. Have several students make a graph of the results. Post this graph on the bulletin board or give each student a copy of it.

Brainstorming

A fascinating approach to oral language is the creative activity of brainstorming an idea, approach, or solution to a problem or a question. The ground rules for brainstorming are very simple:

1. Begin with a problem or question that is as explicit as possible.
2. The emphasis is on generating as many ideas as possible; all ideas are accepted.
3. No criticism of any idea is allowed.
4. Individuals may hitchhike on someone else's idea.

Since evaluation is played down, the creative part of the brain has the opportunity to function. Youngsters do not need to be afraid of coming up with the one right answer, for there may not be any "correct" answer. In general, we have found that individuals at any age tend to enjoy this type of activity, and, before you know it, it is possible to generate a tremendous number of ideas in a relatively short time. These ideas can of course be looked at later with a critical eye and put in order of importance. Some of the more thought-provoking topics, ideas, or problems that we have found include the following:

- Ask the children to think of as many different kinds of animals as they can in a period of five minutes. You can write these down or, if possible, upper-grade youngsters can be brought in and used as scribes.
- Ask the class to think of as many different titles for stories as possible. This is a practical idea in many ways, since these titles can be used for many different room activities, writing exercises, or impromptu speaking.
- Take a common object, like a newspaper, and see how many different uses the class can find for it. You might bring the newspaper to class to help the youngsters in their problem solving of this question.
- Ask youngsters to suggest as many "what ifs" as they can.

- Brainstorm solutions to class problems like excessive noise during free time or arguments about sports.
- Discuss possible solutions to issues studied in social studies, such as pollution or overpopulation. After several large-group practice sessions, the class can be broken into smaller groups which allow each individual more speaking time. Each group can select the most promising solution to present to the rest of the class.

One-sided Conversations

Tape one side—and one side only—of a phone conversation. You can place about five of these monologues on one tape, leaving space between the conversations. The students listen to the tape, hearing one side of the conversation, and try to determine what the other side of the conversation would sound like. Working in pairs or small groups, the youngsters can invent what the other person was saying.

Quotes and Quips

Each day write a provocative quotation on the board or on a chart so that the class can see this quotation all day. At the conclusion of the day, discuss the students' impressions of this quotation. What does it mean to them? How does it apply to their lives? What can they learn from this quotation?

At the end of the week see which quotations children remember. Encourage students to contribute quotations to be displayed. Examples that you might use include:

- *Common sense is not so common.*   Voltaire
- *Everything has its own beauty, but not everyone sees it.*   Confucius
- *Life is either a daring adventure or nothing.*   Helen Keller
- *No bird soars too high if he soars with his own wings.*   William Blake
- *The things that were hardest to bear are sweetest to remember.*   Seneca
- *A mouse never trusts his life to one hole only.*   Plautus

Tape-a-letter

Instead of writing letters to pen pals, students may send a tape from the class. Have all the students tape their letters and then play the tape for the class to hear. The class members can discuss in general what they like and dislike about hearing themselves on tape and make suggestions for future recordings. The class may have other ideas for tapes to send to their pen pals, such as a class discussion or reading parts of their favorite books. Choral speaking and singing also add to this method of sharing.

What You Said!

Every day you speak 4,800 words.

Sharing Time

The sharing period has many distinct possibilities for both oral language learning and listening skills. To develop these skills, however, it is essential that you use this time for more than grading papers or counting milk money and that the experience not become routine. The following suggestions may be helpful to enliven this period:

- Jot down a quick question about each presentation. Keep these questions simple (*What color is Satsuko's new rabbit?*) and alternate between oral and written answers.
- Choose a reporter to ask one question after each presentation. A real or pretend microphone will make the role playing more enjoyable. Model this role yourself to show students appropriate questions.
- Select an idea or theme for each sharing period, for example:
  What older person do you admire most?
  What's the day that you'll never forget?
  What makes a good friend?
- Change the seating arrangement. One possibility is to put the chairs in a circle and pretend that the class is sitting around a campfire. Use this for a sharing period theme, too, as children tell tall tales.
- Correlate other subjects with the sharing period. For example, it might be combined with a current events period, where students can share news that they have observed on television.
- Tell the children which days they will be responsible for sharing.
- Have the children share their favorite books.

Choric Speaking

Choric speaking is an excellent device to develop poetry appreciation. Students have the opportunity to learn poetry in a pleasurable way. Many poems are appropriate for choric speaking. "Poor Old Woman" is a poem that has all the elements to make speaking an enjoyable experience. It is included here as an example to help you get started. Turn this into an even more creative activity as the class writes new verses for the poem.

Poor Old Woman

Leader:	There was an old woman who swallowed a fly.
Chorus:	What, swallowed a fly? (Great amazement)
	Poor old woman, she surely will die! (Sadly, slowly)
Leader:	There was an old woman who swallowed a spider
	Right down inside her she swallowed a spider. (Pointing)
Small Group:	She swallowed the spider to kill the fly. (Aside)
Chorus:	What, swallowed a fly?
	Poor old woman, she surely will die!
Leader:	There was an old woman who swallowed a snake
	Oh, my, her stomach did ache!
Small Group:	She swallowed the snake to kill the spider
	She swallowed the spider to kill the fly.
Chorus:	What, swallowed a fly?
	Poor old woman, she surely will die!
Leader:	There was an old woman who swallowed a bird
	How absurd to swallow a bird.
Small Group:	She swallowed the bird to kill the snake;
	She swallowed the snake to kill the spider;
	She swallowed the spider to kill the fly.
Chorus:	(Repeats same two lines as above)
Leader:	There was an old woman who swallowed a duck
	Wasn't that just terrible luck?
Small Group:	She swallowed the duck to kill the bird;
	She swallowed the bird to kill the snake (and so on)
Chorus:	Two lines as above
Leader:	There was an old woman who swallowed a dog
	She went the whole hog; she swallowed a dog!
Small Group:	She swallowed the dog to kill the duck (and so on)
Chorus:	Two lines
Leader:	There was an old woman who swallowed a pig
	She swallowed the pig while dancing a jig.
Small Group:	She swallowed the pig, etc.
Chorus:	Two lines
Leader:	There was an old woman who swallowed a cow
	I don't know how, but she swallowed a cow!
Small Group:	She swallowed a cow, etc.
Chorus:	Two lines

Leader: There was an old woman who swallowed a horse
                   (Long pause) SHE DIED, OF COURSE!

Tongue Twisters

These tongue twisters are not only a challenge for students to do, but they also improve the students' diction. Clear enunciation is important in effective communication.

Choose one day a week to be Tongue Twister Day. Practice the tongue twister as a group in the morning. Performance of the tongue twister could be the ticket to recess or PE. Your students will enjoy collecting tongue twisters from parents and friends to add to the collection. Examples:

- Big Bad Bob boldly bit the bodyguard to bruise that buffoon.
- Crazy Callie couldn't collect the clickish crickets croaking classically in the creek.
- Dizzy Don delivered the dollars to diehard detectives to detain devilish doctors.
- Friendly Frieda fondly flashed a frivolous filly in front of a four-footed fly.

Small-group Compositions

Students can compose exciting stories if you give them a little help. Show them, for example, that the essential parts of a story tell *who, what, where, when,* and *why.* Divide the class into small groups of five people each. Give each person in a group a card with the key W-word for which they are responsible. The person with the *who* card supplies the character, and the person with the *what* card describes the action. The setting, time, and motive are provided by children who hold *where, when,* and *why.*

After each small group composes its short story, the stories can be shared aloud. Usually they turn out to be very funny, so the composition experience is highly enjoyable. Repeat the experience by exchanging cards so students have to supply a different part of the story each time. Each group will create five different stories in a very short time.

This oral activity can also be developed through writing because students will be interested in recording their stories. Compile a *Big Book of Short Stories* to place in the Reading Center or in your school library. Everyone will enjoy reading these humorous class-composed tales.

Object-ive Stories

Have children bring in all sorts of small, strange objects, and bring in some yourself. Pile them in one central area: a table, corner, or closet. When a youngster is ready for this activity, blindfold the youngster with a piece of cloth and instruct him or her to pick five objects out of the pile and guess aloud what they are. When the child has completed this exercise, he or she can write down what was picked, and then tell a story that includes all five objects that were picked. Then the next child can proceed.

If the whole group is participating, each child should be blindfolded (or just have eyes closed) as he or she picks one object out of the pile. Once each child has tried to guess what it is, he or she can take the blindfold off and share individual objects with their classmates. One child can begin with a story that includes his or her article and the story can be continued in round-robin fashion, with each child adding to the previous story and including the new-found object. The story can be recorded with a tape recorder or by another classmate. Sample objects include:

long kidskin glove	coral	braille book
red bandana	butter mold	shells
well-chewed pencil	cookie cutter	silver dollar
horseshoe	seeds	box of buttons
petrified wood	old-fashioned hat	

Your Wordless Book

Prepare a blank book to use for stimulating open storytelling activities. Begin this exercise by briefly introducing the topic of the story, and then simply pass the book to a child who continues the story and passes it on to another individual. After this has been done as a total class activity, several wordless books can be placed in the Learning Center so that students can dictate stories into a cassette recorder. Give each Wordless Book a story title; for example, "An Adventure Story," "A Tale of a Dog," or "My Most Exciting Gift."

Commercial Wordless Books

Wordless books that are printed commercially are very useful in the primary grades. In these books, illustrations tell the story. Here are four good examples:

Raymond Briggs, *The Snowman* (New York: Random, 1978).
Donald Crews, *Truck* (New York: Greenwillow, 1980).
Tomie de Paola, *Pancakes for Breakfast* (New York: Harcourt, 1978).
Peter Spier, *Peter Spier's Rain* (New York: Doubleday, 1982).

Puppets for Language Development

Many students who are too shy to talk in class will open up when they can talk through puppets. Use hand puppets that look like different kinds of people or animals. Divide the students into small groups to work with the puppets, and give some short assignments to get them started.

The first step is for each student to introduce his or her puppet to the others. The puppets can ask each other's names and ask questions about the other puppets. All the puppets in the group can have a conversation together.

Students can also use puppets to act out events. Have the students use several puppets to act out the most important thing that ever happened to them. They can also act out favorite activities with their puppets.

The group members can work together to create a play for their puppets. (Suggest topics if necessary.) After they have decided what they want to do, the students can present the puppet play to the class. If the children in a group are interested, ask them to write their play so that others can read it, and so they can present it again.

Stick Puppets

The stick puppet is versatile and can be created easily by primary grade children. Popsicle sticks or tongue depressors can form the base of the puppet. Children can use the heads of people or animals or they may wish to develop fully drawn figures to glue on the sticks.

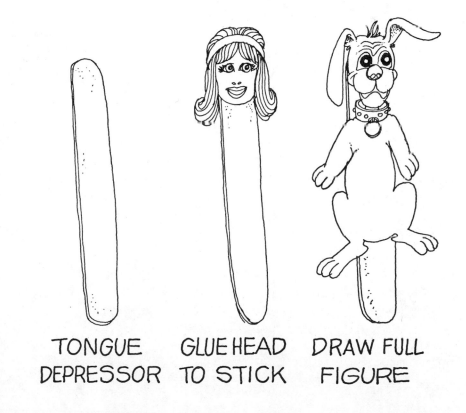

TONGUE DEPRESSOR   GLUE HEAD TO STICK   DRAW FULL FIGURE

Finger Puppets

Finger puppets are easy puppets to make, and they can be used by the youngest of children. They can be made in various ways, as shown.

1.

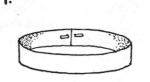 

BAND FOR
FINGER

ANIMAL HEAD
STAPLED TO BAND

2.

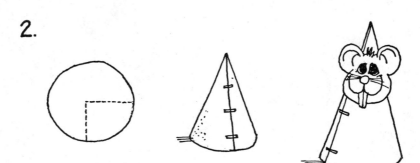

A Simple Hand Puppet Pattern

Give students a piece of paper 8½ × 11 inches, which is more than long enough for any students in your class. They can measure their hands from the tip to the wrist and add three inches to cover the arm.

The pattern is cut on the folded paper, as shown. When opened, of course, the full puppet shape looks like this:

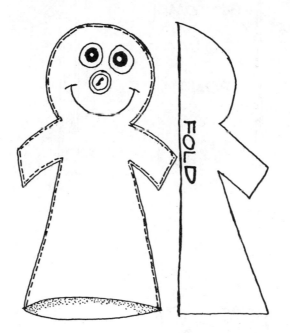

Children may cut two pieces of cloth using this pattern. They can sew these pieces together for an interesting experience in using needles and thread. Hair, ears, button noses, and other features can be added as desired to create a character for the puppet.

Paper Bag Puppets

Puppets can be constructed quickly and easily by using readily available paper bags.

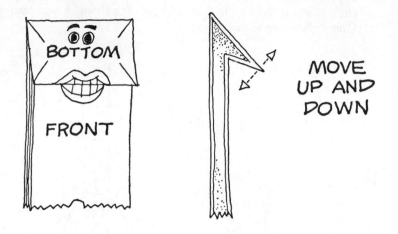

ORAL COMPOSING

As students begin to use oral language for increasingly complex purposes, they practice and refine the skills learned in the previous section. As a result of the activities in this section:

- Students will use oral language for different purposes.
- Students will learn information and solve problems through oral language.
- Students will create individual oral compositions.

Group Picture Stories

Collect magazines for pictures, getting contributions from the students and other people. Give the magazines to the students and ask them each to cut out one picture that especially appeals to them. The students can then work in small groups to create a story out of the pictures they have, using each one's picture. Have each child tape the story and play it for the class while holding up the pictures that illustrate the story.

Key Words for Stories

Write words or groups of words on 4 × 6 inch cards. Place the cards in a box, and ask each student to select a card. Give each child a few minutes to look the card over, and then for three minutes (an egg timer here is very handy) the child should use these words in a story to the class. The youngster has the card to hold on to, which gives some security.

Here are five examples of groups of words that could be put on cards to lead to a story:

1	2	3	4	5
anteater	flute	letter	rainbow	book
volcano	child	tunnel	cape	shadow
banana	danger	jar	chair	moth
rope	chocolate	frog	magic	laughter

The Class Mascot

Choosing a class mascot, an imaginary classroom pet, brings the class together as a group since a mascot gives all the children something in common. Give the mascot a name. On weekends, each child gets a turn to take the imaginary class mascot home.

On the following Monday, the student is expected to share with the class his or her adventures with the mascot. This sharing can be done orally or in written form. You can collate all of these adventures and put them in a book along with pictures that the students might submit illustrating their adventure.

The collected adventures could be used for a number of things. Students might portray the adventures in a film. They might tape the adventures with the mascot, in chapter form ("to be continued . . .").

A special feature of this activity is that it allows the student to have a whole weekend to think of something to share on Monday, whether it is a true experience or totally fabricated. And the audience is motivated to listen to these adventures!

Improvisations

This activity provides students with improvisational experiences, making up stories spontaneously. The students may choose from any of the following lists of words to make up an impromptu story in front of the class or on tape. These lists may be prepared on sheets of paper, or the words can be listed on cards to be placed in a Story Treasure Chest.

- rubber chicken, orange juice, seven, chair, jumping frog
- comet, ice cubes, prism, sinking, yellow
- eight gloves, blue face, Sears Catalog, beef stew
- moose, islands, lemon, green bag, fishing pole
- jump rope, jigsaw puzzle, chocolate cake, sack of coins, pony
- circus tent, lions, tuba, 21 balloons, explosion
- chairs, 9 kazoos, blind, machete, fire, heavy
- three-footed, binders, Saint Patrick, fierce, telephone booth
- square, fleece, scrambled eggs, Mrs. Maloney, friendly

Help!

Use Story Starters to stimulate student imaginations for class storytelling. Suggest a few beginnings and let students choose one to develop as a story and present to the class.

One day I was walking along the beach when I saw something shiny in the sand. Looking closer, I discovered it was a bottle buried in the sand. When I dug it out, I could see there was something buried inside. I opened the bottle to find a message. It said. . . .

There is no gift like the gift of speech; and the level at which people have learned to use it determines the level of their companionship and the level at which their life is lived.

PATRICK GROFF

On the Ball

Give each child a ball to hold while he or she tells a big whopper, tall tale, or story. This is an excellent oral activity and the fact that the youngsters have an object to hold in their hands helps alleviate their nervousness. After the story teller has finished the whopper, he or she picks someone else in the group to receive the ball, and that person tells another story.

A simple modification of this idea is a continuous story. The first student begins a tall tale, passes the ball, and the next person continues.

Talk Boxes

The purpose of this oral language activity is to provide stimulus to students as they compose a story to tell to the class. Use four shoe boxes. Mark each box with a different label: Setting, Character Trait, and Problem. In each of these boxes put suggestions written on slips of different colors, thus:

- red: setting
- blue: character
- green: character trait
- orange: problem

The student selects one slip from each of these four boxes and develops a one-minute story that she or he can relate to a small group, a tape recorder, or the whole class. (The colors of the slips make returning them to the right box easier.)

Students may choose slips presenting situations like the following:

- red: small sailboat
- blue: magician
- green: stubborn
- orange: everything begins to shrink

- red: the bottom of the ocean
- blue: blind person and seeing eye dog
- green: courageous
- orange: all machines stop working

This type of oral activity gives students a chance to use oral language creatively. The structure helps by giving them some idea of what to talk about.

Oral Commercials

Have individuals or pairs of students select from a stack of magazines and newspapers an advertisement they would like to rewrite or remake. They cut out this advertisement, decide how they are to redo it, and present the new advertisement as a commercial to the class. Students can develop some very humorous commercials. This activity gives them a chance to talk and to role play before the class.

Students can also select commercials seen on television or heard on radio, and modify them as oral commercials. For a different kind of discussion, you might tape the presentation to the class and then conduct a discussion of what makes a good commercial, what students enjoy about a commercial, and what devices are used in commercials.

Students will also enjoy creating commercials to "sell" favorite books. The success of the commercial can be judged by the number of students wanting to "buy" (read) the book.

Broadcasting

Many schools have a public address system. This is an excellent device to give students an opportunity to practice and refine their oral language skills. One simple way to use the system is to have students make announcements to the school. Some schools extend this idea by also allowing students to present school news or other items of interest. Students could form a broadcasting group for various activities:

- Read poems.
- Read stories.
- Read a story starter for all students to complete individually or as a class.
- Invite other classes to special performances.

Phone Conversation

This activity encourages oral language and develops skill in the use of the telephone. The materials used include two telephones. It is sometimes possible to obtain phones from the local telephone company, but toy telephones can be used.

Develop a series of cards that give examples of phone calls that are to be made. For instance, one card might require a student to make a phone call to the veterinarian to ask about a shot for a pet dog. One student can fill in the detail (the dog's name and what's wrong with it), and the other student can play the role of the vet. Another card might require a student to make a call to a local radio station requesting a particular song, while another student can be the disc jockey, answering the phone.

Here are some phone conversations to use as starters:

- Ordering ice cream for a birthday party
  (student and ice cream vendor)
- Calling satellite for weather report
  (student and astronaut)
- Arranging class field trip to museum
  (student and docent)
- Reporting escaped tiger
  (student and zookeeper)

After the phone conversation has finished, the students should critique the activity. What would they have added to the conversation? How was it carried out? What were the good points? What might be improved? From this experience, the students could generate a list of dos and don'ts for phone etiquette.

Role Playing

Give students the chance to play different roles in hypothetical situations by encouraging them to respond spontaneously, both with words and action. This type of oral expression is important in a number of ways:

1. It allows students to play different roles while still being themselves.
2. It gives them the chance to create in an instant or spontaneous manner.
3. It gives them a chance to express themselves orally.

The following are examples of situations that might be used:

- Parent explaining Halloween safety rules to small child
- Two people going on a fishing trip
- Three people, two of whom are new to the community, with the other person showing them the sights
- One person teaching another person how to fly a kite
- Officer asking child about bicycle safety
- Student applying for job as pet sitter for six cats

A Talk Show with Character

Create a classroom event by arranging for several students to play a variety of favorite characters. Have another student play the role of Talk Show Host. The host introduces the guests to the "studio" audience and gets them to talk about what is interesting about each one of them.

This activity would be a good review of characters studied during a social studies unit, such as the American Revolution. Discussion topics should be agreed upon in advance so that students have time to consider their character's position.

Coping with Problems

This activity can be done with the whole class or a small group. Each youngster is assigned a role to play. Possible role-playing situations are the following:

- Joe is riding his bike and runs a red light—a policeman sees him.
- Mary comes home too late for supper and her family has already eaten.
- Bill is assigned to do the family shopping and when he gets to the checkout counter he finds he forgot his money.
- Linda brings home a report card with Cs and Ds.

Table Topics

We have to structure opportunities where talking takes place. One way is to provide a topic and then break the class into small groups. Groups should contain no more than five students so that each individual has an opportunity to speak. Possible topics might include:

- The best pet for a small apartment
- Ways to conserve energy in our school

- New games for PE
- A fair method for assigning classroom jobs
- The best way to spend a rainy afternoon at home

After each group has had a talking time, a checklist should be used to determine whether everybody had an opportunity to talk. The class could then develop guidelines for talk etiquette.

Impromptu Speeches

The ability to give an impromptu speech is a very important skill to develop. To stimulate this type of talk, have a number of 3 × 5 inch index cards with a "What If" idea on each; for example, "What if a magician made you two inches tall?" The students select one of the cards, have a few minutes to study the "What If" they have selected, and then deliver a two- or three-minute impromptu talk. The following are additional examples of "What Ifs" to use in your file:

What if . . .

- you became twenty years older?
- there was no summertime?
- you could swim like a fish?
- you were allergic to ice cream?
- you lived inside a cave?
- everything you touched turned to gold/jello/an animal/a rock/another "you"?
- you were the only person left on Earth?
- you had your own children to take care of?
- you lived by yourself?
- animals could talk?
- people could fly?
- you learned by taking pills?
- you could read minds?
- you didn't need food?
- you had two lives?

True Experiences

Give students a chance to retell one of their experiences: an athletic event, a trip, a visit, or any interesting adventure. Begin this activity by brainstorming possible topics with the class. These topics can be recorded on tagboard or kept in a notebook.

- *Exciting experiences*
  First plane ride
  Vacations
- *Scary experiences*
  First Halloween
  Recital
- *Happy experiences*
  Birthday party
  New baby
- *Sad experiences*
  Moving
  Losing a pet

Students can include visual aids related to their experience—graphics, games, maps, pictures, objects—that would help in the explanation. You might also set a time limit for these talks.

A Menu of Topics

Motivate all students to participate in oral activities by having each one suggest a topic for the weekly discussion period. Write the topics on the board or on a chart and then have the class vote to determine which one of the topics will be used. The discussion period could be on Monday or Friday, possibly the first ten or fifteen minutes of the afternoon. Using student suggestions and a class vote ensures a high interest level in the discussion.

What Kids Talk About

- Making money
- Jobs they have
- Monsters
- Movies and TV
- Favorite people in sports
- Musical groups

Provocative Statements

The following topics can be used for debate, roundtable discussion, or talks to convince. Your students may want to suggest other topics as well.

- Dolphins are as intelligent as people.
- Television causes crime.
- There is intelligent life on other planets.
- All families should have guns in the home.
- A woman should be elected President of the United States.
- We should revise the English spelling system.
- Young people our age should be more considerate of their parents.
- Capital punishment should be abolished.
- Driver's licenses should be issued to people when they are fourteen years old.
- "Pushers" of narcotics should be executed.
- People should not travel to the stars.
- No one should listen to a Walkman while riding a bike.
- Every child should have a computer.
- Students would learn more if school were held twelve months a year.

Talk-abouts

Have students create a book of ideas for discussion or subjects for presentations they are to make. Make one page for each topic. This same book can be employed to suggest ideas for writing.

Amusements

- Reading the Sunday funnies
- Playing hide and seek
- Making home-made ice cream
- Chinese checkers with a friend
- Swinging in a hammock
- Building a sand castle
- Watching a kitten play
- Riding a ferris wheel
- Learning magic tricks
- Going to a school dance

Education

- Science experiments in space
- A good teacher
- More schooling or work?
- The value in experience
- A well-rounded education
- Does business want bright students?
- A practical education
- The value of art and music
- Preparing for responsibility
- How to make school more exciting

Customs

- Prayers at mealtime
- Saluting the flag
- Celebrating holidays
- Shaking hands
- Honking horns after a wedding
- Sending valentines
- Wearing ties
- Planting trees on Arbor Day
- Birthdays
- Shopping on Saturday

Friends

- Friends for life
- I wonder what happened to . . .
- The beauty of friendship
- So comfortable to be with
- Talking on the phone
- A friend in need
- The art of being a friend
- The friends I miss the most
- Sharing almost everything
- My dog, Scottie, is always there

Nature

- What is a biologist?
- Identifying birds
- Understanding ecology
- Dolphins and porpoises
- Underwater creatures
- Winter feeding stations
- Hiking in the forest
- Edible plants
- Bee language
- Mountain trout fishing

Occupations

- I want to be a pilot
- Going on a job interview
- Work can be fun
- Working with people
- Scientific research
- Working in a foreign country
- I like the outdoors
- Computer programming
- Music as a career
- Teaching is rewarding

Organizations

- Anti-pollution groups
- Charitable organizations
- Are unions necessary?
- Business groups
- Wildlife preservation
- Community theater groups
- I'm a nonconformist
- Senior citizens
- Religious membership
- Magicians

Pets

- Animals have personalities
- Training tropical fish
- Cats are night creatures
- Parakeets are clowns
- Dogs can be protective
- Problems in raising exotic pets
- Unusual pets
- Keeping your pet healthy
- The perfect hamster habitat
- Trust and wild animals

Hobbies

- Photographing wildflowers
- Playing music with friends
- Profitable hobbies
- My hobby helped me meet people
- Building strange kites
- Sharing a hobby
- Inexpensive hobbies
- Outdoor hobbies
- Collectors' items
- Collecting stickers

Manners

- Going out to eat
- Writing thank-you notes
- Manners at home
- Dressing for the occasion
- Courtesies are appreciated
- Remembering a sick friend
- What are good manners?
- How manners can make a difference
- A time when *please* helped me
- Things I am thankful for

Home

- Picking out a new house
- Who does most of the work at home?
- Family discussions
- Sharing experiences
- Planning for a holiday
- A new brother or sister
- My family traditions
- Father likes to go to the beach
- Mother enjoys working
- Learning responsibilities

Morals

- Cheating on tests
- My personal philosophy
- Respect for law and order
- Earning trust
- Being self-reliant
- What is an honor code?
- Is winning more important than playing?
- Are chaperones needed?
- Is honesty the best way?
- The importance of loyalty

Reading

- My favorite stories
- Are bookstores or libraries more fun?
- Learning from biographies
- Story hour at home
- Appealing adventure stories
- Books my teacher read
- My favorite character
- Magazines on newsstands
- Comic book collections
- Funny and sad poems

Travel

- Discovering new cultures
- Exploring America
- Coastal cruises
- Historical American Indian dwellings
- Favorite camping spots
- Sailing the Mediterranean Sea
- Hazards of traveling
- Communication problems
- Hitchhiking through Europe
- Vacation on the moon

Sports

- Are team sports more fun than games?
- Enjoying the Olympics on TV
- Jogging
- I'd rather go sailing
- Bicycle trips
- My favorite PE activity
- Water ballet
- Tennis fanatics
- Archery for the whole family
- Sportsmanship

A person's conversation is the mirror of his thoughts.

4 Words and More Words

Each new word . . . increases the scope of thought.
BERGEN EVANS

Why study words? Words are the building blocks for all aspects of the curriculum. One of the most important contributions we can make is to provide students with the ability to use and enjoy words. By developing their vocabulary resources, students are able to express their ideas with force and clarity.

Recent research has demonstrated the direct and positive relationship between vocabulary development and reading comprehension. Vocabulary can be studied as a subject on its own, with a special time slot for topics such as word origins or morphology. Or words can be discussed and practiced as they come up in a lesson or a story. Vocabulary is also taught through word games, which develop lively interest in words. All of these opportunities should be employed to teach vocabulary both systematically and incidentally.

This chapter is divided into three parts. As a result of the activities in this chapter:

- Students will recognize new words.
- Students will identify patterns in words.
- Students will discuss words and their meanings.

INTRODUCING VOCABULARY

The first step in vocabulary development is to bring new words into the classroom. Then, to incorporate words into their vocabulary, students need multiple opportunities to practice these words in a variety of contexts. Finally, the teacher checks students' vocabulary development to assess their progress. As a result of the activities in this section:

- Students will define new words.
- Students will use new words in speaking and writing.
- Students will compile word lists.

A Word a Day

A special section of the bulletin board can be devoted to featuring a new word every day. These words should be discovered by students, although you may occasionally feature a word that is especially relevant to a current topic of study. Have the student who provides the word prepare a card with the word and its pronunciation and definition.

Mount the card on the bulletin board and have the class discuss it. At the end of the week, review the five words that have been presented. Throughout the week, try

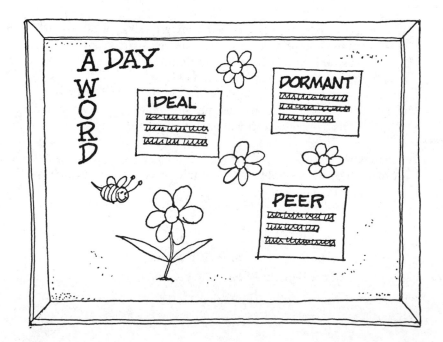

to slip some of these words into your conversation with the class. Reward students who use any of these words, in speaking or writing, by putting their name on the board.

Keep these student-produced word cards in a Word File, for easy student reference and review.

Vocabulary Wordlists

Have students compile wordlists centered around specific topics. Students can work alone to develop personal lists or as a small group to stimulate discussion and vocabulary development. Suggested topics are:

- *Animals:* horses, cats, dogs, tigers
- *Places:* school, home, playground, city
- *Media:* TV, books, movies, music
- *Jobs:* teacher, president, doctor
- *Recreation:* games, toys, parks, sports

These lists develop children's knowledge of categories. Encourage students to help build each other's lists.

A Class Word File

As your class becomes more interested in words, the students can maintain a class word file. Each new word that is talked about or introduced or that children find necessary in their writing can be put in this file. The box contains words on cards with a simple definition and the word used in a sentence.

Students can use this file for writing assignments. They can also develop various word games where they can ask each other a word and see if they can spell it or define it. Students have the opportunity to see their class word file increase as the school year progresses.

Teacher as a Source of Vocabulary

Students will be more likely to remember new words if you try to use them in talking to the class as often as possible. In fact, you are a major source of new words. "Advanced" words quickly become part of the student vocabulary when you use them in contexts where the meaning is clear. This makes new words sound more interesting and students will enjoy discovering the meaning from the context. Make the introduction of new vocabulary part of your daily routine, thus:

- People who procrastinate never get their work done.
- What loquacious students you are this morning!
- I want some volunteers to clean up the chaos in the Learning Center.
- Can anyone tell me why Robert's experiment was a fiasco?
- You should try not to provoke students when they're pugnacious.
- Please line up with alacrity.
- Let's try to think of a rule to end this controversy.

New Words

Always be alert for the opportunity to introduce a new word, whatever subject the class is studying. If the discussion is about health, you could supply the word *ailment* as a synonym for illness. Ask if anyone knows the word and have a student write it on the board as you discuss its meaning. Have the class develop a definition for the new word and ask a volunteer to record in the class Word File. Provide a sentence using the word in context or an illustration to further clarify the meaning.

Outrageous Definitions

Sometimes students find new words especially funny because they see funny meanings in analyzing the parts of the word. As a teacher, you can catch their interest to motivate the learning of new vocabulary. Give them words they may or may not know and ask them to write a humorous definition based on the parts of the word. Afterwards, they should look the word up in a dictionary just to see how outrageous their definitions were. Here are some examples to get you started:

- *Extent:* when you've given away your camping equipment
- *Hallucination:* the country of people called halluces
- *Mushroom:* a place to store oatmeal
- *Enterprise:* an award for attending
- *Cannibals:* what you need to play tennis
- *Shamrock:* a fake stone
- *Palindrome:* a place where they keep elephants

In many cases, knowing the meaning of the parts of a word provides a clue to the meaning. This kind of exercise will encourage students to be aware of meanings of the parts of new words (morphemes) that they encounter.

Good words are worth much and cost little.
GEORGE HUBERT

Word Sleuth

In this activity the players can be divided into groups or the whole class can partici-pate. Each student comes to class with a new word that he or she has written in a sen-tence. If you divide the class into two teams, Team A would listen carefully as a member from Team B says a new word and gives a sentence using that word. Team A tries to determine the meaning of the word from the sentence given. If Team A is success-ful, they receive a point and then present the next word.

What's that Word?

Here is a game designed to increase student vocabulary and to help review words that students can play in small groups and on their own. Using a stack of 3 × 5 inch cards, print a word on one side and its definition on the other. To play the game, divide the cards randomly into six stacks. The players roll a die and pick up the card on top of the stack corresponding to the number on the face of the die. They read the word aloud and then give a definition. If the definition is correct, which they check by look-ing at the back of the card, they get to keep the card and the turn passes to the next person. If they gave the wrong definition, the card is replaced at the bottom of the stack. When a stack is depleted, any player who rolls that number gets a second turn. The game ends when all the cards are used.

You can make a basic set of these cards and add to them every time you introduce new vocabulary. If there are words on the cards that no students can define, you may want to review these words with the class. This game is most useful when the students play it frequently.

Vocabulary Inventory

Another technique for reviewing new vocabulary is the Inventory. This simple vo-cabulary quiz can be compiled by several students. Inventories can be questions such as these:

- If you made a *serendipitous* discovery, would you be (1) pleased or (2) dis-gusted?
- A *neophyte* is a person who is (1) young, (2) pretty, or (3) new?

Students will gain useful knowledge about words by creating these Inventories as well as by answering them. Duplicate the sheets for the Learning Center so students can complete them independently.

Jeopardy

Give students a word that is easily defined and allow a short period of time for them to prepare as many specific questions as possible with that word as the answer. For example, for the word *carrot,* some questions might be:

- What is Bugs Bunny's favorite food?
- What is orange and grows underground?
- What vegetable is rumored to improve eyesight?

If you wish to adapt this activity for small groups, give each leader a pile of word cards with a sample question written on the back. The first player to create three correct questions becomes the new leader. Word cards can be sorted by categories (vegetables, state capitals) to review specific vocabulary.

What a Card!

This game is best played in teams. Pin to each student's back a card with an interesting word printed on it. The object of the game is for each person to guess the word on his or her back. Each student is allowed a specified number of questions that can be answered *yes* or *no*. The player who guesses the right word in the fewest number of questions wins. If someone cannot guess the word in the time limit, the others on the team are allowed to give clues.

Use this game to encourage students to remember new vocabulary words. You can also play the game with titles and authors of books as students guess who they are.

We think with words.
ANATOLE FRANCE

Guess My Word!

One student writes a selected word on a sheet of paper which is shown to the audience. Then a panel of five students takes turns attempting to guess the word selected. The panelists ask questions that can be answered only *yes* or *no,* for example:

Word chosen: Python

- Is it a noun?   (*yes*)
- Does it have more than one syllable?   (*yes*)
- Does it begin with a vowel?   (*no*)
- Is it in this room?   (*no*)

The panelists get twenty chances to narrow down the field so they can guess the word. If they do not guess correctly, the other team wins.

Little Words; Big Meaning

If
it
is
to
be,

It
is
up
to
me
to
do
it.

Malapropism

This strategy derives its name from Mrs. Malaprop, a character in a play by Richard Brinsley Sheridan called *The Rivals,* who was always getting her words just slightly mixed up. An example of this is the sentence, "John is not in school because he is *guaranteed* with the measles." Or, "She took the *subscription* to the druggist."

The following are examples of malapropisms spoken by Archie Bunker, in the television show "All in the Family." Have students underline the malapropism in each and write the correct word above.

- Don't take everything so liberally.
- Forget it. It's irrelevant. It ain't German to the conversation.

- Whoever sent them obviously wanted to remain unanimous.
- You're invading the issue.
- It's a proven fact that capital punishment is a known detergent to crime.
- Well, goodbye and good ribbons.

After you give youngsters some of these examples, they can create their own malapropisms to share with the class. They can try to trick the other students who have to spot the malapropism and supply the correct word. This idea sensitizes youngsters to language and to the use of words. It also results in vocabulary development and the use of the dictionary.

LOOKING AT PATTERNS

Students' vocabulary can be developed by drawing their attention to the patterns in words. Talking with students about compound words, rhyming words, and word roots encourages them to search out more examples and provides a framework to organize the words they know. As a result of the activities in this section:

- Students will arrange words in alphabetical order.
- Students will classify rhyming words.
- Students will categorize words according to number of syllables.
- Students will identify roots and morphemes.

ABC Challenge

Have students make various lists of words that follow the order of the alphabet. This is a good small-group or individual activity for expanding vocabulary, motivating students to use the dictionary, and also for practicing spelling.

Easy Words		*Longer Words*	
Ant	Nail	Accordion	Nonsense
Bed	Owl	Butterfly	Ostrich
Cap	Pin	Crimson	Pinnacle
Doll	Quit	Dolphin	Quotation
Ear	Run	Eclipse	Rainbow
Foot	Star	Fantastic	Saxophone
Goat	Top	Glitter	Tarantula
Hair	Under	Harmony	Umbrella
Ice	Voice	Imagine	Vampire

Jacks	Whale	Jungle	Wintergreen
Kite	X-ray	Kangaroo	Xylophone
Light	You	Luminous	Yearling
Mouse	Zoo	Magician	Zigzag

Vary the wordlists by focusing attention on a particular subject, for example:

Plants	*Animals*
Acacia	Aardvark
Birch	Buffalo
Calendula	Cougar
Dahlia	Deer
Endive	Emu

Other categories might be: titles of books, names of characters, boys, girls, adjectives, nouns, cities, and countries.

Hidden Word Puzzles

Using a puzzle frame, the student fills in names or words related to a single topic. After placing as many words as possible forward, backward, up, down, and diagonally, the student fills in the blank spaces with random letters. The solution of the puzzle is to find the hidden words.

The words to look for can be printed at the bottom of the page or the directions might be like this: "Thirty-four pieces of clothing are hidden in this puzzle. See how many you can find." Possible topics for the puzzle's focus include:

cities	song titles
authors	space
countries	automobiles
students' names	plants
clothing	food
colors	vocabulary words

Encourage students to work together to create these puzzles as well as solve them. Use the following example "Hidden Clothing," to show students how this type of puzzle works.

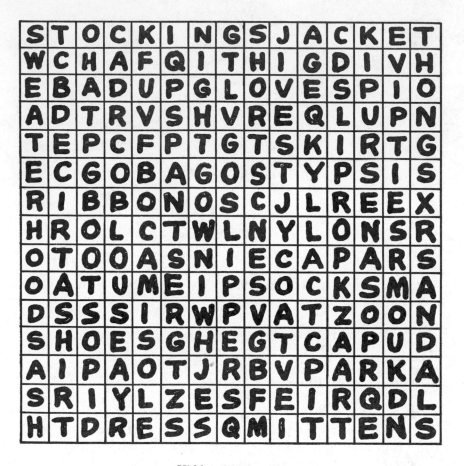

Hidden clothing

Hidden words:

stockings	vest	shorts	hood	leotards
shoes	scarf	jacket	slippers	tie
blouse	shirt	coat	nightgown	camisole
pants	sandals	thongs	purse	slip
sash	skirt	nylons	bag	cap
ribbon	dress	boots	sweater	parka
socks	mittens	hat	gloves	

Creating Puzzles

Draw a puzzle frame on a duplicator master so that you can produce a number of these frames on which students can make their own puzzles. Children have to know much more about spelling in order to create a puzzle than they do to solve one that someone else has created. They can make Hidden Word Puzzles or Crossword Puzzles on different topics or themes: transportation, winter, sports, South America, or music. Use a smaller number of squares for younger children and make the whole frame larger.

Word Search
Hi Tech
All Apples (printer required)
Grades 1 to Adult, depending on content

This program makes and prints word search (Hidden Word) puzzles, using words chosen by the teacher. A puzzle can include up to forty words. When the puzzle is printed, the answer sheet is also provided.

Words with Imagination

Show students a few examples of these funny ideas. Then encourage them to make additional examples. Students can use different kinds of printing, such as manuscript, to suggest the meaning.

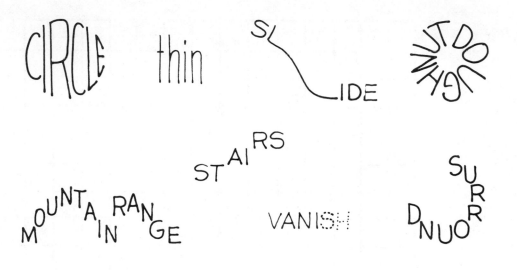

Riddle

Many riddles must be read aloud because they depend on word play based on sound. A classic example is:

What's black and white and read (red) all over?
(a newspaper)

Try this on your students. Did they think of both meanings for the homonym red/read? How did the riddle influence them to interpret the word as a color, *red?*

Read other riddles to the class to encourage them to pay attention to the sounds of words, as well as the meanings. Here are some books to get you started:

William Gerler, *A Pack of Riddles* (New York: Dutton, 1975). Illustrated by Giulio Maestro.

Alvin Schwartz, *Unriddling* (Philadelphia: Lippincott, 1983). Illustrated by Sue Truesdell.

Joanne Bernstein, *Fiddle with a Riddle: Write Your Own Riddles* (New York: Dutton, 1979). Illustrated by Giulio Maestro.

Sound Power

Draw the students' attention to the following words/phrases:

- humpty-dumpty
- namby-pamby
- mumbo-jumbo
- roly-poly
- helter-skelter

Ask the class what they find unusual about these examples. They should be able to recognize that these words differ only in the first letter/sound and that they rhyme. Ask them to suggest similar sets of words. They might come up with examples such as:

- thick and thin
- spic and span
- chitchat
- knickknack

Can students identify the difference between the first list and the second? All of these words are examples of reduplication, where a word or part of a word is repeated and sometimes changed slightly. If only the beginning is changed, the words rhyme. If the ending is changed, the words are alliterative. Examples of simple reduplication are *choo-choo* and *boo boo*. The reduplication gives the words a humorous effect and makes them appealing to say aloud.

Have students listen for more examples of these patterns.

Hinky Pinky

This game is also called Jingo Lingo or Terse Verse. Students think of pairs of rhymed words that create a picture, for example:

hefty lefty	cow chow
bog fog	river sliver
bloom room	bitter quitter

As students think of these two-word "poems," they can have fun making up humorous definitions.

- Maze craze: puzzle fad
- Steel heel: a nasty robot
- Crime chime: a burglar alarm

With this game, students learn to see new relationships between words and to create new ways of looking at the world. Students can use rhyming lists to suggest words. The class could supply definitions after the lists are compiled. Students will also enjoy finding examples of Hinky Pinkies in advertising and in the media.

fat cat	hitch pitch
spring fling	shirt flirt
sheet meet	slender spender
feather weather	trim limb

Word Display

Use the bulletin board to feature words in groups. A good way to emphasize knowledge of syllables and to stretch vocabularies is this display, called Five Syllables, using words that children have discovered. Naturally, children will be intrigued about the meaning of these different words. The person who discovers the word can print a short definition on the back of the leaf. If leaves are pinned on the tree, students can easily remove them while they read the definition and replace them when finished. Notice that emphasizing five-syllable words stresses prefixes and suffixes because that is one way of producing long words. Students will pore over the dictionary to discover words that begin with *un, pre, ex,* and other prefixes they know.

Compound Lingo

Compound Lingo is a bingo game with a twist. It will provide students with lots of fun, plus good exercise with compound words. The teacher can prepare in advance some cards in bingo form.

Let the children select the cards of their choice. Then inform them that you will read an unfinished sentence, and they must listen and try to see which word will fit the sentence. The twist in this game is that after each sentence is read, each player passes his or her card to the left, and continues the game on the card that was just passed. (It would be helpful to have the players sit in circles, either in small groups or as one class.) The first player to cover words in a straight line calls *Lingo,* and if all the answers are right, that player wins.

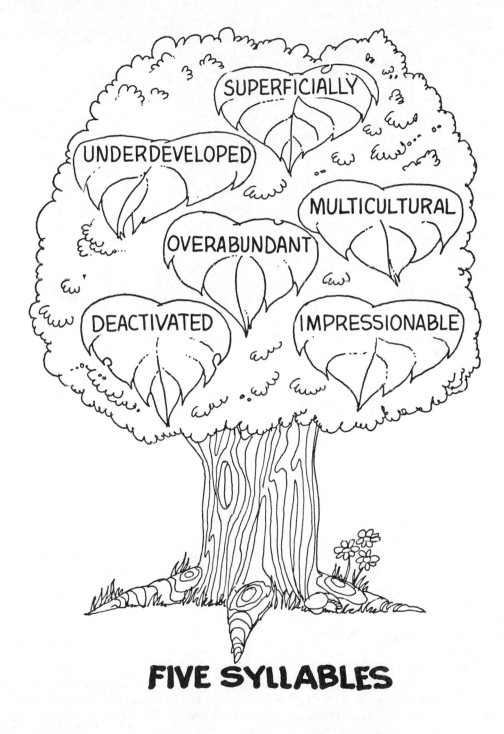

FIVE SYLLABLES

Examples:

bathtub	foursquare	toolbox
toothpaste	railroad	halfway
faraway	seaweed	washcloth
leapfrog	hardware	foxhole
farmland	pawnshop	moonlight
midday	automobile	popcorn

1. A tub that you can take a bath in is a _____.
2. Cleaning paste to scrub your teeth with is _____.
3. Looking away to a far place makes you look _____.
4. A game in which you leap like a frog is called _____.
5. Good land that you can farm is _____.
6. The middle of the day is sometimes called _____.
7. One ball game that four of you can play in a square is called _____.
8. A road that is built for the rails of a train is a _____.
9. A green weed that grows in the sea is _____.
10. The wares that you can buy to do hard work with are _____.
11. A shop in which you can pawn your goods is a _____.
12. A mobile that drives automatically is an _____.
13. Your tools can be stored in a box called a _____.
14. If you've gone only half of the way, you've gone _____.
15. A cloth to wash yourself with is a _____.
16. A hole for a fox to hide in is a _____.
17. The light that is shining from the moon is _____.
18. The corn kernels that can pop make _____.

Place the words in different arrangements for various Lingo cards. You'll also need to provide something for players to cover their words with. Hopefully, the children will learn the concept of "winning with the winner," since everyone is contributing to everyone else's cards.

Picturesque Words

Invite children to play with language as they observe the potentially funny meanings of compound words such as *horsefly* or *catfish*. They can create a humorous poster illustrating this type of play with words, as shown in the picture on page 77. Other words that you can suggest include *boardwalk* and *wristwatch*.

Have you ever seen a horse fly?

ANTics

ANTics is a good way to expand student vocabulary while having fun. You can play this game with the class divided into small groups or you can give each student a list of questions to fill in.

Student A: What kind of ant would you like to have?
    B: Plant. What kind of ant is something to wear?
    C: Pants. What kind of ant is something you would say?
    A: Chant. What kind of ant is on a diagonal?
    B: Slant. What ant means barely enough?
    C: Scant. What ant means something given?
    A: Grant.

Other words that can be used in a list are: *can't, rant,* and *implant.* You can also vary the game by encouraging the use of such words as *lantern, mantel, shanty, frantic, plantation,* and so on.

Giving the Students a Hand

Give students this quiz to increase their vocabulary. They will have fun figuring out the words to answer each question.

1. What you learn after you learn to print   Hand_____
2. A good-looking person is   Hand_____
3. Someone who is good at repairs around the house is   Hand_____
4. Something you did yourself is   Hand_____
5. When someone talks about you behind your back, you say they are _____hand_____
6. Clothes you get from your older brother or sister are   Hand_____ or _____hand
7. A very generous person is called   _____hand_____
8. When you hear about an event from someone who was there, the account is   _____hand
9. A person who works on a farm is a   _____hand
10. The square of material you use to blow your nose on is a   Hand_____
11. A purse is also a   Hand_____
12. What the police put on prisoners   Hand_____
13. Where you would look for information about the basic rules of behavior   Hand_____
14. Embroidery, needlepoint, and knitting are all   Hand_____
15. Someone who cannot see normally has a   Hand_____
16. If you stick your fingers in a bag of candy and pull out as much as you can hold, how much do you have?   Hand_____
17. What might you do if someone gives you what you most want in the world?   Hand_____

Students can make up quizzes like this using other words such as *pan* or *car*.

Answers:

1. handwriting
2. handsome
3. handyman
4. handmade
5. underhanded
6. hand-me-downs or second-hand
7. open-handed
8. firsthand
9. fieldhand
10. handkerchief
11. handbag
12. handcuffs
13. handbook
14. handicrafts, handiwork
15. handicap
16. handful
17. handsprings

Palindromes

A palindrome is a word that reads the same backward and forward. You have probably noticed some of these words, which are interesting to collect. Examples are:

level	Hannah
eye	madam

Even young children will be able to think of a number of palindromes.

Mom	dud	Bub	pop
did	bib	Bob	nun
Dad	Sis	gag	pep
wow	Nan	tot	tat

Some less common examples are:

Anna	radar
ewe	kayak
deified	

A clever use of palindromes is to create sentences that read the same forward and backward. Some examples are:

- Able was I ere I saw Elba
- Madam I'm Adam
- A man, a plan, a canal: Panama!
- Too bad I hid a boot.

IXOHOXI

This palindrome by W. R. Crittenden is the ultimate: it reads the same backwards, forwards, upside down, and reflected in a mirror!

Word Puzzles

Keep a file of interesting and unusual language puzzles on cards for students to answer. (Newspaper columns are often a good source of examples.) Paste the questions on cards and put the answers on the back for students to check.

Students can work on these individually or in pairs. They can also bring in their own examples to share with the class. Start with the following examples:

- What sentence reads the same backward and forward?

  RISE TO VOTE, SIR
- What sentence reads the same upside down?

  NOW NO SWIMS ON MON

  James Thurber

- What is the longest word in the English language?

  pneumonoultramicroscopicsilicovolcanoconiosis
- Reconstruct this English word: the first two letters signify a male; the first three letters signify a female; the first four letters signify a great man; and the whole word signifies a great woman.

  heroine

- What word, when printed in capitals, reads the same forward, backward, and upside down?

  NOON

- What five words, written in capitals, read the same forward, backward, and in the mirror?

  TOOT   WOW   MOM   TOT   OTTO

Root Families

Groups of words are related in meaning through their root. Students can expand their vocabularies just by learning a few common Latin and Greek roots. Give them a root and a few examples and see how many other words they can find, as shown here:

ped—Gr. foot	*port*—L. move
pedestrian	import
pedestal	transportation
impede	portable
scribe—L. write	*graph*—Gr. write
inscription	autograph
scribble	grapheme
prescribe	graphic

You can also give them definitions of several words with the same root and have them figure out the meaning of the root.

- Pentagon—a figure with five sides
- Pentangle—a five-pointed star
- Pentameter—a line of verse with five feet

Word Challenge

Give the class a word and ask them to write down as many words of five or more letters they can find within the given word. For example, in the word *improvisation* the following shorter words can be found:

impart	provision	stair	vision
import	ration	strain	visit
maroon	smart	strap	visor
mason	snort	strip	
ovation	spoon	tapir	
piston	sport	train	

The Word Tree

This bulletin board display will arouse interest in word families. Use a large tree shape for the display, and at the bottom place a root word such as *Scribe* written on a piece of construction paper. Branches of the tree hold examples of English words derived from this Latin root: *describe, inscribe, prescribe, subscribe, transcribe,* and *scribble.* Students can discover new examples of derivatives to add to the tree.

There are many common Greek and Latin roots for you to explore with the class. Some of these are:

- *Auto:* automatic, automobile, autobiography, autograph
- *Mal:* malady, malpractice, maladjusted, maltreated, malice
- *Photo:* photogenic, photography, photosynthesis, photosensitive

Students can sometimes figure out what the root words mean from the words derived from them.

An excellent book to use with the students when discussing roots and word origins is *Word Origins and Their Romantic Stories* by Wilfred Funk, available in most public libraries. You may want to have a copy available for students to examine. This book lists many Greek and Latin roots and their derivatives.

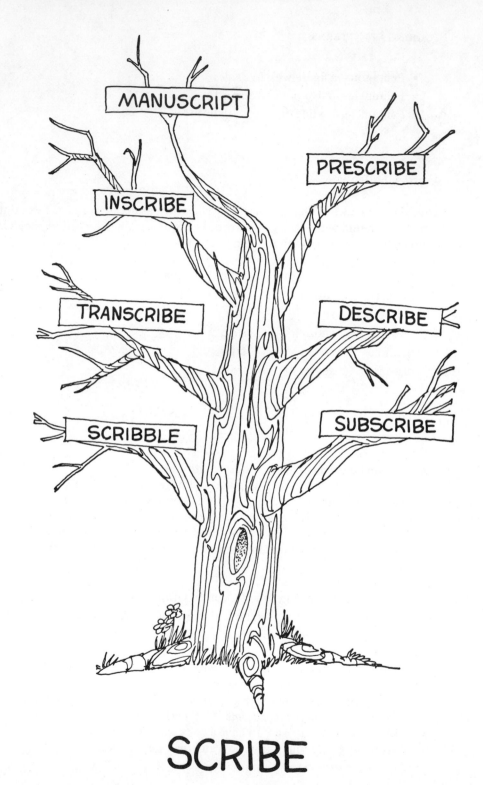

SCRIBE

Root!

Make sets of four cards based on roots and derived words; for example:

- *scope:* telescope, microscope, periscope, stethoscope
- *graph:* phonograph, photograph, telegraph, autograph
- *meter:* diameter, perimeter, kilometer, millimeter
- *cent:* century, centigrade, percent, centipede

A set of fifty-two cards is enough for four players to play Root. This game is played like Fish, with each player trying to complete sets of four cards which are laid down as a book. Each player in turn calls for the root desired, for example, *graph,* while other players turn over the cards that go in that set.

A more complicated version of Root requires students to pronounce each word by asking for a specific card. Holding the card below, a player might ask, "Teresa, do you have *equinox* from the *equi* family?"

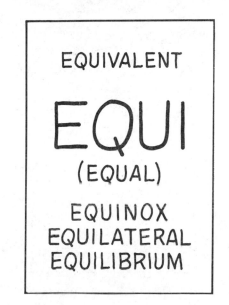

Prefix-Root Wheel

Help students build vocabulary by manipulating a Prefix-Root Wheel. As students move the prefixes, they will form such words as *pretend, discover,* or *unfold.* Make the outside wheel nine inches in diameter. The inside wheel is five inches across.

Students will learn a lot by making these wheels themselves. They need to use the dictionary to check on possible words because not all combinations form new words. They will encounter new words such as *depose* and *deduce.*

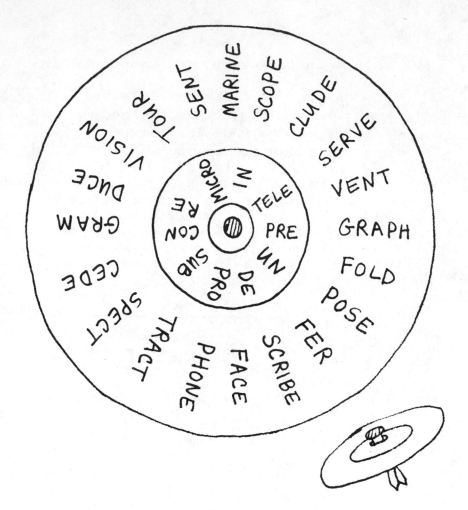

Long Words

sesquipedalian
sesquicentennial
hippopotomonstrousesquipedalian
pneumonoultramicroscopicsilicovolcanoconiosis
floccinancinihilipilification
antidisestablishmentarianism

The Con Game

This game reviews prefixes orally and helps develop vocabulary. A class leader says a prefix, and then quickly counts to 100, while a student names as many words as possible that begin with that prefix. The leader might say *con,* for example, and then point to a student. The student then names words like *convict, contender, conduit,* and *conclusion.*

The class can be divided into teams and the score can be kept by counting one point for each word mentioned. Make a list of common prefixes to use during the game. Lists of words beginning with prefixes can also be developed.

Here is a useful list of prefixes for such activities as The Con Game.

auto	ob
bene	post
contra, counter	pre
de	proto
ex	re
fore	sub
im, in	semi
mis	trans
multi	un

Inventing Scientific Words

Students can participate in the delight of developing a word that is just right for something. Talk about important scientific inventions and what they are called. How was the name invented? If it comes from Latin or Greek roots, what do the roots mean?

Many inventions expand on the possibilities introduced by previous inventions. The *telephone* was an example of the expansion of communication, an advance over the *telegraph,* and *television* was a step beyond. Talk about current popular gadgets and mechanisms, such as calculators and transmitters. What possible future inventions might grow out of these? What might these inventions be called?

How do science-fiction writers invent words for their strange and unusual gadgets? If students are creating a realistic-sounding story of the future, it is important to have "real" sounding names for things. Give students lists of useful prefixes, roots, and endings; for example:

manu	graph	istic	trans
andro	port	tion	able
neo	fact	ness	bio
sub	scope	ator	
phobia	bio	ology	

The following paperback books list words that "don't exist but should." Use them to inspire students to create their own examples.

Rich Hall and friends, *Sniglets* (New York: Collier/Macmillan, 1984).
Rich Hall and friends, *More Sniglets* (New York: Collier/Macmillan, 1985).
Rich Hall and friends, *Unexplained Sniglets of the Universe* (New York: Collier/Macmillan, 1986).

Teaching Orthography

Most students will not be familiar with the scholarly word for spelling, *orthography.* Teach orthography for a change in your classroom, just to break the monotony of routine. Begin by discussing the meaning of this word, "the art of spelling words according to accepted usage."

Students can also examine the two parts of this word that come from the Greek language. *Ortho* means "straight, upright, correct." This element appears in many other English words, for example:

orthodontist	orthodox
orthopedics	orthogenesis

Graphy is used to describe some form of "drawing, writing, or recording." This root word is used widely in words that students may know, for example:

geography	biography
photography	autobiography
choreography	lithography

Other related words that use the root *graph* include:

graphics	grapheme
graphite	graphic

An intriguing book that serves as a launching pad for activities that encourage children to explore their language is *Ounce Dice Trice* (Atlantic Monthly Press, 1958) by Alastair Reid. Here is an author who has a feeling for words and the pleasures entailed in exploring them; he encourages the reader to look at words in unusual ways such as in a mirror or backwards, and sets them the example of inventing new words and fascinating phrases such as: "A Humbuggle of Packages, A Gundulum of Garbage Cans, A Scribbitch of Papers, A Tumbletell of Church Bells, A Snigglement of String, A Tribulation of Children."

THE SEARCH FOR MEANING

Although meaning is central to any discussion of vocabulary, the term disguises a variety of complex tasks. Not only must students pick their way through multiple meanings of the same word, but they must also learn the subtle differences in usage among synonyms.

The activities presented in this section provide opportunities for students to try out the new words they are learning. As a result:

- Students will locate the appropriate word meaning in a dictionary.
- Students will put word meanings in their own words.
- Students will list synonyms and antonyms.
- Students will determine the relationship between pairs of words, or among words in a series.
- Students will research origins of words.

My First Dictionary

Early primary students will enjoy creating personalized dictionaries to illustrate new vocabulary words. On each page, have them put the word, a simple definition (created by the class), and a picture (drawn or cut out). These dictionaries can be prepared individually or as a class, with each student contributing a particular word. Putting the pages in order as new words are added throughout the year is good practice in alphabetizing. Future writing activities can be based on the words in these dictionaries.

The Month Dictionary

Each month is characterized in many different ways: by the color that the month is indicative of (Spring—green—April), the holidays of each month, school activities, and so on. This idea can be used to help increase students' vocabulary and can also be used as a good writing resource for writing stories.

The class can make a dictionary that is divided into the months of the school year. Within each month, words can be included that have something to do with that month; and the paper used can be the color that the month is characterized by. Words can be added to the lists according to the needs of the children or their interests. Children should be encouraged to use this dictionary as a writing tool and also as an alternative dictionary. The words listed may also have a simple definition next to them. Example:

January (white)	February (gray)	April (purple)
winter	homework	Easter
weather	blizzard	vacation
New Year's Day	education	spring
school	chimney	renewal

In Other Words

Instead of having students write out the dictionary definition of words, have them use their own words to explain new words.

Give students sentences like the one below and ask them to rewrite the sentence so that it is easier to understand.

- The servant smiled *obsequiously* at his master.
- The servant smiled *in a sickeningly respectful way* at his master.

The Dictionary Game

Students learn to use their knowledge of word meanings and dictionaries in this challenging game of definitions. Have the students divide into groups of about five. Each group selects a leader to begin playing. The leader uses the dictionary to choose a short, simple word that no one knows, for example, *hovel*. (You may prefer to hand out a list of possible words to choose from in order to save time.) The leader reads the word to the group members and asks them to write down a suggested definition, while he or she writes the correct one. Guesses usually range from obvious to outrageous. Set a time limit and have the leader collect all the definitions. The leader then reads the definitions aloud, including the real dictionary definition, and the group votes on which definition they think is right. After everyone has voted, the leader surprises the group by telling them which definition was from the dictionary. One point is awarded to the leader for each person who did *not* guess correctly and also to the member(s) who fooled someone with a definition. Two points are awarded to the person who guesses the *correct* definition. Then a new leader is chosen to begin the next round.

Besides encouraging dictionary use and vocabulary development, this game challenges students to make intelligent guesses about the meaning of words, and rewards them for writing definitions that sound like reasonable dictionary entries. You can adjust this game to play with the whole class if you keep the number of suggested definitions small. Vary the difficulty of the game by choosing longer or shorter words. In general, the shorter words are more difficult because there are fewer clues to their meaning. For example:

Hovel:

1. a tool used to place cement around tiles
2. a small, miserable dwelling
3. to humble yourself in front of others
4. adjective used to describe someone who makes strange faces

---

An intriguing book of curious words (like *gerrymander*) and their origins is *The Abecedarian Book* by Charles Ferguson (Boston: Little, Brown, 1964).

A Herd of Children

We all use different words for groups of particular objects without thinking. Have students list examples of phrases we use all the time, for example:

- School of fish
- Herd of elephants
- Flock of birds
- Pack of wolves

Some less common terms you might add include:

- Rabble of butterflies
- Pride of lions
- Covey of quail
- Gaggle of geese
- Brace of partridge

Once the students understand the idea of these terms for groups, invite them to think up their own. Start them out by giving them phrases to fill in:

- A _____ of teeth
- A huddle of _____
- A _____ of students
- An entanglement of _____
- A _____ of dragons
- A shushing of _____
- A _____ of penguins

After this stimulating beginning, they will be eager to think of their own unique examples. Have them illustrate their suggestions for a display that others can appreciate. Maybe your class will think of a term that everyone will adopt.

An Exaltation of Larks by James Lipton (Penguin, 1984) contains a multitude of examples of these group words, with illustrations. Students will enjoy poring over the book and discovering unusual phrases.

Go-Together Words

Ask students if they can guess a word that goes with each example given here:

- day and _____
- father and _____
- knife and _____
- table and _____
- back and _____

Can they think of other Go-Together Words? Have them create more examples to try out on the class.

Seeing Relationships

Students are accustomed to sequences of words in alphabetical order or to numbers that have clear relationships, for example: 1, 3, 5, 7. Provide exercises in which one word, letter, or number is omitted to see if the students can supply what is missing based on the relationship they see.

- a e i __ u
- 1 2 4 8 __
- apple bear candy _____ elephant
- farm cow zoo tiger ocean _____
- cub bear _____ duck colt horse
- lazy industrious happy _____ old young
- bone crowd baby corn _____ cork
- O T T F F S S E __ T

Answers:

(o)   (duckling)
(16)   (sad)
(any word that begins with *d*)   (any word beginning with *b*)
(any animal seen in the ocean)   (N; letters begin words for numbers 1–10)

Word Webbing

Illustrate the ramifications of a word by writing the word in the center of the board and drawing a circle around it. Ask students to suggest related words. Place examples provided by students around the circle and draw lines to connect related words.

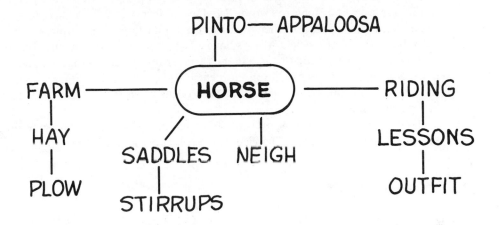

This graphic representation of a word helps students remember new words and incorporate these words into their working vocabulary. Use this activity regularly in your reading program to expand student awareness of multiple meanings.

Ways of Saying

Tell the students that they can't use the words *say* and *said* for a day. Brainstorm lists of possible substitutes. Encourage students to use the thesaurus, a dictionary of synonyms.

whisper	mutter	shout
holler	cry	murmur
call	question	complain
ask	grumble	giggle
proclaim	assert	promise

Another word that could be retired is *walk*. Have students suggest synonyms. Students then choose a synonym to act out, and challenge the class to guess which word best describes their *walk*.

Thesaurus

This book is invaluable because it contains lists of synonyms for most common words. The word *thesaurus* means *treasure* in Latin, so this book is a *treasury of words,* a synonym dictionary.

Pass a copy of a thesaurus around the class and discuss how the book is organized. Some editions have the words listed by subject, so that you have to look up the word in the index first and then find it in the book. Others are alphabetical and are used like other dictionaries. Always have a copy available to students for use during writing periods or to look through in their spare time. Students may also be interested in purchasing a paperback edition for themselves. A class set or at least a set of ten inexpensive editions is recommended in classrooms from fourth grade up for vocabulary development.

A good beginning thesaurus is *In Other Words* by W. Cabell Greer, William Jenkins, and Andrew Schiller (Glenview, Ill.: Scott, Foresman, 1968).

Making a Class Thesaurus

After the class has been introduced to the use of a thesaurus, have students compile a personal version for class use. Each student can take one word that has been overused in class writing and develop a list of synonyms for it. Examples are:

big	nice
red	good
girl	like
run	old

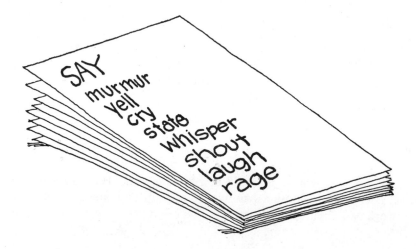

Collect the individual pages and staple them together in alphabetical order for a Class Thesaurus. Make sure that all the words included are useful ones. Then encourage students to consult the thesaurus and share their words. They will learn more from compiling their own synonym dictionary than if they had copied lists of words from another source.

The Synonym Wheel

One way to display synonyms is on a large wagon-wheel shape on the bulletin board. Cut a wheel from brown paper or use a real wheel, if you can get one. At the center, place a common word such as *little*. Have the students write synonyms—*small, tiny, diminutive, miniscule, petite*—for this overworked word on slips of paper and mount them on the spokes and the rim of the wheel. New words can be featured on the wheel as you study vocabulary for reading and writing. Other words to use are: *big, pretty, run, say,* and *good*.

Attach the paper wheel to the bulletin board with a thumbtack so students can turn the wheel to read new synonyms. Display a different synonym every week, helping students find new words to use instead of the common ones. Make sure that students understand the differences between the synonyms (connotations) and the proper contexts for their use by illustrating the words in sentences until students are comfortable with the new words.

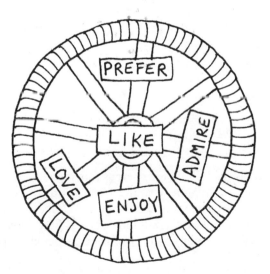

Color Me Red

Color words are useful for students of all ages. Have the class work in small groups to brainstorm all the synonyms for one color, for example, red, yellow, blue, or green.

Notice all the different shades of red that are listed here:

scarlet	ruby	claret
vermilion	garnet	russet
crimson	maroon	magenta
cerise	rust	carmine

When students write after this exercise, they will be able to use less common adjectives to provide a more exact picture for the reader.

Words, when well chosen, have so great a force in them that a description often gives us more lively ideas than the sight of things themselves.

JOSEPH ADDISON, *The Spectator* No. 416

Antonyms

Antonyms are pairs of opposites. Students are very familiar with sets of opposites. Think of as many pairs as you can.

over—under	tall—short	rich—poor
old—new	thick—thin	slow—fast
full—empty	cheap—expensive	happy—sad

Antonyms can be expressed in the form of a ratio, as shown here:

$$\frac{old}{new} :: \frac{thin}{?}$$

The ratio is read: "Old is to new as thin is to _____?" The first step in solving the ratio is to determine what the relationship is between the first two words. Since they are opposites, the second pair must be opposites as well. The answer may be *thick* or a synonym of *thick,* or it might be *fat.* In some cases, there are many right answers when there are many synonyms for a particular opposite.

$$\frac{add}{subtract} :: \frac{?}{little}$$

Here the answer could be *big, gigantic, immense, large, huge,* or *tremendous.*

Jigsaw Opposites

Students can practice using opposites with this game. Select a simple jigsaw picture puzzle and turn it over. On the pieces write pairs of opposites so that the opposites touch. When the students play the game, they try to match the opposites to complete the puzzle. When finished, they turn the puzzle over, and they will have a complete picture.

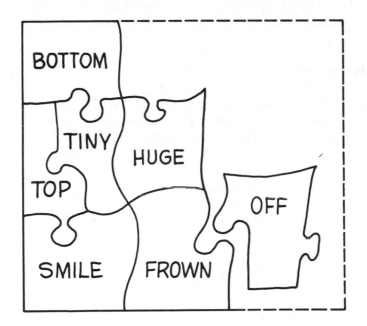

Word Volleyball

Pupils line up in two rows so that they are facing one another. The first group starts out by giving a word such as *good*. Then the first person on the other side must give a synonym for the word *good* such as *excellent*. Then, as in volleyball, the ball or word is passed back to the first team, and they must think of another synonym for *good*. These words, then, are bounced back and forth until one group cannot give a synonym. If you wish to score in this game, the team giving the last synonym would have a point. (You may need to enforce a time limit for answering and have a judge to decide if words are acceptable.) The group that was successful in coming up with the last synonym selects a new word, and play continues again.

This game can also be used for antonyms of the same words or word chains. It can be played without keeping score but with the two teams seeing how long they can keep the "volley" going.

Warm—Hot—Boiling!

This activity requires students to determine the relationship between the words given in order to choose the correct word to complete the sequence.

- cool, warm, _____   (*tepid, hot, cold*)
- sand, pebble, _____   (*mountain, rock, salt*)
- large, gigantic, _____   (*enormous, big, small*)
- tree, sapling, _____   (*forest, seed, pine*)

Playing with Words

There are many interesting ways to represent words. Here we are exploring the meaning of the word through illustration. Encourage students to discover new ways to represent the meaning of their favorite words.

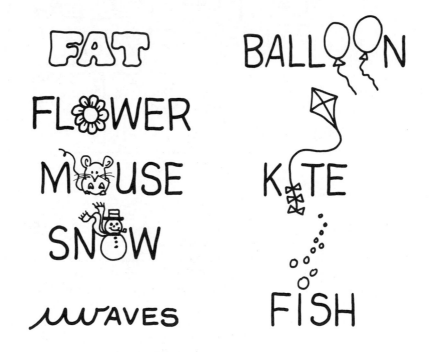

Borrowed Words

One way to encourage vocabulary development is to introduce the students to the many words in English that are borrowed from other languages. Develop this aspect of language in connection with the study of a particular country or language as you feature words borrowed from that language.

For the study of French words, place a map or outline of France on the bulletin board. To this map attach yarn leading to words mounted on pieces of paper around the bulletin board. Possible words to display include:

chic	nation	azure
cuisine	liqueur	ennui
embarrass	à la mode	ballet
compliment	silhouette	

Discuss how borrowed French words are sometimes pronounced differently than English words. An example is *massage* in which the final sound (spelled *g*) is different than it is in *message*. Here are two phonemes: /j/ and /ž/. For *garage* you may hear people using either of these phonemes. The word *page* has been completely anglicized so only /j/ is used by speakers of English. Words that were borrowed from French recently show less adjustment to the usual patterns of English pronunciation than those borrowed some time ago.

Have a small group of students create a world map illustrated with borrowed words from many different countries. Encourage them to discover words from such unexpected languages as Japanese (bonsai), Hindi (khaki), and Dutch (yacht). The students will also enjoy figuring out where some of these languages are spoken.

- Celtic—clan, whiskey
- Spanish—cargo, alligator
- Aztec (by way of Spanish)—tomato, chocolate
- Dutch—cruise, landscape
- Persian—bazaar, caravan, sugar
- Arabic syrup, algebra
- Hindi—bungalow, shampoo
- Russian—samovar, steppe
- Italian—cello, crescendo

Acronyms Create Words

Some acronyms have become words and are no longer capitalized. The most familiar example is *radar,* originally from *radio detecting and ranging.* Many of us have forgotten that these words were once acronyms. Other such examples are:

- Laser—*l*ight *a*mplification by *s*timulated *e*mission *o*f *r*adiation
- Snafu—*s*ituation *n*ormal: *a*ll *f*ouled *u*p

- Scuba—*self*-*c*ontained *u*nderwater *b*reathing *a*pparatus
- Loran—*l*ong *ra*nge *n*avigation
- Sonar—*s*ound *n*avigation *a*nd *r*anging

Through the Looking Glass by Lewis Carroll

". . . There's glory for you!"

"I don't know what you mean by 'glory,'" Alice said.

Humpty Dumpty smiled contemptuously, "Of course you don't— till I tell you. I meant, 'There's a nice knock-down argument for you!'"

"But 'glory' doesn't mean 'a nice knock-down argument,'" Alice objected.

"When I use a word," Humpty-Dumpty said in rather a scornful tone, "it means just what I choose it to mean, neither more nor less."

"The question is," said Alice, "whether you can make words mean so many different things."

"The question is," said Humpty-Dumpty, "which is to be Master—that's all."

New English Words

Have students prepare a list of words that are new in the English language. Many that have been invented during their lifetimes include:

debug	sol (a day on Mars)
waterbed	marsquake
byte	yuppie
frisbie	hacker
splashdown	chip

Word People

The following English words all come from someone's name. Challenge students to research how these words originated.

- Diesel—Rudolph Diesel
- Guillotine—Dr. Joseph Ignace Guillotin

- Leotard—Jules Léotard
- Nicotine—Jean Nicot
- Sandwich—John Montagu, 4th Earl of Sandwich
- Silhouette—Étienne de Silhouette

Invented Words

Invite your students to try to match these words with the authors that created them. (Answers are at the bottom of this page.)

1. scrooge   a. Francois Rabelais
2. ogre   b. Karel Capek
3. robot   c. Charles Perrault
4. moron   d. Molière
5. gargantuan   e. Charles Dickens
6. serendipity   f. Horace Walpole

Crossword Magic
L & S Computerware
All Apples, Atari (graphics printer required)
Grades 1 and up, depending on content

This program allows the teacher to create a crossword puzzle with words and clues of the teacher's choosing. It provides a fast and easy way to develop and use crossword puzzles in all subject areas.

Creating New Words

Using made-up words to spur children in creative writing is a good way to bring out the individuality in every child, since the more conventional titles (i.e., happiness, friendship, etc.) sometimes bring very conventional compositions.

Write the made-up word on the board and pronounce it for the students. Have them think about the word through their senses: What does it smell like? Can you eat

Answers: (1—e, 2—c, 3—b, 4—d, 5—a, 6—f)

it? What does it taste like? How does it feel on your cheeks? Does it make a noise? Can you do anything with it? Here are some sample words:

shoop   oversnod
glunch   jengier
salagango   poubalistic
erpted

Commercial Word Games

There are many word games on the market today that will aid students in building vocabulary and reading comprehension.

- UPWORDS (Milton Bradley, $14.95, 2–4 players)
  In this crossword game, players earn extra points by stacking new letters on previously played words to create new words.

  L   P̄
  M A K E   M A K E
  K   N̄
  E   E

- WORD CHESS (Enigmatics, $12.95, 2 players)
  Players place or move four tiles each turn so that words are formed diagonally. The game ends when a player moves an X to the last rank, or captures the opponent's X by surrounding it.

- IPSWICH (Selchow & Righter, $19.95, 2–4 players)
  All players create a crossword pattern on individual boards within a certain time limit. Bonus points are scored for long words and special squares. The letter tiles can also be used to play anagrams.

- BALI (Avalon Hill, $6.50, 1–4 players)
  Players collect letter cards which are combined into strings and finally into words. Words are scored by multiplying the number of letters by the total point value. Players saving strings to make longer words (MENT) risk losing the letter strings to an opponent who can use them first.

- BIG BOGGLE (Parker Brothers, $18.95, 2 or more players)
  Good large-group game. The 5 × 5 box of letter cubes is shaken and a time limit set for noting words formed by adjacent letters. Points are scored only for unique words.

- DUPLICATE SCRABBLE BRAND CROSSWORD GAME (Selchow & Righter, $10.95, 1 or more players)
  Each player has a score sheet to try and plan for future use of high-scoring tiles and bonus squares.

5 Reading, Literature, and Children

*Read, mark, learn and
inwardly digest.*
BOOK OF COMMON PRAYER

It is with good reason that teaching reading and learning through reading take up most of the school day. With an increasing awareness of the interconnectedness of reading and the language arts, plus renewed interest in reading as comprehension, it is vital that we have access to strategies that enable us to implement these concepts.

This chapter is divided into three sections. The first covers word recognition, auditory/visual discrimination, and general readiness skills. We next look at activities to develop and test students' comprehension of material they read. The third section provides strategies for presenting literature in the classroom. As a result of these activities:

- Students will associate printed words with their sound.
- Students will understand what they read, on both literal and inferential levels.
- Students will read literature for information and pleasure.

READING READINESS

Learning how to read is founded on a variety of crucial skills. Students need adequate preparation and practice in skills such as auditory and visual discrimination before they can begin to associate letter symbols and sounds. With the following activities, you can help students make the leap from speaking the language to unraveling the intricacies of print. As a result of the activities in this section:

- Students will distinguish between different sounds.
- Students will identify letters and sounds associated with them.
- Students will recognize the same sound in different words.
- Students will match rhyming words.
- Students will link blends/digraphs with phonograms.
- Students will categorize consonants and vowels.
- Students will list sight words.

Same or Different?

One of the first steps in learning to read is to learn to distinguish different sounds. Students also learn to recognize the same sound when it occurs in different words. Give them practice in auditory discrimination by providing oral/aural exercises. Read a series of words as they listen carefully to the sounds in the words. Have them clap their hands or stand up when they hear the word or words that answer your question.

- Which word begins with a sound that is different from the first sound in *corner?*
  cat
  cuddle
  teapot
  cotton
- Which words have the same vowel sound as in *met?*
  lend
  sat
  pen
  roar
- Which words end in the same sound as *flash?*
  dish
  jest
  reached
  wash
  glass

To make this exercise more difficult, you can include contrasts such as final *k* versus *g* or *t* versus *d,* and vowel differences such as short *i* versus long *e.*

The Collector

Label brown lunchbags with a beginning consonant sound. In each bag place an object that begins with that sound or a picture of an object. The bag labeled "B" might include a book and a balloon, along with pictures of birds, butterflies, and bats.

   Attach the bags to the bulletin board and encourage students to contribute objects and pictures. Give a "Collector" reward to the student who contributes the most items or the most unusual object/picture.

Focus on Rhymes

Students' awareness of word sounds, as in rhyme and alliteration, can help them develop the auditory discrimination necessary for effective reading. Use the following activities to focus student interest on similar and different sounds:

- How many words can you name that rhyme with *least?*
- In this list of rhyming words, which one doesn't fit?
  flank, prank, rang, sank
- How many words can you name that begin with the same sound as *chime?*
- What sound does your name begin with? Name some words that begin with the same sound.
- What sound does your name end with? Name some words that end with the same sound.

Auditory Discrimination

For a quick review of auditory skills, read the students a list of words in which you include one word that does not fit. Ask them to tell you the word that doesn't belong.

pound	found	long	round

   To introduce students to this exercise, begin with rhyming work. Increase the difficulty of the task as they gain experience and confidence.

loaf	cough	if	bat
blade	mend	sweet	time

These lists can be put on tape and kept in a Listening Center for independent review. Provide answer sheets and an answer key so that students can work alone or in small groups.

Answers: long; bat; mend (not a long vowel)

Visual Discrimination

Ask your local library or senior center to save old copies of large-print newspapers. Give each student a page, a crayon, and an activity like the following:

- Circle all words beginning with *f.*
- Circle all the words that are plurals.
- Underline all the words that begin like *bassoon.*
- Circle all the capital letters.
- Draw a box around the words with prefixes.
- Draw a line to divide all the compound words.

Letter Discrimination

To help students distinguish similar letters, prepare a ditto with outline drawings of the letters *p, q, b,* and *d.* Ask students to color the vertical stems a light color and the curved parts a darker color. Students will then be able to see more clearly the direction the letters should be. Use the same colors to make large chalk letters on the board and ask the students questions: "Who can point to the *p* that starts *pig?*" "Who can point to the letter that begins *baseball?*"

The Library of Congress now grows by two volumes a second.

Letters with Texture

Familiarize students with letter shapes and sounds by making a nameplate for each student. Form the letters by dribbling glue on oaktag, then sprinkling sand or glitter over the glue. The raised letters appeal to students and the texture encourages them to trace the letter shapes repeatedly.

Labels for objects or pictures can be prepared in this fashion and mounted where students can feel the letters. Have the students copy the words on a piece of paper.

Learning the Letter Symbols

The purpose of this activity is to help students recognize the letters of the alphabet. This is obviously an important concept for all students to learn. After students learn any five letters through this color-keyed activity, use the same technique as you gradually add all twenty-six letters. Later directions might read: *Make* A, G, M, *and* Z *red.*

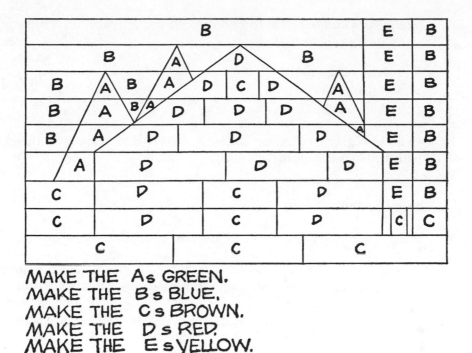

MAKE THE As GREEN.
MAKE THE Bs BLUE.
MAKE THE Cs BROWN.
MAKE THE Ds RED.
MAKE THE Es YELLOW.

Alphabetical Order

Provide a variety of activities to help children learn how to alphabetize.

- Make sets of capital letters and small letters. Have students match the pairs and then put them in order.
- Place a set of alphabet cards in mixed order on a table, and have the youngsters arrange them in correct order. Children can work in pairs as one shuffles the cards and the other puts them in order with his or her partner doing the checking.
- Put letters on a flannel board and have youngsters put them in the correct order.
- Have cut-out letters arranged on an overhead projector in a mixed-up manner. Students can put the letters in order as they are projected. This can be done in small groups, as all students will be eager to see their letters projected on the screen.

ABC Books

A variation on the usual alphabet format is *Pooh's Alphabet Book* (New York: Dutton, 1975) which uses humorous quotations from A. A. Milne's *Pooh* books to illustrate the letters of the alphabet. This example can stimulate student interest in preparing similar ABC books that focus on specific characters or familiar literature, as in the following examples:

- Henry Huggins' ABC's
- Aslan's Narnia
- Authors, Books, Characters

As students generate ideas for special projects in collecting ABCs, they will also be motivated to read more in these areas.

Initial Sounds

Young children need lots of practice associating sounds and symbols. Try these ideas.

- Print a large *T* on the board. Give the children five minutes to name words that begin with *T.* Everybody takes a turn suggesting words that are then printed on the board: *toy, turtle, top, table, television, telephone, tadpole,* and so on.
- Print a large *D* on the board. Again, give the children five minutes to name words that begin with the *D* sound, but this time every word must contain more than four letters. More advanced students can suggest *dandelion, determine, disaster, decorate, destination, diamond,* and so on.

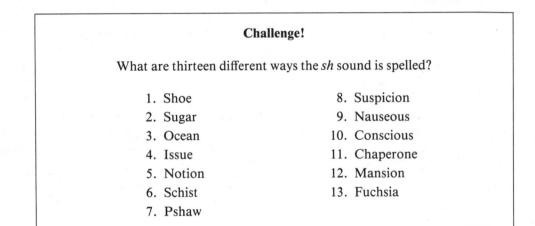

Challenge!

What are thirteen different ways the *sh* sound is spelled?

1. Shoe
2. Sugar
3. Ocean
4. Issue
5. Notion
6. Schist
7. Pshaw
8. Suspicion
9. Nauseous
10. Conscious
11. Chaperone
12. Mansion
13. Fuchsia

Focus on the Phoneme

Constructing word lists helps develop students' spelling abilities as well as vocabularies. Challenge students to think of words beginning with a particular sound. Small groups of students can work together with the dictionary to add words to their list.

This is an excellent word game for practicing spelling as students learn to pay attention to alternate spellings that represent the same sound.

Have the students think of many words beginning with the letter *c*. Then group these words into those pronounced with the /s/ sound and those with a /k/ sound.

	C	
/s/		/k/
cent		cow
cinnamon		caught
cellar		cabbage
cement		cucumber
center		cold
cypress		concrete
cipher		cuff
cylinder		crime
ceiling		climb

As students observe these words, have them make a generalization about these spellings, for example:

- *C* represents the /s/ phoneme before the letters *i, e,* and *y.*
- *C* represents the /k/ phoneme before *o, a, u,* and in the blends *cl* and *cr.*

Important Consonants

Show students how essential consonants are in the structure of a word. Print long words on the board omitting the vowels, thus:

__r__thm__t__c

g__ __gr__ph__

__ __t__m__b__l__

Most of the students in an upper elementary classroom will be able to identify these words rather quickly as *arithmetic, geography,* and *automobile.* This exercise demonstrates how important consonants are in helping children read words. It also points out the structure of the spelling pattern.

For an interesting experiment, print this message on the board without saying anything to the class. See what happens.

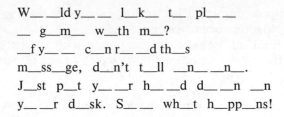

W__ __ld y__ __ l__k__ t__ pl__ __
__ g__m__ w__th m__?
__f y__ __ c__n r__ __d th__s
m__ss__ge, d__n't t__ll __n__ __n__.
J__st p__t y__ __r h__ __d d__ __n __n
y__ __r d__sk. S__ __ wh__t h__pp__ns!

Working with Short Vowels

Encourage beginning spellers to become more aware of the simple vowel sounds in short words by developing a chart like this:

	a	e	i	o	u
hit					
pan					
ten					
him					
sang					
lock					
slip					

Children can fill in the chart as they test the vowel sounds to see if new words can be found. None of the words will work in all slots, so there will always be some empty spots. In the first list, for example, children can insert: *hat, hit, hot,* and *hut.* (Someone may try to make a case for *het,* but you can always use the dictionary as the final test.)

Making Rhyme Lists

Developing rhyme lists is an excellent way of becoming aware of variations in spelling. Using a common phonogram, students can insert consonants in the initial position to test whether a word is created.

Teach children to go through the alphabet as they test these words. The letters marked out are not consonant sounds, or else they repeat sounds.

x̶ b x̶ d x̶ f g h x̶ j k l m
n x̶ p q(u) r s t x̶ v w x̶ y z

Using a regularly spelled phonogram *at,* ask students to say these combinations to themselves. Some are words to be listed; others are nonsense syllables and would be ignored.

bat	jat	pat	vat
dat	kat (cat)	quat	wat
fat	lat	rat	yat
gat	mat	sat	zat
hat	nat (gnat)	tat	

Blends and Digraphs

Further development of these rhyme lists includes trying blends and digraphs. Provide students with a chart like this:

bl	fl	sl	str
br	gl	sm	spr
cl	gr	sn	tr
cr	pl	st	ch
dr	sc	sw	sh
			th

As students try these blends and digraphs with the phonogram *at,* they can add *brat, flat, scat, Sprat* (Jack), *chat,* and *that* to their lists.

Chain "Letters"

This activity gives students the chance to work on initial consonants and medial vowels. Each child can observe this "chain" individually, and create a variety of combinations between the consonant letter and the phonogram. Two strips of tagboard, 3½ x 9 inches, should be made. On one strip print phonograms, and on the other print initial consonants (see the example). Make loops with both of these strips and link them together so that the letters face the reader. Then move either circle so that different combinations of words and sounds can be made.

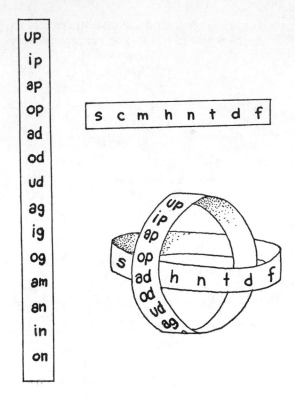

Developing Word Attack Skills

As students learn to read and spell consonant blends, prepare a tape of words that begins with the common blends. Ask students to write just the first two letters that begin each word. This practice helps children learn to attack words they don't know how to spell when they are writing. Deliberately include words that children probably don't know how to spell, as in this list:

spindle	broadcast
sniffle	blastoff
snapdragon	frizzy
slippery	flicker
grasshopper	pretend
glutton	transplant

Encourage students to try spelling the rest of the word without fear of making mistakes. Have a list available to which they can refer to see how close their guesses were.

> *Reading with Your Child: Number One Priority* by Jane Ervin (available in lots of thirty from Allyn and Bacon) includes practical and flexible ideas for parents to make reading rewarding for their children.

Vowel Sounds

Using a chart is helpful in teaching the basic relationships between the vowel sounds. Display this chart prominently so that students can refer to it when they are confused. Be sure to explain that these sounds are not the only ones associated with these letters.

	Long	Short	Followed by *r*
a	cake	bat	far
e	bee	net	her
i	nice	mitt	fir
o	so	mop	for
u	use	fun	purr

Use this chart to help students learn that one letter can represent three different sounds. From this base you can proceed to the study of other vowel sounds.

Y as a Vowel

Some charts list *y* as a vowel. This is confusing to students because *y* is also a consonant. As a vowel, the letter *y* can represent three phonemes: long *i*, short *i*, and long *e*. Examples are:

Long *i*	Short *i*	Long *e*
dye	crypt	happy
my	rhythm	baby
type	lynch	sadly

Have students list all the words they can think of that contain the letter *y* as a vowel. Grouping them into columns as shown helps the students become aware of this letter's function as a vowel.

Challenge older students to develop a generalization that describes when the letter *y* is pronounced as a short *i*, long *i*, or long *e*. (Hint: Look at the letter's position in the word.)

Word Attack Skills

Assign students activities like those below to maintain and improve word attack skills.

- List all the words from this story that contain a diphthong. Underline the diphthongs with your favorite color.
- List all the words from this story that have long vowel sounds. Write the pronunciation symbol for this vowel after each word. (Check your dictionary for the correct symbols.)
- List all the words in this story that have suffixes. Underline the root words with a bright color.
- List all the words in this story that have prefixes. Underline the root words with a cool color.
- List all the contractions in this story.
- List all the compound words in this story. Circle the two words that make up each compound word.

Sight Words

Provide your students with a list of sight words. Split the class into groups and assign each group a story from a basal reader. Ask the groups to list the sight words used in their story and to tally the number of times each word appears. The results can then be graphed and used as a basis for a class discussion about the importance of sight words.

You may wish to continue your sight word investigation by asking the groups to choose chapters from library books and repeat the sight word count. These results can then be compared to the basal reader graphs.

Some California real estate offices post student reading scores of the district where they have homes to sell. The higher the scores, the higher the real estate prices.

EXPRESS News, Vol. 44, August 1982, p. 4

IMPROVING COMPREHENSION

Teaching students to comprehend what they read is a major goal of the reading program. However, many different skills are included under the term *comprehension*. As students practice a variety of reading tasks, you can focus on developing particular skills. Reading is primarily a cognitive skill—students need to be able to make and test hypotheses. Therefore, what students bring to the reading task—their previous reading experience and their knowledge of the world—greatly affects their ability to comprehend fully what they read. As a result of the activities in this section:

- Students will state the main idea of a story.
- Students will associate causes and effects.
- Students will put events in the correct sequence.
- Students will read critically to interpret information and distinguish fact and opinion.
- Students will apply syntactic and semantic context clues to understand what they read.
- Students will categorize concepts to identify similarities and differences.

Find the Similarity

Give your students short lists with something in common and ask them to identify the similarity. (There will usually be more than one right answer.) Students will enjoy small or large group discussions of possible answers.

- whale, dolphin, seal, otter
  (These all live in the ocean.)
- ice skates, skateboard, roller skates, skis
- spring, summer, fall, winter
- ghost, bat, vampire, witch
- rain, snow, hail, sleet

Students who guess the relationship quickly can be challenged to suggest another item that belongs with the group.

Find the Oddball

Give your students short lists with all but one word sharing a similarity. Ask students to identify the similarity and circle the oddball word that does not belong.

- ball, globe, box, grapefruit, orange
  (All the objects are round except the box.)
- fog, mist, haze, ice, smog
- tiger, bear, jaguar, lion, panther

- carrot, cheese, potato, onion, radish
- shirt, sweater, shoes, jacket, coat

These problems can be adapted to challenge even your most able students. For example:

- tiger, lion, jaguar, leopard, ocelot
  (The lion's coat is not patterned.)
- carrot, potato, onion, cucumber, radish
  (The cucumber does not grow below the ground.)

Analogies

Language plays an important part in the development of a child's cognitive processes. Introduce students to the concept of relationships or analogies. You will need to go through several of these with the class to show how this works. Provide worksheets with more examples for them to work on for practice. Read the first example: *Finger is to hand as toe is to what?*

finger : hand	:	toe : _foot_
car : road	:	train : _rails_
lamp : light	:	_radio_ : sound
kitten : cat	:	_puppy_ : dog
book : library	:	horse : _stable_
window : glass	:	_table_ : wood
chair : leg	:	tree : _branch_
cat : animal	:	rose : _flower_
sugar : sweet	:	lemon : _sour_

Students may need help verbalizing the relationship between the items in order to be able to complete the blank.

Of course, students should be encouraged to use the dictionary when they do not understand a word. In some of the examples, several answers are possible. As the students become accustomed to this exercise, provide more difficult examples.

First Sentences

For early primary sentence skills, make large tagboard shapes (such as a train or an elephant) and word cards with tabs that will make a sentence. Cut slots in the shape for cards.

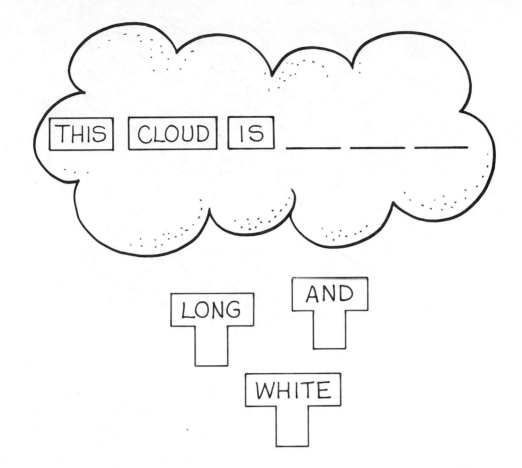

Jigsaw Sentences

An excellent puzzle activity that requires reading ability is this game to play with the class as a whole or in small groups. Each student puts four sheets of paper together and cuts out a large shape. Still keeping the four copies together, each one cuts the shape in half, using some kind of irregular line. Now, separating the copies, each student writes the first half of a sentence on the top half of the shape and the second half of the sentence on the bottom half, so that when the shapes are put together properly, they make a sentence.

Have the students exchange their sets of eight pieces, all mixed up, with the other students in the group or the class. The object of the game is to find two pieces that fit together and also make a sentence.

If you prepare the game in advance, you can create more difficult sentences to test reading ability and knowledge of what makes sense. Cut shapes from tagboard so students can use them over and over again for practice.

Guess the Hidden Word

Prepare sentence strips from three-inch posterboard. Try to use about the same amount of space for each word. Make sliders from two pieces of construction paper by taping the top and bottom. Attach four-inch end strips to prevent the slider from slipping off the posterboard.

Divide the class into small groups. Give each group a stack of sentence strips. Each player reads the top sentence and guesses the hidden word. The slider is moved to verify the guess. If correct, the player earns a token and moves the slider to hide a new word. If incorrect, the slider is kept on the same word and the used strip is placed at the bottom of the stack.

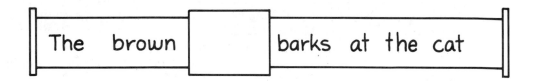

The brown ____ barks at the cat

Basic Cloze

The cloze procedure, a popular diagnostic and instructional tool, can be easily used by any teacher with any group of students. In order to assess student reading level, choose a passage of approximately 250 words that is unfamiliar to the students. Leave the first and last sentences intact. For the rest of the passage, systematically delete every fifth word. (Leave a space the same size for every blank.) Ask students to fill in the word that was deleted.

To obtain a student's score, add up the responses that are exactly the same as in the original. Interpret scores as follows:

57% correct (and above)	Independent Reading Level	Student can read easily as this level.
45–56% correct	Instructional Reading Level	Student can read with teacher assistance.
44% correct (and below)	Frustration Reading Level	Student cannot read at this level, even with assistance.

Writing and reading are reciprocal processes of meaning construction which mutually reinforce one another.

DAVID ELKIND

Cloze Variants

Alternative forms of this sentence completion technique also provide excellent strategies for teaching reading comprehension. The following are examples of cloze variants:

- Delete only words of a particular category (for example, prepositions or content words).
- Allow synonyms (or words that fit the sentence) as correct responses.
- Give the passage orally and have students respond either orally or in writing.
- Provide multiple choice options from which to select an answer (sometimes called Maze).
- Cue students by giving part of the word (for example, all consonants, prefix, first letter, etc.)
- Let students read the passage first without blanks, or give them a cloze on a passage they have seen before.
- Discuss why students chose particular completions.
- Use cloze as a pretest/posttest to check student comprehension of a topic.

All of these exercises help develop student ability to use syntactic and semantic context clues in interpreting what they read.

Cloze Practice

The following is a sample cloze, taken from *The Velveteen Rabbit* by Margery Williams (New York: Doubleday, 1926). Have the students read the sample over once and then try to fill in the missing words. Score the students' responses according to the chart on page 117.

The Boy was going to the seaside tomorrow. Everything was arranged, and _____ (1) it only remained to _____ (2) out the doctor's orders. _____ (3) talked about it all, _____ (4) the little Rabbit lay _____ (5) the bedclothes, with just _____ (6) head peeping out, and _____ (7). The room was to _____ (8) disinfected, and all the _____ (9) and toys that the _____ (10) had played with in _____ (11) must be burnt.

"Hurrah!" _____ (12) the little Rabbit. "Tomorrow _____ (13) shall go to the _____ (14)!" For the Boy had _____ (15) talked of the seaside, _____ (16) he wanted very much _____ (17) see the big waves _____ (18) in, and the tiny _____ (19), and the sand castles.

_____ (20) then Nana caught sight _____ (21) him.

"How about his _____ (22) Bunny?" she asked.

"That?" _____ (23) the doctor. "Why, it's _____ (24) mass of scarlet fever _____ (25)! Burn it at once. _____ (26)? Nonsense! Get him a _____ (27) one. He mustn't have that any more!"

Answers

1. now	8. be	15. often	22. old
2. carry	9. books	16. and	23. said
3. They	10. Boy	17. to	24. a
4. while	11. bed	18. coming	25. germs
5. under	12. thought	19. crabs	26. What
6. his	13. we	20. Just	27. new
7. listened	14. seaside	21. of	

> *M-SS-NG L-NKS: A Game of Letters & Language*
> Sunburst
> All Apple computers
> Grade 3 to Adult
>
> The purpose of this software is to improve student reading and writing skills through the appreciation of syntax and the mechanics of writing. The material used comes from children's literature classics such as *Wind in the Willows* and *The Secret Garden*. You may also add your own selections.

Story Analysis

Use a familiar fairy tale or read your students a short story. Write the column headings below on the chalkboard. Ask the students to retell the story as you fill in the chart. For example:

Somebody	Wanted	But	So
Cinderella	to go to the ball	no dress or coach	Fairy Godmother helped

Tell your students that almost all stories have this logical mapping, and that they can use this chart both to analyze stories and to write their own original stories.

Provide your students with a Somebody/Wanted/But/So ditto each time you read a story aloud. When students become proficient, ask them to map a story of their own.

You recreate the meaning of everything you read.
NORTHRUP FRYE

Writing Main Ideas

Asking students for the main idea in different stories will often help them grasp the concept. For basal reader stories, book reports, and discussions following read-aloud sessions, ask students questions like those on the next page.

- What was the most important idea of this story?
- What was the moral of this story?
- What did you learn from this story?
- What do you remember most about the story?
- If you had to tell the whole story in one sentence, what would you say?
- If you were asked to draw the cover for this story, what would you draw?

Main Idea Pictures

Teaching the skill of identifying the main idea should begin in kindergarten. Each year, students can practice this skill with longer and more complex material. Activities like those below will help early primary students grasp the concept of main idea.

- Display an interesting picture and ask your students what story the picture is telling. Try to get your group to agree on one main idea. You might then ask your students to draw their own picture of the main idea.
- Read a simple paragraph to your students. Discuss the main idea and ask students to draw a picture.
- Read short fables to your students and ask them to identify the main idea (moral) and draw a picture of it.
- Ask students to draw a picture of the main idea of a story in their reading books. Discuss the pictures and help the students write a sentence to amplify their picture. Group discussion will help those still having trouble identifying the main idea.
- Ask your students to suggest possible titles for a picture. Write suggestions on the board and have the group decide which comes closest to stating the main idea.

Speed Reader II
Davidson & Associates
Apple II series, Commodore 64, IBM, PC, PC Jr.
Grades 4 to Adult

This software program increases the learners' reading speeds as well as comprehension. Rates go from 100 words per minute to 2,000 words per minute. An instructional manual is included.

Narrative Story Map

Use a familiar story to create a group story map on the board. You may need to prompt with questions like: *What did the goats do first?*

- Setting:
  Bridge
- Characters:
  3 billy goats, troll
- Problem:
  Goats want to cross the bridge guarded by troll.
- Goal:
  To reach greener grass.
- Events:
  First goat tells troll to wait for fatter brother.
  Second goat tells troll to wait for fatter brother.
  Third goat vanquished troll.
- Resolution:
  All goats feast on greener grass.

Cause and Effect

Introduce students to the concept of cause and effect by asking simple questions about familiar stories. Folk or fairy tales work well.

- The dwarves think Snow White is dead. Why do they think that?
- The mirror says Snow White is the most beautiful woman in the kingdom. What effect does that have on the evil witch?

Ask your students to listen for examples of cause and effect relationships throughout their day.

Cause and Effect Sentences

Ask students to list events from the story you are reading aloud. Show them how to make cause and effect sentences from the events. It is helpful to point out that either the cause or the effect may begin the sentence.

- James went to live with his awful aunts (effect) because his parents were eaten by a rhinoceros (cause).
- James tripped (cause) and spilled his magic potion (effect).

Discuss the importance of cause and effect relationships in the plot of a story.

Matching Cause and Effect

You can prepare simple matching worksheets to monitor and expand student comprehension of cause and effect relationships.

	Cause		Effect
c	1. Pippi Longstocking rescues two boys from a burning building.	a.	Pippi takes a ride on the bull to teach it a lesson.
a	2. The bull chases Tommy and he falls.	b.	The tramps decide to break into Villa Villekulla.
b	3. The tramps see Pippi counting her gold pieces.	c.	The townspeople cheer Pippi.

A variation is to give your students only half of the cause and effect relationship and have them complete it. You can accept any answers that make sense.

Cause	Effect
1.	1. Pippi Longstocking draws on the floor when she goes to school.
2.	2. Two policemen come to see Pippi.
3. Pippi is invited to a coffee party at Tommy and Annika's.	3.
4. Pippi's mother is dead and her father was lost at sea.	4.

Sentences in Sequence

After the students have read a story, lead a discussion of story events, in order, and write down each major event as a sentence. Later, to review the story, duplicate the set of sentences in mixed order and ask the students to cut them out and arrange the sentences in sequence.

Talk with the students about how and why they arranged the sentences as they did.

5. The wolf tries to eat little Red Riding Hood.
3. Little Red Riding Hood arrives at her grandmother's house.

   1. Little Red Riding Hood's mother gives her a basket to take to her grand-
      mother.
   6. The woodsman rescues little Red Riding Hood.
   4. Little Red Riding Hood thinks the wolf is her grandmother.
   2. The wolf eats little Red Riding Hood's grandmother.

Story Graph

Graphing the plot of a story often helps students see the progression from one event
to another. You may wish to add a graph like the one below to your book report format.

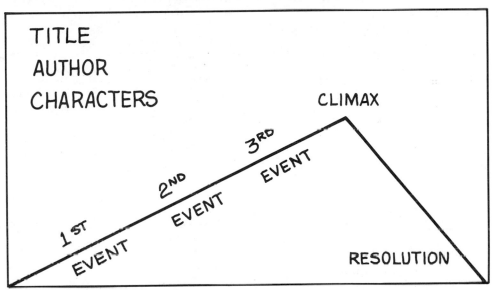

Levels of Questioning

Help students develop skills in asking and answering different types of questions.
Start by modeling for students both literal questions (where the answer is explicit in
the text) and inferential or evaluative questions (where the student must interpret the
material). After reading the first two chapters of *The Phantom Tollbooth* written by
Norton Juster (New York: Random House, 1964), ask the students the following
questions:

1. Why was Milo dejected as he walked home from school?
2. Did Milo have friends he usually played with after school?
3. What were the Doldrums?
4. Why were the Lethargians afraid of the watchdog?
5. How did Milo get out of the Doldrums?
6. Do you think the watchdog is going to be an important character in the rest of the story?

Discuss the questions and how to answer them. For some questions, the answer appears in the book—students can underline it or point to it, even if they have to look in more than one place. There is usually only one right answer. Other questions require students to think about what they read and develop an answer based on their own ideas and experience. In this case, several answers may be equally correct. Have students sort the questions into these two categories, justifying their selection as they make it.

In the Text	On Their Own
Q#1.　Two to three lines; several possible answers	Q#2.　No mention in the book; students must interpret information given
Q#3.　One line	Q#6.　Prediction; students answer based on their experience of reading books
Q#4.　Information given in two places; students must connect these	
Q#5.　One line	

Question Practice

Divide the students into small groups for more practice in asking and answering questions. Select a short passage from a book and have each group write a list of questions about it. Then have the groups exchange their lists so that another group tries to answer the questions.

Discuss the questions produced by the groups. Were both literal and inferential types of questions represented or only literal questions? Which questions required more thought? Which questions had more than one answer? What makes a good question?

Following this discussion, repeat the exercise so that the students can immediately try out what they have just learned. This skill of asking and answering questions on material read is fundamental to higher-level comprehension.

> *Good readers, like good listeners, have to be simultaneously passive and active.*
>
> DAVID ELKIND

First Impressions

Before reading a book, have the students read the title and look at the cover of the book. They can form an idea of what a book might be about before they even open it. Ask them these questions:

- Who might the characters be?
- Where might the story take place?
- What feeling do you get when you read the title or look at the cover?

Discuss the students' experiences with the topic or setting of the book briefly before reading. Why might they be interested in reading this book? Student comprehension will be increased if they have some familiarity with the background of the story.

Where and When?

Select a portion of dialogue from a story or write a short passage yourself. Present the dialogue to the class either on the chalkboard or on duplicated sheets. After the students read this conversation, discuss it together, asking for suggestions about what might have preceded the conversation and what might follow, who is speaking, what kinds of people the speakers are, and so forth.

Each student then composes a story and fits this dialogue in as appropriate. Comparing the results will impress the students with the many possibilities for developing a story from a single situation. Here is a sample dialogue:

"Quick, duck down behind these boxes," Bess hissed. "Who knows what will happen if they catch us here!"

Using Suspense

When reading a book to the class, use high points in the book to create suspense. Choose an exciting moment or decision point, stop reading, and ask the students what they think will happen next. Have them discuss various possibilities and what clues affected their choice.

A variation is to have each student draw three pictures representing possible outcomes. After you resume the story, students can circle the picture that best matches the solution given in the book.

Interpreting Motives

Introduce the concept of motive through a discussion of a book you are reading. Use the following questions with students:

- How did the main character feel at the beginning of the story? Why? Did the main character feel differently at the end of the story? How can you tell? What caused the change?
- Choose an important thing the main character did in the story. Tell what you think the reasons were for his or her action.
- Why did the main character choose that way of solving his or her problem? Do you think it was a good solution? Would the same solution have worked for you, or for a character in another book?

Similar questions could later be added to book report forms.

Evaluating Ideas

Ask students to bring in a variety of newspapers and magazines. Discuss the different appearance of these magazines and newspapers. Do students think that everything printed in the media is true? Are there some newspapers and magazines that they trust more than others? Use activities like the examples below to help your students improve their critical reading skills.

- Read the "Letters to the Editor" column. Find a letter that contains a good idea. Tell why you think it is a good idea.
- Read an article. List five factual sentences. List five sentences that seem to be the personal opinion of the author and that may not be factual. Optional: Find out from another source if these ideas are factual.
- Read an article about a place you know well. List three statements you know are true. List any statements you know are false. List three statements about which you are unsure. How can you verify them?
- Read an article that tries to persuade you to do something or believe a certain way. Tell why you think the author is trying to persuade you. List two good arguments the author uses. List two arguments that don't seem to be based on fact. Tell why you agree or disagree with the author.

An excellent source book for the teacher is *Human Values in Children's Books* (New York: The Council on Interracial Books for Children, 1976). This book deals with biases based on sex, race, age, handicap, or social class. It includes checklists to use in evaluating classroom materials as well as lists of nonbiased materials.

LITERATURE IN THE READING PROGRAM

Students learn to be readers by reading. A teacher who reads to students, shows children's literature on film or video, and supplies students with exciting books will produce a class of fluent readers. Your example will show students the importance of reading, both for a purpose and for pleasure. As students read more widely, they will begin to realize that books are by people. Students will also begin to make the connection between reading and writing as they recognize the role of the author's craft in the story. As a result of the activities in this section:

- Students will react and respond to books, orally and in writing.
- Students will identify authors and their books.
- Students will retell a story from a different point of view.
- Students will recognize the role of characterization in a story.

Read-a-thon

Students are surprisingly motivated to read during a Read-a-thon. The length of time designated for this marathon may be a single afternoon or several days. The rules are simple:

- Students must read books.
- Participants are to read without interruption (except for periodic breaks every hour for a stretch, drink, or bathroom visit, and, of course, lunch).
- Books are selected by the students.

The purpose is to see how many students can keep reading to the end of the Read-a-thon. Students who get tired may drop out at any time. If the whole school is participating in the Read-a-thon, special classrooms and work are provided for those who quit reading. As the number of students who are reading becomes fewer, they may read in the library. You may wish to permit students who drop out to reenter the Read-a-thon, making note of the number of hours they were out.

The Book Exchange

To help encourage children's reading activities, create a book exchange. On a regularly scheduled day have each child bring his or her own book to class. Make a list of your students' names to make sure that each child receives a book. A student will always pass a book to the student that follows his or her own name on the list. The number of days or weeks between the book exchange will depend on the needs of the class.

> An excellent source book for children's trade books is *Reading Ladders for Human Relations,* 6th ed., edited by Eileen Tway (Washington, D.C.: American Council on Education, 1981).

Sustained Silent Reading

Set aside a regular time for free-choice silent reading, either daily or several times a week. Insist that everyone read at this time—including yourself and any classroom visitors. The sustained silent reading period should be about ten minutes for grades 1–3, and twenty minutes for grades 4–6. This regular silent reading time gives students practice in reading for pleasure, improves fluency and comprehension, and broadens reading interests. Some suggestions for a successful program follow:

- Give students five minutes to gather reading material.
- Provide a variety of reading material.
- Set up a regular schedule.
- Let parents know about the program. Ask for contributions to your classroom library.

The Classroom Library

A library can be created in any corner of the classroom. Perhaps an old carpet will be available to make the corner attractive and comfortable. Encourage students to enhance the library by constructing bookshelves, painting chairs, or making pillows to sit on.

Students can also serve as librarians to check books out for reading at home. They can also make book covers for older books and mend those that become torn. Often students can contribute reading material for the library such as paperback books or magazines.

Storytelling Time

Share books with your students by reading aloud to the class. Not only will you model reading as a pleasurable activity but you will also arouse student interest. Choose a picture book, like *Sam, Bangs, and Moonshine* by Evaline Ness (New York: Holt, Rinehart, 1967), for younger students, or keep a book such as *From the Mixed-up Files of Mrs. Basil E. Frankweiler* by E. L. Konigsburg (New York: Atheneum, 1968) going, reading a chapter a day, as students eagerly await the outcome.

Students will quiet down quickly if you establish a special signal for Storytelling Time. Use a special costume, such as a cape or hat, or sit in a certain chair to indicate that you are about to enter a different world. As you read, insert names of students in the class or other familiar references to keep students involved.

Fables

A book that all ages can enjoy is Arnold Lobel's *Fables* (New York: Harper & Row, 1981), with its beautiful illustrations. Discuss the stories with the students. What is the story about? How can they apply the story to their own experience? Students will learn as well as laugh after reading these fables. Other fables to stimulate discussion include:

- Jack Kent, *Fables of Aesop* (New York: Parents, 1972).
- Isaac Bashevis Singer, *The Fools of Chelm and Their History* (New York: Farrar, 1973). Illustrated by Uri Shulevitz.

After reading fables, children can write their own. Provide a list of endings (moral sayings) to start students thinking.

- Curiosity killed the cat.
- A stitch in time saves nine.
- Too many cooks spoil the broth.
- A bird in the hand is worth two in the bush.
- Every cloud has a silver lining.

To Read and Discuss

Many simple stories will stimulate thoughtful discussions. The following books are meant to be read and talked about, as everyone will respond personally to the ideas and feelings.

- Shel Silverstein's modern parable, *The Giving Tree* (New York: Harper, 1964) describes a companionable relationship between a boy and tree. Although the tree gives of itself unselfishly until it is only a stump, even the stump offers a resting place for the boy, now an old man. The touching story will provoke extensive discussion about the value of giving and receiving.

- A classic book, *The Velveteen Rabbit* by Margery Williams (New York: Doubleday, 1958), offers another perspective on human values. In this story, the toy Rabbit asks "What is Real?" How he finds the answer to his question is lovingly described in the book and its illustrations.

The Bookfinder: A Guide to Children's Literature about the Needs and Problems of Youth Aged 2-15, by Sharon Spredemann Dreyer (Washington, D.C.: American Guidance Service, 1981) is an extensive reference book with an unusual format that allows the reader to leave the subject index open to a page, while reading the annotations of specific books.

Category Reading

To encourage students to broaden their reading, provide each student with a list of categories to complete. Leave space to write the name of the book next to the category. Sample categories might include:

- Science fiction
- Nonfiction
- Mystery
- Humor
- Historical fiction
- Fantasy
- Biography
- Adventure

Students who complete the first category chart by reading one book of each type may move on to the bonus chart, which could include:

- Poetry
- Mythology/Folktales
- Sports

Book Fair

Sponsor a Book Fair in conjunction with the school library or local PTA. Classes can create a variety of displays, such as a mural of historical fiction, collected student writing, mobiles or dioramas of favorite books, and book covers made by students. If you hold the fair during Book Week (the third week in November) you will be able to obtain posters, bookmarks, and other materials through The Children's Book Council (67 Irving Place, New York 10003). You can also contact local bookstores and publishers to see if they would like to cooperate with a display. Be sure to include plenty of paperbacks and children's magazines, as students will not be able to resist taking a look inside. Prepare handouts for parents that include suggested books for different grade levels as well as recommendations for reading aloud. Book Fairs can generate a great deal of enthusiasm for reading in the school and in the home.

Reading Log

Have the students keep a record of all the material they read in a single day. Encourage them to think about the different kinds of things they read, especially outside the classroom. What might they be reading without really thinking about it? Some examples might be road signs, billboard slogans, cereal boxes, and TV advertising. The class can discuss the results of these logs. Were they surprised to see how much they read? How do they learn new words when they read?

Students can also interview adults to find out what they read in a typical day. Many adults regularly read specialized material, such as memos, reports, or instruction manuals, that students may not be aware of.

Ad Reading

Advertising copy can be an excellent source for reading activities in the classroom. Bring in examples of newspaper or magazine ads and discuss them with the students. Many ads depend on *multiple meanings* for their effect. Can students spot the different meanings involved? How are words with multiple meanings effective? Are they humorous? Attention-getting? Students can also look for *word play* in ads. How many examples can they find? Are these examples of puns? Many ads will include words unfamiliar to students. Can students guess the meaning of a word from the *context?* What clues help them guess? (There may be visual as well as syntactic and semantic context clues.)

Expanding Reading

Enlarge student horizons by showing them that reading is not something they do only in the classroom. Bring in items from the following list of free or inexpensive materials to encourage students to read and increase their ability to understand different kinds of text.

Tickets	Songs (songsheets)
Candy wrappers	Recipes
Postcards	Comic strips, cartoons
Train/bus/plane schedules	Clothing tags
Coupons	Telephone directories
Catalogs	Grocery lists
Want ads	TV program listings
Restaurant menus	Record/cassette labels
Game instructions	Instructions for operating something
Cereal boxes	Maps

Encouraging Student Reading

Maintain a classroom environment that stimulates student interest in reading. Brainstorm with the students different ways to obtain reading material for the classroom library. Use the following suggestions to promote a positive attitude toward student reading.

- Talk to the class about what you are reading.
- Give parents a list of suggested gift books.
- Join a book club (see Chapter 10).
- Have an author or illustrator come and talk to the class.
- Distribute a list of suggestions for summer reading.

Children's Choices

Books selected by children are listed every year in the October issue of *The Reading Teacher,* a publication of The International Reading Association. The list may also be obtained by writing The Children's Book Council, 67 Irving Place, New York, N.Y. 10003.

Summarizing Stories

Students need experience in summarizing information and connecting details before they can write coherent book reports. After reading a selection, have the students practice retelling the story or text. Make sure they include all the important information, by writing the elements of the story on the board. Then help them organize this information as the class puts events in order and selects the main idea. Guide the students by asking questions such as the following:

- Who were the important characters in the story?
- Where and when did the story take place?
- What happened at the beginning of the story?
- What did the characters do?
- Why did they do that?
- What happened at the end of the story?
- How did the characters feel?

Read Me a Story

When students enjoy books, they also enjoy telling others about the books and telling the stories. For older students, arrange with teachers of lower grades to have your students visit their classes and tell stories to the younger students. Students should pick a story that they are enthusiastic about. Have them practice in front of their own class, a small group, or with a tape recorder, before they go to the other class. Small groups of younger students can be brought to your classroom at first if storytelling in front of another class is too frightening. Storytelling is great practice in oral language skills, with the added bonus of near-guaranteed audience appreciation.

If your class is younger, explore the idea of having older students tell stories to your class.

There is more treasure in books than in all the pirates' loot on Treasure Island . . . and best of all, you can enjoy these riches every day of your life.
WALT DISNEY

Group Reading

A small group of children who are interested in reading the same book may choose to share the story by reading aloud together. Let them decide how the reading will be done. Perhaps each one will take a turn reading a page as the book is passed from person to person. Or the group may decide to let people who like to read aloud volunteer to do the reading while the others listen. After the story is completed, this group can share the story with the class by dramatizing a portion, painting a small mural, or by some other interesting method that seems appropriate.

Keys to Successful Oral Presentations

In order to sell other students on books, oral book reviews need to be stimulating. Presentations should be short and should employ varied approaches. The following tips will liven up the traditional report.

- Show the class the book cover. How does it relate to the story?
- Read an especially interesting or vivid passage to the class. Be sure to tell the audience what has led up to this scene.
- Talk about the author. What other books has he or she written? Is the story based on something that happened to the author?
- Talk about a suspenseful part of the book. Ask the class what they think will happen next.

Seminar Report

When students are not comfortable giving oral reports before the whole class, set up an alternative informal environment. Organize the class into small groups. Have the groups meet regularly to talk about books they have read or are reading. These groups may then choose to share books with the class through a panel discussion or a bulletin board, for example. Positive experiences at this level will lead to greater confidence and ease in speaking to a larger group.

Puppet Talk

Students can produce a puppet show version of their favorite book. Have the puppets enact an interesting incident from the book or use the puppets to introduce several of the characters. Whether you have a puppet stage ready or not, you can always have simple hand puppets for the students to use while standing up.

Puppets are an effective means of presentation even when only one student is presenting the book. The student can use one puppet to tell the story from that character's point of view.

See Chapter 3 for examples of easily made puppets.

Flannel Board Stories

Have students work in pairs to present a story on the flannel board. One student can tell the story to the class while the other student moves the characters on the board. This method helps students visualize the sequence of events.

In order to develop an effective flannel board presentation, students will need to make a list of characters and other plot elements. Then they can outline the events of the story. They must also decide how to illustrate these events so that the class will be able to follow the story action.

Students will want to rehearse their presentation at least once before going in front of the class. A successful flannel board presentation can go "on tour" to other classes or grades.

Book Jacket

To combine an art activity with a book report, have students make book jackets for the books they read. They can draw a picture for the cover that says something about the story and is designed to get people to read the book. They should also make a jacket *blurb* that summarizes the book and gives information about the author and illustrator.

These book jackets can be displayed on the bulletin board or they can actually be put on the book. They are effective in motivating other students to read the books.

Make a Mobile

A mobile provides a particularly striking visual display of a book. Students can make mobiles illustrating events or showing characters from a book they have read. Each mobile can be hung from the ceiling, to stimulate interest in the book on the part of other students.

Almost any art technique could be used for the mobile. Be sure to have the students include the title and author of the book. The simplest way to hang the mobile is with thread and sticks of wood. The heavier the pieces used by the students, the easier it will be to balance the mobile properly.

Cover Puzzles

Collect book covers from the books you have in the classroom, books that come to the library, or covers that students bring in. Glue the paper covers to any heavy material, such as cardboard, and cover them with plastic. With a sharp knife, cut the boards into puzzle shapes. The pieces can be kept in boxes for students to play with in their spare time as they put the pieces together to create a book, title, and author. Students will enjoy the puzzles of their favorite books, and they may become interested in reading new books that they encounter in a puzzle.

Tips for Sharing Books

Give students a choice of alternative ways to report on and react to books they have read. Some activities may be more appropriate for particular books.

- Write a new ending for your book.
- Report on the author of the book.
- Compare this book with another book on the same topic or by the same author.
- Write a letter to your favorite character in the book. Send it to the author (in care of the publisher).
- Choose your favorite character and write a description of him or her.
- Read a selection from the book to a lower grade class.
- Tell a friend or write about your favorite part of the book.
- Write down some new or unusual words from your book.
- Illustrate a scene from the book.
- Prepare a selection from the book for dramatic presentation. Enlist the help of a friend or two to act out the scene.
- Write an incident from the book as a newspaper article. Include an eye-catching headline.
- Write yourself into the book. Give yourself a name and a role to play. What would you say to the other characters? What would you do?

Advertising Posters

Interest students in reading by selling a book through a poster. Display book advertising posters on the bulletin board to catch students' attention. Include catchy slogans and attention-getting artwork and lettering on these posters, as well as the author and title of the book.

Meet the Press

Have the students interview a character from a book they have read. After reading Marjorie Sharmat's *Maggie Marmelstein for President* (New York: Harper and Row, 1975), for example, one student can play Maggie while the others write questions they would like to ask her. Have the student interviewers and interviewee sit in front of the class for a panel presentation.

This would be an excellent activity to videotape for later reshowing.

Name the Character

Names often bring a picture to mind. Ask the students to list several unusual names they have heard or read, or you may supply fictitious names such as Ruby Lowery, Gerald Higgins, Diana Tate, Mike Barrows. Discuss the students' reasons for matching certain characteristics with the names used. Have each student choose one name as a character about whom to write. Then have them list ten characteristics of that person, including physical appearance, personality, and behavior patterns.

This exercise is useful for vocabulary development. Before listing characteristics, you could suggest interesting new words to stimulate student thinking, such as *gregarious, lanky, brazen, drab, downtrodden, nocturnal,* and so on.

After students develop their list of characteristics, have them consider how to describe this person to another student. How can they *show* what the character looks and acts like rather than *tell?* The awareness the students develop from writing their own characterizations should lead to an increased understanding of the importance of character development in the books they read.

Character Role Playing

Have the students present a critical situation that a character faces in a book. Students will need to pay particular attention to the clues given by the author in order to get inside the character's skin. They can pretend to be the character and describe how they felt and what they did in that situation, or they can present a hypothetical situation and predict what the character would be likely to do.

This activity works best with students who have read the same book. You may wish to begin by providing a list of role-playing situations for a book you have read aloud to your class. After sharing A. A. Milne's *Winnie-the-Pooh* (New York: Dutton, 1961), you might ask students to role play:

- How Eeyore felt about his birthday
- How Piglet felt about being Henry Pootel
- What Owl might do if Pooh gave him a book to read aloud
- What Kanga might do if she saw the mess in our art corner

Dear Diary

Read a story in the form of a diary, such as *Dear Mr. Henshaw* by Beverly Cleary (New York: Morrow, 1983) or *A Gathering of Days* by Joan Blos (New York: Scribner's, 1979), to show the importance of the narrator's point of view. Does it make a difference who is telling a story? Would another character in the same story tell it differently? What information about the main character is missing when we read his or her diary?

Students will enjoy looking at stories from a different point of view. Practice with familiar tales such as Beatrix Potter's *Peter Rabbit* (New York: Putnam, 1981). Have students tell the story from a character's outlook—for example, from Mr. McGregor's point of view.

Students can select a character from a book they have read and write entries for a diary kept by that character. How would this person see the events in the book? What would he or she think about the other characters? This kind of exercise gives students insight into the concept of characterization.

Fractured Titles

Students can have fun rewriting the titles of familiar books, which is a good way to encourage and maintain interest in reading. Give the students a list of book titles that are familiar names in disguise, as shown here. Have them match the "improved" titles with the original versions. Once they have completed this list, students can make up their own examples to enjoy with the rest of the class.

Familiar Titles	*Fractured Titles*
a. *Wind in the Willows*	__Trip to the Middle of the World
b. *The Red Balloon*	__Ice Crystals and Flatfish Skeletons
c. *Hailstones and Halibut Bones*	__Breeze in the Trees
d. *Journey to the Center of the Earth*	__Into the Mirror
e. *Kidnapped*	__The Happy Exploits of Bird Hat
f. *Through the Looking Glass*	__Cry of the Untamed
g. *Call of the Wild*	__Abducted
h. *The Merry Adventures of Robin Hood*	__The Ruby Inflatable

As a variation, write one or two fractured titles on the board for a warm-up during roll call. Students may wish to sign up for the responsibility of providing the next day's title.

Word Crossings

In this game, a puzzle is constructed by crossing the key word, running vertically, with related words. The students are given clues to help them figure out the related words and fill in the blanks.

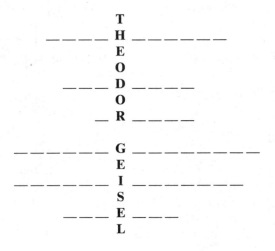

Clues:

1. The first name of the boy who had lots of hats.
2. The name of the kind-hearted moose.
3. Who stole a holiday from the children?
4. The title of a book about breakfast.
5. Who came back?
6. Theodor Geisel's pseudonym.

Answers:

1. Bartholomew
2. Thidwick
3. Grinch
4. *Green Eggs and Ham*
5. The Cat in the Hat
6. Dr. Seuss

Students will enjoy thinking up Word Crossings to stump their friends. They may choose this as a way of sharing a book they have read or describing the life of a favorite author.

BOOKO

Small groups of students can play BOOKO and learn about authors and titles of books at the same time. Prepare five or six large bingo cards marked off into squares.

Roller Skates	Will James	*The Dark Frigate*	Rachel Field	*Jacob Have I Loved*
Onion John	Ellen Raskin	*Ginger Pye*	*...And Now Miguel*	*Rabbit Hill*
Esther Forbes	*A Gathering of Days*	Lois Lenski	*Miss Hickory*	*Call It Courage*
Scott O'Dell	*The High King*	Betsy Byars	Free	*Westing Game*
Sounder	Joan Blos	*The 21 Balloons*	Katherine Paterson	Monica Shannon

Newbery Award winners

Write the title or author of a book in each square. Make a card for each title and author to use for calling. Make slips for covering the bingo card. After you have taught the students to play the game, you can leave the cards in a Learning Center for small groups of students to play.

You can make separate games for titles, authors, and author-titles. Encourage reading by using books from the school library. Students will be curious about books that they have not heard of, and you can take advantage of their interest by taking them to the library. You might make a set of cards featuring the Caldecott or Newbery Award winners.

Author-Title Dominoes

Construct this game by cutting out thirty cardboard rectangles. Use a colored pen to draw a line dividing each rectangle in half. On each half write the author or title of a book. Use about ten different authors with matching titles from books in your class library. Dominoes is an easy game for students to play on their own and is motivation for further reading. Encourage students to add dominoes to the set.

Newbery Winners

Sunburst
All Apple computers
Grades 3 to 8

Each book is accompanied by software that contains programs for vocabulary, comprehension drills, and games. Some of the books included are *Sounder, A Wrinkle in Time,* and *Bridge to Terabithia.*

Books Are by People

When students read books, encourage them to think about the person on the other side of the book—the author (or illustrator). Challenge students to find out more about favorite authors/illustrators. Give them a list of questions to answer and some suggested sources to research, and then post the results on a bulletin board. You might ask the following questions:

- Can you find a picture of the author?
- When was he or she born? (When did he or she die?)
- Where does the author come from?
- Why did the author write this book (or these books)?
- When was the book written?

Sources that students can investigate for more information include:

- Book jackets. (Biographical information and a photo are often given.)
- The publisher. (Students can also write to the author in care of the publisher.)
- Reference books available in the library (such as *Contemporary Authors* and *Current Biography*).
- Two books by Lee Bennett Hopkins are also recommended: *Books Are by People* (New York: Citation, 1969) and *More Books by More People* (New York: Citation, 1974).

Check with the children's librarian at your local library to see if there are any authors who live locally. Invite one of them to speak to the class, perhaps during Book Week in November.

When you read *If I Ran a Zoo* by Dr. Seuss (New York: Random House, 1950), you might tell your students that Dr. Seuss's father was a zoo director.

Pseudonyms

Pseudonym means *false name* but it does not always mean a hidden identity. Pseudonyms used to be popular among writers, not necessarily because they were ashamed of their works. The most familiar pseudonym or pen name is Mark Twain (Samuel Clemens). Clemens chose his name from the riverboat custom of marking off the depth of the Mississippi River.

Early women writers commonly used male names for their books because they were afraid that books by women would not be published or taken seriously. Examples of pseudonyms that may be familiar to some students are:

- O. Henry—William Sidney Porter
- Saki—H. H. Munro
- Andre Norton—Mary Alice Norton
- Dr. Seuss—Theodor Geisel
- Lewis Carroll—Charles Dodgson

Children may enjoy making up their own pseudonyms to use on their writing. Some may choose a name that refers to an interest or a physical characteristic. Others may choose a nickname or a name they've always wanted to be called. Encourage the children to share their names with the class and explain why they chose them.

Students will find other pseudonyms as they read more. Have them present these to the class when they discover the author's real name.

A selected list of classic stories that are available on videotape from Weston Woods Films (Weston Woods, CT):

- *Harold and the Purple Crayon,* animated, color, 8 minutes
- *Curious George Rides a Bike,* iconographic, color, 10 minutes
- *Where the Wild Things Are,* animated, color, 8 minutes
- *Make Way for Ducklings,* iconographic, color, 11 minutes
- *The Swineherd,* animated, color, 13 minutes

6 Putting Words to Use

Two of the greatest stumbling blocks in writing are spelling correctly and using the language properly. This chapter provides activities that attack these difficulties and help students solve the problems involved.

As children enter school, it is essential for us to build on the skills students already have. Furthermore, it is important that positive attitudes be stressed from the beginning. As children learn to write alphabet letters, they will learn to spell simple words and soon put these words together in sentences. These first experiences in spelling and usage should be highly satisfying and functional. Gradually, children learn the more difficult spelling patterns of English words and, at the same time, they begin to handle more complex sentence patterns easily as they write.

This chapter is divided into two parts. The activities in the first section focus on teaching spelling. The last half of the chapter provides strategies for presenting grammar and usage to students. As a result of these activities:

- Students will learn to spell correctly.
- Students will learn to assemble sentences properly.

TEACHING SPELLING

Recent studies have shown that English spelling is more systematic than teachers once thought. However, the words that are learned first and used most frequently are the irregular ones and, naturally, the most troublesome to spell. The teaching of spelling should emphasize the relationship between the sounds that children know and the letters or combinations of letters that spell those sounds, in such a way that students can discover the patterns.

As a result of the activities in this section:

- Students will recognize the relationship between sounds and symbols.
- Students will identify patterns of English spelling.
- Students will employ varied approaches to learning how to spell English words.
- Students will analyze English as a code.

Alphabetical Lists

A good first activity that stresses alphabetizing is to list words in alphabetical order. Try making a list of alphabetical foods from *asparagus* to *zucchini*. Later, list all animals from *ant* to *zebra*. Another list could be names of people from *Alice* to *Zeb*. Many other lists can be developed from the alphabet. Students should have a chance to discuss their lists and to compare what they have come up with and what others have discovered. Display these lists where children can read them easily.

Spelling Race

Have each student write the letters *A* to *Z* down the left-hand side of the paper. At the start of the race, each child has this piece of paper with the alphabet on the left. The purpose of this game is to see how many words students can write for each of the alphabet letters. They must have a word for each of the letters; then they can go back and write a second word or a third word. What an incentive to learn *xylophone* and *zebra!*

The teacher determines the length of time allowed for this activity. The first time the game is played it might be necessary to allow more time so that each student can succeed at some level. After the game has been played several times, children can count the number of words they have written. Scoring by teams alleviates personal competition.

Another modification of this activity is to say that each word has to be at least five letters long. The important thing, however, is that every student has an opportunity to write words and to succeed at a personal level of proficiency. Sample lists look like this:

Easy List	*Advanced List*
aim	aardvark
black	bumpity
care	calendar
dear	destroying
eagle	equal
farm	fantasy
go	ghostly
her	horrendous
ink	irresistible
jelly	journey
kitten	kitchen
lame	loosely
meow	menacing
now	nuisance
open	organized
pin	placid
quit	quake
rat	righteous
soon	shuffling
tame	tedious
under	understanding
vase	virile
wagon	whimsy
x-ray	xylophone
yell	youth
zoo	zipper

Common Phonograms

Students can make lists of common word endings (phonograms). These lists help students to become more conscious of patterns in the English language and to improve their spelling abilities. They may also learn new words. Here are a few phonograms:

ack	ate	el	ite, ight	ote, oat
ale, ail	ean, een	in	oar, ore	ub
ang	eed, ead	ine	ong	ug
at	eg	ing	ort	ule

Give students a list of phonograms and a beginning consonant or blend. Ask students to combine the consonant or blend with the phonograms to make as many words as possible. For example, *b* + the A phonograms would make words like: *back, bat, bang, bail, bale,* and so on. Students may find this activity more exciting if you draw the beginning consonant or blend from a box or use a spinner to determine the phonogram list.

Spelling Sheets

Create Assignment Sheets focusing on variant spellings of common phonograms.

Eek!

How many words can you list that rhyme with *eek?* You can find at least ten and perhaps more than twenty!

_____

_____

Group the words you have discovered according to their spelling. Match them with these spellings.

> *SLEEK*   *SNEAK*   *Others?*

Examine the lists you have made. Answer these questions.

1. What are the two common spellings for this phonogram (word ending)?
2. How many sets of homonyms can you find?

_____

_____

_____

_____

_____

_____

Useful Phonograms

This list of phonograms will be helpful in developing activities for students.

	A		E	I	O	U	
ab	awl	ead		ib	oad	ost	ub
ace	awn	eak		ibe	oat	ot	uck
ack	ax	eal		ice	ob	ote	uct
act	ay	eam		ick	obe	ouch	ud
ad	aze	ean		id	ock	oud	ude
ade		ear		ide	od	ought	udge
aff		ease		ie	ode	ounce	uff
aft		eat		ife	og	ound	ug
ag		eave		iff	oil	ount	um
age		eck		ift	oin	our	ump
ail		ect		ig	oke	ouse	un
ain		ed		ight	old	out	unch
air		ee		ike	ole	ove	ung
aise		eed		ile	oll	ow	unk
ake		eek		ill	olt	owl	unt
alk		eel		ilt	olve	own	urch
all		eem		im	ome	ox	ure
am		een		ime	on	oy	url
ame		eer		imp	ond		urn
amp		eese		in	one		urt
an		eeze		ince	ong		us
ance		eet		inch	oo		usc
and		ell		ind	ood		ush
ang		em		ine	oof		ust
ank		en		ing	ook		ut
ant		ence		ink	ool		utch
ap		ench		int	oom		ute
ape		end		ip	oon		
ar		ense		ipe	oop		
ard		ent		ire	oose		
are		ept		irl	oot		
ark		er		irm	ooth		
arm		erb		irt	op		
art		erse		isk	ope		
ash		ert		iss	opt		
ast		erve		ist	ord		
aste		esh		it	ore		
at		ess		itch	orm		
atch		est		ite	orn		
ate		et		ive	ort		
ave		ew		ix	ose		
aw				ize	oss		

Searching for Owls

The letters *owl* can be found in many words, and of course, these letters spell the name of a bird that hoots at night. Challenge students to see how many owls they can find, for example:

- fowl
- cowl
- jowl

They can write their findings like this:

- An expression of displeasure__ __ __ __ __
- A deep, threatening sound__ __ __ __ __
- To cry loudly__ __ __ __
- A baby owl__ __ __ __ __

Students can search for cats and other animals, too.

Patterns of Vowel Spellings

You can help students become aware of different patterns by having them develop rhyme charts that involve spelling variations like this one.

Spelling the phoneme /iy/ long e

eek	eak	eet	eat	eer	ear	eel	eal
leek	beak	beet	beat	deer	dear	feel	deal
meek	leak	feet	heat	beer	fear	heel	heal
peek	peak	meet	meat	jeer	gear	keel	steal
reek	teak	fleet	pleat	peer	hear	kneel	real
seek	weak	greet	seat	leer	near	peel	seal
week	sneak	sleet	peat	cheer	rear	wheel	peal
cheek	speak	sweet	neat	sneer	sear	reel	meal
creek	freak	street	treat	steer	year	steel	
Greek		(mete)	bleat	(mere)	smear	(spiel)	
sleek		(Pete)	wheat		spear		
(eke)							
(pique)							

Be sure that students generate these lists themselves rather than use reading lists you have prepared. Creating such rhyme lists helps students contrast the alternate spellings of common phonograms. Students will find a number of homonyms across these lists. Talk about the spellings as students read the words they have listed.

Rhyme Roots

You may wish to have a rhyme root of the week posted on tagboard. Ask students to contribute words to the list throughout the week. At the end of the first week, create a group poem using as many of the contributed words as possible. After practice with group poems, students may prefer to create small group or individual poems.

Students will also enjoy seeing who can come up with a sensible sentence using the most rhyming words. For example:

> The sleek Greek mouse went once a week to take a meek peek at the creek and seek a leek and carry it away in her cheek before it began to reek.

Guess the *ie/ei* Word

Jointly brainstorm several lists of words designed to show patterns or spelling rules. Use this list to demonstrate when to use the spelling *ie* or *ei*.

ie	*ei* (after *c*)	*ei* (long *a*)	*ei* (long *e*)	*el* (long *i*)
chief	receive	eight	seize	height
genie	deceive	rein	weird	sleight
believe	conceive	neigh	caffeine	neither (regional
babies		feign	neither	variant)
relieve		neighbor		
niece		weight		
ladies				

Divide your class into two teams to review these words. One team begins by saying, "We are thinking of a word where *ie* sounds like long *e*." The other team has a certain number of guesses to discover the word; for example, "Does your word come out of a bottle and give three wishes?" You may wish to cover your class list after a few practice rounds.

Riddle-Me-Ree

Students love riddles. Here the riddle is used to teach students patterns of English spelling. The form of the riddle is a poem, with each line providing a clue for one letter of the answer.

> *My first is in* awl *but not in* all;
> *My second is in* car *but not in* bike;
> *My third is in* tea *but not in* coffee;
> *My fourth is in* pet *but not in* animal;
> *My fifth is in* air *but not in* sky;
>   Riddle-me-ree;
>   What can it be?

The clues tell us that the first letter is *w.* The second letter can be *c, a,* or *r,* while the third letter is *t* or *a.* The fourth is *p, e,* or *t* and the fifth is *a, i,* or *r.* Although the clues seem confusing as they are listed, the students can reason that since the word begins with *w,* it can't be followed by *c,* possibly might be *r,* but is most likely *a. Wa* can't be followed by another *a,* so the next letter must be *t.* The fourth letter then can't be *p,* but it can be *e* or *t.* Finally, the word can't end in *ea, ei, ta, ti,* or *tr* but only *er.* The answer is *water.*

This game can be used with younger students as well by making the examples easy. Here is a simpler example that would be good for slow readers.

> *My first is in* cave *but not in* brave;
> *My second is in* ask *but not in* question;
> *My third is in* take *but not in* give;
>   Riddle-me-ree;
>   What can it be?

The answer can only be *cat.*

Encourage students to prepare their own riddles to use in teams. Everyone will benefit from the vocabulary development and spelling practice.

Jumblies

Jumblies is a simple word game that students of any age can enjoy playing. Give the students a joke or a riddle and provide the answer, only with the letters scrambled. They will know when they have unscrambled the letters correctly because they will have the answer to the question.

You can use this technique on test questions or any time you are reviewing the students' knowledge. Knowing that they can discover the answer provides the motivation for working the puzzle. Conundrums are excellent for this purpose, for example:

- *What is worse than raining cats and dogs?*
  (giahinl xatabcsi)
  hailing taxicabs

Hole in One!

To play Golf, open a textbook to a page of print. Place a slip of paper along the left side of the page so only three letters show, as in the illustration. On a score sheet record the data collected for each game of nine holes.

The student tries to make a word beginning with the letters given by adding as few letters as possible. The score equals the number of letters added. As in golf, the object is to get a low score.

To encourage students to write longer words, play *Basketball.* The object then is to get a high score.

Hole		Play	Strokes
1	che	cheer	2
2	hea	head	1
3	don	donate	3
4	pas	pass	1
5	On	On	0
6	pro	problem	4
7	suc	such	1
8	tuc	tuck	1
9	hun	hunt	1
TOTAL			

Key Words

Show students a puzzle based on a key word like the one shown here. Then challenge them to create more puzzles based on key words they select, such as *happy, success,* or *create.*

1. __T__   ____   ____   ____
2. ____   __H__   ____   ____
3. ____   ____   __I__   ____   ____
4. ____   ____   ____   __N__   ____   ____
5. ____   ____   ____   ____   __K__   ____

1. Used for camping
2. To demonstrate
3. To fool someone
4. Two times ten
5. A way of eating

Growing Words

Beginning with a one-lettered word such as *i, a,* or *o,* make a word grow by adding one letter at a time. Each time, of course, you must make a new word, thus:

a	o
an	do
ant	nod
pant	node
paint	nodes
paints	

Challenge students to see how long a list they can make. One of the longest is the following:

I
in
sin
sing
swing
sewing
stewing

strewing

wrestling

sweltering

Add-a-Letter

This is a stimulating word game especially interesting for advanced students. Give the students a list of words that can be changed into new words by the addition of a single letter. Duplicate several lists of words and have answer sheets ready for the students to check themselves. Always leave room for the students to add new examples.

In this example, the Add-a-Letter is *e*. The student is to add an *e* anywhere in the word without changing the order of the letters.

far (fare, fear)

spar (spear, spare)

plan (plane)

on (one, eon)

man (mean, mane)

fat (fate, feal)

chat (cheat)

par (pare, pear)

fat (fate, feat)

hat (hate, heat)

ban (bane, bean)

star (stare)

brad (bread)

mad (made, mead)

fast (feast)

bar (bare, bear)

pal (peal, pale)

mat (mate, meat)

hat (hate, heat)

at (eat, ate)

Here are examples for the letter *i:*

run (ruin)

her (heir)

plan (plain)

bran (brain)

pad (paid)

sad (said)

pan (pain)

Challenge students to discover new examples of words that can be changed by adding one letter:

even (event, seven)

tar (star, tear)

sing (sling, sting)

bed (bred, bead)

Key Letters

Students become aware of the structure of words through an activity focusing on letters in sequence. If you give them the letters *v* and *n,* they can supply words in which these two letters appear in that order, for example:

van	event
vane	evasion
vine	valentine
even	

Giving students three letters makes the task even more interesting as students search for words that fit patterns as shown here:

- *mbr:* amber, lumber, member, jamboree
- *smn:* jasmine, submarine, superman, smiling
- *ftr:* feather, father, after, faster
- *rnd:* rend, round, grind, rendition

Notice that three letters often appear on license plates, so this is a good game to play when traveling in a car.

Off to Washington!

Challenge students to see how many words they can find in the word *Washington.* The letters may be arranged in any order, but they may not be used more than the times they appear in this word. Examples include:

wash	as	tan
sing	ton	ant
wing	tin	want
ash	win	wag
sang	sin	sag
hang	hint	tag
tang	song	nag
saw	tongs	snag

Obviously many words will do. As you do more of these you might challenge students to list only words of at least four letters.

Word Family Chain

Children who are beginning to read and spell words will be intrigued by this kind of chain.

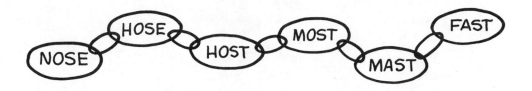

Notice that only one letter in the chain is changed each time in order to form a new word. Challenge children to create as long a chain as possible on the board as a group project. Or, start several chains at different places on the chalkboard at which children can work. This activity can also be developed as individual sheets that children can complete. Good beginning sets of words are the following:

cat	slip	less
fat	ship	loss
far	shop	lost

Challenge more advanced students to create chains with longer words, for example, *short, shirt, shire, share*. The longer the words are, the harder the task.

Transformations

A word game that fascinates students is to change one word into the opposite by changing one letter at a time. Each time you must have a real word. The object is to reach the other word in as few steps as possible. See how you change *cold* into *heat* in as few moves as possible. Notice that there is no single answer.

cold	cold
colt	hold
coat	held
boat	head
beat	heat
heat	

The longer the word, the more difficult the task is. Show the class how to work the example and then challenge them to produce others. Have a student test pairs of words to make sure the transformation is possible before you challenge the rest of the class. Remember that there may be several different ways of reaching the end word.

work	work
pork	pork
perk	perk
peak	peak
beak	peat
beat	plat (surveyor's map)
seat	play
slat	
slay	
play	

Word Building

Students need experience in building words. Give them u-shaped blocks to fill in with three-lettered words that contain the short sound of *u*. Have the students fill in as many u blocks as they can. This activity can be made into an Assignment Sheet.

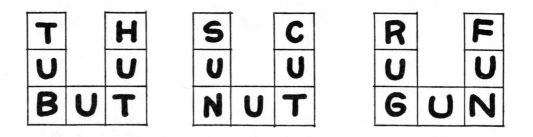

Mouse Maze

Letters can be connected in many different ways to spell different words. See how many words your students can spell from the mice below. Students must stay on the maze paths and cannot jump over a mouse.

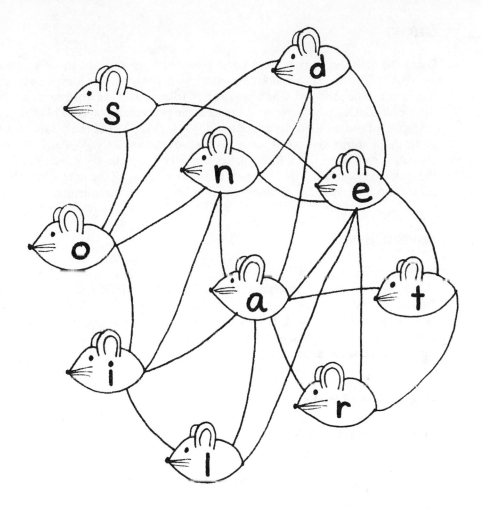

real line soil dear

Spell a Word

Prepare fifty one-inch cardboard squares on which the letters of the alphabet are printed. Make extra squares for more common consonants that begin many English words; for example, *b, l, m, n, p, s,* and *t.* These squares can be used in many ways. Encourage students to develop spelling games, such as drawing ten squares and seeing if they can spell a word with the letters drawn.

GHOST

Using the alphabet squares from the previous activity, turn the squares so the letters are visible. The first player chooses a letter to start a word. The players in turn add letters to continue the word. The player forced to complete the word earns a letter from the word GHOST. A player who suspects the preceding player is bluffing can challenge the player to spell the entire word. (V-A-L-L = ?) If the player was bluffing and cannot complete a word, or spells the word incorrectly (V-A-L-L-Y), he or she also earns a GHOST letter. If the player correctly completes the word (V-A-L-L-E-Y), the challenger earns a GHOST letter. A player earning all the letters in GHOST vanishes from the game. The dictionary may be used to settle challenges.

SUPERGHOST

In this version, letters may be added at either end (B, B-O, L-B-O, E-L-B-O, E-L-B-O-W). This variation is much more difficult. SUPERGHOST is a good review of affixes since strategy demands escaping into longer words (R-E-A, E-R-E-A, E-R-E-A-D, E-R-E-A-D-I, . . . R-E-R-E-A-D-I-N-G). Challenges occur more often in this version, but players have five extra letters before becoming a SUPERGHOST and vanishing from the game.

Beginning and Ending Chain

Groups of children can play this game on sheets of paper or at the chalkboard. It also makes a good relay. The first person writes any word, for example, *ball*. The next person must begin the next word with the letter that ends the first, in this case, *l*. If that person writes *lark*, the next word must begin with *k*, and so on, thus:

ball—lark—kitchen—nice—easy—yes

For variety, chains can be printed in this form:

ballarkitcheniceasYesnowinter

To make the game more difficult for advanced students, specify that words must have at least four letters. Another variation would be that the words must contain three or four syllables.

Using a Code

Language is a kind of code. We can send and receive messages only with people who know the same code: English. Part of the process of teaching children to read and to write is teaching them how to encode their knowledge of the spoken language into the written code, and how to decode written messages.

You can introduce the idea of encoding and decoding with a simple written code.

A = 26	N = 13
B = 25	O = 12
C = 24	P = 11
D = 23	Q = 10
E = 22	R = 9
F = 21	S = 8
G = 20	T = 7
H = 19	U = 6
I = 18	V = 5
J = 17	W = 4
K = 16	X = 3
L = 15	Y = 2
M = 14	Z = 1

Using the key to this code (above), can you decode this message?

"11 15-22-26-8-22, 14-26-8-7-22-9," 8-26-18-23/7-19-22/24-26-7, "4-18-15-15/2-12-6/24-19-26-13-20-22/14-22/18-13-7-12-/26/14-26-13?"   15-15-12-2-23/26 15-22-3-26-13-23-22-9, 7-19-22/24-26-7/4-19-12/1 18-8-19-22-23/7-12/25-22/26/14-26-13.

You should read:

"Please, master," said the cat, "will you change me into a man?" Lloyd Alexander, *The Cat Who Wished to Be a Man.*

Code Variations

Once students have become familiar with the operation of a code, they can begin to construct more complex coding systems. There are many simple variations on the basic code that even slower students can use:

$$A = 1 + 3 \qquad A = Z$$
$$B = 2 + 3 \qquad B = Y$$
$$C = 3 + 3 \qquad C = X$$
$$D = 4 + 3 \qquad D = W$$

Students can also create codes in which nonletter symbols are used to represent letters, for example:

$$A = \triangle \qquad A = \mathcal{M}$$
$$B = \triangle \qquad B = \circ\!\!-\!\!\circ$$
$$C = \square \qquad C = \rightarrowtail$$
$$D = \boxdot \qquad D = \frown$$

The relevance of using codes to teaching spelling and reading is that every time we use a code, we are encoding English spelling. To use the code properly, students must know how to spell the words correctly. Playing with codes, therefore, adds variety and interest to spelling lessons.

Encoding Quotations

Have a student write a quotation in code every day on the board. This could be a quote from a famous person, a favorite saying, or a passage from a book the class is reading. Provide keys to the code for everyone and let students work out the solution. Encourage students to develop their own codes.

Students will be motivated to continue code study on their own once they realize the possibility for complexity. Some students will notice that each code is an algebraic statement. Even the most complex codes are related mathematically to basic codes. They can develop codes such as these:

- $A = N + 3$
- $A = 2N + 4$
- $A = 3(N - 2)$
- $A = N \div 2$

A Code Wheel

A useful code device is based on the idea of a circle within a circle. The larger circle is mounted on heavy paper or cardboard. The smaller circle is attached to the larger by a brad or tack through the center of both circles so that the inside moves around freely. The bank around the rim of both circles is divided into twenty-six spaces and the lines separating the spaces must extend evenly from the small to the larger circle. Write the twenty-six letters in alphabetical order counter-clockwise around the edge of the larger circle.

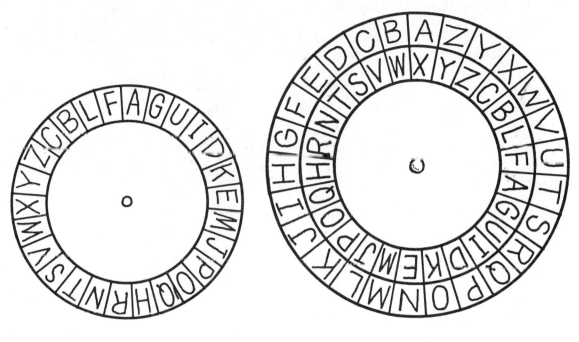

Part 1   *Part 2*

AHQG DQYYX BIITTJ MXPTG MT HFFRUZ!

Translation: This pizza wheel makes me hungry!

Students can create a personal secret cipher by writing the letters of the alphabet around the smaller circle in any order. One way to do this is to pick a key phrase or word with a variety of letters. A possible key phrase is the student's name (see part 1). Arrange the key around the smaller circle in alternate spaces. Then fill in the empty spaces with the remaining letters in alphabetical order.

To write in this cipher, first place the A in the outer circle against the X in the inner one (see part 2). After writing out the message in regular spelling, find each letter in the outer circle and write the corresponding letter in the inner circle.

To decipher the message, you use the same wheel, of course, as you reverse the process. Students can work in pairs for this activity. Round pizza boards make excellent wheels.

The English Code

After the students have worked with coded messages, introduce the idea of a phonetic code. English can be represented by a phonetic alphabet. Once you know how to read the symbols, there is no possible confusion over two sounds being represented by the same written letter or two letters representing the same sound because this expanded alphabet provides a symbol for each sound we use in English.

Learning the phonetic alphabet is useful in sorting out the intricacies of English spelling. Symbols placed between slashes indicate a sound (phoneme), not a letter of the alphabet. Here is a sample phonetic alphabet:

Consonants

/b/ bill
/d/ do
/f/ fight
/g/ go
/h/ hi
/j/ jam
/k/ key
/l/ low
/m/ more
/n/ no
/p/ pot
/r/ red
/s/ sit
/t/ to
/v/ van
/w/ will
/y/ yell
/z/ zoo

Digraphs
/č/ chew
/š/ shoo
/ž/ Asia
/θ/ thing
/ð/ the
/ŋ/ sing

Vowels

Diphthongs
/iy/ see
/ey/ bay
/ay/ I
/ow/ oh
/yuw/ use*
/oy/ toy
/aw/ now
/uw/ too

Simple Vowels
/i/ hit
/e/ Ed
/æ/ at
/ə/ nut
/a/ ah
/u/ put
/ɔ/ jaw
/ɨ/ her

*This sound is actually two phonemes /y/ and /uw/. We include it here so that all five long vowel sounds are represented.

Students will notice that there are twenty-four consonant sounds and sixteen vowel sounds. What letters of our alphabet are missing? Why? What phonetic symbols do we use that are not letters of the English alphabet? As students practice using this code for English words, they will learn to pay more attention to how the words sound and also to the different ways of writing (spelling) the same sounds.

Using the Phonetic Alphabet

Give the students a copy of the phonetic alphabet and a worksheet of activities like the following:

- Use the phonetic alphabet to write your first name.
- Use the phonetic alphabet to write your favorite color.
- Use the phonetic alphabet to write your favorite game.
- Use the phonetic alphabet to write your favorite food.

These papers can be posted on the bulletin board with questions like:

- What is Rod's favorite color?
- Who wrote the answers in green ink?
- How many people chose pizza as their favorite food?
- What is Kyra's favorite game?

Another worksheet for students is:

- Here are five of your spelling words. Can you crack the phonetic code?

/č/	/ey/	/n/	/j/	(change)
/š/	/aw/	/t/		(shout)
/t/	/iy/	/θ/		(teeth)
/š/	/ae/	/k/		(shack)
/r/	/iy/	/č/		(reach)

Coding and Dialects

As students practice using a phonetic alphabet, they will soon notice that people in the class pronounce the same words in different ways. When they try to encode English words in phonetic symbols, they must learn to listen carefully to their own speech. Here is a sample of phonetic writing from Astrid Lindgren's *Pippi Long-stocking* (New York: Viking, 1950). Ask students to read aloud.

/Wey owt æt ðə end əv ə tayniy litəl town wəz æn old ovərgrown gardən, ænd in ðə gardən wəz æn old hows, ænd in ðə hows livd Pippiy Loŋstakiŋ./

Ask the students, "Does this paragraph sound like the way you talk? Would you change any of the symbols to match your speech more precisely?"

Although it may seem difficult at first to read these symbols, you will find it easier as you become more familiar with them and with the sound each one represents.

Researching Codes

Encourage students to research information about the history of codes. There are many historically important codes they could look up and learn to use, for example, the Morse code.

Books about codes that children could use include:

Helen Jill Fletcher, *Secret Codes* (New York: Watts, 1980).

Martin Gardner, *Ciphers and Secret Writing* (New York: Simon & Schuster, 1974).

John Peterson, *How to Write Codes and Send Secret Messages* (Englewood Cliffs, N.J.: Four Winds, 1970).

Joel Rothman and Ruthven Tremain, *Secrets with Ciphers and Codes* (New York: Macmillan, 1969).

Homonyms

Homonyms are words that sound the same but are spelled differently and have different meanings. The English language has many homonyms, and students are always intrigued to discover them. Have a contest to see who can list the most number of homonym pairs. For example:

hare-hair	blue-blew	stationery-stationary
bare-bear	deer-dear	stair-stare
bee-be	so-sew	son-sun
know-no	vane-vein	fair-fare
red-read	eye-I	principle-principal

There are even homonym triplets. Students probably know some of them:

pear-pair-pare	four-for-fore
to-too-two	aisle-I'll-isle
rain-reign-rein	carrot-caret-carat
they're-their-there	

Direct the students' attention to the spelling patterns shown by these homonyms. Many pairs end in air/are, ea/ee, ail/ale. Have students become more aware of homonyms and their spellings by writing sentences that contain both words:

- The bear that I found was completely bare.
- May I have a knife to pare this pair of pears?
- That last storm blew down the blue sign.

Dictate these sentences for spelling practice.

In discussing homonyms with the class, it is important to remember that some speakers pronounce vowels differently and words that are homonyms for many students in the class may not be homonyms for everyone, for example, *Mary, merry,* and *marry.*

The Pair Tree

Create a large tree by anchoring a branch in a coffee can filled with gravel. Cover the can with colored paper and the words *The Pair Tree,* as shown. This tree will be used to display pears cut from yellow construction paper on which different pairs of homonyms are printed.

The tree can also be used to emphasize other pairs of words, such as:

- Antonyms (full–empty; sharp–dull)
- Expressions (cats and dogs; beep and creep; P's and Q's; ladies and gentlemen)
- Verbs and Nouns (deceive–deception; explain–explanation)

Be sure to add a partridge to your pair tree!

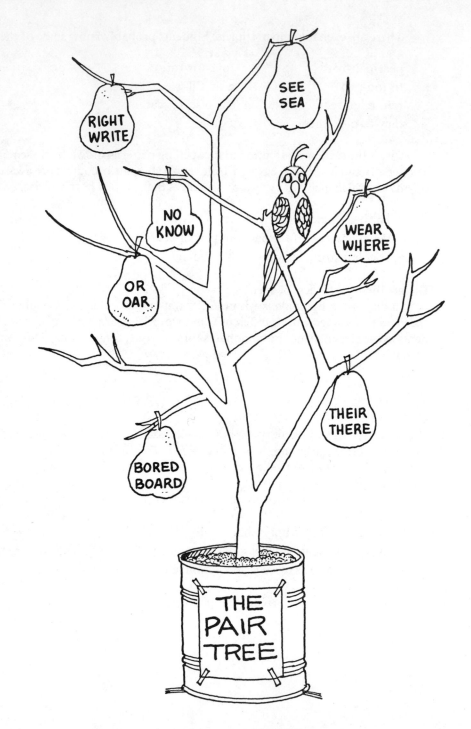

Hidden Homonyms

Increase students' awareness of homonyms (or homophones) in our language by playing this game. Give them a sheet of sentences in which words have been left out. The missing words in each sentence are homonyms. The goal is to guess the words and fill them in, including spelling them correctly. Of course, once the student has guessed one of the words, the other should be obvious. Here are some sentences (with answers indicated) to start with:

* Have you _____ the book with the _____ cover?
            (read)   (red)

* The _____ people in the hospital all _____ from the same dish.
      (eight)   (ate)

* They were surprised to _____ that the ship was already at _____.
                        (see)   (sea)

* I can't _____ the way everybody goes _____ foot in summer.
          (bear)   (bare)

* Would you like to _____ the author of *100 Ways to Cook Snake* _____?"
                    (meet)   (*Meat*)

* When they arrived at the camping _____, they found an unforgettable
                                   (site)

_____.
(sight)

Have duplicated sheets of these sentences available for students to work on when they choose. Students will also enjoy thinking up examples to try on the class.

Homonyms

Here is a useful list of less common homonyms to use with the suggested activities:

metal, mettle	cast, caste	write, right, wright, rite
horse, hoarse	waive, wave	carrot, carat, caret
aloud, allowed	dough, doe	cite, site, sight
knew, gnu, new	mete, meet, meat	censor, censer
raze, raise	colonel, kernel	climb, clime
knight, night	mane, main, Maine	complement, compliment
dew, due, do	you, ewe	stationery, stationary
feint, faint	all, awl	council, counsel
mist, missed	flair, flare	baron, barren
hew, hue	paced, paste	roe, row

gage, gauge

core, corps

whet, wet

wails, whales, Wales

suite, sweet

assent, ascent

sty, stye

faun, fawn

choir, quire

magnet, magnate

barer, bearer

pier, peer

sold, soled, souled

pique, peek, peak

foul, fowl

sign, sine

idle, idyl, idol

so, sow, sew

bald, bawled, balled

heroine, heroin

great, grate

cede, seed

wile, while

tear, tare

sloe, slow

knave, nave

wind, whined, wined

seine, sane

not, knot

Homonym Play

This poem demonstrates the humorous effect achieved by deliberately using the wrong homonym. Ask students to identify the correct spellings for each homonym.

A Tail of Whoa (Two bee red allowed)

Eye stood before the window pain
To stair out on the stormy seen.
  The wind it blue
  With grown and mown
As rein pored threw the lain.

Eye razed my head to view the cite
And new my hart wood brake
  Four rested from hour would
  Were awl the furs sew tall and grate
Know more too waive the see.

Aisle ne'er forget that dreadful knight—
A quire of desolation maid
  Buy hale and creek of bows—
  Yet still no paws or lesson.
The whether it was fowl!

Then shown at last the mourning son.
The heir now boar the fare suite cent
  Of rows and hair belle whet.
  At piece the wind; knot sew my sole,
Fore their the land lei waist.

IRIS M. TIEDT

Spelling Search on the Bulletin Board

Give students the chart below. Let them find as many words as possible by drawing a circle around any words they use. Make a board with small finishing nails tacked into each letter glued on the board. Provide a box of yarn for the children to connect the letters of a word by wrapping the yarn around each letter. You can use rubber bands as well.

Timed Spelling

Ask your class, "How many words that begin with *p* can you write in sixty seconds?" As the stopwatch ticks, children should write quickly without the aid of dictionaries. Then they break up in small groups to check each other's words. They can keep score if the words are given values according to length, thus:

Length	Value
1–2 letters	0
3	1
4	1
5	3
6	4
7	6
8	7
9	7
10	10
11 +	20

They spell it Vinci and pronounce it Vinchy; foreigners always spell better than they pronounce.

MARK TWAIN

Spelling Who Am I?

Use the current spelling list for this game. Start the game by picking a word from the list and asking the students to guess the word. Give identifying clues to help them figure out the word you have in mind. Examples are:

I have three syllables
I contain a prefix
I have a short vowel sound
I can be used as an adverb
One synonym for me is . . .
One antonym for me might be . . .
    Who am I?

The student who guesses the word first can select the next word and prepare the clues. Help students by suggesting useful clues. Students can also play this game in teams. Each team vies with the other for the most interesting and difficult clues.

Scrambled Words

Challenge the more able students in your class by asking them to develop an activity sheet that the rest of the class can use. They can scramble ten of the current spelling words and supply synonyms as clues, thus:

- wroth   (toss)
- thogs   (spook)
- arhic   (seat)
- soecl   (shut)
- nayrg   (mad)
- phapy   (glad)
- kistc   (twig)
- molob   (flower)
- disel   (skid)
- ghaul   (giggle)

The Word Loop

Find as many words as possible in the word loop, going clockwise. All letters are to be used. Do not list any word more than once. Sometimes small words may be found within bigger words. There are more than forty words in this loop. Note that a particular letter may be part of more than one word.

The size of the loop and the words used can be varied to suit any grade level. This game encourages students to use the dictionary to check words they think might be in the loop.

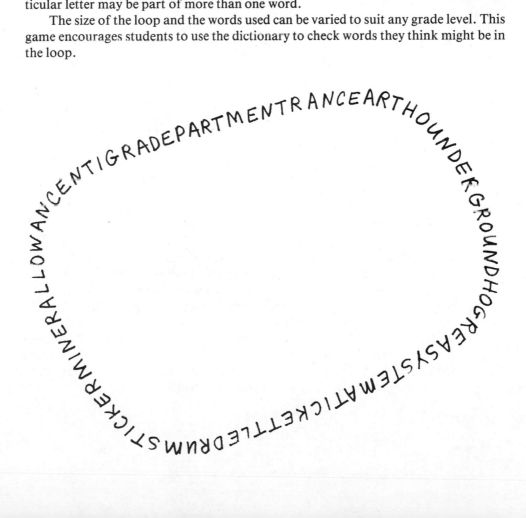

Categories for Beginning Spellers

Choose several categories and write them on strips of tagboard. Some examples are: names in our class, animals, ice cream flavors, colors, and so on. Give a category and a selection of letters, such as Scrabble squares, to each small group. Each player in turn draws a letter and gives a word beginning with that letter that belongs in the category. If the player cannot supply a word, the alphabet square is returned to the pile. Players get one point for correctly naming a word. To make the game more difficult, the player may be required to spell the word.

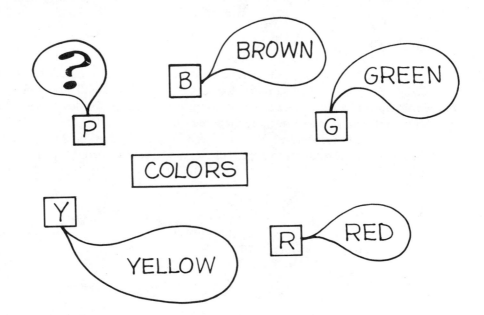

Categories for More Experienced Spellers

This game is played in groups of five. Each player will need a category chart. Each group will need a pile of letters of the alphabet from which to draw. Each player nominates one category which all group members write on their charts (or you can provide five categories you wish to emphasize). Each player then draws one letter which all write on their charts. Then students compete to see who can fill in the most spaces on the chart. A kitchen timer can be used to set a time limit. One point is scored for each correctly spelled answer. (Pass charts to player on the left for scoring. Dictionaries and other references may be used to verify answers.) A scoring variation is to double the score of any category completely filled.

	Rivers	Countries	Mammals	Fruit	Insects
P					
A					
L					
T					
R					

Spelling Doozers

accent, ascent, assent
dessert, desert
loose, lose, loss
accept, except
they're, there, their
you're, your
whose, who's

Mnemonics

Children are intrigued by the word *mnemonics*. Even though these memory devices don't always work, they have a strange fascination. Talk about these aids to memory.

- *arithmetic*   A rat in the house may eat the ice cream.
- *almost*   Almost always spelled with one l.
- *balloon*   A balloon is like a ball.
- *parallel*   All railroad tracks are parallel.

- *superintendent*   There is a *dent* in superinten*dent*.
- *principal*   The princi*pal* is a prince of a *pal*.
- *all right*   *All* right is like *all* wrong.
- *chocolate*   There is a second *o* in chocolate.
- *familiar*   There is a *liar* in fami*liar*.
- *separate*   There is *a rat* in sep*arate*.
- *cemetery*   Watch the e's in c*e*m*e*t*e*ry.

Our Queer Language

When the English tongue we speak,
Why is "break" not rhymed with "freak"?
Will you tell me why it's true
We say "sew" but likewise "few";
And the maker of a verse
Cannot cap his "horse" with "worse"?
"Beard" sounds not the same as "heard";
"Cord" is different from "word";
Cow is "cow" but low is "low";
"Shoe" is never rhymed with "foe."
Think of "hose" and "dose" and "lose";
And think of "goose" and yet of "choose."
Think of "comb" and "tomb" and "bomb";
"Doll" and "roll" and "home" and "some."
And since "pay" is rhymed with "say,"
Why not "paid" with "said," I pray?
We have "blood" and "food" and "good";
"Mould" is not pronounced like "could."
Wherefore "done" but "gone" and "lone"?
Is there any reason known?

And, in short, it seems to me
Sounds and letters disagree.

ANONYMOUS

Important Words

Ask the students, "What are the ten most important words in our language? What are the ten most crucial words—words that we cannot do without?" List all the words suggested. Then have students vote on the ten most crucial or important words. How did they define *important* or *crucial?*

Encourage students to argue for or against the inclusion of certain words before voting takes place. This list can be displayed as a chart: The Ten Most Important Words in English, Selected by Room 27. Incorporate these words regularly in your spelling list.

Word Treasures

Have each student keep a small book of words based on his or her interests. These are words that they have heard in class or found while reading. Pages can be allocated for:

- Words I Need to Write
- My Favorite Words
- Interesting Words I Found
- Strange Animals

GRAMMAR AND USAGE

Grammar and usage are two distinct aspects of language. The first is the study of how language is organized, and the second is the effective and appropriate use of language. Practice in both areas is essential to strengthen students' language development. The following activities are designed to teach students how to manipulate their language for greater effect. As a result of the activities in this section:

- Students will identify words as nouns, verbs, and the like.
- Students will create new and varied sentences.
- Students will select precise and appropriate language.

Word Classes

Rather than teach students definitions of classes of words that they must memorize, have the students discover on their own what characteristics can be used to group particular words together. Give the students five minutes to think of as many words as possible. You can do this as a group activity, writing the words on the board as the students think of them, or you can have them write their lists individually. Now divide your list by asking a series of questions:

- What words can be made plural? (*tree, book, radio*)
- What words can be possessive? (*girl, mother, cat*)
- What words can be changed from present to past tense? (*ask, see, laugh*)
- What words can have *-ing* added to them? (*listen, make, speak*)
- What words can follow *very*? (*old, stupid, big*)
- What words can fall in several of these groups? (*turn, head, paper*)
- What about the words left over? (*the, never, quickly*)
- Are there any words we use commonly that were not on the list? (*my, not, really*)

Once you have seen how the list can be divided, explain to the students that the words we use are divided into classes depending on how we can use them in a sentence.

Sentence Frames

Students can learn to test words to determine the word class they fit in by using such frames as these:

Noun:

- I need some _____.
- This is a _____.

Verb:

- Everyone _____ at home.
- What is he _____?

Adjective:

- It is very _____.
- The _____ children run.

Such exercises are useful in primary grades as children are developing sentence sense. This simple framing test continues to serve older students as they work with grammar.

Parts of Speech Chart

Prepare a large chart to display in your room to aid students in recognizing different parts of speech. It is not necessary that students memorize such definitions, but using these terms makes it easier for them to talk about their writing. Use such terms as *noun* and *verb* incidentally, even in primary grades.

Language Terms

- *Noun:* A noun is a word that can be made plural or possessive and it may follow *the, a,* or *an.* (flower, happiness)
- *Verb:* A verb is a word that can be changed from present to past, and *-ing* may be added to it. (speak, hear)
- *Adjective:* An adjective is a describing word that can follow the word *very* or a form of the verb *be* (is, are, was, were). (easy, tired)
- *Adverb:* An adverb is a word that can follow a verb and tell how a thing is done. (quickly, well)
- *Determiner:* A determiner signals that a noun follows. Included are articles, demonstratives, possessive adjectives, numbers, and so on. (the, my)
- *Pronoun:* A pronoun substitutes for a noun but does not follow a determiner. (it, him)
- *Intensifier:* An intensifier precedes adjectives and adverbs. (very, really)
- *Auxiliary:* An auxiliary signals that a verb follows. Some auxiliaries may also be verbs by themselves. (is, has)
- *Subordinator:* A subordinator connects an independent clause with a subordinate clause. (but)
- *Conjunction:* A conjunction joins equal groups of words (and)
- *Preposition:* A preposition usually introduces a phrase and signals that a noun follows. (of, in)

Vocabulary Classes

Tell the students to write the word *Vocabulary* down the left-hand side of a piece of lined paper. Across the top of the page should go the words *Adjective, Noun, Verb,* and *Adverb.* They will head for the dictionary to find unusual words that fit the slots. Encourage them to work together on looking up the meaning, spelling, and parts of speech of these words.

	Adjective	Noun	Verb	Adverb
V	vermilion		vilify	
O			open	
C		catamaran		casually
A	antique		ache	
B		byte		
U	unusual		unify	usefully
L	laborious	lift		
A		anemone	alight	abruptly
R	rambunctious			rudely
Y		yacht	yodel	

You can vary this activity by having students write their name down the left-hand side of a sheet of paper and try to fill in the boxes with words to make a sentence.

	Noun	Verb	Noun
B	Bob	builds	barns
A	Anna	ate	ants
R	Richard	robbed	Randy
B	Bill	borrowed	bolts

Lingo

This game, played like Bingo, will provide small groups of students with practice and review of the parts of speech. Prepare a set of large cards, marked off in squares, with LINGO written across the top. Fill in each square with different words that are nouns, verbs, adjectives, or adverbs. Make small squares for the caller that are labeled L-Adjective, G—Noun, G—Adverb, and so on. Also cut squares of paper for students to use to cover their cards. These should be labeled *Adjective, Adverb, Noun,* and *Verb.*

L	I	N	G	O
paint	quickly	game	purple	cast
create	dawn	forest	rocky	strange
volcano	bright	catch	surround	take
soft	fine	narrowly	candle	mineral
difficult	pencil	forget	short	slowly

As in Bingo, the caller shuffles the slips and calls them out, one at a time. The students look down the column to see if they have a word that belongs to the category called (noun, verb, adjective, or adverb). If they find a word that fits, they cover it with the corresponding marked square. The first person to cover a row, column, or diagonal can check to see if the words were identified correctly as a part of speech.

You can make the game more difficult by including words that can be different parts of speech, for example *paint* or *fine.* Then the students must justify their answer by using the word correctly in a sentence.

Word Cubes

Students can construct Word Cubes (dice) by cutting this pattern from any stiff paper and folding it as indicated in the illustration.

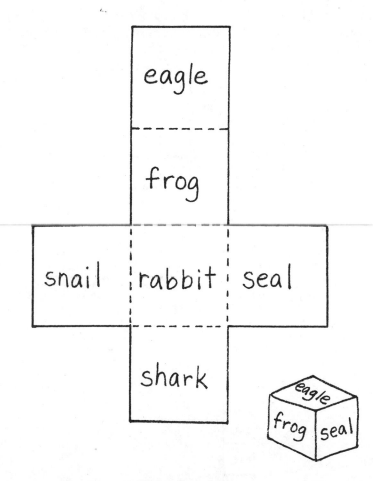

A "Nouns" word cube

Ask students to work together in small groups to create four cubes on which they list (1) nouns, (2) verbs, (3) adjectives, and (4) adverbs. They can then use the cubes like dice to create sentences by rolling the four dice. They can add any structure words needed to create a sentence. If, for example, they rolled the words *eagle, flew, brave,* and *slowly,* they could create the sentence: *The brave eagle flew slowly.*

If you want to encourage students to write long sentences, let them add as many words as possible to the four core words. Then the score is determined by the number of words written by each student. You might have such sentences as: *The brave old eagle flew slowly over the small town, looking for the mountains in which he had spent the happy days of his youth with brothers and sisters who loved to hide deep in the rocks so he couldn't find them.*

Name Crossword

Ask each youngster to write his or her name across a sheet of paper. Then construct a puzzle by using adjectives that describe this person. For example:

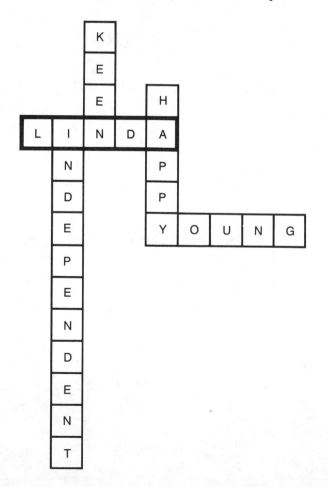

Adjective Story

Here is an activity that allows children to be as silly as they want, yet learn how to use adjectives creatively. Students can prepare a list of adjectives beforehand from which to choose or fill in whatever comes to mind as they read the story.

When Sally woke up this _____ morning, her _____ hair was in a _____ mess. She used a _____ brush to clean it up a bit, but it was still too _____. She asked her _____ mother to help her out, but her _____ mother was _____. Sally went across the _____ street to ask her _____ neighbor, but her _____ neighbor wasn't home. Sally sat on the _____ curb, wondering what to do next. Along came a _____ dog, who licked the _____ mess on Sally's _____ head. Hooray! The dog licked the _____ mess right out. Sally patted the _____ dog's _____ head, and the dog said, "I sure showed you a lick or two!"

Acrostic Names

One version of acrostics is based on a person's name. Students can use their own first or last name or the name of a friend. The words chosen to fill in horizontally may be personal characteristics or adjectives that apply generally.

A   musing
M   ild
I   maginative
R   owdy

R   ambunctious
Y   oung
A   mbitious
N   oisy

Once students become accustomed to these acrostics, they can scramble the adjectives so that the others have to figure out whose name is being used.

Picture This!

Have students write a noun at the top of a sheet of paper. Then ask them to list at least ten words that could describe the noun. Of course, they have made a list of adjectives or adverbs. As a follow-up, students create a picture outline of the noun using the descriptive words they have listed. A student who chose *tree,* for example, might create a picture from his or her list, as illustrated.

Tree

green	brown	graceful	tall	slippery
shady	hard	gnarled	cool	rough
leafy	scratchy	ancient	twisted	

Post the students' illustrations and note imaginative choices of words.

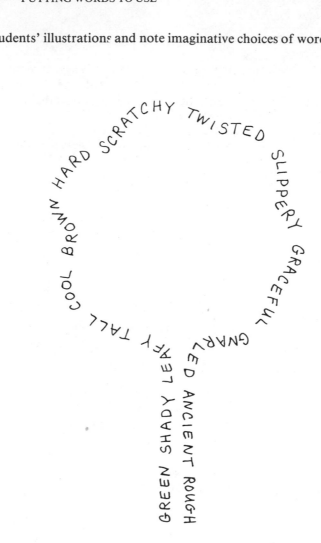

Tom Swifties

This activity allows students to play with language and at the same time teaches them verbs and adverbs. The best explanation is a set of examples:

- "I'll hurry," said Tom swiftly.
- "Be careful with that knife," he said sharply.
- "I wish it would rain soon," he said drily.
- "I can't see the point," he said bluntly.

- "I think there are moths in my sweaters," he said airily.
- "I've always wanted to go up in a balloon," he said lightly.
- "I can never remember the two times tables," he said evenly.
- "I'm taking up medicine," he said cuttingly.

Tom Swifties are made by combining an adverb with an action or comment to produce a humorous effect. Notice that writing the examples also requires students to use quotation marks.

Heteronyms

Heteronyms are words that are spelled alike, but by a slight change, usually a shift in stress, signal a change in meaning, for example:

- She likes to keep the papers *separate*.
- I will *separate* the correct words from the incorrect.

Many heteronyms are noun-verb pairs.

- The administration will not *permit* this behavior to continue.
- He got the *permit* for the car today.
- I would like to *address* the conference next month.
- I never write because I don't have your *address*.

Examples of heteronyms are the following:

content	record	entrance
desert	subject	rebel
object	present	produce
project	reject	bow
tear	refuse	use

Have students write sentences including pairs of heteronyms like those above. They can practice listening for heteronyms and using them correctly.

Sentence Wheel

Use a set of wheels to help students produce sentences as well as review parts of speech. You can use determiners, nouns, and verbs, or adjectives, nouns, and verbs. In this example, we have used nouns, verbs, and adverbs. Directions for making these wheels appears on page 165.

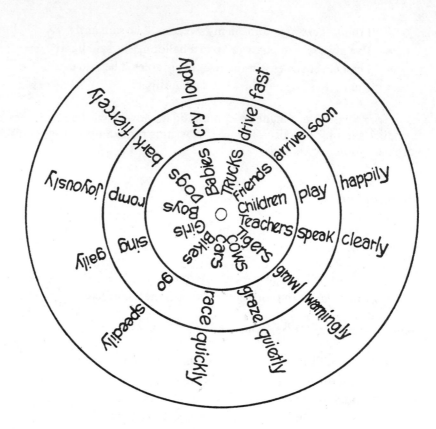

Understanding Grammar

Explain that we all have a "sentence-making machine" in our brains that enables us to create new sentences any time we need them. Demonstrate this knowledge of English grammar by having students identify which of these groups of words is an English sentence and which is not.

- rode the boy park
- the boy the park
- the boy rode through the park

Almost every child will quickly identify the third group as a sentence. How do they know? Their sentence-making machines allow them to recognize something is missing without knowing the proper names for word classes.

Word Order

Merely including all the right words is not enough to make a sentence. Show the students how important word order is in English by having them compare these two sentences:

- The girl sat on the friendly horse.
- The horse sat on the friendly girl.

Ask the students if the two sentences mean the same thing. What's the difference? Can students understand these sentences?

- Maria to each speak Luis and often other.
- sick the today are teachers all.
- radio from music the comes.

What must we do to make sentences comprehensible? Note that a group of words may make several possible sentences.

Scrambled Sentences

Ask the children to unscramble these sentences to make them grammatical.

- spaghetti supper Marty for made
- dove waves The the under seal
- broken the mended She vase
- planted a Mike garden vegetable
- Sally two younger has sisters

Occasionally include an extra word so students really have to think.

- the Gail in bowl radio oranges the put
- from picked garden his newspaper Walt squash ten
- pictures Jennie pretty cooked draw can
- her to wrote a Nancy letter car friend
- on sandcastle built they a beach wave the

The basal reader is a good source for the construction of more examples. The ability to make these groups of words into sentences illustrates a student's knowledge of grammar.

Original Sentences

Give students practice in producing new sentences. Print a word on the board and ask each student to suggest a sentence using that word. Don't try to record them, but point out that each sentence is an individual production and each student can produce many different examples. Try these words for starters: *tiger, submarine, jump, wheels.*

After practicing sentences from one word, your students will enjoy the challenge of creating original sentences from two or more words: *sandwich–table, elephant–tree, school–fish, picture–red–dog, shark–cold–teeth.*

The Basic Sentence

Show students the simplest sentence pattern, which is only two words—a noun and a verb:

- Babies cry.
- Cars honk.
- People shiver.

Have the students write a number of two-word sentences. Then ask them to expand one of their two-word sentences. They can add words before or after the two words as they make the sentences as long as possible. This demonstration of how we add modifiers, clauses, and additional ideas shows students how easy it is to write longer sentences. For example:

> As I wait outside the door, I look up at the stars and wonder what I'm doing standing outside in the cold and dark while all around me people shiver in line so that they can buy tickets to the concert in the morning.

Underlining the original two-word sentence is an effective way of showing how the sentence was developed.

More Sentence Patterns

The most common sentence pattern is a noun subject followed by an active verb and an object (SVO). Have children generate sentences like these examples:

- Naomi asked a question.
- The girl raised her hand.
- Lee studied gymnastics.

Discuss with the students the need for an appropriate article.

Mount a large picture on the bulletin board. Have everyone write a sentence in the SVO pattern to display with this picture. Everyone will be pleased to see and read the sentences displayed.

To Be a Sentence . . .

Another common pattern is the sentence with a form of *to be,* followed by an adjective or a noun, thus:

- Pablo has been sick.
- Alex is a student.
- We were late.
- Mrs. Okawa is our teacher.

Have students generate a number of sentences using *am, is, are, was, will be, shall be, were, has been, have been,* or *had been.* Notice that such forms as *is playing* or *was going* are aspects of the verbs *play* and *go,* not the verb *to be; be* can be used as an auxiliary to make progressive forms of other verbs.

Formula Sentences

Print sentence formulas on strips of paper that students can pull from a sentence dispenser made from a paper towel tube, a box that held long fireplace matches, or a painted coffee can. Use sentence formulas like this:

- Adj & N & V & Adv = S
- D & Adj & N & V & Obj = S
- N & V & I & Adv = S

Appropriate sentences that students might write for the formulas above include:

- Young children smile gracefully.
  New babies wail loudly.
- The inexperienced waiter spilled the drinks.
  A black dog chased a squirrel.
- Teachers work quite hard.
  Birds chirp very often.

Abbreviations for parts of speech are:

- D—Determiner
- Adj—Adjective
- Adv—Adverb
- N—Noun
- V—Verb
- I—Intensifier
- Obj—Object

Build-a-Sentence

Prepare a chart that lists words in different categories that students can use in sentences, as shown here:

Determiner	Adjective	Noun	Verb	Adverb
The	ravishing	chefs	growled	stupidly
Several	confused	flowers	screeched	ferociously
These	scrumptious	princes	gobbled	hastily
Three	gallant	typewriters	burned	slowly
Those	humorous	ropes	scurried	happily
Six	realistic	tigers	examined	hopefully
Forty	delighted	ostriches	slid	heartily
Several	dilapidated	racers	gasped	mournfully
Nine	handsome	tables	exploded	menacingly
Many	strong	owls	floundered	helplessly

For example, the students might create these sentences:

- Several ravishing princes floundered slowly.
- Forty gallant tigers gobbled heartily.

Sentences created can be used as Story Starters. They might stimulate students to draw humorous illustrations.

Focusing on Problem Areas

As students write, you will find that different students need help in particular areas. Don't drill the whole class on the uses of *their* and *there* if most of them already know how to use these words correctly. If, however, you note that one student or a small group of students needs this information, teach it to those students in an individualized approach.

Obtain a set of ten language workbooks. Take the books apart and reassemble into little booklets covering related skills. Color code the covers and key the booklets to student needs, so that you can refer a student to the green set, for example, to practice verb forms. Or students can work on these booklets in small groups. If some of the students continue to make errors, have other booklets of lessons available for additional practice. Students can also correct each other's work, which reinforces the skills learned.

Synonyms

Synonyms are words with the same meaning, but we must remember that no words mean precisely the same thing. The differences in use of synonyms depend on their different connotations. In certain circumstances, some words are more appropriate than others, for synonyms may have a positive or negative connotation. For example, if you agree with people you might say they have the courage of their convictions. If you disagree, you might call them stubborn. Ask your students, "Which of these terms would you call yourself? A friend? An enemy?"

- Pig-headed
- Obstinate
- Strong-minded

The thoughtful use of synonyms adds precision to our speech as well as descriptiveness.

Silly Sentences

Give students sentences that contain words that do not make sense in context. Have the students cross out the silly word and make a written or oral substitution. Allow for individual creativity and accept any substitution that makes sense. Students will enjoy creating their own silly sentences to share.

- The baby slept on the roof.
- The moon was very square last night.
- Isabel played the banana after school.
- The dog had brown and blue fur.
- The rock floated in the air.
- Jesse drank the chocolate cake.

British and American English

We say that the British and Americans speak the same language, but do they? Americans visiting England often have trouble with all the differences in vocabulary. Explore these differences with the students by researching English vocabulary. Here are some examples to get you started:

British English	American English
underground	subway
sweet	dessert
biscuits	cookies
bonnet	hood
petrol	gasoline
wireless	radio
lift	elevator
dustbin	garbage can
geyser	hot water heater

Students may have encountered some of these English words in books they have read without understanding what they meant. It is important to realize that different groups may have different words for the same thing and that one is no more correct than the other. The American word is appropriate in the United States and the English word is appropriate in England. Children will also notice differences in spelling, for instance, colour and color.

An excellent children's book for upper grades that includes examples of British English is *Children of Green Knowe* by Lucy Boston (New York: Harcourt, 1954). You can read this book aloud as children enjoy the story but also note differences in language used. This English author is a fine writer, so you will also find many examples of good writing style that you can draw to children's attention.

Making a Dialect Atlas

One of the best ways dialectologists have found to demonstrate dialect differences is to construct a map that shows the geographical distribution of different words or their different pronunciations. Your class can construct a smaller version of an atlas by giving a dialect questionnaire to all the students.

Give everyone a sheet of paper with this sentence to complete: *Harry and Maria went to play on the* _____. On the board, draw a picture of a *seesaw.* Instruct the students to finish the sentence, providing the word for the object on the board, without talking to any other person. Be careful not to use any word for the object. Then ask the students to write down where they were born and where they have lived since then, as well as where their parents are from.

After you collect the papers, you can use the information on the paper to create a map. Print each answer on a card, including the ones that list the same word. Pin the card to the map in the area where the student is from. You should have clusters of particular answers. If a different word shows up in the middle of a group, look for an explanation in the student's background. Discuss with the class why people's language might change when they move to a different area.

Your class could also exchange answers with a class in another area of the country. The more answers that can be placed on the map, the more accurate it will be. Students could ask their parents what word they can remember first using.

Answers that are in the first atlas of the United States, *The Linguistic Atlas of New England* by Hans Kurath (Providence, R.I.: Brown University Press, 1943), include:

teeter board	cock horse
teeter-totter	riding horse
tinter	hick horse
tippity-bounce	tilter board
dandle	

There are linguistic atlases for most areas of the country. Look up one of them for more examples of words to try.

Language Reflects Values

Children become more aware of how language reveals values when they compare and discuss such words as the following:

mailman	businessman
policeman	chairman
mankind	

Why would people prefer not to use some of these words? Contrast the previous words with alternatives such as *letter carrier* and *peace officer.* Can a woman be a *businessman?* Can a man be a *secretary?* Or a *stewardess?* (Note that both men and women are now called *flight attendants.*)

Students might also want to consider which adjectives are traditionally applied to women and which to men. For example:

sweet	sensitive
delicate	pretty
strong	handsome

How and why are these words used? Are there more precise or descriptive words we could use? Do we want to have different words for men and women?

Cataloguing English Idioms

Every language has colorful expressions that are part of everyday speech. These expressions, called *idioms,* would not make sense, however, if translated into another language. Some of the most familiar are:

- It's raining cats and dogs.
- He was hot under the collar.
- That's the last straw!
- I could eat a horse!

None of these, of course, are meant to be interpreted literally.

Anyone learning English, whether a child or a foreigner, has to learn what these idioms mean and the appropriate contexts in which to use them. We have heard them so often ourselves that we forget what they sound like to someone hearing them for the first time.

Your students can develop a catalog of idioms. You may want to spread this activity over several days, so that the students can enlist their parents' help in providing less familiar examples and unique regional idioms. Students will enjoy discovering idioms they have never heard before. Some idioms on your list may be:

- Butter wouldn't melt in his mouth.
- To have a finger in the pie
- To jump out of one's skin
- To pull another's leg

Collect these idioms in a book for the class to share. Students can add to this compilation as they find more unusual idioms.

Ask your students to practice using some of these idioms in their descriptive writing. Encourage them to develop their use of figurative language by using idioms from their list and by making up new expressions.

Translating Idioms

Challenge students to translate English idioms for a person who is just learning to speak English. Give students sentences like these which they are to explain:

- The family had a hard time keeping the *wolf from the door.*
- Joe was always *barking up the wrong tree.*
- Bess advised her friend not to *burn the candle at both ends.*
- Don't get your *feathers ruffled* if you aren't chosen first.
- The detective suspected the butler mainly because he looked like the *cat that swallowed the canary.*
- Ralph decided to *butter up* his parents before showing his report card.

Ask students to list other idioms they observe in their own speech.

Illustrating Idioms

Have students illustrate their favorite idioms. The literal idea behind each of the following makes a humorous picture:

- To rake up the past
- To have something up your sleeve
- To get down to brass tacks
- To weigh your words
- To turn the tables
- To be a stick in the mud
- To be on the tip of the tongue
- To steal one's thunder
- To fly into a rage
- To have bats in the belfry
- To be completely in the dark
- To know which way the wind is blowing
- To be all wrapped up in your work
- To be up the creek without a paddle
- To be caught red-handed
- To lean over backwards

Dictionary of Slanguage

Because slang is everywhere, students can easily develop an interest in studying it. Have students list as many slang words as they can to be defined, categorized into word classes, used in sentence patterns, and compiled by several "lexicographers" into a class *Dictionary of Slanguage*. For example:

- *hacker* (hak´ ĕr), n. 1. an expert computer programmer. 2. a person with little sense of right and wrong; as, having the morals of a hacker.
- *tight* (tɪt), adj. 1. very strict. 2. unfair.

Will the words in this dictionary become dated? Discuss this with the students.

The Lore and Language of Schoolchildren (New York: Oxford, 1959), by Iona and Peter Opie, is a classic book that reports the results of a nationwide study of children's folklore in Great Britain. For the first time, children's rhymes and games were taken seriously as worthy of study. The Opies found that children's stories are remarkably similar across Great Britain, that particular topical rhymes spread incredibly fast, and that adults have no role in the development and dissemination of children's folklore. The examples given in the book are especially fascinating for their resemblance to children's rhymes and stories in the United States. Use children's own lore in the classroom for reading and oral language activities. Collect, for example, a book of *Children's Sayings* or *Jump Rope Jingles*.

7 Children Can Write

Students learn to write by writing. Our task as teachers is to provide them with the opportunities and experiences necessary to express their thoughts and feelings in a clear, coherent manner.

Young writers are often intimidated by the finality of putting words on paper. We can encourage fluency and self-expression by teaching students that editing is a natural process that comes only after our ideas have been recorded. Once students are accustomed to constructing connected sentences, they will learn to control more sophisticated skills, such as using descriptive language and writing for different purposes.

Writing can be a lengthy, even difficult, task, but students are always thrilled to see their words on paper, and perhaps in print. This final stage of the writing process can be the motivation to learn editing skills as the teacher guides students through the intricacies of grammar, style, and word choice.

Learning to write, like learning to think, is a never-ending process of growth. However, use of the stimulating strategies in this chapter will enable students to write better at the end of the year than at the beginning. In order for students to see their own growth, collect a writing sample in the fall. Throughout the year, place examples of writing in each student's folder. When you have individual conferences, point out ways in which the student's writing has improved. Through the activities in this chapter:

- Students will put sentences together to make stories.
- Students will practice different modes of writing.
- Students will express their ideas in writing, using precise and descriptive language.
- Students will learn to polish their writing in order to share it with others.

ENCOURAGING WRITING

Students can begin to compose their own stories as soon as they enter school. As they contribute to group stories and dictate stories to others, students are building positive attitudes toward writing. We must encourage students in their initial efforts through use of varied experiences and strategies that stimulate students to write. As a result of the activities in this section:

- Students will write simple sentences.
- Students will construct stories when given a title or first line.
- Students will practice writing on different topics.
- Students will contribute to group stories.

Story Scribes

Even the youngest students can "write" a story if they have someone to dictate it to. Use aides, parents, or even upper-grade students to sit with students and type or write the story as it is told. If you establish a special "story chair" for this purpose, students will vie for the opportunity to have their words recorded.

Since the student composed the story, it is easy for him or her to read it back. At the same time, students are learning the conventions of writing without having to worry about correct spelling. Duplicate the stories for class reading material or staple them together in book form for pride of authorship. Story dictating will help students develop a positive attitude toward communicating through writing.

Beginning to Write Independently

As soon as first graders learn the rudiments of printing, they are fascinated by printing words. They can soon compose a sentence or two, for example, expressing ideas they have drawn in a painting. They can also compose sentences based on a topic introduced by the teacher:

- *What do you like to do?*
  I like to play ball.

- *What do you like to eat*?
  I like to eat ice cream.

Help the students with spelling by printing words they need on the board. Many teachers encourage students to leave a blank space where they do not know the spelling of a word so that they are not inhibited by the need to make every word perfect. The ideas students express are more important than the form they use. Interest and need will lead to greater awareness of meaning and proficiency in spelling as the student gains fluency in writing.

All about Me

This inventory can be given to youngsters of any age. They can write their responses or tell them to the class. Each item can be used separately and carried out over a week. The inventory can also be used at the beginning of the year and at the end of the year, as children compare their responses.

- What arc three things I enjoy?
- What are three things I don't enjoy?
- What are three things I like to do alone?
- What am I proudest of?
- What would I like to change about myself?
- What would I change about the world?
- What job do I do best?
- What person do I admire the most?
- What special talent would I most like to have?
- If I had one wish, what would I wish for?

Afterwards, ask the students what they learned about themselves by answering the questions.

Group Dictation

The dictated sentence story or poem lends itself to beginning writing. Students can compose sentences, telling personal news or describing class experiences. As an imaginative teacher you may extend this technique to record more creative expression by introducing such phrases as: *Snow is* . . . or *The funniest thing happened to me* . . . .

Group dictation can also result in a story or poem that a class composes orally. Record this story as it develops sentence by sentence. Begin by asking the class members what animal they would like to write about. The students get ready to write by talking about the selected animal. If they choose a hippopotamus, they might discuss places they have seen hippos, and then decide on a specific one in terms of size, color, name, location, and habits. The story grows as each child is encouraged to participate. Then it can be typed or printed on a large sheet for use in reading activities.

A "Holey" Story

Give each child a piece of white construction paper, 9 × 12 inches or larger, in which you have cut scattered circles of various sizes. Have the students draw a picture around the circles utilizing them in some way. They can then write or dictate a sentence(s) about their pictures. Have them discuss their pictures with the class. Put finished drawings together to form a book, with the titles and sentences.

Use Your Senses

Use this idea at the beginning of the year to familiarize students with their senses: hearing, seeing, smelling, tasting, and touching. Ask the children to be as creative as they can when they jot down their responses to the following questions:

- How many bright red things can you name?
- Name two sounds that make you feel happy.
- What tastes make you think of summer?
- What is the fuzziest thing you can think of?
- What smells would you most like to find when you go home tonight?
- What makes you feel really cold when you see it?

Simile and Metaphor

My foot is asleep and my toes feel like ginger ale.

Color is a grease puddle: a dead rainbow.

Story Skeletons

This writing activity involves completing a set of sentences that form a story when read in sequence. Use a pattern like the following example:

- One morning I was on my way to _____.
- I saw a huge spotted _____.
- It was sleeping under _____.
- I didn't want to wake it because _____.
- Suddenly I heard _____.
- I began to run toward _____.
- Just as I got there _____.
- I'm lucky that _____.

After all the sentences have been completed, tell the students to add a title at the top of their papers. They can read some of the versions of this Story Skeleton. Present this exercise orally with the whole class so all students finish the eight sentences at about the same time. For an individualized activity, the sentences can be duplicated with several lines allotted for the completion of each sentence.

Creative Writing

One way to motivate students to write is to present something that is totally different from what they're used to doing. "Take a piece of paper out and start writing" is a pretty ordinary instruction, but "Draw a circle in the middle of the sheet and start writing around in circles" intrigues children. The circle in the center could contain a picture of what the story is about, or it could be the title of the story. Instruct the youngsters to write in a circular motion, so that the reader has to turn the sheet around to read the story.

Chalkboard Writing

Children love to write on the chalkboard, especially with colored chalk. Designate a corner of the chalkboard for free writing where children can write a riddle to mystify their friends, a favorite line of poetry, or a question they wonder about.

At times you might label the corner for a specific activity such as:

- Animals and their babies
- What does *horse* make you think of?
- Words of five syllables

Picture That!

A simple device for motivating student writing is to show a large picture from a calendar or magazine and discuss it with the entire class. Before the students begin to write, take a few minutes to discuss the activities portrayed in the picture. Encourage students to give names to the people pictured. Point out that the people can have any names that they, as authors, choose. Write words around this picture on the board to assist spelling and to suggest ideas to be used in individual stories. Pass the picture around so students can examine it.

After this "warm-up" period, let students begin writing independently. When everyone has completed at least a portion of his or her story, have some stories read aloud, noting the different approaches used by the authors, making the point that no two people see the same situation exactly the same way.

As a variation, you could present several pictures and have students write about the one they prefer.

Hot Air Stories

Give each student a balloon to blow up. Have the students pretend they are inside the balloons and write group or individual stories. Here is a sample story:

> Something strange is happening. I can't hear anything. I wonder where I am? The last thing I remember is blowing up the balloon Mrs. Richardson gave me. I was glad that she handed me a red one since that's my favorite color. Wait a minute! That's why everything looks so rosy. I'm INSIDE THE BALLOON! It's sort of fun in here; really slippery in some spots and (yuk!) *damp* in other spots. I think I'll slide down to the bottom. Whoops! It's hard to stop! Hey! I can jump on the bottom and touch the top. This is more fun than a trampoline. Oh, oh, the walls are starting to cave in. I'd better get out of here before I'm smothered!

Shapes and Things

Give children a sheet of paper with objects drawn on it to write about, or draw objects on the board that they can write about. You can also ask children to think of objects and draw them in front of the class to entice their classmates to write about. For example:

These objects have been adapted from Native American artwork illustrated in *Authentic Indian Designs*, edited by Maria Naylor (New York: Dover Publications, 1975). (Up to ten illustrations can be reproduced free and without special permission.)

Peculiar Animals

Have the students draw a picture of the most peculiar animal they can imagine. Then they can write stories about the adventures of their animal. What is the animal's name? Where does it live? What does it like to eat? Would it make a good pet?

This is also a good activity for oral conversation. After a student has described the animal to the class, the other students can ask questions about the animal's habits and adventures.

Snabbit

It's a Bear's World

Display several stuffed bears around the room or place a box of them in a special location. Let the students choose one of them and pretend the bear has come to life. What would its adventures be? Where would it live? What would it eat? What kinds of things would it do?

Creature Features

One day after school, cut giant footprints out of heavy paper and arrange them across the walls, floor, and ceiling of your classroom. When the students arrive, have them try to imagine what kind of creature made these prints. What does this creature look like? Where does it live? What does it eat? They can write stories about the creatures they imagine.

Post the stories on the board and use them to extend the learning experience. Give students an exercise sheet with questions on it like the following:

- List four synonyms for *scary*.
- List five synonyms for *big*. Circle the one that's the *biggest*.
- Give a recipe for your creature's favorite dish.
- How does your creature celebrate a birthday?

- Look up the following words and circle the one that best describes your creature: *herbivorous, carnivorous, omnivorous.*
- What's your creature's favorite color and why?
- If a movie was made about your creature, what would it be called? Who would star in it?
- Write a bedtime story for your creature.

The Touch Box

Inside the Touch Box is a hidden object. From what the children imagine the object to be and from its texture, they can begin to create a story or poem. An ordinary shoe box can be the Touch Box. Cut a hole in the front of the box big enough for a child to reach inside to feel the object. Attach a sleeve around the hole so the child cannot see what is inside the box. Write "Touch Box" on the lid. Print instructions with a felt pen on a 12 × 18 inch sheet of paper or tagboard, as shown in the illustration.

The Touch Box

Put your hand in the box.
Feel what is inside.
What do you think it is?
Write your answer on a sheet of paper.
Tell what the THING looks like.

After three days, open the box. What is it: A Christmas decoration? A funny-shaped sweet potato? A sock filled with interesting objects? Let the children discuss their guesses.

What If?

A favorite stimulus for writing is the "What if" idea that encourages students to use their imaginations. Read a few of these to students:

What if . . .

- All of the television sets vanished overnight?
- You could buy gills to breathe underwater?
- Everyone looked exactly the same?
- You never needed to sleep again?
- People were really the pets of animals?

Encourage students to suggest other "What if" ideas that can be used.

Trading Places

Here is an activity that combines both writing and imagination. Pose some questions for your class, beginning with the phrase, "How would you feel if . . . ?" and have them write down their responses. Try to provide some illustrations of each question so that the children can visualize the situations. For example:

- How would you feel if you were looking at your goldfish and all of a sudden you became the goldfish swimming around in the fishbowl, and the fish was looking at *you*?
- How would you feel if you woke up one morning in a strange bed in a strange house and then looked in the mirror and realized you had turned into your best friend and you were living with his or her family?

Cat Tales

Make a bulletin board display of cats. Include Story Starters that are related to cats. For example:

- Last night my cat jumped up on the table and said _____.
- This morning I woke up and felt really strange. I jumped out of bed and found myself standing on four feet. I had turned into a cat!
- On Halloween night, my black cat always disappears.
- My neighbor's cat has the funniest pet.
- I think that my cat is getting much smarter since I showed him how to turn on the computer.

Each child should choose one of these sentences to begin a story. Attach the completed stories to the bulletin board display or compile a *Big Book of Cat Tales*.

The idea is to get the pencil moving quickly.
BERNARD MALAMUD

Plot Situations

Here are some Story Starters put in a plot situation form. This technique immerses the child in a situation, and the child is encouraged to get totally involved in whatever situation he or she is interested in.

Easy

- Betty Lou got an animal for her birthday. What is it and where will she keep it?
- Stan hates to eat cooked carrots. Today he has decided to pretend the carrots are something else. What will he do to fool himself? Will his trick work?
- While Lynn was eating breakfast, a bird began to peck on the window. What does the bird want Lynn to do?
- While Justin was taking a bath today, he thought of a nice thing to do for his sixty-year-old neighbor. What will he do? What will his neighbor do?
- Robin looked out the window today and was so happy that it was raining. She knew that she'd do her favorite thing in the rain. What is it?
- The ice cream man said that he had a new flavor today. What is it? How does he make it?

Hard

- When Jeanne got dressed this morning, she noticed that her clothes were much too big. Why is Jeanne getting smaller? Can she do anything to stop shrinking?
- Alec painted a picture of two horses. When he showed the picture to Sasha, they noticed a shadowy boy standing next to one of the horses. As Sasha examined the painting, the boy in the painting began to look more like Alec and the real Alec began to become transparent. Why is this happening to Alec? Can Sasha save Alec? Does Alec want to be saved?
- When you woke up this morning and walked out the door to go to school, a crowd of people was waiting outside to get your autograph. What are you famous for?
- Last night, Bob baked some magic cookies that would grant any wish that a person had, but warned everyone against eating too many of them. What *would* happen if you ate too many? Can you guess what happened when Fat Albert came to visit?

- Every day, Sally ate her lunch in the park by a statue. Today, the statue tapped Sally on the shoulder. What did the statue want? How did the statue communicate with Sally?

Unfinished Stories

Prepare assignment sheets on which Unfinished Stories are printed. The first paragraph sets the stage and suggests what might happen, but students will produce different endings. For example:

> Joy wanted to show her friends her brother's new motor scooter. She sat on the scooter and began to explain how it worked. As she was talking, the scooter suddenly began to move. Soon it was rolling quickly down the hill. Joy was terrified. She tried desperately to remember what her brother had said about stopping the scooter.

- Did Joy manage to stop the scooter? How?
- What did her friends think?

Leave space on the sheet for students to illustrate their story.

Bank Street Writer (School version, revised 1984)
Scholastic Inc.
All Apple computers
Grades 4 and up

This is one of the best pieces of software for the beginning writer. It allows the writer to edit, revise, and produce a printed copy. *Bank Street Writer* includes three disks and a teacher's manual.

Supposing

Encourage students to write intriguing paragraphs that begin with "Supposing . . . ." For example:

- Supposing I fed some cows carob pods and all the milk came out chocolate.
- Supposing I woke up in the morning and I was smarter than everybody, including the teacher.

Students can illustrate their examples and bind them in a class book.

A book that presents these kinds of ideas is *Supposing* by Alastair Reid (Boston: Little, Brown, 1960).

Tomorrow's Headlines

Ask the children to write five headlines they would like to see in tomorrow morning's newspaper. Examples that you might mention are *Bill Rasmus Wins the Lottery* or *Sally Thompson Inherits Half Million Dollars*. After writing the five headlines, the students take one of them and write a story just as a newspaper story might run. Have newspapers on hand so students can see examples of how the headline describes the story.

Last Lines

Last sentences can serve as Story Starters and, just like beginning sentences and titles, stimulate interest and motivate writing. Place last lines in a notebook or box where students can look at several and select one that suggests a story. The following are examples to start you off:

- Suddenly the wind stopped and everything was still.
- Emily thought she saw the cat wink as it left.
- The music faded away as the sun rose.
- "I guess it was only a dream," thought Dale. Then he noticed the purple feather on his pillow.
- Caroline blinked twice and the mouse vanished.

Students can brainstorm new ideas whenever the supply runs low. These endings could also serve for an impromptu storytelling session.

A Day in the Life of a Doorknob

Good writers will sometimes immerse themselves in an idea to write more creatively about the subject. This activity will allow children to really get behind an object—paintbrush, doorknob, soccer ball, umbrella—and then write about it. Objects can be personified by having the children pretend that they are one of these objects (or any object they choose). The stories can be entitled "A Day in the Life of a _____."

Use a variation as an excellent follow-up to a science activity. Have students pretend to be the object or animal studied. Ask stimulating questions such as, "How did the lake feel when it began to rain?" "What does the plant sitting on the ledge think about the classroom it's in?"

Happiness Is . . .

Use *Happiness is a Warm Puppy* by Charles Schulz (San Francisco: Determined Productions, 1962) as motivation for writing about happiness. Other abstract nouns—*sadness, friendship, love, fear*—can also be used. Ask students to list what happiness is to them. For example:

- Happiness is sharing warm cookies with my friends.
- Happiness is coasting down a steep hill.
- Happiness is finding a new book by your favorite author.
- Happiness is holding a sleeping kitten.

Students can then choose one of their statements as the base for a story.

Variations of this theme make interesting group project books for lower primary students. Children can transfer drawings and sentences onto dittos divided in halves or quarters. Themes might include:

- *Thanksgiving*: "I am thankful for . . ."
- *Father's Day*: "A Dad is someone who . . ."
- *Valentine's Day*: "I love my _____ because . . ."

Literature and Writing

Read the story of Tom Thumb. (One source is the version by the Brothers Grimm, *Tom Thumb* [New York: Atheneum, 1973]. Illustrated by Felix Hoffman.) Then ask students to make up adventures for Tom in addition to the ones that they've already heard. What would life be like if you were only as tall as one of your fingers? What adventures would be available to you if you were small? How would your life be different if you were small? One variation of this theme is a game like "What if you were 10 feet tall?" What would your life be like? Another variation is "Which would you rather be? Small like Tom Thumb, or 10 feet tall, and why?"

My Favorite Food

This activity allows students to write directions and explain a process. Ask the students to think of their favorite food. Next, they can interview their mothers or fathers (someone who cooks for them), or, better still, they can watch how that food is prepared. The students then write their version of the recipe for My Favorite Food (My Favorite Potatoes, My Favorite Apple Pie, My Favorite Hamburgers, etc.).

The results can be delightfully humorous. Some examples are:

- My Favorite Hamburgers: You make hamburgers with grease in it.
- My Favorite Chocolate Cake: Put all the stuff in first in a bowl, and then you crack an egg in it.

These recipes can be put on ditto sheets and fastened together as a book. The students then have a present for a special occasion.

Mud Pies

Marjorie Winslow's *Mud Pies & Other Recipes* (New York: Macmillan, 1961)* is a delightful recipe book made for children or anyone. Winslow includes recipes for such tantalizing dishes as "Roast Rocks" and "Crabgrass Gumbo," all written with explicit instructions and utilizing the simplest ingredients. A favorite with many dolls is "Marigold Madness: Shred several marigolds into a pan and fill with water; set in sun to simmer; when the liquid has turned to gold, strain into bowls and put in the shade to cool; serve chilled." Besides becoming "connoisseurs of fine dining," children learn about their environment in a highly innovative way. Children can invent their own recipes for mud pies or other interesting concoctions.

Me Collage

Here is a creative way to get acquainted during the first week of school. Have students make a collage about themselves—who they are and what they like. Ask them to bring in materials for everyone to share as they make the collage. Have magazines, newspapers, pictures, paints, and crayons on hand. They can cut out pictures and words, illustrating their ideas any way they want. Give students large pieces of cardboard on which to mount their collages so that you can display the results on the bulletin board.

After they think about what they want to express through their collages, have the children write something about themselves. They can write a short description or a series of phrases in poetry form. If they feel comfortable talking about what they write, you can have students read what they wrote as they show their collages. Students are curious to hear what others wrote and what kinds of things everyone thought of. This is a good way for students to find out what the other students are interested in.

*From *Mudpies and Other Recipes*. Copyright © 1961 by Marjorie Winslow. Reprinted by permission of McIntosh and Otis, Inc.

What I Would Miss Most

Ask the students to think for a minute about what they would miss most if it were taken away. Anything they wish to ponder can be used: an object (television), an idea (friendship), a person (Grandma), and so on. The purpose of this activity is not only to have students write but to motivate them to think for a minute about their own lives, their values, and what is important to them. After a brief discussion, they write about "What I Would Miss Most." (If students feel comfortable, they might share their ideas.) The composition can be merely a paragraph, or it might be a page, but the children are to explain why they would miss this thing, or idea, or person in some detail, and why it is important to them.

Dreams

One of the most creative sources of ideas for all writers is the unconscious. Dreams provide a fertile source of ideas for writing. To free students to write about their dreams, it is imperative that you create an atmosphere of trust in the classroom. Students must be assured that private dreams will remain private. You may wish to begin this topic with a description of a dream you had recently. Ask students to describe vivid dreams they have had. Some students will protest that they never remember their dreams. You can then mention that many people keep a dream journal next to their bed so that they can make notes as soon as they awake. You may wish to have students begin a Dream Journal with topics like:

- My Favorite Dream
- My Scariest Dream
- My Most Common Dream

Almost Like Me

Sometimes, in our urge to have students write creative stories, we forget that they are also interested in everyday activities. Students often enjoy writing adventure stories about children their own age. The fictional character might live in your town, go to your school, and perhaps even meet the author of the story. The use of personal experiences often helps the novice author become comfortable with the art of writing. Students will find it easy to create a hero/heroine by exaggerating their own strengths and interests. Writing about someone the same age and sex as themselves will make it easy for students to insert a note of reality into their story. You may wish to prompt your students with titles like these:

- The New Student in Room 14
- The Day I Moved to San Francisco
- The Soccer Player
- The Checkers Champ of Fairmeadow School

Tombstones and Epitaphs

Tell students something about epitaphs, the short statements that appear on tombstones. An interesting one, for example, was written by Robert Louis Stevenson, a poet and author students may know. The words on his tombstone are taken from one of his poems, "Requiem."

Here he lies
  Where he longed to be;
Home is the sailor,
  Home from the sea,
And the hunter,
  Home from the hill.

Ask students what they would like to have written on their own tombstones. They can write their own epitaphs—funny, poetic, serious—in any style they choose. This is an interesting activity since the students take a look at themselves and consider how they would like to be remembered or how other people may view them.

A Potpourri of Titles

Develop a file of provocative titles that you and the students can add to periodically. The student who needs an idea for writing can consult this source.

The Cave	Kitchen Chemistry
Dreams for Sale	Lost in the Computer
Walk into the Future	The Homework Machine
Forbidden Island	Storm of the Century
Fur or Feathers?	The Great Science Experiment
The Worst Day of My Life	The Hundred Year Old Egg
My Undersea Adventure	Ice Cream Madness
Alone on a Sunny Beach	The Cosmic Zoo

The Mysterious Man Next Door	Magic and Mystery
My Closest Friend	Inside the Outside
The Best Time I've Ever Had	Room for One More
Why I Always Wear a Hat	No More Room
The Ticklish Fish	Factory of Fun
Adventures of a Banana Slug	Sneaky Sneakers
The Secret Life of Plants	Flying High
The Caterpillar's Secret	The Teacher's Room
The White Tiger	One More Winter

WRITING SKILL DEVELOPMENT

When students want to express more complex and sophisticated ideas in writing, they begin to see the need to develop specific writing skills. Exposure to different genres of writing will expand their concept of what can be accomplished through writing. Focus on word choice will demonstrate the importance of clarity and description in effective writing. As students write more often and compose longer stories, they are necessarily practicing advanced thinking and writing skills. As a result of the activities in this section:

- Students will write fluently.
- Students will express their thoughts and feelings in writing.
- Students will write for different purposes and different audiences.
- Students will write varied sentences.
- Students will use words effectively.
- Students will write stories with a clear beginning, middle, and end.

A Commonplace Book

Start students off on the right foot for writing by encouraging them to keep their own Commonplace Book. A Commonplace Book is a journal or log that many professional writers use to record ideas for stories, notes (of characters, details, etc.) to include in future work, or bits and pieces of writing. Like an artist's sketchbook, it is a collection that a writer can refer to later to construct longer, more polished writing.

Give students a fixed amount of time every day to write in their Commonplace Book. They can record potential story titles, story starters, what if's, and other imaginative stimuli. They can also experiment with different forms of writing, from letters or descriptions to poetry or jokes. If students have difficulty thinking of subjects to write about, you can put a topic on the board as a suggestion. Every two weeks or so, have students select a passage from their notebook to revise and polish up to turn in.

Regular writing in these books develops fluency and increases the quality of student writing. Students write more freely because they are not afraid of being corrected. They can communicate thoughts, ideas, and feelings that are usually not shared with others.

This notebook can also be used for a teacher-student dialogue on the nature and purpose of writing. If the students agree, collect the journals weekly and make comments in them in response to the *content* of each student's writing—perhaps a reaction or a question. Then return the journals so that the students have a chance to write their responses. In this fashion, a dialogue can be developed that will lead students to improve their writing, without judging their grammar, spelling, or punctuation.

Endless Writing

Divide the class into four or five teams. At the instruction "Go," every member of the class begins to write. The purpose of this game is to see how many words each person can write in his or her story during a set period of time. (Five minutes might be a good time to start with.)

When you call, "Stop," have each youngster total up the number of words in his or her story, and then add them together for a team score. The team with the most words wins. If the students find that they are running out of ideas during this time period, they can repeat the last word that was written until a new idea comes along, or they can write about what they're thinking when they can't think of anything to write.

For the first few times, list several suggestions on the board before the game starts, for instance:

- A funny thing happened to me on the way to school this morning.
- If my pet could talk, what would it say?
- What if we could read other people's minds?

Sentence Strategy

Write five letters on the chalkboard. Have the youngsters write several five-word sentences using only words that begin with those five letters. For example:

S   O   A   E   M

- Many sweet oranges are enormous.
- Ellen stepped on a mouse.

Set a time limit and see how many sentences students can create. Students will also enjoy competing to produce the funniest or wildest sentence.

The "I's" Have Had It

One of the problems that children have with writing is falling into the trap of starting each sentence with *I*: *I* went shopping, *I* went downtown, *I* went to the show, *I* went to the ball game. The object of this activity is to develop new ways of starting sentences so that youngsters have the opportunity to read and observe sentences that start in ways other than *I*. Encourage them to experiment with new ways of writing sentences. *I went to the show*, for example, might be rewritten: *Bill and I went to the show, My friend and I went to the show, Going to the show with my friends was great fun.*

Have your students see how many different ways they can write the sentence: *I saw my friend*. Samples include:

- My friend looked nervous when I saw her at the band concert!
- My dog licked my friend when I saw him downtown yesterday.
- While I was eating breakfast, I saw my friend jog by my window.
- Yesterday I saw my friend playing soccer in the park.
- Wait! I just saw my friend's face in that movie!

Fortunately and Unfortunately

A good motivation for writing sentences is the Fortunately and Unfortunately game. Read a few of these examples to your students to get them started with this humorous approach to writing.

- Fortunately, I bumped the car in front of me very gently.
  Unfortunately, it was a police car!
- Fortunately, I spilled the paint on an ugly shirt.
  Unfortunately, it belongs to Mr. Adams!
- Fortunately, I found my dog before it turned dark outside.
  Unfortunately, he was chasing a cat up a tree!
- Fortunately, I stopped the egg before it hit the floor.
  Unfortunately, I stopped it with my foot!
- Fortunately, there was an ice cream shop nearby.
  Unfortunately, it was closed!
- Fortunately, I stopped the door from slamming.
  Unfortunately, I stopped it with my finger!
- Fortunately, my grandfather's antique radio works.
  Unfortunately, it gets only one station.

A nice illustration of this exercise is Remy Charlip's *What Good Luck, What Bad Luck* (New York: Parents Magazine Press, 1964). The book takes the reader through a stream of occurrences that are classified as good luck and bad luck. You'll find that children will turn the pages faster and faster to see how Ned will get out of the *next* one!

Importance of Punctuation

How important is punctuation in expressing what we really mean? Show students what kinds of confusion might result if we did not use the rules of punctuation consistently and accurately. Give them a list of sentences like the following and ask them if these sentences mean the same thing.

- No, help is coming!
  No help is coming!
  (Which would you use to calm a struggling swimmer?)
- Quiet—hospital zone.
  Quiet hospital zone.
  (Which one specifies the kind of hospital?)
- *The Day the Flying Saucer Landed.*
  The Day the Flying Saucer Landed.
  (Which one makes you want to go outside and check?)
- He knows, John.
  He knows John.
  (Which one means flee, all is discovered?)
- Who put this in the wastebasket?
  Who put this in the wastebasket!
  (Which is more likely to be said by an irate parent?)
- Uncle George's cat knows its master.
  Uncle George's cat knows it's master.
  (Which one reflects the independence of a cat?)

The class will enjoy trying to find or invent more examples. The exercise will increase their awareness of the necessity for punctuation in their own writing.

Quotation Marks

One effective approach to teaching the use of quotation marks is to provide a sheet with no marks, capitals, and so on, and ask the students to put in the necessary punctuation. After this has been done as a total class activity, sheets like this can be placed in a skill center for additional work when it is required.

THERE ARE VERY FEW RULES FOR USING QUOTATION MARKS SO YOU MIGHT AS WELL GET BUSY AND LEARN THEM NOW SAID MRS AMOND-SEN CANT WE JUST LOOK IT UP IN OUR BOOK BLURTED OUT LITTLE

HELIOTROPE RAISE YOUR HAND BEFORE YOU SPEAK SAID MRS
AMONDSEN STERNLY HELIOTROPE RAISED HER HAND YES HELIO-
TROPE SAID MRS AMONDSEN SWEETLY WHY CANT WE JUST USE OUR
BOOKS WHILE WE WRITE ASKED HELIOTROPE YOU WONT HAVE THEM
WITH YOU WHEN YOURE TAKING COLLEGE FINALS FOR ONE REASON
ANSWERED MRS AMONDSEN HOW MANY CRUMMY RULES ARE THERE
MUTTERED JONATHAN GEORGE WEATHERBEE UNDER HIS BREATH
MRS AMONDSEN HAD HEARD HIM WHISPER ALTHOUGH HE WAS SIX
ROWS AWAY AND SAID JONATHAN GEORGE PLEASE DO NOT MAKE FA-
CETIOUS REMARKS YOU ARE DISTURBING THE CLASS THE FIRST RULE
IS THAT YOU ENCLOSE ALL CONVERSATION IN QUOTATION MARKS
AND BEGIN IT WITH A CAPITAL LETTER THEN YOU MUST REMEMBER
TO SET THE CONVERSATION ASIDE FROM THE REST OF THE SENTENCE
WITH SOME OTHER MARK OF PUNCTUATION YOU MUST NOT FORGET
THE RULE THAT SAYS THE QUOTATION MARKS GO OUTSIDE THE OTHER
MARKS OF PUNCTUATION AND THE RULE MOST OF YOU FORGET ON
YOUR WRITTEN WORK IS THAT YOU HAVE TO START A NEW PARA-
GRAPH FOR EACH NEW SPEAKER OTHERWISE IT WOULD BE DIFFICULT
TO KNOW JUST WHO IS SPEAKING SUPPOSE I WROTE DOWN WHAT WE
HAVE BEEN SAYING FOR THE LAST FEW MINUTES DONT YOU THINK IT
WOULD BE DIFFICULT TO READ IF IT WERE NOT ALL SEPARATED YEAH
SAID THE WHOLE CLASS EMPHATICALLY DID YOU RAISE YOUR HANDS
ASKED MRS AMONDSEN

Punctuation Skills
Milton Bradley Company
All Apple computers
Grades 4 to 9, Enrichment to Remedial

This program includes quizzes that can be used as pretests, instructional material, a mastery test for each lesson, and a review test. A game follows the
cumulative review test, and the better the student does on the test, the more
time he or she has to play the game.

All Time Excuses

Ask students to write creative excuses like the following:

Excuses for when I'm Late:

- My cat died and I had to bury it.
- The sun kept shining hotter and hotter and I had to keep coming home to take
  off some of my clothes.

- A boxcar train stopped the traffic on Main Street and my brother told me to count the cars.
- A firecracker accidentally blew up in the boys' bathroom and I had to make sure everything was OK.
- Yesterday there were only two hopscotches on the sidewalk, and today there were three new ones, so I had to see which was the best.

Excuses for when I Forget to do Something:

- By the time I got home, I was too tired.
- My foot fell asleep.
- I forgot to brush my teeth (hair).
- There was a good show on TV and I didn't want to miss it.

Excuses that Never Work:

- The hot water heater blew up so I couldn't do the dishes.
- The eclipse happened right when I wanted to mow the lawn, so I couldn't see a thing.
- I got called by Dialing for Dollars for the magic combination, so I had to turn on the TV for the answer.
- Last weekend, I went skiing with my folks and got in a car accident on the way; I broke my jawbone and ankles, and sprained my elbow; plus my eye's all puffy from hitting the dashboard. No, I can't go dancing with you.
- Sorry, I have a headache.

Now have students write their own excuses. Each one must be a complete sentence.

What Happened Next?

Write an active sentence on the board, for instance: *The horses dashed madly across the field*. Encourage students to speculate about the story situation that might include this sentence. The sentence is then used as the first line in a story. Other sentences you might wish to use include:

- The flames crackled ravenously through the forest.
- The prairie dog scurried frantically into the grass and dove into a hole.
- The coiled rattlesnake struck with deadly swiftness.
- The hissing kittens tumbled down the hall in a blur of fur and claws.

Encourage students to imagine similar sentences that can be used in the same way. They can also examine first lines that authors have used in books.

Teaching students to write clearly and effectively should be a central objective of the school.

DR. ERNEST L. BOYER

Headliners

Give the students stories from the newspaper with the headlines cut off and have them write the headlines. Keep the real headline so students can compare their suggestion with the one the reporter wrote. Or give each student a headline and have him or her write a news story to accompany the headline.

Use this technique to discourage students from copying reports or information from encyclopedias. When you ask them to research topics, have them write up the results as newspaper stories with headlines.

Story Plotting

Use the chart on this page to stimulate writing ideas. The students can pick one item from each column and write a story. The possibilities are endless. When students exhaust this chart, have them make up new charts for different combinations.

Setting	Character	Character Trait	Problem
Dark basement	Scientist	Playful	Character suspects foul play.
Space shuttle	Panther	Intelligent	Character is lost and hungry.
Museum of Natural History	Secret Agent	Timid	Character is given the power to become invisible.
Island in the tropics	Unicorn	Knowledgeable	Character discovers two others in danger.
Fire station	Dalmation	Helpful	Character finds a time machine.
Orchestra pit	Bassoon player	Heroic	Character is trapped by an enemy.
The 99th floor of a building	Explorer	Reliable	Character has to do three good deeds before dawn.
Jungle	Detective	Cautious	Character must act quickly to prevent disaster.
Airport	Alien being	Stubborn	Character wants to play a trick on friends.
Sunny meadow	Mystery writer	Conceited	Character loses a vital object.

Paragraph Writing

Have your students write a paragraph using all the words listed below. They can add articles, verbs, and prepositions. They should have fun with this exercise.

surprise	uncle
eleven	string
Floyd	riddle
daisy	helicopter
San Francisco	yesterday
telephone	clarinet
bagel	carrot
amazing	dolphin
historian	enormous

What a Card!

Select words from your vocabulary review list or reading word cards for this activity. Pass out three words to students so that each one has a noun, an adjective, and a verb. After reading the words, each student writes a story inspired by them. Including challenging words motivates students to stretch their imagination and incorporate these words into their vocabulary.

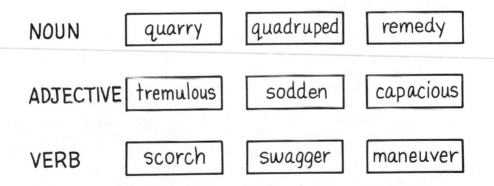

NOUN	quarry	quadruped	remedy
ADJECTIVE	tremulous	sodden	capacious
VERB	scorch	swagger	maneuver

The following is a sample story:

I was on my way to the old *quarry* when I saw the strange man. Since the quarry had been shut down many years ago, I was the only person I knew who still went there. From a distance he seemed bewildered, and as I approached, he asked in a *tremulous* voice "Where am I?" . . .

Exploring Words

Use a class writing period to motivate students to learn new vocabulary. If the class is writing on a particular topic, first ask the students to brainstorm words associated with that topic. Have students suggest as many words as they can while you insert a few more difficult words. For example, here are some words that might appear in a class list on the topic of "Winter":

slope	toboggan
snowplow	apple pie
icicle	chill
shiver	maple syrup
frost	frigid
ski	parka
fireplace	glacier
reindeer	numb

This technique is an effective way of getting students to use the new words they learn. Students who have trouble finding ideas for writing will see possible topics in this list, and students with smaller vocabularies will quickly expand their knowledge. Developing the word list also serves as a warm-up period so students are ready to write and have the vocabulary to enable them to be successful.

Pictures Tell a Story

Ask the children to bring in pictures of people. They can be pictures of people who are happy, sad, angry, and so on. It is helpful if some pictures are large and colorful. The pictures can be mounted on a sheet of paper placed on a bulletin board. Depending on the space available, five or ten pictures can be mounted.

As a daily oral exercise, students can contribute descriptive words about each of the pictures. You can write down the students' words or a scribe from the class can perform this task. Words are then placed under each picture.

At the end of the week, each child has the opportunity to select one of the pictures and to create a story, giving his or her ideas about what might have led to the picture and why this person is acting this way. Of course, the descriptive words are available to aid the children in writing their stories. Each student writer has the option of utilizing these words or thinking of new ones.

The advantage of this approach to writing from pictures is that the youngsters learn to "read" pictures. They develop a vocabulary for each of the pictures. It might be interesting for the children to discuss why they selected certain pictures to write about.

Sensible Language

Stimulate students to think about how they perceive objects through their senses: sight, hearing, touch, taste, and smell. Select an object such as a strawberry and place it in front of the class so that everyone can see it. Now have the students suggest words that describe how they *see* the strawberry, how they hear the strawberry, and so on, through the senses. Write the suggestions on the board, thus:

Strawberry:

- sight—red, green, spotted
- touch—soft, bumpy
- hearing—squishy, plop
- taste—sweet, juicy
- smell—fresh, sweet

Notice that words such as *sweet* can be applied to more than one sense. We all have trouble distinguishing the role the different senses play in perception. Some senses are used much less frequently than others. While we almost always use the sense of sight, we exercise our sense of taste less often. Other objects for class exploration of the language of the senses include:

raisins	watermelon
cloves	coconut
almonds	pomegranate
kiwifruit	mint leaves
chives	garlic

Painting Word Pictures

To stimulate the use of adjectives and adverbs, discuss with the class how terribly dull writing would be if we eliminated all colorful words from our language. No one would bother to read stories if they read like this:

Yesterday I went to the beach. It was cold. There were waves. I saw some birds. I saw a seal. I played in the sand. I found a shell. Then I came home.

Give the students a worksheet with several ordinary, colorless sentences written on it. Tell the class to add color, sparkle, and excitement by substituting more interesting words and phrases.

- The bird flew into the tree.
  (What kind of bird? How did it fly? What kind of tree?)
- The truck went down the street.
  (What kind of truck? How was it being driven?)
- They were eating ice cream.
  (Who is *they*? Describe the ice cream. How was it being eaten?)
- The lion jumped.
  (Describe the lion, how it jumped, and why it jumped.)
- The butterfly sat on the flower.
  (What did the butterfly look like? What kind of flower?)

You might then ask the students to write three ordinary sentences of their own and rewrite the sentences to make them more exciting.

Improving Word Choice

To help the students see the importance of word choice, give them sample paragraphs for editing. Select a passage and underline words that may be replaced because they are trite, vague, or nondescriptive. Provide a list of suggested substitutions that includes a variety of synonyms for each word. As students read over the story, they can search the list for a synonym that fits the story. Since they can use each word only once and some alternatives may be more appropriate than others, students will have to consider the possibilities carefully.

Students will learn editing skills to apply to their own writing when they perform this activity as a class, individually, or in small groups. Advanced writers will also enjoy creating sample passages for the class to work on, particularly developing the list of synonyms.

Whale Hunt

When I woke up that morning, the ocean was <u>calm</u>. I <u>got</u> out of my bunk and <u>got</u> into my clothes. I took a glass of orange juice and <u>went</u> up on deck. The sun felt good on my back and the breeze was <u>warm</u>. I pulled out my binoculars and began to <u>look</u> for spouts. I felt sure that today I would find my first whale. Then I <u>saw</u> a thin line in the distance. I told the captain to <u>go</u> to the left. As we got <u>closer</u>, I was sure I had finally <u>found</u> a humpback. Then a <u>large</u> body <u>came</u> out of the water. It was in the air long enough for me to snap a picture. Then it <u>fell</u> back into the water. What a <u>noise</u>! I was glad our boat had not been any closer to that <u>big</u> show of strength. I <u>saw</u> my whale spout once more as our <u>small</u> boat rocked in the waves the humpback had made, but I was too busy <u>holding on to</u> the rails to take any more pictures!

Words to Choose from

serene	splashed	reaching for	huge
spotted	clinging to	occupied	drew near
suddenly	balmy	climbed	racket
steer	scrambled	soothing	encountered
tiny	leapt	streaked	enormous
observed	scan	titantic	approached
suspended	identified	slipped	clambered
relieved	turn	tremendous	slid
vaulted	crept	insignificant	watched
search	met	knifed	tremor
tore	miniscule	sparkling	noticed
peaceful	soft		

Pen Pals Abroad

An excellent motivation for children to practice expressing themselves in writing is a class pen pal project. Many English-speaking countries are good sources of pen pals (for example, Australia, India, Scotland, Ireland, and some countries in Africa). Older students might be interested in corresponding with students who are studying English as a foreign language.

The first letters students write should include some basic information about themselves: name, age, school activities, interests, hobbies, and sports. Later letters can provide information about their city, state, and country. Some students will benefit from a structured framework to help them write, particularly for the first letter.

The class can discuss what they want to say in their letters and then write them individually. What do they think students in another country would want to know about the United States? What do their pen pals probably already know about the United States?

Letter Writing Center

Set up a Letter Writing Center in the classroom, equipped with paper, pencils, and fancy felt-tip pens. Add a list of addresses of individuals and places that would interest students, such as Congressmen and Congresswomen, local newspapers, authors and their publishers. A typewriter is a definite asset to your Writing Center. A phone book for acquiring local addresses is also essential.

Cheerful Greetings

Patients in hospitals and convalescent homes appreciate receiving cheerful notes and letters. Discuss the kinds of information that these individuals would probably enjoy sharing. Many older people appreciate and get enjoyment from communicating with young children. Addresses of people who are bedridden or housebound, either temporarily or permanently, can usually be obtained from local service groups like Meals on Wheels, Senior Citizen Centers, and disabled groups. When appropriate, include the students' artwork with their letters.

Write a Letter to the Editor

Ask each student to create a letter to the editor by filling in the blanks and underlining words or phrases for emphasis where appropriate.

Dear Editor:

_____ is an issue of concern for all of us. Every person in _____ should (view with alarm/point with pride at/be puzzled by/be grati-
(city or state)
fied by) this latest development, which comes at a time when _____ faces
(city or state)
the darkest day in its history.

All people of goodwill should band together to (see that it doesn't happen again/perpetuate it/encourage it/discourage it/deplore it/praise it). Only in this way can we

assure continued (progress and prosperity/justice and freedom/peace and joy) in
_____ which is faced with a new crisis as never before.
(city and state)
        We must all (get behind/oppose) this latest development in order that the
_____ may continue to _____. As
_____ has said so well, "_____." The future of
_____ hangs in the balance. We must not fail.
(city and state)

                                       Sincerely,

                                       _____
                                              (Your name)

Dear Dragon

Enliven your students' letter-writing activities by introducing Sesyle Joslin's book,
Dear Dragon (New York: Harcourt Brace Jovanovich, 1962). These examples of outrageous circumstances followed by a meticulously written letter can lend humor and
enjoyment to teaching letter writing.

Dear George

Combine historical reading and research with letter writing. Have the students select
an historical individual and do the research necessary to find out more about this person through books, encyclopedias, and magazines, so they learn about his or her life
and times. Then they write a letter to the figure they have chosen. For example, the
letter might be addressed to George Washington, Abraham Lincoln, Harriet Tub-
man, or Florence Nightingale. This can be a serious or humorous letter; but it should
be based, in part, on facts that they have learned about this individual.
        If two students research the same historical figure, they can exchange letters and
answer them.

Postal Cards

Have your students cut out slips of paper the size of postal cards and practice writing
addresses. Provide tagboard if they are actually to be mailed. You might ask students
to bring a stamped postal card to class to send to a friend or a relative.

Send a Telegram

Make copies of telegram forms (from your local telegraph office) and have students send telegrams to other students in the class. Students should invent fictitious information to be sent via the telegram and write their messages using brief and complete information. Encourage students to create their own stories to go along with the message that was sent to them.

Autobiographical Timelines

Most children have difficulty writing autobiographies. Ask them to list the five most important (happiest) things that ever happened to them. Each one can make a scroll that presents these happenings in order. Most children begin with their birth.

As children create this *Scroll of Life*, they are putting things in a time sequence. They will naturally add things that came in sequence as they begin to think about their lives, and they will add words to help explain the events depicted. Older students can write a more detailed autobiography after making this concrete timeline of their lives. This activity works well orally, especially for younger children as they tell the group about what happened in their lives.

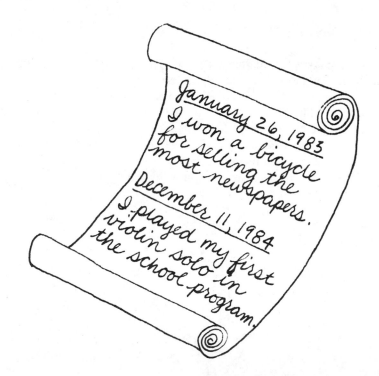

Writing Television Scripts

Students can create their own television show to present to the class. Use an original script or base it on a story the group has read. Students must first decide what events from the story they want to show and then list them in sequence. Next, they divide a roll of paper (shelf paper, for example) into the proper number of frames and create an illustration for each scene. They then write a narration for each scene, numbered to correspond to the frame on the roll. As students read the script or tell the story from brief notes, others pull the roll through a box decorated to look like a television set (as shown in the illustration).

Conundrums for Writing

A conundrum is a kind of riddle that usually features a pun or other play on words. Students will learn what the word *conundrum* means by working these examples. The riddles may sound hard at first but once you know the answer, they're really very simple. Here are some samples to get you started:

- To what question can you only answer no?
  (*Are you asleep*?)
- What tastes best at dinner?
  (*Your tongue.*)
- To what question can you only answer yes?
  (*What does y-e-s spell*?)
- On what side do you wear your coat?
  (*On the outside.*)
- What is the beginning of happiness?
  (*The letter* h.)

- What most resembles half a sandwich?
  (*The other half.*)
- What makes more noise than a baby crying?
  (*Two babies crying.*)
- Why is tennis such a noisy game?
  (*Because each player raises a racket.*)
- What has teeth but cannot eat?
  (*A comb.*)
- What is the best way to makc a coat last?
  (*Make the pants first.*)
- What has four legs but only one foot?
  (*A bed.*)

Keep copies of conundrums for the students to add to as they discover and invent new ones. Display a weekly conundrum on the bulletin board and have students write suggested answers. This is an excellent way to motivate both reading and writing.

Problem Solving

In a problem-solving exercise, children can think of something that they would most like to change in their lives. Each child states the problem and what he or she could and would do to solve that problem. *After* the problem has been stated, give the child some object (a banana, a pencil, an eraser, a shoe) and instruct the child to apply that object toward solving his or her problem. Example:

Problem:

I wish my brother's friends would stop picking on me.

Solution:

- I could avoid them totally.
- I could pick on them too.
- I could tell my Mom or Dad to make them stop.
- I could wait till I'm old enough to handle it.

Exercise:

Solving the problem with a shoe

- The shoe is made of leather—tough, brown, smooth.
- The shoe has shoelaces to tie it up with—secure, knot, different ways to lace, tight, loose, bows, two-sides, etc.

- The shoe keeps my feet warm.
- The shoe has a left and right foot.
- There is a toe, heel, tongue, and sole.

New Solution:

All of my brother's friends are "tough," but they're pretty nice sometimes. Just last week Billy helped me get my cat down from the tree, even though he did trip me as I was walking into the house. Inside, I know that I really like them, but I always get mad everytime they make fun of me. Well, I could either tighten my shoelaces and always hurt my foot, or I could loosen them and be a little more comfortable. To loosen myself, I could laugh back and joke around with them. I would feel warmer if I could be friends with them rather than enemies.

Ann Landers

This activity is appropriate for upper-grade youngsters. Bring in Ann Landers or Abigail Van Buren articles from the newspaper, and read them to your students. After the youngsters are familiar with the column, and the type of topics that are dealt with in the column, divide the class in half. Half of the youngsters write letters to Ann Landers, stating their problem or situation. They exchange their letters with the other half of the class who answer the letters in the Ann Landers and Abigail Van Buren style. For example:

Dear Ann:

Everytime I go bike riding with my friends, I always get left way behind because I keep accidentally bumping into things in the road, like cars, fire hydrants, gutter grills, and dogs. My bike's in pretty bad shape, and I'm getting a little banged up myself. How can I solve this problem?

John Black (and blue)

Dear John:

Next time you go riding with your friends, try opening your eyes.

Ann L.

Getting to Know You

At the beginning of the school year, it is important to have a number of writing activities that allow students to express themselves. Such writing gives you an opportunity to become acquainted with the class. The following examples are questions that might be asked of students at the beginning of the year:

- If you were a food, what food would you be? Why?
- If you were an animal, what animal would you want to be? Why?
- If you could be any kind of machine, what machine would you be? Why?
- If you were a character from a book, which character would you be? Why?
- If you could be any age, what age would you choose? Why?
- If you were a haiku, what season would be your theme? Why?

Twenty Things about Me

Ask students to list the numbers from 1 to 20 on a sheet of paper. (For younger children, this might be adjusted to 1 through 10.) Then ask the students to write down the first twenty things that come into their heads that describe who they are. An example might be: love baseball, like to eat, hate girls, fat, don't like school. (Don't list these examples before the students have a chance to do it; we only list these as examples to you.) This activity has the advantage of making students more aware of themselves, and also gives students the opportunity to look at their thoughts and ideas about who they are. In order to encourage honest thinking on the part of the students, emphasize that no one else will read the papers unless students wish to share.

I Resolve

Give students the opportunity to think about areas where they would like to improve in their work, in their lives, or with their families and friends. This activity works well not only at the beginning of the year, but also as New Year's resolutions, at mid-year time, or at the start of a new semester.

Students write their resolutions in the form, "I Resolve . . . ." The resolutions can involve any areas they wish. The students' resolutions should be confidential, but you might share some of your resolutions with the class. These sheets can be kept in a safe place and taken out every month or fixed period of time to see if students want to make revisions, and to see how they are doing on their resolutions.

A Gift

Students can use writing to express their individuality. Ask students to write down one gift that they would give themselves if they could give themselves anything. Then have them write their explanations of why they selected this gift. The gift may be real or intangible, but give them the opportunity to justify their selection. They can share this information with their classmates, if they wish.

- I would give myself 10 pomegranate trees so I could eat them every day. I would also make them a different kind so they wouldn't make red spots everywhere and I wouldn't have to eat them on the front porch.
- I would give myself the power to play chess better than anyone else in the world. I would do this so I could beat my brother Stan. Also I could probably be famous for beating those chess computers.

A modification of this idea would be to ask students what they would give someone else. To whom would they give it? Follow the same rules to justify or explain why they selected this person and what they would give this person.

- I would give my Grampa one of those lawn mowing machines that you can ride on because it hurts his back to use the pushing kind.
- I would give my mom a dishwasher because she is always too tired to wash the dishes and I break things sometimes. Then we wouldn't have to talk about the dishes all the time.

The *Teachers & Writers Collaborative Newsletters*, published quarterly, is a collection of articles and journals written by writers/educators. Based in New York, TWC believes in creating a curriculum that is relevant to students, and the group places professional writers in classrooms to encourage students to create different uses of language. The articles provide a personal insight into teaching creative writing, and include such titles as "The Tree of Possibilities," "Garbage Picking," "On Not Correcting Children's Writing," and "How to Make Videotapes When You Don't Know the First Thing About It." These are good publications to provide a take-off base for your own ideas. (Teachers & Writers Collaborative, c/o P.S. 3, 490 Hudson Street, New York, NY 10014.)

SHARING AND EVALUATING WRITING

When students can express themselves fluently and have experience with varied types of writing, they are ready to select examples of their work to refine in order to share with others. Like professional writers, students can now learn to step outside their own work and approach it from the point of view of a reader. Through the editing experience, students will begin to understand the reciprocal relationship between writer and reader. As a result, they will become better writers as well as better readers. As a result of the activities in this section:

- Students will share their writing with others.
- Students will proofread and critique their own writing.

- Students will discuss what makes writing effective.
- Students will evaluate the writing of others in pairs and small groups.

Analyzing Student Mistakes

As you read a set of writing papers, prepare a typed or printed ditto master. Copy sentences exactly as they appear in a student's story, being careful to include no more than one example from any child's paper.

Use the duplicated sheet in class to assist students in analyzing faulty usage or punctuation. Examine together the words that present difficulty. Review rules for using punctuation correctly.

You may also note words that are repeatedly misspelled. Add some of these words to the weekly spelling list.

Individual Conferences

One means for guiding student development in writing is the individual conference that is held for a few minutes each week. You may choose to confer with each student about a specific piece of writing as the student analyzes strengths and weaknesses. Together you decide on one or two suggestions for improving his or her work.

At this time you may note, for instance, that a child does not know how to use quotation marks, possessives, or the correct usage of *your* and *you're*. Don't tell a student too many things; it is usually wiser to make only a few points at any one conference.

You may focus a conference period on each student's writing folder, commenting on the variety of the writing, on the general types of errors that have been marked, and on improvements made. Make several suggestions for future work; you may, for instance, share an interesting word that might be particularly useful.

The personal conference shows each student that you are interested in what he or she is doing. It helps motivate student interest in improving, in trying different types of writing, and in telling you about plans for writing.

You're Great!

Remember that evaluation is more effective if you concentrate on emphasizing the positive aspects of student performance. Recognize student efforts and show them that you appreciate their work by presenting awards like the following:

A DOLPHIN SALUTE

FOR _____

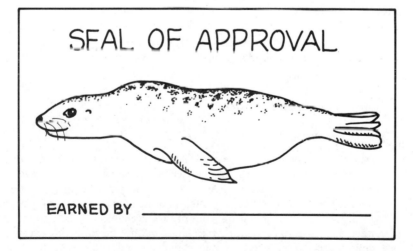

SEAL OF APPROVAL

EARNED BY _____

Beyond Teacher Evaluation

Checking every paper of every student can be very time-consuming. The following are some suggestions to help you eliminate some of this work:

- Students read their papers to the class or a small group.
- Students write in journals and you don't have to read it all.
- Let students choose which paper will be checked.
- Use symbols (√, W.W., and E all signify error) in the margin of student papers to encourage self-editing. Allow students time to identify their errors before dividing into small groups to correct the mistakes.
- Experiment with coauthorship. Students working together often catch mistakes more readily.

. . . the mere act of reading aloud put his work before him in a new light and by constraining his attention to every line, made him judge it more rigorously.

SAMUEL BUTLER

Writing Evaluation Policy

Many teachers feel obligated to read and correct every student paper because they think parents will insist on this. The following is an example of a letter you might send to parents explaining your writing evaluation policy and the reasons for it. If the parents are made aware of the procedures used in your class, they are less likely to misunderstand or complain.

Anywhere School District

Dear Parents:

In my writing program this year, I will be teaching and guiding your child as she or he writes. I have established a classroom environment where I hope students will be confident enough to try out new ideas. Because the goal of writing is communication, I am primarily interested in the content, not just the mechanics of expression. Therefore, I will be emphasizing only one or two mechanical skills at a time (periods, capitals, subject-verb agreement, etc.) and I will not be correcting every error on your child's paper. I will also be writing comments and reactions to the child's ideas. Recent research in writing has shown these teaching strategies to be most effective in developing fluency and competence in writing skills.

Your child's writing will be kept in a folder here at school. Although it is my goal to have students writing every day, they will not be perfecting or revising every paper. They will choose their best papers from the folder to revise. If you wish to see the folder, please send a note, and I will send the folder home for a night so you may look over the work.

Your encouragement and positive attitude toward your child's continued progress in writing will do much to hasten improvement.

Sincerely yours,

On the Bulletin Board

Quotations provide inspiring captions for displays of student writing. Use the following:

- "Imagination is more important than knowledge."   (Albert Einstein)
- "The world of reality has its limits; the world of imagination is boundless." (Jean Jacques Rousseau)
- "Anything one man can imagine, other men can make real."   (Jules Verne)
- "Never say NO to adventures."   (Ian Fleming)

Another interesting idea for your bulletin board is to place this caption in the upper left corner of the board. Display student stories of dragons and monsters.

```
TALES
E
R
R
I
F
Y
I
N
G
```

For a Halloween theme, "Wily Witches" is a good bulletin board caption for stories. Scatter torn paper witches among the papers displayed.

"Able Authors" or "Write On!" can be captions to feature student writing. Place each selection on a piece of brightly colored construction paper cut in an irregular shape.

This Is Our Best

Students will enjoy compiling a book of their writing efforts. Unless the book becomes a schoolwide project, you will probably not be able to produce it frequently, but two or three efforts a year will serve as an outlet for student endeavors.

Even a simple book is an excellent type of material to distribute to parents at an open house. You may also consider a book of writings as an especially good gift for parents for holidays or birthdays.

Our Tallest Tale

This activity is a natural follow-up for a lesson on tall tales such as those about Paul Bunyan. After youngsters have heard many tall tales, ask them to write some of their own. One teacher organizes what she calls the "Liar's Club," and has certificates to give each child who completes a yarn or tall tale.

Write the tall tales on tall thin paper, and put them in a tall thin book. Then the Tall Tale Book can be a class project. Youngsters enjoy this activity, for they don't frequently have the opportunity to tell outlandish tales, and of course, everyone likes to hear these humorous stories.

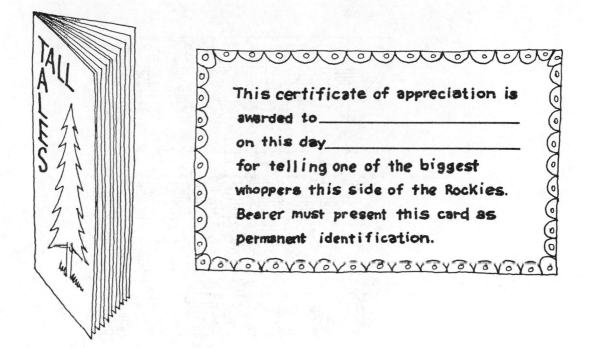

This certificate of appreciation is
awarded to_____
on this day_____
for telling one of the biggest
whoppers this side of the Rockies.
Bearer must present this card as
permanent identification.

Bookbinding

Here is an easy technique that students of all ages can use to produce neatly bound books. Supplies required are yarn and a tapestry needle.

1. Punch holes 1½ inches apart along the margin of the book cover and pages.
2. Measure and cut a length of yarn three times the size of the side of the book. If the yarn is thin, double it first.
3. Thread the needle with the yarn and pass the needle down through the first hole.
4. Bring the yarn up across the back and down through the first hole again.
5. Pull all the yarn through, leaving only a short piece hanging to tie later. Keep the binding loose.
6. Pass the yarn to the second hole and go up through the hole, bring the yarn across the back, and draw it up through the hole again.
7. Repeat step 6 until the yarn has passed twice through every hole. (See illustration #1.)
8. When you come out of the last hole, bring the yarn up and down alternating through the holes, so that a solid line is formed across the top and bottom. (See illustration #2.)
9. Tie the two ends together at the top in a knot or bow. (See illustration #3.)

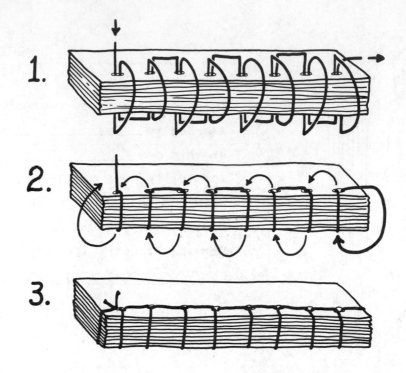

Book Covers

Older students can bind original stories for added interest and motivation as shown here.

Cut

- Cloth or contact paper 11″ × 25″
- Child's story on 8″ × 10″ paper
- Colored paper 7″ × 21″ (2)
- Cardboard 8″ × 10″ (2)
- Cardboard for hinge 8″ × ⅜″ (1)

Fold

- Colored paper in half

Staple

- Sandwich style: one folded colored piece of paper on top, the stack of white paper in middle (the story), and one folded colored piece of paper on bottom
- Then fold colored piece on very top and very bottom, back ¼", then forward ¼"

Tape (vinyl)

- Hinge between covers to form back

Glue

- Cloth on covers plus hinge. Can add tape all around at hinge. Glue colored paper to inside covers. Trim colored paper to be even with first colored page.
- This makes a book that is 8" × 10".

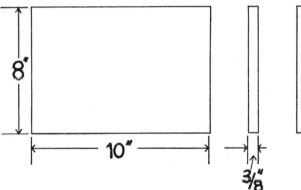

Sharing Writing

The following suggestions are designed to encourage students to write more and improve their skill at communicating:

- Invite older students to read their stories to primary grades.
- Display stories on library and office bulletin boards where everyone can read and appreciate them.
- Hold bookbinding parties at regular intervals to encourage students to finish masterpieces.
- Collect the best of the class writing in a small three-ringed notebook. Students can easily revise and change their contributions. This collection can be bound at the end of the school year.

How Books Are Written

Pencil to Press (New York: Lathrop, 1963) is a book about itself. Marjorie Spector follows a book from the time she first thought of writing it to the book's being sold to readers. The book achieves a special interest by showing the different versions the text went through.

The film *Story of a Book* (Pied Piper, 1962) is narrated by Holling C. Holling, who describes how he and his wife produced a book. The book *Pagoo* began with searches in southern California tidepools to capture hermit crabs to study. The processes of writing and illustrating are described, then the production of the book, until finally the book appears on bookstore shelves.

8 Teaching Poetry

Instead of painting a picture which tells more than a thousand words, the poet tries to make one word invoke a thousand pictures.

GEORGE RUSSELL HARRISON

Poetry is an important part of our cultural heritage. Before children come to school, they may already have been exposed to poetry, through counting rhymes and jump-rope chants, for example. But all students need to know the poems that form part of our common lore, from *Mother Goose* to "Casey at the Bat." Teachers can prepare students for poetry by sharing favorite poems, reading poems aloud, and using poems in all areas of the curriculum.

Modern poets such as Shel Silverstein open up a new world for students when they realize that poems can be about a messy room or a baby brother. From there, it is only a short step to students writing their own poems. Student poets can be successful with a variety of forms and patterns, even in the primary grades, and writing poetry helps students appreciate that poetry is a special way of seeing. As a result of the activities in this chapter:

- Students will listen to poetry read aloud.
- Students will read poetry for pleasure.
- Students will write different types of poetry.

READING AND LISTENING TO POETRY

Poetry is meant for the ears as well as the eyes; it is a natural form for reading aloud. Children learn to hear poetry by listening to you and others read it aloud, by sharing poetry orally, and by listening to poetry on tapes and records.

The activities in this section are organized to provide for the appreciation of poetry. As a result of these activities:

- Students will recognize and enjoy the rhythm and language of poetry.
- Students will respond to poetry in various ways.
- Students will interpret poetry as individuals and as groups.

Jump Rope Rhymes

Have the children collect the rhymes they chant as they jump rope. Make a book of *Rhymes for Jumping Rope*. Boys and girls can join in compiling this book as the children all interview friends and family to learn new rhymes. For example:

> *Teddy Bear, Teddy Bear, I am sick*
> *Send for the doctor, quick, quick, quick.*
> *Teddy Bear, Teddy Bear, turn around,*
> *Teddy Bear, Teddy Bear, touch the ground.*
> *Teddy Bear, Teddy Bear, are you lame?*
> *Teddy Bear, Teddy Bear, spell your name.*
> *Teddy Bear, Teddy Bear, has much to do,*
> *Teddy Bear, Teddy Bear, you are through.*
>
> *Monkey, monkey in the tree*
> *How many monkeys do I see?*
> *1, 2, 3, 4, 5, 6, etc.*
>
> *Down by the meadow where the green grass grows,*
> *There sat _____, sweet as a rose.*
> *She sang, and she sang, she sang so sweet,*
> *Along came _____ and*
> *Kissed her on the cheek.*
> *How many kisses did she get?*
> *1, 2, 3, 4, 5, 6, etc.*

The Rhythm of Poetry

Students will become aware of the rhythms of poetry by singing rounds. Each group must sing the same rhythm or the round doesn't come out right. The following songs are good for all ages: "Row, Row, Row Your Boat," "Three Blind Mice," and "Are You Sleeping?"

White Coral Bells

Children who have had experience with rounds will be able to sing the lovely song, "White Coral Bells."

Discovering Couplets

Studies have shown that youngsters enjoy hearing rhymed verse. One of the simplest types is the couplet. Youngsters use this rhyming form in their own play, in jump rope games, and in jingles. Encourage students to find examples of couplets such as these:

January brings the snow,
Makes our feet and fingers glow.

MOTHER GOOSE

Star Light; star bright;
First star I see tonight.

OLD SAYING

Poetry is not irregular lines in a book but something very close to dance and song, something to walk down the street keeping in time to.
NORTHROP FRYE

Quatrains

One of the most commonly used poetry forms is the quatrain, a four-line poem. Children can find many examples of quatrains in Mother Goose poems. For example:

> *Simple Simon met a pieman*
> *Going to the fair.*
> *Said Simple Simon to the pieman,*
> *"Let me taste your ware."*

Other verses familiar to children are quatrains with different rhyming patterns:

> *There was a crooked man, and he went a crooked mile;*
> *He found a crooked sixpence against a crooked stile;*
> *He bought a crooked cat, which caught a crooked mouse,*
> *And all lived together in a little crooked house.*

> *Pat-a-cake, pat-a-cake, baker's man,*
> *Bake me a cake as fast as you can;*
> *Pat it and prick it, and mark it with T,*
> *Put it in the oven for Tommy and me.*

As students identify quatrains, have them examine the rhyme scheme to see how many different arrangements they can find.

Combining Quatrains

The quatrain is often used in combinations to form longer poems. Present examples like "A Bird" to the children. Check the rhyme scheme in this quatrain.

> *A Bird*

> *A bird came down the walk,*
> *He did not know I saw;*
> *He bit an angleworm in halves*
> *And ate the fellow, raw.*

And then he drank a dew
From a convenient grass,
And then hopped sidewise to the wall
To let a beetle pass.

EMILY DICKINSON

Poetry Doesn't Have to Rhyme

Show the children examples of poetry that doesn't rhyme to dispel the idea that rhyming is a necessary aspect of poetry. Poets whose work is in anthologies of poetry for children include Hilda Conkling, Carl Sandburg, e. e. cummings, and Walt Whitman—all of whom write free verse.

How to Eat a Poem*

Don't be polite.
Bite in.
Pick it up with your fingers and lick the juice that may run down your chin.
It is ready and ripe now, whenever you are.

You do not need a knife or fork or spoon or plate or napkin or tablecloth.
For there is no core
or stem
or rind
or pit
or seed
or skin
to throw away.

EVE MERRIAM

Learning Limericks

Children love limericks. Here are two they can learn quickly.

There once was a lady from Niger
Who smiled as she rode on a tiger
They came back from the ride
With the lady inside
And the smile on the face of the tiger.

COSMO MONKHOUSE

*From *It Doesn't Always Have to Rhyme* by Eve Merriam. Copyright © 1964 by Eve Merriam. All rights reserved. Reprinted by permission of Marian Reiner for the author.

There was an old man of Blackheath,
Who sat on his set of false teeth.
Said he, with a start,
"Oh, Lord, bless my heart!
I've bitten myself underneath!

UNKNOWN

Alliteration

Alliteration, the repetition of initial consonants, contributes to the musical quality of poetry. Encourage your students to identify examples in word play and poetry. Notice how alliteration (and assonance, the repetition of vowel sounds) is used in the following poems to provide rhythm and humor.

Betty Botter bought some butter,
But, she said, the butter's bitter;
If I put it in my batter
It will make my batter bitter,
But a bit of better butter
Will make my batter better.
So she bought a bit of butter
Better than her bitter butter,
And she put it in her batter
And the batter was not bitter.
So 'twas better Betty Botter bought a bit of better butter.

How much wood would a woodchuck chuck
If a woodchuck could chuck wood?
A woodchuck would chuck as much as he would chuck
If a woodchuck could chuck wood.

Onomatopoeia

Talk about words that sound like what they mean (onomatopoeia). Children will soon list a number of familiar words such as:

slush	sizzle
sneeze	roar
crackle	splash
meow	beep
hiss	chomp

As you read poetry together, encourage students to note other examples of such words. Help children observe how this effect adds to the music of language.

An excellent poem to use with students is "Galoshes," by Rhoda Bacmeister (in Jean Thompson, comp., *Poems to Grow On,* Boston: Beacon, 1957), which describes the sounds of mud and slush.

"Poems for the Very Young" is an excellent record that encourages children to listen to poems. The poetry is read by Marni Nixon and Donald Murphy. Available from Bowmar Records, 10515 Burbank Boulevard, Los Angeles, California.

Metaphors in Poetry

Children will find many examples of metaphors (direct comparison without the words *like* or *as*) in poems they read. As you read poems aloud to children, talk about the comparisons that are being made. Children will be able to identify what is being compared in these poems because it is very clear.

The Garden Hose*

In the gray evening
I see a long green serpent
With its tail in the dahlias.

It lies in loops across the grass
And drinks softly at the faucet.

I can hear it swallow.

BEATRICE JANOSCO

Other Comparisons

Personification is another kind of comparison—one in which something that is not human is described in human terms. Many poets use personification to make their images more vivid. Read "Dandelion," in *Poems by a Little Girl* by Hilda Conkling (New York: Stokes, 1920) and discuss how the personification creates a strong impression. Tell the students that the poet was a little girl when she wrote this and other poems.

---

*Reprinted with permission from Beatrice Janosco.

Discovering Images

Children can find many examples of similes, metaphors, and personification in the poems they read. Encourage them to copy examples like "The Eagle" on strips of art paper to display.

The Eagle

He clasps the crag with crooked hands;
Close to the sun in lonely lands,
Ringed with the azure world, he stands.

The wrinkled sea beneath him crawls;
He watches from his mountain walls,
And like a thunderbolt he falls.

ALFRED TENNYSON

Story Poems

Make poetry a part of your classroom as you read students a poem such as "Casey at the Bat" (first published in 1898 in *San Francisco Examiner*). Students can also learn this poem to recite to the class, as its rhyming structure makes it easy to memorize. Other enjoyable narrative poems found in most anthologies include:

- "Antonio, Antonio" by Laura E. Richards
- "The Shooting of Dan McGrew" by Robert Service
- "Paul Revere's Ride" by Henry Wadsworth Longfellow
- "The Highwayman" by Alfred Noyes

Casey at the Bat

It looked extremely rocky
  for the Mudville nine that day;
The score stood two to four,
  with but one inning left to play.
So, when Cooney died at second,
  and Burrows did the same,
A pallor wreathed the features
  of the patrons of the game.
A straggling few got up to go,
  leaving there the rest,
With that hope which springs eternal
  within the human breast.

For they thought: "If only Casey
      could get a whack at that,"
They'd put even money now,
      with Casey at the bat,
But Flynn preceded Casey,
      and likewise so did Blake,
And the former was a pudd'n,
      and the latter was a fake.
So on the stricken multitude
      a deathlike silence sat;
For there seemed but little chance
      of Casey's getting to the bat.
But Flynn let drive a single,
      to the wonderment of all.
And the much-despised Blakey
      "tore the cover off the ball."
And when the dust had lifted,
      and they saw what had occurred,
There was Blakey safe at second,
      and Flynn a-huggin' third.
Then from the gladdened multitude
      went up a joyous yell—
It rumbled in the mountaintops,
      it rattled in the dell;
It struck upon the hillside
      and rebounded on the flat;
For Casey, mighty Casey,
      was advancing to the bat.
There was ease in Casey's manner
      as he stepped into his place,
There was pride in Casey's bearing
      and a smile on Casey's face;
And when responding to the cheers
      he lightly doffed his hat,
No stranger in the crowd could doubt
      'twas Casey at the bat.
Ten thousand eyes were on him
      as he rubbed his hands with dirt,
Five thousand tongues applauded
      when he wiped them on his shirt;
Then when the writhing pitcher
      ground the ball into his hip,
Defiance gleamed from Casey's eye,
      a sneer curled Casey's lip.

And now the leather-covered sphere
came hurtling through the air,
And Casey stood a-watching it
in haughty grandeur there.
Close by the sturdy batsman
the ball unheeded sped;
"That ain't my style," said Casey.
"Strike one," the umpire said.
From the benches, black with people,
there went up a muffled roar,
Like the beating of the storm waves
on the stern and distant shore.
"Kill him! Kill the umpire!"
shouted someone on the stand;
And it's likely they'd have killed him
had not Casey raised his hand.
With a smile of Christian charity
great Casey's visage shone;
He stilled the rising tumult,
he made the game go on;
He signaled to the pitcher,
and once more the spheroid flew;
But Casey still ignored it,
and the umpire said, "Strike two."
"Fraud!" cried the maddened thousands,
and the echo answered "Fraud!"
But one scornful look from Casey
and the audience was awed;
They saw his face grow stern and cold,
they saw his muscles strain,
And they knew that Casey wouldn't let
the ball go by again.
The sneer is gone from Casey's lips,
his teeth are clenched in hate,
He pounds with cruel vengeance
his bat upon the plate;
And now the pitcher holds the ball,
and now he lets it go,
And now the air is shattered
by the force of Casey's blow.
Oh, somewhere in this favored land
the sun is shining bright,
The band is playing somewhere,
and somewhere hearts are light;

And somewhere men are laughing,
*   and somewhere children shout,*
But there is no joy in Mudville—
*   mighty Casey has struck out.*

ERNEST LAWRENCE THAYER

Favorite Poems to Read Aloud

Keep a poetry book on your desk so that you always have a poem handy for a spare moment. Mark some of your favorites or any poems that tickle your imagination. Students of all ages will enjoy the following poem.

*Eletelephony**

Once there was an elephant,
Who tried to use the telephant—
No! No! I mean an elephone
Who tried to use the telephone—
(Dear me! I am not certain quite
That even now I've got it right.)

Howe'er it was, he got his trunk
Entangled in the tetephunk;
The more he tried to get it free,
The louder buzzed the telephee—
(I fear I'd better drop the song
Of elephop and telephong!)

LAURA E. RICHARDS

Speaking Poetry Together

Use a humorous poem to help children learn to speak a poem together. Mother Goose books are good sources of poems that children enjoy. They can sing the verses, too, of poems like this one:

Sing a Song of Sixpence

Sing a song of sixpence,
*   A pocket full of rye,*

*From *Tirra Lirra: Rhymes Old and New* by Laura E. Richards. Copyright 1932 by Laura E. Richards; copyright © 1960 by Hamilton Richards. By permission of Little, Brown and Company.

Four and twenty blackbirds
Baked in a pie.
When the pie was opened,
The birds began to sing.
Wasn't that a dainty dish
To set before the King?

The King was in his counting house
Counting out his money;
The Queen was in her parlor,
Eating bread and honey;
The maid was in the garden,
Hanging out the clothes,
Down came a blackbird
And snipped off her nose.

MOTHER GOOSE

Poems with pronounced rhythms are also good choices for speaking aloud.

The Pirate Don Durk of Dowdee*

Ho, for the Pirate Don Durk of Dowdee!
He was as wicked as wicked could be,
But oh, he was perfectly gorgeous to see!
The Pirate Don Durk of Dowdee.

His conscience, of course, was as black as a bat,
But he had a floppety plume on his hat
And when he went walking it jiggled—like that!
The plume of the Pirate Dowdee.

His coat it was crimson and cut with a slash,
And often as ever he twirled his mustache
Deep down in the ocean the mermaids went splash,
Because of Don Durk of Dowdee.

Moreover, Dowdee had a purple tattoo,
And stuck in his belt where he buckled it through
Were a dagger, a dirk, and a squizzamaroo,
For fierce was the Pirate Dowdee.

So fearful he was he would shoot at a puff,
And always at sea when the weather grew rough
He drank from a bottle and wrote on his cuff,
Did Pirate Don Durk of Dowdee.

*From *Child Life Magazine,* Copyright 1923, 1951 by Rand McNally & Company.

Oh, he had a cutlass that swung at his thigh
And he had a parrot called Pepperkin Pye,
And a zigzaggy scar at the end of his eye,
  Had Pirate Don Durk of Dowdee.

He kept in a cavern, this buccaneer bold,
A curious chest that was covered with mold,
And all of his pockets were jingly with gold!
  Oh jing! went the gold of Dowdee.

His conscience, of course, it was crook'd like a squash,
But both of his boots made a slickery slosh,
And he went through the world with a wonderful swash,
  Did Pirate Don Durk of Dowdee.

It's true he was wicked as wicked could be,
His sins they outnumbered a hundred and three,
But oh, he was perfectly gorgeous to see,
  The Pirate Don Durk of Dowdee.

MILDRED PLEW MERRYMAN

Children who have *heard* poetry are more eager to *read* books of poetry. Play record selections from "Poetry Parade: Poets Read Their Poetry for Children," edited by Nancy Larrick, which includes poems by David McCord, Harry Behn, Karla Kuskin, and Aileen Fisher. A two-record set is available from Westin Woods Studios, Weston, Connecticut.

Folk Songs Are Poetry, Too

Provide the printed words of songs that children sing to show them that a song is a poem. They will also be interested in reading the words they sing. One good example is the folk song "The Erie Canal."

The Erie Canal

First Verse

I've got a mule, her name is Sal,
Fifteen miles on the Erie Canal.
She's a good old worker and a good old pal,
Fifteen miles on the Erie Canal.
We've haul'd some barges in our day,
Fill'd with lumber, coal and hay,

And we know ev'ry inch of the way
From Albany to Buffalo.

Refrain

Low Bridge, ev'rybody down!
Low bridge, for we're going through a town,
And you'll always know your neighbor,
You'll always know your pal,
If you ever navigated on the Erie Canal.

Second Verse

We better get along on our way, old gal,
Fifteen miles on the Erie Canal,
Cause you bet your life I'd never part with Sal,
Fifteen miles on the Erie Canal.

Git up there, mule, here comes a lock,
We'll make Rome 'bout six o'clock,
One more trip and back we'll go
Right back home to Buffalo.

A Light in the Attic by Shel Silverstein (New York: Harper and Row, 1981) is a wonderful collection of humorous poems for children of all ages.

Riddle Poems

Many old poems set up riddles to be answered. Answering correctly usually depends on unraveling the metaphor. Can your students follow the riddling metaphors in these examples?

Little Nancy Etticoat,
With a white petticoat,
And a red nose;
She has no feet or hands,
The longer she stands
The shorter she grows.

   (A candle)

As I was going to St. Ives,
I met a man with seven wives;
Each wife had seven sacks,

Each sack had seven cats,
Each cat had seven kits:
Kits, cats, sacks, and wives,
How many were there going to St. Ives?

 (One)

Printing Poems

Let children select a poem they especially like and have them print it on a Poetry Poster. They can use manuscript printing or try other styles of calligraphy to create an artful presentation, such as the illustration of "Morning," by Emily Dickinson.* Simple drawings enhance the poem and suggest its content.

MORNING

by Emily Dickinson

Will there really be a morning?
Is there such a thing as day?
Could I see it from the mountains
If I were tall as they?

Has it feet like water lilies?
Has it feathers like a bird?
Is it brought from famous countries
Of which I've never heard?

Calligraphy by Cat

How to Teach a Poem

As you talk about a poem with children, there are various levels of sophistication that you can operate on. It is important to focus student attention not only on the literal

*Reprinted from *Reading Ideas,* September 1975. Reprinted by permission.

elements of the poem, but also on the inferences and implications important to the comprehension of the poem.

The Wind

I saw you toss the kites on high
And blow the birds about the sky;
And all around I heard you pass,
Like ladies' skirts across the grass—
 O wind, a-blowing all day long,
 O wind, that sings so loud a song!

I saw the different things you did,
But always you yourself you hid.
I felt you push, I heard you call,
I could not see yourself at all—
 O wind, a-blowing all day long,
 O wind, that sings so loud a song!

O you that are so strong and cold,
O blower, are you young or old?
Are you a beast of field and tree,
Or just a stronger child than me?
 O wind, a-blowing all day long,
 O wind, that sings so loud a song!

ROBERT LOUIS STEVENSON

Questions that might be asked regarding this poem are suggested for each level.

Literal Level

- Who was the poet?
- What is the title?
- Tell one thing the wind did.

Inferential Level

- What is the poet saying in this poem?
- In what different ways does the poet picture the wind?
- How would you compare Stevenson's style of poetry to that of Carl Sandburg?

Creative Level

- Write a poem on how you feel about the wind.
- Do you enjoy being outdoors? What is it that makes you feel good?
- Describe a place or experience in the outdoors that you remember clearly.

What Is Poetry?

When I feel physically as if the top of my head were taken off, I know that is poetry.

EMILY DICKINSON

Poetry for Children to Read

Order a number of poetry books that children can read themselves. *Knock at a Star: A Child's Introduction to Poetry,* edited by X. J. Kennedy and Dorothy Kennedy (Boston: Little, Brown, 1982), is an excellent collection of more than 150 poems, many of which are not found in other anthologies. Especially suited to reading aloud are *Jamboree: Rhymes for All Times* by Eve Merriam (New York: Dell/Yearling, 1984) and *Snowman Sniffles and Other Verses* by N. M. Bodecker (New York: Atheneum, 1983). Include a few light-hearted collections such as *Tiny Tim: Verses for Children,* a collection of British and American poems chosen by Jill Bennett (New York: Delacorte, 1982), or books on special interests such as *A Dog's Life,* contemporary poems selected by Lee Bennett Hopkins (New York: Harcourt, 1983).

A Poetry Collection for You

Each teacher needs a good collection of poetry from which to draw. The following books are recommended for the quality and variety of their selections.

- May Hill Arbuthnot and Shelton Root, *Time for Poetry* (Glenview, Ill.: Scott, Foresman, 1968).
- Jack Prelutsky, *The Random House Book of Poetry for Children* (New York: Random House, 1983). Illustrated by Arnold Lobel.
- Joanna Cole, *A New Treasury of Children's Poetry: Old Favorites and New Discoveries* (New York: Doubleday, 1985). Illustrated by Judith Gwyn Brown.
- Edward Blishen, *Oxford Book of Poetry for Children* (New York: Watts, 1963). Illustrated by Brian Wildsmith.

WRITING POETRY

Children need many opportunities to write poetry and practice its various forms. Students respond with enthusiasm to the structured task of writing a cinquain or haiku, while free verse or unrhymed poetry releases their desire to experiment.

The following activities provide examples of poetry forms that students can write successfully:

- Students will express ideas through rhyming and unrhyming poetry.
- Students will recognize and produce examples of the following: alliteration, onomatopoeia, imagery, simile, and metaphor.
- Students will share and enjoy their poetry.

Rhyming List

Words that rhyme usually have the same ending—*rain, stain, gain*—but it is good to remember that rhymes are sounds and that words don't need the same ending to rhyme, for example: *said, head.*

Here are examples of words that are easy to rhyme. Challenge students to find five rhymes for each word.

- mean
- sat
- pan
- cup

Each student can make a rhyme list for several words, such as *bend, light, round.* The class can assemble a rhyme dictionary to help each other when they write poetry.

First Poems

After you explore rhymes and rhyming, select a topic and use this theme to create couplets about a month, a season, a holiday, an event, or the weather. Then explore what possibilities this exercise offers. Provide the first line for a poem, and then have the class suggest the next line. Some examples of first lines are:

- What do you do in the spring?
- I woke up early one day.
- Across my face came a smile.
- We ran on the sand.

Limerick

The limerick consists of a triplet and a couplet. The triplet is lines 1, 2, and 5; the couplet is lines 3 and 4. Limericks can be written about anything: people in the classroom, famous people, or people from literature. This is a simple form of poetry, but everyone can have a lot of fun with it. One way of beginning is to give students a series of beginning lines which they can use as starters, for example:

- There once was a doggy named Rover . . .
- There was a young bookworm called Booky . . .
- There once was a girl dressed in pink . . .

Use one of these lines to compose a group poem like this:

> *There once was a doggy named Rover*
> *Who rolled in a patch of green clover.*
> *His master came out;*
> *Said he with a shout,*
> *"Look! Rover's got clover all over!"*

Alliterative Phrases

Students will enjoy writing phrases that contain words beginning with the same sounds, for example:

- Fancy fringed feathers
- Reasonably red raspberries
- Lithe leaping lizards

Some students will be motivated to write whole sentences in this manner. This is a good small-group activity.

- Black-browed bears bowled briskly before breakfast.
- Aunt Agatha asked angrily and agile Abraham answered anonymously.

Composing such sentences will lead students to the dictionary as they pore over words listed under one letter. They will encounter new vocabulary in this way, too.

Number Poem

Numbers form the structure for interesting poems that students can write, thus:

> *One is only, the most, the best;*
> *One is lonely, rejected, alone;*
> *One is a baby's first birthday party;*
> *One is the power atop the throne.*

Alliteration Number Poems

More advanced students might enjoy the challenge of creating alliterative lines for an unrhymed number poem. Notice that alliteration is based on sound, not spelling.

> *One whistling wild warbler winged westward.*
> *Two trembling timid turtles tiptoed to town.*
> *Three throbbing thrushes threaded through thrillingly.*

Terse Verse

Just two words can form a poem that has meaning, for instance:

Go	*Hot*	*Snack*
Slow	*Shot*	*Pack*

Students can discover many such pairs as they play with rhyming words. They can present such poems artfully for display.

Two-word Lines

A simple, but effective, poetry pattern consists of just two words on each line. No rhyming is required although it could be added in different ways.

> *Fun*
>
> *Bikes racing;*
> *Balls batting;*
> *Skateboards swishing;*
> *Hoops twirling.*

Noise

Bells, yells;
Waves, raves;
Sports, snorts;
Clouts, shouts.

Free Verse

Free verse is a style of poetry that children can write very successfully. The reason is that there are few restrictions in the writing of free verse; there is no set pattern of rhyme, no set length of line or content, and any topic can be written about. Free verse can consist of one line or twenty. One way of helping youngsters to create free verse is to show them a group of pictures or slides on a theme. Then have them describe this idea with one, two, three, or four words. Having the whole class participate in this beginning experience of writing free verse is an excellent strategy for introducing this form.

Another method is to present a familiar concept. For example, have students list all things that are hard. Begin a group poem, thus:

What is hard?
Hardness is a baseball.
Hardness is doing homework.

Other useful topics include: "Summer Is . . ." or "A friend Is . . . ." Students might suggest lines like this:

Vacation Is . . .

   swimming in the pool,
   going camping.

Poetry Takes Shape

Help students think of poetry in concrete terms. Have them draw a large shape on a sheet of colored construction paper—an animal, an object, or an imaginary shape—and cut it out. Ask them to tell the class about the shape by writing a poem on the paper. Encourage them to perceive this shape with all their senses. They can write their poems on the shape they have cut. Mount the picture poems on the bulletin board for everyone to enjoy.

THIS LITTLE BLUE LAKE
CONTAINS A THOUSAND WONDERS.
THE FISH NO NOISE MAKE
AS THEY GO SWIMMING BY.

Green Is . . .

Give students an opportunity to discuss some of their favorite colors. For motivation, you could use *Hailstones and Halibut Bones* (New York: Doubleday, 1961), the poetry book by Mary O'Neill, or the film *Hailstones and Halibut Bones* (Sterling, 1963), in which the poetry is read and illustrated. Ask the students what their favorite color is and have them break up into small groups by color. Each student in the group can describe something that is their favorite color. Or they can discuss why a specific color is their favorite. The group can prepare a color collage featuring clippings of pictures and words that depict, for example, the color green. They can also write a poem about the color similar to those by Mary O'Neill, beginning "Green Is . . . ."

Developing Sensory Awareness

Take a poetry field trip or display colorful pictures that appeal to each of the five senses for this discussion. Discuss these questions, followed by the experiential activities suggested here:

- What do you taste when you think yellow?
  Pass around pieces of lemon to taste.
- What do you see when you think green?
  Take a walk around the school. Come back to class and share all the things that you saw that were green.
- What do you smell when you think purple?
  Provide things that have different fragrances for students to experience—lavender, ripe purple grapes, grape juice.

- What do you feel when you think?
  Include discussion of emotional feelings as well as touch. Bring objects for tactile sensations.
- What do you hear when you think blue?
  Provide a tape of ocean sounds, birds, or anything else you feel would be appropriate.

Wishes, Lies, and Dreams: Teaching Children to Write Poetry (New York: Vintage Books, 1970) is Kenneth Koch's account of his work with children in P.S. 61, New York City. Examples of children's writing are included.

Similes and Metaphors

Introduce students to similes and metaphors as an effective method to improve their writing, particularly the writing of poetry. Both similes and metaphors compare two dissimilar objects, but similes include the words *like* or *as*. Many similes have become cliches, such as "busy as a bee," "wise as an owl," and "big as a house."

Have students brainstorm fresh comparisons. Students can create colorful similes and metaphors that open up the mind to new ways of looking at the world, as in Eve Merriam's poem, called "Metaphor."

Metaphor*

*Morning is
a new sheet of paper
for you to write on.*

*Whatever you want to say,
all day
until night
folds it up
and files it away.*

*The bright words and the dark words
are gone
until dawn
and a new day
to write on.*

EVE MERRIAM

*From *It Doesn't Always Have to Rhyme* by Eve Merriam. Copyright © 1964 by Eve Merriam. All rights reserved. Reprinted by permission of Marian Reiner for the author.

A Listing Poem

An easy kind of poem for children to write is a list of related words. The topic could be animals, automobiles, or favorite things. This poet describes "swift things."

Swift Things Are Beautiful*

Swift things are beautiful:
Swallows and deer,
And lightning that falls
Bright-veined and clear,
Rivers and meteors,
Wind in the wheat,
The strong-withered horse,
The runner's sure feet.

ELIZABETH COATSWORTH

Acrostic Poem

The acrostic poem can be of varied length. It might be only a couplet, or a group of words, and it can vary in rhyme scheme. The special characteristic of the acrostic poem is that the first letters of each line are part of a word that can be read vertically. Poems like this can be used to honor a famous person, spell a subject, or celebrate a season, as in this example:

Sleepy blue lake
Unveiled by disappearing mist;
Memories of summers past
Make permanent the
Etchings; while I sit here
Reclined before a warm winter fire.

The possibilities for a poem like this are endless. Develop a class poem around a word. Print the letters at the left first, and then fill in the poem. Students can develop individual acrostic poems.

Cinquain

The cinquain is a poem consisting of five lines. There are many varieties of five-line poetry, but the cinquain is one that both teachers and students seem to enjoy. Easy to compose, one cinquain form follows these specifications:

*Reprinted with permission of Macmillan Publishing Co., Inc., from *Away Goes Sally* by Elizabeth Coatsworth. Copyright 1934 by Macmillan Publishing Co., Inc., renewed 1962 by Elizabeth Coatsworth Beston.

- Line one: one word (usually the title)
- Line two: two words (describing the title)
- Line three: three words (an action describing the title)
- Line four: four words (feelings describing the title)
- Line five: one word (refers back to the title)

Compose a class cinquain as the whole class contributes to the writing of one poem. Then each youngster can compose cinquains independently.

Students of all ages are able to write the cinquain form, as shown in this example:

Puppies

Snuggly, cuddly
Jumping, rolling, chasing
They always love you
Dogs

JEFF, GRADE 3

Stars

Twinkling bulbs
Brighten the sky
Glowing, blinking all night
Diamonds

KATIE, GRADE 6

Vacation

School's out!
Swimming, camping, fishing
I can hardly wait
Summer

ROBERT, GRADE 4

Winter

Icy cold
Freezing, blowing, snowing
It lasts so long—
Spring?

SUE, GRADE 6

Syllabic Cinquains

Another form of the cinquain follows a syllable form, as outlined here:

- Line one: two syllables
- Line two: four syllables
- Line three: six syllables
- Line four: eight syllables
- Line five: two syllables

The syllabic cinquain, illustrated in the poem that follows, provides an excellent lead-in to the writing of haiku, another syllabic form of poetry.

Today

Never ceasing
Passes sometimes hurting
Changing with every moment
Silent

JOHN KIMBALL

Writing Haiku

A beautiful unrhymed poetry form, the Japanese haiku, originated in thirteenth-century Japan. Haiku is a three-line verse form, with the three lines totaling seventeen syllables, thus:

- Line 1: 5 syllables
- Line 2: 7 syllables
- Line 3: 5 syllables

The topic of haiku poetry is usually related to nature and the season is indicated. There is no rhyme, and articles and pronouns are rarely used. Like all poetry, haiku is subtle and symbolic. American haiku has been written by a variety of people on a number of topics. The lines have not always been the classic length.

Students are very successful with this brief form. Their poems are often as subtle as those of adults, as shown in these examples by students from Alberta, Canada:*

---

*From *An Ice Cream Cone Feeling: In the Dark of December, An Anthology of Writing from the Students of Alberta* (Edmonton, Alberta: The Alberta Teachers' Association). Reprinted with permission.

Here comes a sunset
Pulling a blind over me
Making a dark orange.

GEOFFREY DELVES

The sun goes to bed
Leaving the scorched horizon
To nurse its sunburn.

LAUREN ATKINSON

Group Composing of Haiku

Begin composing haikus by working together as a group. Examine a classic haiku to observe the form it follows. Show children how the season is indicated and the way nature is stressed.

Suggest topics that children might find familiar, ones that are associated with nature, for example:

- water: stream, river, ocean
- rain: storm, drops, wind
- trees: pine, roots, leaves
- flowers: daisy, pansy, fragrance

Thinking about one selected topic, help the children develop the image before they write anything. Thinking of the pine tree, for instance, discuss where the tree is, what it looks like, and what might be happening around it. Then encourage children to suggest lines for the poem. Don't worry about the exact number of syllables at first as this can be developed as part of polishing the poem. The group might gradually create a poem like this together:

Pine tree—tall, bold, strong;
Lean into the wind
Or you will be uprooted.

Haiku by the Masters

Share examples of haiku written by the ancient Japanese masters. Print them on posters for display. Here are several that children can understand and enjoy.

*It is nice to read
news that our spring rain also
visited your town.*
ONITSURA*

*Over the wintry
forest, winds howl in a rage
with no leaves to blow.*
SOSEKI*

Collections of Haiku

Short forms of poetry such as haiku lend themselves to long slender books that your class can create easily. Type one haiku by each child in two columns on a duplicating master. The sheets can then be folded vertically to form the pages for a booklet of poetry, as shown here:

These booklets make attractive gifts for holidays or birthdays, and everyone is represented. Illustrations can be added around the poems and on the cover.

*From *Cricket Songs,* Japanese haiku translated by Harry Behn. © 1964 by Harry Behn. All rights reserved. Reprinted by permission of Marian Reiner.

Tanka

The tanka is a 5-line Japanese poem that contains a haiku in the first three lines. Similar to the haiku, the tanka's lines are unrhymed and contain a total of 31 syllables for the poem. Like the classic haiku, it usually has something to do with nature. The form of the poem is:

- Line one: 5 syllables
- Line two: 7 syllables
- Line three: 5 syllables
- Line four: 7 syllables
- Line five: 7 syllables

Some people maintain that the original form was the tanka and that the haiku is, in effect, an abbreviation of this form. The tanka represents to us an advanced form of the haiku and can be an extension of the haiku form. After youngsters have experienced writing haiku, they can then go on to the tanka.

Poetry is my kind of fooling.
ROBERT FROST

Diamante

The diamante, as its name indicates, is diamond-shaped. Created by Iris M. Tiedt, it follows these specifications:

- Line one: subject = one word
- Line two: adjectives = two words
- Line three: participles = three words
- Line four: nouns = four words, to begin the transition
- Line five: participles = three words
- Line six: adjectives = two words
- Line seven: noun = the opposite of the subject = one word

This 7-line diamond-shaped poem gives youngsters an opportunity to contrast two moods or two opposite ideas in one poem.

Diamond

Light
all-colored, bright
dazzling, flashing, flickering
daybreak, dawn, sunset, twilight
falling, slowing, dying
heavy, awful
Darkness

SHEILA, GRADE 6

Sneaky Poems

Children love writing sneaky poems because the subject "sneaks" up on the reader. The 5-line poems are composed according to the following formula:

- First line: word related to the subject
- Second line: adjective plus noun about subject
- Third line: two action words
- Fourth line: descriptive phrase
- Fifth line: subject

Here are some examples written by sixth graders.

Oval
Unpredictable path
Spiraling, flashing
It's an odd shape
Football.

RYAN

Steel
Hesitant smile
Binding, grinding
Sparks off of teeth
Braces.

MICHELLE

9 Language Arts in the Content Areas

The simplest schoolboy is now familiar with the truths for which Archimedes would have sacrificed his life.

JOSEPH ERNEST RENAN

The language arts of listening, speaking, reading, and writing are used in all areas of the curriculum. Many opportunities exist for developing language abilities in all of the content areas. The more we are aware of these possibilities, the more effective our teaching will be—not only of the specific content areas, but of all the language arts.

The activities in this chapter are organized to emphasize the language arts in the areas of science and math, social studies, and music and art. After completing the activities in this chapter:

- Students will learn through reading and listening.
- Students will learn to express their ideas through speaking and writing.

SCIENCE AND MATHEMATICS

Science and math are fascinating subjects to youngsters. Both fiction and nonfiction children's literature provide excellent material to promote and encourage this interest. As we delve into such studies as ecology, space exploration, metrics, and plant and animal life, youngsters will have many opportunities to use the language arts in all its forms. As a result of the activities in this section:

- Students will formulate good questions.
- Students will read widely.
- Students will develop expository writing skills.

Science Crossword

Ask each youngster to write the word *science* across the page. Then have them construct a crossword puzzle using words that describe science. For example:

Class Word List

Before beginning a science topic, list some related vocabulary words on the board. For example:

- tide
- bathysphere
- oceanographer
- current
- scuba

Ask the students what these words have in common. If they guess that the words are all related to the *sea,* does that help them figure out what *oceanographer* means? Challenge students to uncover the meaning of any new words on the board. As they look up the words, they will run across others to add to the list. The class can prepare a poster or a book showing the words and definitions, which can be consulted during their study of this topic.

It's in the Bag

Early in the school year, give each student a paper bag. Individuals collect ten items to put in the bag while taking a walk around the school neighborhood. When the students return to the classroom, they sit in a circle and remove their ten items from the paper bags. Each child selects one unusual item that she or he has collected to discuss with the group.

After students have described the objects they found, have them classify them in some way. Students discuss the various groupings and why they put certain items together. This should be an open-ended activity where there are no specific answers, but students have an opportunity to describe, discuss, and to generalize about their findings. This activity could be repeated. It is also an activity that can be carried out on different levels.

Observing and Recording

Encourage students to look at their environment for examples of nature and seasonal changes. Have them record their observations as a group in a Class Nature Log or individually in a journal or diary. Students can note changes in plants and animals according to the seasons, and record weather data such as temperature, rainfall, and wind direction from appropriate instruments. At the end of the school year, students can review their data and chart the seasonal variation. What was the coolest day? The warmest day? On what day did the first leaves fall? If you keep a journal each year, students can compare their information to that of previous years.

Acrostic Poems

The acrostic makes a different kind of poem. One word is written vertically and the beginning letters of each line are used to fill in words related to the topic, as shown here. Explain to your students that each letter of the word will begin a line of the poem. Encourage your students to suggest ideas for your collective acrostic, which might go like this:

> **W**ild winds blowing,
> **I** cicles hanging from the roof,
> **N** oses are red from the cold.
> **T** he tinkle of sleigh bells is heard.
> **E** agerly children await
> **R** eindeer and Santa Claus, too.

Students enjoy creating their own acrostics. Have students make acrostics to fit a book they have read, seasons, or current events. Acrostics relate spelling and vocabulary development to student interests.

The Sky Is Full of Song, collected by Lee Bennett Hopkins (New York: Harper, 1983), contains poems for children that celebrate the variety of seasons.

I've Got the World on a String

Give each student a piece of string approximately two feet long. The ends of this string are tied together to make a circle. When each student has completed a circle, the class goes outside, preferably to a grassy area, although it can be anyplace on the playground. Each person chooses a place to lay his or her string to form a circle. Each student then studies and observes the world within this circle. Depending upon the maturity of the student and the time available, students can observe what's going on not only on the surface but below the surface. They can record how many things there are in this little world. On returning to the classroom they can describe either orally or in written form what they have just observed in their circles. They can also draw a picture or map of their world developing the idea as much as they like.

Familiar Animals

Have students make lists of all the animals that live in your area: rats, mice, squirrels, seagulls, pigeons, and so on. Use this list to discuss how the students think the animals got there and what purpose they serve. Students might be interested in doing research on this topic to learn more about animal life around them. Once the class has discussed this information, the students can write stories based on what they have learned about the animals. Possible topics might include:

- A Pigeon's View of Our Town
- My Life as a Fly
- A Worm's Eye View of the World
- My Friend, the Squirrel
- If I Were a Hawk

A Bug's Eye View

A variation of the previous activity is to inform the class that they are to be a bug, a worm, or any insect. They are to *be* that animal and tell what their world would look like: where they would live, what they would eat, what they might see and do. They can tell what the world would look like from an ant's point of view or from the point of view of a butterfly. Encourage students to use the first person as they write for real involvement.

Which Animal Would You Like to Be?

After discussing animals with the class, have students select an animal that they would like to be. Students should tell why they would want to be that animal, what kind of adventures they would have, what they would be able to do, how they would live, what part of the world they would live in, and what they would eat. This activity requires that students research background information on animals and their habitats. They can use this information to write stories or descriptions.

Have the students read their stories in small groups so that the other students can ask questions about their life as an animal. Students could illustrate their stories and put them where everyone else can read them. As a follow-up, students can draw pictures of their animals for a bulletin board, "Who Am I?" which can be developed into an oral language activity.

Air, Land, or Sea!

Play this game in pairs or small groups. A student selects one of the categories: *air, land,* or *sea.* Then she or he points to another student and counts to five. The person pointed to must name an animal, for example, that lives on land: rabbit, pig, elephant. If the person names an appropriate animal before the number five is reached, then she or he is the next one to select the category. A particular animal or creature or species can be named only once. This activity can be developed on different levels of sophistication and can be played on a point basis if the group plays for some time.

Modified Cloze

This procedure forces your students to read carefully. Ask students to fill in the blanks with words that make sense. Discuss their responses to show that many answers will work and that some answers work better than others in context. Personalizing the paragraphs will help to motivate your students.

> Lucinda has many fish. She keeps them in a _____ tank. The fish tank is full of _____. She also has snails _____ plants in the fish tank. The snails keep _____ glass clean. Lucinda's cat likes to watch the fish _____. Sometimes the cat puts his _____ in the water. He tries to catch _____ fish.
>
> Michael has a pet cat. He feeds his _____ every day. The cat's _____ is Tiger. Tiger has orange stripes on her _____ and black stripes on _____ face. Tiger likes to _____ on Michael's bed. Sometimes she sleeps on _____ pillow and sometimes she sleeps under _____ covers.

Create an Animal

What might animals be like that live on other planets? Your discussion might take the following path: "Most animals we know have two eyes. Can you imagine an animal with five eyes, or one eye? How would this animal make use of its eye(s)?" After discussing some ideas as a group, have students begin to sketch their imagined animal. Continue the discussion as students decide how their animal will move, eat, and communicate.

When students have finished inventing their animal, they can give it a name and write a story about where it lives and how it behaves.

Animals in Our Language

Have the students consider how many of our expressions refer to animals, for example: *blind as a bat, sly as a fox,* and so on. Ask the students how many of these expressions they can list.

Busy as a bee	Happy as a lark
Hungry as a bear	Roars like a lion
Eats like a bird	Stubborn as a mule
Thirsty as a camel	Strong as an ox

Cat-like walk	Vain as a peacock
Runs like a deer	Struts like a rooster
Slippery as an eel	Wolf in sheep's clothing
Wild as a March hare	A whale of an appetite

Help your students become aware of the richness of our language by discussing how these expressions might have originated. What characteristics of animals are represented in these phrases? Some animals appear in many expressions; for instance, cats and dogs. What different pictures of the animals' behavior do the expressions imply?

Have students select different animals and describe them. Then ask them to invent expressions that we might use, referring to these animals. After everyone has shared these creations, you can talk about the importance of using fresh expressions in writing and not the familiar cliches such as "quiet as a mouse."

Science Acrostic

At the end of a unit, give students a thematic word or phrase, and ask them to make an acrostic and construct sentences beginning with each letter. Here are two examples done by students who completed a unit study on seasons.

> *Seasons change according to nature's timetable.*
> *Each season is about three months long.*
> *Autumn is when plants die and animals store food to prepare for winter.*
> *Spring is the season of new life.*
> *Old Man Winter brings cold weather and ice and snow.*
> *Nice, sunny weather makes summer the favorite season.*
> *Seasons are different in different parts of the world.*
>
> JULIE

> *Flakes of snow fall from the sky.*
> *Everyone has to shovel their sidewalks.*
> *Bright sunshine can't melt the snow away.*
> *Ride your sled down the long hill.*
> *Use Dad's old hat for your snowman.*
> *Ask Mom to make hot chocolate.*
> *Remember February. . .*
> *You and I can be valentines!*
>
> MICHAEL

Know What You Eat

Introduce students to the study of nutrition by having them read the list of ingredients on packaged foods. Assign the students to read all the ingredients of the foods they eat in one day. Discuss the results the next day. How many of the foods had sugar in them? Did they know what all the words meant? Has reading the list of ingredients changed their ideas about any of the foods?

Free Food Information

Have groups of students compose letters to ask for information from food advisory boards. Many organizations will send nutritional information, recipes, botanical charts, and posters. This would be an appropriate time to discuss propaganda techniques and critical reading skills. Students will enjoy checking the daily mail for responses and presenting the material to the rest of the class.

Kansas Wheat Commission
2630 Claflin
Manhattan, KS 66502

National Peanut Council
1000 16th Street N.W., Suite 700
Washington, DC 20036

The Rice Council
P. O. Box 22802
Houston, TX 77027

California Olive Advisory Board
516 North Fulton Street
Fresno, CA 93728

Science and the Cinquain

The cinquain form lends itself to discussions of science topics, for example, ecology and pollution. This type of writing is a good way of summarizing what students have learned in a particular science unit. The students can write the cinquain poem and then illustrate it with their own pictures or pictures they select from magazines. A collage used to illustrate and summarize the end of a science unit might include this poem:

Pollution
Unhealthy Litter
Human Garbage Heaps
Man's Inhumanity to Life
Ugly

Study Color

Utilize your students' interest in color to motivate writing and speaking. The following are suggestions that you might use to elicit student reactions to color:

- What is your favorite color?
- What color makes you feel good?
- What color makes you feel bad?
- What color is happiness?
- What color is pain?
- What color is Sunday?

Use these questions to begin a study of color as a science unit.

Flannelboard Review

Students will enjoy reviewing basic concepts in science when you illustrate them with flannelboard figures. For example, make a flannelboard cut-out for each stage of the butterfly's life cycle and use it to teach students the concept. Then students can use the same figures to retell the story to each other or to other classes.

Combining oral language tasks with illustrations that can be manipulated helps key students' memories and reinforces concepts learned.

Science Facts

Science can help students learn to distinguish between facts and common misconceptions. Is Mt. Everest really the tallest mountain? Students can find out by reading *The Dinosaur Is The Biggest Animal That Ever Lived, And Other Wrong Ideas You Thought Were True,* by Seymour Simon (New York: Lippincott, 1984). Have students prepare a "Science Trivia" bulletin board with questions such as "What's the biggest animal that ever lived?" written on cards that they can turn over to find the answer.

Inventing the Year 2000

This activity helps students project their lives into the future. It can also lead to other studies of the future as students develop their ideas. Students gain practice in applying concepts of cause and effect as they discuss the consequences of present activities.

How to Invent the Year 2000*

2000 A.D.
Subtract this year   _____ A.D.

Answer   _____ Years until 2000 A.D.
Add your age   _____

_____ your age in 2000 A.D.

In 2000 A.D.
I will be living in

_____

In 2000 A.D. I will be spending most of my time

_____

_____

In 2000 A.D. my most significant relationship will be with

_____

_____

In 2000 A.D. our planet's most troublesome problem will be

_____

_____

In 2000 A.D. the schools will be
_____ About the same as they are now.
_____ Totally different than they are now.
_____ I don't know; I just can't imagine.

*From Tom McCollough, *Education in the Year 2000*. Reprinted by permission of the author.

Individual Lists

Have every child choose one topic that interests him or her. For one week the children search diligently, using varied sources, to develop their individual word lists. They can also help each other. For example, if everyone knows that Chuck is collecting horse words, they will pass any they happen to find on to him.

These lists can be used to develop word collages including pictures related to the theme chosen. Or each student can copy his or her list on pages for a class book entitled "Master Word Lists."

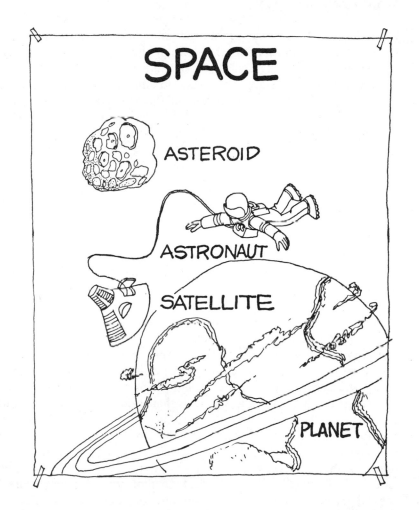

Star Trek

The year is 2267 A.D. You are captain of a space ship from the planet Earth. You and your crew have the task of exploring new life forms in outer space. You have just discovered a planet that you believe is inhabited. Construct a ship's log for your adventures.

This activity is an excellent device for integrating science and writing. Students are naturally fascinated by the possibilities of space exploration, so they can bring together what they know about the field of science and use their imagination. This can be a small-group effort or each student can write a space log.

Word Brackets

Motivating students to explore the dictionary is easy with this game. Students work by themselves and with each other to think up longer and more obscure words. The game is set up by writing a word vertically down the left side of the paper and then reversing it up the right side. The object is to think of words that begin with the letter in the first column and end with the letter in the other column.

S	impl	**E**
P	icni	**C**
A	rom	**A**
C	atni	**P**
E	xactnes	**S**
	Score:	*25*

The word that forms the frame can be chosen to fit a school subject, such as *Science,* or a particular topic like *Mexico* or *Winter.* Vary the difficulty of the game by limiting the meaning of the words used to fill in. If your class is studying the sea, use *Ocean* for your bracket, and ask students to think of the sea's inhabitants, ocean-related occupations, and descriptive terms for the ocean.

Score this game by adding up the number of letters between the vertical columns. You may also wish to develop a way of rewarding the more unusual responses. Students are encouraged to develop their vocabulary by looking for longer and longer words and they will become interested in the meaning of these words.

Another advantage of this game is that students become more aware of spelling rules and word endings. We are accustomed to thinking of the beginnings of words but not of how they end. The letter *s* at the end is easily seen as a plural. Letters *g* and *d* can be used for *ing* and *ed.* Knowing suffixes (and prefixes) adds to the skill of playing the game. Students will begin to pay attention to less obvious suffixes such as *al* (seasonal), *ment* (enjoyment), and *tion* (exploration). Students will observe that the same letter can represent different sounds, for example, an *h* at the end can be preceded by *c* (church) or by *g* (rough).

Display the longest and most creative solutions to motivate further vocabulary development. Students can discuss the meaning of these words and the patterns of spelling and suffixes. Everyone has an opportunity to learn new words.

This game can be made easier by allowing students to use words that include the letter in the right hand bracket without ending in it. In this case, the score includes only the letters inside the brackets. The letters extending beyond them do not count.

When Stars Come Out

When the class is studying space, have each student choose a constellation to research. Draw each star of the constellations with luminous paint on black paper. You can also use polyester cloth cutouts with a black light. Darken the room and let students tell the story of their constellation. They should discuss what the name means and how it got its name.

Scrambled Words

For a quick review of words learned in a science unit, mix up some familiar words and put them on the board for students to unscramble.

losra tesysm	solar system
aletspn	planets
leecospet	telescope
apecs	space
ultop	Pluto
onortasym	astronomy
uoatstrna	astronaut

Balloons

This activity involves science, writing, and (hopefully) a lot of wind. Provide a number of balloons that can be inflated with helium gas. Each balloon has a card attached to it with a student's name, address, and phone number on one side, and information giving the day of the launch, the time, and a request to the finder of the balloon to communicate where this balloon came down, who found it, and when it landed. When these notes are returned to the students, brief thank you notes should be sent to the finders. A book that might be used with the class during this activity is *The Red Balloon* by Albert Lamorisse (New York: Doubleday, 1957). (This is also available as a film by Macmillan, 1956.)

After some of the notes have been returned, students are well-primed for a discussion of wind and wind currents and how winds carry not only balloons but seeds, birds, and airplanes. This could lead to interesting and extensive discussions of science topics such as meteorology and plant germination.

Picture This

One creative way to end a science unit is to have students draw a picture of what they have studied and then write related words around the picture. For example, after studying the sun, students can draw a picture and write words (adjectives, nouns, and verbs) like *sunspot, glow, ray, star, shine, dawn,* and *yellow.*

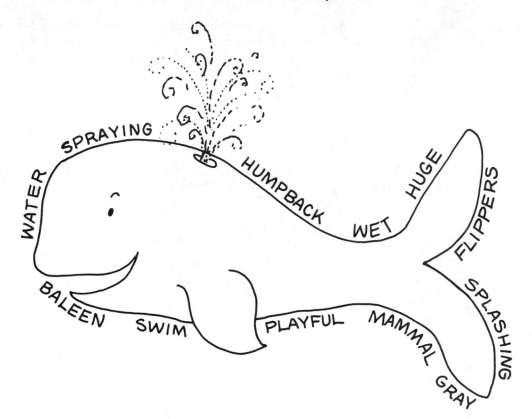

Science and Poetry

Students will enjoy writing poetry about science-related topics. The limerick is an easy form to use, as in this example by an anonymous writer:

> *Relativity*
>
> *There was a young lady named Bright,*
> *Who traveled much faster than light,*
> *She started one day*
> *In a relative way,*
> *And returned on the previous night.*

Discuss other scientific topics about which poems can be written, such as: animals, plants, trees, birds, fish, magnetism, or electricity.

Word Bingo

Use this game to review new vocabulary. Provide students with a list of at least 30 words you wish to practice. Have the students write 24 words at random on a bingo grid. You can pronounce the words or give definitions or synonyms.

BOTANY BINGO

STEM	OVARY	ZYGOTE	CORK	RHIZOME
LEAF	FLOWER	BULB	SEED	OSMOSIS
NODE	PETAL	FREE	NEEDLE	FRUIT
SPORE	BARK	BUD	ROOT	PITH
TUBER	CLONE	PISTIL	POLLEN	VEIN

Word People in Science

One of the ways of improving youngsters' knowledge about science and also enlarging their vocabulary at the same time is to introduce them to the concept of Word People. Many terms and names in science come from the name of the person who developed or discovered them. For example, Alexander Garden, a botanist, developed the gardenia flower which is named after him. The volt, a measure of electricity, is named after Alessandro Volta, an Italian physicist.

As an activity, you might develop a list of people and the students could research what terms came from the people's names. Here are a few more names of people and what they gave their name to.

- J. G. Zinn, German botanist   (zinnia)
- George Ohm, German physicist   (ohm)
- James Watt, Scottish inventor   (watt)
- Joel R. Poinsett, U.S. Ambassador to Mexico   (poinsettia)
- John McAdam, Scottish engineer   (macadam)

The Marvelous Inventions

This idea makes reading, writing, and inventing fun. Read *The Marvelous Inventions of Alvin Ternauld* by Clifford B. Hicks (New York: Scholastic Book Services, 1960) to the class. This provides an inventive, experimental atmosphere for students to

dream up their own creations. They could write a description of their invention and answer questions about their invention. What does it do? Who is it made for? Does it take much maintenance? How much does it cost? Can anyone use it? Some examples of inventions that students create are:

- Chocolate Vegetables
- Instant Cookie Maker
- Pocket Future Predictor
- Automatic Kickball Kicker
- Room Straightener and Bed Maker
- Homework Machine

It would also be fun to illustrate the inventions. A variation would be to have the students do an oral presentation and try to "sell" their inventions.

An excellent resource for teachers to keep on their desk is *Words of Science and the History Behind Them* by Isaac Asimov (Boston: Houghton Mifflin, 1959).

Science and Creative Thinking

One excellent device for challenging youngsters to think about science in different ways is to ask them some provocative "What ifs": What if the oceans started drying up? What if dolphins could talk? Some additional examples are given below to help your youngsters get started on this activity. They will, of course, be able to think of many more once they are started. Some can be used in oral discussions; others can be written about in a creative writing period. The important thing is that this strategy allows for thinking.

What if . . .

- it was always cloudy?
- it never got dark?
- you were a dolphin?
- all the planets switched positions?
- you could talk to insects?
- plants could talk?
- there was no gravity on earth?

- there was no rain?
- the world was flat instead of round?
- all plants began to die?
- all the rivers stopped running?
- you discovered the skeleton of an unknown animal?
- you could grow a fantasy garden?

Encourage children to use any means necessary to express their ideas and thoughts for their stories (tape recorders, art, drama).

Books about Scientists

The following children's books should be shared with your class to help motivate student interest:

Edward Holmes, *Great Men of Science* (Danbury, Conn.: Warwick Press, 1979).
Tillie S. Pine, *Scientists and their Discoveries* (New York: McGraw-Hill, 1978).
Vernon Pizer, *Shortchanged by History: America's Neglected Innovators* (New York: Putnam, 1979).

The Question Box

The purpose of this idea is to encourage children to ask questions, which is an important skill to develop. Provide a box where students can place questions that they want answered. They can also indicate topics that they want to know more about. These questions can be signed or unsigned. Provide opportunities for students to write questions.

These questions provide input to the teacher about areas of interest and concern to students. Periodically, questions should be pulled from this box and used as class discussions or as suggested areas for further study. This is a strategy that can be conducted throughout the year.

Group Decision Making

This task requires group decision making, which involves individual decisions, group discussion, and group consensus. It is very important that students have this type of small-group experience. Although this is a somewhat artificial situation, it stimulates the type of activity that students will be involved in throughout their lives: decision making.

Decision by Consensus
Prepared by NASA

1. Individual Decision

Instructions:

You are a member of a space crew originally scheduled to rendezvous with a mother ship on the lighted surface of the moon. Because of mechanical difficulties, however, your ship was forced to land at a spot some two hundred miles from the rendezvous point. During the landing much of the ship and the equipment aboard were damaged, and since survival depends on reaching the mother ship, the most critical items still available must be chosen for the two-hundred-mile trip. Below are listed the fifteen items left intact and undamaged after landing. Your task is to rank them in order of their importance in allowing your crew to reach the rendezvous point. Place the number 1 by the most important item, the number 2 by the second most important, and so on through number 15, the least important.

_____Box of matches
_____Food concentrate
_____50 feet of nylon rope
_____Parachute silk
_____Portable heating unit
_____Two .45-caliber pistols
_____One case of dehydrated milk
_____Two 100-pound tanks of oxygen
_____Map of the stars as seen from the moon
_____Life raft
_____Magnetic compass
_____5 gallons of water
_____Signal flares
_____First-aid kit containing injection needles
_____Solar-powered FM receiver-transmitter

2. Group Consensus

This is an exercise in group decision making. Your group is to employ the method of group consensus in reaching its decision. This means that the prediction for each of the fifteen survival items *must* be agreed upon by each group member before it becomes a part of the group decision. Consensus is difficult to reach. Therefore, not every ranking will meet with everyone's complete approval. Try, as a group, to make each ranking one with which *all* group members can at least partially agree. Here are some guides to use in reaching consensus:

1. Avoid arguing for your own individual judgments. Approach the task on the basis of logic.
2. Avoid changing your mind only in order to reach agreement and eliminate conflict. Support only solutions with which you are able to agree to some extent, at least.
3. Avoid conflict-reducing techniques such as majority vote, averaging, or trading in reaching decisions.

4. View differences of opinion as helpful rather than as a hindrance in decision making.

On the Group Summary Sheet place the individual rankings made earlier by each group member. Take as much time as you need in reaching your group decision.

GROUP SUMMARY SHEET
INDIVIDUAL PREDICTIONS   GROUP
                                PREDICTIONS

	1	2	3	4	5	6	7	8	9	10	11	12	
Box of Matches													
Food Concentrate													
50 Feet of Nylon Rope													
Parachute Silk													
Portable Heating Unit													
Two .45-Calibre Pistols													
One Case Dehydrated Pet Milk													
Two 100-lb. Tanks of Oxygen													
Stellar Map (of the Moon's Constellation)													
Life Raft													
Magnetic Compass													
5 Gallons of Water													
Signal Flares													
First Aid Kit Containing Injection Needles													
Solar Powered FM Receiver-Transmitter													

Group_____

Key.   Take the difference between your ranking and the ranking on the key. Add the differences. The lower the score the better. These answers are based on the best judgments that are now available to you. They are not absolute answers.

15	Box of matches	Little or no use on moon.
4	Food concentrate	Supply of daily food required.
6	50 feet of nylon rope	Useful in tying injured together; helpful in climbing.

__8__	Parachute silk	Shelter against sun's rays.
__13__	Portable heating unit	Useful only if party landed on dark side of moon.
__11__	Two .45-caliber pistols	Self-propulsion devices could be made from them.
__12__	One case of dehydrated milk	Food; mixed with water for drinking.
__1__	Two 100-pound tanks of oxygen	Fills respiration requirement.
__3__	Map of the stars as seen from the moon	One of the principal means of finding directions.
__9__	Life raft	CO_2 bottles for self-propulsion across chasms, etc.
__14__	Magnetic compass	Probably no magnetized poles; thus useless
__2__	5 gallons of water	Replenishes loss by sweating, etc.
__10__	Signal flares	Distress call when line of sight possible.
__7__	First-aid kit containing injection needles	Oral pills or injection medicine valuable.
__5__	Solar-powered FM receiver-transmitter	Distress-signal transmitter— possible communication with mother ship.

3. Critique

Following the exercise, discuss the sources of the problem-solving techniques. How often did individuals use the affective domain in working out the problem? How often did the cognitive domain dominate? What kind of balance existed? How did their knowledge of the extensional world allow them to work with the unknowns? What did they learn about their own learning styles? Did they work better in groups or alone? Did they score higher as a group, or was the individual score better? How did the scores compare with the group average? Did they enjoy the individual work more than the group work?

I Can Guess Your Age

There are many tricks that students can learn to do with numbers that will make the unsuspecting think they are mental wizards. Show students how to guess another person's age.

- Multiply your age by 10.
- Now multiply 9 by any lower number.
- Subtract this product from the first product.
- What's the answer?

(To get the person's age, you add the two digits of the answer together. If it is three digits, the first two digits are one number that is added to the third digit, to get the age.)

Calculators

These two sequences always produce the same number, no matter what number the person starts with. Tell someone that you will guess his or her secret number by guessing the result of a series of calculations.

- Choose a number from 1 to 8.
- Add 9.
- Double the sum.
- Subtract 4.
- Divide by 2.
- Subtract the chosen number.
  (The answer is always 7.)

- Choose any number.
- Multiply it by 5.
- Add 25 to the product.
- Divide the sum by 5.
- Subtract the chosen number.
- Multiply the remainder by 3.
  (The answer is always 15.)

Students can amaze their friends and astonish enemies with these simple mental math tricks. They will be so enthralled to see these tricks work that they will be motivated to learn *how* they work.

Number Lore

A numerologist is someone who believes in the power of numbers. But we all have associations with the power of various numbers. Discuss with students the different expressions we have that use numbers. For example:

- It takes 2 to tango
- 10 gallon hat
- 6 of one, half a dozen of the other
- On cloud 9

- To kill 2 birds with 1 stone
- The 11th hour

Another aspect of the power of numbers is that we think some numbers are lucky and others unlucky. Ask students to provide examples. Some numbers have mathematical powers. There is always something special about primes, for example, and squares. Introduce these concepts to students and discuss some examples.

Prepare a bulletin board featuring a number. "All about 7" could include expressions featuring the number 7 and facts about 7.

All about 7

- 7th heaven
- 7 league boots
- the 7 Wonders of the World
- at 6's and 7's
- 7 is a prime
- the square of 7 is 49

There's luck in odd numbers.
SAMUEL LOVER, 1836

Adventures of a Number

Ask the students to pick a favorite number and write an adventure about that number. You may wish to help students begin the adventures of their numbers by asking questions like:

- How is your number special?
- Is your number old or young?
- Does the shape of your number influence its movement?
- How was your number invented?
- What is your number's favorite operation? (+ , − , x , ÷)
- What does your number like or dislike about its job?
- Is your number lucky or unlucky?
- Is your number magical?

Number Hunt

Divide your class into small groups to investigate the numbers in your classroom. Give each group a list of categories to fill. For example:

- List 3 things that come in pairs.   (shoes, socks, barettes)
- List 1 thing that comes in 16s.   (crayons)
- List 1 thing that comes in 12s.   (numbers of a clock, eggs)
- List 1 thing that comes in 6s.   (jacks)

Expensive Words

Have fun and motivate interest in both spelling and math by giving letters monetary values, as follows:

A	1	J	6	R	1
B	2	K	4	S	1
C	4	L	2	T	1
D	2	M	2	U	1
E	1	N	2	V	7
F	5	O	1	W	6
G	3	P	1	X	10
H	4	Q	9	Y	5
I	1			Z	8

Because the less commonly used letters are given higher values, students will be encouraged to spell more difficult words. Longer words also carry higher value just because they contain more letters. A word such as xylophone would be a very high-priced word, worth 27 cents.

Give students assignments designed to use this monetary system. For example:

- What is the most expensive holiday you can think of?
- Spell at least three animals worth more than one dime.
- How much is this lunch worth: peanut butter and jelly sandwich, milk, orange.
- You have $1.00 to buy four words. List your four words and the price of each.

Compute This Riddle!

Students will enjoy this self-checking activity and quickly learn to recheck their computations if the numbers do not translate into sensible words. After students become familiar with the format, you may wish to organize a Riddle Workshop by providing riddle books and asking pairs of students to create computation riddles for the rest of the class.

A	12		N	21
B	4		O	14
C	1		P	26
D	18		Q	11
E	9		R	24
F	23		S	7
G	2		T	20
H	16		U	13
I	5		V	22
J	25		W	8
K	10		X	19
L	15		Y	6
M	3		Z	17

Riddle

How many elephants can you put in an empty boxcar?*

7	16	17		6	30	12	7	12		14	8	10	30
+7	+5	−8		+6	−7	+8	+2	+12		+6	+8	+2	−10

————————— ,   ——————————————   ——————————————

14	11		4	13		17	16	13		18	6	30	10	14
−9	+9		+1	−6		+4	−2	+7		−9	−3	−4	+10	−8

————— ————— ————— ——————————————— !

Math Terms

Students can compile a math dictionary with definitions of terms in their own words. They will find their own definitions easier to remember than those memorized from a book. For example:

*Answer: One, after that it is not empty!

- Triangle: It always has three sides, but it can be different shapes.

Creative Math Writing

Have students write letters explaining the concept or process they are learning. These letters can be addressed to real or imaginary beings. The letters should be used to monitor concept comprehension and should not be corrected for spelling or grammar.

Dear Hamlet Hamster,

This is a picture of a right triangle. The little square means that the angle is exactly 90°, like one of the corners of a square. The other two angles also add up to 90° since all three angles of a triangle must equal 180°.

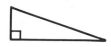

Personalized Math

To maintain student interest in written and oral word problems, create problems featuring your students.

The sunflower Demian planted in his garden began growing this morning. If Demian's sunflower grows an average of 3 cm a day, how tall will it be in two weeks?

Rava and her family are going to Disneyland during vacation. Rava's father will wake her up at 6:00 A.M. Rava's mother will serve breakfast 30 minutes later. Write the time that Rava should be at the breakfast table on your paper.

Students will enjoy suggesting new situations for word problems and creating problems of their own.

Divergent Problems

Challenge your students by presenting them with problems that require careful reading and thinking. Practice strategies for identifying and solving each type of problem before mixing the problems on challenge worksheets.

- *Problems with extra information:* Ask students to cross out the unnecessary details and to circle the important ones.

Michael and Vincent went to the store to buy vegetables for supper. Artichokes were 4 for $1.00. Corn was 8 ears for $1.50. Celery was 49 cents a bunch. Radishes were 39 cents a bunch. Lettuce was 79 cents a head. How much change did Michael and Vincent get if they paid $5.00 for 2 heads of lettuce and 6 artichokes?

- *Insufficient information:* Ask the students to explain the data needed to complete the problem.

Emily rode her bike to the store to buy supplies for her birthday party. She bought 20 balloons for 2 cents each, 2 packages of paper plates for 79 cents each, 3 bags of peanuts for $1.29 each, and 2 sacks of mints for 89 cents each. How much change did Emily get?

- *More than one answer:* Show your students that some problems have several right answers.

David got a 10-gallon fish tank for his birthday. He can put about 1 inch of fish per gallon in his new tank. David wants to buy some Pearl Gourami and some Bala Sharks. The Pearl Gourami are about 1 inch long and the Bala Sharks are about 1½ inches long. How many of each should he buy?

Break Out of Your Box!

Present this 9-dot problem to encourage divergent thinking. Provide each student with several copies of the problem and encourage experimentation.

•   •   •

•   •   •

•   •   •

Directions: Draw 4 straight lines connecting all of the dots without lifting your pencil. Each dot must be touched only once.

Most students will try to stay within the array and will not discover the solution. After allowing time for experimentation, you may wish to draw the first line on the board and discuss the importance of trying different solutions when the obvious ones do not work.

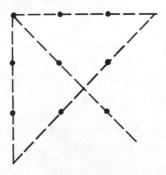

> One excellent source of provocative math problems is *Aha! Gotcha: Paradoxes to Puzzle and Delight* by Martin Gardner (San Francisco: W. H. Freeman, 1982).

Mental Math

Mental Math is another game that can be played with the class. Give students an oral arithmetic problem that they must not only listen to, but solve mentally. This approach can be adapted to any level. A simple problem to start with is the following:

> Take two. Add four. Subtract three. Multiply by two. Subtract one. What's your answer?

This activity reinforces listening skills as well as basic arithmetic facts as students learn them. You can also make a tape of addition or multiplication facts so that students can listen to it whenever they need to review independently.

Estimation Game

Give the students oral or written problems to demonstrate the importance of estimation. Use examples that show the value of this process in daily life.

> The PTA will give out juice bars to celebrate our first 2-mile jog. They have 400 juice bars and want to know if that will be enough for everyone. Here is the enrollment for each class: 28, 23, 29, 27, 24, 32, 29, 26, 28, 31, 27, 23, 22, 28. Does the PTA have enough juice bars?

> Kipp saw that he had exactly $10.00 when he opened his wallet. Does he have enough money to buy all of this?

> | orange juice | $1.29 |
> |---|---|
> | apples | $1.89 |
> | crackers | $1.85 |
> | carrots | $ .79 |
> | soap | $2.19 |

Record Mistakes

Have the students analyze their own mistakes on quizzes and homework papers. By writing out the reasons for their errors, students will become aware of facts that need to be reviewed and will begin to read problems more carefully. For example:

> On number 4, I circled a rectangle instead of a square. I read the question too fast.

Graphing Your School

Divide your class into small groups to survey another class or the entire student body. Conduct a workshop to decide the best format for presentation of each topic (bar graph, pie graph, etc.) after data have been collected. Display results in a central location. Topics might include:

- Number of students in each grade
- Favorite school lunch
- Favorite subject in school
- Hours spent on homework
- Favorite after-school activity
- Favorite musical instrument
- Favorite color
- Favorite animal

Graph Search

Ask the students to collect graphs from newspapers and magazines. These graphs can be posted on a bulletin board and discussed. How are graphs used? Do they help you understand the subject better? Why are graphs important? How many different ways to present information (graphs) can you find?

> *Dot and Line: A Romance in Lower Mathematics* by Norton Juster (New York: Random House, 1977) is an engaging book that deals with the concepts of "same" and "different." Also available as a film.

How Much Is It?

What can you buy with one dollar? Have students guess what this amount would purchase. List the following amounts on the board. Estimate what you could buy with each. Do students agree on how much things cost? Discuss.

$1.00
$10.00
$100.00
$1,000.00
$10,000.00
$100,000.00
$1,000,000.00

Divide students into small groups. Each group has a certain amount of money to spend. Give each group some newspapers and magazines and have them cut out examples (words or pictures) of objects they could buy and the price. Afterwards, discuss whether their estimates matched their selections of what they could really buy.

Money Talks!

Have the students examine U.S. coins for a few minutes. List all visual symbols on the board (profile of Lincoln, 1984, ONE CENT, etc.). Discuss why these symbols were included on the coin. You may want to divide the list into two columns—information about the coin and information about the country. Provide examples of coins from other countries and have small groups list all printed symbols. Provide time for library research to verify guesses about people and mottos. Have each group present its coin to the rest of the class.

Money Makes the World Go 'Round

Ask if anyone in your class is a numismatist, and explain that this is someone who collects rare money pieces. What other words are related to money? What expressions do we have that refer to money?

- Down to your bottom dollar
- Dollars to donuts
- A penny for your thoughts
- A penny saved is a penny earned

Pesos or Pounds?

Provide your students with a currency conversion chart from the newspaper and a list of problems. For example:

- Would you rather have 100 pesos or 100 pounds?
- How many Canadian dollars would you get for 10 U.S. dollars?
- How many francs would you get for 150 lira?

Bring in examples of money from other countries. Prepare tags listing the name of the money and the country of origin. Include a sample of U.S. currency. Ask students to rank the money by value. Provide conversion charts (or display U.S. equivalents for younger children) and discuss relative values.

England: pence, pound	France: centime, franc
Mexico: peso	Italy: lira
India: rupee	Austria: shilling
USSR: ruble	Germany: mark
Japan: yen	

Discuss the monetary system of the United States in comparison with other countries. The U.S. system is based on the decimal principle. Are there any other systems based on the decimal?

SOCIAL STUDIES

Studying the social sciences provides rich opportunities for developing the language arts skills. Youngsters can listen to taped discussions, talk about current events, write reports on specific countries, and read biographies about a particular person in history. As a result of the activities in this section:

- Students will comprehend social studies material through listening.
- Students will describe topics in oral discussion.
- Students will classify and describe material for written reports.

Who's Who in Room 14?

Ask your students to interview each other to find out different kinds of information. For example:

- Who was born in this state?
- Who is the oldest person in the room?
- Who has a birthday this month?
- Who has lived in another country?

Each student selects one specific question to investigate. After collecting this information, the students compile charts, graphs, or maps to display on a large bulletin board as an innovative way to get acquainted.

Class Directory

Class lists can be useful for many different classroom activities. Children have the opportunity to see their own name as well as the names of their classmates. They have a chance to try out different language activities with their names. The following is just a sample of some of the activities that you can use.

- Write the names of all the girls in the class.
- Arrange the class in alphabetical order by last names.
- Find names with double letters (for example, Bill).
- Write names that start with a certain letter (for example, *S*).

These activities also help children become acquainted with each other. For this reason, these activities are especially helpful at the beginning of the school year.

Celebrating People

To help children be more aware of the contributions of Great Americans, make a point of celebrating birthdays. Children can research the birth dates of specific people, for example:

Great American Women

March 11—Wanda Gag (1893–1946)
April 3—Jane Goodall (1934–   )
June 24—Amelia Earhart (1898–1937?)
June 27—Helen Keller (1880–1968)
October 11—Eleanor Roosevelt (1884–1962)
December 25—Clara Barton (1821–1912)

Challenge able students to discover the birthdays of little-known or modern American women. The birthdays of these women are probably not listed in your school encyclopedia.

Maya Angelou
Dr. Sara Josephine Baker

Elizabeth Blackwell
Deborah Sampson Gannett

Create a calendar on which these dates can be noted. Each month, a committee can make a large calendar on the bulletin board on which to feature birthdays of famous people, thus:

	S	M	T	W	Th	F	S
J			1	2	3	4	5
U	6	7	8	9	10	11	12
N	13	14	15	16	17	18	19
E	20	21	22	23	24	25	26
	27 HELEN KELLER 1880-1968	28	29	30			

Here are a few biographies to get your students researching:

Eleanor Coerr, *Jane Goodall* (New York: Putnam, 1976).

Margaret Davidson, *Helen Keller* (New York: Hastings House, 1969).

Barbara Shook Hazen, *Amelia's Flying Machine* (Garden City, N.Y.: Doubleday, 1977).

Deloris L. Holt, *The ABC's of Black History* (Los Angeles: Ward Ritchie Press, 1971).

Johanna Johnston, *Women Themselves* (New York: Dodd, 1973).

Norah Smaridge, *Famous Author—Illustrators for Young People* (New York: Dodd, 1973).

Bennell Wayne, ed. *Four Women of Courage* (Champaign, Ill.: Garrard, 1975).

Biographical Interviews

Ask students to interview an adult they know well (for example, one of their parents or grandparents) in order to learn about change in people's lives. Students can develop a list of questions as a group. Possible questions to ask include:

- How long have you lived here?
- What changes have you seen in the area?
- What was it like when you were a child?
- Is life different for children today?
- What kind of work do you do?
- Is it easier or harder than when you first started? Why?
- Have machines or appliances changed what you do? Did you have them 10, 20, 30 years ago?
- What's the most significant change that's taken place in your lifetime?

Students will practice important listening and writing skills as they ask questions, take notes, and write up their report. Discussion afterwards can focus on categorizing types of changes or describing how the local neighborhood has changed as students summarize their findings.

Biography Writing

As a follow-up to their interviews, students can collect more information (or interview another person) and write an account of that person's life. Students can tell about where their subject was born; where he or she has lived; what his or her hobbies, accomplishments, or talents are; and who is in the family. Other information might include: a description of a typical day, pictures or illustrations, a map tracing various moves, or a timeline of important events.

Who in History?

Write on the board: *If you could be anyone in history, who would you like to be? Why?* Students select a person from history and tell why they would like to be that person. In order to do this, they must be familiar with the person and the time in which they lived.

If students have not had experience with this type of activity, you might suggest some names or have the class suggest historical figures as you write them on the board. It is not necessary for every member of the class to select a different person. In fact, it is interesting when several students select the same historical figure because they can compare their reasons, which might be entirely different.

What's My Name?

Begin by selecting a group or panel of five to seven students, and somebody to be the "mystery person." The "expert" panel sits facing the class so its members cannot see the chalkboard. The mystery person signs the name of the individual that he or she represents on the board, and the panel tries to determine who this person is by asking questions that can only be answered "yes" or "no." The mystery person can be an individual from history, a person from literature, or a famous contemporary individual. This is an excellent teaching strategy, for it reinforces the importance of asking good questions, and is a follow-up on this inductive approach to learning. It also provides a good review for the class studying a particular period of history to focus on a person from that period and that time.

George Washington Sat on Me

Have the students pretend to be an inanimate object such as a chair. Pretending to be, for example, George Washington's chair, they write a story from the chair's viewpoint. The chair might complain about being sat upon or having rough shoes scrape its rungs. The story might be an account of the chair's day. Encourage students to illustrate the story.

A Mouse on the Mayflower

Tell the students to pretend they are a mouse on the Mayflower. What would they see? What would their trip be like? What kinds of experiences would they have? Describe the landing. Describe the people. This is an excellent device for personalizing history. After students have written this experience, you might want to read the story of *Ben and Me,* by Robert Lawson, in which a mouse tells about its life with Ben Franklin (Boston: Little, Brown, 1951).

A Time Machine

Instruct the students that they are going to enter a time machine and they can set the time back to any period in history. Students choose the period they would like to go back to and then select a day in this period. Discuss possible sources of information as you gradually saturate your classroom with appropriate books and resources. Then describe what a day would be like on April 22, 1861. What would be happening at that time? What would it be like to be a ten-year-old child in 1861? What might people have then that they wouldn't have now? What did they wear and eat? What was the furniture like? Each student can write a diary entry for that day.

This is a good way to personalize history and sensitize students to historical fact. After they have written their diary, discuss how they felt and what twentieth-century things they missed most. They can also read some historical fiction set in this period.

Social Studies Categories

This game is useful because it can be adapted to whatever subject the class is studying. Use the word *History* to send children exploring books.

The object of the game is to fill in as many spaces as possible with a word beginning with the letter on the left. Encourage students to think of different possible answers. You can increase interest by limiting the answers to Europe or the United States.

	Countries	People in History	Cities
H	Hungary	Hitler	Helsinki
I	Ireland		
S	Spain		Seattle
T	Turkey	Thoreau	Toledo
O	Oman		
R	Romania	Roosevelt	Rome
Y	Yugoslavia		Yorktown

Bon Voyage

Tell the students they can take a trip anywhere in the world for one month. After they have chosen a place from the map, they can begin planning their trip by writing for information to the Tourist Office of that country. They will need to do research to find out how to get there and how long it would take. Then they can write themselves a ticket to get there and back. The next step is preparing an itinerary. Travel brochures will help them decide where to go and what to do. When they have finished, they can write a travelogue of the sights, food, transportation, activities, and weather, along with a map, some illustrations, and maybe even a few words of the language.

Cards from Afar

Collect picture postcards from as many places as possible. Mount them around an outline map of the world. Attach yarn from the card to the place pictured. If students' parents are traveling, encourage them to send cards to the class. Note the settings of books read together in class. This display adds reality to the study of geography.

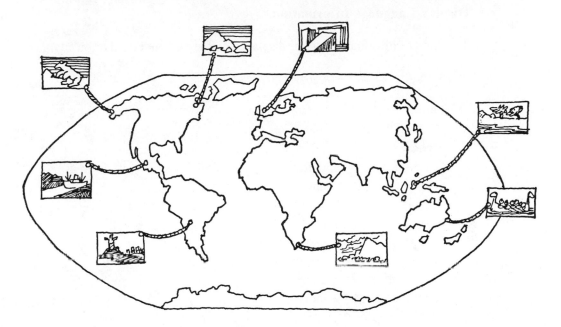

Languages of Other Countries

As you talk about various countries in social studies or in connection with a pen pal project, take the opportunity to discuss the languages spoken in different countries. Can the students name other countries where English is spoken? Find out what the students know about the languages spoken in other countries. Perhaps some of your students know other languages such as Spanish, Italian, or an oriental language. They probably know that German is spoken in Germany and French in France, but what is spoken in Belgium, Argentina, Brazil, Egypt? Some countries have two or more official languages, for instance, Canada (French and English) and Switzerland (French, Italian, German, and Romansch). Even in a country with only one official language, the people usually speak several different languages. Ask students if they can name some of the languages spoken in the United States besides English.

On a world map have students list the language(s) spoken in each country. In some countries several languages will be listed. How many countries are there for English? What language is spoken by the most people?

Display Language Information

This kind of information can be displayed on the bulletin board or on a large chart.

M Is for Mother—In Any Language

Latin:	mater
Greek:	meter
French:	mère
German:	mutter
Spanish:	madre
Russian:	maty
Italian:	madre
Polish:	matka
Persian:	mader
Armenian:	mair
Danish:	mor

Hidden Words Puzzle

A Hidden Word Puzzle can be correlated with any social studies lesson. Words and names related to U.S. history are hidden in this example. The words may be horizontal, vertical, or diagonal, and either forward or backward. Students may wish to construct their own puzzles and try to stump the class.

Key

Washington
Patrick Henry
Boston Tea Party
Louisiana Purchase
Abe Lincoln
Whig
Railroad
Tom Paine
Democracy
Civil War
Plymouth Rock
Constitution
Hancock
Paul Revere
Minutemen
Nixon
Strikes
America
Independence
Colony
Patriot
Rights
Scout
Harbor
North
Role
Garlic
Slavery

C	O	N	S	T	I	T	U	T	I	O	N
K	C	O	R	H	T	U	O	M	Y	L	P
H	A	R	B	O	R	L	Q	K	O	R	L
N	P	A	T	R	I	O	T	C	N	Y	I
L	N	E	M	E	T	U	N	I	M	E	G
C	O	L	O	N	Y	I	O	S	B	K	H
Y	R	O	L	E	L	S	S	C	O	U	T
C	T	N	D	E	E	I	R	P	S	P	I
A	H	H	B	S	N	A	S	A	T	S	N
R	W	A	S	H	I	N	G	T	O	N	D
C	H	N	T	L	A	A	Y	R	N	F	E
O	I	C	R	N	P	P	S	I	T	L	P
M	G	O	I	I	M	U	T	C	E	A	E
E	A	C	K	X	O	R	H	K	A	M	N
D	R	K	E	O	T	C	G	H	P	E	D
N	L	Z	S	N	A	H	I	E	A	R	E
C	I	V	I	L	W	A	R	N	R	I	N
O	C	L	N	D	Y	S	T	R	T	C	C
P	Q	S	L	A	V	E	R	Y	Y	A	E

Imaginary Journeys

Use creative writing to reinforce your students' understanding of geography. Provide maps and story starters like the examples on the next page to help the students plan their trips. Encourage them to describe what they would see, feel, hear, smell, and taste on their travels.

- If I had wings, I would fly to . . .
- If I were a dolphin, I would swim to . . .
- If I had a magic carpet, I would travel to . . .
- If I had my own airplane, I would fly to . . .
- If I were an eagle, I would fly over . . .
- If I were a horse, I would gallop to . . .

Create a Country

Creating a country correlates with a number of subjects, but it emphasizes particularly the social studies and the language arts. The students, either in groups or as a class, create a country. They decide on its area, climate, people, history, government, industries, monetary system, and so forth. Students can begin by sketching out what the country might look like from an aerial point of view. They begin to think about what its geography and topography would look like. It is easier to create a small country than a large one, so many teachers use the idea of creating an island that is a self-contained country.

After the whole class has had a chance to talk about the country, and some ideas are outlined on the board, divide the class into groups and have each group develop one component of the country. The class can list the various components that need to be dealt with: location, topography, climate, government, schools, industry, economics, number system, and communications. As groups go to work in these areas, they can develop varied projects; for instance, in communication, students can develop a newspaper or create examples of the literature, perhaps a series of legends that explain how the country came into being.

Because all of these topics are interrelated, it is important to have some way of correlating the work of the various committees. A means of presenting the report for each of the groups also needs to be selected. This can be a written activity or verbal activity, such as the chapter of a book, or it could be a combination of language and art, for example, an extensive bulletin board display.

Obviously, this idea is open-ended. It has the advantage of allowing students to see the various aspects of a country and how they all are interrelated—something that may be better observed with an imaginary country than with an existing one. This activity could precede or be the culmination of a series of studies of real countries.

Cooperation

Here is an intriguing small-group activity that requires cooperation. As it is described here, five people may play. If you want to use the game with more students, produce multiple sets of materials as instructed.

Each of the five players is given an envelope containing several pieces of construction paper. The shapes in all five envelopes potentially can make five squares, as shown in the illustration.

No one player, however, has enough pieces to form one square. Since the object of the game is to have everyone construct a square, players must cooperate. Rules for the game are:

- There is absolutely no talking.
- A player may give away pieces *only*. No player may take another player's pieces.

After the game is over, discuss how players felt during this experience, and the problems they encountered.

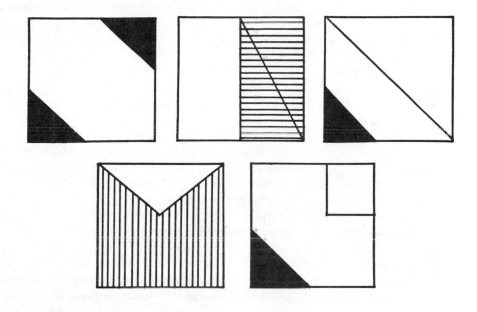

Time Capsule

Tell the students that they are going to bury a space capsule in the corner of the schoolyard. This space capsule will be opened in 100 years. The class must select the ten things—objects, ideas, letters—that should be placed in this capsule to tell the people 100 years from now what life was like in your community. Don't give too many examples that might limit the students' thinking.

One approach to this task is to have all the students write down the ten things they would like to see in this time capsule and why each one should be included. Then groups can be formed to see if there is any consensus. After each group compiles its list of ten items, the class could decide on a class list. This activity has many purposes. It forces students to examine what is happening around them; it allows students to decide what things are important to our society now that need to be explained to a group 100 years from now; and it gives students experience in oral discussion and in arriving at group consensus.

Notables

A class project that focuses on current events is useful for practicing writing skills. Have each student pick a person currently in the news to follow for several weeks. The students are to find out information about that person from television, radio, newspaper, and magazines and take notes on the material to keep in a folder about the person. At the end of the research period, each student writes a summary of all he or she learned and presents it to the class, along with pictures or other materials.

Meet the Press

Focus attention on student speaking and listening by holding a mock press conference. Students can work in pairs or in small groups with one person at a time being the interviewee. Students can pretend to be one of the people they are studying in history or someone currently in the news. They will need to do research to prepare for the press conference. Talk about methods of note-taking and discuss ways to conduct research. Also discuss the important characteristics of an interview. The goal is for the interviewee to know what she or he wants to say, and for the interviewer to have questions prepared to ask the "famous" person. The interviewer must listen closely to the interviewee's responses because she or he will write up the conference as a contemporary newspaper article complete with headline.

If the persons interviewed all come from the same country or time period, you might collect the newspaper articles into a class booklet or a single newspaper. The class could work on filling out the newspaper with other items of interest from the same period.

Headliner

Ask students to bring a short item from the newspaper to class. The item can be from any section of the newspaper. It may be related to a subject the class is studying. Each item should include the headline it was given in the newspaper.

In small groups, have one student read the item that she or he brought to the group, minus the headline. Then each person in the group writes a possible headline for the item. The person who read the item writes down the headline that really appeared. The papers are all passed to the leader, who shuffles them so that no one can tell which is the real headline. The leader reads the articles aloud, one by one.

The students vote on which headline they think actually appeared in the newspaper. The leader records the votes and then tells the group which was the real headline. Each student whose headline was voted for gets a point. Then the next student becomes the leader.

Our Future Newspaper

After students have studied the newspaper as a class project, they can prepare a newspaper for the year 2000. Divide the class into groups with each one taking a section of the paper; for example, one group might take the national news for the year 2000. Set a specific date, for example, May 15, 2000. Then students can create a full newspaper including all sections: sports pages, comic pages, national news, international news, solar system news, want ads, or a "Dear Abby" column. After the groups have completed their parts, the proofreaders and copyeditors go to work. This paper can be published if facilities are available, or it can be displayed on a large bulletin board area.

ART AND MUSIC

Art and music offer stimulation and creative ideas that children will enjoy. Emphasizing the arts in the language arts can provide exciting, aesthetic experiences for youngsters. As a result of the activities in this section:

- Students will experience their own creative talent.
- Students will identify music through listening.
- Students will describe ideas in art and music.

Alphabet Books

Primary students will enjoy making their own alphabet books. They can draw an illustration for each letter on a page, label the illustrations, and then staple the pages together into a book. These books can later be used for reading and writing practice.

Older students can choose a favorite person or object—their teddy bear, a pet cat, or a baby brother—and make an alphabet book of the world as seen by that individual. They can draw pictures of their examples and write definitions representing their character's point of view.

ABC Art

Letters of the alphabet can be considered visual symbols and art forms as well as letters to be used in writing and reading. Groupings of letters or words can be used to produce pictures of animals, people, or whatever students can imagine.

Students can use letters to develop fascinating pictures or designs. Begin by having students bring in newspapers and magazines. They can cut out letters and words of varying sizes and shapes. Give students large sheets of construction paper and paste to see how they can incorporate these letters and words in pictures. The goal of this assignment is to have students become involved with letters so that they are aware of the abstract symbols but they also see letters and words as having artistic value, as shown in these illustrations.

Inversions by Scott Kim (New York: McGraw-Hill, 1981) provides examples of words that read backwards and forwards, upside down and right side up, and in circles.

On the Bulletin Board

Feature art and language on the bulletin board as students create designs based on related words, thus:

Letterhead Notes and Cards

Encourage letterwriting by having students make personalized stationery. They can write their name at the top, using distinctive lettering copied from calligraphy books. Another possibility is to create a monogram from their initials, working with the shapes of capital letters. Or they can print a word (such as *hello*) as a heading or border, using printing press letters and a stamp pad.

> *Words and Calligraphy for Children* (New York: Van Nostrand Reinhold, 1969) by John W. Cataldo is a large art book that presents examples of children's interpretations of words and language through art. Cataldo discusses the need to have children express themselves this way in order to learn the expressiveness of language. Beautiful pictures are accompanied by quotes and comments on the origins of the work shown and its relationship to adult creativity.

Happy Grams

Let children create Happy Grams on which to write messages to friends in the classroom or to their parents to tell them what they have been doing. Use one like the example on the next page yourself to write messages to your students. This kind of positive reinforcement gives children a real boost as they struggle to learn to cope with everything they're expected to know. Encourage students to create individual designs.

What Is It?

This creative writing idea involves both art and creative writing. Have the children make an ink blot figure and then ask them to write about it. Blowing on the ink blot will make interesting spike patterns. You may want to guide them with questions such as:

- Where did you find it?
- What was it doing?
- How does it move?
- What does it eat?
- Where do you keep it?
- Where does it sleep?
- What would happen if it got wet?
- What does it do when you go to school?
- Can it fly?
- Can it change shape?
- Is it magical?
- Does it need your help?
- Is it lost?
- Is it in danger?
- What is it afraid of?

Storytelling Strings

When students prepare stories to tell to the class, help them remember the major events and their sequence by preparing a Storytelling String. Each student illustrates several important scenes from the story, cuts them out, and ties them to a piece of rope. The student who tells the story holds the rope so that he or she has a reminder of the sequence of events and a series of illustrations to show the class.

The Illustrator's Art

Show students the work of one illustrator, such as Brian Wildsmith or Uri Shulevitz. Let them compare the different styles of art used in various books illustrated by one author. They may discover that an illustrator uses a very distinctive style consistently which they can recognize.

Illustrations play an important part in the reader's reaction to a story. Select several editions of familiar works illustrated by different people to share with students (*Grimm's Fairy Tales* or *A Child's Garden of Verses,* for example). Discuss how the illustrations made them feel. What was each illustrator trying to do? Compare the illustrators' styles, use of color, subject matter, and emotional tone. Which did the children prefer and why?

The film *The Lively Art of Picture Books* shows author-illustrators Maurice Sendak, Robert McCloskey, and Barbara Cooney at home and at work. Available from Weston Woods, Weston, Connecticut.

Get into the Picture

It is often difficult for children to focus on works of modern art long enough to build any appreciation. You can help your students understand what is happening in a painting by preparing questions to guide discussion or writing. Your local library will often lend you posters that you can post on a bulletin board with guide questions like those below.

The Three Musicians by Pablo Picasso

- How many people do you see in this painting?
- What do you think they are doing?
- Describe the clothing that the guitarist is wearing.
- What are the other two musicians wearing?

- Which musician looks like he might be wearing dark glasses?
- What do you think is on the table?
- Which musician would you rather be? Why?
- What would be a good name for this painting?

Starry Night by Vincent van Gogh

- What is the first thing you noticed about this painting?
- How does the painting make you feel? Why?
- What time of day is it in the painting?
- Can you identify any of the buildings?
- What do you think the orange thing is in the upper right hand corner?
- What do you think the other yellow swirls are?
- If you were in the painting, would you be inside or outside? Why?
- What would be a good name for this painting?

What's Your Color?

Ask the students to choose their favorite color. Provide watercolors (and color wheels or paint test strips for unusual colors) and show students how to make a wash of the color they have selected. While the watercolor backgrounds are drying, have students compose a first-person account of their color's experience and feelings.

> My name is Yellow. I am bright and happy. I am the color of the moon and the sun. I am the color of the first flowers in spring and new baby chicks. I am the color of the banana peels that clowns slip on.

These essays can be copied onto the watercolor washes, or shapes can be cut from the washed paper and used to border the essay.

Some students may prefer to turn their essays into cinquains or free verse before copying onto the colored paper.

> *Yellow*
> *Sun bright*
> *Soft baby chicks*
> *Banana peels tripping clowns*
> *Golden*

Young fuzzy chicks
Endless desert sands
Long summer days
Lovely bright moons
Old faded books
Windows at night.

Medallions with Character

This simple art idea is useful for sharing books the students have read. Have students draw pictures of their favorite book characters on plastic lids with felt pens. Punch a hole in the lids so that you can hang them. Then place the lids on aluminum foil in a pan in the oven. Bake at 400 degrees for 2 to 3 minutes to melt the plastic slightly. When cool, hang them with string for a display with character!

Stuart Little

Animal Characters

Students can create their favorite animal characters from layers of newspaper glued over a two-pound coffee can or a large plastic bottle. After the newspaper has dried, facial features, legs, arms, and tails may be added. Could this be Wilbur?

Creative Book Covers

As students write original stories or reports, have them create beautiful book covers as art projects. Try a variety of these activities:

- Fold a sheet of white construction paper in half. Place bits of yarn dipped in different colors of tempera randomly on one half. Fold the other half over and press firmly while pulling the yarn out. Unfold and let dry.
- Use bright crayons to draw heavy lines or an abstract shape on a sheet of 9 × 12 inch paper. Then cover the sheet with thin black tempera paint. The bright crayon shows through.
- Drop several colors of oil-based paint, diluted in a little paint thinner, on water in a pie pan. Stir. Lay a sheet of paper (9 × 18 inches) on the water to pick up the enamel. Fold into a booklet.
- Drop several colors of tempera on a dampened sheet of paper. Tip the paper to encourage the colors to run together and mix, creating attractive colored designs. Fold as a cover.

Guess Who?

Have the students prepare a display featuring their favorite literary personalities. They can draw a character and cut it out with a ring base so that it will stand up. Number each entry and give prizes to students who guess the identities of your literary Who's Who.

Now Showing

Feature student work in the arts with distinctive bulletin board displays. For example, a collection of silhouettes might be titled "Me and My Shadow." Other examples include:

- "Atlantis" or "20,000 Leagues Under the Sea" (featuring undersea scenes)
- "A Rose Is a Rose Is a Rose . . ." (displaying repeating motifs)
- "Artichokes to Zucchini" (illustrating a vegetable alphabet)

Books about Artists for Children

The following children's books are excellent sources for generating interest about artists:

- Alice Elizabeth Chase, *Famous Artists of the Past* (New York: Platt, 1964).
- Ann Margaret Mayer, *The Two Worlds of Beatrix Potter* (Mankato, Minn.: Creative Education, 1974).
- Ernest Raboff, *Pablo Picasso: Art for Children* (New York: Doubleday, 1968).

The Sounds of Music

Instruments have distinctive sounds, and composers combine instruments in particular ways for distinctive sound effects. Teach students to listen to music with discrimination by teaching them to listen for particular instruments. Before you listen to a piece of music, write the names of some of the instruments on the board. Ask students to think of what these instruments remind them of. What feelings and images does a trumpet call up? Then have them list words that describe the sounds these instruments make. Is a trumpet shrill or brassy? After you have developed a list for each of the instruments, discuss the differences between these instruments. Why would some instruments be used for certain effects and not others?

Now have students listen to a piece of music. Have them shut their eyes to listen to the music better and name an instrument for them to listen for. When they hear the instrument, they are to raise their hands. After the listening period, discuss how they recognized the instrument. Was it by the visual or emotional images evoked by the instrument or did they recognize the instrument by the sound-words that describe it?

Musical Listening

Play a recording of Prokofiev's *Peter and the Wolf* for students. Ask them to identify the musical instruments and what animal they represent. Students can select a particular animal, listen for their instrument, and raise their hand when they hear the appropriate instrument or stand up when their animal comes in. This activity involves the students and it sharpens their listening skills.

Instruments

As students listen to music and become familiar with the instruments, they will be curious to find out more about particular instruments. They can research the history of an instrument such as the guitar, drum, trumpet, or flute, and answer the following questions:

- Where does the name come from? What does it mean?
- How has the shape changed over the years?
- When and where was it invented?
- How is it used?
- What kind of sound does it make?

This kind of research is most effective when students are divided into small groups and each group takes responsibility for an instrument. When the groups have completed their reports, they can decide on an interesting way to present the information to the class—play the instrument, play a record, make a poster, design a bulletin board, and so on. Later, each group develops an exercise to check students' understanding of the information presented. Having to construct a true-false, matching, or question-and-answer exercise reinforces students' grasp of the concepts involved.

Who's Who in Music

Whenever you play a particular piece of music, tell the students about the composer—his or her name, nationality, and date and place of birth. After the class has heard a selection, discuss the music. Ask them what would help them listen to the music. Would knowing more about the composer's life help them understand or appreciate the music better? What would they like to know?

Divide the students into groups and have each group use a different source to research and read about the composer and the piece of music. Ask them to answer these questions:

- Where and when was the composer born?
- Who or what was the music composed for?
- Where and when was it first performed?

330 CHAPTER 9 LANGUAGE ARTS IN THE CONTENT AREAS

Assemble the information gathered by the students into a report. Discuss whether the groups found different answers in their research. Why might this be? Share the results and then listen to the music again.

Cloze Lyrics

Promote good listening skills by having students listen to familiar or favorite songs. Invite them to bring in a special song. Make a copy of the lyrics but leave blanks for every fifth word, as in a cloze test, or once in every phrase. Students must listen carefully to the song to fill in the missing words. Play the song again and check the answers. Did everyone hear the same word? Was it easy to decide which word was heard?

After this exercise, discuss how singing a sentence is different from speaking it. Students can take passages from textbooks and practice singing them in the style of their favorite singing star or other singing model. Give the students an object to hold (such as a crayon or spoon) so that they can pretend it is a microphone.

Writing Song Titles

For practice with writing capital letters, encourage students to write song titles. This not only provides practice for handwriting but helps students learn which words require capitalization in a title. Have students create lists of their favorite songs to display on the board. Everyone has a number of titles to share. This list will introduce new vocabulary, too, and may lead to an interesting exchange of music as students bring in their records or sing a song for the class. Examples of possible titles to get them started are:

- "America the Beautiful"
- "I've Been Working on the Railroad"
- "God Bless America"
- "Row, Row, Row Your Boat"

An extension of this idea might be to have the students make up their own song titles. For example:

- "Let's Play Ball"
- "My Day"

Write Poetry to Music

Music has many similarities to poetry. After your students have had some experience with music, talk with them about what they think music and poetry have in common. Some musical selections are *tone poems,* which describe a setting and/or a feeling; some portray events; and others are more complex, combining all elements. Play music for the class—a dreamy fantasy like DeBussy's *La Mer,* or something emotional like Stravinsky's *The Rites of Spring.* Ask students to write a poem about what the music made them see. They can list the images that the music conjured up for them or express the musical themes in words.

After students have written their poems, discuss how the music made them feel. Did some people react very differently? Why? Trying to capture the spirit of the music in a poem helps students to understand the richness of feeling expressed in music.

Play the record again. Ask if anyone notices new aspects of the music that they had not heard before. A piece of music can be a new experience every time it is played. You may want to have students read their poems to the class while you play passages from the music. In this way, the music is illustrating the poem and the poem is illustrating the music.

Setting Poems to Music

Help children create a melody for poems they enjoy. Have melody bells or a simple xylophone available to aid them in picking out the notes that match their singing. Several students may work together on this project.

Duplicate wide-lined music staffs and show students where to place the notes they play, thus:

You need not worry about the music notation being exact at this state. Permit free adjustment of the rhythm as students sing or play the notes they have written.

Encourage students to select short poems to produce songs like the following which you may enjoy singing together.

Who Has Seen the Wind

Christina Rossetti   Iris M. Tiedt

Who has seen the wind?
Who has seen the wind?

Nei-ther you nor I
Nei-ther I nor you

But when the leaves hang trem-bl-ing
But when the trees bow down their heads

The wind is pas-sing by.
The wind is pas-sing through.

Language Experience Songs

Students like to make up songs and enjoy the music of repeated phrases and rhythms. Encourage them to express their ideas through music by writing class songs about experiences you have shared. Brainstorm a list of words and phrases on the board. Pick a well-known tune such as "Farmer in the Dell" or "She'll Be Coming Round the Mountain" to set your song to. Students suggest different ways to assemble the words to fit the rhythm pattern, in order to come up with a satisfying arrangement. They will learn that in composing songs, as in writing stories, sometimes you have to try a number of different possibilities before you find something that seems right.

Music Sets a Mood

Playing a record while students write is often an excellent way to set a mood for writing. Records such as *Zen Meditation and Other Joys* are outstanding for motivating the writing of Haiku poetry. A series of records on the seasons is available from Windham Hill Records (P.O. Box 9388, Stanford, California 94305).

Word People in Music

What do the following people have in common?

- Adolph Sax
- John Philips Sousa
- Nellie Melba
- Luisa Tetrazzini

They're all people from the world of music whose names have entered the language. Ask students if they know what instruments are named after the first two people. Do they know the foods named after the other two people? Investigate how *saxophone, sousaphone, melba toast,* and *turkey tetrazzini* got their names.

People in the Orchestra

Students will be fascinated to see that the musicians in an orchestra are people, too. Read Karla Kuskin's *The Philharmonic Gets Dressed* (New York: Harper, 1982) to the class when you are talking about the orchestra. Students will learn more about the different musicians and what they do.

Books about Composers

The following children's books are excellent sources for the children in your class:

Helen L. Kaufmann, *History's 100 Greatest Composers* (New York: Grosset & Dunlap, 1964).

Dorothy Samachson, *Masters of Music: Their Works, Their Lives, Their Times* (Garden City, N.Y.: Doubleday, 1967).

Harold C. Schonberg, *The Lives of the Great Composers* (New York: Norton, 1981).

10 A Guide to Instructional Resources

Resources can be extremely helpful for the teacher because they are sources of new ideas and they can save teacher time. Because no teacher can buy or use all the materials available, we present in this chapter resources that we especially recommend. Our selection is based on quality, significance, and usefulness. The books and resources listed here were selected to aid you in discovering new ideas and enlivening your teaching. The major areas of the language arts are represented. In addition, we offer a special section on computer software. The chapter is organized by the following categories:

For Teachers

- Idea Books
- Language Books for Your Library
- Periodicals of Interest to Teachers

For Students

- Books that Stimulate Thinking Skills
- Poetry for Children

- • Award-Winning Books—Caldecott and Newbery Medalists
- • Read Alouds
- • Published Writing by Children
- • Kids' Magazines
- • Pattern Books

Multimedia

- • Selected Children's Video Titles
- • Selected Films to Motivate Students
- • Selected Computer Software for the Language Arts

FOR TEACHERS

Idea Books

Allen, Roach Van, and Allen, Claryce. *Language Experience Activities*. Boston: Houghton Mifflin, 1976, paperback.

Resources for creating Learning Centers.

Arnstein, Flora J. *Poetry and the Child*. New York: Dover, 1970, paperback.

Awakening children's ability to write poetry.

Calkins, Lucy McCormick. *The Art of Teaching Writing*. Portsmouth, N.H.: Heinemann, 1986.

Excellent, detailed description of strategies for teaching writing as a process.

Carlson, Ruth K. *Writing Aids through the Grades*. New York: Teachers College Press, 1970, paperback.

A variety of ways to stimulate student writing.

Chihak, Mary K., and Jackson Heron, Barbara. *Games Children Should Play*. Glenview, Ill.: Goodyear-Scott Foresman, 1980, paperback.

Sequential lessons for teaching communication skills.

Coody, Betty. *Using Literature with Young Children*. Dubuque, Iowa: Wm. C. Brown, 1983, paperback.

A practical idea book in its third edition.

Croft, Doreen J., and Hess, Robert D. *An Activities Handbook for Teachers of Young Children*. Boston: Houghton Mifflin, 1985, paperback.

An excellent collection of ideas for the young child in all areas of the curriculum.

Elmore, Dana T. *Creative Writing Activities for the Elementary School Classroom*. San Jose, Calif.: Teaching/Learning Press, 1980, paperback.

Ideas for the Learning Center.

Fader, Daniel, and McNeil, Elton. *Hooked on Books: Program and Proof*. New York: Berkley Medallion, 1982, paperback.

Motivating reluctant readers.

Goodman, Yetta M., and Burke, Carolyn. *Reading Strategies: Focus on Comprehension*. New York: Holt, Rinehart and Winston, 1980, paperback.

A practice book with specific lesson plans.

Graves, Donald H. *Writing Teachers and Children at Work*. New York: Heinemann, 1982, paperback.

Ideas and inspiration in the teaching of writing.

Griese, Arnold A. *Do You Read Me?* Glenview, Ill.: Goodyear-Scott Foresman, 1977, paperback.

Approaches to teaching reading comprehension.

Hansen-Krening, Nancy. *Language Experiences for All Students*. Reading, Mass.: Addison-Wesley, 1982, paperback.

A practical idea book on the language experience approach to teaching.

Henderson, Edmund. *Teaching Spelling*. Boston: Houghton Mifflin, 1984, paperback.

A developmental approach to spelling.

Hennings, Dorothy Grant. *Content and Craft*. Englewood Cliffs, N.J.: Prentice-Hall, 1973, hardbound.

Suggestions for working with language arts.

Hennings, Dorothy Grant, and Grant, Barbara Moll. *Written Expression in the Language Arts*. New York: Teachers College Press, 1981, paperback.

Ideas and skills for the writer.

Hopkins, Lee Bennett. *Pass the Poetry, Please*. New York: Citation, 1972, paperback.

More ideas about teaching poetry.

Johnson, Dale D., and Pearson, P. David. *Teaching Reading Vocabulary.* 2nd ed. New York: Holt, Rinehart and Winston, 1984.

A good collection of ideas to teach vocabulary.

Karlin, Muriel Schoenbrun. *The Parker Treasury of Elementary Classroom Activities*. West Nyack, N.Y.: Parker, 1981, hardback.

This guide contains a galaxy of classroom ideas.

Kirby, Dan, and Liner, Tom. *Inside Out*. Upper Montclair, N.J.: Boynton/Cook, 1981, paperback.

Strategies for teaching writing.

Koch, Kenneth. *Wishes, Lies, and Dreams*. New York: Vintage, 1970, paperback.

Great ideas for motivating the writing of poetry.

Koch, Kenneth. *Rose, Where Did You Get That Red?* New York: Random House, 1974, hardbound.

Teaching classic poems as models for student writing.

Mattes, Larry J. *Classroom Oral Language Development*. Springfield, Ill.: Charles C. Thomas, 1982, paperback.

An elementary oral language curriculum.

Milone, Michael. *Every Teacher's Guide to Word Processing*. Englewood Cliffs, N.J.: Prentice-Hall, 1985.

Assortment of practical activities and positive approaches.

Mueser, Anne Marie. *Reading Aids through The Grades*. New York: Teachers College Press, 1981, paperback.

Presents individualized reading activities for beginning and advanced readers.

National Council of Teachers of English. *Ideas for Teachers from Teachers: Elementary Language Arts*. Urbana, Ill.: National Council of Teachers of English, 1983, paperback.

A collection of ideas from individual elementary teachers.

Nessel, Denise D., and Jones, Margaret B. *The Language-Experience Approach to Reading: A Handbook for Teachers*. New York: Teachers College Press, 1981, paperback.

This book presents ideas for the primary classroom.

Norton, Donna E. *Language Arts Activities for Children*. 2nd ed. Columbus, Ohio: Charles E. Merrill, 1985, paperback.

Presents ideas in a lesson plan format.

Pearson, P. David, and Johnson, Dale D. *Teaching Reading Comprehension*. New York: Holt, Rinehart and Winston, 1978, paperback.

Presents research and ideas to improve reading comprehension.

Petty, Walter T. *Slithery Snakes and Other Aids to Children's Writing*. New York: Meredith, 1967, paperback.

Stimulating creative writing.

Pilon, Grace H. *The Workshop Way*. New Orleans: Xavier University, 1970, paperback.

Motivating student learning through a new approach.

Raymond, Dorothy. *Individualizing Reading in the Elementary School*. West Nyack, N.Y.: Parker, 1973.

A step-by-step guide to individualizing a reading program.

Rico, Gabriele Lusser. *Writing the Natural Way: Using Right-Brain Techniques to Release Your Expressive Powers*. Los Angeles: J. P. Tarcher, 1970, paperback.

Uses right brain techniques for teaching writing.

Siks, Geraldine Brian. *Drama with Children*. New York: Harper Row, 1983, hardback.

A second edition of one of the classics in the field.

Smith, Charlene W. *The Listening Activity Book*. Belmont, Calif.: Fearon, 1975, paperback.

Teaching literal, evaluative, and critical listening in the elementary school.

Smith, James A. *Creative Teaching of the Language Arts in the Elementary School*. 2nd ed. Boston: Allyn and Bacon, 1973, paperback.

Creative approaches to speaking, listening, and writing.

Spache, Evelyn. *Reading Activities for Child Involvement.* 3rd ed. Boston: Allyn and Bacon, 1982, paperback.

Variety of teaching strategies for developing reading skills.

Stauffer, Russell G. *The Language-Experience Approach to the Teaching of Reading.* New York: Harper & Row, 1970, paperback.

This book gives teachers ideas as to how they can teach the language experience approach.

Stott, Jon C. *Children's Literature from A to Z.* New York: McGraw-Hill, 1984, paperback.

A guide to children's literature for parents and teachers.

Temple, Charles A., Nathan, Ruth G., and Burris, Nancy A. *The Beginnings of Writing.* Boston: Allyn and Bacon, 1982, paperback.

A practical guide to a young child's writing.

Thompson, Richard A. *Energizers for Reading Instruction.* West Nyack, N.Y.: Parker, 1973.

Many reading games and activities are listed in this book.

Tiedt, Iris M. *The Language Arts Handbook.* Englewood Cliffs, N.J.: Prentice-Hall, 1983, hardback.

A collection of many ideas in all of the language arts.

Tiedt, Iris, and Tiedt, Sidney. *The Elementary Teacher's Ideas and Materials Handbook.* Englewood Cliffs, N.J.: Prentice-Hall, 1983, hardback.

A comprehensive collection of ideas for every subject in the curriculum.

Tiedt, Pamela, and Tiedt, Iris. *Multicultural Teaching: A Handbook of Activities, Information and Resources.* 2nd ed. Boston: Allyn and Bacon, 1986.

Gives practical ideas for K–8 classrooms on incorporating multicultural strategies across the curriculum.

Trelease, Jim. *The Read-Aloud Handbook.* New York: Penguin Books, 1982, paperback.

An excellent introduction to children's books.

Whitehead, Robert. *Children's Literature: Strategies of Teaching.* Englewood Cliffs, N.J.: Prentice-Hall, 1968.

Activities for using books in the classroom.

Language Books for Your Library

The following books are recommended for your school library. They include reference books, children's books, and books to help you in planning language lessons.

Asimov, Isaac. *Words from the Myths.* Boston: Houghton Mifflin, 1963.

Asimov, Isaac. *Words of Science and the History Behind Them.* Boston: Houghton Mifflin, 1959.

Asimov, Isaac. *Words on the Map.* Boston: Houghton Mifflin, 1962.

Basil, Cynthia. *Nailheads & Potato Eyes.* New York: Morrow, 1976.

Bolinger, Dwight. *Language: The Loaded Weapon.* New York: Longman, 1980.

Brandreth, Gyles. *The Joy of Lex*. New York: Morrow, 1980.

Cataldo, John W. *Words and Calligraphy for Children*. New York: Van Nostrand Reinhold, 1969.

Dickson, Paul. *Words*. New York: Dell, 1982.

Dugan, William. *How Our Alphabet Grew*. Racine, Wisc.: Golden Press, 1972.

Epstein, Samuel, and Epstein, Beryl. *The First Book of Words*. New York: Franklin Watts, 1954.

Epstein, Samuel, and Epstein, Beryl. *What Is Behind the Word?* New York: Scholastic Books Services, 1964.

Ernst, Margaret S. *In a Word*. New York: Knopf, 1939.

Ernst, Margaret S. *Words: English Roots and How They Grew*. New York: Knopf, 1937.

Evans, Bergen. *Comfortable Words*. New York: Random House, 1962.

Fadiman, Clifton. *Wally the Wordworm*. New York: Macmillan, 1964.

Ferguson, Charles. *The Abecedarian Book*. Boston: Little, Brown, 1964.

Funk, Charles E. *Heavens to Betsy*. New York: Harper & Row, 1955.

Funk, Charles E. *Hog on Ice and Other Curious Expressions*. New York: Harper & Row, 1948.

Funk, Charles E. *Thereby Hangs a Tale*. New York: Harper & Row, 1950.

Funk, Charles E., and Funk, Charles E., Jr. *Horsefeathers and Other Curious Words*. New York: Harper & Row, 1958.

Funk, Wilfred. *Word Origins and Their Romantic Stories*. New York: Grosset and Dunlap, 1950.

Heatherington, Madelon E. *How Language Works*. Cambridge, Mass.: Winthrop, 1980.

Hofsinde, Robert. *Indian Picture Writing*. New York: Morrow, 1959.

Juster, Norton. *The Phantom Tollbooth*. New York: Epstein and Carroll, dist. by Random House, 1961.

Kaye, Cathryn Berger. *Word Works*. Boston: Little, Brown, 1985.

Laird, Charlton, and Laird, Helene. *Tree of Language*. New York: World Publishing Co., 1957.

Lambert, Eloise, and Pei, Mario. *Our Names: Where They Came from and What They Mean*. New York: Lothrop, Lee and Shepard, 1960.

Maleska, Eugene T. *A Pleasure in Words*. New York: Simon and Schuster, 1981.

Merriam, Eve. *A Gaggle of Geese*. New York: Knopf, 1960.

Michaels, Leonard, and Ricks, Christopher, eds. *The State of Language*. Berkeley: University of California Press, 1980.

Nilsen, Don L. F., and Nilsen, Alleen Pace. *Language Play an Introduction to Linguistics*. Rowley, Mass.: Newbury House, 1979.

O'Neill, Mary. *Words Words Words*. New York: Doubleday, 1966.

Partridge, Eric. *A Charm of Words*. Salem, N.H.: Ayer, 1960.

Pei, Mario. *All about Language*. Philadelphia: J. B. Lippincott, 1954.

Pei, Mario. *Our National Heritage*. Boston: Houghton Mifflin, 1965.

Pinnell, Gay Su, ed. *Discovering Language with Children*. Urbana, Ill.: National Council of Teachers of English, 1980.

Rand, Ann, and Rand, Paul. *Sparkle and Spin*. New York: Harcourt, Brace, 1957.

Rawson, Hugh. *A Dictionary of Euphemisms and Other Doubletalk*. New York: Crown, 1984.

Reid, Alastair, *Ounce, Dice, Trice*. Boston: Little, Brown, 1958.

Rossner, Judith. *What Kind of Feet Does a Bear Have?* Indianapolis, Ind.: Bobbs-Merrill, 1963.

Schwartz, Alvin. *A Twister of Twists, a Tangler of Tongues*. Philadelphia: J. B. Lippincott, 1972.

Shipley, Joseph T. *Playing with Words*. Englewood Cliffs, N.J.: Prentice-Hall, 1960.

Shipley, Joseph T. *Word Play*. New York: Hawthorne Books, 1972.

Spector, Marjorie. *Pencil to Press: How This Book Came to Be*. New York: Lothrop, 1975.

Sperling, Susan Kelz. *Tenderfeet and Ladyfingers: A Visceral Approach to Words and Their Origin*. New York: Penguin Books, 1982.

Steig, William. *CDB!* New York: Simon Schuster, 1984.

Wilbur, Richard. *Opposites*. New York: Harcourt Brace Jovanovich, 1973.

Zim, Herbert S. *Codes and Secret Writing*. New York: Wm. Morrow, 1948.

Periodicals of Interest to Teachers

Included on this list are those magazines you'll want to subscribe to. Write to the address given for full subscription information.

Early Years
Allen Raymond Inc.
Box 1266
Darien, CT 06820

Instructor (and Teacher)
Harcourt Brace Jovanovich
Box 6099
Duluth, MN 55806

Language Arts
National Council of Teachers of English
1111 Kenyon Road
Urbana, IL 61801

Learning
P.O. Box 2589
Boulder, CO 80321

The Reading Teacher
International Reading Association
800 Barksdale Road
Newark, DE 19711

FOR STUDENTS

Books that Stimulate Thinking Skills

Included here are books to use with your class that encourage students to speculate and think in different ways.

Anglund, Joan. *A Friend Is Someone Who Likes You.* New York: Harcourt, 1958.

Anno, Masaichiro, and Anno, Mitsumasa. *Anno's Mysterious Multiplying Jar.* New York: Philomel, 1983.

Barrett, Peter, and Barrett, Susan. *The Line Sophie Drew.* New York: Scroll, 1972.

Belting, Natalia. *The Sun Is a Golden Earring.* New York: Holt, 1962.

Borten, Helen. *Do You See What I See?* New York: Abelard, 1959.

Borten, Helen. *Do You Hear What I Hear?* New York: Abelard, 1960.

Bradfield, Roger. *There's an Elephant in the Bathtub.* Chicago: Whitman, 1964.

Brown, Margaret. *The Important Book.* New York: Harper, 1949.

Burgess, Anthony. *A Long Trip to Teatime.* New York: Stonehill, 1976.

Charlip, Remy, and Joyner, Jerry. *Thirteen.* New York: Parents' Magazine, 1975.

Ciardi, John. *The Wish-Tree.* New York: Crowell, 1962.

Cleary, Beverly. *The Real Hole.* New York: Morrow, 1960.

Emberly, Edward. *The Wing on a Flea.* Boston: Little, Brown, 1961.

Fago, Vincent. *Here Comes the Whoosh!* Racine, Wisc.: Golden, 1960.

Fleming, Ian. *Chitty-Chitty Bang-Bang.* New York: Random, 1964.

Garelick, May. *Where Does the Butterfly Go When It Rains?* Glenview, Ill.: Scott, 1961.

Jonas, Ann. *Round Trip.* New York: Greenwillow, 1983.

Joslin, Sesyle. *Dear Dragon . . .* New York: Harcourt, 1962.

Joslin, Sesyle. *What Do you Say, Dear?* New York: Harcourt, 1962.

Juster, Norton. *The Phantom Tollbooth*. New York: Epstein, 1962.

Keats, Ezra Jack. *Regards to the Man in the Moon*. New York: Four Winds, 1981.

Klein, Leonore. *What Would You Do If* . . . Glenview, Ill.: Scott, 1961.

Krauss, Ruth. *A Hole Is to Dig*. New York: Harper, 1952.

L'Engle, Madeleine. *A Wrinkle in Time*. New York: Ariel, 1962.

Livingstone, Myra C. *See What I Found*. New York: Harcourt, 1962.

Munari, Bruno. *Who's There? Open the Door*. New York: World, 1957.

Myers, Walter Dean. *The Golden Serpent*. New York: Viking, 1980.

O'Neill, Mary. *Hailstones and Halibut Bones*. New York: Doubleday, 1961.

Reid, Alastair. *Ounce, Dice, Trice*. Boston: Little, Brown, 1958.

Reid, Alastair. *Supposing*. Boston: Little, Brown, 1958.

Roberts, Cliff. *The Hole*. New York: Watts, 1963.

Scheer, Julian. *Rain Makes Applesauce*. New York: Holiday, 1964.

Schulz, Charles. *Happiness Is a Warm Puppy*. San Francisco: Determined, 1963.

Seuss, Dr. *McElligott's Pool*. New York: Random, 1947.

Van Allsburg, Chris. *The Mysteries of Harris Burdick*. Boston: Houghton, 1984.

Wolff, Janet, and Owett, Bernard. *Let's Imagine Thinking Up Things*. New York: Dutton, 1961.

Zolotow, Charlotte. *Do You Know What I'll Do?* New York: Harper, 1958.

Poetry for Children

These collections of poems include poems for beginners as well as more advanced students. Keep a number of books of poetry around for students to browse through.

Adoff, Arnold, ed. *I Am the Darker Brother: An Anthology of Modern Poems by Black Americans*. New York: Macmillan, 1970.

Baron, Virginia Olsen, ed. *The Seasons of Time: Tanka Poetry of Ancient Japan*. New York: Dial, 1968.

Behn, Harry, trans. *Cricket Songs*. New York: Harcourt, Brace, World, 1964.

Behn, Harry, trans. *More Cricket Songs: Japanese Haiku*. New York: Harcourt Brace Jovanovich, 1971.

Benet, Rosemary, and Benet, Stephen Vincent. *A Book of Americans*. New York: Holt, Rinehart Winston, 1933.

Bennett, Jill, comp. *Days Are Where We Live and Other Poems*. New York: Lothrop, 1982.

Bodecker, N. *"Let's Marry," Said the Cherry, and Other Nonsense Poems*. New York: Atheneum, 1974.

Bontemps, Arna. *Hold Fast to Dreams.* Chicago, Follett, 1969.

Brown, Marcia. *Peter Piper's Alphabet.* New York: Scribner, 1979.

Ciardi, John. *Fast and Slow.* New York: Houghton Mifflin, 1975.

Ciardi, John. *The Man Who Sang the Sillies.* Philadelphia: Lippincott, 1961.

Clifton, Lucille. *Some of the Days of Everett Anderson.* New York: Holt, Rinehart Winston, 1970.

Cole, William, comp. *Beastly Boys and Ghastly Girls.* New York: World, 1964.

De La Mare, Walter, comp. *Come Hither.* New York: Knopf, 1957.

Dunning, Stephen, Lueders, Edward, and Smith, Hugh. *Reflections on a Gift of Watermelon Pickle, and Other Modern Verse.* Glenview, Ill.: Scott Foresman, 1966.

Frank, Josette, ed. *Poems to Read to the Very Young.* New York: Random House, 1982.

Frost, Robert. *You Come Too: Favorite Poems for Young Readers.* New York: Holt, Rinehart Winston, 1959.

Giovanni, Nikki. *Spin a Soft Black Song: Poems for Children.* New York: Hill & Wang, 1971.

Hopkins, Lee Bennett, ed. *Girls Can Too!* New York: Watts, 1972.

Jordan, June. *Who Look at Me.* New York: Crowell, 1969.

Kuskin, Karla. *Near the Window Tree.* New York: Harper and Row, 1975.

Larrick, Nancy. *On City Streets.* New York: Bantam, 1969.

Larrick, Nancy. *Room for Me and a Mountain Lion: Poetry of Open Space.* New York: Lippincott, 1974.

Lear, Edward. *The Complete Nonsense Book.* New York: Dodd Mead, 1948.

Lewis, Richard, ed. *I Breathe a New Song: Poems of the Eskimo.* New York: Simon & Schuster, 1971.

Livingston, Myra Cohn, ed. *O Frabjous Day! Poetry for Holidays and Special Occasions.* New York: Atheneum, 1977.

Lobel, Arnold. *The Book of Pigericks.* New York: Harper and Row, 1983.

McCord, David. *Every Time I Climb a Tree.* Boston: Little, Brown, 1967.

Merriam, Eve. *Out Loud.* New York: Atheneum, 1973.

Nash, Ogden, comp. *The Moon Is Shining Bright as Day.* Philadelphia: Lippincott, 1953.

O'Neill, Mary. *Hailstones and Halibut Bones.* New York: Doubleday, 1961.

Prelutsky, Jack. *Nightmares: Poems to Trouble Your Sleep.* New York: Greenwillow, 1976.

Silverstein, Shel. *A Light in the Attic.* New York: Harper and Row, 1981.

Silverstein, Shel. *Where the Sidewalk Ends.* New York: Harper and Row, 1974.

Viorst, Judith. *If I Were in Charge of the World and Other Worries.* New York: Atheneum, 1982.

Zolotow, Charlotte. *All That Sunlight.* New York: Harper and Row, 1967.

Award-Winning Books

Caldecott Award Books

The Caldecott Award is given annually for an outstanding picture book. Because this award goes to an illustrator, these books tend to be for primary grade children.

1985 Hyman, Trina Schart. *Saint George and the Dragon*. Boston: Little, Brown & Co.

1984 Provensen, Alice, and Provensen, Martin. *The Glorious Flight*. New York: Viking.

1983 Brown, Marcia. *Shadow* by Blaise Cendrars. New York: Scribner's.

1982 Van Allsburg, Chris. *Jumanji*. Boston: Houghton Mifflin.

1981 Lobel, Arnold. *Fables*. New York: Harper & Row.

1980 Cooney, Barbara. *Ox-cart Man* by Donald Hall. New York: Doubleday.

1979 Goble, Paul. *The Girl Who Loved Wild Horses*. Scarsdale, N.Y.: Bradbury Press.

1978 Spier, Peter. *Noah's Ark*. New York: Doubleday.

1977 Dillon, Leo, and Dillon, Diane. *Ashanti to Zulu* by Margaret Musgrove. New York: Dial Press.

1976 Dillon, Leo, and Dillon, Diane. *Why Mosquitos Buzz in People's Ears*. New York: Dial Press.

1975 McDermott, Gerald. *Arrow to the Sun*. New York: Viking.

1974 Zemach, Margot. *Duffy and the Devil* by Harve Zemach. New York: Farrar, Strauss.

1973 Lent, Blair. *The Funny Little Woman*. New York: Dutton.

1972 Hogrogian, Nonny. *One Fine Day*. New York: Macmillan.

1971 Haley, Gail E. *A Story, A Story; An African Tale*. New York: Atheneum.

1970 Steig, William. *Sylvester and the Magic Pebble*. New York: Windmill Books.

1969 Ransome, Arthur. *The Fool of the World and the Flying Ship*. New York: Farrar, Straus and Giroux.

1968 Emberly, Ed. *Drummer Hoff*. Englewood Cliffs, N.J.: Prentice-Hall.

1967 Ness, Evaline. *Sam, Bangs and Moonshine*. New York: Holt, Rinehart and Winston.

1966 Hogrogian, Nonny. *Always Room for One More*. New York: Holt, Rinehart and Winston.

1965 De Regniers, Beatrice Schenck. *May I Bring a Friend?* New York: Atheneum.

1964 Sendak, Maurice. *Where the Wild Things Are*. New York: Harper & Row.

1963 Keats, Ezra Jack. *The Snowy Day*. New York: Viking.

1962 Brown, Marcia. *Once a Mouse*. New York: Scribner's Sons.

1961 Sidjakov, Nicholas. *Baboushka and the Three Kings*. Emeryville, Calif.: Parnassus.

1960 Ets, Marie Hall. *Nine Days to Christmas*. New York: Viking.

1959 Cooney, Barbara. *Chanticleer and the Fox*. New York: Thomas Crowell.

1958 McCloskey, Robert. *Time of Wonder.* New York: Viking.

1957 Simont, Marc. *A Tree Is Nice.* New York: Harper & Row.

1956 Rojankovsky, Feodor. *Frog Went a-Courtin'.* New York: Harcourt.

1955 Brown, Marcia. *Cinderella.* New York: Scribner's Sons.

1954 Bemelmans, Ludwig. *Madeline's Rescue.* New York: Viking.

1953 Ward, Lynd. *Biggest Bear.* Boston: Houghton Mifflin.

1952 Mordvinoff, Nicholas. *Finders Keepers.* New York: Harcourt.

1951 Milhouse, Katherine. *The Egg Tree.* New York: Scribner's Sons.

1950 Politi, Leo. *Song of the Swallows.* New York: Scribner's Sons.

1949 Hader, Berta. *Big Snow.* New York: Macmillan.

1948 Duvoisin, Roger. *White Snow, Bright Snow.* New York: Lothrop, Lee and Shepard Co.

1947 Weisgard, Leonard. *Little Island.* New York: Doubleday.

1946 Petersham, Maud. *The Rooster Crows.* New York: Macmillan.

1945 Jones, Elizabeth Orton. *Prayer for a Child.* New York: Macmillan.

1944 Slobodkin, Louis. *Many Moons.* New York: Harcourt.

1943 Burton, Virginia Lee. *The Little House.* Boston: Houghton Mifflin.

1942 McCloskey, Robert. *Make Way for Ducklings.* New York: Viking.

1941 Lawson, Robert. *They Were Strong and Good.* New York: Viking.

1940 Aulaire, Ingrid. *Abraham Lincoln.* New York: Doubleday.

1939 Handforth, Thomas. *Meili.* New York: Doubleday.

1938 Lathrop, Dorothy. *Animals of the Bible.* Philadelphia: Lippincott.

Newbery Award Books

The Newbery Award is given annually for an outstanding book written for children by an American author. Because the award stresses story content, these books tend to be for older students.

1985 McKinley, Robin. *The Hero and the Crown.* New York: Greenwillow Books.

1984 Cleary, Beverly. *Dear Mr. Henshaw.* New York: William Morrow.

1983 Voight, Cynthia. *Dicey's Song.* New York: Atheneum.

1982 Willard, Nancy. *A Visit to William Blake's Inn.* New York: Harcourt Brace Jovanovich.

1981 Paterson, Katherine. *Jacob Have I Loved.* New York: Crowell.

1980 Blos, Joan W. *A Gathering of Days.* New York: Scribner's.

1979 Raskin, Ellen. *The Westing Game.* New York: Dutton.

1978 Paterson, Katherine. *Bridge to Terabithia.* New York: Crowell.

1977 Taylor, Mildred D. *Roll of Thunder, Hear My Cry.* New York: Dial.

1976 Cooper, Susan. *The Grey King.* New York: Atheneum.

1975 Hamilton, Virginia. *M. C. Higgins the Great*. New York: Macmillan.

1974 Fox, Paula. *The Slave Dancer*. Scarsdale, N.Y.: Bradbury Press.

1973 George, Jean Craighead. *Julie of the Wolves*. New York: Harper & Row.

1972 O'Brien, Robert C. *Mrs. Frisby and the Rats of NIMH*. New York: Atheneum.

1971 Byars, Betsy. *The Summer of the Swans*. New York: Viking.

1970 Armstrong, William Howard. *Sounder*. New York: Harper & Row.

1969 Alexander, Lloyd. *The High King*. New York: Holt, Rinehart and Winston.

1968 Konigsberg, Elaine E. *From the Mixed-up Files of Mrs. Basil E. Frankweiler*. New York: Atheneum.

1967 Hunt, Irene. *Up a Road Slowly*. Chicago: Follett Educational Corp.

1966 De Treviño, Elizabeth B. *I, Juan de Pareja*. New York: Farrar, Straus, and Giroux.

1965 Wojciechowska, Maia. *Shadow of a Bull*. New York: Atheneum.

1964 Neville, Emily. *It's Like This, Cat*. New York: Harper & Row.

1963 L'Engle, Madeleine. *A Wrinkle in Time*. New York: Farrar, Straus, and Giroux.

1962 Speare, Elizabeth G. *The Bronze Bow*. Boston: Houghton Mifflin.

1961 O'Dell, Scott. *Island of the Blue Dolphins*. Boston: Houghton Mifflin.

1960 Krumgold, Joseph. *Onion John*. New York: Thomas Crowell.

1959 Speare, Elizabeth. *Witch of Blackbird Pond*. Boston: Houghton Mifflin.

1958 Keith, Harold. *Rifles for Watie*. New York: Thomas Crowell.

1957 Sorenson, Virginia. *Miracles on Maple Hill*. New York: Harcourt Brace.

1956 Latham, Jean L. *Carry On, Mr. Bowditch*. Boston: Houghton Mifflin.

1955 De Jong, Meindert. *Wheel on the School*. New York: Harper & Row.

1954 Krumgold, Joseph. *. . . .And Now Miguel*. New York: Thomas Crowell.

1953 Clark, Ann N. *Secret of the Andes*. New York: Viking.

1952 Estes, Eleanor. *Ginger Pye*. New York: Harcourt Brace.

1951 Yates, Elizabeth. *Amos Fortune, Free Man*. New York: Aladdin.

1950 De Angeli, Marguerite. *Door in the Wall*. New York: Doubleday.

1949 Henry, Marguerite. *King of the Wind*. Skokie, Ill.: Rand McNally.

1948 DuBois, William Pène. *The 21 Balloons*. New York: Viking.

1947 Bailey, Carolyn S. *Miss Hickory*. New York: Viking.

1946 Lenski, Lois. *Strawberry Girl*. Philadelphia: Lippincott.

1945 Lawson, Robert. *Rabbit Hill*. New York: Viking.

1944 Forbes, Esther. *Johnny Tremain*. Boston: Houghton Mifflin.

1943 Gray, Elizabeth J. *Adams of the Road*. New York: Viking.

1942 Edmonds, Walter. *The Matchlock Gun*. New York: Dodd, Mead.

1941   Sperry, Armstrong. *Call It Courage.* New York: Macmillan.

1940   Daugherty, James. *Daniel Boone.* New York: Viking.

1939   Enright, Elizabeth. *Thimble Summer.* New York: Farrar, Straus, and Giroux.

1938   Seredy, Kate. *White Stag.* New York: Viking.

1937   Sawyer, Ruth. *Roller Skates.* New York: Viking.

1936   Brink, Carol R. *Caddie Woodlawn.* New York: Macmillan.

1935   Shannon, Monica. *Dobry.* New York: Viking.

1934   Meigs, Cornelia. *Invincible Louisa.* Boston: Little, Brown.

1933   Lewis, Elizabeth F. *Young Fu of the Upper Yangtze.* New York: Winston.

1932   Armer, Laura. *Waterless Mountain.* New York: Longmans.

1931   Coatsworth, Elizabeth. *The Cat Who Went to Heaven.* New York: Macmillan.

1930   Field, Rachel. *Hitty: Her First Hundred Years.* New York: Macmillan.

1929   Kelly, Eric. *The Trumpeter of Krakow.* New York: Macmillan.

1928   Mukerji, Dhan G. *Gay-Neck, The Story of a Pigeon.* New York: Dutton.

1927   James, Will. *Smoky: The Cowhorse.* New York: Scribner's Sons.

1926   Chrisman, Arthur Bowie. *Shen of the Sea.* New York: Dutton.

1925   Finger, Charles J. *Tales from Silver Lands.* New York: Doubleday.

1924   Hawes, Charles B. *The Dark Frigate.* Boston: Little, Brown.

1923   Lofting, Hugh. *The Voyages of Dr. Dolittle.* New York: Stokes.

1922   Van Loon, Hendrik W. *The Story of Mankind.* New York: Liveright.

Read Alouds

Here are twenty outstanding books for young people that teachers have used successfully for reading aloud.

Alexander, Lloyd. *The Book of Three.* New York: Holt Rinehart, 1964.

Babbitt, Natalie. *Tuck Everlasting.* New York: Farrar Straus, 1975.

Banks, Lynne Reid. *The Indian in the Cupboard.* New York: Doubleday, 1981.

Blume, Judy. *Tales of a Fourth Grade Nothing.* New York: Dutton, 1972.

Cleary, Beverly. *Ramona the Pest.* New York: Morrow, 1968.

Galdone, Paul. *Henny Penny.* New York: Scholastic, 1968. (primary)

George, Jean Craighead. *Julie of the Wolves.* New York: Harper and Row, 1972.

Haas, Irene. *The Maggie B.* New York: Atheneum, 1975. (primary)

Konigsburg, E. L. *Jennifer, Hecate, Macbeth, William McKinley, and Me, Elizabeth.* New York: Atheneum, 1967.

Lewis, C. S. *The Lion, the Witch, and the Wardrobe.* New York: Macmillan, 1970.

Lindgren, Astrid. *Pippi Longstocking.* New York: Viking, 1950.

McCloskey, Robert. *Homer Price.* New York: Viking, 1943.

McCloskey, Robert. *Make Way for Ducklings.* New York: Penguin, 1981. (primary)

McGovern, Ann. *Stone Soup.* New York: Scholastic, 1968. (primary)

Milne, A. A. *Winnie the Pooh.* New York: Dutton, 1926. (primary)

Ness, Evaline. *Sam, Bangs, and Moonshine.* New York: Holt Rinehart, 1966. (primary)

O'Dell, Scott. *Island of the Blue Dolphins.* Boston: Houghton Mifflin, 1961.

Rawls, Wilson. *Where the Red Fern Grows.* New York: Doubleday, 1974.

Twain, Mark. *The Adventures of Tom Sawyer.* (any edition)

White, E. B. *Charlotte's Web.* New York: Harper and Row, 1952.

Published Writing by Children

This list includes books that contain poetry and prose by children. These selections are especially good for showing students that people their age really can write.

Baron, Virginia. *Here I Am.* New York: Dutton, 1969.

Poems by minority children.

Children of Cardozo Tell It Like It Is. Washington, D.C.: Education Development Center, 1968.

Washington, D.C. children's writings on the assassination of Martin Luther King and subsequent riots.

Clegg, Alexander. *The Excitement of Writing.* London: Chatto and Windus, Clarke, Irwin and Co., 1965.

Poems by English children from a wide age range.

Dorothy. *How the World Began.* New York: Pantheon Books, 1964.

One child's picture in words and art of how the world began.

Ford, Boris. *Young Writers—Young Readers.* New York: Hutchinson, 1963.

Stories, poetry, and art are included along with critical essays.

Grossman, Barney, and Groom, Gladys. *Black Means . . . .* New York: Hill and Wang, 1970.

Children from the Bronx give their definitions of black.

Holland, John. *The Way It Is.* New York: Harcourt, 1969.

Children describe the world they live in with prose and photographs of Brooklyn.

Hopkins, Lee Bennett, *City Talk.* New York: Knopf, 1970.

Here are cinquains about city life from children all over the country.

Jordan, June, and Bush, Terri. *The Voice of the Children.* New York: Holt, 1968.

These stories and poems reflect the concerns of urban black and Puerto Rican children.

Joseph, Stephen M. *The Me Nobody Knows.* New York: Avon, 1970.
  Children's voices from the ghetto.

Kojka, Sherry. *I Will Always Stay Me.* Austin: Texas Monthly Press, 1982.
  Writings of migrant children.

Larrick, Nancy. *Green Is Like a Meadow.* Champaign, Ill.: Garrard, 1970.
  Children respond to poems about colors and animals with poetry of their own.

Larrick, Nancy. *I Heard a Scream in the Street.* New York: Evans, 1970.
  Examples of urban poems, by children and young people.

Lewis, Richard. *Journeys.* New York: Simon and Schuster, 1969.
  Prose by children of the English-speaking world.

Lewis, Richard. *Miracles—Poems by Children of the English-speaking World.* New York: Simon and Schuster, 1966.
  Poems by children from many different cultural backgrounds.

Neville, Mary. *If a Poem Bothers You.* Washington, D.C.: New Day, 1980.
  Collection of children's writings.

Pellowski, Anne. *Have You Seen a Comet?* New York: John Day Co., 1971.
  Children's art and writing from around the world.

Prague. *I Never Saw Another Butterfly.* New York: McGraw, 1964.
  Poems by children in concentration camps during WW II.

Schaefer, Charles, and Mellor, Kathleen. *Young Voices.* New York: The Bruce Publishing Co., 1971.
  Highly original poems by elementary children from New York City.

Kids' Magazines

Magazines published for children are a bargain because they provide information, teach students skills, and hold student interest. The following is a list of recommended magazines. Write for sample copies.

Boy's Life, ages 8–13
1325 Walnut Hill Lane
Irving, TX 75062

Child Life, ages 7–9
Benjamin Franklin Literary & Medical Society
P.O. Box 567
1100 Waterway Blvd.
Indianapolis, IN 46206

Cobblestone, ages 8–13
Box 959
Farmingdale, NY 11737

Cricket, ages 6–12
Box 100
LaSalle, IL 61301

Highlights for Children, ages 3–12
803 Church St.
Honesdale, PA 18431

Peanut Butter, ages 4–7
Scholastic Home Periodicals
P.O. Box 1925
Marion, OH 43302

Penny Power, ages 9 and up
Consumers Union
256 Washington St.
Mount Vernon, NY 10550

Ranger Rick, ages 5–12
National Wildlife Foundation
17th and M Streets NW
Washington, DC 20036

Sesame Street, ages 2–6
P.O. Box 2895
Boulder, CO 80321

Stone Soup, ages 5–13
Children's Art Foundation
P.O. Box 83
Santa Cruz, CA 95063

Pattern Books

The following list offers books that manipulate language in predictable ways. Students are encouraged to apply familiar oral language strategies and experiences that will help them develop and enjoy the ability to read.

Aliki. *Go Tell Aunt Rhody*. New York: Macmillan, 1974.

Aliki. *Hush Little Baby*. Englewood Cliffs, N.J.: Prentice-Hall, 1968.

Bonne, Rose, and Mills, Allan. *I Know an Old Lady*. New York: Rand McNally, 1961.

Brown, Marcia. *The Three Billy Goats Gruff*. New York: Harcourt Brace Jovanovich, 1957.

Brown, Margaret Wise. *Goodnight Moon*. New York: Harper and Row, 1947.

Brown, Margaret Wise. *Home for a Bunny*. Racine, Wisc.: Golden, 1956.

Charlip, Remy. *Fortunately*. New York: Parents Magazine, 1964.

Charlip, Remy. *What Good Luck! What Bad Luck!* New York: Scholastic, 1970.

de Regniers, Beatrice Schenk. *May I Bring a Friend?* New York: Atheneum, 1972.

Emberley, Barbara. *Simon's Song*. Englewood Cliffs, N.J.: Prentice-Hall, 1969.

Galdone, Paul. *Henny Penny*. New York: Scholastic, 1968.

Galdone, Paul. *The Little Red Hen*. New York: Scholastic, 1973.

Galdone, Paul. *The Three Bears*. New York: Scholastic, 1972.

Keats, Ezra Jack. *Over in the Meadow*. New York: Scholastic, 1971.

Lobel, Arnold. *A Treeful of Pigs*. New York: Greenwillow, 1979.

Martin, Bill. *Brown Bear, Brown Bear*. New York: Holt Rinehart Winston, 1970.

Martin, Bill. *Fire! Fire! Said Mrs. McGuire*. New York: Holt Rinehart Winston, 1970.

Peppe, Rodney. *The House that Jack Built*. New York: Delacorte, 1970.

Quackenbush, Robert. *She'll Be Comin' Round the Mountain*. Philadelphia: Lippincott, 1973.

Quackenbush, Robert. *Skip to My Lou*. Philadelphia: Lippincott, 1975.

Scheer, Jullian, and Bileck, Marvin. *Upside Down Day*. New York: Holiday, 1958.

Spier, Peter. *The Fox Went Out on a Chilly Night*. Garden City, N.Y.: Doubleday, 1961.

Viorst, Judith. *Alexander and the Terrible, Horrible, No Good, Very Bad Day*. New York: Atheneum, 1972.

Zaid, Barry. *Chicken Little*. New York: Random House, no date.

Zemach, Margot. *Hush, Little Baby*. New York: Dutton, 1976.

Zemach, Margot. *The Teeny Tiny Woman*. New York: Scholastic, 1966.

MULTIMEDIA

Selected Children's Video Titles

More and more teachers are discovering that the videocassette is an excellent way to present children's literature, due to its flexibility and ease of operation. The following are just a few of the quality children's stories available on video. Check your local library to see what they have. You can also request that they purchase some of these.

20,000 Leagues Under the Sea

Adventures of Huck Finn, The

Alice in Wonderland

Captains Courageous

Charlotte's Web

Doctor Doolittle

Goldilocks and the Three Bears

Heidi

Hobbit, The

Horton Hears a Who

How the Grinch Stole Christmas

Jack and the Beanstalk

Jungle Book, The

Legend of Sleepy Hollow, The

Lord of the Rings, The

Mary Poppins

Princess and the Pea, The

Rapunzel

Secret of NIMH, The

Snow White and the Seven Dwarfs

Swiss Family Robinson

Tale of the Frog Prince

Thumbelina

Watership Down

Where the Red Fern Grows

Wind in the Willows

Winnie the Pooh

Wizard of Oz, The

Selected Films to Motivate Students

Showing films is an excellent way to stimulate student thinking, reading, and writing. Here is a list of ten classic films with which all teachers should be familiar.

Red Ballon, 34mm, color, 1956.

Snowy Day, 8mm, color, 1964.

Hailstones and Halibut Bones, 6mm, color, Part I 1964, Part II 1967.

Rikki Tikki Tavi, 26mm, color, 1976.

The Snowy Day, 6mm, color, 1964.

In a Spring Garden, 6mm, color, 1967.

A Chairy Tale, 10mm, black and white, 1957.

Loon's Necklace, 11mm, color, 1964.

William's Doll, 18mm, color, 1981.

Where the Wild Things Are, 8mm, color, 1974.

Selected Computer Software for the Language Arts

The following software programs have been carefully chosen to represent the best available. They provide practice and reinforcement in writing, reading, spelling, and thinking skills. Many professional journals regularly review and update lists of recommended software. Because it is difficult for you to determine whether a particular program will be suitable, you need to arrange to preview software before purchasing it.

Bank Street Writer
Broderbund Software
1938 Fourth St.
San Rafael, CA 94901

Build a Better Paragraph
McDougal, Littell & Co.
5401 Old Orchard Rd.
Skokie, IL 60077

Build a Better Sentence
McDougal, Littell & Co.
5401 Old Orchard Rd.
Skokie, IL 60077

Build a Book About You
Scarborough Systems, Inc.
25 N. Broadway
Tarrytown, NY 10591

Capitalization
Microcomputers Corp.
34 Maple Ave.
P.O. Box 8
Armonk, NY 10504

Cloze Plus
Milliken Publishing Co.
Computer Products Div.
1100 Research Blvd.
Saint Louis, MO 63132

ClozeMaster
Skillcorp Software, Inc.
3741 Old Conejo Rd.
Newbury Park, CA 91320

Composition Strategy
Behavioral Engineering
230 Mt. Hermon Rd., #207
Scotts Valley, CA 95066

Comprehension Power
Milliken Publishing Co.
Computer Products Div.
1100 Research Blvd.
Saint Louis, MO 63132

CompuPoem
South Coast Writing Project
UCSB Dept. of English
Santa Barbara, CA 93106

Electric Poet
International Business Machines Corp.
Entry Systems Div.
P.O. Box 1328
Boca Raton, FL 33432

Factory, The
Sunburst Communications
39 Washington Ave.
Pleasantville, NY 10570

Friendly Filer
Grolier Electronic Publishing, Inc.
Suite 407
95 Madison Ave.
New York, NY 10016

Gertrude's Secrets
The Learning Company
Suite 170
545 Middlefield Rd.
Menlo Park, CA 94025

Grammar, What Big Teeth
Krell Software Corp.
Suite 219
1320 Stony Brook Rd.
Stony Brook, NY 11790

Hartley Courseware
Hartley Courseware, Inc.
123 Bridge St.
Dimondale, MI 48821

HomeWord
Sierra On-Line, Inc.
Sierra On-Line Bldg.
Coarsegold, CA 93614

KidWriter
Spinnaker Software Corp.
215 First St.
Cambridge, MA 02142

Magic Slate
Sunburst Communications
39 Washington Ave.
Pleasantville, NY 10570

Mastertype's Filer
Scarborough Systems, Inc.
25 N. Broadway
Tarrytown, NY 10591

Micro-Read Spell
American Educational Computer, Inc.
2450 Embarcadero Way
Palo Alto, CA 94303

Milliken Word Processor
Milliken Publishing Co.
Computer Products Div.
110 Research Blvd.
Saint Louis, MO 63132

Missing Links
Sunburst Communications
39 Washington Ave.
Pleasantville, NY 10570

Newbery Winners
Sunburst Communications
39 Washington Ave.
Pleasantville, NY 10570

NewsRoom
Scarborough Systems, Inc.
25 N. Broadway
Tarrytown, NY 10591

Note Card Maker
Grolier Electronic Publishing, Inc.
Suite 407
95 Madison Ave.
New York, NY 10016

Pick a Path Series
Scholastic, Inc.
2931 E. McCarthy St.
P.O. Box 7502
Jefferson City, MO 65102

Print Shop
Broderbund Software
1938 Fourth St.
San Rafael, CA 94901

Punctuation I and II
Educational Activities, Inc.
P.O. Box 392
Freeport, NY 11520

Puzzler
Sunburst Communications
30 Washington Ave.
Pleasantville, NY 10570

Readability Calculations
Micro Power and Light Co.
12820 Hillcrest Rd., #219
Dallas, TX 75230

Secret Filer
Scholastic, Inc.
2931 E. McCarthy St.
P.O. Box 7502
Jefferson City, MO 65102

Sentence Combining
Milliken Publishing Co.
Computer Products Div.
110 Research Blvd.
Saint Louis, MO 63132

Story Machine
Spinnaker Software Corp.
215 First St.
Cambridge, MA 02142

Story Maker
Scholastic, Inc.
2931 E. McCarthy St.
P.O. Box 7502
Jefferson City, MO 65102

Story Tree
Scholastic, Inc.
2931 E. McCarthy St.
P.O. Box 7502
Jefferson City, MO 65102

Subject-Verb Agreement
Microcomputer Workshops
225 Westchester Ave.
Port Chester, NY 10573

Wordsearch
Hartley Courseware, Inc.
123 Bridge St.
Dimondale, MI 48821

Wordstar
MicroPro International Corp.
33 San Pablo Ave.
San Rafael, CA 94903

Index

"Casey at the Bat," 254–257
Cataldo, John W., 322
Category reading, 130
Cause and effect, 121–122
Charlip, Remy, 220
Chase, Alice Elizabeth, 328
Child Life Magazine, 258
Children's Book Council, 131, 132
Choric speaking, 39–41
Cinquains, 270–272, 284
Ciphers and Secret Writing, 168
City Noisy Book, The, 11
Classroom library, 128
Classroom organization, 1–7
    language arts, 2–7
    teacher's role, 1–2
Cleary, Beverly, 139
Cloze procedure, 20, 116–118, 282, 330
Coatsworth, Elizabeth, 270
Codes, 163–168
Coerr, Eleanor, 309
Cole, Joanna, 263
Collages, 214
Commercial word games, 100
Composers, 329, 333
Compound words, 74
Comprehension (*see* Reading
    comprehension)
Computer software, 69, 99, 119, 120, 143,
    211, 222, 354–359
Conferences with students, 238
Conkling, Hilda, 251, 253
Consonants, 107–108, 166
Contemporary Authors, 143
Conundrums, 154, 233–234
Cooney, Barbara, 324
Couplets, 249
Crews, Donald, 42
Cricket Songs, 274
cummings, e. e., 251
Current Biography, 143

"Dandelion," 253
Davidson, Margaret, 309
Dear Dragon, 231
Dear Mr. Henshaw, 139
Definitions, 64
Delves, Geoffrey, 273

de Paola, Tomie, 42
Dialects, 33, 167, 194–195, 198
Diamante, 275–276
Dickinson, Emily, 250–251, 261, 263
Dictation, 201
Dictionaries, 87–88
Digraphs, 109, 166
*Dinosaur Is the Biggest Animal That Ever
    Lived, And Other Wrong Ideas You
    Thought Were True, The,* 285
Directions:
    following, 23–24
    remembering, 26
Disney, Walt, 133
Dog's Life, A, 263
*Dot and Line: A Romance in Lower
    Mathematics,* 305
Dreyer, Sharon Spredemann, 130

"Eagle, The," 254
Education in the Year 2000, 286
Einstein, Albert, 241
"Eletelephony," 257
Elkind, David, 117, 125
"Erie Canal, The," 259–260
Ervin, Jane, 111
Evaluation policy, 240–241
Exaltation of Larks, An, 90

Fables, 129
Fables of Aesop, 129
Famous Artists of the Past, 328
*Famous Author-Illustrators for Young
    People,* 310
Feedback, 2
Ferguson, Charles, 89
*Fiddle with a Riddle: Write Your Own
    Riddles,* 72
Films, 353–354
Fisher, Aileen, 259
Fleming, Ian, 241
Fletcher, Helen Jill, 168
Food advisory boards, 284
Fools of Chelm and Their History, The, 129
Foreign languages, 97, 313–314
Four Women of Courage, 310
France, Anatole, 66
Free verse, 267

THE

COMPLETE

EVANGELISM

GUIDEBOOK

THE

COMPLETE
EVANGELISM
GUIDEBOOK

EXPERT ADVICE on
REACHING OTHERS
for CHRIST

EDITED BY SCOTT DAWSON

FOREWORD BY LUIS PALAU

BakerBooks
Grand Rapids, Michigan

Published by Baker Books
a division of Baker Publishing Group
P.O. Box 6287, Grand Rapids, MI 49516-6287
www.bakerbooks.com

Second printing, October 2008

Printed in the United States of America

Library of Congress Cataloging-in-Publication Data
        The complete evangelism guidebook : expert advice on reaching others for Christ / edited by Scott Dawson ; foreword by Luis Palau—2nd ed.
            p.   cm.
        Includes bibliographical references (p.   ) and indexes.
        ISBN 978-0-8010-7185-0 (pbk.)
        1. Witness bearing (Christianity)—Handbooks, manuals, etc. 2. Evangelistic work—Handbooks, manuals, etc. I. Dawson, Scott.
        BV4520.C66 2008
        269'.2—dc22   2008020159

Correspondence may be sent to:
Scott Dawson
P.O. Box 380653
Birmingham, AL 35238
http://www.scottdawson.org
info@scottdawson.org

This book is published in association with the literary agency of Sanford Communications, Inc., 6406 N.E. Pacific St., Portland, OR 97213.

Contents

Foreword

Have you ever tasted a nice, cool, refreshing Coke? Congratulations! So have hundreds of millions of other people all around the world. And it's all Robert Woodruff's fault.

Well, not all his fault. But he's largely to blame.

You see, Woodruff served as president of Coca-Cola from 1923 to 1955. While Chief Executive of that soft drink corporation, he had the audacity to state, "We will see that every man in uniform gets a bottle of Coca-Cola for five cents wherever he is and whatever it costs."

After World War II ended, he went on to say that in his lifetime he wanted *everyone* in the world to have a taste of Coca-Cola. Talk about vision!

With careful planning and a lot of persistence, Woodruff and his colleagues reached their generation around the globe for Coke.

Say, how big is your vision? Have you ever thought about what God could do through you to influence our own generation? I'm not kidding. Neither was the Lord Jesus Christ kidding when he called his disciples to gain a vision of impacting the world for his name.

Jesus made his mission very plain: "For the Son of Man came to seek and to save what was lost" (Luke 19:10). We know his final command to "go and make disciples of all nations" (Matt 28:19) as the Great Commission, not the Great Suggestion. I believe evangelism is the main work of the church of Jesus Christ.

I am proud to preach the gospel, the power of God, because I cannot imagine anything that helps people more than introducing them to Jesus Christ. Evangelism saves people not only from dying without Christ but also from living without him. And as they live with him and for him, they become salt and light in a world lost in darkness, sorrow, conflict, violence, and fear.

To be giving out the gospel, leading people into the eternal kingdom of God Almighty—you can never have more fun. There's no greater thrill. Give evangelism all you've got. This life is your only chance.

Are you expecting great things from God? Or are you letting the opportunities pass you by? If it's true that the Lord wants the gospel preached worldwide, then we can't remain passive. Whatever our gifts or abilities or resources, we need to work together as faithful stewards of what God has bestowed on us.

Start doing something by making specific plans of action. That's what this book is all about. I pray that you will find it helpful as you seek to share the life-changing message of the gospel with your friends, family, neighbors, co-workers, and many others.

The Good News of Jesus Christ is for everyone in every segment of society. God wants to use you to reach *your* world for Jesus Christ. Let him!

Luis Palau, author, evangelist, and broadcaster (www.palau.org)

Acknowledgments

A mentor of mine once told me: "A self-made man doesn't make much!" I can honestly agree that this resource would not be much if it included only my thoughts and words. It is with my sincerest gratitude that I thank all of those who have contributed to this work.

It all starts with my helpmate and best friend on this planet, my wife, Tarra. She is the picture of Proverbs 31 and also a great writer. Hunter and Hope gave up their dad for this project with the understanding that these words would be read for a long time. My parents have lived out before me the principle that "there is no success without sacrifice," for which I am forever indebted.

Another friend of mine often quotes an Irish proverb: "The best thing you can do for a friend is to introduce him to your friends." I believe this is true for evangelism, but I also believe this to be true in this work. Encompassed in these pages, you will read the very heartbeat of men and women, whom you may not know but whose introductions and words will challenge you. I thank every contributing author who stayed up late, got up early, and met every challenge with a smile for the good of this book.

My personal assistant, Cary Greer, worked nights, weekends, and holidays to make sure every item of the project was completed. She has gotten to know some of the authors very well with her timely emails and commitment to excellence for every chapter submitted.

Linda Marcrum, our project editor, who was flawless in her editing, tenacious in her deadlines, and gracious in correcting my grammar, is one of the great MVPs of this project. I do not think she will ever forget the day when she agreed to work on this project—no matter how hard she tries!

I thank Josh Malone and Jan White for their help in researching, interviewing, and developing several key parts of this project and for not giving up or in to obstacles. Additional thanks are due to Saint Green, Jane Young, and Christy Foster.

In addition, the entire team at Scott Dawson Evangelistic Association knows how important this project is to evangelism, especially Keny Hatley, Mike Greer, Dwayne Moore, Gina Handley, Trey Reynolds, and Stephanie Drew, all of whom took the stress from my life and worked tirelessly for the ministry.

I want to thank the Board of Directors of our ministry who have co-labored with me for twenty years in sharing the Good News across the planet. Thank you so much for your love and support for me, but especially for the Lord.

I also want to thank David Sanford and his team at Sanford Communications, without whom this project would not have materialized. I thank you, David, for believing and sharing my vision to reach the world with the message of Christ. I praise the Lord for bringing you into my life! Additional thanks go to Brian Peterson at Baker, who championed this project from the start.

Finally, but most important, I thank the One who makes this book relevant and possible. If there were no resurrection, we would not be developing a resource on how to share Jesus Christ with the world. If Christ had not changed my life, I would not have bothered to write such a book.

Like you, I have the message of Jesus Christ that needs to be delivered to this world with a passion, an eloquence, and a burden that I pray this book brings into your life. My prayer is that we will link arms and commit our lives to share the greatest message this world will ever hear!

Introduction

Why or Why Not Witness?

Scott Dawson

A few years ago I surveyed more than six thousand Christians from sixteen states on why people have a hard time sharing their faith. After the survey was complete, a team placed the answers in corresponding categories. It's interesting that all of the answers given revolved around three basic issues for the nonwitnessing Christian.

The response most often given was *ignorance*. A majority of believers in this country do not have enough confidence in their knowledge of their faith to share it with another individual. Could it be that we have assigned evangelism, which is the natural outflow of knowing Christ, to an elite class of believers who have achieved something special? My fear is that programs that were developed to enhance evangelism have now elevated evangelism to a level that intimidates most believers.

Evangelism in its purest form is *me* sharing with *you* what Christ has done in my life. Anyone who has begun a relationship with Christ can be involved in evangelism. As we grow in our faith, we should grow in our ability to evangelize. Being able to explain terms such as *sin, gospel,* and *atonement* may give the soul-winner eloquence and poise when sharing his faith, but even if you have never heard of *propitiation, election,* or other theological terms, you can still be an evangelist.

The goal of this book is to place the theological basis of evangelism alongside the practical methods for evangelism. More than sixty authors from all walks of life have accomplished this task. The professors, pastors, and laypeople represented here share one passion—evangelism—and their desire is for you to be involved in it. To us, it is not *if* you are involved, but *how* you are involved! This book does not offer another program of evangelism but is a tool to be used in evangelism. There are at least three ways to use this resource.

First, use it to sharpen your own skills in evangelism. Allow it to awaken the burden in your soul for those around you. Second, use it as a guide for interacting with someone who belongs to a distinct people group. I promise you that in the next thirty days you will meet someone who is discussed in this book. The world is no longer across the ocean but across the street. Third, in conversations with other Christians, you will hear concern for friends whose lifestyles or situations are discussed in this book. Through this resource you will be ready to give an answer. This is not intended to be an exhaustive study of every people group, just a means to equip someone like you with the unique nuances and understanding needed to share the gospel with the various people who live around you.

Our survey found that the second reason people have a hard time witnessing is *fear*. Our team categorized answers like "fear of rejection," "fear of the unknown," and "lack of boldness" all under this topic. I suspect every Christian has been afraid to share Jesus with someone at one time or another. All of us encounter this natural emotion. How can you overcome fear? Allow me to use this example of my daughter, who is presently five (and a half, according to her). She is afraid of the dark. Why? Because she cannot see in the dark; therefore, she does not know what is in a dark room. Now, when we leave the light on, she is fine. "What is the difference?" you may ask. *Light always dispels darkness.* Jesus is the light of the world (John 8:12), and he will always conquer any fear we may have in sharing our faith. The challenge is for us to know him in his fullness (17:3) and discover that he who is in us is greater than he who is in the world (1 John 4:4).

The third answer given in our survey for not witnessing is related to *friendship*. Many people do not evangelize their friends because they think (not know) it will *turn off their friends* and end their friendship. The problem with this thinking revolves around integrity. If you are dealing with this personally, then remember the foundation of friendship. Friendship is about wanting the best for your friend—thinking more about your friend than about yourself. If this is true (and it is), what is better than sharing Jesus Christ? How can you call yourself a friend and not share the best thing that has happened to you and could happen to your friend?

Friendship is often referred to as two friends on the same ship going in the same direction. If a person is truly a friend (rather than just an acquaintance), are you both going in the same direction spiritually and eternally? Too many of us have sacrificed our integrity on the altar of compromise with our friends. Personally I have concluded that when someone will not share with a friend because of the risk of losing that friendship, her reluctance to share has little to do with the friend and more to do with the Christian's personal comfort getting in the way of fulfilling God's command.

Why We Witness

In Matthew 22:36–37 Jesus was asked, "Which is the greatest commandment in the Law?" Do you remember how Jesus answered? He replied, "Love the Lord your God with all your heart and with all your soul and with all your mind." Notice that he first mentioned the heart. Throughout Scripture the heart is the key to all emotions, beliefs, or actions. Evangelism starts in our hearts. Why? Because people talk about what is in their hearts not what is on their brains. Sports, children, destinations, or whatever are issues in your heart and will eventually come out in every conversation.

So it is with Jesus. He has changed my life! I have to talk about him!

The debate over evangelism is sometimes ridiculous. The desire to evangelize should not come out of duty or devotion but out of delight. Psalm 37:4 says, "Delight yourself in the LORD and he will give you the desires of your heart." If Christ lives in you, whose heart is it? How can we keep him from our conversations if he is truly in our hearts? We cannot! The reason we are able and energetic about sharing Christ is because of the place he holds in our hearts.

However, Jesus did not stop at the greatest commandment. He continued, "And the second is like it: 'Love your neighbor as yourself'" (Matt. 22:39). The other reason we witness is that we have concern for people. In logical conclusion, Christians should care for people more, longer, and better than anyone else on the planet. The old song lyric "They will know we are Christians by our love" should not be used as a comedic line but as our theme in living. Contrary to popular opinion, it is all right (and commanded by Christ) to care for one another. This care should be focused in two areas: eternal concern and temporal concern.

Eternal Concern

All of us come to this project with certain theological differences. This is not only healthy but also helpful in many conversations concerning evangelism. However, we must all agree on the basic belief that, apart from Christ, all men and women are eternally separated from God. I understand even that sentence can be discussed and (unfortunately) argued in classrooms across the country; however, this starting point is still necessary.

Scripture uses different terms to describe the godless eternity commonly referred to as "hell." Here are a few:

- "But the subjects of the kingdom will be thrown outside, into the darkness, where there will be weeping and gnashing of teeth" (Matt. 8:12).
- "Then he will say to those on his left, 'Depart from me, you who are cursed, into the eternal fire prepared for the devil and his angels'" (Matt. 25:41).

- "Then they will go away to eternal punishment, but the righteous to eternal life" (Matt. 25:46).
- "They will be punished with everlasting destruction and shut out from the presence of the Lord and from the majesty of his power" (2 Thess. 1:9).

As you can see, hell is described as "everlasting" and "eternal." It is apparent in Scripture that eternity offers no second choice for our destination. In addition, the hardest part for me to imagine is being separated from Christ for eternity! Can you imagine a place without at least a remnant of Christ? As bad as the backstreets of America are today, at least there is a lighthouse in every community. A Christless eternity is what makes hell, hell for the unbeliever.

Temporal Concern

The wrath of God is twofold: One aspect is eternal wrath (hell) and the other aspect is temporal. Your friend without Christ is experiencing God's wrath right now! You may not see fire and brimstone surrounding him or her, but the wrath is just as real. The worst part of life is emptiness, and without Christ the emptiness cannot be filled. Often I say that everyone without Christ goes to bed at night and thinks, *I made it another day.* How do I know? Because everyone has done it, including me! I just got sick of it and knew there had to be something more to this life. I found it in Jesus Christ!

Now that you have read reasons why we do not witness and even reasons why we do witness, the next stage is learning how to witness. Over the next pages you will discover a world of new ideas and timeless principles to help you share the gospel of Jesus Christ.

Use this book as a source for new ideas if you already have an active evangelistic lifestyle. Or use this resource as an introduction to your new adventure in evangelism. If you are fearful, ask God to calm you. If you are apathetic, ask God to burden you. If you are ready, ask God to use you to share his wonderful message.

My prayer is that you and I will always desire to be like Andrew, Jesus's disciple, who was often *bringing someone to Jesus*! (See John 1:41; 6:8–9.)

Part I

Sharing
Your
Faith

Defining Your Faith

1

What Faith Is

Using Your Evangelism Muscle

Luis Palau

When you plant vegetable seeds, you are exercising faith that, in time, you'll enjoy homegrown vegetables from your garden. When you sit in a chair at your kitchen table, you are exercising faith that the chair will support your body. When you board a jet, you are exercising faith that the jet will hold together and the pilot will direct it safely to your destination.

Although faith is essential to everyday life, you seldom think about it because you've learned to put your trust in what you believe to be trustworthy objects and people. But sometimes putting our faith in Someone is a matter of life and death.

Good works aren't good enough to earn God's acceptance, to find peace with God, or to pay the debt for sin. No matter how hard we try and how sincere our efforts, our consciences will never be cleansed "from acts that lead to death" (Heb. 9:14). Instead we must come to God on his terms—not by our works but by trust in the finished work of his Son.

The Trustworthy Object of Our Faith

The important question isn't how much faith we need. What matters is this: Who is the object of our faith? Only the God of the Bible, the One who sent his Son, Jesus Christ, to die on the cross for our sins, is fully trustworthy. Faith trusts him to always be who he says he is. Faith believes that the Promiser keeps his promises. Your faith is enough if your faith is in him.

God's work of salvation in Jesus Christ was finished nearly two thousand years ago—before I was born, long before I committed my first sin, let alone before I repented and believed. It is finished, and there's nothing I can add to my salvation.

Although we commonly trust chairs to support our weight and airplanes to arrive at the destination city, these things can let us down. It doesn't take much to make these objects of our faith untrustworthy. God is always trustworthy; we can put our faith in him and know with certainty that he will be who he says he is and do what he said he would do.

Lamentations 3:21–23 says, "Yet this I call to mind and therefore I have hope: Because of the LORD's great love we are not consumed, for his compassions never fail. They are new every morning; great is your faithfulness." Our hope is based in a God whose mercies are constantly renewed; we can rest our whole being in his faithfulness.

Faith Required

Faith is essential to eternal life; it is the way we have a relationship with God. First, when we receive Jesus Christ as Savior, we are exercising faith that he is the way to heaven, the one who makes us God's child. Second, because we cannot see God now, we live our lives by faith. We make our decisions and follow desires based on God's character and his promises.

During one evangelistic crusade, I counseled people who called our television program in search of spiritual help. As I prayed on the air with those who wanted to receive Christ, the station manager standing in the studio listened intently.

"I don't understand it," he said to me as the program signed off. "I attend church every Sunday. I partake of Holy Communion. I do confession at the stated times. And yet I have no assurance of eternal life."

Unfortunately, millions of Americans share that station manager's uncertainty and are on a long quest, because they are trusting their own efforts—especially religious observances—to get them into paradise. This kind of thinking permeates all religions, including traditional Christianity.

From the moment Adam disobeyed God in the garden, man has sought his own way to cover his sin and cleanse his conscience. We desire *to do*. We ask the same question the crowd asked Jesus: "What must we do to *do the works* God requires?" (John 6:28).

And God has always replied, "There's nothing you can do. You must trust me to do it for you." Jesus answered the crowd: "The work of God is this: to believe in the one he has sent" (v. 29).

It seems so easy! God requires only faith for our salvation, but it is the way that we live that enables us to grow in our relationship with him. Ephesians 2:8–9 says, "For it is by grace you have been saved, through faith—and this not from yourselves, it is the gift of God—not by works, so that no one can boast."

Faith Proven by How We Live

It is after conversion that we are to "spur one another on toward love and good deeds" (Heb. 10:24). Good works are the *outcome* of faith. Good works are a logical, loving response to the mercy and grace of God, and a fruit of the Holy Spirit who has now come to live within us. "For we are God's workmanship, created in Christ Jesus to do good works, which God prepared in advance for us to do" (Eph. 2:10). True saving faith leads inevitably to good works—doing the revealed will of God. Obedience is faith in action.

"But someone will say, 'You have faith; I have deeds.' Show me your faith without deeds, and I will show you my faith by what I do" (James 2:18). Good works reveal our faith. "As the body without the spirit is dead, so faith without deeds is dead" (v. 26). We work for God and for good because we are saved, not seeking to be saved.

A good deed in the eyes of God is not something we choose to do. Good works are obedience to God's revealed commands. An honest Christian will always feel that his good works are certainly less than perfect. But he's at peace with imperfection because he's not basing his right standing with God on his good deeds. Daily he proclaims, "My soul will boast in the LORD" (Ps. 34:2)—in him alone. That's what salvation is all about.

Growing Faith

Our faith in God does not grow without careful attention. Like the vegetables in your garden, your faith needs deliberate care. A bodybuilder cannot lie in bed and dream of growing strong and thus develop muscles. Neither can we leave our faith on the shelf and expect it to grow.

God does not ask us to work the "muscle" of faith on our own. The father of the demon-possessed boy who brought his son to Jesus Christ said, "I do believe; help me overcome my unbelief!" (Mark 9:24). What a beautiful thing to tell the Lord! God does not expect us to mature alone but commands a few things that will aid in the development of our faith.

Read over the list below. Where do you stand? What steps can you take to develop your faith muscle?

1. Experience fellowship with other believers (Heb. 10:25) so that you can sharpen each other's faith on to greater maturity. Commit to a church home and get involved with a Bible study, Sunday school class, or ministry. You cannot grow alone!

2. Commit to reading and studying God's Word to know him better. David says in Psalm 119:11: "I have hidden your word in my heart that I might not sin against you."

3. Choose to pray for a particular person, situation, or even a country. Praying for others will not only increase your faith but also increase your love for people. God loves to answer the prayers of his children!

2

What Faith Isn't

Six Mistakes That Keep People from Christ

Timothy George

The New Testament uses the word *faith* in two different ways. When it speaks of "the faith" with the definite article, it is referring to the content of what is believed, the apostolic message of God's love and grace revealed in Jesus Christ. One place where we find *faith* used in this way is Jude 3. Here believers are encouraged "to contend for the faith that was once for all entrusted to the saints."

More commonly, however, the word *faith* is used to describe not *what* we believe but rather the means *by which* we believe the gospel message. Thus Paul says in Ephesians 2:8: "For it is by grace you have been saved, through faith—and this not from yourselves, it is the gift of God."

Both meanings of the word *faith* are very important, indeed essential, for the Christian life—the faith that we believe is the Good News of the gospel itself. It is summarized many times in the New Testament (see John 3:16; Rom. 1:1–3; 1 Cor. 15:1–4; 1 Tim. 3:16). But the bare knowledge of the content of the Christian message does not make one a Christian. Other chapters in this book will describe in a positive way what it means to "believe on the Lord Jesus Christ," to have the sort of faith in him that leads to salvation. In the next few lines, I want to do something different. I want to talk about what faith isn't, to look at six bypaths that actually will lead one *away* from Christ not *toward* him. It is important to avoid these pitfalls if we are to know and claim Jesus Christ as the Lord and Savior of our lives.

Not Mere Mental Assent

Often when people hear the story of Jesus, when they read about his life and death on the cross or even his resurrection from the dead, they find themselves in complete agreement with the historical facts they have encountered. They can nod and give mental assent to such propositions. This is good and necessary but by itself it is not sufficient to lead one to living faith in Christ. Why not? Because the basic human problem is not mere lack of information. What we need is not more data but rather an inner transformation. Merely saying yes to the facts cannot by itself bring about such a change of heart and will.

Not Allegiance to a Church or Denomination

Most Christian churches and denominations have a stated set of beliefs, a confession of faith, officers, programs, patterns of worship, and social activities of various kinds. These are not evil things in themselves, and many people do become believers in Christ through the outreach of local congregations. But my point is this: To know Jesus Christ is not the same thing as belonging to the church. Jesus Christ is a real person not just an idea or a doctrine. We come to know Jesus the same way we come to know any other person—personally, through personal encounter, in a relationship that begins by acknowledging who he is, talking with him one-on-one, and opening the door of our life for him to come in (Rev. 3:20).

Not Hereditary Endowment

Some people think that, because their parents or grandparents were believers in Jesus, they are automatically Christians by virtue of this family connection. But a relationship with Jesus is not something that can be inherited like blue eyes, big feet, or the family farm. Jesus once had a famous meeting with a very religious man, Nicodemus, and he said to him: "You must be born again" (John 3:7). Nicodemus wondered how it could be possible for a grown man to be unraveled, so to speak, to be taken back through all the stages of his life to the very point of conception. Jesus explained that he was not talking about a new physical birth but rather a new birth, a new beginning, "from above." Jesus was talking about a spiritual birth, one that can be brought about only by the Holy Spirit. National loyalties, ethnic pride, and family ties can never substitute for the new life Jesus brings.

Not an Emotional State

Some people equate the Christian life with a certain emotional state, a condition of heightened religious consciousness or a sense of self-esteem, feeling good about oneself. One theologian described religion as "the feeling of absolute dependence." There is some truth in this, of course. When Jesus enters a person's life, his presence affects everything, including the emotions. A sonata by Bach or a beautiful painting by Rembrandt can fill us with a sense of awe or bring a flood of tears to our eyes. Feelings are not bad, but they are flimsy. Our emotions ebb and flow with the circumstances of our lives. Godly feelings flow from faith, but they can never be the foundation for it. As Martin Luther once wrote, "Feelings come and feelings go, and feelings are deceiving; my warrant is the Word of God, naught else is worth believing."

Not a System of Good Works

Faith is sometimes equated with outward behavior, a code of ethics, a life lived by high moral principles. Indeed, the Bible does teach that there is a close relationship between faith and works. "Faith without works is dead" (James 2:17). Good works are to spring from a life of faith, just as fruit appears on the branches of a well-planted tree. But the sequence of that analogy is important: first the roots, then the fruits. The problem is that none of us can live a life good enough, free enough from sin and selfishness, to be accepted by God on the basis of our meritorious behavior. "All have sinned and fall short of the glory of God," the Bible says (Rom. 3:23). To believe on the Lord Jesus Christ means to cast ourselves on his mercy, to trust in his atoning sacrifice on the cross, to surrender ourselves to his will, and to embrace his lordship over our lives. On the basis of this relationship, we learn to walk in the light and to grow more fully into the kind of person God wants us to be.

There is another subtle danger at this point. Many people know that the Bible teaches that we are saved by grace, through faith, and not by any good works that we have done. We are sometimes tempted, however, to treat faith itself as though it were some kind of good work, a meritorious act we can perform to bring ourselves into right standing before God. Nothing could be further from the truth. This is why the Bible emphasizes so strongly that faith itself is a gift, something we have received directly from God, not a service we render to God to secure his mercy or favor on us. Only when we realize that grace is the unmerited, unprovoked favor of God and that faith is a free gift bestowed by the Lord, apart from anything we do to deserve it, can we truly appreciate the extent of God's amazing love for us. In writing to the Corinthian Christians, Paul asked this question: "What do you have that you did not receive?" (1 Cor. 4:7). The proper answer to this question for every Christian is, "Nothing, nothing at all." Perhaps the old hymn says it best: "In my hands no price I bring, simply to thy cross I cling."

Not a Passive, Inert Condition

To become a Christian involves a twofold movement on our part, both prompted and enabled by the Holy Spirit: repentance and faith. To *repent* is to turn around, to change direction, to forsake one way of thinking for another. *Faith* is the positive side of this movement—to embrace Jesus Christ, to trust in him alone, to cling to his cross, to rest in his promise of forgiveness and new life. Even though we receive faith as a radical gift from God, faith itself is not a passive, inert condition that leaves us unmoved and unchanged. Faith is an active, dynamic reality that propels us forward into the Christian life. Faith belongs to the basic triad of Christian virtues—faith, hope, and love. None of these are self-generating qualities or mere human possibilities. They are gifts of God actualized in the lives of his children by the presence of his Spirit in their hearts.

Faith's True Meaning

It is important to sort through these various mistaken understandings of faith to grasp its true reality. Here are some steps you can take to explore the meaning of faith more fully:

- Meditate on the life, death, and resurrection of Jesus Christ. Look at the ways in the Bible that men and women came to faith in Christ. Jesus always dealt with those he met on a personal level, extending a hand of compassion, calling them by name. "Mary," he said to a forgiven woman. "Lazarus!" he called out to a dead man. Jesus still calls us by name and wants us to reach out in faith to him.

- Spend time alone with God in prayer. While we are not saved by our praying, Jesus does promise not to turn away anyone who comes to him. Our prayers need not be sophisticated or long-winded. When we are not sure what to say, something as simple as "Jesus, have mercy on me!" will do.

- Ask a Christian friend to tell you how he or she became a believer in Jesus. Here is my story, briefly told. When I was eleven years old, I knew that I needed to believe in Jesus and that I had never taken that step. After hearing a message from the Bible on Psalm 116, I went home that night and knelt beside my bed. I said a very simple prayer, something like this: "Oh, Jesus, forgive my sins. Come into my life. I want to know you and follow you." This was not a dramatic experience but a simple surrender of a young boy to the living Christ. From that day until now, my life has been different and, though I have failed Christ many times, he has never failed me. My confidence today, and for all time, is in him alone.

3

Know the Difference

Christianity Is Not Just a Religion

Rick Marshall

And they will call him Immanuel —which means, *"God with us."*

Matthew 1:23

At the heart of the Christian faith is the *incarnation*, and at the heart of the Christian Way are the *followers* of the Way.

Os Guinness (italics added)

Christianity is unique, different from all other faiths for many reasons but supremely for one. Put simply, the Christian Way teaches that God became a man!

The word *incarnation* means "endowment with a human body, appearance in human form." This is an amazing concept. If it is true that God became a man, it must be considered the most significant event in world history. The great Cambridge and Oxford University professor C. S. Lewis wrote more than sixty years ago in his classic *Mere Christianity*: "I have to accept the view that Jesus was and is God. God has landed on this enemy-occupied world in human form."

God's strategy for revealing his true nature and his care for lost humanity was not through an organization, media outlet, ad campaign, TV miniseries, or Academy Award winner. It was through a flesh-and-blood human being, Jesus Christ. To put this idea in movie terms would be to say that there has been only one historically verifiable ET! John, the friend and disciple of Jesus, wrote an

29

eloquent description of this great revelation: "The Word became flesh and made his dwelling among us. We have seen his glory, the glory of the One and Only, who came from the Father, full of grace and truth" (John 1:14).

God the Father sent his Son on a rescue mission for all humanity—for all women and men of every race, every language, every class.

And yet a great many doubters remain. We know people who ask the question "What is the difference between Christianity and all other faiths?" This is an important question, especially in an age when tolerance is considered one of the greatest virtues.

When my second daughter, Jessica, was a senior at Millersville University in Pennsylvania, working on her teaching degree, she had an encounter that changed her thinking about evangelism and challenged mine. As an English literature major she participated in a weekly reading group. Passages were read aloud, then discussed and debated passionately but never vindictively, that is, until the day when religion came up. Jessica has forgotten the literary subject but not the tone the discussion took. A group member blurted out, "Jessica, you're the Christian. You tell us what this means!" She was shocked and speechless at the hostility and bitterness in her friend's voice. Before finishing the story, Jess said, "Dad, I don't call myself a Christian anymore!" My worried look brought a smile to her face as she explained, "Dad, don't worry. I still believe in Jesus."

Then she told me that two weeks later, when discussing a different passage from an assigned book, a spiritual matter could not be avoided. This time Jessica took the lead and said, "For me, on this subject, Jesus is the Master and I'm his disciple."

"How did they respond to that?" I asked.

With a grin Jessica replied, "They just nodded and said, 'Cool.'" Just a matter of semantics? I think not.

The religion—Christianity—was "out," but the person of Jesus was "in"!

Sources of Confusion

Os Guinness, renowned author and thinker, has written insightfully: "We are never more powerful witnesses to the gospel of Jesus than when we ourselves are changed by following Jesus." As we have seen, God's strategy was to send to earth his personal, in-the-flesh representative in the person of Jesus. Now you and I, his followers, are also his representatives, part of his strategy! For two thousand years of church history, Jesus's followers have been his representatives. But despite this, it is still difficult for people to take the claims of Christianity seriously. What has happened in our day to make this increasingly so?

First, the times have changed. There have been cultural shifts of seismic proportions in our lifetime. *Second*, the impact of these changes has, perhaps without our realizing it, profoundly affected the way we live and think. Consider the following:

- dramatic increases in life expectancy in the United States since 1900, from age forty-one to age seventy-seven
- significant increase in the standard of living and rise of the middle class
- serious decline in global natural resources
- globalization of the world economy
- work relocation from rural to urban and loss of community
- breakup of the family in the aftermath of liberalized divorce laws
- spread of virulent diseases
- global dominance of "pop" culture
- growing levels of fear and anxiety following 9/11
- explosive growth of technology

This last change, the impact of technology, cannot be overstated. We are the first two or three generations to be raised in a predominately electronic environment.

In 1922 President Warren Harding was the first Chief Executive to bring a radio into the White House. Today, according to a March 2005 Kaiser Family Foundation survey—"Generation M: Media in the Lives of 8–18 Year-Olds"[1]—the average U.S. home has:

- four CD or tape players
- three TVs, with one home in five owning five or more
- three VCRs/DVD players
- two computers
- two video game players

Students use electronic media an average of six and a half hours per day. That is more than forty-five hours per week!

It may be too early to know the full impact of this kind of media saturation, but what is known for certain is that all North Americans have access to an unprecedented amount of media and technology. And to be sure, it is not all good.

The Use of Technology

Of course, technology can be used to communicate the gospel and advance the kingdom of God, but this can come at a price, a terrible price. Today, if a visible and well-known Christian leader succumbs to temptation and breaks either the moral law of God or the law of the land or both, what happens? After the news breaks, at nearly the speed of light, news organizations tell the story to millions of people around the world via the Internet, cable, satellite, or TV and radio broadcasts.

We jump on the "information superhighway" every day. Remember that one hundred years ago, it took more than three weeks for a handwritten letter in New York City to reach London. Not today and not ever again. The late New York University professor and author Neil Postman understood the effect of unbridled media: "It is simply not possible," he wrote, "to convey a sense of seriousness about any event if its implications are exhausted in less than one minute's time."[2] This has strong implications for the Christian's use of the media. The timeless, deep message of the gospel takes time to tell, but media limit the time any communicator has to tell it. Postman writes: "[Television preachers] have assumed that what had formerly been done in a church or a tent, and face-to-face, can be done on television without loss of meaning, without changing the quality of the religious experience."[3] Every form of media can manipulate, but especially the electronic media. A studio-produced Christian TV program requiring makeup, lighting, and staging and being edited for time, with frequent interruptions during the taping, will distort the biblical story. Call it "sound bite" faith—the attempt to communicate biblical truth in under thirty seconds. You can plant a seed in thirty seconds, but you can't cultivate, nurture, or harvest in that amount of time.

Christianity's Media Image

Sadly, too often the negative image of Christianity that the watching world gets from the media is accurate. The image is not who we should be, but it's a form of reality TV. We can't eliminate from the public memory our public failures. Our assertions and claims must be matched by evidence. We must be *seen* as true followers of Jesus. Confidence in the church has been lost because of our greed, hypocrisy, harsh language, anger, and terrible misdeeds. I will never forget seeing the bumper sticker that read: "Jesus Save Me From Your Followers!"

Trust, which can be lost in thirty seconds, can take years to restore. The public's loss of confidence is played out in the media every day. Our faith demands honesty and consistency and the watching world demands it too. If we fail, we need the courage and humility to admit it. The three hardest words to say in any language are "I was wrong!"

On another, more important level, the world does not receive an accurate image of Christianity from the media. It is tragic headline news when a passenger plane crashes, but the fact that each day thousands of planes take off and land safely is not news. In the same way, it is not news that every day across the globe, millions of followers of Jesus live their lives and speak the truth with courage and compassion, grace and love, performing countless acts of sacrificial generosity.

The average person never sees God at work through these lives and never hears the gospel message of hope through the media.

Despite this silence, however, the followers of Christ have changed the course of history! Many of the great ideas and institutions of the Western world had their inspiration and origins in the Christian faith. Consider, for example:

- great music, paintings, sculpture, literature, and architecture
- establishment of hospitals, orphanages, and hospices
- caring for the poor and philanthropy
- abolition of slavery, civil rights movements, and the spread of freedom

In a way, the apparent weakness of God's working through *human vessels* is also the greatest strength. We are not only the objects of God's love but also the prime carriers of his message. Indeed he is the Master, and we are meant to be his followers. Therefore, as his followers we must speak and act as closely as possible to his claims and his call on our lives. In an open letter to Christians, Os Guinness wrote about this: "In a day when religion is tied to hatred and violence—we must show love. In a day of mediocrity and corruption—we must be a people of integrity and excellence."

Billy Graham was once asked at a press conference: "Where can we go for inspiration and instruction on how to renew the church?" He replied, "Back at least two thousand years, to the Bible and the early church leaders who showed us how to follow Christ with dedication and faithfulness." This is what the watching world needs to hear and, I believe, longs to see.

A Unique Story

The Christian story is unique in the world. G. K. Chesterton, the celebrated Englishman of the early twentieth century, wrote, "I had always felt life first as a story—and if there is a story, there is a story teller."[4] In a similar way, J. R. R. Tolkien, in his classic book *The Lord of the Rings: The Two Towers*, says this through the character Samwise Gamgee to Frodo Baggins: "I wonder what sort of tale we've fallen into?"[5]

God, the storyteller, created a world of beauty and goodness. In the opening chapters of the story, in Genesis, we are told that nothing was evil anywhere in creation. In its original design, the world was a perfect garden, our home made by God. Since Eden we have dreamed about and searched for the echo of this time and place. But in this life it is not to be. The Bible teaches us that something has gone wrong within us and among us. Tragically, sin came into God's perfect world. Theologians call this tragedy the fall. And we see its effects every day.

As I write this paragraph, I can see the March 14, 2005, *Time* magazine cover with a haunting black-and-white photograph of a desperate and nearly lifeless woman, a mother perhaps, with three small children clinging to her. The headline reads: "How to End Poverty: Eight million people die each year because they are too poor to stay alive." It grips my heart, and I think, *How can this be, in a world with so much wealth?* But this is our reality. We live on a ravaged planet, affected in every part—the earth, the sky, the sea, the animals, and especially the human family, who were created in the image of God (Gen. 1:27).

There is another poverty that grips everyone. It is a poverty of the soul—where longings are never satisfied, desires never fulfilled, hopes never realized, and fears ever growing. C. S. Lewis felt this keenly: "If I find in myself a desire which no experience in this world can satisfy, the most probable explanation is that I was made for another world."[6]

We know that Earth is not our ultimate home, because God has "set eternity in the hearts of men" (Eccles. 3:11). Every day we strive to change our surroundings for the better or live in denial that we are not displaced. But this is an inescapable biblical truth: We were made by God to be and do something better. As Bono of U2 sings in the song "Yahweh," we are "stranded in some skin and bones." The well-known words of St. Augustine, written more than sixteen hundred years ago, are still true: "Our hearts are restless until they find their rest in thee."

At the end of the millennium, MTV counted down the top one hundred rock songs of all time. Number one was "Satisfaction" by the English rock group The Rolling Stones. The opening line became the anthem of a displaced generation: "I can't get no satisfaction, though I tried and I tried and I tried and I tried. . . ." Nothing will ever completely satisfy our hearts unless it comes from the heart of God.

Jesus is no "rolling stone." He is the Rock of our salvation and the Cornerstone of our faith. And he still calls out to restless hearts: "Come to me, all you who are weary and burdened, and I will give you rest. Take my yoke upon you and learn from me, for I am gentle and humble in heart, and you will find rest for your souls" (Matt. 11:28–29).

God's creation encourages us: "Be grateful." The fall of humanity says, "Be sad." But the incarnation, a story of redemption, declares, "Be glad!" It is the story of my wife's friend Joy, who wrote of her encounter with the Savior: "All of my life built up to that one moment, when I ran out of myself, and God took over." Only the intervention of God through his Son Jesus Christ put Joy's world right—and mine and all who "were redeemed from the empty way of life . . . with the precious blood of Christ" (1 Pet. 1:18–19).

C. S. Lewis called this "the good invasion." God in a rescue mission came to planet Earth. Peter and Matthew, disciples and friends of Jesus, described Christ's mission in the New Testament: "The Son of Man did not come to be served, but to serve, and to give his life as a ransom for many" (Matt. 20:28). "For Christ

died for sins once for all, the righteous for the unrighteous, to bring you to God"
(1 Pet. 3:18).

God's Work through Us

The incarnation—God becoming a man—I believe, is the ultimate example
to follow. This central truth and claim make Christianity unique and the most
powerful force for good on the planet. We are the hands, feet, and voice of Jesus—
his storytellers—called to bring love, wisdom, and holiness into our turbulent
and technologically chaotic world. Christianity is not just a religion—it is about
relationship. One transformed life, made for eternity, touches another. This is
God's work in us and through us, with the hope that everyone in our world will
know the difference that Jesus can bring. But first, Jesus must become our center
and passion. Only then will we be changed—and that is what a lost world is
craving to behold.

4

Show the Difference!

It's Impossible Not to Shine

─────────────────────

Lon Allison

Those who are wise will shine like the brightness of the heavens, and those who lead many to righteousness, like the stars for ever and ever.

Daniel 12:3

There is something about a star. I'm writing this chapter for *The Complete Evangelism Guidebook* as Christmas fast approaches. Homes in the Chicago area are decorated with an enthusiasm and dedication approaching fanaticism! Our street, with more than fifty homes, finds fewer than five without outdoor lights. The houses with the white lights are the brightest. There are hundreds and thousands of these little stars on Carpenter Drive. It is wonderfully bright. There is no room for darkness.

Daniel suggests that God-followers shine with a similar light. His language is exuberant. The wise are like the brightness of the heavens. Those (wise ones) who lead people to righteousness are "forever stars." It's impossible not to shine if we are in Christ and walking in the fullness of the Holy Spirit. In this chapter I will describe this brightness in some theological detail. Now, don't get worried. This is not a biblical theology of "stardom." What I will attempt is to detail the difference between Christ-followers and those yet outside the kingdom. Why? Not to separate us from the world but rather to help us better love it with all the distinctives the Spirit expresses through us.

The inheritance we have in Christ provides a contagious lightlike uniqueness as we reach the world. Sometimes we forget that. I can certainly understand how. This is a pretty dark world. Dark language and dark stories fill the communication between humans at every conceivable level. And even the "stars" have lapses. Sin creeps and crawls, insidiously challenging us to deny God and our truer selves. Worst of all, every believer is tempted to rely on self, instead of on the indwelling Spirit who makes us shine. That's why we need a thorough dose of biblical reality as we engage the world Jesus loves. He hates darkness. The Bible tells me, in fact, that he won't stand for darkness. Wherever he is, light consumes darkness (John 1:5). Wherever he goes, light is in his train.

I will attempt to define this brightness in the Christ-follower in four dimensions. Think of them as points on a star. The top point of the star is the brightness of Christ in our lives. From that we can trace four other points that each further describes the brightness we have as Christians.

The first is our *coherence*. To be coherent is to be logically consistent. Any person who thinks at all about life develops his or her own worldview. However, the key is not whether a person has a worldview but whether it makes sense when examined. Is it, therefore, coherent? The Christian has a coherent worldview because of a standard text of truth—the Scriptures.

The second dimension is our *character*. We will review the reality of Christ in us and how that transforms us. Sin's power is broken, and new winds of holiness are blowing in our souls.

The third reality is in the area of *competency*. The Bible describes this as the impartation of special capacities (spiritual gifts) that express and spread the kingdom throughout the planet.

Finally, there is a unique *chemistry* that is organic in Christ-followers. There is to be a divine romance, if you will, a love affair between followers of every color and creed that defies human explanation. Each of these star points pours witness-light into our lost neighborhoods and cities. It is *impossible*, therefore, *not* to shine, or show the difference!

Coherence

The spiritual man makes judgments about all things, but he himself is not subject to any man's judgment: "For who has known the mind of the Lord that he may instruct him?" But we have the mind of Christ.

1 Corinthians 2:15–16

I spoke with a young man not long ago who told me he was developing his own worldview. As the discussion progressed, I understood his method. He saw the world of ideas like a grocery store, where he could pick from any aisle and shelve any notion of truth that suited him at a particular time. Tossing each idea into his cart, he would have a shopping bag full of philosophies and beliefs. The outside of the bag would be labeled "worldview."

The trouble is some things just don't go together. For instance, in our Western world, the notion of tolerance may be the highest of values. The trouble is tolerance falls apart when one asks if everything is to be tolerated. Should murder be tolerated? Should date rape be tolerated? Of course not. Well then, perhaps tolerance must be qualified. But who does the qualifying? There is the rub. The young man would probably say each individual is to define what is to be tolerated. Rather than coherence, what is left is chaos. Everyone does what is right in his own eyes.

Christians have the mind of Christ. The Spirit within us leads us to all truth (John 16:13). The Scriptures teach truth about God and humanity. What a light-source! Coherence is attainable because of the consistent worldview taught by the Spirit and revealed in the sacred text. I am so grateful that I don't have to struggle with issues such as when life begins or how the universe came into existence or man's place within the created order or how to act within relationships. I have a consistent and quite brilliant position on all those issues, not because I am brilliant but because the God who reveals truth is. This is the first great point on our shining star, a coherent worldview.

Character

> For we know that our old self was crucified with him so that the body of sin might be done away with, that we should no longer be slaves to sin.
>
> Romans 6:6

Whether you look at goodness from the starting point of a virtue or a vice, people end up losing the race. We believe (our coherent worldview) that every human being is addicted to sin. There is no part of us that couldn't be better. And, if we are honest, most human beings will admit it's easier to be bad than good because at our core resides the disease of sin; that is, until Jesus Christ immerses us in his own goodness. Paul explained that we (our old sinful selves) were killed when Christ died. And his new resurrection life indwells us now, giving us a new life (Rom. 6:8). What an incredible advantage! The tables have turned. It used to be we couldn't help but sin. Now, with Christ within us, sin is a foreigner, a virus that disrupts but doesn't belong. I'm not saying we don't sin anymore, because we do. It's just that it is not comfortable to do so. Where sin once fit me like a glove, now it just doesn't feel right.

In my early thirties I had a huge crush on Porsches. I dreamed of owning a Porsche (a used one, of course, to display good stewardship). They were sleek, fast, classy, and the perfect wheels for a young California pastor. But there was a whole lot of "prestige sin" going on inside me. Now, some readers would have no sin problem with a Porsche at all. But I did. Quite honestly I was obsessed. Thank God that is over. Twenty years later a Porsche can't even turn my head. It's not that I'm denying myself. I just no longer want something like that. I'd be nuts to trade our 95 GMC van for a Porsche! A silly illustration perhaps, but I hope the point is clear. Sin is no longer master. Sin is a visitor and, thanks be to God, someday will be only a distant memory. Talk about light! Honest to goodness, goodness is wonderfully attractive to an addiction-driven world.

Competency

> Now to each one the manifestation of the Spirit is given for the common good.
>
> 1 Corinthians 12:7

Thus Paul begins his teaching on the spiritual gifts. Do we really grasp how different this makes us from a nonbelieving world? Each believer is given at least one special capacity from God for making the world better (Rom. 12:6–8; 1 Cor. 12:4–11; Eph. 4:11–13). Have you ever been around someone with the gift of mercy? They are unique people. They stop for strangers, work in rescue missions, and open their homes to people in need. They won't stand for AIDS and weep openly for the pain it causes. Christians with the gift of mercy care deeply without selfish hidden agendas. That is what God does in his followers.

Mercy is just one of twenty or so special capacities God gives to his people. These competencies are supernaturally given and, when deployed, have supernatural impact. We are to use our gifts for the common good. They are God's means of extending his kingdom-light into every corner of the planet.

Chemistry

> For we were all baptized by one Spirit into one body—whether Jews or Greeks, slave or free—and we were all given the one Spirit to drink.
>
> 1 Corinthians 12:13

This worldwide family thing is intoxicating. As I write these words, my memories are floating toward the Philippines, Thailand, England, and Scotland. But I'm not remembering places. I see faces. I see brothers and sisters I've met in the last year, and my heart swells with joy. God has made us family. Within a few hours of meeting, there was a connection, chemistry only the one whom we call *Father* could initiate.

The church is foremost a family of believers. In some ways it is stronger than blood. This family is destined to live together forever, while sadly, some of our earthly blood relations may be separated from God and also us, if they say no to

Jesus. I don't mention that to create sadness as much as to point out the eternal nature of the family of God. It may be that the global family of God, loving each other deeply, is the greatest witness of Christ next to the proclamation of the gospel.

Imagine the power of this point of the star. Some of humanity's strongest divisions, like nationalism, race, gender, and class, are literally erased by the all-encompassing reality of the family of God. This is not to say we break down the walls of separation perfectly. But when we are filled with the Holy Spirit, the walls come tumbling down. What a light to the world! This week I spoke with the leadership of a church in Santa Cruz, California, which employs a staff person to help coordinate the efforts of sixty churches in their city. They believe there is one church in that city. It goes by different names and meets in different places, but it is the *one* church.

Are you overwhelmed by all we have in Christ? This short chapter only brushes across each of the points of light. But perhaps that is adequate. My hope is that these realities don't lead us to hoard our good things but rather to wish them for every person in the world. And remember, these four realities are witnesses of the top point of the star—the great light of Jesus Christ. Let's go shine the light and show the difference that Christ makes!

SECTION B

Demonstrating Your Faith

5

Extraordinary Lifestyle

*Servant Evangelism—Using God's Kindness
to Reach the Human Heart*

Steve Sjogren

I came to Cincinnati, Ohio, some twenty years ago after being a part of several church-planting teams in various parts of the United States and in Europe. I had met with both great success and spectacular failure prior to coming to Cincinnati and when arriving here was surprised to find such high levels of conservatism. I had helped start a church in Oslo, Norway, yet the resistance found in Cincinnati was greater than that in Europe. People in this midwestern city were very wary, constantly asking if this new church was a cult! It seems that if you aren't a Roman Catholic or a Baptist in this city, then you are suspect.

Eventually their resistance was worn down as we went into the city doing acts of generosity that is now called servant evangelism. To make a long story short, this church has served between four and five million people in the Cincinnati area. People have responded in a big way. The church has grown to some six thousand on weekends, with a large percentage coming from a completely unchurched background.

Servant evangelism is based on the following principles or perspectives:

- Anyone can be kind.
- The average Christian is able to do highly effective evangelism—anyone can sow a seed (see Matthew 13).

- Effective evangelism is a process and does not produce an immediate flip-flop from the kingdom of darkness into the kingdom of light. "I planted the seed, Apollos watered it, but God made it grow" (1 Cor. 3:6).
- Evangelism happens in an atmosphere of acceptance of new people who are coming in—loving them just as they are, just where they are. The story of the prodigal son is a model of this acceptance (Luke 15:11–32).
- We can begin effective evangelism now, right where we are. It doesn't take any further training. We've all received the training we need to be effective evangelists if we have spent six months in the church and in reading our Bibles. It's very simple! Just do it—as Matthew 28:19 directs.
- It is the kindness of God that leads to repentance (Rom. 2:4).

Let the Seed Planting Begin

Start flinging seeds of God's love and kindness boldly in your city. Don't be an overly cautious seed planter like many Christians of this generation. There is a fear that there is a limited amount of seed to go around. That's a misunderstanding about the abundance of God on earth. He isn't stuck in scarcity. There is plenty of money to plant seeds of his love in our cities. I am often asked, "Won't it be expensive to do the things you are talking about?" (for example, give away bottles of water or give away hot chocolate with marshmallows). My response is, "Whoever said that it would be inexpensive to win our cities to Christ?" Of course, it's going to cost us something. In my last book, *Irresistible Evangelism*, we quote a source that claims that the church now spends $330,000 per convert worldwide. That's a lot of money on any scale! The projects I am suggesting are super cheap by comparison.

As I see it, we need to raise up in each city many churches that are filled with seed flingers, people who will go out and broadcast their seeds of kindness, generosity, and love. For example, at our church it is second nature for people to pay for the meal of the person behind them when they drive through a fast-food line. They simply ask the cashier, "How much is the meal in the car behind me?" They pay for the meal and give the cashier a "connection card" (this is a business-sized card that has all the pertinent information about the church on it—map, website, phone number, service times, logo, and a little saying such as, "This is to show you God's love in a practical way. If we can be of more help, please don't hesitate to give us a call!").

Our church gives away close to two hundred thousand of these cards each year—many at drive-through windows—to surprised, hungry people on their lunch breaks. Each time a seed like that is planted, we are nudging that person a step closer to Christ. In my estimation it takes between twelve and twenty of these anointed moments where God breaks through and makes the connection between that act of love and that person's heart before the person in question comes to Christ. That's a lot of free lunches!

As we raise up many churches like this in each city and as they develop atmospheres of acceptance in their weekend celebrations (they throw a party instead of a funeral), we will steadily change the perception of the city toward the church. The church's voice will be heard once again. People will listen to Christians as they say the simple truths of the Message, such as, "Jesus is in love with you!" And people will begin to believe us because they have seen that love in action from many, many Christians all around the city.

I know it's a simple strategy, but it works. I've seen it work. Over the last twenty years we have come a long way toward redefining our city's perception of God and many, many churches are benefiting. Before this new understanding began to take shape, there was just one church with more than one thousand attenders, and it was that size because it bussed people in from around the city. Now, after many churches have gotten on board with the giving away of God's love in practical ways all over the city, there are some twelve churches of over one thousand attenders and about three pushing four thousand or more. That's progress in an objectively measurable package.

Show, Then Tell

As I see it, the evangelism models that we have had to work with in America have been based on a win-lose proposition. It's as though we have based our evangelism thinking on coach Vince Lombardi's philosophy: "Winning isn't everything—it's the only thing!" We have created a culture of winning at all costs within the church world. We go out and we take on the heathens. We argue them into submission, and eventually they must give in because we have brought them to their knees intellectually. We think, *Yes, that's how we gain converts into the kingdom.* But nothing could be further from the truth.

The truth is people are yearning to be convinced that Jesus is real and that what he stands for is good and right. But these days none of them are going to be argued into the kingdom. They are going to be escorted or nudged into God's kingdom by fellow travelers who are willing to make changes to become just like them. Perhaps Vince Lombardi wasn't a Christian. Did you ever stop to think about that? We have adopted an approach to ministry that is based on something that isn't Christian in its basic approach. Jesus never approached situations with a win-lose perspective (except with the Pharisees perhaps). He got down on people's level and spoke their language, so they could easily understand.

We are living in an age that isn't exactly postmodern, but it is influenced by postmodern thinking to a large degree. I believe this is true across the United States right now, in small towns and large cities alike. For example, people are saying, "If I can't experience it first, then it's not real." They are saying (and thinking),

"It has to touch my heart before I will allow it to invade the space of my head." A few years ago the Canadian rock group Rush had the hit song "Show Don't Tell." That song could have easily been a prophetic song for the church, but we missed the moment. That's the sentiment of the watching world: "Show, don't tell." Or at least, "Show first before you attempt to tell."

People do not really need a clean car. But most of us like a clean car, and few of us enjoy doing the cleaning.

A small country church in the Northwest decided that dirty cars made a wonderful evangelism opportunity. Their little town of 3,500 has only three grocery stores. Most of the town's cars show up at one of these three parking lots at least once a week.

Everyday after school for a week, the church's youth group divided into three groups and went after cars in the parking lots. The assignment was simple enough: put a little slip under the windshield wipers. The message read, "We are the high school youth of XYZ church. This Saturday we want to wipe the dirt out of our town. Your car is invited to a free and superb wash job at ABC gas station." This gas station chosen for the wash sits next door to the largest of the grocery stores. Patrons could leave their cars off to be cleaned while they did their shopping.

The turnout, as you would guess, was tremendous. And there were no nasty surprises—you know, tracts stuffed into glove boxes, under seats, inside air-conditioning vents or the spare-tire hub. No, all that was offered was a respectful, free service.

From Tony Campolo and Gordon Aeschliman, *Fifty Ways You Can Share Your Faith.* (InterVarsity, 1992), 27–28. Used by permission of the authors.

6

Extraordinary Actions

Adapted from Evangelism That Works

George Barna

Every revival in the history of the modern world has been grounded in an explosion of prayer and evangelism.

During this past quarter century or so, Christianity in America has withstood a powerful challenge to its strength and supremacy as the basis of its law, order, virtue, and purpose. The Christian church in this country continues to be rocked by the social forces aligned against it.

The results of the relentless battle to destroy the centrality of Christianity are evident: media mockery of Christians and their faith, declining church attendance, a shrinking pool of people who are ardently committed to their faith, history books and political debates that eliminate or deny the positive influence of Christianity, the reduction of religious liberties (ironically conducted in the name of religious freedom), a diverted national focus away from the things of God to the vices and pleasures of humankind, the waning influence of religious institutions and spokespersons, and severe "legal" restrictions against the application of the Christian faith to all dimensions of life.

A Time for Revival

Our present circumstance is not unprecedented in human history. A comforting realization is that, historically, conditions often reach their nadir just before the dawning of a period of awakening or enlightenment. Often matters must become so deplorable that not even those who helped to engineer such circumstances maintain an interest in continuing the course they charted.

The result is a rapid transformation from decadence to repentance and cultural renewal. From a Christian perspective, we are immersed in a bruising but exciting time because the social and moral conditions are right for spiritual revival. There is something missing, however. Students of church history and contemporary culture will immediately see the problem with the proposition that America is on the precipice of revival. Every revival in the history of the modern world has been grounded in an explosion of prayer and evangelism.

In the time directly preceding an outbreak of spiritual revival, churches focus their energy and resources on congregational repentance, personal commitment to outreach, and preparation for the potential outpouring of God's Holy Spirit on the land and the influx of new converts. The hole in the hypothesis that America is living on the edge of revival is that as matters stand today, the church is not poised to initiate and sustain a revolution of the human heart and soul.

No one can deny, however, that our present cultural and spiritual conditions are ripe for a massive return to God by the people of America. Today approximately 295 million people live in the United States. By my calculations, based on large-scale surveys of the population, about 190 million of those people have yet to accept their Lord and Savior.

Responsibility for Sharing the Gospel

Our research also shows that evangelism is not the revitalizing factor many Christians wish it were. How ironic that during this period of swelling need for the proclamation of the gospel and the healing powers of the church, the ranks of the messengers have dissipated to anemic proportions.

Why does this paradox exist—the growing need for God's love and truth in a culture where the church seems less emphatic about communicating and demonstrating that love? I believe it has to do largely with our misperception of circumstances and misinterpretation of responsibilities. For example, most Christians believe (incorrectly) that evangelism is meant to happen primarily during the Sunday morning worship. Amazingly, just one-third of all adults contend that they personally have any responsibility or obligation to share their religious views with other people.

Most people are content to let the church do the work of spreading the religious party line. Consequently, as long as numerous churches are accessible to the populace, Christians tend to feel secure that evangelism is happening or, at least, can happen. The fact that we have about 320,000 Protestant and Catholic churches in the United States has seduced the Christian community into complacency regarding the necessity of enthusiastic, multifaceted, aggressive evangelism outside of church services.

In our well-intentioned but ultimately harmful simplification of Christian experience and responsibility, we have become accustomed to thinking of evangelism as the exclusive domain of three types of people: pastors, missionaries, and people who have the spiritual gift of evangelism.

Even if we exaggerate the numbers, we still could not honestly claim the existence of a pool of more than five million of these alleged outreach specialists. That leaves an enormous majority of Christians who feel mentally and emotionally freed from the concern and responsibility for ongoing evangelistic efforts.

Given that more than eighty million adults contend that being on the receiving end of an evangelistic pitch is "annoying" and knowing that several million born-again Christians refuse to describe themselves as born again for fear of becoming social outcasts, Christians and non-Christians alike opt for a nation in which people are free to practice their religion as long as it is done in secret (or quietly).

Public outbursts of religiosity, whether through public prayer, exhortations to operate with biblical values and principles, or interpersonal proselytizing, are looked on as evidence of inappropriate and crude behavior. In this environment, a "real Christian" is defined as a person who is compassionate enough to keep his beliefs private. And so the world's greatest gift is now faced with becoming the world's greatest secret. Many of the people whom Christ is counting on to spread the gospel have succumbed to pressures from the target population to maintain a reverent silence about a matter as personal as spiritual belief.

Rather than commit to the hardships associated with being influence agents, Christians have become influenced agents—influenced by the very society they have been called to transform with the love of Christ, for the glory of God and the benefit of those who would be transformed.

Just as Jesus's coming some two thousand years ago was no accident, we must also understand that his example (and that of the apostles) is a perfectly adaptable model for us to institute today. The apostle Paul, the world's first great itinerant evangelist, provided us with the cornerstone principle, drawn from the example of Jesus's ministry, for effectively communicating the gospel. Paul admonished the believers in the church of Corinth to contextualize the message—that is, to share the gospel with a culture so that it could be understood without compromising or reshaping the work of Christ (1 Cor. 9:19–23). The apostle understood that he was called to be a faithful messenger of a timeless message and that the message would be relevant to all people in all walks of life. He also understood that the manner in which the information was proclaimed might have to shift from one cultural context to another.

Evangelistic Truths Still Apply

Consider some of the central tenets of evangelism prepared for us in the Bible. These principles are every bit as dynamic and pertinent to us as they were to Peter, John, Matthew, James, and the rest of the ragtag army who followed Jesus and then turned their world upside down by retelling his story.

- The message is God's. The means of getting the message to those who need to hear it is people communicating through words and actions that are consistent with the lessons in the Bible.

- God can, has, and will use anybody who is open to serving him to convey the gospel. He will bless the efforts of his servants whether they are gifted as evangelizers or not.

- We are called to take advantage of opportunities to share our faith in Christ and to make the most of those opportunities. However, the act of converting a person from condemned sinner to forgiven and loved disciple of Christ is the job of the Holy Spirit. The evangelizer plays a role in the conversion process but will not be held accountable for the choices made by those who hear the gospel.

- The life of someone transformed by the reality of the gospel is a powerful attraction to a nonbeliever. Although a verbal explanation of faith is helpful toward facilitating a nonbeliever's decision to follow Christ, a verbal proclamation without a lifestyle that supports that proclamation is powerless.

- The most effective evangelists are the most obedient and committed Christians. They need not have formal theological training, a full-time position in a church, or credentials such as ordination. They need a passion for Christ, a desire to make him known to the world, and the willingness to be used in any and all situations to help usher others into the kingdom of God.

- Evangelism is the bridge we build between our love for God and our love for other people. Through the work of the Holy Spirit, through us, God can complete his transformation of a person for his purposes and glory.

- We cannot give away what we do not have. Therefore, we must be in close relationship with God and must be open to being used by him as a conduit of his grace.

- Effective outreach always involves sincere and fervent prayer that God will bless our efforts, although there is no guarantee that the nonbeliever will make the right choice.

- Knowing, trusting, and using God's Word is central to leading a person to a lifesaving faith in Jesus.

- When we intelligently share our faith with nonbelievers, it pleases God.

- Every Christian must be ready at all times and in all situations to share his or her faith in Christ with those who do not have a relationship with Christ.
- Evangelism is not meant to be limited by human convenience or preference. It is to be done with obedience and faith.
- The most effective evangelistic efforts are those that are simple and sincere.
- Evangelism that starts at the nonbeliever's point of felt need and ties the gospel into that area of need has the greatest capacity for capturing the mind and heart of the non-Christian.

There can be no denying—though some people have tried—that you and I as believers in Jesus Christ have a responsibility to share the Good News of this free gift of ultimate love with the rest of God's creation. The motivation must not be whether people are anxious to hear the gospel, but whether we have been called to deliver the message to the unbelieving world.

The Harsh Side of Success

In America today, as in many nations around the globe for centuries, success has been defined in earthly, material ways: comfort, longevity, popularity, emotional peace, intelligence, freedom, and financial independence. Increasingly, we see our country turning to the notion that it takes a combination of these conditions to achieve real success, which is sometimes mistakenly labeled as "happiness."

In heaven today, success is defined the same way Jesus Christ defined it two thousand years ago during his earthly ministry or thousands of years before that as God revealed his will to Israel. Success is faithfulness and obedience to God. Everything else is a diversion. In the end, all that matters is whether we have given God control of our lives and have been faithful to him.

As we strive to understand what faithfulness means, the Bible is our best and most authoritative source of study. Obedience is defined as:

- a personal commitment to Christ in which we acknowledge him to be our one and only Savior (see John 3:16–18)
- a personal commitment to holiness, perhaps best defined by Paul as the fruit of the Spirit (see Gal. 5:22–24; 1 Thess. 4:7)
- a personal commitment to pleasing God, not for the purpose of salvation but as a way of bringing him glory, honor, and pleasure through our obedience to his commands (see Exod. 20:1–21; Rom. 12:1–2)
- a personal commitment to consistent worship of God alone (see Matt. 4:10)

- a personal commitment to performing selfless acts of service for others, motivated by the exemplary love of Christ and conducted to reflect our love for God and his creation (see John 13:1–17)
- a personal commitment to share the Good News of Christ's sacrificial life, death, and resurrection (see Matt. 28:19)

Why have forty million people been martyred since the death of Christ? Because at least forty million people had their faith radically challenged and they refused to back down from following Christ no matter the cost of that relationship. To those saints, the very purpose of life was wrapped up in their understanding of the fullness of the Christian life. These martyrs viewed their relationship with Jesus Christ as one worth dying for. Their faith was more than a simple series of religious truths that enabled them to gain earthly riches, to be seen in the right places at the right times, or to gain new insights into human character. Their faith was the defining thread of their lives and dramatically illustrates how they defined success and purpose in life.

What do these martyrs' examples say to those of us in a different milieu, where people may be ridiculed for their public commitment to Christianity but certainly not threatened with physical death for their allegiance to Jesus Christ? Their examples represent nothing less than a standard for comparison of how deeply committed we must be to Christ, of how passionate we are to be about our faith, and of how completely we must be willing to trust in the promises of God.

Do you buy the notion, beyond a morsel of doubt, that "in all things God works for the good of those who love him, who have been called according to his purpose" (Rom. 8:28)? Do you truly believe that his grace is sufficient for you (2 Cor. 12:9)? Do you really accept the idea that the greatest end of humankind is to "love the Lord your God with all your heart and with all your soul and with all your mind" (Matt. 22:37; also see v. 38)?

Evangelism in Perspective

Evangelism, then, is one of the most important elements of being faithful and obedient to God. But it is not the only aspect that makes us valued servants of the Father. Some people may consider this a heresy, but I suggest that evangelism may not be the single most important activity in life.

Evangelism is critically important, but so are other elements of the Christian life. Christianity that focuses exclusively on evangelism and ignores the other critical factors of faithfulness is a dangerous, unbalanced Christianity. A life of devotion to Christ that does not include a focus on evangelism is similarly unbalanced.

The emphasis we place on evangelism depends on many elements: the opportunities we have, our ability to communicate clearly, our maturity as believers, the spiritual gifts and special talents God provides, and so forth. Balance, then, does not necessarily mean that you and I have to spend an equal amount of time on evangelistic efforts as, for example, on discipling, serving, praying, and worshiping.

As a useful analogy, I think about the meaning of chemical balance in a swimming pool. Could you imagine swimming in a pool comprised of equal amounts of water, chlorine, acid, ash, and each of the other key chemicals? Jump into such a concoction and you would have a memorably painful swim! The chemicals must be balanced in a way that creates a viable environment.

In the same way, leading a truly balanced Christian life requires that we understand ourselves and our calling and be true to both. As we share our faith with others, we must ensure that evangelism is coming from a heart that wants to engage in it as an act of love for God and service to humanity, and that it is done in the context of our efforts to be complete and diligent agents of God.

The Question of Relevance

Some people ask if evangelism is still relevant today. The question does not so much inquire about the utility of sharing the gospel as it questions the validity of the Christian faith for an age that is more complex and perhaps more perverse than any previous one. The question alludes to a crisis of faith rather than to a true concern about the value of exhorting others to follow Christ.

The fact that many Christians even raise such a question, however, points out the importance of a dogged commitment to balanced Christianity. People must hear the gospel proclaimed. They must study the foundations of the faith. They must see the faith through constant devotion to spiritual growth.

Evangelism is relevant only as long as the Christian faith is relevant to the people of the earth. Toward that end, I suggest that, if properly understood and explained, the gospel is equally relevant in all ages and perhaps is needed more now than ever, given the conscious depravity of our culture.

The message of God's love for his creation is more relevant than the messages communicated in today's most popular songs and movies, more relevant than the major political issues that are being debated so hotly on Capitol Hill, and more relevant than many of the decisions that seem like life or death choices at our places of work. The task that you and I have is to think and to pray about how God might use us most effectively and significantly in spreading the Good News.

Whether a need exists today for evangelism is not really the issue. Whether we will be committed to a continual and relevant presentation of the gospel to those who are not followers of Christ is the real challenge for us to accept.

7

Extraordinary Prayers

Adapted from Sharing Christ When You Feel You Can't

Daniel Owens

Becky has seen many people come to Christ through her personal witness, but according to her the key to evangelism isn't necessarily how much you know. "I've discovered that good evangelism does not always require great theological knowledge," she says. "But one thing it definitely does require is prayer. In all the opportunities I have had to speak of my faith, my strongest asset has been purposeful, daily, diligent, persevering prayer. People are not 'skins' to be caught. They are searching for answers. So, I pray that they will not run from Jesus, that they will be freed of their misconceptions of him, and most of all, that they will experience his love."

You may already pray about many different things. You may ask God's blessing on your food before every meal. You probably have prayed for other Christian brothers and sisters who have been sick or have undergone surgery. You may even pray with your kids every night before they go to bed.

But do you ever pray that someone in your neighborhood would come to know Jesus as their Savior? Have you ever prayed with your kids that their friends might trust Jesus too? Have you ever prayed that the person working next to you at your job would recognize his or her sinfulness, and that you could build a bridge into that person's life that would allow you to share the good news of the gospel?

I confess, I struggle to keep prayer a consistent part of my Christian life. I'm a highly motivated reader—I love to sit for hours and read the Bible, or other books on biblical subjects. But when it comes to prayer, I flounder.

I was with a Christian businessman awhile back who showed me his prayer journal, and I was so impressed. In this compact notebook, he kept the names of people for whom he was praying, opportunities when he had actually shared the gospel with these people, and notes about how God was answering prayer as he built bridges into their lives. He even noted when he was able to lead some of these people to Christ.

At first this man's diligence was very intimidating to me, but then I was so encouraged that he had his priorities straight about prayer. His example motivated me to pray, "Lord, help me to be more disciplined in prayer as I reach out to others."

E. M. Bounds used to say, "It is a great thing to talk to men about God. It is greater still to talk to God about men." Let me encourage you to begin to build your bridges to non-Christians through prayer. Honestly ask yourself, "Do I really pray for those who don't know the Lord? Will I pray for the members of my family, coworkers, teachers at my kids' school, neighbors, my auto mechanic, or the person who cuts my hair?" Bridges begun with prayer don't crumble like those begun without it.

We could talk all day about prayer in general, but here are a few specific areas that we should be praying about.

Pray for the Messenger

The messenger who carries the gospel to someone you know can be you, but it also could be some other Christian coming into the life of the person to whom you are building a bridge.

A woman came to me one time and said, "Dan, I've been praying for years for my son to come to Christ. I prayed that the Lord would use me to bring him to faith. For years nothing ever happened. But one day in prayer the Lord inspired me with the idea, 'Why don't you pray for someone else to come into his life? Pray for another Christian messenger who will become his friend. Some colleague, some neighbor who will share the gospel with him.'"

She continued, "I started praying that way, and several weeks later my son called and talked about a new friend that had come into his life through his work situation." The son described how he had built a new friendship with this person, and that this guy was just a bit "different."

"It was only a few weeks after that," the mother said, "that my son called back and said that he'd opened his heart to Jesus Christ—because of this new Christian friend."

That mother was not at all disappointed that someone else, and not her personally, had led her son to faith. In fact, she was thrilled! She had said as much as she could say to her son, and then God used someone else—someone she was praying for—to enter his life and lead him to the Savior.

Pray for Opportunities

We need to pray for opportunities to speak with our non-Christian friends, so that when the opportunity comes we see it as an answer to our prayer, and know that the Lord has prepared the way for our words.

Christian author, teacher, and theologian Norm Geisler relates how he was teaching in a Bible college, surrounded by only Christians day after day, when God began to teach him that he needed to do the work of an evangelist, even if he didn't have the "gift" of evangelism. An old hymn came to his mind, "Lead me to some soul today, O teach me Lord, just what to say."

Geisler later wrote, "I thought to myself: Did I ever pray that prayer? Even though I'm surrounded by Christians and don't have the gift of evangelism, did I ever actually ask God to lead me to some non-Christian? That began the change in my life toward the other direction."

The next morning Geisler prayed, "Lord, I never see a non-Christian during the daily course of activities. Lead me to someone." Just as the day was ending at the college, one of the students came up to him and said, "I am really embarrassed to bring up this question. But my pastor thinks I am, this school thinks I am, I've told everybody I am, and here I am studying for the Lord's service—and I don't think I'm a Christian. What should I do?" Geisler had the privilege of leading that young lady to Christ that afternoon, and she later became a missionary to South America.

Pray for Boldness

I need boldness. Many times the opportunity that I have been praying for comes along, and I say, "Boy, Lord, this is a great opportunity, but I think I'll pass on this one. Maybe you could bring another opportunity along later, all right?"

The Lord brings opportunities, and we need to pray for boldness to take advantage of them when they come. Our heart may well be pounding wildly when we pray, "Lord, this is a great opportunity. Help me to speak, because here I go."

Even the great apostle Paul asked his friends to pray that he would be bold in sharing the gospel. "Pray also for me, that whenever I open my mouth, words may be given me so that I will fearlessly make known the mystery of the gospel, for which I am an ambassador in chains. Pray that I may declare it fearlessly, as I should" (Ephesians 6:19–20). If Paul asked for prayer so that he could proclaim the gospel fearlessly, then I am in good company.

The Extraordinary Power of Prayer

Becky, whom I mentioned at the beginning of this chapter, had a high school friend, Steve, who confided he had a problem with alcohol. He had struggled with it since high school, never intending for it to become an addiction. He was leaving the next day to enlist in the Navy, so little was done beyond talking about the problem.

From that day, Becky began to pray for Steve. Three years later she appeared on a TV interview in the east during which she related how God had helped her overcome an addiction to alcohol years before. Steve saw her on TV that day and left a message on her office's answering machine. He had responded to her invitation to give his life to God, and he wanted to talk to her! Now Steve serves as a rehabilitation counselor for the Navy.

Amazing, isn't it? After praying for three years, Becky saw her friend come to Christ. Now she says, "Experience has shown me that without purposeful, diligent time spent with God, we will not have the purity or the passion necessary for evangelism. Once you start praying and staying alert to the people God sends into your life, God will begin to use you. You don't have to be a full-time evangelist, or even in ministry. All you need is a willingness both to know God better and to make him known."

William Carey, the great missionary to India, once said, "Work like everything depends on you. Pray like everything depends on God." If there is a "secret" to leading people to Christ, that may be it

Declaring
Your
Faith

8

Your Testimony

Sharing Your Life Message

Rick Warren

Your lives are echoing the Master's Word. . . . The news of your faith in God is out. We don't even have to say anything anymore—*you're* the message!

1 Thessalonians 1:8 Message

God has put a life message within you. When you became a believer, you also became God's messenger. God wants to speak to the world through you. Paul said, "We speak the truth before God, as messengers of God" (2 Cor. 2:17 NCV). You have a storehouse of experiences that God wants to use to bring others into his family. The Bible says, "Those who believe in the Son of God have the testimony of God in them" (1 John 5:10 GW).

There are four parts to your life message:

- your testimony—the story of how you began a relationship with Jesus
- your life lessons—the most important lessons God has taught you
- your godly passions—the issues God shaped you to care about most
- the Good News—the message of salvation

Sharing Your Testimony

Your testimony is the story of how Christ has made a difference in your life. Peter tells us that we were chosen by God "to do his work and speak out for him, to tell others of the night-and-day difference he made for you" (1 Pet. 2:9 Message).

61

This is the essence of witnessing—simply reporting your personal experiences with the Lord. In a courtroom, a witness isn't expected to argue the case, prove the truth, or press for a verdict; that is the job of attorneys. Witnesses just tell what happened to them. Jesus said, "You will be my witnesses" (Acts 1:8). He did *not* say, "You must be my attorney." He wants you to tell your story to others. Sharing your testimony is an essential part of your mission on earth, and I believe it is an essential part of being a pastor. In many ways, your personal, authentic testimony is more effective than a sermon.

Personal stories are also easier to relate to than principles, and people love to hear them. They capture our attention, and we remember them longer. Unbelievers would probably lose interest if you started quoting theologians, but they have a natural curiosity about experiences they've never had. Shared stories build a relational bridge that Jesus can walk across from your heart to theirs.

Another value of your testimony is that it bypasses intellectual defenses. Many people who won't accept the authority of the Bible will listen to a humble, personal story. That's why on six different occasions Paul used his testimony to share the gospel instead of quoting Scripture (see Acts 22–26).

The Bible says, "Be ready at all times to answer anyone who asks you to explain the hope you have in you, but do it with gentleness and respect" (1 Pet. 3:15 TEV). The best way to "be ready" is to write out your testimony and then memorize the main points.

Divide it into four parts:

1. What my life was like before I met Jesus
2. How I realized I needed Jesus
3. How I committed my life to Jesus
4. The difference Jesus has made in my life

Of course, you have many other testimonies besides your salvation story. You have a story for every experience where God has helped you. You should make a list of all the problems, circumstances, and crises that God has brought you through. Then be sensitive and use the story that your unbelieving friend will relate to best. Different situations call for different testimonies.

Sharing Your Life Lessons

The second part of your life message includes the truths that God has taught you from experiences with him. These are lessons about God, relationships, problems, temptations, and other aspects of life. David prayed, "God, teach me lessons for living so I can stay the course" (Ps. 119:33 Message).

It's sad that we never learn from a lot that happens to us. Of the Israelites, the Bible says, "Over and over God rescued them, but they never learned—until finally their sins destroyed them" (106:43 Message). You've probably met people like that.

While it is wise to learn from experience, it is wiser to learn from the experiences of others. There isn't enough time to learn everything in life by trial and error. We must learn from the life lessons of each other. The Bible says, "A warning given by an experienced person to someone willing to listen is more valuable than . . . jewelry made of the finest gold" (Prov. 25:12 TEV).

Write down the major life lessons you have learned so you can share them with others. We should be grateful Solomon did this, because it gave us the books of Proverbs and Ecclesiastes, which are filled with practical lessons on living. Imagine how much needless frustration could be avoided if we learned from each other's life lessons.

Mature people develop the habit of extracting lessons from everyday experiences. I urge you to make a list of your life lessons. You haven't really thought about them unless you have written them down.

Here are a few questions to jog your memory and get you started:

- What has God taught me from failure (Psalm 51)?
- What has God taught me from a lack of money (Phil. 4:11–13)?
- What has God taught me from pain or sorrow or depression (2 Cor. 1:4–10)?
- What has God taught me through waiting (Psalm 40)?
- What has God taught me through illness (Ps. 119:71)?
- What has God taught me from disappointment (Gen. 50:20)?
- What have I learned from my family, my church, my relationships, my small group, and my critics?

Sharing Your Godly Passions

God is a passionate God. He passionately loves some things and passionately hates other things. As you grow closer to him, he'll give you a passion for something he cares about deeply so you can be a spokesperson for him in the world. It may be a passion about a problem, a purpose, a principle, or a group of people. Whatever it is, you'll feel compelled to speak up about it and do what you can to make a difference.

You cannot keep yourself from talking about what you care about most. Jesus said, "A man's heart determines his speech" (Matt. 12:34 TLB). Two examples are:

- David, who said, "My zeal for God and his work burns hot within me" (Ps. 69:9 TLB).

- Jeremiah, who said, "Your message burns in my heart and bones, and I cannot keep silent" (Jer. 20:9 CEV).

God gives some people a godly passion to champion a cause. It's often a problem they personally experienced, such as abuse, addiction, infertility, depression, disease, or some other difficulty. Sometimes God gives people a passion to speak up for a group of others who can't speak for themselves: the unborn, the persecuted, the poor, the imprisoned, the mistreated, the disadvantaged, and those who are denied justice. The Bible is filled with commands to defend the defenseless.

God uses passionate people to further his kingdom. Don't be afraid to preach on your passions. God gives us different passions so everything he wants done in the world will get done. You should not expect everyone else to be passionate about your passion. Instead, we must listen to and value each other's life message, because nobody can say it all. Never belittle someone else's godly passion. The Bible says, "It is fine to be zealous, provided the purpose is good" (Gal. 4:18).

Sharing the Good News

What is the Good News? "The Good News shows how God makes people right with himself—that it begins and ends with faith" (Rom. 1:17 NCV). "For God was in Christ, reconciling the world to himself, no longer counting people's sins against them. This is the wonderful message he has given us to tell others" (2 Cor. 5:19 NLT). The Good News is that when we trust God's grace to save us through what Jesus did, our sins are forgiven, we get a purpose for living, and we're promised a future home in heaven.

There are hundreds of great books on how to share the Good News, but all the training in the world won't motivate you to witness for Christ until you learn to love lost people the way God does. God has never made a person he didn't love. Everybody matters to him. When Jesus stretched out his arms on the cross, he was saying, "I love you this much!" The Bible says, "For Christ's love compels us, because we are convinced that one died for all" (2 Cor. 5:14). Whenever you feel apathetic about your mission in the world, spend some time thinking about what Jesus did for you on the cross.

We must care about unbelievers because God does. Love leaves no choice. The Bible says, "There is no fear in love; perfect love drives out all fear" (1 John 4:18 TEV). A parent will run into a burning building to save a child because the love for that child is greater than the fear. If you've been afraid to share the Good News with those around you, ask God to fill your heart with his love for them.

The Bible says, "God does not want anyone to be lost, but he wants all people to change their hearts and lives" (2 Pet. 3:9 NCV). As long as you know one person who doesn't know Christ, you must keep praying for that person, serving him or her in love, and sharing the Good News. And as long as there is one person in your community who isn't in the family of God, your church must keep reaching out. The church that doesn't want to grow is saying to the world, "You can go to hell."

What are you willing to do so that the people you know will go to heaven? Invite them to church? Share your story? Take them a meal? Pray for them every day until they are saved? Your mission field is all around you. Don't miss the opportunities God is giving you. The Bible says, "Make the most of your chances to tell others the Good News. Be wise in all your contacts with them" (Col. 4:5 TLB).

Is anyone going to be in heaven because of you? Will anyone in heaven be able to say to you, "I want to thank you. I'm here because you cared enough to share the Good News with me"? Imagine the joy of greeting people in heaven whom you helped get there. The eternal salvation of a single soul is more important than anything else you'll ever achieve in life. Only people are going to last forever.

God created you to fulfill five purposes on earth: He made you to be a member of his family, a model of his character, a magnifier of his glory, a minister of his grace, and a messenger of his Good News to others. Of these five purposes, the fifth can only be done on earth. The other four you'll keep doing in eternity. That's why spreading the Good News is so important; you have only a short time to share your life message and fulfill your mission.

9

Everyday Illustrations

Sharing the Gospel Right Where You Are

Mike Silva

This is the secret of evangelism: Tell me and I will forget. Show me and I will remember. Involve me and I will understand.

It takes more than a clear understanding of the life-changing gospel message to experience the needed epiphany that comes through a picture, which we know is worth a thousand words. It's vitally important to know how to explain the basic gospel message, but is it enough to simply say the right words? More than ever, we need to shine the light on Jesus and the gospel message so others may *see*. Not unlike the first century, we live in an increasingly visual age. God has hardwired us to be visual creatures. Before people can *hear* the gospel of Jesus Christ, they need to *see* it.

Everyday Places

You don't need to travel to a Third World country to share the gospel. You can do it while opening the door for a friend as you walk into a restaurant, attending a sporting event with a co-worker, or fishing on the river with an unsaved family member. Opportunities to illustrate the Good News are all around you. For example, as you hold a door open for someone, you might remember that Jesus uses the picture of a door to illustrate the way he stands at the door of our hearts and knocks. We can stay locked inside and hope he goes away, or we can open the door and invite him in.

God can be involved in sports too. As you walk into a baseball stadium and hand your ticket to the attendant, you can reflect on what it will be like to enter heaven. This is a great opportunity to ask your companions if they have thought about their "ticket" to heaven. We might ask what would happen if God looked at us and said, "Why should I let you into my heaven? Do you have a ticket?" As a Christian, we can answer, "Yes, Sir, it is Jesus Christ—he alone is my ticket to heaven." Then our heavenly Father will say, "Come on in! And enjoy the game!"

Maybe you are the kind of person who likes to fish on a quiet river with a close friend. Jesus enjoyed being out on the lake with his disciples. You could use the fish, the boat, the rod, and many other things to start up a conversation about Jesus's life.

Whether you are indoors or out, at work or at home, exercising or relaxing around the dinner table, take a minute to look around you. An opportunity to share the greatest message of all may be presenting itself to you!

Everyday Objects

When Jesus wanted to illustrate the kingdom of heaven, he used objects that were well known to the Israelites, like a mustard seed (Matt. 13:31) or a fishing net (v. 47). You can do the same. Things you use every day can become illustrations of salvation.

Gift certificates have become popular in our society. People enjoy getting them because they can choose the gift they really want. However, one thing to remember about gift certificates is that they often come with expiration dates. A gift certificate can be worth one hundred dollars one day, and then the next day you might as well throw it in the garbage because it's expired and you've missed the opportunity to spend it.

God's gift of forgiveness is like a gift certificate that's more valuable than anything we can imagine. He paid for it with his Son's life. God is holding that priceless gift certificate out to us, waiting for us to take it. However, if we don't accept it and use it, then it's of no value to us. The next time you buy a gift certificate for someone, think about how you could use it to illustrate the greatest gift of all.

Do you know someone who enjoys reading best sellers? Every week there may be a different title at the top of the *New York Times* best-seller list, but not one of them has ever sold more copies or been printed and translated into more languages than God's Word, the Bible. The Bible is truly the number one best seller of all time—year after year, decade after decade, century after century, millennium after millennium.

The next time someone asks you what you've been reading lately, mention that you're in the middle of the world's best seller of all time. Maybe the person will want to see what all the excitement is about!

Nearly everyone has some empty boxes lying around the house or office. When I see an empty box, I often think of the way I feel about religion. Many people are "religious." They pack into their lives a load of rules and regulations that say you have to live a certain way and be a certain kind of person to please God. However, in the end, hollow religion leaves you feeling dissatisfied and empty, like an unused box.

We can be thankful that Jesus did not come to impose a religion on us. He wants a *relationship* with us. Instead of struggling to abide by a long list of dos and don'ts, trying to be good enough for heaven, we can place our trust in Jesus Christ and what he did for us on the cross.

Evangelism doesn't have to mean walking around with a big black Bible under your arm. The best witnesses are not the ones who wear T-shirts that say, "If you're not a Christian, you're going to hell!" You can be an effective witness by using items you have lying around the house to illustrate the gospel message.

Everyday Situations

Jesus never left the land where he was born. He didn't travel to the social center of the world, Rome, or make great journeys to faraway places. Instead, he took advantage of the place where God had placed him and used the situations around him to win people for the kingdom.

Don't wait for an earthquake or a national disaster like 9/11 to draw people to God. You can be God's tool today, whether you're driving in your car, walking through your neighborhood, or sitting at a restaurant. It doesn't matter if you're a construction worker, a CEO, or an elementary school teacher, God will use you right where you are.

Picture your favorite fast-food restaurant and imagine that you are standing in line to order. Not being overly hungry, you plan to order just a bacon cheese-burger. Then the person behind the counter smiles and asks, "Would you like fries with that?"

"Oh, sure," you say. Now that she mentions it, fries do sound good. Think about how many times you have ordered fries or super-sized your meal just because the person behind the counter "invited" you to do it.

In a similar way, many lost and hurting people out there are just waiting in line for an invitation—a gentle tug from a trusted friend! A friendly dinner out, a concert, or special event at your church may be just the thing to lift their spirits and get them interested in Christianity.

We've all found ourselves standing in line at a convenience store. While you wait, have you ever glanced behind the counter and been tempted to buy a lottery ticket? Every day thousands of people give in to that temptation. But did you know that the odds of winning an $84-million jackpot are 1 in 515,403,500?

Still, many people will spend several hundred dollars to purchase tickets when the jackpot gets high.

All I can say to a person who buys a lottery ticket is, "Good luck!" because that is all you have—luck. There is no guarantee you will win anything. There's not even a good chance you will win.

For the person who seeks Jesus Christ, the odds of finding him and receiving eternal life are 1 in 1. Jesus told us that *whoever* seeks him will find him!

Everyday People

When you're at an everyday place, with an everyday object, in an everyday situation, whom do you run into? Everyday people! Men and women who need to hear the gospel are all around us. They pour our coffee, they work in our offices, they bag our groceries, and they live in our neighborhoods.

Evangelism isn't difficult, but it does take effort. Here are some steps you can take:

1. Select three visuals or word pictures that you like and feel comfortable using. For ideas, see my latest book, *Would You Like Fries with That?*[1] which explains how to use more than a hundred everyday visuals to present the gospel message.
2. Practice how to use your favorite visuals to present the gospel. The best way to practice is using them with several of your Christian friends.
3. Once you master a gospel visual, use it to share the Good News with a not-yet-saved family member or friend. You might even say, "I'm trying to learn how to explain what I believe. May I share an illustration with you?" Then ask for feedback. Thank the person, especially if he or she offers any constructive criticism. More likely, the person will ask questions and may even show an interest in knowing more about the Savior.
4. Don't stop! Keep adding new visuals to your repertoire. You'll never run out of creative new ways to share the Good News.

10

Gospel Presentation

Sharing the Gospel Clearly and Effectively

Larry D. Robertson

Since "the gospel . . . is the power of God for the salvation of everyone who believes" (Rom. 1:16), it is incumbent on the Christian witness to present that gospel clearly. Of course, a person must have a clear understanding of the Christian gospel to be able to present it clearly.

The apostle Paul defined the gospel in 1 Corinthians 15:1–4 (NASB): "Now I make known to you, brethren, the gospel which I preached to you . . . that Christ died for our sins according to the Scriptures, and that He was buried, and that He was raised on the third day according to the Scriptures." In short, the gospel is the simple, historic message of Jesus's death and resurrection.

The term *gospel* literally and appropriately means "good news," since it is a message of hope, speaking to the human condition of sin and promising forgiveness, purpose, and eternal life to those who believe. But the gospel has a logical "dark side." While the gospel promises heaven to those who believe, those who reject the gospel (and consequently God's salvation) are destined for hell.

There is no set formula, no sinner's prayer per se, no mandated approach prescribed in Scripture for sharing the gospel. Every person is unique; thus it follows that not every evangelistic conversation will be the same. Certainly there are key concepts that must be communicated if we're going to be true to the gospel, but how those concepts are transferred will vary. The witness must pray for discernment and tact in every situation.

While flexibility in how we share our faith is important, witnesses must be careful in how they get decisions. We must remember that the ends don't always justify the means. Our goal is to "make disciples" (Matt. 28:19) not just get decisions.

Unfortunately, sometimes our spiritual zeal (at least I want to believe it's always spiritual) has led to disappointing evangelism results in the long term. We see people make their "decisions for Christ," but they do not go on to make a public confession of their faith through baptism (see 10:32–33) and become fully devoted followers of Christ.

I have heard more than my share of preachers defend sloppy evangelism—what Dietrich Bonhoeffer called the preaching of "cheap grace"—by contending that normally we can expect only about 25 percent of those who "pray the sinner's prayer" to follow through with baptism. Some even use Jesus's parable of the soils (13:3–8, 18–23) to prove their point! How did we ever come to think of this as normal?

Jesus's words about bearing fruit that will last (John 15:16) haunt much of our contemporary evangelism. While a multitude of factors could contribute to decisions for Christ that don't seem to last (see, for example, 1 John 2:19), clarity in the gospel presentation can only increase the quality of such decisions.

Peter's Pentecost sermon (Acts 2:14–41) presents an excellent example of the gospel being shared with clarity and effectiveness. Several distinctive features of Peter's presentation of the gospel are worthy of discussion.

Practice What You Preach

When Peter and the other apostles stood to declare the Good News of Jesus on the day of Pentecost, they did so as men whose lives had been dramatically changed by the death and resurrection of Jesus. They were so different because of the empowering of the Holy Spirit that some in the crowd accused them of being drunk! Peter began his sermon by explaining that the noticeable difference in the people was the work of God.

In most instances, we witness with our lives before we witness with our lips. So the need for authenticity and credibility in our witness cannot be overstated. Remember the old saying: "Actions speak louder than words."

St. Francis of Assisi used to say, "Preach the gospel at all times. If necessary use words." This is not to suggest that words are unnecessary but that our conduct and character contribute significantly to our effectiveness as witnesses. If what people observe in our lives contradicts what they hear from our lips, our presentation of the gospel becomes distorted.

Use Scripture

One of the most notable qualities of Peter's sermon was his use of Scripture. In other words, as he interpreted and applied the Scriptures, he presented them as authoritative. God's Word is far more powerful than human wisdom and eloquence, regardless of how innovative or creative they might seem.

The use of Scripture as we present the gospel does not necessitate a seminary degree or the use of a ten-pound Bible. Our witness can be contained in such media as conversations, gospel tracts, emails, books, websites, audio recordings, or wireless transfers between handheld computers. The point is not the medium in which the Word of God is presented but *that* the Word of God is presented. "For the word of God is living and active and sharper than any two-edged sword, and piercing as far as the division of soul and spirit, of both joints and marrow, and able to judge the thoughts and intentions of the heart" (Heb. 4:12 NASB).

Talk about Jesus

There were many topics that Peter could have addressed and many arguments that he could have made as he spoke to the crowd gathered in Jerusalem that day. He talked, though, about Jesus. But he spoke about more than Jesus's life and ministry; he emphasized Jesus's death and resurrection.

To say that a clear presentation of the gospel focuses on Jesus's death and resurrection might sound like stating the obvious, but not everyone agrees on what the gospel is. If you ask some people to define the gospel, they will tell you it is the love of God or the wrath of God. Others will describe the gospel in terms of Jesus's teachings or his ethics. Still some will describe it as service to others.

Some people try to evangelize with some other message than that of the death and resurrection of Jesus, and they do so to the detriment of their witness. Some people are offended by the facts of the gospel and prefer a "bloodless gospel" or a "nicer gospel." But the gospel is what it is. We can't re-create it or revise it. It just *is*.

The fact that *Christ died for our sins* means that Jesus made atonement for our sins as our substitute. Since our unrighteousness prevented us from satisfying God's demand for holiness and perfection, God credited Christ's righteousness to the sin debt of those who believe.

The resurrection completes the equation. The Christian faith rises or falls on the resurrection of Jesus Christ. The cross is powerless without the empty tomb. If Jesus was not raised from the dead, he was nothing more than a revolutionary martyr for his cause. But *he was raised on the third day!*

Christ's resurrection brings hope despite the terminal factor—that everyone is going to die. We know of at least three people that Jesus raised from the dead, but

Jesus was the first to be raised from the dead never to die again! The resurrection brings hope and meaning to this life and the life to come.

Never shy away from focusing on Jesus as you share your faith. Since he is *"the Savior of the world"* (John 4:42), what else could you share with a person that would be more important than the gospel story?

The Holy Spirit's Role

When men demonstrably changed by the power of the gospel presented the message with clarity, something unusual happened. People "were pierced to the heart" and cried out, "What shall we do?" (Acts 2:37 NASB). When was the last time you heard a congregation respond like that to a sermon?

Jesus said that the Holy Spirit is responsible to "convict the world of guilt in regard to sin and righteousness and judgment" (John 16:8). Methods and techniques abound to get a response out of people, but what have we accomplished if the person has no brokenness over his or her sin?

The witness must be careful not to rely on fleshly tactics but to trust in God's Spirit to convince people of their need for Christ. Peter declared the truth of the gospel, trusted the Holy Spirit to convict, and saw three thousand people become followers of Christ in one day! Today's witness must share the gospel with clarity and trust the Holy Spirit to bring conviction.

The Invitation

When the crowd asked what they should do in response to the gospel message, Peter called them to repentance and public confession of Jesus as Savior and Lord. Often the invitation is the point at which many evangelistic conversations fall apart. Many witnesses can share the facts of the gospel with clarity and conviction, but they falter when it comes time to invite the person to receive Christ.

The story has been told that Henry Ford had a friend who was in the insurance business. When Mr. Ford bought a million-dollar policy from another agent, his friend asked him why he had not purchased the policy from him. Mr. Ford replied, "You didn't ask."

The message of Jesus's death and resurrection, by necessity, begs for a response. The invitation, therefore, is the logical and practical conclusion to the presentation of the gospel. The goal of the gospel witness, however, is far more than simply getting people to pray a prayer. The goal is for people to turn *from* their sin and *to* God (Acts 26:20). By necessity, therefore, to be saved, a person must grasp at least three concepts: sin, repentance, and lordship. The terms, as such, may not be used, but the concepts must be understood.

Jesus said that repentance is a nonnegotiable in salvation: "I tell you, no! But unless you repent, you too will all perish" (Luke 13:5). But how can people repent if they have no awareness or understanding of their sin? And the confession of Jesus as Lord mandates a surrender to his lordship (see 6:46). Thus repentance is turning away *from* sin and turning *to* God in surrendered faith.

While presenting the gospel message is intimidating to many witnesses, it need not be. Evangelism can be (and should be) a natural, normal part of every believer's Christian experience. The gospel can be weaved into virtually any conversation. Scripted gospel presentations can be helpful, but many witnesses have experienced the frustration of memorizing and reciting gospel monologues. Still, having direction in our conversations is a good idea.

Remember, not every evangelistic conversation will be the same. Be careful that the witness of your life does not contradict the witness of your lips. Use Scripture as you focus on Jesus's death and resurrection. And trust the Holy Spirit to bring conviction as you urge the person to receive the gospel. "How beautiful are the feet of those who bring good news!" (Rom. 10:15).

11

The Scriptures

The Power That Transforms Willing Lives

Floyd Schneider

At sixty, Max was still working as a mountain guide leading groups into the Austrian mountains. He didn't want to come to the church. He wasn't saved yet, but we did finally talk him into coming to our weekly Bible study in the Gospel of John. His salvation came gradually, as God's Word bored deep into his heart. When he finally did get saved, he told us that the Bible study had made him realize that he had been seeking God for a long time. Eventually, through more Bible reading, it became clear to him that God had been seeking Max!

Leading Us to Salvation

God wants to save everyone. "God our Savior . . . wants all men to be saved and to come to a knowledge of the truth" (1 Tim. 2:3–4) Where do the Scriptures enter into God's plan to bring people to himself? There are four parts to the answer.

First, the Lord told the Samaritan woman that God is seeking a certain kind of people to worship him. "True worshipers will worship the Father in spirit and truth, for they are the kind of worshipers the Father seeks" (John 4:23). Although God wants everyone to be saved, Proverbs 8:17 emphasizes God's passion for seekers: "I love those who love me; and those who diligently seek me will find me" (NASB).

Second, no one seeks God on his own initiative. "The LORD looks down from heaven on the sons of men to see if there are any who understand, any who seek

God. All have turned aside, they have together become corrupt" (Ps. 14:2–3). Therefore, Jesus sends the Holy Spirit to draw the unsaved to himself. "When [the Holy Spirit] comes, he will convict the world of guilt in regard to sin and righteousness and judgment" (John 16:8). Both the Lord Jesus and the Holy Spirit are of the same essence; they are both God. If a person reacts favorably to the Holy Spirit, that person will do the same with the Lord Jesus. The drawing of the Holy Spirit makes it possible for every human being to begin to seek God. Then man's God-given free will must decide. What do I really want in life? Do I *want* to have the void in my heart filled?

Third, the Holy Spirit inspired the text of the Bible (2 Pet. 1:21). The term *inspired* (NASB) or *God-breathed* (NIV) in 2 Timothy 3:16 means literally that God "breathed out" the words that the apostles used to write the text of Scripture. The Bible is the only book that God has ever written directly. The Bible is the only supernatural book in the world. The Muslim Qur'an, the Hindu scriptures, the Book of Mormon, and every other piece of religious literature are all dead writings that keep people in darkness. The Bible alone is alive and has the power to change a heart and draw a person to Christ.

> For the word of God is living and active and sharper than any two-edged sword, and piercing as far as the division of soul and spirit, of both joints and marrow, and able to judge the thoughts and intentions of the heart. And there is no creature hidden from His sight, but all things are open and laid bare to the eyes of Him with whom we have to do.
>
> Hebrews 4:12–13 NASB

The Holy Spirit wields the Scriptures like a knight uses a sword. The sword slices through the thoughts and intents of the heart, revealing to the unbeliever his problem of sin deep within his soul. It wakes him up to the fact that he is spiritually dead to God.

Fourth, the Holy Spirit uses the Scriptures to draw people to Christ. We want people to come to Jesus, but we can't invite them to our house and introduce them to him physically, as Matthew did (Luke 5:29). However, since the Holy Spirit inspired the Bible, the Bible is God's supernatural tool that he uses to introduce people to Jesus. If a person rejects the Bible, he is rejecting the witness of the Holy Spirit in his life.

We have discovered in our ministry of evangelism and church planting that people who reject the Bible—who do not want to read it or take it seriously—also reject anything that we tell them about God or the Lord Jesus. We discovered that the way people react to the Bible shows us if they are seeking God or not. In some cases we gave the gospel to people without first showing them the verses in the Bible. When they responded positively to the gospel message, they wanted to start reading the Bible immediately.

God is seeking seekers. He draws seekers to himself through the Scriptures, and by using the Scriptures we can discover who they are.

Sanctifying Believers

The Lord uses the Scriptures in a second way in evangelism. The apostle John writes, "Dear friends, now we are children of God, and what we will be has not yet been made known. But we know that when he appears, we shall be like him, for we shall see him as he is" (1 John 3:2). The process whereby the believer reaches this incomparable finished product is called sanctification, and the Scriptures play a crucial role in this process.

"From infancy you have known the holy Scriptures, which are able to make you wise for salvation through faith in Christ Jesus" (2 Tim. 3:15). This salvation refers to the three-step process of moving from our unregenerate state to perfection in heaven. The first step occurs when a person accepts Christ as her Savior. This step frees the believer from the penalty of sin. The second stage of salvation, the process of sanctification, frees the believer from the power of sin. The third step, arriving in heaven, frees the believer from the presence of sin.

During the second stage of a believer's salvation, God has more in mind than the believer becoming a better person. Once we accept Christ as Savior, we begin to change. The Holy Spirit begins working in us to produce the fruit of the Spirit: love, joy, peace, patience, kindness, goodness, faithfulness, gentleness, and self-control (Gal. 5:22–23). Our sin nature has been nailed on the cross with the Lord Jesus, and God has given us his nature. "You may participate in the divine nature and escape the corruption in the world caused by evil desires" (2 Pet. 1:4). Now the battle begins!

As the believer struggles to obey God, Jesus reveals himself to him or her through the Scriptures. This stimulates the believer to change. "Therefore, putting aside all malice and all deceit and hypocrisy and envy and all slander, like newborn babies, long for the pure milk of the *word*, so that by it you may grow in respect to salvation" (1 Pet. 2:1–2 NASB).

When this transformation begins to take place, unsaved relatives and friends begin to notice the changes in the believer's speech, behavior, and attitude. And because these changes are supernatural, they can't be overlooked. The world will not understand what has happened to the believer, but these relatives and friends will begin to ask questions. Now the new believer will have the opportunity to reach others, fulfilling God's first purpose! "Sanctify Christ as Lord in your hearts, always being ready to make a defense to everyone who asks you to give an account for the hope that is in you, yet with gentleness and reverence" (3:15 NASB).

As the believer grows more and more in knowledge of the Scriptures, the Word becomes "profitable for teaching, for reproof, for correction, for training in righteousness; so that the man of God may be adequate, equipped for every good work" (2 Tim. 3:16–17 NASB). At some point in the believer's growth process, he or she will discover an ability to do what Apollos did when he was witnessing to the Jews: "demonstrating by the Scriptures that Jesus was the Christ" (Acts 18:28 NASB).

I sat in Max's kitchen, drinking tea and eating Austrian pastries. He had just finished explaining how every single one of his family members had recognized that he had changed. He told me that he hadn't noticed the change so much, until his relatives began pointing things out. He no longer cursed. He no longer lied about his exploits in the mountains. He had become far more hospitable and giving. And his family had become divided. Some had started to hate him. Some had begun reading the Bible with him.

God's cycle continues.

The Scriptures transform lives. Using any method possible, persuade your unsaved friends and relatives to saturate their minds with God's Word. The Holy Spirit will do the rest.

Defending
Your
Faith

12

Welcome Common Questions

Four Questions I've Encountered While Witnessing

Jay Strack

God knows our faith will be questioned. In 1 Peter 3:15 we are told to "set apart Christ as Lord. Always be prepared to give an answer to everyone who asks you to give the reason for the hope that you have. But do this with gentleness and respect." Many Christians are intimidated by the questions thrown at them by unsaved friends and family. How can we have an answer to every question? How can we respond without destroying relationships?

Types of Questions

To give defense with meekness we can't be discouraged or distracted by the questions we are asked. Instead, anticipate the following types of questions that true seekers will ask:

- *Smoke screen questions.* Many times people will ask a question to get the pressure or conviction off themselves. If you haven't been asked already, it won't be long before you are faced with the old "What about the people in Africa? What about life on other planets? Do you believe in evolution?" Often these are all smoke screen questions—questions people ask even when they aren't interested in the answers—but you can use the answers to these questions to touch on important issues.

- *Seasonal questions.* Certain questions come at specific times of the year. For example, Christmas and Easter precipitate questions concerning the virgin birth and the resurrection of the dead. Halloween may bring up questions of evil. As a resident of Florida, I'm often asked during hurricane season why bad things happen to good people.
- *Current events and pop culture questions.* World and national events can also bring about questions. When America is involved in a war, a frequent question is whether a Christian should serve in the military. A new book, movie, or television program can also spark questions. In the 1980s Erich von Daniken's *Chariots of the Gods* caused people to wonder about aliens and how life on other planets would affect Christian beliefs. More recently we've been faced with questions streaming from Dan Brown's work of fiction *The Da Vinci Code*, which claims that Jesus and Mary Magdalene were married and had a child.

Second Timothy 2:15 says, "Do your best to present yourself to God as one approved." This means we need to study and learn God's Word, but we can't expect to have every answer. When I've been faced with a question that I'm unable to answer completely, I admit that I don't have all the information, but because I care about the person asking the question, I will go to others or spend more time in study to get a more complete answer. For now, we will concentrate on the four common questions I've been asked when talking to others about Christ.

The Four Common Questions

1. *Do you honestly believe in the virgin birth?*
Our first question is often a seasonal question; however, it's not asked just around Christmas. Larry King has interviewed Billy Graham on several occasions. On one particular show Billy Graham asked Larry, "If you were able to interview Jesus face-to-face and could ask only one question, what would you ask?"

Larry King responded without hesitation, "I would ask him, 'Were you born of a virgin?'"

Billy Graham was a bit surprised. "If you don't mind my asking, why would that be the question?"

"Well," Larry replied, "if he was born of a virgin, that would answer all the other questions I had."

As a Christian, I believe you need to be prepared to respond to this common question. The first time I encountered this question was in my early twenties while I was a student at Charleston Southern. I was speaking to various groups around the Southeast and was called to speak to a large assembly at the University of Florida. It intimidated me somewhat to speak to my peers and the professors at the university, but I faced the challenge. After giving my presentation, a professor stood and complimented me, and then he asked a question. "I understand that you are going to school in South Carolina. What if a young girl from North Carolina came down out of the mountains, was obviously pregnant, and claimed that she'd never been with a man—would you believe her?" The people in the room started snickering because they knew what he was getting at.

My reply to the professor was honest. I told him that because of my background I don't tend to trust people without some sort of proof, so I'd probably not believe the girl. However, because my wife and I place a high value on life—both unwed mothers and their unborn children—we would offer to help her. When the child was born, I would keep my eye on the child to see if there really was anything extraordinary about him. If he started performing miracles, speaking like no other child had spoken, acting like no other man had acted, lived and died in an extraordinary way, and then rose from the dead . . . well, I would have to be man enough to admit that I must have been wrong because there was no way an ordinary man fathered this child.

We must keep in mind when answering this question that the proof that Jesus was the Son of God is not just in the words of Mary but in the remarkable life he led. Jesus had no equal. And if God could create man out of dust and create the entire world around us, why should it be beyond our comprehension that he's also able to cause a young lady to be with child?

2. What about those who have never heard the gospel?

When we look at the mind and heart of God expressed through the Bible, we easily discover that he is more concerned about people than we are. In Matthew 10:29–31 we read: "Are not two sparrows sold for a penny? Yet not one of them will fall to the ground apart from the will of your Father. And even the very hairs of your head are all numbered. So don't be afraid; you are worth more than many sparrows." And in 2 Peter 3:9 we read: "The Lord is not slow in keeping his promise, as some understand slowness. He is patient with you, not wanting anyone to perish, but everyone to come to repentance." God places a high value on men and women. It is his promise that everyone has the opportunity to choose to live with him in eternity.

After the disciples met the resurrected Christ, they had a passion to tell the world about him. The longest continual Christian church can be traced back to Acts 8 when Philip led a man of Ethiopia to the Lord and baptized him. Thomas is credited with bringing Christianity to the people of India. And in Acts 2:5 on the day of Pentecost, "there were staying in Jerusalem God-fearing Jews from every nation under heaven." God is concerned for people of all nations, which is why we are told to go into the world and make disciples.

Being mindful of what I shared at the start of the chapter about smoke screen questions, when I'm asked the question about those who have never heard the gospel, I often say that I am touched by the person's care about others, but my first concern is her need for Jesus. I suggest that she allow me to lead her in the sinner's prayer, follow through with discipleship, and then we can both go into mission work. If the person is not willing to be saved, how can she lead others to be saved? It's like the person who doesn't know how to swim, standing on the shore, helplessly watching others being swallowed by the riptide. It doesn't matter how concerned you are; you aren't able to help.

3. *So where does evolution come in?*

When I first became a Christian, this was the question that caused me the most concern. Having been taught in the public schools about evolution, I wasn't sure how it worked with what the Bible was telling me. It was difficult for me to get my mind around it, so I understand why this is an important issue for many.

After looking at the explanations for evolution that were offered and comparing them with the truths of the Bible, I easily came to the conclusion that the Bible was right. Now, when I'm asked this question, I answer with my own question: Have you read Darwin's *Origin of the Species*? Every time I read Darwin's work I have a curious habit. I get a highlighter and mark certain words and phrases: *maybe, perhaps, could have been, seems to be, plausible, feasible,* and *possible*. These words and phrases appear 188 times. This book has been long considered a basis for evolution; however, you can't build a solid argument on that many *maybe*s and *could have been*s.

In comparison, the Bible states more than two thousand times "thus says the Lord." And the Bible can be used as an authority on science. The Scripture says in Isaiah 40:22 that the Lord sits above the circle of the earth. This was written seven hundred years before Christ and thousands of years before people began to really believe that the earth was round.

You probably don't want to get into a scientific debate, however, or a game of "he said-she said." Back when I was a seeker and asked this question of a wise man of faith, he replied, "Are you more worried about where you came from or where you are headed?"

4. *Do I have to go to church to worship God?*

The New Testament word translated "church" is *ekklesia*, which is derived from two words: *ek*, meaning "out," and *kaleō*, meaning "to call." Originally, it referred to an assembly of people "called out" from their homes to a gathering place for discussion. In time it was applied to Christians who gathered for public worship and discussion of Christian issues. A popular definition today for the local church is a body of baptized believers in Jesus Christ who band together to carry out Christ's commission.

The word *church* is used many times in the New Testament. In several instances it refers to the total body of redeemed believers; however, the word is often used for local congregations meeting regularly for worship. The church is God's appointed instrument for fulfilling the Great Commission—by preaching, teaching, discipling, baptizing, and ministering (Matt. 28:19–20). We read in 1 Timothy 3:15

that the church is also "the pillar and foundation of the truth." In the Scriptures the church is called a body (1 Cor. 12:12–31), a building (Eph. 2:19–22), and a bride (2 Cor. 11:2; Rev. 19:7).

Not everyone who belongs to a visible church is a true Christian, but every Christian should belong to a visible New Testament church, that is, a congregation of believers. A description of a New Testament church is given in Acts 2:40–47. In Hebrews 10:25 we are instructed to "not give up meeting together, as some are in the habit of doing." To be a Christian is to follow Christ's example. In Luke 4:16 we see that "on the Sabbath day he went into the synagogue, as was his custom. And he stood up to read." Jesus went to a building, a place of worship. In this act Jesus is our great example.

The Need for Meekness

No matter what questions you are asked, always remember to treat the person asking with dignity and respect. Don't try to belittle a seeker. Remember that you were once a seeker yourself. Use your own examples, experiences, and questions to bring God's promise to your friends and family in an exciting and welcoming way. The only way we learn is by asking questions, and as Christians, our main goal should be to help others learn about the promises we have in Christ.

If you question your urgency to share with others about Christ, give yourself the following test:

1. Am I grateful for what the Lord Jesus Christ did for me on the cross and through his bodily resurrection? Do I understand that he did something for me that I did not deserve, nor could I ever repay?
2. Do I believe the Scripture when it teaches that life is tissue-paper thin and there are consequences to being separated from God? Does this truth break my heart for those who don't know Christ?

I have found that a testimony with sincere tears is the most powerful witness. "He who wins souls is wise" (Prov. 11:30).

13

When You Have the Answers

Adapted from More than a Carpenter

―

Josh McDowell

The distinct claims of Jesus to be God eliminate the popular ploy of skeptics who regard Jesus as just a good moral man or a prophet who said a lot of profound things. So often this conclusion is passed off as the only one acceptable to scholars or as the obvious result of the intellectual process. The trouble is, many people nod their heads in agreement and never see the fallacy of such reasoning.

It was of fundamental importance to Jesus who men and women believed him to be. To say what Jesus said and to claim what he claimed about himself, one couldn't conclude he was just a good moral man or prophet. This conclusion is not possible, and Jesus never intended it to be.

C. S. Lewis, who was a professor at Cambridge University and once an agnostic, understood this issue clearly. He writes:

> I am trying here to prevent anyone saying the really foolish thing that people often say about him: "I'm ready to accept Jesus as a great moral teacher, but I don't accept his claim to be God." That is the one thing we must not say. A man who was merely a man and said the sort of things Jesus said would not be a moral teacher. He would be either a lunatic—on a level with the man who says he is a poached egg—or else he would be the Devil of hell. You must make your choice. Either this man was, and is, the Son of God: or else a madman or something worse.[1]

Jesus claimed to be God. He didn't leave any other option open. His claim must be either true or false, so it is something that should be given serious consideration.

Jesus's question to his disciples, "Who do you say I am?" (Matt. 16:15), has three possible responses.

First, consider that his claim to be God was false. If it was false, then we have two and only two alternatives. Either he knew it was false or he didn't know it was false. We will consider each one separately and examine the evidence. Then we must consider the possibility that his claim to be God was true.

Was He a Liar?

If when Jesus made his claims, he knew that he was not God, then he was lying and deliberately deceiving his followers. But if he was a liar, then he was also a hypocrite because he told others to be honest, whatever the cost, while he himself taught and lived a colossal lie. More than that, he was a demon, because he told others to trust him for their eternal destiny. If he couldn't back up his claims and knew it, then he was unspeakably evil. Last, he would also be a fool, because it was his claims to being God that led to his crucifixion.

Many will say that Jesus was a good moral teacher. Let's be realistic. How could he be a great moral teacher and knowingly mislead people at the most important point of his teaching—his own identity?

You would have to conclude logically that he was a deliberate liar. This view of Jesus, however, doesn't coincide with what we know either of him or of the results of his life and teachings. Wherever Jesus has been proclaimed, lives have been changed for the good, nations have changed for the better, thieves have become honest, alcoholics have been cured, hateful individuals have become channels of love, and unjust persons have become just.

If Jesus wanted to get people to follow him and believe in him as God, why did he go to the Jewish nation? Why go as a Nazarene carpenter to a country so small in size and population that so thoroughly adhered to the undivided unity of God? Why didn't he go to Egypt or, even more logical, to Greece, where they believed in various gods and various manifestations of them?

Someone who lived as Jesus lived, taught as Jesus taught, and died as Jesus died could not have been a liar.

Was He a Lunatic?

If it is inconceivable that Jesus was a liar, then couldn't he actually have thought himself to be God but been mistaken? After all, it's possible to be both sincere and wrong. But we must remember that for someone to think himself God, especially in a fiercely monotheistic culture, and then to tell others that their eternal destiny depended on believing in him, is no slight flight of fantasy but the thoughts of a lunatic in the fullest sense. Was Jesus Christ such a person?

Someone who believes he is God sounds like someone today believing he is Napoleon. He would be deluded and self-deceived, and he would probably be locked up so he wouldn't hurt himself or anyone else. Yet in Jesus we don't observe the abnormalities and imbalance that usually go along with being deranged. His poise and composure were certainly amazing if he were insane.

In light of the other things we know about Jesus, it's hard to imagine that he was mentally disturbed. Here is a man who spoke some of the most profound sayings ever recorded. His instructions have liberated many individuals in mental bondage. Clark H. Pinnock asks, "Was he deluded about his greatness, a paranoid, an unintentional deceiver, a schizophrenic? Again, the skill and depth of his teachings support the case only for his total mental soundness. If only we were as sane as he!"[2] A student at a California university told me that his psychology professor had said in class that "all he has to do is pick up the Bible and read portions of Christ's teaching to many of his patients. That's all the counseling they need."

Psychiatrist J. T. Fisher states:

If you were to take the sum total of all authoritative articles ever written by the most qualified of psychologists and psychiatrists on the subject of mental hygiene—if you were to combine them and refine them and cleave out the excess verbiage—if you were to take the whole of the meat and none of the parsley, and if you were to have these unadulterated bits of pure scientific knowledge concisely expressed by the most capable of living poets, you would have an awkward and incomplete summation of the Sermon on the Mount. And it would suffer immeasurably through comparison. For nearly two thousand years the Christian world has been holding in its hands the complete answer to its restless and fruitless yearnings. Here . . . rests the blueprint for successful human life with optimism, mental health, and contentment.[3]

C. S. Lewis writes:

The historical difficulty of giving for the life, sayings and influence of Jesus any explanation that is not harder than the Christian explanation is very great. The discrepancy between the depth and sanity . . . of his moral teaching and the rampant megalomania which must lie behind his theological teaching unless he is indeed God has never been satisfactorily explained. Hence the non-Christian hypotheses succeed one another with the restless fertility of bewilderment.[4]

Philip Schaff reasons: "Is such an intellect—clear as the sky, bracing as the mountain air, sharp and penetrating as a sword, thoroughly healthy and vigorous, always ready and always self-possessed—liable to a radical and most serious delusion concerning his own character and mission? Preposterous imagination!"[5]

Is He Lord?

Personally I cannot conclude that Jesus was a liar or a lunatic. The only other alternative is that he was the Christ, the Son of God, as he claimed.

When I discuss this with most Jewish people, it's interesting how they respond. They usually tell me that Jesus was a moral, upright, religious leader, a good man, or some kind of prophet. I then share with them the claims Jesus made about himself and then the material in this chapter on the trilemma (liar, lunatic, or Lord). When I ask if they believe Jesus was a liar, there is a sharp "No!" Then I ask, "Do you believe he was a lunatic?" The reply is, "Of course not." "Do you believe he is God?" Before I can get a breath in edgewise, there is a resounding "Absolutely not." Yet one has only so many choices.

The issue with these three alternatives is not which is possible, for it is obvious that all three are possible. But rather, the question is, Which is more probable? Who you decide Jesus Christ is must not be an idle intellectual exercise. You cannot put him on the shelf as a great moral teacher. That is not a valid option. He is either a liar, a lunatic, or Lord and God. You must make a choice. "But," as the apostle John wrote, "these have been written so that you may believe that Jesus is the Christ, the Son of God; and"—more important— "that believing you may have life in His name" (John 20:31 NASB).

The evidence is clearly in favor of Jesus as Lord. Some people, however, reject this clear evidence because of the moral implications involved. They don't want to face up to the responsibility or implications of calling him Lord.

14

When You Don't Have the Answers

Adapted from How to Respond to a Skeptic

Lewis Drummond

In a university philosophy class, a mismatched debate erupted between the professor and a freshman. The professor had been lecturing for several days on various world religions. In this particular discourse, Christianity became the topic. He made it clear he was not a believing Christian as he spiced up his lecture with irreverent jokes and sarcastic comments about the Christian position.

Most of the students laughed at the professor's clever and caustic comments about what he called the "myth of faith." Even though I was a Christian and something of a trained debater, I offered no defense. I simply sat and listened transfixed, perhaps a little chagrined, by the professor's sophisticated and pungent oratory. Suddenly, however, a freshman girl in the class surprised us all. Although she had said absolutely nothing during the previous six weeks of class discussion, this day she dramatically broke her silence and triggered a confrontation with the professor by asking him a simple yet quite profound question: "Why are you so biased against the Christian religion?"

The professor, noticeably startled by her blunt, forthright question, paused for a moment. He then replied in a courteous but slightly condescending manner, "Well, as far as I can tell, Christianity and all religions are nothing but mythological, illogical philosophies that are beyond belief."

Perhaps he thought that would end the conversation, but the girl pressed on undaunted. In a calm yet passionate voice she said, "What I believe may seem foolish to you, but to me it is far more true than anything I have heard or read in this class."

"Okay," the professor responded, "let's talk about your faith." It resulted in a question and answer period of unusual intensity on the part of the combatants and unusual interest on the part of the class. The professor sat down on his desk and posed the question, "Do you really believe in someone you cannot see? If so, surely you realize that you are not being scientific but simply superstitious."

The student answered immediately, "Can you deny that the wind is real? Can you see the wind? You believe it is real because you feel its effect. Maybe not in the same way, but I feel God's effect on my life. I can see the fingerprints he has left on the world: the beauty of nature, the songs and tunes. There is no other way the universe could exist without a God who made it all. You talk of science, but there is no purely scientific explanation for Christian experience, for beauty, for music, for intelligence, for love, and for the very first cause of the universe itself. But these things are real, and the Bible explains what science does not."

What a mouthful, I mused, *and quite truthful; what will the professor say now?*

There was no rebuttal to the student's lengthy answer; rather, a second question was posed: "I suppose you believe in obeying archaic Victorian morality as part of your Christian beliefs?"

The freshman hesitated before saying, "If you are referring to moral laws like the Ten Commandments, then I do believe in them; but I am not sure that is the same thing as Victorian morality. I believe we should do our best to obey God's moral laws as we must obey scientific laws. When you break a scientific law you hurt yourself, and when you break a moral law, you hurt yourself. More than five thousand years of history show that when societies honor the Ten Commandments, they usually prosper, and when they do not, they normally decay and fall. This fact is a partial explanation why our own campus is plagued with problems of dishonesty, drugs, alcohol, and venereal disease. If the Ten Commandments were obeyed, would we have these problems?"

The professor challenged the student's historical analysis. He also tried to score some points by thrusting her in a corner with a reference to the German Christian pastor Dietrich Bonhoeffer, who involved himself in the plot to assassinate Adolf Hitler. "Was he justified in ignoring the prohibition against killing?" the professor asked. "If not, are not the commandments too inflexible?"

Just when it seemed the student was going down for the count, she came up swinging: "I am not familiar with the Bonhoeffer affair, but as a Christian I believe there are basic rules of morality just as there are basic rules of grammar. But when I read the Bible I do not feel that I must wear a straitjacket. What I need is a God-guided conscience that will help me in my real-life situation."

After a few minutes of lingering debate over morality, the professor turned the topic with another question: "Do you believe in immortality? If so, how can you believe that we who die and decay can live again?"

"I do and I can," came the reply. With a sense of exasperation the professor declared, "This is unbelievable! It simply means you have never faced the finality of death."

A long, tense silence followed. Then, with tears glistening in her eyes, the young girl stunned the class: "Sir, both of my parents were killed in a car accident last year. I watched as their bodies were lowered into the grave. I cried and cried. And then I cried some more. It still hurts deeply when I think about it; but I know that my father and mother were more than a few pieces of mangled flesh and bones. They were human beings. And just as energy cannot be destroyed, life cannot by destroyed. Physically we die, but there is much more to life than that. During this time I experienced something that you may not understand but something that you and no one else can deny. That something was the 'peace that passes all understanding.' God made all the difference in the world to me then. He does now."

That ended the discussion. A telling witness for Christ had been made, even if all the questions were not fully answered.

It may sound rather incredible. I too was amazed by the incident, but that is the way it actually happened. As a timid "silent debater," I was never the same after hearing an unsophisticated but earnest girl for all practical purposes out-debate her professor. True, there were some "holes" in her arguments. A sophisticated, argumentative philosopher could have latched on to them. But she tried—and her arguments were not too bad. The point is, every person probably left class that day having a higher opinion of Christianity. No one may have been directly converted as a result of the student's stand, but everyone heard an unashamed Christian challenge the arguments of a good but skeptical thinker. And that in itself may well have given birth to many second thoughts and a new curiosity about the things of God. If that occurred, a successful witness had taken place.

That is what all believers must learn to do—even if they are not philosophical or very able in argumentation. And it can be done. People can, in love, be helped to reevaluate their position and become more open to the gospel of Jesus Christ. But should Christians really attempt to witness if people are blasé and skeptical?

Why Witness?

Whether or not we find witnessing comfortable, there is a rapidly increasing and compelling need for believers to have the courage and ability to defend and commend the Christian faith to the doubter. The reason is obvious. We are living in an age of escalating skepticism, humanism, scientism, and materialism where more and more people have difficulty believing in a God they cannot see. Not only that, many doubters and unbelievers feel that the church, although it is a believing community, is not a thinking community. Consequently, the skeptical thinker may assume he has to surrender his mind to believe in the God of the Bible.

Also we must honestly face, as Langdon Gilkey points out in his book *Naming the Whirlwind*, that even in our churches there are those with serious doubts.[1] All this points to the compelling need to learn how to answer doubting questions. That is why we should learn to witness effectively to the skeptic.

The church needs concerned Christians who possess some expertise in presenting helpful answers to the arguments against their faith. Our responsibility is to offer some sensible reasons for what we believe. The apostle Peter stated it: "Sanctify Christ as Lord in your hearts, always being ready to make a defense to everyone who asks you to give an account for the hope that is in you, yet with gentleness and reverence" (1 Pet. 3:15 NASB). If people choose to ignore or reject Christ after being confronted with the reasonableness of Christianity, then it is their responsibility. But they have the right to hear a coherent presentation of the faith. That puts the burden on us who believe. Our responsibility is to help them work through their honest doubts. Until that is done, we are to that extent culpable for their rejection of Christ. Therefore, we must try to answer whatever doubt or skepticism separates them from a saving knowledge of Jesus Christ. This brings us to the second basic question: How do we carry out our responsibility?

How to Witness

Answering skeptical doubters involves not only knowing *what* to say but *how* to say it. In the first place, a Christian must pray for God's guidance, patience, and understanding; this goes without saying. Anyone who would communicate Christ effectively must do it in the wisdom and power of the Spirit of Christ—and with love and concern. Mere argument rarely convinces or wins anyone, especially if a person is close-minded and his doubts are not truly *honest* doubts. Our argumentation will rarely touch or move such a person. Quite often this brand of skeptic has some sort of moral problem and, rather than face it, tends to retreat into skepticism.

Many, it seems, reject Christ because they still prefer to remain in sin and refuse the leadership of Jesus in their lives. If this situation persists, their doubts and skepticism are hardly honest, which is another problem to be dealt with forthrightly. But if a person has honest doubts, we believers can help. Through God's guidance and loving patience, we can find a way into the very heart, mind, and soul of the sincere skeptic. To reach this person, therefore, we must learn to identify with the problems he or she expresses. This is what love demands.

Moreover, the incarnation, "God with us," is not a mere theological proposition; it is a practical principle to be understood and applied. As Christ became flesh to reach out and save us, we must exemplify the same attitude. To impact others, a willingness to identify with them in the spirit of the incarnation is vital. The challenge for all Christians is to thrust ourselves in the worst of all places—among the poorest of the poor, the sickest of the sick, the loneliest of the lonely, and the most skeptical of the skeptics—just as Jesus did.

Often we Christians seem to be too interested in protecting ourselves from every form of pain and doubt. Instead, we should find ourselves in the poverty-stricken ghettos, pain-wrenched hospitals, and doubt-ridden circles of the skeptics wherever they are found. Picking up one's cross and following Christ results in experiencing the joys, sorrows, faith, and doubts of people whom we seek to reach and touch with God's love. There is no cross without identification and no identification without sacrifice.

An Answer for the Skeptic

It is not easy to learn how to identify with and talk to a skeptic. Paul Tournier said, "Listen to the conversations of the world. They are, for the most part, dialogues of the deaf. A person speaks in order to set forth his own ideas, in order to justify himself, in order to enhance himself."[2] Is this what the skeptic sees in the witnessing of high-pressure Christians? Hopefully not! We are to be willing to listen to and empathize with people. Paul Tournier knows that communicating effectively with people requires Christian sensitivity in which one identifies with "the innumerable throng of men and women laden down with their secrets, fears, sufferings, sorrows, disappointments and guilts."[3] To reach the doubter demands that we become genuinely concerned with the flesh-and-blood skeptic.

In learning how to share with the skeptic, the foundational question we face is why so many reasonable, able, and thinking people—not to mention many who are less able—have been so dogmatic in their denunciation of belief in God. For example, Thomas Edison declared that "religion is all bunk."[4] Edison's denunciation seems quite unreasonable when he admitted how little he knew about the universe. He stated, "We don't know the millionth part of one per cent about anything. We don't know what water is. We don't know what light is. We don't know what gravitation is. We don't know what electricity is. We don't know what heat is. We have a lot of hypotheses about these things, but that is all."[5] Yet he outright denied the Christian faith. Why? The answer to that fundamental question is first found by seeking to understand the heart, mind, and inner soul of such skeptical personalities. Something has brought them to their doubts. Some experience—probably negative—gave birth to their skepticism. Therefore, we must try to grasp their subjective philosophy, that is, their personal convictions.

John Warren Steen, in his book *Conquering Inner Space*, cites several possible reasons people become skeptics. He gives examples such as the absence of a child-father relationship, a rebellion against an overly strict home, disillusionment with organized religion, excessive egocentricity, a genuine problem reconciling the reality of evil with a good God, and so on.[6] Once we penetrate the surface of what we may perceive as hard-boiled or blasé skepticism, we will soon see a person who needs to be understood, loved, and respected—not rejected. In a word, we must love him or her, yet at the same time not be intimidated by the skeptical line.

We Christians have some helpful answers to doubts, but first we must learn to love the doubter and accept him or her as a personality created in God's image and for whom Christ died. If we keep that fact before our spiritual eyes, we will discover that we can learn to care for even the most militant anti-Christian, not because he may become a mere trophy to be won in a religious debate, but because we see him without Christ, lost and lonely. The principle is plain: People are reached primarily through love not insensitive argumentation alone. We learn to "argue" well because we love them and seek to win them to Jesus Christ.

Further, dealing with the doubter demands self-confidence, but that must not be tainted with any form of self-righteousness or intellectual pride. The normal but harmful temptation to preach at and argue against the various forms of skepticism and atheism must be resisted. "Don't preach to me!" is the cry of rebellion when one tries it.

At a civic club luncheon one day, the conversation centered on atheism. One rather sanctimonious saint recited Psalm 14:1: "'The fool says in his heart, "There is no God."' So saith the Word of God," he arrogantly stated, implying that all atheists are fools. In a sense that is true, but it is doubtful that our Lord Jesus Christ would quote such a Scripture when trying to reach an atheist. Jesus never preached down to anyone or belittled anyone's personhood. He was firm and frank, but he did it all in humility and love.

We must have an answer for the skeptic. It will not do to be loving and silent. Much good can come from a positive presentation of our faith that makes sense to the doubter's mind. The skeptical arguments may seem formidable, but we have no reason to fear; our faith is rooted in truth. Our only problem arises when our ignorance of the available weapons leaves us defenseless. And in the light of today's world we cannot afford the liability of being illiterate, powerless Christians. A believer must know the arguments for and against the faith.

15

When to Raise New Questions

How to Reach Out to the Hard-to-Reach

Alvin L. Reid

In the New Testament the witness of believers always demonstrated fearless, intentional, passionate sharing about Jesus out of the overflow of radically changed lives. No one had to stay long with an early believer to know there had been a life-changing encounter.[1] In fact over and over in Acts, one can read of the persistent witness of not only the apostles but others as well (see 6:10–12; 8:1–3; 11:19–26, for example). In their day and ours, the reason many have not been saved is because no one has told them how!

Even when we intentionally, boldly, compassionately share Christ, some will be resistant. Others, although a smaller percentage, will be hostile. What should be the approach of the witness when the gospel has been shared and rejected? When do you raise new questions for these people?

First, note some general guidelines:

1. Remember, with adults, 70 percent come to Christ out of a crisis or a significant lifestyle change. Be aware of what is going on in their lives as you share.
2. Be their friend regardless of their response. Jesus was called a friend of sinners (note: not a friend of sin). You can show genuine, Christlike love and interest in people's lives without compromising your own convictions. People don't care how much you know until they see how much you care about them!

3. Have confidence in the gospel—it, Paul tells us, is the power of God to salvation. Often the Spirit is working in ways we cannot see.

4. Live out the changed life Christianity is! Remember the New Testament does not emphasize raising questions with the lost but being ready to answer the questions the lost have for us when they see the changed lives we live (1 Pet. 3:15). The Bible never tells us to answer every person's questions. But we should answer legitimate concerns.

Knowing When to Raise Questions

There are several circumstances in which it is appropriate to raise questions with people who have already rejected your witness. Here are four of them:

1. *In response to questions they have.* The first excuse people give is virtually never the real reason they reject Christ. However, any legitimate question they raise concerning Christ should be answered before taking the next step.

2. *When the conversation moves to spiritual issues.* Christianity is not simply a spiritual part of a person's life that relates only to religious issues. It is a way of life. Virtually any issue can move to a spiritual theme. If there is a problem, the gospel has an answer. If there is an objection, truth can meet that.

3. *When you feel compelled by the Spirit to ask.* Acts 8 records the account of Philip and the Ethiopian. Philip approached the Ethiopian's chariot at the Lord's bidding and asked the man a question. Be sensitive to the work of the Spirit.

4. *Whenever there is a crisis or a time of change in the life of the other person.* If the other person has seen you as a person who lives out the changed life of a genuine Christ-follower, it would only make sense for you to raise spiritual questions in such times.

How to Raise Questions

A friend named Jack Smith, in his book *Friends Forever*, outlines a simple, doable approach to help build that kind of relationship where questions normally flow in a gospel context. He uses the acrostic S-H-O-T:

Someplace. Invite a person for whom you are concerned to go someplace with you. This allows you to spend time with the person. Questions could naturally come up in conversation.

Help. Ask the person to help you in something. Do not ask only questions of a spiritual nature. Ask for help, show you are not one of the "holier-than-thou" believers who turn off lost people. This is exactly what Jesus did with the woman at the well. He asked her for a drink.

Our place. Invite the person to your home. The better the relationship, the more natural the questions.

Their place. Visit the other person's home.

You could seek to implement one of these elements each week over a four-week time period. However, given today's hectic lifestyles, it might be better to spread it out over a longer period. Also you might repeat any or all these over time. Here are suggestions for each step:

Someplace. Invite the person to meet you at Sunday school, at a church musical, for lunch, or to go on a shopping trip or a golf outing.

Help. Ask the person to help you at a church function. Or, if he or she has a skill, ask for help at your home. You might ask the person to help out with a ministry project, such as repairing the roof of an elderly person.

Our place. Invite the person to a meal, for dessert, to see something new (such as a car or flower garden), to watch a ball game, or to study the Bible.

Their place. Visit the person during church visitation. Take a gift to him or her.

Smith also notes stages through which relationships move. The level of your relationship can affect your effectiveness in sharing Christ. Please note: At *any* level you can and should offer Jesus, but in long-term relationships in which a person is not readily open to receiving Christ, understanding these approaches can be of great help in raising new questions.

16

Don't Be Afraid!

Becoming a Bold Witness

Scott Dawson

The subject of fear is pervasive in every aspect of society. Humans are prone to have a fear of almost everything. When we are young, we are afraid to take the first step or take the first jump into the pool. As we age, the fear remains when we apply for a job or give or accept a proposal for marriage. In fact someone told me recently that there are more than three thousand phobias known to man. The phobias range from a fear of the dark to a fear of watermelons! It is safe to assume that we live in fear of fear!

Recently I was on a plane with a very successful salesman. During our conversation, I asked him a pointed question regarding sales. "Do you ever get scared during your presentation?" His answer came with complete honesty. "When I first started with the company, my focus was too much on me during my presentation. Now, I focus on the need of the company for which I am presenting and the quality of the product being offered."

Do you see the point? When this salesman learned that the real value of his presentation is not found in him but in the needs of others and the quality of his product, he was set free from fear.

I will state the obvious: I do not think we can remove fear from evangelism, but we can control it. Let me explain. A quarterback for a football team is usually smaller than all of the defensive players on the field who want to tackle him. The quarterback should have fear, but the real success of the quarterback comes if he can control his fear and funnel it into having a positive outcome. When I share my faith in a world with more hurt, questions, and anger than I could ever imagine, I should have fear. However, like the salesman, when I stop focusing on me and start focusing on the needs of the individual and the quality of my product, the fear is funneled into a positive energy.

The Role of the Holy Spirit

Paul states, "I consider everything a loss compared to the surpassing greatness of knowing Christ Jesus my Lord. . . . I want to know Christ and the power of his resurrection" (Phil. 3:8, 10). Paul was someone who had experienced the "products" of his day. Paul was from a good family, had a great education, and was apparently very popular before he received Christ. But in his opinion, nothing the world could offer compared to the sufficiency of Christ.

Paul wants to know the power of the resurrection. Why? It is in the resurrection where a believer finds boldness. As horrific as the cross was, if Jesus only died, then we would still have a problem. It is the resurrection that validates our faith, secures our future, and forgives our sins. First Corinthians 15:3–4 says, "Christ died for our sins according to the Scriptures, . . . he was buried, . . . he was raised on the third day according to the Scriptures."

To understand the power of the resurrection, we must look at the significance of the cross. It was on the cross where Jesus suffered. It was on the cross where we find a peculiar paradox. God, who is infinite and eternal, somehow is found between two thieves. God, who cannot die, somehow is crucified for our sins. Since God cannot die and God cannot sin, we must turn to the resurrection to find sorrow turned into joy. The resurrection informs us that we are not alone in this world. Through the resurrection we understand that God is not dead, sick, or worried but is alive. In addition, John 14 tells us he will not leave us but will send his Spirit to dwell in our hearts (vv. 23, 26).

Jesus promises us that his Spirit will empower us, enable us, and encourage us in our daily lives. To be overcome with fear in evangelism is to take the focus off Christ and place it on us. The Holy Spirit goes before us to prepare the hearts that will be open to the gospel. There are two reasons I do not believe this means we share Christ only with people who *seem* to be open. First, we cannot determine whom God is speaking to at any given time. I was sharing Christ in a McDonald's with some students who should have been listening. When I gave the appeal, I received negative responses and sarcasm from the group of boys. Feeling rejected, I was about to leave when an elderly lady approached me. She said she had overheard me talking and was very interested in Jesus. I had been concentrating on some young people, but God was preparing the heart of a grandmother who looked like a Sunday school teacher.

The second reason we share Christ with people who may not *seem* to be open is that, before we can harvest a crop, we must plant seed. What if farmers never prepared the soil, planted the seed, or watered the fields, but just waited for a harvest? The farmer would be disappointed . . . and hungry! If we witness with a focus only on salvation, we will constantly be discouraged. The salvation of others is our hope but not our responsibility. Even Paul states, "I planted the seed, Apollos watered it, but God made it grow" (1 Cor. 3:6). Many times we are fearful when we become focused on success or failure instead of on faithfulness. What scares us most—having someone ridicule us or feeling that we've let Christ down? This is not intended as a theological statement but a practical application. It may be that I am the one to introduce someone to the *thought of Jesus* not to salvation. The Holy Spirit nudges us to witness at the right time. I have never known a *wrong time* to witness, only a *wrong way* to witness.

Stephen Olford shares incredible insight into the role of the Holy Spirit in witnessing. He becomes vulnerable when he states, "I am scared to witness, guilty because I do not witness. . . . I feel like a failure." But then, to our relief, he states, "Good news, you are a failure. Only God through His Holy Spirit can change a life."[1] In essence, as a follower of Christ, I do not have to *try to witness*; I must trust that I will *be a witness*. It is not trying to live for Jesus, but Jesus living through me.

A Fail-Proof Understanding

What can happen when we share our faith? There can be only three results: we could see someone come to Christ; we could plant a seed; we could be rejected. As I have studied human nature, I realize the fear of rejection overcomes most people's aspirations of success. As a result, we only dabble in witnessing and rationalize most people's spiritual condition. Allow me to turn the tables in the next few paragraphs.

What if there was a way for you to conquer your fear of witnessing? In order for this to happen you must ask yourself, *What am I afraid of*? Usually the response is once again rejection. However, what if rejection, for the right reason, is something we should strive for? Would that make it a little easier to handle?

First Peter 4:14 states, "If you are insulted because of the name of Christ, you are blessed, for the Spirit of glory and of God rests on you." Wow! Here Scripture tells us that our fear is misplaced. It is not when we are rejected that we should fear, but when we are silent. The next time a door is slammed, dirty words shouted at you, or a resounding rejection given to your gospel presentation, do not despair or hang your head low. Rejoice because you are blessed by your faithfulness to Christ.

Above anything else, the change in your life represents the greatest amount of strength you possess. Have you noticed how bold some people are in their witness? Is this due to a personality trait or too much caffeine? There was a time when I thought only "super" believers could be bold witnesses. Then I regressed to thinking only those who had a "real" testimony could witness. I believed this because I had received Christ as a young person and never experienced any issues or addictions I thought were bad in society's eyes. However, now that I've studied evangelism for nearly two decades, allow me to share with you my main insight into bold witnessing. The one who understands the *price* that was paid for our salvation lives a life of gratitude. To be a bold witness you must discover the "why" of the cross not just the fact of the cross. With your guilt, you were hopeless, but according to Romans 5:8, God demonstrated his own love toward *you* in that while *you* were a sinner, Christ died for *you*!

I have seen drug dealers come to Christ and become bold believers, but I have also seen sweet grandmothers boldly tell their story of salvation to complete strangers as well as close friends. What is the similarity? It is the recognition of what Christ has done for them. Most people do not believe they have done bad things, but when they come face-to-face with their evil—not only that which is birthed in them but evil thoughts and deeds that they do every day that caused Jesus's death on the cross—they realize how much they owe him. Once this realization penetrates our minds and hearts, our attitude is that of gratefulness to Christ, who has changed our life. It does not matter how bad we may have been. What matters is that we were lost and he found us.

Answering Their Needs

A well-known movie star was asked in an interview to name one thing he wanted that he did not have. His answer was *peace*. Think about that statement. Does it not reflect the heart of the Lord when he says, "Peace I leave with you; my peace I give you" (John 14:27)? We must realize that our generation is searching for peace. The greatest need of people today is not economic, political, educational, or even emotional, but it is to have a personal relationship with the God who loves them.

The salesman, whom I mentioned earlier, realized that he had to focus on the needs of others to sell his product. In witnessing, we must do the same. The needs may not always be as obvious as after an accident occurs or an illness is diagnosed, but the basic needs of everyone's life must be addressed in evangelism.

The most basic need in a human's life is to be loved. As most of us know, people do some weird things to show love and to be loved. However, most love we experience is temporary and conditional.

God's love for us is unconditional. We cannot do anything to make God love us more or less. Therefore, to be a bold believer, we must find security in the greatest theological discovery of all time. God loves us!

A second human need is forgiveness. Over time, guilt can ravage a soul. Men, engulfed by guilt and looking for relief, can become like beasts searching for food. But for this problem, you and I have the greatest message the world can hear. Not only is there forgiveness available for all but reconciliation as well! In Hebrews 10:17 the Bible says, "Their sins and lawless acts I will remember no more." Forgiveness can be found in the One who loves us unconditionally.

Another vital need of humans is security. We realize the need for financial, relational, and physical security, but our greatest need is spiritual security. My son is an avid sportsman. He loves to play sports all the time. On one of his many teams was a kid from a family that was in total disarray. It seemed that turmoil was involved in every area of their lives. After many conversations, I understood the problem. The dad was insecure. He had tried money, drugs, pornography, gambling, and other things to quench his desire for security. In one vulnerable moment he confessed, "I feel so alone." In a world that is filled with hurt, people are in search of a place where they can feel secure. Christians have the message, the tools, and the opportunity to be a bold witness for Christ.

Do you feel like you are ready, with no fear? Probably not. One chapter will not take all the apprehension out of sharing your faith. Allow me to conclude with one final practical thought. You have asked God to live through you today. Now, ask a friend to be your accountability partner. Ecclesiastes 4:12 says, "A cord of three strands is not quickly broken." Ask a spiritually mature friend to pray for you and go with you during some of your encounters. You may want to start keeping a journal of all the opportunities you have to share Christ. It will be amazing how the Lord will show you how far you have grown in a short time. It is like the growth chart in the hall of our house. Every month we check our children to see if they have grown an inch or two. With your journal, you can check your "growth chart" and see if you have grown in your witnessing.

Now, in the words of my high school English teacher, "Practice makes perfect!" Don't expect to be Billy Graham or Mother Teresa the first time you witness. You were not Fred Astaire when you took your first step, Peyton Manning on your first football throw, or Tiger Woods with your first golf shot. These people practiced to become the best. You can become a bold witness if you will take the first step.

17

Spiritual Warfare

Reaching People by Taking on the Enemy

Chuck Lawless

I t seemed to me that Greg was completely closed to the Good News of Jesus. No matter how much I shared the gospel, he had no interest in following Christ. The Bible meant little to him. The arguments about Christ carried no weight for him. He was, as one church member put it, "just living in the dark."

Have you ever found personal evangelism to be difficult like that? Does it sometimes seem as though you are fighting against forces that are stronger than you? Maybe you are facing the reality of spiritual warfare in your attempts to be an effective personal evangelist.

Spiritual warfare has become a hot topic in the last few years, but much of the current teaching lacks a biblical foundation. Our goal in this chapter is to examine what the Bible says about the warfare we face as we try to reach unbelievers.

Blinded to the Gospel

The apostle Paul told the Corinthians that unbelievers are blinded by the "god of this age" (2 Cor. 4:3–4). The god of this age is Satan, who is also called the "prince of this world" (John 16:11) and the "ruler of the kingdom of the air" (Eph. 2:2). He operates in the "dominion of darkness" (Col. 1:13; see also Acts 26:18).

The persons we seek to reach—like Greg—are in spiritual bondage, and our task is to proclaim a message of liberation and freedom. The enemy counters, striving to hold his captives in chains. Though God has already defeated Satan and secured salvation for his own through the cross (Col. 2:15), the battle is nevertheless a real one. This is Samuel Wilson's conclusion: "We are forced, given the nature of evangelism and spiritual struggle associated with it, to military metaphor. . . . This is the language of scripture, because it is the reality of our engagement with real spiritual enemies."[1]

Satan's strategies for keeping unbelievers blinded are numerous. The enemy provides the lies to which unbelievers cling, such as "I'm good enough" and "I can always wait until tomorrow to follow God." He makes sin attractive and alluring, convincing the unbeliever that following God will mean a loss of pleasure. He snatches away the Word of God before it takes root in an unbeliever's heart (see Matt. 13:3–9, 18–23). More specifically, Satan blinds unbelievers to the gospel by promoting distorted views of the gospel itself.

What does this reality mean for us as we try to reach lost people? Simply, *we do not have the power in ourselves to reach people blinded by the enemy.* Nothing we can do in our own strength is sufficient to open blinded minds. For this reason, evangelism must be accompanied by *prayer.* Evangelism is the task, but prayer is the power behind the task. If only God can open blinded minds, does it not make sense to seek his guidance and intervention as we evangelize lost people?

As you train church members to evangelize, be sure to train them to pray also. Raise up intercessors, and put them to work. When you send members out to do evangelism, secure a prayer team to support them. If you do not do so, you may be sending the evangelists into a spiritual battle unarmed. The result is too often a defeated church member who loses the passion to do evangelism.

Targets for the Enemy

Scripture affirms that Satan continues to attack people who become believers. Jesus warned Peter that Satan had asked for permission to "sift you as wheat" (Luke 22:31). Peter himself later warned believers, "Be of sober *spirit,* be on the alert. Your adversary, the devil, prowls around like a roaring lion, seeking someone to devour" (1 Pet. 5:8 NASB). The apostle Paul likewise admonished believers to "put on the full armor of God so that you can take your stand against the devil's schemes" (Eph. 6:11). James too called believers to resist the devil, presupposing that the enemy would attack (James 4:7). If Satan does not attack believers, such recurrent warnings would seem irrelevant and unnecessary.

Maybe your story is like mine. I became a believer as a teenager, but nobody taught me to be a disciple of Christ. My church told me what I needed to do (read the Bible, pray, and witness), but they did not show me how. Nobody told me how to walk in truth, righteousness, and faith (see Eph. 6:11–17). The "armor of God" meant little to me. As a result, I lived a defeated Christian life for far too many years.

As my story—and perhaps yours—illustrates, the enemy aims his arrows especially at young believers who have not been discipled. He strikes them with doubt and discouragement. Sometimes he hits them with loneliness, as they move away from their non-Christian friends and try to fit into a church that is unfamiliar to them. At other times, he lures them with the same temptations they faced as nonbelievers. Whatever his strategy may be, he wants to strike at new believers before they get solidly planted in the church.

Our response to Satan's strategy is simple: *We must teach new believers intentionally to put on the armor of God.* The essence of "putting on the armor" (Eph. 6:11–17) is not about magical prayer that applies the weaponry to believers' lives; rather, it is about discipleship and spiritual growth that affect all of one's life. Wearing the armor is about daily living in truth, righteousness, faith, and hope, while always being ready to proclaim the gospel of peace found in the Word.

But will a new believer understand how to live as a Christian if we do not teach him or her? To lead your church in overcoming the enemy, enlist a group of faithful church members and train them to be disciplers. Assign a trained mentor to each new believer. Develop an intentional strategy for leading a new believer toward maturity in Christ, and use the mentors to guide converts through the process. Be willing to start small, but do not give up—the enemy delights when discouragement sets in.

An effective evangelism strategy simply must include an uncompromising commitment to discipleship for both the evangelist and the new convert. In the spiritual battles we face, discipleship means the difference between victory and defeat.

Proclaiming the Word

In my work as senior associate dean of the Billy Graham School of Missions, Evangelism, and Church Growth, I have worked with research teams that have studied thousands of evangelistically growing churches. Each of our studies has shown that proclaiming the Word has been a primary factor in the churches' effectiveness in evangelism and assimilation.

That finding should not surprise us though. The Word is alive and powerful (Heb. 4:12), converting the soul (Ps. 19:7), and protecting us from sin (Ps. 119:11). The Word is the "sword of the Spirit" (Eph. 6:17). It is the weapon to which Jesus turned when he faced temptation (Matt. 4:1–11). Three times the devil tempted Jesus in the wilderness, and three times the Son of God responded by quoting God's Word. Ultimately the simple phrase "It is written" was enough to cause Satan to back down from the battle. The enemy is no match for the Word. If you want to grow a church that overcomes the enemy, *take up the sword of the Spirit and proclaim the Word.*

To illustrate this truth with regard to evangelism, it is clear that the enemy seeks to undermine the biblical truth that personal faith in Jesus Christ is the only way to God. The belief that salvation is found in Christ alone is largely rejected.[2] A growing number of American adults believe that "all good persons" will go to heaven whether or not they know Jesus Christ as Savior.[3] While the church buys the lies of pluralism and inclusivism, Satan disguises himself as an angel of light (2 Cor. 11:14) and lulls unbelievers into a false sense of spiritual security.

We prepare for and counter this strategy by passionately proclaiming the biblical truth that personal, explicit faith in Jesus is necessary for salvation (John 14:6; Rom. 10:9–10). Consider doing a theological survey in your church, and find out what your members *really* believe about this important topic—then proclaim the message again and again to drive it home. It is, after all, the truth that can set free people like Greg (John 8:31–32).

Evangelism is more than a strategy, technique, or program. Instead, it is taking the gospel of light into the kingdom of darkness. Prepare for this battle by taking the following steps:

- Make certain that you are wearing the armor. Be a fully devoted disciple of Jesus.
- Mentor new believers.
- Lead your church to develop a comprehensive evangelism and discipleship program.
- Enlist prayer warriors to support your church's evangelistic efforts.
- Proclaim the truth!

Part II

Ordinary
People

Ordinary People by Relationship Group

18

Family

Spreading Your Faith to Your Family Members

Tarra Dawson

The family was the first institution ordained by God in the Garden of Eden and is the very basic unit on which our society is built. Today, however, the family unit is under attack, and many influences compete for the interests and time of our children. So what do we do? How do we win our families to Christ? You've heard the catch phrase, "It's more caught than taught." In striving to lead our family members to Jesus, faith is both caught *and* taught.

Faith Is Caught

Leading by example is not a new concept. However, to win our family members, specifically those living under our roof, to Jesus, this principle is imperative. Our families see our true character, godly or ungodly, revealed in everyday life situations. When the air conditioner in the family car goes out and you owe the mechanic fifteen hundred dollars for repairs, do you give thanks in everything (1 Thess. 5:18)? When the boss calls you into his office to inform you the company is downsizing and your job is no more, do you claim that all things work together for good to those who are called according to his purpose (Rom. 8:28)? When the kids' grades are good and you've just been able to purchase that new vehicle you've dreamed of having, do you recognize that every good and perfect gift is from above (James 1:17)?

My point is this: Do your family members see an authentic faith being fleshed out in you? Do they see you go to the Lord in prayer about everything and look to the Word for direction? Do they see the divine inner strength that sustains you? Do they see you share your faith in Jesus with others because you're so convinced your life is better because of Jesus and that the lives of others would be too?

If your answers are yes, stay the course. Jesus says if he is lifted up, he will draw men to himself (John 12:32).

If your answers are no, are you willing to examine yourself honestly before the Lord and change through his power so that you can pass on to your family a legacy of authentic faith in Jesus Christ as Savior and Lord?

Faith Is Taught

A godly example is not enough to ensure that our family members will come to know Jesus as Savior and Lord. We must also teach them about Jesus and their need for him. Let's look at some ways to do this.

Unconditional Love

I was on my way into Wal-Mart one morning when I overheard the conversation of a man and woman walking behind me in the parking lot. The woman said that she didn't know anyone who had children that was happy. The man agreed and explained that everyone he knew just wanted their children to grow up and get out of the house. What a tragedy!

As believers seeking to lead our children to Jesus, we must not fall into this trap of selfishness. Rather, we must remind ourselves that our children are a treasure from the Lord and that he has entrusted us with one of his most prized creations (Psalm 139). And just as God has loved us unconditionally (Rom. 5:8), we must love our children just because of who they are—a masterpiece of God. Nothing they do should make us love them more, and nothing they do should make us love them any less. Their worth is not based on achievement or lack thereof. By loving our families in this manner, we help them understand how valuable they are to our heavenly Father—so valuable, in fact, he would allow his one and only Son Jesus to die for them.

Relational Love

The dictionary defines the word *relate* as "getting along well together or understanding each other." However, just below *relate* is the entry *related*, meaning "to be part of the same family." Do you see the stark contrast in definition?

To lead our families to Jesus, our relationships must be much more than sharing a name or being part of the same unit in one house. We must establish a "getting along together and understanding of each other." Our message carries very little weight if no relationship exists behind the words.

How do we develop healthy relationships? Of course, we must provide the basic needs of living, such as food, clothing, and shelter, but we must also get involved in the lives of our children. In fact I would dare to say that most children spell *love* t-i-m-e. Help with their homework; have their teenage friends over for pizza; take them on errands so you can talk one-on-one and just let them know you like having them around; be at that championship game; plan family fun time—whether it's a big vacation or a simple game of cards after dinner; send frequent notes and emails to your college student for encouragement.

Whatever stage your children are in, find ways to stay connected. Then your relationship will allow you to have great influence in sharing the gospel and discipleship, simply because they know you care. The greatest example of this is Jesus. He related to individuals and then met their spiritual needs.

Tough Love

Another way to lay the foundation for leading your family to Christ is to exercise tough love. This does not mean that you exhibit a tough, gruff demeanor. Actually, tough love is displayed when, with great gentleness and self-control, you as a parent do what is best for your child and not what is easiest for you. Let me illustrate.

When our son was three years old, we had been to the grocery store one morning, and he had gotten a helium-filled balloon. He was having great fun playing with this balloon. However, he kept wanting to bite it. I explained to him that he shouldn't do this because it could be dangerous if the balloon popped and some of the pieces got in his mouth. I added that if he tried to bite it again, I would have to take it from him and pop it.

Well, you know exactly what he did. He put the balloon up to his mouth. At that moment I realized that I was actually going to have to do what I had said. I didn't want to do it! The easiest thing would have been to just tell him again and let him keep playing. Then I could get all my groceries put away. But because I love him and want the best for him, I also knew that it was more important to teach him through this.

Teach him what? One, he should listen to Mom's voice and obey. Two, his choices have consequences. Three, Mom doesn't give empty promises. So, I did the tough thing. I took the balloon and popped it. Then, as the tears flowed (his and mine), I held him and reassured him of my love for him. And the groceries still hadn't been put away!

Let's look at the spiritual implications of this illustration. First, as we keep our word, whether it is to bring a gift to our children or take disciplinary action like popping a balloon, we teach them that God is true to his Word. We are laying the groundwork for how our children will view God. Therefore, we have a great responsibility to help them understand that they can always trust their heavenly

Father. And should we mess up (and we will because we're not God), we must readily admit it and ask for our children's forgiveness, at the same time reminding them that God never messes up—he's perfect!

Second, by insisting gently but firmly on obedience, we teach our children to obey. The way we train them to respond to us as parents will likely be the way they respond to God. John 10:3–4 says that the shepherd's sheep hear his voice and obey. Do we want God to have to raise his voice, do something drastic, to get the attention of our children? Or can he simply speak to their heart and they obey?

And third, by holding our children accountable for disobedience, we help them see their sin nature. Romans 3:20 tells us that the whole purpose of the law was to make man conscious of sin. Sinners need a Savior. The members of our family will receive Jesus only when they realize they need him.

Practical Love

If we are truly seeking to lead our families to Jesus, it makes sense that we talk with them about him, read God's Word with them, actively participate in a local body of believers, and pray. In other words, we must involve our families in the basic spiritual disciplines of our lives. We cannot depend on the church to grow our children spiritually. We can depend on the church to reinforce what we are already teaching in the home.

In Isaiah 55:11 God says this about his Word: "It will not return to me empty, but will accomplish what I desire and achieve the purpose for which I sent it." Are we faithfully reading God's Word with our families so he can accomplish his purpose in each of them? Are we helping our family members memorize God's Word, hide it in their hearts so as not to sin against him (Ps. 119:11)? Are we fervently petitioning the Holy Spirit to show up and do what only he can do in their lives? I remember a quote from a Sunday school class attributed to *Common Sense Christian Living* by Edith Schaeffer: "Prayer makes a difference in history. Interceding for other people makes a difference in the history of peoples' lives." Why? How? Ephesians 3:20 makes that very clear. God "is able to do immeasurably more than all we ask or imagine."

Seizing teachable moments is another practical way of leading your family to Jesus. For example, your child wants to watch a television show you know contains questionable language and attitudes. Don't just say no, but in love explain why your answer is no, based on the principles in God's Word. Or your child has deliberately disobeyed your instruction. In love explain to your child that his or her disobedience is sin.

Finally, we must also remember that each person has a free will to choose or not choose Jesus. Let us be faithful to do all we can to lead our family to Jesus, and then do what Corrie ten Boom says: "As a camel kneels before his master to have him remove his burden, so kneel and let the master take your burden."

Other Family Relationships

You may see other relatives—cousins, aunts, uncles, grandparents— often, or you may see them only at Christmas. How can you have an influence for Christ in their lives?

Many of the same principles already addressed in this chapter can be applied .to more distant family relations too, like being a godly example and praying for them. A Scripture we should take particular note of in these relationships is 1 Peter 3:15: "But in your hearts set apart Christ as Lord. Always be prepared to give an answer to everyone who asks you to give the reason for the hope that you have. But do this with gentleness and respect." Be ready! Use those family parties and holiday gatherings to count for eternity!

19

Friends

Don't Let Friends Go to Hell

Greg Stier

Why is it so tough to share Jesus with those who are closest to us? Maybe we are afraid of losing them. I mean, what if we share the gospel with them and they abandon us because they think we've become some religious freak?

Or perhaps we are secretly terrified that if we start "preaching" to our friends, they will point out an area of our lives that is inconsistent with our faith. They are the ones who know us best, after all. They know our dirty laundry, and if we start trying to push Jesus on them, they could start asking a lot of uncomfortable questions, questions about our own ability to practice what we preach.

Sharing Christ with our friends can be tough. There's no doubt about it. But we must gather courage from the Holy Spirit to overcome these fears so that our friends can know Jesus in the way we know him. I mean, if you think about it, if your friends trust in Christ, your friendships could become even closer. Christians can relate to each other on the deepest spiritual level. So if your friends become believers, you will have a new depth in your relationships.

The question is how. How do we bring up this tough subject in a way that doesn't turn them off? How do we reach out without freaking out? Here are a few practical action steps to help you on this exciting and scary journey.

Realize the Urgency

My mom went to be with the Lord exactly a year ago. I watched as she died a slow, painful death from cancer. This devastating disease ate away at her body for eighteen months before she finally succumbed and was ushered into the presence of the Lord Jesus.

If, a few years ago, through some weird experiment, I had discovered the cure to cancer, I would have stopped at nothing to get my mom to take the cure. If she resisted, I would have persisted. Any protest she made would have been met with an answer. I would have used all of my powers of persuasion to make her give in to my plea. My prayers would go up for her in the nighttime, and my cure would be offered to her in the daytime. I love my mom too much to have given up.

So why are we waiting to share the cure with our friends? Our friends who don't know Christ have something infinitely worse than cancer and are headed somewhere infinitely worse than death! And what kind of friends are we if we let them pass into eternal hell without doing our best to get them to take the cure?

Don't Buy the Lies

Satan will do his best to keep your mouth shut about Jesus, especially with your friends. He will whisper lies in your ear like:

"Now is not the time. Just build the relationship a little longer."

"Let them see Jesus in your life before you talk about him."

"If you share the gospel, they are going to reject you and Jesus both!"

"Your life is not consistent with your message anyway. They won't believe you!"

The list of lies goes on and on. And the way that Satan lies is by taking a partial truth and then mixing in a little arsenic. For instance, we should be living a life for Jesus, and our friends should be seeing evidence of him in our lives, but whether or not they can see him at work in us shouldn't keep us from sharing the cure. And, yes, we mess up as Christians. Get it out of your mind that you have to be perfect to share your faith. We've all said or done something inappropriate in front of our friends that we wish we could take back. But we can't. We are sinners too. That's why my favorite definition of evangelism is "one beggar showing another beggar where to find the bread."

Don't let Satan shut you up. Reject his lies. Say, along with Jesus, "Away from me, Satan!" (Matt. 4:10).

Look for Opportunities

This should be easy. We live in a spiritual culture (not necessarily a Christian spirituality but spiritual nonetheless) where it should be easy to talk about our spiritual beliefs, especially with our friends.

Whether it's a movie like *The Lord of the Rings* or a book like *The Da Vinci Code*, this culture affords us a lot of opportunities to talk about life and afterlife. Go into a bookstore and just check out how many books deal with spiritual subjects. Spirituality is everywhere.

How can you bring it up with your friends? Just ask a question like, "What do you believe about (insert spiritual subject here)?" For instance, let's say you just watched a movie where someone dies. You could ask your friend, "What do you think happens to people after they die?"

Or let's say that your friend read *The Da Vinci Code.* You could ask, "So do you think that Jesus was God or just a man?"

However you bring it up, you always follow up with a question like, "Would you mind if I shared with you what I believe about that?"

If you think about it, there are a whole lot of opportunities to bring the subject of spirituality up with our friends. That is not the problem. The problem is that we pass up opportunities every single day because we forget what is at stake and we are listening to the lies of the Evil One.

Just Do It

If you think about it, the gospel message is a simple story. The plot goes something like this:

- God created humanity.
- Humanity rebelled against God.
- God sacrificed his Son to be reconciled to mankind.
- Those who believe go to heaven.
- Those who reject go to hell.

It's not as though we Christians have some complicated, convoluted belief system that is difficult to understand or articulate. Jesus summed it up when he told Nicodemus, "For God so loved the world that he gave his one and only Son, that whoever believes in him shall not perish but have eternal life" (John 3:16).

That's it! Salvation from sin is as simple as putting your faith and trust in Jesus, based on the fact that he died in your place for your sins. That's it! It's not a matter of being good or doing good. It's a matter of simple faith.

So why can't we explain that message to our friends? The message is simple, and yet we are afraid to share it.

Get Creative

There are a lot of creative ways that you can share the gospel with your friends. Here are a few:

- *Write a letter or send an email.* Why not just sit down and pour out your heart to your friends about the gospel? The great thing about writing things out is that you can craft your letter and make it sound just right. You can pray over it as you ponder what to say. You can run it by someone else before you send it, to make sure it is clear and compelling.
- *Invite them to church, to a small-group activity, to a Christian concert, or to a gathering.* If you invite your friends to go to some kind of Christian gathering with you, they are on your turf. There is something about the body of Christ uniting in the power of the Spirit to hear the Word of God and do the works of God that can be powerful and compelling. Afterward go out to lunch or dinner or coffee with them and talk to them about what they just experienced. Answer any questions that they may have and share your spiritual journey with them.
- *Give them a book to read or a CD to listen to that shares the gospel.* Whether it is Lee Strobel's *A Case for Faith*, Josh McDowell's *More than a Carpenter*, or some book or CD from a preacher who shares the gospel message in a powerful way, pass it on to your friends! Later on, ask them what they thought of it.

Love Your Friends

Friends don't let friends go to hell.

I considered Pat a friend. I talked to her almost every day. She worked at the restaurant I frequented, where I would read, write, and study for sermons. She knew that I was a preacher, and we talked around the gospel but never directly about it, because I didn't want to push it on her. *I'll build the relationship and then when the time is right, I'll share the gospel,* I thought, figuring I had plenty of time. Then one day I walked into the restaurant and she wasn't there to greet me. She would never be there again. The night before, she had taken her own life. Little did I know that behind that smiling facade that met me every day was a boiling cauldron of worthless feelings that were assaulting her soul and mind.

I guess I wasn't her friend after all. If I had been, I would have shared Jesus with her.

So what kind of friend are you?

20

Co-workers

Building Bridges to Share Christ

Daniel Owens

Why is sharing our faith so difficult? What makes it so hard to give our testimony to somebody or to quote a few Bible verses to him or her? What scares many people is the idea that we have to go down on the street corner, confront someone with a gospel presentation, and keep prompting until he prays the sinner's prayer.

Confrontational evangelism works for some people, but most of us are relational. That's why I like to do what I call *conversational evangelism*—establishing friendships, developing relationships with others, building bridges into people's lives. What better place to start than at your job, with the people you see five or even six days a week?

Sometimes we have become so preoccupied with our own lives, our own Christian world, that we neglect the people we see nearly every day who are without hope. We may be teaching children's church, leading the youth choir, or hosting a Bible study—but what are we doing to reach out to those people who need to hear the message of salvation? We can't get so caught up in doing good things that we ignore the Great Commission. So the only question is, how do we get started?

Begin with a Plan

When I was growing up in the San Francisco Bay area, my uncle worked for a steel company that built bridges. I would often listen to my uncle's incredible stories about building those bridges—the kind of stories a little kid loves to hear. He would remind me, "Dan, whenever you build a bridge, there is always a plan. You don't just go out and say one day, 'Well, I think I'll build a bridge right here.' You have to study the geology of the area, the traffic patterns, the water currents—everything. Building a bridge requires detailed analysis that leads to a plan."

It's embarrassing to admit that when we begin to build a bridge into someone's life, too often we jump in without a plan. When I do that, I always fall flat on my face. I don't stop to say, "God, I need a plan to reach this person. What should my plan be?"

Let me encourage you to begin building your bridges to non-Christians through prayer. Honestly ask yourself, *Do I really pray for those who don't know the Lord? Can I make a commitment to pray for my co-workers, even the ones I don't get along with?* Bridges begun with prayer don't crumble as easily as those without it.

One time I had the privilege of seeing the prayer journal of a Christian businessman. In this compact notebook, he keeps the names of people for whom he is praying, a list of opportunities when he has actually shared the gospel with these people, and notes about how God is answering prayer as he builds bridges into their lives. He even notes when he was able to lead some of these people to Christ.

At first, this man's diligence was very intimidating to me, but I was encouraged that he had his priorities straight about prayer. His example motivated me to pray, "Lord, help me to be more disciplined in prayer as I reach out to others."

E. M. Bounds said, "It is a great thing to talk to men about God. It is greater still to talk to God about men."[1]

Develop a Relationship

Sonja is a vice president of a Seattle-based company and has led hundreds of people to the Lord by using what she calls "lifestyle evangelism." She reads a lot and keeps up with the times, and as her co-workers bring up moral issues or personal problems, she chimes in at the right time, "You know, our pastor was just talking about that this Sunday, and he said . . ."

Sonja has tried to develop a reputation at work of being someone who listens to people's problems. Her kindness is well known throughout the company, and when the staff brings problems to her, conversations often turn into discussions about faith.

Another Christian businessman shared this tip: "When I see a person reading something on the economy, I ask, 'Things like that make you wonder what's in store for the future, don't they?' I've found many opportunities to use that question to begin a discussion about spiritual things."

A woman told me she had come to Christ because of a booklet that someone had left on her desk at work. A colleague of this woman had been concerned about her and wanted to talk with her about the Lord, but she was too timid. She bought the gospel booklet and put it on the woman's desk one morning, during a particularly difficult time in the woman's life. The woman began to read the booklet and got interested because it addressed problems she was having at that time, and she opened her heart to Christ.

It usually takes seven to nine contacts with the gospel before people make a decision for Christ. Relationships take time to grow, to develop depth and trust. There isn't a shortcut or an alternate route. Plan to spend time if you plan to build relationships.

Share Your Story

Once you've established a friendship, be ready to share your testimony. You don't have to memorize fifty Bible verses, and you don't have to be afraid of mixing up the points in your gospel presentation. Your personal story is very nonthreatening to the person listening to you.

It's also conversational. When your co-worker listens to your testimony, it isn't like sitting in church listening to a sermon. You may be hanging out in the break room or having lunch together. She can stop you and ask questions. You don't need a soapbox, a microphone, or a pulpit. It's just you and the other person in a conversation.

Another great thing about your testimony is that no one can dispute it. How can anyone argue that what you are saying about yourself didn't really happen? If you have joy and peace and love in your life as a result of knowing Christ, that will be evident and people will notice.

Finally, your testimony is interesting. When people are friends, it is natural for them to want to know more about each other. Here are some principles for sharing your testimony:

- *Keep it simple.* Although the story of how you came to Christ may still be very exciting to you, even if it happened many years ago, curb the temptation to extend it into a detailed, minute-by-minute account of your life from birth until your conversion. Most people can successfully concentrate on someone else talking for about ten minutes at a time.
- *Point to Jesus Christ.* It's your story, but it has meaning only because of Jesus. The apostle Paul, after describing his life, says, "But whatever was to my profit I now consider loss for the sake of Christ. What is more, I consider everything a loss compared to the surpassing greatness of knowing Christ Jesus my Lord, for whose sake I have lost all things. I consider them rubbish, that I may gain Christ" (Phil. 3:7–8).
- *Identify why you needed Christ.* This could be your need for love, for forgiveness, or for assurance of heaven when you die. If your co-worker is feeling the same need, you are showing the way to fulfill that need.

- *Clearly explain the gospel message.* If you are going to point the way to Jesus Christ, take pains to keep the gospel simple so that you can explain it clearly. As you present your testimony, it's easy to get caught up in the emotion of reliving your life-changing story, and it's common to be just plain nervous! Either way, I suggest a rehearsed gospel presentation to keep you from saying too much and to help you cover all the vital facts. Watch out for "Christianese." Terms like *born again, repent,* and *eternal life* may be confusing to a non-Christian. You can also share some key Scripture verses, especially if you have a "life verse." If you really want to be prepared, consider memorizing a key verse on a few topics that are common felt needs, such as guilt, forgiveness, love, and fear.

From the Workplace to the Church

Once you have built a good relationship and your co-worker has come to respect and trust you, look for opportunities to take the relationship outside the workplace. The following ideas can be very effective in exposing your co-worker to the gospel message in a nonthreatening way.

- Invite him or her to a church outreach event—concerts, potlucks, drama performances.
- Invite your co-worker to dinner and to a crusade.
- Invite your co-worker's children to VBS or other children's programs at your church.
- Give your co-worker appropriate Christian materials, such as books, magazines, or tracts.

Often we give ourselves only one serious shot at sharing the gospel with someone, and if it doesn't work we say, "Well, I tried my best." This relationship that we are so carefully building is worth far more than one try.

21

Couples

Creating an Earthly Bond with Heavenly Power

From an interview with Les and Leslie Parrott

For the last decade and a half, Leslie and her husband, Les, have been actively involved in helping couples find a pathway to a healthy relationship. Both of them had faith demonstrated to them through their parents, and they have set their course to help couples discover spiritual intimacy in their marriage. They have written twenty books, have been involved in hundreds of seminars, have spoken to thousands of students, and have had an infinite number of late-night discussions on the subject. They are confident that God has a plan for spouses.

Although evangelism is not the direct focus of the Parrotts' ministry, it is the purpose. They attempt to transcend the four walls of the church to communicate with the world. In their books, seminars, and discussions, they are intentional about using words that everyone can understand.

When believers are light in a dark place, what they offer can be very attractive to others. As a result of the Parrotts' new television show, people have asked them about their faith and beliefs, not because of their words but because of their actions and the way they treat their guests.

The Parrotts have seen and personally experienced the benefits of a marriage that has spiritual intimacy. When Christ is the center of the relationship, it is a beautiful picture of God's love. Often in Paul's writings, salvation is compared to marriage, because both are built on a relationship. A Christ-centered relationship teaches couples the meaning of a covenant. The expression of faithfulness that is paramount in a successful marriage is seen in the life of Christ.

In a Christ-centered marriage there is a true understanding of forgiveness. When a person experiences the love of God and the forgiveness he offers, he is, or should be, more forgiving of others.

A most important benefit of a Christ-centered marriage is spiritual intimacy. One of the questions in a class offered by the Parrotts' ministry is, "On a scale of one to ten, how important is spiritual intimacy?" The answers are usually a "three" or "four." Surprisingly, the "three" and "four" answers are given by those in both Christian and non-Christian marriages.

If spiritual intimacy is a benefit of a Christ-centered marriage, why are most marriages not experiencing it? One possible answer to this question is that most couples learn on their own, and they do not transfer what they learn into their marriage relationship. The Bible teaches us that husband and wife are "one flesh," and seeing a spouse blossom into the person God desires him or her to be ultimately blesses both partners and blesses the marriage as a whole.

Sharing Christ with Your Spouse

After having read some of the benefits of a Christ-centered marriage, you may be wondering how to share Christ with your spouse. What should a believer say and how should he act in front of the spouse who is not a believer?

First, we must understand that having a spouse who is not willing to participate in the most sacred and important aspects of life is a very lonely and fragile place to be. It can be very disappointing and it could be so easy to translate those feelings into bitterness and contempt toward a spouse. But, of course, that is not the answer! Intercessory prayer is critical for this situation. It is an active part of evangelism. As a spouse who is a believer, you must realize that *you* cannot change your husband or wife. Only God can do that.

Also, be careful not to become distant from your spouse. Pray that God will bring (or keep) you together. Your prayer should be twofold, asking God to help your spouse be responsive to him and to help you display the fruit of the Spirit. *The Message* describes this so well: "What happens when we live God's way? He brings gifts into our lives, much the same way that fruit appears in an orchard—things like affection for others. . . . a sense of compassion in the heart. . . . We find ourselves involved in loyal commitments . . . able to marshal and direct our energies wisely" (Gal. 5:22–23 Message). When we are active in our prayer life, we will discover that our testimony may be less about what we say and more about how we act.

It is also important to learn how to best approach our spouse concerning spiritual issues. Gary Thomas gives an excellent study on this topic that is defined as "sacred pathways." Basically, just as in school we learn in different ways, we learn spirituality through different means. It is important to discover what would attract our spouse to Christ. Is our spouse more responsive to a naturalist, traditionalist, or enthusiast? (Find out more at www.garythomas.com.) Most spouses will reach out only in the path that is their favorite, not in their partner's path. Consequently, what brings one spouse the most joy may bring only emptiness and confusion in the life of the other.

Finally, above all else, we must love our spouse. We must stop trying to change our spouse and focus instead on his or her positive qualities. As followers of Christ, we have experienced unconditional love. God loved us before our relationship with him ever started. We must love our spouse in the same way. This means respecting her likes, dislikes, interests, and choices. It means being willing to be involved in and support his commitments and dreams, unless these things would violate biblical teachings. Once again, it is how we live out our life—by our words, actions, and attitudes—that will influence our spouse.

Making It Right

There have been many times that Leslie and Les have spoken to couples who are living together but are not married. They handle these situations with much care and gentleness. When one partner enters into a relationship with Christ, it brings pressure on the relationship. There are many advantages to living our lives the way God has instructed, especially in the marriage relationship. It is the conviction of most Christians that cohabitation before marriage is not biblical and thus is not God's plan.

Along with the desire to follow God's plan for marriage, there are social advantages for not cohabiting before marriage. The main advantage is in the area of divorce. Although common thinking says that cohabitation will help a couple know if they are compatible enough for a marriage relationship, ironically, the divorce rate for couples who live together before they are married is extremely high.

If you are a believer who has found yourself in this situation of cohabitating before marriage, here are a few thoughts. First, think of the road ahead. You and your spouse want your relationship to be the best it can be. For that to be accomplished, you must have spiritual intimacy. Without becoming soul mates, you can have everything (cars, home, children, and so on) but still ache on the inside until you walk with God together. To be soul mates, there must be unity in your relationship. It will be difficult for this to happen while you cohabitate. You must tell your partner of your commitment to Christ and your expectation for the future. You want to experience everything God desires, and that means learning his ways and living his principles. Separating from your partner may seem like one step backward in your relationship, but you can go twenty steps forward by following God's plan.

How should you approach your partner about this? There is no formula that spells this out. Above all else, pray. Pray for wisdom, grace, and discernment to speak the truth with grace.

A Christ-Centered Relationship

An overwhelming majority of couples get married in a church. Even those with no church involvement seek out a church in which to say their vows. Because of this fact, the Parrotts have started the class "Save Your Marriage before It Starts." The class is designed for couples who have not yet had a marriage ceremony. During the seminar a plethora of issues is covered. Afterward, the couples are connected to mentor couples in the community. The mentor couples model what is experienced in a marriage that has Christ at the center.

A Christ-centered marriage is neither perfect nor built overnight. Just as we are growing in Christ, we are growing together. During conflict or tension, there may be times when we fail. We all make mistakes in our walk with Christ, so it is important that we respond to our spouse as God responds to us—with unconditional love, infinite forgiveness, and a concern for what is best for us.

When we share a spiritual relationship with our spouse, it gives us incredible energy to walk with Christ. This cannot happen when we are bonded with a nonbeliever (see 1 Corinthians 6). If you are a single person, develop a relationship with an individual who is walking with Christ and encourage each other in spiritual growth. If you are married to a nonbeliever, remain committed to him or her. Follow the guidelines offered above, learn more about the God you follow, and learn more about your spouse. Do not become stagnant in your spiritual journey, but also do not leave behind the one to whom you said, "I do."

22

Neighbors

Taking the Gospel Next Door

Josh Malone and Mark Cahill

It has been said that the hardest people to witness to are the ones that you know best. We can tell you this is true from personal experience. Many times our fear comes not from the fact that we know the other person but because that person knows us so well! When it comes to sharing Christ with our neighbors, two things are a must.

First, we actually need to know them. It is very easy in our day of busy lives not to know the people who live in the apartment, condominium, or house next door. Second, we must have a lifestyle that will make them curious about our faith not roll their eyes in disbelief about our faith.

Live the Message

A pastor once told of a time he witnessed to his new neighbors. He had recently taken a new pastorate and moved into the house that the church provided. He began to build a relationship with his neighbors. One day this pastor talked with his neighbors about their faith and found that they were attending a Jehovah's Witness assembly. He invited them to visit his church. When he did this, he found out just how big an impact the previous pastor and his wife—who had lived in the same house beside the same people for a few years—had had on this family. The one thing they noted about the previous pastor was the profanity they had heard from his wife at the local Little League baseball field. That had a major impact on this family.

If we are going to reach our neighbors for Christ, we are going to have to live in such a way as to spark interest in our faith. We cannot offer them the hope found in Christ when we live as though we have no hope. Our lifestyle must not contradict our message; it must support our message. Vance Havner once said, "The greatest advertisement for Christianity is a Christian." How true that is when we live out what Christ has done in our lives, but how dangerous it can be when we claim to know him but we have an undetectable, dead faith. We have an incredible opportunity to see our daily faith in Christ impact the life of another if we will simply live out what we believe. If we do this, we are sure to get the opportunity to share the reason for our hope.

Tell the Message

Many of us have been guilty of hoping that those closest to us would "catch" our Christianity. We seem to think that if we live out our faith, then we have done our "duty." While living a surrendered Christian life is a must and is commendable, it is not the end of our responsibility to a lost world. An evangelist once shared an illustration that really drives this point home. He told the audience to imagine that everyone in the room had cancer, a terrible disease by which we all had been affected in some way. He had us imagine that someone had given him the cure without us knowing. He had been healed and was walking around the room, obviously healthy. We all noticed his health and were astonished at the difference in his health compared to ours. Here was a man who had once been sick like us but now was healthy.

Obviously we would be eager to know how this happened. We would long to know how he got better. The fact remained though that no matter how much we wanted to be better, we would not get better until he shared the cure with us. The same is true with our faith. We must live it, but people will not become followers of Christ by just seeing our obedient Christian life; they must also hear the good news. So how do we get to the point of sharing the message of Christ with our neighbors?

Build the Bridge

We live in a day when people say, "Don't just tell me, show me." The best way to show people our Christianity is to develop a conversational relationship with them. We must learn our neighbors' interests and know the names of their spouse and children. If we want our neighbor to be interested in what we have to say, we must be interested in our neighbor.

People long for relationships. They like friendships. Most of us want to get to know our neighbors and build a friendship with them, but sharing the message of Christ is where we tend to have trouble. Just remember, in building a relationship with our neighbors, if we become genuinely interested in them, we have an automatic common interest—because I can promise you that your neighbors are interested in themselves! We should make our conversations less about ourselves and more about them. This will help them like us, and this is essential if they are going to listen to us.

Cross the Bridge

At some point in our relationship with anyone, neighbor or not, there comes a time when we need to ask the important questions. Why spend our time building a bridge of friendship with our neighbor if we are not going to cross it to share our faith? In *One Thing You Can't Do in Heaven*, Mark Cahill gives some great questions we can use to help us cross the bridge.

- *Where are you on your spiritual journey? What is happening spiritually in your life?* Everyone is on a spiritual journey of some sort, but the question is, what will be the final destination of that journey? Carl Sagan, a renowned atheist, was on a spiritual journey during his life. Now that he is dead, he is 100 percent assured of what is out there—but it's too late for him to do anything about it. We want to be sure that people know what is awaiting them before they leave the planet.
- *If you died tonight, are you 100 percent sure that you would go to heaven?* Is it possible that the people you talk with could die today? The answer is yes. The only question is, where will they be if they do die today?
- *If you were to die tonight and stand in front of God, and he asked, "Why should I let you into heaven?" what would you tell him?* This is a great follow-up to use with the previous question. Since it doesn't have a yes or no answer, it will draw out more information from the person so you can know how to direct the conversation.
- *When you die, what do you think is on the other side? What do you think is out there when you leave here?* When you ask this question, you will hear all kinds of answers—heaven and hell, heaven and no hell, nothing, reincarnation, unsure, and energy sources such as white light, among others.
- *Do you want to go to heaven?* This is a great question because everyone answers "yes" or "if there is one." Then you can follow up with "Do you know how to get there?" or "Can I show you how to get there?" Within a couple of questions you can be sharing the gospel with someone.

- *What is the most important thing in the world to you? On the day you die, what do you think will be the most important thing to you?* The answer lets you know immediately what people value in life. To the first question, people often give answers like money, family, or health. Many times people will give the same answer to the second question as they did to the first.

Once you have confronted your neighbor with life's toughest questions, you will have a wide-open door to give him or her the answers that only Jesus Christ can provide.

Confront Their Needs

If we are at a point with our neighbor that we have sparked interest in spiritual things, how do we convince him or her that Christ is the greatest need, that he holds the answers to life's deepest questions? The law is a great tool to reveal to people their need for Christ.

Galatians 3:24 explains: "Therefore the Law has become our tutor to lead us to Christ, so that we may be justified by faith" (NASB). That's its purpose: The Law carries us right to Jesus. People attempt to be justified by their works, but the Law leads us to Jesus so that we can be justified by our faith not by our works.

Greek is a very descriptive language. The Greek word for "tutor" in Galatians 3:24 is also translated "schoolmaster" or "teacher." It describes someone who walked or carried a child to school to make sure he arrived. Now do you see how the Law works? It will literally carry someone right to the cross, which is where we want to go in any witnessing conversation.

A pastor who used to work in advertising made an interesting statement. In commercials, he explained, advertisers never say their product is better than the competition. Instead, they create a desire for their product so people will want to buy it. Why, in commercials, do they place an attractive woman next to the car? They are trying to create a desire in you so that you will buy their product. This is exactly what the law of God, the Ten Commandments, does for a sinner. Helping sinners see their personal guilt before a holy, just God will create in them a desire for whatever can get rid of their sin. They will have a desire for Jesus and his cleansing blood.

Once your neighbor has had his interest piqued by your lifestyle, his thoughts provoked by your questions, and his conscience pricked by God's law, share with him the only solution—Jesus Christ.

23

Classmates

Seven Tips for Reaching Students

Jose Zayas

The numbers are in your favor. According to the October 2004 survey by Christian pollster George Barna, 64 percent of people who made commitments to follow Jesus Christ did so before they turned eighteen. That means six out of ten people who trust in Jesus Christ will do it before they get their high school diploma!

So, what's it going to take to see your fellow students reached? It's going to take a change in perspective. You and I are going to have to see our campuses as more than a place to read a book or get a degree. It's your mission field.

If you're ready to be used by God, consider the following seven tips for reaching students around you.

Call on God

"Where do I start?"

Pray. There's a real battle going on. God wants to rescue your classmate. Satan wants to keep him in the dark. You're in the middle of a battle for souls.

Pray. Don't try to witness in your own strength. Here's an encouragement: You're not powerful, smart, or savvy enough to convince any other student that Jesus is the only way to God (hint: neither am I).

Pray. God wants your friend to be rescued more than you do, so call on him now, often, always.

Start praying for your not-yet-Christian friends, *by name*, asking God to open the door for them to receive his offer of salvation. Not the creative type? Don't worry—the Bible tells us exactly what to pray for:

- more workers (Matt. 9:38)
- more opportunities (Col. 4:3–5)
- more boldness (Acts 4:29)

That's what we need! Consider Jesus's promise to you: "Ask and it will be given to you.... For everyone who asks receives" (Matt. 7:7–8). As James 5:16 reminds us: "The prayer of a righteous man is powerful and effective." Call on God. He's listening.

Count the Cost

"But what if my friend doesn't listen to me? Or worse, what if he doesn't want to hang with me once he finds out I'm a Christian?"

Good questions. Admittedly, there is a risk, a cost in following Jesus. Look at what Jesus told his first followers, "No servant is greater than his master. If they persecuted me, they will persecute you also. If they obeyed my teaching, they will obey yours also" (John 15:20). Most of the people that Jesus spoke to rejected him. Only a few followed. No matter what happens to us, it happened to Jesus first.

You and I are not called to win a popularity contest. We're called to fulfill God's purposes on the earth. And to do that, we've been given precious promises:

- Jesus is with us every time we share his name (Matt. 28:18–20).
- We have the Holy Spirit's power to be a witness (Acts 1:8).
- God's Word always accomplishes God's objectives (Isa. 55:11).

So count the cost. Choose to be used by God, no matter how difficult the challenge.

Conquer Your Fears

"How can I overcome the fear I have of witnessing?"

Have you ever taken a test without studying? I can remember my heart pounding as I walked into the classroom, totally unprepared for a test, wondering if I would know the answers.

The same can be said about our witness to students. First Peter 3:15 reminds us to "always be prepared to give an answer to everyone who asks you to give the reason for the hope that you have." It's our job to be ready. It's God's job to give us the power when we need it.

The guaranteed way to a fear-filled witness is to do nothing. Want to break those fears? Learn what you believe. Study the chapters in this book on other religions. Read. Ask other Christians to help you. Ask your not-yet-Christian friends what questions or objections they have to following Jesus. Then do some research and get back to them.

I'm always nervous when I share my faith. It's never easy. But you don't have to let fear keep you from taking the first step.

Connect the Dots

"I'm having trouble getting a spiritual conversation started. How do you bring it up?"

Your friends will listen to you when they know that you really care. First, you need to connect with your schoolmates. What do you like to do? What are you good at? Whatever it is—skating or BMX, for example—you have instant credibility with other students who like to do the same thing. Our job is to connect with our friends, build sincere friendships, and establish a level of trust.

What if they find out I'm not a perfect Christian?

There are no perfect Christians! What you want your friends to see is the "authentic you." As a follower of Jesus, you have ups and downs, victories and failures. Following Jesus doesn't mean that everything is perfect in your life—it simply means that you're following the Perfect One, who promises to forgive you and be with you through life's storms.

Next, our goal is to help connect our friends with the good news of Jesus Christ. It's like the connect-the-dots drawings I used to do as a kid. You probably did them too. Remember, you'd have the bunch of dots with numbers under them and you'd take your pen and draw a line from one to two. Then from dot two to three. Finally, when you connected lines between all of the dots, you could see the picture clearly.

What's your classmate's spiritual IQ? What does he know about God, the Bible, or Jesus? Find out and make that "dot number one." Don't assume that he believes that the Bible is the Word of God or that God created the heavens and the earth.

The best way to find out a classmate's spiritual IQ is to ask open-ended questions like, "Who do you think Jesus is?" or "What are your spiritual beliefs?" This is a nonthreatening way to start a spiritual conversation.

Ask what she believes and, chances are, you'll get the question right back at you. Now you have an open door! The goal is for your schoolmate to understand who Jesus is, what he did to rescue us, and what he offers to those who trust in him. Learn to "connect the dots."

Combine Your Gifts

"Can I really be involved in evangelism?"
Evangelism is a team sport! Don't buy into the lie that you're the only person who will share with the person you're praying for. More than likely, there are other students who love Jesus and want to reach out on your campus. Find them!

You may have the gift of evangelism, and sharing your faith comes easily. Great! Go for it! If not, begin to look for open doors to partner with other Christians and "tag team" it. You may want to invite the person you're praying for to a Christian club on your campus. Look for the right event at your youth group to plug him into. Take a friend to a Christian concert or get her hooked on your favorite Christian band. Watch a movie, like *The Lord of the Rings*, and talk about the spiritual symbolism. The options are endless!

If you don't feel comfortable talking yet, look for another Christian to do the talking. Next time, ask God for the boldness to share his message yourself. Don't go at it alone. Combine your gifts.

Clarify the Message

"But what if they ask me what I believe? What do I say?"
The good news is so rich and profound that we will never fully comprehend it. Yet it's so simple that a seven-year-old child can grasp it and believe (that's my story!). Reread the first section of this book, "Defining Your Faith" (part I, section A), for a better understanding of what the gospel message is. Allow me to summarize with two cornerstone verses:

- John 3:16: "For God so loved the world that he gave his one and only Son, that whoever believes in him shall not perish but have eternal life."
- 1 Corinthians 15:3–4: "For what I received I passed on to you as of first importance: that Christ died for sins according to the Scriptures, that he was buried, that he was raised on the third day according to the Scriptures."

Jesus died and rose again to save sinners. That's our message.
Now, some practical tips to clarify the message with your classmates:

- *Start in Genesis.* God made it all. Until they know that God made them to know him, what Jesus did may not make sense.
- *Use class lessons as "starting points."* So much of what is taught in school contradicts a biblical view of life. Make the most of what is taught to contrast what the Bible teaches.

- *Share what God is doing in your life.* Keep your testimony current. Focus on how God rescued you and what he's doing in your life right now. They may not believe the Bible yet, but God's work in your life is undeniable—God's Word in and through you.

- *The Good News leads to a decision.* It's not enough to know *about* Jesus Christ. We are called to surrender and follow him personally. Don't shy away from asking other students if they are ready to receive God's gift of forgiveness. The Holy Spirit does the convincing, but we do the asking!

Continue to Share

"What do I do when I'm ready to give up?"

Don't give up! Your schoolmates may not be ready to respond at the exact moment you attempt to share with them, but you never know how open they may be next week, next month, or next year. I tried to share with other students in high school, often with little visible results. During my senior year, a popular student suddenly committed suicide. The doors were wide open and I was able to clearly share with many students about my personal relationship with Jesus. I have a schoolmate that I'm still sharing Christ with ten years later. He isn't a follower yet, but he's much closer than before.

Your friendships shouldn't end when people reject the message. Hold on. Keep praying. Try again. Remember, God wants to reach your schoolmates more than you do.

24

Strangers

Making the Most of Every Opportunity

―――――――――――

Phil Callaway

How do you witness to strangers when often you have just enough time for one conversation?

Be Yourself

I've found that when I am myself, people talk to me. On one particular flight, I sat down next to a psychologist who introduced himself to me and asked, "What do you do?"

"I am a speaker and I write books," I said. I also told him what I write and speak about. Within thirty seconds, he diagnosed me as a Christian and said, "I've had bad experiences with Christians."

I stuck out my hand and replied, "Really? Me too!" He laughed and I laughed, and we had a four-hour conversation about Jesus on that plane.

One of the greatest stresses in my life has always come from something Christians call "witnessing." I would sit on an airplane knowing that if it crashed and the guy beside me went to hell, it would be my fault alone. When I told others about my faith, I was as clumsy as a carpenter with ten thumbs. I took a personal evangelism course once to try to get over my fear, then I tried preaching on the street. A little girl threw rocks at me. I decided to throw *Four Spiritual Laws* booklets from a moving car, but I couldn't bring myself to do it. I knew they might throw me in jail for littering and I'd have to witness there. In those days, I operated out

139

of guilt not love. Finally, I realized that a closed mouth gathers no foot, so I kept mine shut.

A few years ago, I made a surprising discovery. When I simply tell others what I have seen or what God has done, they listen. When I incorporate some humor, their faces light up, and sometimes their hearts do too.

I used to count conversions, but now I count conversations. Sometimes I wish I were a Billy Graham or that I had the wisdom of a Charles Colson, but God has given each of us different gifts and different ways of getting into people's lives.

I just love a conversation, though I usually don't force conversations with strangers. "Remember, everyone on earth is just a little bit lonely," my mother used to tell me when I was a little boy. We need to remember that as believers. A smile can go a long way with people, as well as standing to give someone else your place on the bus. Asking someone, "How's it going?" and genuinely listening to his or her answer is important.

People are either open-faced or closed-faced. Christians need to be those open-faced people with a kind word for the stewardess or bus driver. There's this joy Christ alone can give. If people can't see within the first five minutes of meeting us that we are joy-filled people, there's something wrong.

Pray for the Person beside You

Whether you're traveling on an airplane or commuting to work on a subway, take a moment to bring the person next to you before God by praying for him or her. I have found that this can be incredibly effective in opening up an opportunity to talk about God.

Some Christians, like my wife, are shy. Getting into a conversation with someone takes nerve. It doesn't always happen. God made each of us a certain way. Pray and trust him and opportunities will arise.

I don't think anything scares believers or nonbelievers more than witnessing. Honestly, if you looked at me, you'd think I'm fearless, but it's quite the opposite. What I've learned that really helps me is simply this: I am a witness. I'm not here to smack people over the head with the gospel. I'm here to tell them what has happened to me. That's what a witness does in court. I look at my life and I know beyond a shadow of a doubt where I would be were it not for my faith in Christ. So I pray and ask God for opportunities to tell others about what he has done for me.

Strike Up a Conversation

A book or current event on the front page of a newspaper can be a good subject for starting a conversation. While getting into a taxi one day, I chose to sit up front beside the cab driver. I happened to be reading C. S. Lewis's *Mere Christianity*, and he asked me, "What's that?"

"Let me read you a quote." I began explaining that this author was an atheist who became a Christian. Then I posed the question, "What do you think about that?"

The driver was very interested. I didn't tell him my story. I talked about C. S. Lewis. If people I'm sitting beside look at what I'm reading and I make eye contact with them, they'll sometimes ask, "What are you reading?"

When tragedy hits, men and women begin to ask the question, "How could a loving God allow such suffering?" I've found my own story can answer their question. "You know, I don't understand that either. I want to ask God someday." Then I tell them about a difficulty I've gone through, because we've all gone through some troubling times in our lives. It gives us a point of common interest. I don't have all the right answers, but I know and care about the questions.

Find a Connecting Point

Golf or some other hobby can be a connecting point. If I talk about my children, and the person I'm witnessing to has children, suddenly we have much in common. I've discovered a common interest is a much better way to connect than just handing people the *Four Spiritual Laws*. Jesus comes into my conversation about my life because he's the biggest part of it. He's central to everything I do.

There's a liberal media columnist who lives about an hour from me. I liked a column he wrote about a rock star, so I phoned him to say how much I appreciated his article. During our conversation, he learned pretty quickly that I was a believer and said to me, "I used to be a Christian."

I told him I'd be in his city in about a week and asked if I could take him out for lunch. We had a two hour lunch. He asked me to pray before we ate our pizza. We kept in touch often. Frank came to our house for breakfast.

Then I found myself at an Eagles concert with him and seventeen thousand others. Joe Walsh, their lead guitarist, played a beautiful guitar solo of "Amazing Grace." People started singing and Frank knew all the words. Later he attended a Petra concert with me, and their song about the Apostle's Creed offended him. We talked for more than an hour about what I believe. Frank said, "I don't understand it all, but I can't get that out of my mind." He was speaking specifically of my wife and me who have been married for twenty-two years and the difficulties we've gone through for years with her seizures.

"I would give anything for the love you have," Frank said. I told him, "Frank, you can have that love. It's Christ." Several months later, I got an email from him that read, "I did it. I did it. I came to Christ."

Make the Most of Unexpected Opportunities

Even an inconvenience can provide an opportunity. During a two-hour flight delay, I sat in the airport terminal and talked to a fellow traveler. I could have complained to him about our situation. Instead, I turned that around and used our time together to say, "I'm thankful that I'm alive and that our plane got here safely."

When Jesus walked the earth, he was constantly meeting strangers. He always had time for them, even when he was weary. Jesus always had time for two things that really matter—the two things that last forever: God's Word and people.

Ordinary People by Age Group

25

Senior Adults

It's Not Too Late!

Jimmy Dusek and Jim Henry

George Barna's research places elders in two groups: Builders, born between 1927 and 1945, and Seniors, born before 1927. Both groups have a perspective on life that causes them to face more honestly the reality of death and eternity. They have dreamed dreams, accomplished much in their chosen careers, raised a family, succeeded or failed in family and life pursuits, worked hard, fought in wars, attended church, contributed to their communities, then entered retirement and focused on volunteerism.

In matters of faith, most have some background, either in their childhood or when their children came along and they took them to church occasionally. According to Barna's research (2004), the number of Builders and Seniors who declare they are born-again Christians is about 44 percent, yet when asked if faith is important in their lives, 80 percent said yes, with 75 percent believing that God is the all-powerful, all-knowing, perfect Creator that rules the world today. Yet some lack assurance of salvation and are not confident that they have a personal relationship with Christ as Savior and Lord. Therefore, your strategy is to help them know for sure that Jesus is their personal Savior.

The process is similar to processes used with other groups but with an emphasis on assurance of salvation.

Pray for the Person

Before you take a step toward witness and discussion with a senior adult, spend time in prayer. Psalm 126:5–6 says, "Those who sow in tears will reap with songs of joy. He who goes out weeping, carrying seed to sow, will return with songs of

145

joy, carrying sheaves with him." We have a precious message—"good seed"—but the person needs to be "good ground"—ready to receive it. Prayer is vital to God's working in *our* hearts as well as in the person with whom we are sharing Christ.

Build Relationships

Bathe the process in prayer as you begin to share with the individual; then ask the person to tell the story of his spiritual journey. Listen carefully and build a relationship of trust and caring. As you listen, be alert to key points that will help you ask more pointed questions. Some key comments from senior adults may be: "I went to church because my parents made me," "I follow the golden rule," "I live by the Ten Commandments," "I took my kids to church," "I was baptized as an infant," "I worked hard to provide for my family," or "I served in the military." All of these responses focus on what they have *done*. They are implying that their good works or their nominal church attendance should be enough for heaven.

Another key in listening is to find out about health needs. These people, who are often concerned with their health and the possibility of life-threatening illnesses, seem to be more receptive to spiritual matters and more concerned about their eternal salvation than younger people.

Ask Clarifying Questions

Sometimes the answer senior adults give to questions about whether or not they have a personal spiritual relationship with Christ is "I hope so" or "I am trying my best" or "I pray everyday." From this you will realize that clarifying questions need to be asked to help them focus on their spiritual need and certainty that Jesus is their personal Savior.

Evangelism Explosion by D. James Kennedy gives two diagnostic questions that help a person clarify where she is in relationship to Christ. The first is, "If you were to die tonight, where would you spend eternity?" The second asks, "If you died tonight and you came before God and he asked why he should let you into heaven, what would you say?"[1] The answers to these questions will focus either on "works" the person has done or on a "hope-so" attitude, or she will declare her faith and trust in Christ alone and in his saving grace as her only hope for heaven. For those who don't seem sure of their relationship with Christ, John 14:6; Acts 4:12; and Ephesians 2:8–9 are good verses to share.

Patiently help them see that works cannot make us right with God. They need to see salvation as a new-birth experience. Scripture says, "There is no one righteous, not even one" (Rom. 3:10) and "All have sinned and fall short of the glory of God" (v. 23). We need a Savior. Jesus, and a relationship with him, is our only hope of eternal life (John 3:16).

Lead in a Prayer of Commitment

Once the senior adult sees his need, you can offer to lead him in the sinner's prayer of confession and commitment to Jesus as Savior and Lord. If the person agrees to pray with you, ask him to pray out loud as you lead. Clarify that this is a confession, an act of the will to trust in Jesus and Jesus alone for salvation. This will bring assurance that he knows Jesus as his personal Savior and Lord.

A simple prayer would be:

Dear Jesus,

Thank you for dying on the cross for my sins. I am sorry for my sins and repent of them as I now confess you as my Savior. Forgive my sins and come into my heart and save me forever. Fill me with your Holy Spirit and, when I die someday, take me home to heaven with you. Thank you, Jesus, for coming into my heart.

I love you and will serve you.

Amen.

Affirm the Confession

Scripture verses can add to the person's understanding of this eternal transaction of salvation. You can affirm that God and you have heard her confession of a need for salvation through Christ. An assurance that God has heard and answered can bring peace and bless the person's life for whatever years she has left in this world. Read 1 John 5:13: "I write these things . . . so that you may *know* that you have eternal life." Read John 14:1–6, where Jesus promised to receive believers to himself. John 10:28 states: "No one can snatch them out of my hand." Acts 2:21 tells us: "Everyone who calls on the name of the Lord will be saved."

Encourage the new believer to read God's Word daily and to worship the Lord personally and corporately with the people in the church. Help him see the importance of telling others about how they can know Jesus personally as their Savior and Lord.

Three Responses

In witnessing to mature adults, I (Jim Henry) usually receive one of three common responses.

The first one is outright rejection and no interest in spiritual matters. One gentleman I visited was in a hospital and close to death. After some minutes of conversation, we got into a spiritual discussion. He cut me off by saying, "I'm not interested in God or spiritual things. I don't believe in anything beyond death. As far as I'm concerned, a human is like a dog. You die and that's the end of it. Nothing."

Another response is delay. You would think that, as the finish line draws nearer, there would be a sense of urgency, but this is not always true. I remember Buford, who lived fairly close to our church. His wife was a faithful worshiper. One Saturday while out visiting, I drove by their house and felt strongly impressed to go back to the house and make a call. His wife told me he wasn't feeling well, that he was in the bedroom, and she asked me to see him. He sat on the edge of the bed, and we had a friendly chat.

I engaged him in conversation about his relationship to Christ and shared the way home to Jesus. He listened intently and, when I finished, I asked Buford if he would accept Jesus. He said no. I urged again. No. I prayed for him and turned to leave, and he said, "But I will be in church next Sunday."

When I came back to the church the next weekend (I was doing seminary work), I noticed a fresh gravesite, covered with flowers, in the cemetery that was adjacent to our church. I drove into the village and saw one of our members and asked about the fresh grave I had seen. He said, "Haven't you heard? Buford got real sick last Monday. They rushed him to the hospital, but they couldn't help him. We buried him at the church cemetery last Thursday."

I'll never forget walking back to that freshly dug grave, with the flowers draped over the brown dirt, and saying, "Buford, you waited too late. Sunday never came."

The third response is, "I need to be forgiven, but I've messed up so bad, especially when I was younger. I'm too rotten to be forgiven, and it doesn't seem right to ask Jesus Christ to save me now, when I've wasted my life and have so little to give back." What a joy to remind people who say this of the thief on the cross—his repentance and trust in Jesus! Through the years, we've seen scores and scores of older adults come to faith in Christ and become vibrant witnesses and faithful to the Lord and to the church for the rest of their lives. I remember baptizing a man in his nineties. I was talking to him about the process, making sure he felt secure about going in the water. He said, "Son, I swam the river when I was ninety; I can handle this pool!" Their universal response to their salvation is always, "I wish I had done this years ago."

I agree with a cherished brother in Christ who said, "I am convinced that very few people want to die without Christ. Even those who are not altogether sure that there is a Christ fix in their minds the importance of not dying without him. The problem with most of us is that dying remains a future event—we all want to be saved—but not yet—we had rather wait until we've tasted the world's dessert before we begin the feast of God."[2]

Our task is to be faithful in witnessing, steadfast in prayer, compassionate in spirit, believing he, who is not willing that any should perish, does not give up on any, regardless of age, unless they have totally hardened their hearts to the wooing of his Holy Spirit.

26

The Baby Boomer Generation

Reaching Men and Women with the Gospel

Scott Dawson

The statistics are staggering concerning adults coming to know Christ. It is estimated that after a person turns eighteen, the chances of his receiving Christ is less than 15 percent. My intention in this chapter is to offer you practical advice on how to be involved in shattering these statistics with your adult friends. Will it be easy? Probably not. Can it be done? Certainly!

After speaking to a crowd in an arena, my eyes were fixed on one man on a mission. During the invitation after my message, I had suggested, "Ask the person beside you if he or she is willing to follow Christ. If the person says yes, offer to come down with him or her to the front." I saw this distinguished politician ask another public figure the question, and then they both came forward—another illustration of how one person brings another to Christ.

This example is as old as Scripture. When Andrew met Christ, he went immediately to his brother Simon Peter and brought him to Jesus (John 1:41–42). As believers in Christ, our one motivation should be to bring another person to Jesus.

The Difficulty

Why is it so difficult to reach adults? First, adults are usually more cynical in nature than children and teenagers. Most adults have heard sales pitches, quick fixes, and scams for so long that a natural barrier guards them against believing

149

in everything or anything. In comparison, a young child will believe every word of a parent. A teenager evolves into questioning every suggestion a parent offers. This only gets worse as the person grows older. This barrier is difficult to overcome with the gospel, especially when you consider we are speaking about a God people cannot actually see.

Second, most adults have accumulated baggage over the years that serves as a hindrance to the gospel. The term *baggage* refers to emotional, physical, relational, mental, and religious experiences that have formed a kind of bondage. "Can anything set me free?" was the question an adult male asked me one night after a church service. The man explained that his life had been filled with broken relationships that had started with his father and was now involving his third wife in fifteen years. After a long discussion, this man came to understand that his baggage had to be dumped for him to experience true freedom. Although the past cannot be forgotten, the present situation must be accepted, knowing only God can heal the hurt.

Third, adults have moved into a stage of self-existence. They have moved from dating to marriage, part-time jobs to occupations, and from hot rods to SUVs. During this transition, there is tremendous pressure to produce simply to survive. Adults have moved from dreaming of their future to enduring their present. When this happens, many adults lose their "need" for Christ. With a secular mindset, an adult must ask, "What can Christ do for me?"

Fourth, and probably most damaging, is the fact that most adults have seen so much hypocrisy in church that Christ has simply been dismissed. In the age of church scandal and Christian celebrity downfalls, society has looked at the church with a sense of discouragement and, even worse, disdain. In Florida I spoke with a couple about their spiritual condition. I tried to bring up the subject with the following question: "When you and your friends discuss Christ or religion, what do you normally discuss?" The answer was that the subject is never brought up! We must ask ourselves in the Christian community which is worse—to be criticized by society or simply ignored? We must make an effort to discuss spiritual issues with those around us.

While there are many similarities in reaching men and women for Christ, we must note that there are also some differences. Although all adults have the same void and hunger for God in their lives, the trigger points may be different. In general, a woman desires security in her life, while a man is searching for significance. As the woman longs for touch, the man longs for the thrill. A woman desires conversation; the man desires control. When a woman wants to focus on a problem, the man wants to fix the problem.

When it comes to sharing Christ, you may know a person who could fit into either of these stereotypes. The way we reach a person is really driven by the emotional state of the individual, but generally the genders can be effectively reached by considering their differences.

Here is some practical advice: *A good rule is never be alone with a member of the opposite sex when you are sharing Christ.* Take my word for it and don't do it. It's just not a good idea. In addition, avoid any tendency toward emotional manipulation. Provide biblical answers to situations and leave personal nuances out. Always speak the truth. It is impossible to present Jesus who says, "I am the way and the truth and the life" (John 14:6), if we are telling things that are not true. If you are unable to answer questions, admit your lack of knowledge. It is not a sin not to know the answer, but it is a sin to lie!

Reaching a Man

From the time in the Garden of Eden, man has been trying to find peace in his soul. A man has many pressures on his life, and the greatest is to have peace with God. In our culture, men have been trained to be the hunter—the breadwinner—for the household. Due to this fact, men are searching for significance. The first thing that attracts a man in friendship is leadership or success. We all want to be like the star quarterback or know the local celebrity. Why? Significance. So how can we show the significance of Christ to the male culture?

First, be real in your relationship. Have you ever seen one of those movies that has been dubbed into another language? You see the mouth moving, but the audio doesn't fit. In essence, the audio doesn't match the video. In the same way, as followers of Christ, our audio (talk of Christ) should match our video (our walk with Christ). Without it, your friends will not place significance on a relationship with Christ.

Second, be clear. There is nothing worse than trying to drive with fogged-up windows. It's impossible to see where you are on the road. In a similar way, when sharing Christ, you must be clear in your focus or you won't know where you are going. Start with a question like, "Can I share with you something that changed my life?" By all means, until you are comfortable with your own style, use a tract or evangelism piece from your church. Read it beforehand and make sure you understand it before you read it to another person.

Third, be persistent. Men are notorious negotiators. Everything can be cheaper or done better in their eyes. Honestly, it is very rare when I share Christ for the first time with a male that I see him enter into a relationship with the Lord. Usually, he will discuss the topic again (maybe four or five times) before the commitment is made. Do not be discouraged if you are rejected or even ridiculed during your first presentation. Expect ridicule. When (if) it happens, you can smile and say you will discuss it again next week. You will be amazed at how relieved you feel when you are already prepared for the situation.

Finally, be willing. Without your willingness to share Christ, he will not be shared. How else will this world know about Jesus unless we share? God in his sovereignty has given us this task. He is the one who saves, but he uses us to do his work. If you are scared, join the club—we all are. If you have messed up in the past in front of your friends, here is a newsflash—we all have! However, if you are not willing to share the greatest news your friends can ever hear, then God help us all.

Reaching a Woman

As I said earlier, women tend to search for security—the security of a relationship. What better relationship to have than with the Creator of the planet! Think about it. A woman in relationship with the sovereign God will experience a security that is foreign to most people today. To know the very God who issues life and desires a true relationship with her will fill her life with safety. The following principles have been proven to work when sharing Christ with an adult woman.

First, follow the principles above that are used with a man: Be real, clear, persistent, and willing to share.

Second, refer to women of faith in Scripture. Can you imagine a world without Esther's courage, Sarah's faith, and Mary's commitment? Look to the women of faith in Scripture to provide illustrations and bridges for evangelism.

Finally, resolve to be "intrusive" about Jesus. We live in a world where tolerance is overstated and evangelism is under siege. To have the beauty of Christ blossoming in your life and not share this is truly a shame. A friendship is but a little while; however, eternity is forever. I encourage you to ask probing questions about the gospel in your relationships. The best way to start is to plan to do it. I know you will see many people come to Christ!

27

Youth

Hope for Today's Youth

Alvin L. Reid

In the 1700s God touched the American colonies with a mighty revival called the First Great Awakening. Many have heard of this revival, but few are aware that it was most powerfully at work among young people. Jonathan Edwards, a pastor during the revival, observed the role of youth in this revival: "The work has been chiefly amongst the young; and comparatively but few others have been made partakers of it. And indeed it has commonly been so, when God has begun any great work for the revival of his church; he has taken the young people, and has cast off the old and stiff-necked generation."[1]

Youth in the Bible

Young people are often related to the worst problems in society. It's interesting that this is not the picture of youth that the Bible gives. While there are some negative examples of young people in Scripture, the overwhelming majority are positive. For example:

- Isaac, as a young man, simply obeyed his father to the point of being a sacrifice.
- Joseph, at seventeen, was sold into slavery by his brothers but lived for God.

- Samuel, as a lad, heard the voice of God and became a great leader.
- David, as a youth, faced Goliath and led a nation.
- Jeremiah was called to be a prophet as a youth.
- Josiah chose to follow God as a youth and led a revival while a young king.
- Esther, as a young maiden, stood for God.
- Daniel and his friends, possibly middle-school aged, stood for God in the face of the mighty king of Babylon.
- Mary was probably a teen when she gave birth to the Lord Jesus.
- Timothy was told not to let anyone look down on his youth but to be an example.
- And the first recorded words of Jesus, at age twelve, were, "Didn't you know I had to be in my Father's house?" (Luke 2:49).

Youth Today

When treated like young adults preparing for lifelong service to God rather than children emerging from the cocoon of childhood, youth will rise to the level we as spiritual leaders set for them. The coming generation of young people, born after 1982 and dubbed Net-Gens, Generation Y, Mosaics, or Millennials, display some of the most hopeful characteristics of any in recent times.

They are not pessimists; they are optimists. Contrast this with the more pessimistic Generation X that preceded them. In recent surveys nine in ten Millennials described themselves as happy, positive, or confident.

They are not self-absorbed; they are cooperative team players. This generation has been raised on Barney and the Power Rangers, who focused on team activities. This is the generation that has made possible the phenomenal success of Upward Basketball in churches across the land. They have also shown a remarkable commitment to personal evangelism when sent forth in teams.

They are not distrustful; they accept authority. In one study of twelve-to-fourteen year olds, the young people said they looked to their parents the most for answers. George Barna notes, "Family is a big deal to teenagers, regardless of how they act or what they say. It is the rare teenager who believes he or she can lead a fulfilling life without receiving complete acceptance and support from his or her family." He adds, "In spite of the seemingly endless negative coverage in the media about the state of the family these days, most teens are proud of their family."[2]

They are not rule-breakers; they are rule-followers. Over the past decade, most violent crime statistics among youth have actually declined.

They are not stupid; they are very bright. This generation understands technology better than their parents.

They have not given up on progress; they believe in the future. The idealism of the Boomer generation of the sixties is seen in this group without such an anti-authority edge.

They are not unmotivated; they simply want to be challenged. We can decry the low academic standards in our public schools all we want, but the level of expectation for discipleship in our churches is strikingly similar.

Reaching Youth

Reaching youth today includes several general principles:

- *Be real.* This is the generation of reality TV. It is a generation that has a high level of spiritual interest but a low tolerance for hypocrites. Speak to youth straight, giving them the pure truth of the gospel. Emphasize how Jesus changes life now.

- *Equip Christian youth.* One of the most remarkable aspects of this generation of Christian youth is their passion for witnessing when taught how to do it. The best person to reach a young person is another young person. Equip your youth to reach their friends, show them how, and turn them loose.

- *Use adults.* As noted above, this generation actually likes their parents. But remember the wise words a student said recently: "We know how to be teenagers; show us how to be adults." Don't act like a teenager; act like a loving parent. Many youth today, with so many broken or dysfunctional families, long to know a real parent. Someone has coined the term *SOAP*: Significant Other Adult Person. Many unsaved youth can be reached when an adult takes the time to be a significant, caring person in his or her life.

- *Use the arts.* This generation loves the arts, music, drama, media, and so on. This generation is much more right-brained than the last one. Reach them on their turf with the changeless gospel presented in creative ways. Music is an especially powerful medium with this generation.

- *Set the bar high.* Speak and relate to them as young adults not as misfits somewhere between childhood and adulthood.

- *Make sure your church is not just an institution that meets on Sunday but part of a movement.* Show unsaved youth who attend your services authentic worship. Let them know the manifest presence of God.

28

Children

Leading a Child to Jesus

Patricia Palau

Children don't need to wait until they become adults to make the most important decision of their life—to trust Jesus Christ as Savior. The Lord longs to welcome children into his family. "Let the little children come to me," Jesus said, "and do not hinder them, for the kingdom of heaven belongs to such as these" (Matt. 19:14).

But how do you present the gospel to a child? How much does a boy or girl need to know to make an intelligent, valid decision?

Here are five guidelines for helping a child understand and accept the basic truths of the gospel.

Spontaneous Conversations

Conversations with children about spiritual matters often take place spontaneously. Take advantage of the times when a child wants to talk with you.

Children's natural curiosity often leads them to ask a million questions. Our youngest son, Stephen, for instance, was fascinated with heaven. "Where is it?" "Who's there?" "Who'll be waiting?" "How are we going to get there?" These are opportunities for the teacher in you to come forth and start thinking, *Okay, what's a good illustration of that?* Use illustrations from children's lives, from nature, and from things they deal with on a daily basis.

If you say something and later realize a child misunderstood what you meant, don't give up and quit talking with the child about the gospel. Go back and say, "Now remember what we were talking about yesterday?" and readdress the issue in terms the child understands. It's a trial and error process. If you use an expression a child takes the wrong way, don't panic. Our errors and mistakes are not going to threaten God's purposes.

Young children are naturally inclined to trust and believe in God. Though they may sometimes absorb wrong concepts about what it means to "ask Jesus into your heart," there is nothing innately wrong with a child's inadequate concept of God or Christianity. The One who made us understands exactly how children think and doesn't expect us to fully understand the gospel before we commit our lives to Jesus Christ.

The temptation for some adults is to rush or force the decision if a child puts off making a profession of faith in Christ. If anything should happen to a child, we want to know that he or she is going to heaven. It is essential, though, to be sensitive to the Spirit's work in a child's life.

Telling the Gospel Story

For various reasons, some people are reluctant to talk with children about subjects like the cross and the crucifixion of Jesus. Yet the Passion story is profoundly moving to children. Don't shy away from it. Present the gospel, let them ask questions, and then build on that.

Usually, the best approach in teaching about the Lord Jesus is to start at the beginning and proceed chronologically. First, God loves us and entered the human race, born of the virgin Mary. He was named Jesus, the Savior. As a man, Jesus traveled about healing the sick and feeding the hungry. He demonstrated to the multitudes who God is. They marveled at the power of his teaching and the holiness of his life. Nevertheless, Jesus was betrayed, crucified, and buried. Three days later, he rose from the dead and a few weeks later returned to heaven.

It doesn't hurt children's self-esteem to admit they've sinned. Children know they're not perfect, but what's exciting is to tell them about the Savior. Soon, they'll begin asking, "Why is he on the cross?" They likely won't grasp the whole significance, but they can understand that he died on the cross and will continue to ask questions.

Covering the Basics

Our emphasis in presenting the gospel to our children should be that God is our heavenly Father. That is essential. Instead of initially focusing on sin—"We hurt the Lord when we do wrong things"—we should emphasize the fact that our heavenly

Father, who is perfect, loves us with an everlasting love. Yet the issue of sin needs to be addressed.

Many have debated about when children develop a sense of guilt and personal responsibility. No one knows, but it can be much earlier than they ever let on. Many young children are sensitive. That sensitivity may be a seed planted by God in their hearts.

To experience God's love, our children must own up to the things in their lives that hurt him—selfishness, pride, deceit, and all the rest. They need to see that "the wages of sin is death" (Rom. 6:23). They need to learn that "all have sinned and fall short of the glory of God" (3:23). That includes everyone, young and old alike.

The aim, of course, is to show children that Jesus took our sins on himself. The Bible says, "Christ died for sins once for all, the righteous for the unrighteous, to bring you to God" (1 Pet. 3:18). When the Lord died on the cross, he conquered death so that each of us may be forgiven. We deserve to be punished for the wrong we have done in God's eyes, but God sent his Son to receive our punishment in his body on the cross (see 2:24). What he did is like a judge finding a prisoner guilty, taking the prisoner's place, and receiving the sentence himself. What magnificent love!

A child may not completely understand how God places the penalty for his sin on his Son. That's okay. Doesn't God simply ask us to respond to him based on what we *do* know? When someone becomes a Christian, she may not understand it all at the beginning, but as that person reads the Bible and is sensitive to God's teaching, her understanding will grow.

Leading in a Prayer of Commitment

If a child asks, "Well, how do I become a Christian?" turn to Scripture for the answer. I like to use Romans 10:9–10 with children, inserting their names in the blanks. "If you, _____, confess with your mouth, 'Jesus is Lord,' and believe in your heart that God raised him from the dead, you, _____, will be saved. For it is with your heart that you, _____, believe and are justified, and it is with your mouth that you, _____, confess and are saved."

The best way I know to make Jesus the Lord of your life is to bow your head in prayer, confess your sins to God, by faith open your heart to Christ, believe in him, and receive him. If that's your child's decision, then ask him or her to tell God. Here is a suggested prayer:

Heavenly Father, I want to be a Christian. I realize that my sins have separated me from you. Please forgive me. I believe in what Christ did for me on the cross. I don't completely understand it, but I accept it by faith. I want to be a child of yours. Please come into my life, Lord Jesus, and make me your child right now. I'll follow you and obey you forever. Amen.

When leading a child in prayer, explain that you'll say one phrase of the prayer at a time. Then the child can repeat that phrase out loud after you. Emphasize that the prayer is to God not to you.

After you finish praying together, ask several questions to help a child clarify the decision he has just made. Then celebrate that decision! Give him an opportunity to share the joy of his decision with family members and Christian friends.

To help a child look back on and remember the decision, encourage her to write it down in a Bible or New Testament. We suggest children write the date, a statement such as "Today I accepted the Lord Jesus Christ as my Savior," and their name. It will be a great day to remember!

Giving Assurance

Children need assurance of their salvation. Wait for a good teachable moment when the subject comes up naturally, and then say, "When we come to Jesus, we're his forever. Nothing can separate us from God's love." You can move alongside a child and say, "You know, aren't you glad that Jesus will never, ever let you out of his hands? He's never going to let you go. You're part of his family forever."

It's also helpful to memorize biblical promises about assurance, such as John 10:28, with a child. When doubts come, we need to be able to go to the promises of Scripture. You can say to your child, "Remember what we memorized last week?"

It's tragic that some people resist the idea of evangelizing children. In evangelistic campaigns, we've seen men and women holding back their children from going forward to confess the Lord Jesus as their Savior. Other Christians don't talk about the issue of salvation with children, as if it were just a theological matter for adults to discuss at church. The message many children are picking up is, "Wait until you grow up and then you can make your decision." But it's really the other way around. Unless we become like little children, we can't enter the kingdom of heaven. "The kingdom of heaven belongs to such as these," says Jesus (Matt. 19:14). Let's actively, prayerfully encourage children to come to him.

Ordinary People by Vocation

29

Arts

The Role of Creativity in the Expression of Truth

Colin Harbinson

As the biblical story unfolds, it does so in stories and poetry. In fact, approximately 75 percent of Scripture consists of narrative, 15 percent is expressed in poetic form, and only 10 percent is propositional and overtly instructional in nature. As we retell the gospel story, we have reversed this biblical pattern. Today an estimated 10 percent of our communication is designed to capture the imagination of the listener, while 90 percent is purely instructive.

At particular times in history, the arts have played a strategic role in the mission of the church. At other times—when perceived to be morally and spiritually bankrupt—they were largely abandoned. However, in all probability, there has never been a time in which a biblical understanding of the arts by the church has been more needed than in our current postmodern culture with its visual and experiential orientation.

A Biblical Perspective

The Bible begins with the majestic pronouncement "In the beginning, God created . . ." (Gen. 1:1). Stunning in its simplicity yet profound in implication, this statement introduces us to God as the Creator, the original artist. He is the creative imagination and personality behind all things. Creativity is an essential part of his divine nature.

God intended creation to be both functional and beautiful (2:9). Into this world he placed the man and woman created in his image. They had the ability to think, feel, and create. The Cultural Mandate affirms that God intended for human beings to develop and steward his world. We were commissioned to be culture formers (1:28; 2:15).

The specific call of God for Bezalel to make "artistic designs" (Exod. 31:1–6) opens up the possibility of artistic expression as a spiritual calling. Creativity is a gift from God. The best way to thank him is to develop and use our gifts. Unfortunately, many never give themselves permission to begin to develop their creativity because it has not been encouraged or validated by the church. Others either abandon their gifts or abandon the church when told that their artistic motivation and their faith are incompatible.

God told Moses to make a sculpture of a snake because he wanted to use this visual representation as a means to bring forgiveness, healing, and restoration to his people (Num. 21:4–9). Other Old Testament examples abound showing how God commissioned the use of the arts in worship, to remind the people of their story, or to reveal his purposes. The prophets often used stunning visual means with vivid language and miracles to demonstrate God's heart. In the New Testament, Jesus, the master storyteller, ignited the imagination of his listeners through narratives, parables, and metaphors that pointed to spiritual reality.

The Role and Nature of the Arts

The beliefs and values of a community are reinforced and passed on through storytelling, poetry, dance, theatre, music, and the visual arts. Artistic expressions have the ability to influence individuals and cultures in powerful ways because:

- The arts give an experience that impacts the whole person. When *moved* by a story we want to enter into its action and meaning.
- The arts allow us to experience events and situations we would not normally encounter, through *the power of the imagination*. They offer windows through which to observe some aspect of life or human experience.
- In the rush of daily life, we look at many things but see very little. The arts can make the familiar appear unfamiliar, so that we are invited to *see with fresh eyes and receive new insight*.
- Good art is not passive in nature. It asks something of those who engage it. Artistic expression creates a place where artist and audience meet. *Thoughtful reflection is stimulated*. Easy answers are avoided.

When God finished his creative work, he declared it to be *very good*. Our gifts must be developed to reach their fullest potential, with excellence the hallmark of our art and our character. Humility, purity, godly accountability, and the heart of a worshiper will enable the artist to overcome the distortions of idolatry, pride, and sexual impurity that pervade the world of the arts.

Some may wonder, if God's intention for art has been distorted, would it not be wise for the church to avoid it altogether? Absolutely not! The arts are God's good gifts to us. We are to be involved with God in the reclamation process. The arts, though distorted by sin and idolatry (see, for example, Exodus 32; 2 Kings 18:4), can be restored. When we fail to understand that the kingdom of God—his rule and reign—extends to every sphere of life, Christians will be discouraged from "worldly" involvement in the arts.

The Arts as a Witness

Should artists witness through their art? What makes a work of art an authentic witness? The biblical narrative is authentic. It is a true witness of human nature at its best and at its worst, yet it never glorifies the sin and the rebellion that it exposes. Instead, it shows God's broken heart over his creation and points to the possibility of restoration through Christ. For art to be a truthful witness, it must be deeply authentic in its portrayal of life as we experience it, while affirming a biblical worldview.

Given the above understanding of the arts and how art works, the following personal examples and observations, while not exhaustive, will help to identify some of the different ways in which the arts can express the truths of God's kingdom.

- *Create modern-day parables. Toymaker and Son* is an allegory of the gospel set within a world of toys. Using a nonverbal fusion of drama, dance, mime, and music, this theatrical production has been able to cross national and cultural barriers around the globe. Truths creatively expressed in contemporary and meaningful parables will be a key to open the hearts and minds of our communities.
- *Let the church celebrate!* The church should be a celebrative community that reflects the original artist whom we worship and serve. All of the arts should be integrated into the whole life of the church. They should not be just an add-on to the worship service.
- *Act out our stories.* The arts are a powerful way to move the church to action. *Dayuma* is a theatrical reenactment of the modern mission classic told in the book *Through Gates of Splendor*. A powerful show in its own right, when performed in partnership with a Bible translation organization, it resulted in the completion of twenty translation projects.
- *Exchange creative gifts.* The concept of cultural exchange in the arts can facilitate significant relationships and transformation to all involved. International

Festival of the Arts has used the international language of the arts to hold large-scale, cross-cultural festivals. More than seven hundred Christians involved in the arts have participated in high-profile cultural exchanges with Russian, Bulgarian, and Chinese artists that enabled relationship building, respect, trust, dialogue, and the expression of a biblical worldview.

- *Promote creativity in the Christian academy.* Belhaven College, located in Jackson, Mississippi, sent its dance students to China to live and exchange dance forms with the Chinese minority nationalities. This cultural exchange was reciprocated when the Chinese sent their best scholars to Belhaven, where they were exposed to a biblical worldview in their discipline.

- *Be culture formers not culture escapers.* Believers involved in the arts should seek to establish and lead credible cultural institutions, organizations, and performing entities that can contribute to and influence the cultural landscape with artistic expressions that reflect a biblical worldview on all of life. A location containing an artist's café, art studios, and an art gallery, established by believer-artists in China, is now considered *the* place where Chinese artists in the city assemble to paint and dialogue about art, life, and spiritual reality.

- *Be salt and light.* Secular artists are "discipling the nations," because the church has, to a significant extent, abandoned the marketplace. Christians should be encouraged to pursue their artistic calling within the secular culture—to be salt and light on the stage, in the art gallery, or in the film industry.

Reaching Those in the Arts

How would people who are already involved in the arts be reached with the gospel? First, pray for these artists. Instead of degrading anyone who does not have your moral values, pray that God will move in his or her life. Second, live out your faith in front of the individual. In some cases, Christ may speak louder through what you do not say than through the words you speak. Third, ask the person open-ended questions. Allow him or her to express thoughts that will alert you to unique opportunities to witness, especially by reminding the artist that God created the arts. He is the master artist. Speak with the assurance that the gospel is the "power of God for the salvation of everyone who believes" (Rom. 1:16).

Before the arts can take their God-ordained place within the church and in the culture at large, there must be a recovery of a biblical understanding of the arts to the glory of God that ignites the imagination. When this happens, the calling of the artist will be affirmed, recognized, and supported.

The definition of evangelism and mission must be broadened from their narrow confines to embrace the full breadth of God's redemptive purposes. He is seeking to restore all things—every area of human reality—to his original creative intention.

In conclusion, art at its best is a shared experience—no room here for preaching or moralizing but rather a powerful place of potential revelation as truth is uncovered and shown. The church must celebrate its own story and creatively show it to a word-weary and biblically illiterate world.

30

Athletics

The Power of God in Sports

Pat Williams

There is no greater honor than to be the instrument in God's hands of leading one person out of the kingdom of Satan into the glorious light of heaven.

D. L. Moody

If you were to ask any athlete who has the privilege of playing in a championship game to name his main objective for the day, his answer would be, "To impact the outcome of the game." Every athlete wants to win. By simple definition, a *team* is a group of individuals having the same desire or moving toward the same result. For the team to win, all team members must do their job to the best of their ability. The front management, trainers, coaches, players, and everyone else must be intentional and committed to the principle of winning.

The apostle Paul refers to this in his writings concerning evangelism and our involvement in it. If one plants a seed, and another waters, who ultimately brings the seed to harvest? The answer is the Lord. My position as senior vice president may not have me on the court shooting three pointers, but my job is to be the best I can be with the decisions I must make for the Orlando Magic to be successful. If this is replicated throughout the organization, we will be a winning team.

In 1967 I was the president of a minor league baseball team in Spartanburg, South Carolina, and was on the fast lane to success in sports. Although it should have been the season of joy and satisfaction, my life seemed unfulfilled and lonely. The days were spent in hard work, while the nights were filled with baseball games.

As president, one of my roles was to oversee the promotions for each game. As the emptiness loomed, the games rolled on with increasing attendance and new promotions. I remember one evening I had scheduled Paul Anderson, the strongest man in the world, to break boards and to attempt other feats of strength. In pure amazement the crowd sat dumbfounded by the power of this mighty man.

As his performance went on, without warning or precedent, Paul Anderson shared something that brought my personal search for significance to the surface. He said, "I, Paul Anderson, the strongest man who ever walked the face of the earth, can't get through a minute of the day without Jesus Christ." He continued, "If I can't make it without Christ, how would the rest of you?"[1] I remember thinking that though I was a church attendee, I could never discuss the topic of religion openly like Paul. What he had found was the goal of my constant pursuit.

I came to find Christ personally through a young lady who gave me the *Four Spiritual Laws* tract. After I read the tract, it all started making sense, and I knew I needed Christ. The final step took place in a conversation with a pastor, my mentor, and my best friend. Finally, without reservation or hesitancy, I asked God to forgive me and make me brand-new. A team was involved in my journey of faith. God used Paul Anderson, the young lady, my pastor, my mentor, and my best friend to lead me to Christ.

The Power of a Testimony

The role of an athlete does not dissolve when he walks off the floor or out of the stadium. Our professional athletes stand on a platform that society builds for them, and this can be a powerful tool in sharing the gospel. It has been a privilege to know solid believers who are also professional athletes. I thought about this when Reggie White, the Hall of Fame defensive lineman who played primarily for the Eagles and Packers in the National Football League, passed away. Beyond the professional accolades, Reggie will always be remembered as a man who loved God with all of his heart. It is said that when Reggie White tackled the quarterback (numerous times throughout the game), he would say, "Jesus loves you and I will be back to sack you again in a few minutes." Reggie and others who love Christ and have invested their lives in advancing the kingdom of God are powerful tools God uses in our society.

The Attraction

Why do so many athletes seem attracted to the personality and calling of Christ? I believe it is due to the fact that an athlete speaks the language of victory. An athlete understands terms like *discipline, commitment*, and *sacrifice*. When we share the life of Christ with such an individual, the bond is natural.

We see this when Jesus pronounces his call to discipleship. Jesus says, "Deny yourself, take up your cross, and follow me" (see Matt. 16:24). Look at these three traits from the perspective of an athlete's life: Daily the athlete chooses to deny himself. The battle for faster, stronger, and higher is won through self-denial.

When Christ says, "Take up your cross," he is referring to complete surrender. It's his call for us to bear the name of Christ, no matter what. We must be prepared for the journey, knowing that whatever battle we face is no longer our battle but his. The apostle Paul consistently compared the Christian life to that of the athlete, using phrases like "fight the good fight," "press toward the prize," and "I have finished the race." All of these relate to the lifestyle of an athlete. Today athletes will say, "No pain, no gain" and, as believers, we look to the life of Christ and see that it is true.

The final aspect of the call is related to "followership." Jesus tells us to follow him—a direct call to obey, serve, trust, and commit to the claims and commands of Christ. The professional athlete must be willing to submit his goals to the hands of his coach. Tom Landry, the legendary coach of the Dallas Cowboys, said that the role of the coach is "to get men to do what they hate, to become the athlete they have wanted to become."

All of these characteristics do not make an athlete a follower of Christ; only his Holy Spirit can accomplish this task. Nor do they exempt the Christian athlete from facing the temptations of the world. However, when the claims of Christ are shared and explained, athletes are often drawn to him. True, authentic Christianity is attractive to those who do not possess it; I know it was to me.

The Athlete's Mindset

Now, as we seek to impact the athletic culture with the gospel, it is important to understand the mindset of an athlete. First, an athlete is results-driven. To have respect for something or someone, she must be able to see the results. This is important to remember when we are developing a relationship with an athlete for the purpose of the gospel. Our life and reputation will give the athlete the first clue as to our authentic walk with Christ.

Second, to an athlete, time is critical and the use of time often intense. An athlete understands that he has only so many seasons left in his body. As the high school athlete is dreaming of stardom, the professional is living in the reality of that dream. Every athlete knows that one day will be the last day of his or her career.

Third, the higher the level an athlete achieves, the more impersonal life becomes. As an athlete has more success, there is more pressure to please more people, commit to more things, and achieve higher accolades at the cost of real, transparent relationships. Consequently, athletes have in their minds that they are only as good as their last performance.

Bobby Richardson is a great athlete who has modeled Christianity. Now a good friend, Bobby has inspired and challenged me to be all Christ wants me to be in the realm of professional sports. One day Bobby was asked if being a Christian made him a better athlete. In his usual charming manner, Bobby responded, "Being a

Christian makes me a better husband, a better father, even a better citizen of this country. I must think that it makes me a better athlete."

Sharing the Gospel

Here are some practical ideas that will help you share the gospel with an athlete: First, have an active prayer life. As you pray about witnessing to an athlete, allow the Holy Spirit to warm your heart toward the *person* not the *persona*.

Second, use Scripture as a foundation not a soapbox. Allow God's Word to flow naturally into your conversation, not just to prove a point or condemn a lifestyle.

Third, learn the plan of salvation. I have watched individuals who have tried to share Christ but did not have any organized thoughts. I must go back to 1968 when that young lady handed me the *Four Spiritual Laws* that caused everything to make sense. Take time to learn the basics of a gospel presentation. This will improve your confidence and your listener's understanding.

Finally, be concerned about the person. My good friend Rich DeVos, who is a billionaire, is incredibly adept at this. He always says to the person he is talking to, "Tell me about you." Can you imagine the billionaire asking the pauper to share about himself? Rich continues to lead the individual to open up by asking, "Where do you go to church?" or "What do you believe about God?" Godly people, no matter what their financial statement may say, want to help anyone and everyone know Christ.

Russ Polhemus, a former strength coach at several universities, uses an interesting evangelistic approach. Russ shares his faith through an explanation of laws. He explains that there are physical and spiritual laws. In this life both must be understood and both are irrevocable. They will either work for you or against you. He says, "Over 90 percent of the problems we face in training are in the athlete's form not function." If we work against the physical law, we will never get where we want to be in life. The same is true with spiritual laws. Over time, Russ presents the gospel through a presentation of the *Four Spiritual Laws*. Russ concludes, "I see every student as the next Billy Graham not the next great athlete. If they can be both, then my job is absolutely successful."

Trusting Him

Through my many years as a player, manager, and vice president for professional teams, I have witnessed many athletes coming to know the Lord. It is impossible for you or me to save anyone; only God can perform this miracle. However, he has always chosen to use people like us to be instrumental in the miracle. Once we have entered into a relationship with Christ, we discover God wants to advance his kingdom through us.

I close with the thought that we *can trust him*. Salvation cost Jesus his life on the cross, and he calls us to trust him with everything we possess. In the more than forty books and numerous articles I have written, the most powerful topic I have discussed is the integrity of Jesus (see my book *Be Like Jesus*). Salvation is about trust. If Jesus's integrity were ever brought into question, the offer of salvation would be null and void. After Jesus's forty-day fast, Satan tempted him three times in an effort to get him to compromise (Luke 4:1–13). Every time Jesus responded with Scripture. He stood firm and defeated Satan's temptation to take a shortcut to nowhere. If his integrity had cracked at that moment, we would not be concerned with a book on evangelism! *You* can trust him and share him with someone today!

31

Business

Taking Your Faith to Work

Regi Campbell

Abraham was a rancher. Peter had a fishing business. Paul made tents. Matthew was a tax collector. Daniel was a government administrator. Nehemiah was a general contractor, and Joseph was a grain futures trader. Last, but far from least, Jesus was a carpenter.

All through the Bible, the greatest people of our faith were involved in work, the marketplace, and business. Our forefathers weren't monks, priests, preachers, or professors. They were working people, people of commerce, members of organizations, just regular guys.

So how did we get the modern-day perception that people in business aren't "in ministry" and that evangelism is the job of the paid clergy and not the job of the payroll clerk? Well, we certainly didn't get it from Scripture.

In each of the four Gospels and in Acts, Jesus's last instruction to us was to "go and make disciples." There's no gray area. No wiggle room. He didn't say, "Okay, I'm going to call a few of you to be ministers, and those whom I call are to go make disciples." He didn't say, "All you evangelicals, you go and make disciples. You 'mainstream' people, you just light candles, pray the rosary, and repeat the liturgy." He said, "Go and make disciples of all nations" (Matt. 28:19). He said it to all of us. And he sent us out to "all nations," all the world, which includes

173

the world of business. Here are four keys to putting your faith to work as an evangelist in business.

Develop Relationships

The world of business is a world of relationships, and since people and God's Word are the only two things that continue from this life to the next, developing relationships is the most important thing God calls us to do. Remember all of Jesus's instructions? "Love your neighbor" (Matt. 19:19); "love your enemies" (Luke 6:27); "consider others more important than yourself" (Phil. 2:3); "greater love has no one than this, that he lay down his life for his friends" (John 15:13). Jesus was emphatic that relationships were at the center of what he called us to do. And today many of our relationships are derived from business and work. When we go and build relationships, we've actually begun to go and make disciples.

George Barna's organization has done extensive research into the psyche of America. One of the most telling facts that Barna unearthed relates to how adults become Christians. Is it through the church, through televangelism, through gospel tracts, Christian books, and music? No, although these often play a part, the key element—more than 80 percent of the time—is the influence of a "trusted friend." And where do we develop many of our trusted friendships? At the office, at the hospital, at the plant, at the store, at school—at work. So evangelism in the business world begins with building trusted friendships, and those begin when we accept people.

Accept Others

Our natural tendency is to hang out with people who are like us. It's the old "birds of a feather" concept. Problem is, it's not biblical and it's not what Jesus taught or modeled. He was a "friend of sinners," not to mention tax collectors, lepers, and other social outcasts. He entered into relationships with those people to influence them and to accomplish his Father's purpose. I love the story of Zacchaeus, how Jesus picked out this despised man and went home to dinner with him. Jesus's acceptance motivated Zacchaeus not only to repent but voluntarily to make restitution to the people he had cheated.

When we accept people at work who aren't like us—and maybe even people we don't particularly like—then we are obeying our heavenly Father's instructions. He shows up when we do that, and often a door will open into the hearts of people we've befriended. Remember, in the same breath that he told us to go and make disciples, he said, "I am with you always" (Matt. 28:20). Demonstrate your love and acceptance for the people you work with, and God will show you what to do and what to say when they start to ask questions.

Think "Steps"

All too often we have developed relationships with people we work with only to "blow it" by trying to lead them to Christ. I know that sounds heretical, but hang with me!

Suppose your friend's car starts to fall apart. Repair bill after repair bill—tow trucks, garages, bumming rides to work. Yuk! Eventually his mechanic says, "You know, this time it's going to cost more to repair your car than it's worth." Now, he's in the market for another car.

Imagine that another friend just got a new car. She has car trouble. She takes the car back to the dealership to have it repaired. Problem solved. Is she in the market for a new car? Not likely. She just bought one.

You see, these two people are in completely different places when it comes to cars. Your first friend is probably tuning in to the new car ads on TV. Your other friend is probably "tuning out." Both had car problems, but they are in different places when it comes to cars.

Well, I believe it's critical that we recognize that people are in different places when it comes to Christianity. Some are completely apathetic—they don't know and they don't care about spiritual things in general and about Christianity in particular. Others are searching. They acknowledge "God," but they haven't figured out much more than that. But they are curious; they read and they talk. Still others have "figured it out," at least to the point that they aren't actively searching. They may say, "Oh, I believe," and call themselves Christians. And of course, there is a huge number of people who say they have "found it" in some other place—Mormonism, Islam, Eastern mysticism, and all sorts of New Age theologies.

Thinking "steps" means that we must first build strong enough relationships with our colleagues that they will share with us what they believe. Then we try to help them move one step toward Christ—one step and only one step. If they are completely apathetic about spiritual things, we just want to inspire them to start to search. If they are searching, we want to inspire them to consider Christianity. If they say they are Christians, we want to inspire them to take the next step—to become active, growing Christians who are flourishing in their relationship with our heavenly Father. Is there a time for sharing the gospel, giving the *Four Spiritual Laws* presentation, asking the "if you died tonight" question? Absolutely. But it's when God says it's time, not when we get up our courage!

Be Intentional

In business we have tons of relationships. What would happen if Christians all over the world (some two billion of them) began to have a second purpose in every business relationship? Imagine if every salesperson decided to have two purposes in every client or prospect relationship. Yes, the salesperson wants to make a sale and keep the customer happy, but he also wants to know what the customer believes about Jesus. He wants to help that person move one step closer to Christ, regardless of where he is today. Suppose an attorney *intentionally* serves her client well (because the attorney is doing her work heartily as to the Lord) *and* she *intentionally* builds a relationship with the client so that she can have influence with him for Christ. Intentionality leads us to be purposeful in our interactions with people. And intentionality for Christ begins with consistently praying for the people in our business "nation."

Never forget—God saves people; we don't. Jesus took "the monkey off our back" when he assured us that "No one can come to me unless the Father who sent me draws him" (John 6:44). It's our job to love, accept, and serve people, but it's his job to redeem them—when he chooses.

Evangelism in a business context takes patience. People come to a need for God on their time frame not ours. And how many people do you know who accepted Christ as an adult when everything in their world was at the top? I know not one. We don't need God when we're on top—it's when there is *disruption* that we start to look for answers outside ourselves. A disruption could be a health scare, a lost job, a kid that goes off the deep end, a financial setback that turns the world upside down, an accident, or a divorce.

When disruption happens, we turn to our trusted friends. And if we Christians in the business world have built strong relationships by intentionally loving, accepting, and serving our unbelieving co-workers, then we will be the trusted friends they turn to when disruption happens. We will be the people who get the opportunity to point them to our Savior, Jesus Christ. We will get the blessing of being used by God to add a soul to his kingdom.

32

Education

The Worldview Battlefield

Roger Parrott

American education touts its commitment to be the world's great bastion of diversity, and that it is—except for the diversity of ideas. Though the diversity of ideas may appear to be welcomed and encouraged in American education—no matter how unfounded a concept might be or how far out of sync it is with reasoned thought or social norms—this openness does not extend to the tenets of Christian faith. The same vocal leaders who advocate diversity block aggressively any discussion of Christian faith, considering these ideas to be narrow-minded, mean-spirited, judgmental, and antiquated.

God's truth will always stand up to the bright lights of scrutiny, but in the world of American education, God's truth is most often not allowed to see the light of day. It is remarkable that we live in an age where in Russia they use the Bible to teach ethics, in India they use it to teach reading, and in America it is not allowed in the classroom.

The "not welcome" sign is hung with pride by the academy when Christian ideas come to the front door of the school. And through the years, these same "champions of diversity" have used their bully pulpit to convince or intimidate our lawmakers into agreeing that a private silence is the only appropriate application of faith in public education.

So as educators, in a profession where both the laws and the culture are working aggressively against Christian ideas, what can we do to evangelize within our profession?

The Wide Divide

Why is it that a well-trained, intelligent science teacher, who has seen up close the complexities and intricacies of biology, astronomy, and physics, still holds so strongly to a big bang theory of creation and will not waver on the theory of evolution, even when no scientific evidence exists of evolution between species?

Education always comes down to worldviews—developing them, teaching them, and promoting them. Because of that science teacher's circumstances and experiences in life, he holds to a certain point of view—a specific point from which he views life. From this viewpoint he looks at the world through lenses that color how he receives ideas. And while both his worldview and the world shape his thinking, his worldview becomes cemented as he develops assumptions about what is supposed to be in his view at all. Thus, when an idea comes into his view that doesn't fit with his assumptions, he finds ways to dismiss it, explain it, or just belittle it.

Accordingly, if a creator God, who is the source of order, accountability, and absolutes, cannot fit into that science teacher's assumptions of life, no amount of scientific evidence can convince him otherwise. Anything that doesn't fit with his assumptions he brushes off as "bad science" rather than attempting to deal with the breakdown of his secular worldview.

When a worldview's assumptions are built on anything other than absolute truth, they become prejudices, which get reinforced by the network of people in that science teacher's life—whom he self-selects to associate with, because they also share his view from the same point and look through the same tinted glasses. And as those people give him confirmation that he is right in how he sees the world, his assumptions become his truth.

This is what is called a false consensus, and it is why worldviews have become so cemented in more recent years—because we now have the flexibility to connect to only those people who think, act, and believe like we do, and we can avoid the worldview of others who might have ideas that contradict ours.

Over the last quarter century American educators have created a secular worldview that deliberately brings together people who agree with it and marginalizes those who do not. This is a false consensus environment. And this is why education has become the frontline battleground for worldviews and evangelism.

Changing the Core of Education

To combat this relentless force of American education's bias against Christian ideas, we must work to change the core of the problem not just treat the symptoms. Bringing prayer back into the schools might make Christians feel more comfortable, but those thirty seconds in the morning would not offset the impact of textbooks, teachers, curriculum, or school boards who teach against it. And currently we don't need a Supreme Court ruling to ask God to transform the thinking of those who now guide our schools and classrooms.

Addressing the symptoms is the easy way out. Instead, we must be developing teachers, administrators, and school board members who have a solid Christian worldview *and* have the ability to articulate their ideas in the marketplace of ideas as an educational peer—not a combatant. Christian colleges may be one of the most important components of our future, for they are producing the teachers and administrators who have been properly equipped to do just that. Christian principals tell me they come to my campus to recruit, because they know exactly the type of teachers they will be getting, and they want to find teachers grounded in a Christian worldview.

As educators, we must be aggressively working to advocate for Christians to be hired by school districts and universities. This will not happen by rewriting the position profile selection criteria but rather by someone on the inside intentionally looking for quality Christian applicants and working on their behalf to see they are given full consideration in the search process. Human Resource departments cannot ask the "illegal questions" about faith, family, and worldview, but as a "friend" you already know those answers about the potential applicant you've advocated for a position. I've seen public school districts where nearly every teacher is a Christian, simply because someone has gone out aggressively to find that type of educator and has encouraged such people to apply for positions.

When enough Christians are hired into a school or college, the false consensus worldview that is aggressively anti-Christian will begin to lose its grip.

Evangelizing from the Teacher's Desk

If you as a teacher are waiting for the laws or culture to change so you can be free to express your faith in the classroom, you are really only making excuses for not sharing your faith with your students. In point of fact, there are many options for evangelism, even within the restrictive legal environment that has been created around us.

Part of the reason Christians have become so marginalized in education is that we've spent the last two decades pounding on the front door of the school demanding change rather than getting inside the school to share the compassionate love of Christ.

Triggering anti-Christian lawsuits is not the path for most of us, although those who find themselves the victim of blatant discrimination help bring the discrepancies into the public view when they go to court. And surely, making an issue out of trivial issues and cultural icons does not gain Christians anything other than ridicule.

So what can you do?

The model of Mission America, a coalition that includes most American evangelical denominations, has developed a wonderful, simple guideline for Christians to use for their evangelism. And in an educational setting, this plan overrides the restrictiveness of Separation of Church and State laws.

Educators need to live out three simple principles: prayer, care, and share.

1. Begin by praying for those under your care as an educator. Keep a list on your desk of the students in your classroom; or if you are an administrator, keep a list of faculty for whom you will pray regularly. Pray for those facing special challenges, and let God go where you are not yet invited to minister. Pray for those students or peers who are the hardest to get along with, and you'll better demonstrate godly patience as you deal with them. Pray for all students and teachers to discover their gifts, and ask God to help you unwrap and develop the gifts of those under your care.

2. After several weeks of focused prayer for a student or teacher, begin to look for genuine ways to show your care for them. If you are a teacher, get to know the parents of your students; if you are an administrator, find out more about the people you supervise. As you pray for them, God will open doors for you to demonstrate in tangible ways your care for them. Soon you will have more ministry opportunities than you will have hours in the day. And never forget that, as a teacher, the greatest care you can give to a family is your best effort as an educator to their precious child.

3. Only *after* you pray and *after* you care, do you look for opportunities to share your faith. Moments when you can freely discuss your faith will come to you, and you won't have to force them. You can share without pressing the edges of any government laws, teacher association guidelines, or the wrath of those in supervision over you. God will provide opportunities both inside and outside the school building for you to tell others why you are a person whose life is characterized by love, joy, peace, patience, kindness, goodness, faithfulness, gentleness, and self-control.

"Against such things there is no law" is the punch line of that list of fruit of the Spirit given to us in Galatians 5:22–23. And even within the maze of the laws from school boards, state legislatures, and the federal Department of Education, there is no law that can keep you from living out your faith as you demonstrate the fruit of the Spirit.

You don't need posters, preaching, or prayer over the loudspeaker to be an evangelist in your school. Simply live a life worthy of your calling (see Eph. 4:1) by being the finest educator you can be, and then, as you pray and care, our sovereign God will provide a host of opportunities to share Christ, who has transformed your life.

Evangelizing the Educator

How does the evangelism process work on the other side of the desk? Most students are not afforded the luxury of a Christian environment through their years of educational experience; consequently, the Christian student must be the evangelist. Some helpful principles include:

- *Respect the position.* Educators are professionals who have been recognized by educational facilities, peers, and sometimes secular firms for the hard work that was invested in their field of study. The position of teacher also brings a certain respect, not to be intimidating, but a title that should not be discounted. We must give educators the same respect we give to anyone in any position of leadership.

- *The classroom must not be a platform.* Students must recognize that the educator (unless it is his first year) has taught the same course for several years to students similar to them. Usually the debates are the same, the discussions are the same, the coffee in the lounge is the same for the educator. He has studied the subject to the best of his ability and will not be open for discussion of his expertise in front of students over whom he has authority. Be careful that you do not place the educator in such a position that he feels compelled to use the classroom as a soapbox for expressing personal religious preferences or defending religious controversy. Putting a teacher in a defensive stance in the classroom might cause a true witnessing opportunity to be lost forever. Read on.

- *Share the facts about Christ.* Jokes, ridicule, and condemnation at the expense of the organized church are often unfair and unwarranted but still a reality. We should be careful not to concentrate our discussion around the activities or situations of religion. Students must discuss these social/religious ideologies with teachers and, yes, even in class, but our defense should revolve around what we know about the person of Christ not our personal convictions. These comments will be perceived more as showing an attraction to Jesus than changing dialogue into debate.

- *Develop a friendship.* Normally educators like to know the students they are teaching. Make a point of speaking to the teacher after class, extend an invitation to her to join you and your Christian friends for coffee or pizza, when you and your friends can discuss issues with her. Due to all the new guidelines and concerns over the appropriate conduct of an educator (and biblical guidelines for believers like yourself), careful and strict boundaries should always be in place between the educator and student, especially when meeting outside the classroom. Always make it a group discussion.

- *Know the gospel and share Jesus.* Finally, be prepared to share the gospel when given the opportunity to do so. Do not be afraid to share the greatest discovery for any person—the life-changing message of Christ. Know the facts about the gospel. An educator is a person who has devoted his or her life to the pursuit of facts and will usually want to know truth. What better truth can you share with an educator than the truth of Jesus! (John 14:6).

33

Entertainment

Did Somebody Say, "Hollywood . . . Can I Get a Witness?"

Karen Covell

I am writing as a missionary in a faraway land, living with a strange tribe, and engulfed in the foreign culture of Hollywood. Actually, my husband and I are tentmakers. As a film and TV composer and producer, respectively, Jim and I make our living in the secular entertainment industry and minister within the same community, getting paid by and ministering to the Hollywood Tribe, simultaneously.

The Mission Field

Our philosophy of ministry is to live among the tribesmen we are ministering to, as Jesus did, because we love them and we're excited to tell them about the most wonderful news—Jesus! We actually believe that every Christian is a missionary in the workplace, neighborhood, school, and even family environment where the Lord has placed us. For we are all to be his witnesses going out into *all* nations—not just Africa, China, Jerusalem, or Judea, but even Hollywood. In fact we'd love to have every church put a sign at each exit to remind each person leaving the church: *You are now entering your mission field.*

I consider myself a foreign missionary to the people in the entertainment community—*foreign* because our Hollywood culture is like a foreign land to most of the church in America; *missionary* because even though I'm an entertainment

182

professional, I am also here hoping God will use me to tell my peers and associates about the love of Jesus.

The people in the media are feared, not understood, and even hated by much of the Christian community. In fact most Christian parents would be far more comfortable sending their child off to minister in the depths of India than sending them off to Hollywood! But the Christians in Hollywood believe that every group of people who doesn't know about Jesus needs to hear his message of hope and peace, even the people in the entertainment industry.

The Message

So how does the growing community of Christian missionaries in Hollywood communicate the truth of Jesus to media professionals? We follow the ways of Jesus—building relationships and respect, one person at a time. We believe that telling others about Jesus should be natural, and it should be a privilege that is earned. We believe that talking about our faith should be culturally relevant and should be in words that the person we're talking to can understand. And we're committed to the calling because we believe that Hollywood is the most influential mission field in the world. Washington, D.C. is the global seat of power; Hollywood is the global seat of influence.

That's why Jim and I have been teaching the class "How to Talk about Jesus without Freaking Out" for the past ten years in our home to Christian entertainment professionals. Every mission field has its own specific and unique characteristics that any missionary should be sensitive to and understand. And the entertainment industry truly has its own uniquely definitive qualities. For instance, we have our own watering holes, our own language, dress, accessories, morals, ethics, and traditions. We have our own gods that we worship, like the god of the personalized parking space, the Emmy god, the Grammy god, and, of course, the Oscar god.

We are also very nomadic. We work on a project for a few months; then it ends, and we move on to something else, with a whole new group of people. Our executives are bicoastal, and our producers go back and forth between the United States and Canada. Our composers score films in places like Seattle or Budapest, and most studio VPs have worked for quite a few other studios or production companies. Ironically, as a media nerve center, we are closed to outside influence; less than 2 percent of our community attends church or synagogue, and many professionals here have never even seen a Bible.

Our tribesmen are more sophisticated than most but more ignorant of the ways and beliefs of the rest of the country than one would think. They support alternative lifestyles, dysfunctional families, and crude language, because that's all most of them know from their childhoods. Staying a virgin is pointless, living with a girlfriend or boyfriend is expected, and even lying is an accepted part of our culture—because everyone does it.

Their Story

You may ask, "How do you talk about Jesus with people like that?" There are four main ways: First of all, we love them. They are such a creative group of sharp, passionate people. They care about the state of the world, and they want to be loved and accepted for who they are—just like you and me. Love is the key. And the only way to truly love people is to get to know them. Therefore, we tell our class members to ask questions of their friends, peers, associates, and bosses. Then listen to *their story*. Everyone has a story, and once you hear it, you can't hate a person anymore. As we listen to the stories, our compassion grows, their trust in us grows, and friendships usually develop.

Prayer

After we've listened to their stories, we pray for them. We ask the Lord to show us how we can have a positive, eternal impact on our new friends or associates. We pray that the Lord will soften their hearts, that he will bring other solid Christians into their lives, and that he will not let them go until they come to know him. In fact we challenge everyone in our class to choose one pre-Christian in their workplace to pray for every single day for the ten weeks of the class. During that time of disciplined prayer, God always moves mightily, and sometimes in ways we never expected.

Why don't you choose a pre-Christian in the media right now whom you know or enjoy watching or hearing about and commit to pray for that person every single day for a month? Choose someone of your gender and someone you truly care about. Then see how God can do a miracle in his or her life and in your life in the process. Expect miracles! You have just committed to making an eternal difference in the heart and life of an entertainment industry professional through the simple act of prayer. Thank you!

Our Story

We tell the industry professional our spiritual story. After building a relationship with a person, it usually grows into conversations where both people get a chance to share their stories. You should be prepared to express how you chose to have a personal relationship with Jesus and how he's changed your life since you made that choice. That's called *your story*.

We help our class members write out and then tell a three-minute version of their story so that they are prepared to tell the shortest version possible. It's always easy to spend an hour talking about ourselves, but if we can summarize our faith in God and how he's changed us, in three minutes, then we're prepared for anything. Also, when we tell about our love for Jesus, it's a powerful witness that can't be refuted, debated, or denied. It's a firsthand account of a personal encounter with the living God, and all we have to do is tell the facts. Whether someone believes it or not is not up to us. That's between that person and the Holy Spirit.

His Story

Finally, we will at some point get a chance to tell our friend or associate *his story*. That's God's story, including his plan for us and his desire for a relationship with everyone. It's about Jesus and why God sent him to this world to communicate with us. It's how to become a Christian. That's the core of the gospel, the bottom line to salvation, and the hardest thing in the world to calmly discuss with someone who doesn't believe! Telling his story is hard because it's true. It's absolute truth. And we'll experience a spiritual battle in some way every time we tell it. But we have to. The good news is that all we have to do is be honest about what we know. It's not our job to convert anyone. It's only our job to tell people what we personally know, and the rest is up to God.

That's all it takes. That's what Jesus did. We Christians need to study Jesus, read about him, talk to him, and act like him, then treat others just like he did. That's the most effective way to share your faith with anyone. And if it works in Hollywood, it will work anywhere.

In the entertainment industry, the Christians and pre-Christians are all very similar to Jesus. We are all storytellers, Jesus being the first and best of us all. We love to tell stories. In fact that's all we do—we write them, produce them, direct them, act in them, and distribute them around the world. As a Christian missionary in Hollywood, I know that I can talk to my peers about Jesus the same way they talk to me about their work. I tell them stories. In fact that's why I focus on the three specific stories mentioned above—*their story, our story,* and *his story.*

Because I love the people I live and work with in entertainment, I want to learn *their* story. I don't have the right to tell them they need God if I don't know anything about them. I start every relationship by asking questions and then listening to the answers. I ask about people's family background and church background, if any. I ask about what they are passionate about, what their goals are, and what's been hard for them. It doesn't take many questions to make people feel comfortable enough to start talking all about themselves. Everyone has a story and it's up to us to find out what it is. Many people in Hollywood spend hundreds of dollars an hour just to have someone listen to their story. We should be listening for free.

Then, when I've earned the right to tell them *my* story, I tell it in a way that gives the glory to God. Most often, it's in bits and pieces, as the relationship grows. But sometimes, it's all at once. It can be in conversation, or it can be in actions. We can tell about ourselves in many creative and loving ways. Sometimes it's even simply in our work, but it's always about Jesus and it's always honest.

Jim was in London, conducting the London Symphony for one of his film scores, and he decided to read to the orchestra short excerpts from the book *The Spiritual Lives of the Great Composers* between takes. At the end of the session he surprised the players by handing each of the sixty-six musicians a copy of the book as a gift. They were completely blown away by both the fascinating insights into famous composers during the session and the free book that they patiently waited in line to get after the session. As the bus waited to take them to a Paul

McCartney session across town, one musician stopped to talk to Jim. He thanked him, then added, "I didn't know composers had spiritual lives!"

Life-Changing Power

I've been telling my story to some of my industry friends for years, and apparently many of them haven't been interested in making the same spiritual commitment that I have. Two producers in particular have great respect for me, they know my story, they've told me all about theirs, but they haven't been able to let go of their own fears and embrace the God whom I've told them so much about. Finally, after years, I invited both of them to two different events to hear someone else's story. In both situations, just when I was about to give up out of discouragement, their hearts were suddenly ready. Both of these two old friends became Christians within two months of each other, after they had heard the same message told one more time. The power of our personal stories is life-changing.

Sometimes our stories can be told without even using words, and it's just as powerful. As St. Francis once said, "Preach the gospel at all times, and if necessary use words."

Jim had just been hired on as the composer for a new network TV series when he was immediately pushed out of his comfort zone in the second episode. The producers wanted him to write music to reflect the feeling of the desperate lives of young gang members in New Orleans. The show closed with the final voiceover saying, "We don't know what the answer is to gang killings, and we don't even know if there is an answer." It was a depressing ending that would be giving out a message of hopelessness to millions of viewers across the world.

Jim knew he had to find a message of hope, so he came up with a way to change the meaning through a choice of music. He didn't know if the Jewish producers would go for it, but he decided to take the chance.

Soon the hopeless voiceover was followed by the sound of a gospel singer singing the hymn "Softly and Tenderly." As an image of a murdered child appeared, the viewer heard, "Jesus is calling for you and for me to come home." And when the final image of a teenage murderer came on the screen, the singer was singing, "Calling, O sinner, come home."

We thought it was powerful. It gave hope and lifted up the name of Jesus. I was excited—then I freaked out. What in the world was Steven, the Jewish executive producer, going to say? Jim turned in the show late Thursday and at 9 a.m. Friday, prior to the Monday airing, he got a call from Steven. He said, "Jim . . . ?"

I swallowed hard, thinking that this was his second and last episode on the series. Steven said, "I just saw your show and it's *#@&%* incredible! And I don't know what it is, but it's the best show we've ever done! Good job. See you on Monday!"

Jim thanked him and hung up smiling, knowing exactly what "it" was. It was the truth; it was his story told boldly and truthfully, and it touched the producer deeply. It was the power of story at work.

The Work of Prayer

What is the best way for someone outside of Hollywood to "reach" or "change" the people in our mission field? It's prayer. Oswald Chambers said that "prayer is not preparation for the greater work, prayer is the greater work." We will see mountains move, hearts change, and America roll into a full-scale revival—if we pray for Hollywood. Pray for the Christians who are here on the front lines, trying to earn a living and be an ambassador for the Lord. Pray for the pre-Christians who are hard, bitter, unhappy, or hard-hearted. Pray for favor, for hearts to melt, for the Lord to have a bolder presence here. Pray for revival! Replace any anger, fear, or frustration toward the media with prayer. There are even a few established prayer efforts that you can join: MasterMedia International has a Media Leader Prayer Calendar that lists two media influencers to pray for every day of the year (www.mastermediaintl.org).

My ministry, The Hollywood Prayer Network, unifies Christians around the world to pray for Hollywood and the people in it by sending out monthly emails with information, people, and shows to pray for. It currently reaches almost ten thousand faithful prayer warriors who all stand together believing that Hollywood just needs God's mercy. We know that he hears the prayers of the righteous and can bring revival to this place, and through prayer for Hollywood comes cultural revival. I encourage you to join the missionaries in the entertainment industry by praying for the people here. You will then be a part of a global effort of evangelism and prayer. Just go to www.hollywoodprayernetwork.org and get a monthly newsletter on how to pray for Hollywood, a free fifteen-minute DVD called *The Hollywood Crisis*, which tells how to pray for Hollywood, and even free remote prayer stickers that stick on the front of your TV remote, reminding you to pray for the people behind the show you're watching every time you change the channel.

Philemon says in verse 6, "I pray that you may be active in sharing your faith, so that you will have a full understanding of every good thing we have in Christ." So how do you find out all the good things that Jesus has for your life? Share your faith! And how do you do it in Hollywood? Tell stories—true, powerful, and life-changing stories.

Go out and be Mighty Warrior Attack Sheep for the Lord. Remember that you are missionaries, and ask the Lord to use you today to impact Hollywood!

34

Government

Reaching Community Leaders

Tim Robnett

From the earliest days of the church, God has given attention to government officials. Jesus addressed Pilate, the Roman governor; Peter spoke on many occasions to the national leaders of Israel; and Paul dialogued with a number of Roman and Jewish leaders. In Matthew 8:10 Jesus commended the Roman officer for his faith. God called Peter to dialogue with Cornelius, the Roman military official, who, though a God-fearer, lacked the knowledge of the Good News of Jesus Christ. When Cornelius learned about Jesus and the forgiveness of sins through him, he was filled with the Holy Spirit, and he and his household came to faith in Jesus Christ.

Government officials exercise significant authority over many areas of the community. Whether they hold local, regional, or national positions, government officials impact the lives of thousands of people. Because of the unique influence of men and women in government, Christians need to intentionally connect with and minister to them.

During some periods of history, government officials and church leadership have become enmeshed. These periods have often proven unproductive in the growth of the church. However, the Good News is for all people, including politicians and government officials. A Christian must maintain a wise balance—connecting with leaders, while remaining independent of the power of politics. This should not, however, cloud the call to reach our leaders with the message of Jesus Christ.

The Scriptures declare that God has established kings, rulers, and all in authority (Rom. 13:1–4). So, whether God-fearing, atheistic, or followers of Jesus Christ, government officials have a God-ordained role and responsibility. Therefore, they need Christ, and the cause of Christ needs godly leaders in government.

The Responsibility

Why should Christians make an effort to reach government officials with the Good News of Jesus Christ? Here are some important reasons:

- God has put government officials in positions of authority, power, and influence. Because of their unique role in the lives of the whole community, they need to hear the Good News.
- Their influence over thousands of people through policy making, setting community standards, and solving societal issues mandates that the church reach out to these people.
- The need for godly wisdom in developing multiethnic, multigenerational, and economic strategies in society is of paramount importance. Jesus Christ offers peace, joy, and wisdom. Leaders are desperate for this wisdom in their dealing with community issues.
- Government officials are human. Though many people expect them to be in some ways superhuman, the reality is these officials have their own personal struggles and challenges, just like everyone else. They long for respect, personal peace, a sense of purpose and usefulness, and love. In Jesus Christ we experience all of these. In Christ our shame is removed and our lives are infused with hope.
- Government leaders can be filled with pride and arrogance and in some instances have the power to bring great pressure and persecution on people (see Daniel 4; Acts 8:1–3).
- God's Word states that we should pray for government leaders because they can be instrumental in maintaining peace in society (1 Tim. 2:1–4). A peaceful society is more conducive to sharing the gospel. The propagation of the gospel relieves guilt, calls people to a life of serving others, and enhances stability in society.

The Barriers

What are some of the barriers to reaching government officials?

- Ignorance in the church is a barrier. We need to realize that government officials really matter to God and, when reached with the gospel, they can become allies of the church.

- Some government officials fear that Christians have some religious agenda that would compromise their political positions.
- Christians may fear that they will be rejected and humiliated by government officials.
- Ignorance about how to approach government leaders keeps Christians from reaching them.
- Sharing the gospel with government officials is not a priority of Christian ministry.

Some Suggested Methods

How can we reach out to government officials? Here are some suggestions:

- Establish personal communication with them via letter, email, and phone. This personal touch, from Christian to city leader, often gives additional opportunities for serving the government leader and others in the community. Write a personal letter congratulating the official on his election or appointment or a letter sharing positive words of appreciation for the leader's service and sacrifice. To couch the letter in terms of personal concern facilitates the government official's positive response to questions concerning his personal faith.
- First Timothy 2:1–4 commands believers to pray for all government officials. The purpose of these prayers is focused on the desire and abilities of the officials to maintain peace and order in our world. This condition of peace and order promotes the ability of the church to take the gospel worldwide.
- We need to pray not only *for* our leaders but also *with* them. A Christian who makes an appointment with a government official to pray with him or her is often met with openness and affirmation. When the official witnesses the believer's connection with God, it is a powerful example of a living faith.
- Personal contact through a visit to the government official's office will have an impact. Showing personal concern for the welfare of leaders often results in improved relationships with them. Creating special occasions to honor and ask blessings on officials is an effective witnessing tool. When visiting government officials, remember to bring an appropriate gift, wear the appropriate clothes, and address them with the correct title. Use Sir, Your Honor, Chief, and other appropriate titles when initially meeting these dignitaries.
- Inviting a government official to address your church or civic group can be an effective witnessing occasion. Not only will you be honoring him as a guest, but it places you in a position to share the Good News of Jesus with the leader.

A Unique Message

What unique message does God have for Christians to give to government leaders?

- God has chosen them to carry out a special responsibility in their community. When government officials hear us say, "God has placed you in this position for a special purpose," they most often feel that we respect them. This attitude of honor facilitates their willingness to listen to our message. Not only are they chosen, but they are also in positions of significant influence and authority. By acknowledging this fact, we are recognizing their special place in society. Our commitment to pray for, encourage, and stand with them typically motivates them to listen to what God has to say to them. We must let them know that God values them highly and has placed them in a position to benefit others. He wants the best for them so they in turn can work for the welfare of the community.
- Jesus Christ came to earth to give them life, peace, and joy. The questions we need to ask are: "Are you on God's side?" "Have you received Christ?" "Are you allowing God to supply all your needs?" Many officials may not have understood the Good News in these terms. As we share the message of empowerment through the gospel of Jesus Christ, the people of authority can turn to the One of ultimate authority and receive eternal life. Many officials have experienced changed lives and more effective leadership through the gospel. Share the testimonies (stories) of other government officials who are followers of Jesus Christ. Chuck Colson's changed life is a good example of what God can do.

The Benefits

What are some of the benefits of sharing the Good News with government leaders?

- When the church reaches out to government officials, it can create a climate of respect and honor in the community. Even though people may disagree about issues, a culture of respect begins to grow between the church and the government.
- We demonstrate God's love in a personal way. Hearing God's message of salvation enables government officials to understand that God cares about them as people not just about their position of leadership.
- We inform leaders of the resources of God: salvation through Jesus Christ, the prayers of the church, and the people who compose the church. Most

leaders will be happy to know they have a unique support system available to them.

- When Christians reach out to government officials, they initiate a relationship of concern and compassion between the leaders and the church. When the church shows its concern for government officials, they are more likely to call on the church to assist the government when issues call for it. This unique positioning will situate the church to respond to the ongoing needs of the community and nation.

So whether we desire to reach a city counsel member or the President of the United States, obedience to the call of God to reach all people with the Good News of Jesus Christ remains our mandate. Overcoming fear by faith through prayer and having a clear strategy will empower us to be successful in fulfilling God's desire for the church in this ministry. Remember, no matter what one's position in society, we are all people created in God's image, separated because of sin, and empty on the inside until we return to our Creator. You could be the person God uses to reach those who often seem unreachable.

35

Media

Friends or Foes?

David Sanford

Try asking eighty Christian business or ministry leaders if the "secular" media are friends or foes. Every time I take this poll at a conference or seminar, one or two hands go up rather timidly for "friends." The rest go sky high for "foes." What's your vote?

Many Christians feel that the media are the greatest enemies of religion. Unfortunately, they focus on the liberal reporting and the secular biases of some journalists and ignore the positive influence that media can have on Christianity.

By working together with the media, and forming relationships with key media people, Christians can shine the light of Jesus Christ into their world.

Helping Change the Media

Over the past fifteen years, a handful of Christian leaders have helped change the face of the American mainstream media for *good*. Michigan businessman W. James Russell created the Amy Awards, offering cash awards of up to ten thousand dollars per article. Russell's only requirements? That journalists quote at least one verse of Scripture per entry published in a mainstream newspaper or magazine.

The first year, Russell received 154 submissions. Over the next decade, however, he received more than 10,000 qualified entries published in hundreds of periodicals, including the *Atlantic*, the *Boston Globe, Quill, Reader's Digest, Time, U.S. News and World Report, USA Today*, the *Wall Street Journal*, and the *Washington Post*.

After Prison Fellowship chairman Charles Colson won the prestigious Templeton Prize for Progress in Religion, he was invited to speak to members of the National Press Club in Washington, D.C. Colson acknowledged that many Christians "harbor a fear and loathing of the media elite" and that some "show more zeal than thought." He offered an olive branch, however, saying, "Both sides need each other for the greater good of society."

Colson stated, "Christians bring something important to our culture, something that cannot be easily replaced. I want to argue that they deserve an honored place at the table, that in a free, pluralistic society, we can contend in the public square for the truths we cherish without 'imposing' them on anyone."

He added, "Those of us who represent the Christian faith share a common interest with you, the media, in the preservation of America's first freedom. Both of us live or die by the same First Amendment."[1]

Bridging the Gap

Several years ago, *Los Angeles Times* religion writer John Dart and former Southern Baptist Convention president Jimmy Allen released a report titled "Bridging the Gap: Religion and the News Media." The report summarized the findings of journalism researcher Robert Wyatt, who interviewed more than eight hundred editors, journalists, and Christian leaders nationwide to examine the wide degree of distrust between Christians and journalists.

Wyatt documented some important findings: 72 percent of editors and 92 percent of religion writers said religion is very or somewhat important in their lives. More than 80 percent said they didn't feel they were biased against Christianity. Their biggest fear, however, is "making mistakes and incurring religious wrath."

A few months later, world-renowned evangelist Billy Graham spoke to the American Society of Newspaper Editors in Washington, D.C., on the topic "Newspaper Coverage of Religion and How It Can Be Improved." Graham urged editors to recognize that "religion continues to be an important part of American life," to report more news about the positive impact of religion, to reach out to local religious leaders, and to hire qualified journalists to work the religion beat.

Afterward, several major daily newspapers hired full-time religion reporters. And in many markets, religion coverage increased well beyond the traditional calendar of church events.

Sharing Jesus Christ

Over the course of his prolific career, Cal Thomas has been one of America's most popular media commentators on television, radio, and in print. While the mainstream media often *are* biased, Thomas believes the bias "isn't always deliberate." Often a reporter's bias is borne out of a bad church experience or personal tragedy that produced deep feelings of disappointment with God.

In one of his hundreds of articles, Thomas states: "Unlike many Christians I meet, I've decided not to be content with cursing the media's spiritual darkness, but to devise a strategy for doing something."[2] That strategy involves getting to know others in the media, developing genuine friendships, and then sharing the love of Jesus Christ.

"I'm not really advocating anything new. Jesus is the pattern. He spent most of his time with people who didn't know him," Thomas says. "This pattern works with anyone, regardless of profession or position." After all, "You don't have to be a journalist to reach a journalist."[3]

Another Christian leader reaching out to mainstream journalists is former banking executive and evangelist Luis Palau, who has led a growing number of television directors, news anchors, cameramen, editors, reporters, and photographers to Jesus Christ.

Palau says, "Frankly, it grieves me that so many Christians characterize the media as 'the enemy.' Yes, journalists on the whole admit they're rather liberal. Most don't see eye to eye with us on many issues. Many haven't darkened the door of a church since their wedding. But if we'll give them half a chance, they'll do more good for the cause of Christ in one day than we could do in half a year."[4]

It's sad that most Christians don't know anyone in the media, and some refuse to give media professionals the benefit of the doubt. The results can be disastrous.

At the urging of Billy Graham, for instance, the (Portland) *Oregonian* newspaper hired a full-time religion writer named Mark O'Keefe, gave him a great deal of freedom to cover the religious side of news stories, and often featured his articles on page one.

A religion reporter's dream job? Hardly.

O'Keefe started receiving scores of *hate* voice-mail messages and *hate* letters via post, fax, and email from so-called Christians. Many of these zealots completely missed the point of his in-depth articles. And almost all were clueless that O'Keefe himself is a committed Christian.

After O'Keefe moved to Washington, D.C., to work as a national correspondent for the Newhouse News Service, the *Oregonian* hired another religion writer who isn't a Christian—yet. Tragically, she's received the same kinds of *hate* messages once directed toward O'Keefe. Thankfully, a handful of Christians have befriended her and made it clear that the hateful minority don't speak for Jesus Christ or his church.

Stepping Stones to a Media-Friendly Relationship

"It's imperative that Christians build positive relationships with real individuals in the local media," says Palau. How can you do that?

- Recognize your own biases. Ask God to change your heart and give you a love for individuals working in the media.
- Don't forget that fellow Christians probably work at almost every major mainstream media organization in your city. Find out who they are—and support them.
- Ask your colleagues if they know anyone in the media. If so, ask for that reporter's contact information. Then take the initiative to contact him, introduce yourself, and schedule a time to meet. If the reporter doesn't know the Lord yet, that's great. Schedule a second time to get together. Become friends. Pray for him. Expect God to draw that reporter to himself.
- If a journalist calls you for an interview, take a minute to find out who the reporter is and then ask for her contact information. If you need time to gather your thoughts, offer to call the reporter back in an hour. After the interview, immediately send a quick thank-you note to the reporter via email. *Don't* ask to see the story before it runs.

36

Medical Field

Sharing the Healing Message of Christ

Herbert Walker

For more than twenty years I have viewed my vocation as a physician as an opportunity to share my faith as often as the Lord allows with patients and vendors, as well as with other doctors with whom I come in contact. It has always been a joy to see someone come to know Christ through a faithful witness. In this chapter I will address how a doctor can share his faith, as well as how you can share with a person in the medical field.

Early Beginnings

Early in my practice I met with my office manager, who was burdened to share the gospel. She asked if it would be all right to give gospel tracts out in the office. As a doctor trying to build a practice, I was a little concerned about scaring people off with such a bold witness, but my heart resonated with the same burden. I gave the old church answer, "Let's pray about it!" to give me time to get my thoughts together.

I consulted a committed Christian who is an oral surgeon. His response was loud and clear. Dr. Buck said, "Being an oral surgeon, I get my patients from dentists throughout the city. When I share my faith, I could possibly offend not only the patient but also the referring dentist." He said, "There is only one reason I share Christ."

"What's the reason?" I asked.

197

Dr. Buck said, "God commands it."

Immediately the consecration of our office to ministry took on a practical approach. It is a sin not to share the gospel when God commands it. "Therefore go and make disciples" (Matt. 28:19).

Communicating the Message

There was great relief in knowing that since God's name would be so overtly proclaimed in the office, he would take care of what belonged to him. We knew, first, we had to be professional in all we did. There should be no sacrifice in the medical treatment a person receives from an office sharing the gospel. As Paul says, "And whatever you do, do it heartily, as to the Lord and not to men" (Col. 3:23 NKJV). Serving the Lord as a Christian doctor, I have a mandate to provide the best care humanly possible.

Second, it's a team effort. It is a great comfort to know that our staff is united in their passion for sharing Christ. My nurse has given a gospel tract with a brief challenge to practically every new patient for the last twenty years. The gospel is woven through every part of our office. The music we play in the waiting room is quietly orchestrated traditional hymns; the books and magazines available on the tables are uncompromising; and even the artwork on the walls reflects the character of Christ. The employees' dress is modest. The employees voluntarily get to the office early and pray for God's wisdom in the medical decisions through the day, that God would directly appoint each patient visiting that day and that God would protect us.

Third, as a physician, I attempt to communicate every day in a language that people understand. It is vital to translate complicated medical terms into plain English for the patient. The same is true when I share the Lord Jesus Christ—clear communication is critical. The Bible states, "Faith comes by hearing, and hearing by the word of God" (Rom. 10:17 NKJV). Just as a doctor studies the latest news in the medical field, believers should study God's Word to know how to treat man's spiritual condition.

In a practice that has been in existence for a period of years, it could be unnerving for a doctor to begin to share her faith with patients. Doctors must be secure in what they are communicating to people. They are supposed to know the answers. I developed confidence in sharing Christ by using the *Four Spiritual Laws*. This happened through training when I was challenged to go door-to-door to speak with people who did not know me as Dr. Walker but as a young man stumbling through a tract. But God, who is always faithful, delivered his Word to those he chose. If you are not comfortable with what you should say, you will not share the gospel. You may speak *about* God but not present how to *know him personally*. There is a difference between *witnessing* and *soul winning*. By definition we are all witnessing about something, but God gives a special crown to soul winners (1 Thess. 2:19–20).

My worst fear is that I will stop a conversation short of the cross. People talk *about* Christ a lot, but hardly anyone tells you how you can receive him. The gospel climaxes with a call to respond. When Peter preached at Pentecost in Acts 2, the crowd asked, "What shall we do?" Peter responded, "Repent and be baptized, every one of you, in the name of Jesus Christ for the forgiveness of your sins" (vv. 37–38). If the gospel is presented without a call for a response, it is the same as if an illness is diagnosed without giving the medicine to provide the cure!

Steps to Evangelism

I offer four suggestions to anyone burdened to reach people through the medical field.

1. You must humble yourself. The Bible says, "God opposes the proud but gives grace to the humble" (James 4:6). Sharing Christ and receiving him require God's grace. Dr. Stephen Olford says, "Nothing less than the out-living of the indwelling attractiveness and friendliness of the Lord Jesus will succeed in personal evangelism." In other words, when we humble ourselves, the Holy Spirit is free to draw people to himself.
2. Get comfortable with a method of presentation. I use Campus Crusade's *Four Spiritual Laws*. I just read the booklet with people cover to cover.
3. If I'm not in the Word of God daily, then there is no daily drip of his Word into my conversations. I talk only medicine. God's words are not in my mouth. Just as a workman would not part with the essential tools of his trade, so a believer should not be apart from the Word of God. As we live by the Word and daily use it for teaching, rebuking, correcting, and training in righteousness, so we are equipped for every good work (2 Tim. 3:16–19).
4. You must surrender to just do it. For a professional medical person, the thought of treating hypertension is elementary, but to speak to the need of a soul is like bleeding sweat. I think of the many times I did not share Christ with someone, and it breaks my heart. The reality that on Thursday I could be listening to a heart that may stop beating on Friday compels me to share the love of God.

You will face rejection for the cause of Christ. I remember distinctly one lady getting so upset that she stormed out of the examination room, threw the tract down, burst through the front door, and left without paying, causing quite a stir. Six months later she returned to the office. She told us that when she had left the office in such a rage, she started asking herself why she was so angry: *Why did*

I act that way about God? The doctor wasn't mean—why was I? The Holy Spirit led her to a pastor who introduced her to Christ, and she returned to give us the good news.

Negative reactions do not always turn out like that one. However, 1 Peter 2:23 informs us of how Christ responded to criticism: "When they hurled their insults at him, he did not retaliate; when he suffered, he made no threats. Instead, he entrusted himself to him who judges justly." This is the only manner in which a believer should respond to rejection.

Reaching Those in the Medical Field

You may feel burdened for your doctor or someone in the medical field. In my own town the ministry of Mrs. Joyce Yancey has blessed us. During the first week of December every year, she organizes a banquet called Celebration, which is targeted at reaching people for Christ. From its small beginnings, it is now a time when hundreds gather for a two-day event. The first evening is for businessmen, and the second evening is for everyone in the community who has been prayed for regarding salvation. A speaker clearly shares the gospel and the appeal is offered through a prayer for salvation. If a person makes a decision for Christ, the one who invited him to the Celebration follows up. I invite many medical doctors, pharmaceutical representatives, and patients to this event.

There may not be this type of event in your city (maybe you could be the one to start one!), but you can speak with your own doctor about Christ. First, understand that a doctor is used to straightforward discussions. She is comfortable talking about anything and everything. Who better than a physician understands that everyone is terminal? Life is short, and the doctor certainly is aware of that fact.

Don't be afraid to ask probing questions, such as "How would you discuss death with a terminally ill person?" or "What hope can you offer to your patients?" Would the doctor be silent? Would he send for a pastor? The doctor must be able to treat the body, soul, and spirit, and there must be solace for the soul. Once again, the physician knows that time is of the essence.

As for the doctor, what has he done about the problem of sin in his own life? Simple, straightforward questions that allow you to use Scripture are the best way to start sharing with a medical person. Telling briefly and concisely your own personal salvation testimony leads easily into using a tract.

I always try to focus extra attention on someone I am praying for about accepting the gospel. Many times it has been a student who observes our practice. I cannot choose a student; the student always chooses us for one month of training and observation. Throughout this month I focus on either reaching this person for Christ or teaching the student to be a soul winner. I would caution that you must be sensitive to the Spirit and look for a certain openness to Christ in people with whom you share the gospel. We cannot coerce anyone into the kingdom, and our lifestyle must speak the first words of our faith. For every one tongue in the mouth, there are two in the shoes.

Finally, be willing to do whatever God asks you to do in reaching someone for Christ. This is true for any believer in any field at any time. Ultimately, God's concern is to save the lost while conforming us into the image of his Son. Our worth is not found in what we do, but in whose we are.

My journey began two months after I received Christ. I attended a conference where we were challenged to go and tell someone about Christ with tracts that were available. I was so nervous! I remember telling myself that I would not do it. It was not due to apathy but because of all-out fear that I delayed. Fear of rejection and embarrassment kept me in bondage.

Then I passed a man with a long white beard reading a philosophy book when the Holy Spirit seemed to urge me to share Christ. Once again I said no. It was a battle of my will against the prompting of the Holy Spirit. I kept going back and forth until finally the man looked up and asked, "You got something to say?" Because of fear I didn't want to do it, but I sat down and stumbled through the tract and looked up, ready for ridicule. I was shocked to see the man looking at me with tears in his eyes. He said he had always wanted to know, but no one had taken the time to share. Not only was that man saved, but I realized God was doing this for me. I needed that encouragement, and God had arranged our meeting.

Unknown to me, across the street that day was Mrs. Joyce Yancey and her two daughters. She had noticed my situation and stopped to pray for me and my courage (or lack of it!). She and her two daughters prayed that God would give me encouragement and boldness. Although it would be years later, I eventually had all the unique details about this story revealed to me. I married one of the daughters who stopped to pray for me that day! She is the mother of my children and an incredible witness for the Lord. I am so thankful for the leading of the Holy Spirit, and I am thankful that, on that day, I was obedient! Will you be sensitive to the Spirit today?

37

Military

Suggested Opportunities for Evangelism
within the Military Community

Sherman R. Reed

The chaplain has heard and answered the call: "Who will minister to military personnel who train to defend their country and may be mobilized to bear arms against aggression?" Opportunities for evangelism within the military are as numerous as the chain of command and as creativity will permit.

Our nation does not view its military members as soulless tools of the state. Instead, they are respected as created in the image of God and worthy of the best training for defense and survival that can be given them. Spiritual fitness is vital to that preparation. The chaplain is uniquely placed within the military to provide the freedom of the service members to worship and practice their respective religious beliefs as long as they do not interfere with the given mission of the military unit to which the members are assigned. The military chaplain is a staff officer with responsibility to ensure the free exercise of religion. As an integral part of the military, the very presence of the chaplain will prompt the "God question."

Ministries

A number of ministries that encourage spiritual growth are provided to military personnel.

Chapel Worship Services

Chapel services are conducted on a regular basis on military installations. The chaplain may design the services for spiritual growth or for making decisions for Christ. Christian education/discipleship training is also a part of nearly all chapel-life programs. Such ministries, in depth and breadth of evangelism, may mirror those in the civilian community, depending on the chapel leadership.

Bible Studies

Bible studies take place in various forms and places. The chaplain may be invited to have group studies in the home of a chapel family, in a separate area in the worship chapel, or in the barracks (military dormitory) of a single service member. Bible studies may also take place in a tent, in an aircraft hangar or ship, during a field training exercise, or at a proper, designated time in the various phases of combat and combat training.

The tools of Bible study will vary, depending on the situation and setting. The goal of the group or availability of personnel will determine if only the Bible is studied or if very elaborate learning materials are used. There are times when only the Scripture and perhaps a devotional reading are practical. The important ingredients are interested people and a godly leader to guide the group in spiritual formation.

Spiritual Life Retreats

Chaplains work routinely in tandem with quality-of-life and family readiness/support programs. Retreats are very special times and may vary in spiritual intensity. Some are designed for married couples, and the emphasis may range from numerous topics to enrich the military marriage to spiritual inspiration and physical recuperation. The retreat could take place at a rented retreat campus in the remote outdoors, at an urban commercial conference center, or in a motel complex. Other retreats may be tailored for the single service person, whether male or female.

In peacetime retreats may take place at any time. During combat a retreat may be scheduled either after notification of deployment or on returning from combat as a part of the homecoming efforts. The length of the retreat is based on the available time and money committed. Most military services have available "Permissive TDY" during peacetime. This is time that the military person can be away without its counting against his accumulated leave or vacation days and can be used for spiritual retreats at the soldiers' own expense. Planners will know the purpose of the particular retreat, and this determines the speakers and musicians they can invite to come.

Other Ministry Opportunities

Family Support and Readiness

Family readiness is another time of evangelism opportunity for Christian planners and volunteers. In addition to the chaplain, there are many volunteer workers who lend their expertise to the support of the military family. The goal is to have the family at a stage of such preparedness that when the service member is mobilized for combat, the family is properly sustained in her absence. The desire is to minimize concern and worry for both the family and the military warrior. Being left behind when a family member goes off to war is difficult and often brings awesome responsibilities to a spouse or other family members.

A vital portion of the family support training is spiritual preparedness. Most services have a Family Life Chaplain or a chaplain designated for such a role. Evangelism in this setting takes place as spiritual counseling, group Bible studies with family members, worship services, or one-on-one evangelism, as the need and opportunity are presented.

Basic Training Units

In the modern era the chaplain and chaplain assistant are a Unit Ministry Team (UMT). One proven place of assignment for the UMT is the Basic Training Units. A Basic Training Unit is where the newly recruited person receives training and instruction on military life. There is, by nature, much stress, learning, change, adjustment, reorientation of goals, objectives, and desires happening in these foundational and necessary units. The chaplain will have numerous counseling, instruction, and spiritual guidance opportunities. The weeks the new person is in this environment are prime times for prayer, repentance, and discovery of spiritual direction.

Battle Orders

When war is imminent, the intensity of spirituality rises, along with other necessary preparations. The UMT will have many ways to do personal evangelism and encourage spiritual decisions, as military warriors bear the reality of conflict and potential death. At these times services of worship, communion, and decision are often well attended, and service members are very responsive. The need for spiritual decisions and commitment becomes evident. Baptisms have been conducted in jungles, ponds, the sea, rivers, and the desert. Makeshift baptisteries have been survival dinghies, poncho liners in holes in the sand, pouring of water from canteens, and so on. Beyond the public worship services, the chaplain will have opportunities for prayer and evangelism with the troubled soldier in a tent or during walks in the combat preparation area. The observant and approachable chaplain will be in demand at numerous times and places during this special phase of the war.

Special Services

The chaplain may schedule services that are different from the standard chapel or field worship services. The purpose can be varied but may well be for evangelism, discipleship training, or spiritual inspiration.

Music and Testimony Services

In music and testimony services, the aim is to proclaim the gospel message. There may be singers, preaching evangelists, celebrities with special testimonies, or individuals with varied gifts and talents involved. This depends on the purpose of the service and the creativity and location of the particular military units. Planning, coordination, and the available finances and support people also determine the type of service that can be provided.

Funeral and Memorial Services

The very nature and purpose of the military—to fight and win America's wars—entails danger and death. Not all deaths result from acts of war. Whether in times of war or training for war, fatal accidents will occur. The military recognizes two significant services directly connected with the loss of a service member—the funeral service and the memorial service.

Funeral services are momentous and heart-rending times. Military honors alone add a special dimension to this service of honor and spiritual recognition. The military chaplain becomes the expert and pivotal person in the life of the military family at this intersection of life and death, sorrow, and devotion. The times prior to and following the funeral service will be occasions for the chaplain to provide spiritual counsel and guidance.

Memorial services differ from funerals. Memorial services are special services for fallen comrades. They are usually held where the unit is located and may be in formation or in a more relaxed atmosphere. Other times they are conducted in the immediate area where the battle has occurred. In the latter case, safety and mission priority must be considered. In either situation, the chaplain administers the services.

Memorial services are to honor and recognize the fallen unit member and his contribution to the mission, to service, and to country. In some situations, unit members may participate. Brevity and appropriate honor are the two considerations in a memorial service. The chaplain must be available to counsel friends and other unit members affected by the death of the unit member. These moments will be opportunities for spiritual guidance and evangelism.

I recently received an email from a mother who was desperately concerned for her son. She said, "My son joined the army to pay for his college education; I had no idea he would be sent off to war. I know his cause is worthy, but I'm worried about his salvation. How can I share Christ with my son who is across the planet?"

This is too much of a reality for families across our nation today. You may have found yourself in the same situation. Allow me to share some principles with you that I shared with this mother.

Pray

Nothing is more powerful than your prayer life. God knows your soldier's heart and his condition at this very moment. Pray for protection. Pray for peace. Mortality becomes very real to soldiers fighting a war. Pray for the peace that passes all understanding (Phil. 4:7).

Communicate

If at all possible, communicate with your soldier. Some methods of communicating may not always be available due to highly secure areas, but often the soldier can call home on a regular basis. Remind your soldier of your love and also of God's love for her. Explain God's plan for her life and his desire to be in a loving relationship with his children. If you cannot communicate by phone, email and postal letters are the next best methods. Military personnel are seeing evil in the worst human form, so they need to hear or see the opportunity of finding God's goodness during war.

Send Care Packages

Allow people in your church to help with this project of caring. Send articles that will not only be useful but will remind the soldier of spiritual highlights in his life. Tracts like *Steps to Peace with God* or *Four Spiritual Laws* will take up little space and will provide a clear presentation of the gospel.

Contact the Chaplain

Pray for the chaplain assigned to the unit. Ask the chaplain to be sensitive to your soldier's spiritual openness on the battlefield.

Do Not Lose Hope

You may go several days or even weeks without hearing from your soldier. Do not lose heart. Galatians 6:9 says, "At the proper time we will reap a harvest if we do not give up." Do not allow the silence to deafen your prayers. Keep your trust in God, who is faithful to complete the work he started. Finally, remember that there is only one other who cares for your soldier more than you do, and he is the one in whom you put your trust.

Scott Dawson

Ordinary
People
by
Religion

38

Agnosticism

Seven Questions Skeptics Ask

Rusty Wright

How do you deal with questions and objections to faith that your agnostic friends pose? First, pray for wisdom, for God's love for inquirers (Jer. 29:13), and for your questioner's heart. If appropriate, briefly share the gospel first. The Holy Spirit may draw your friends to Jesus Christ. Don't push though. It may be best to answer their questions first.

Remember that some questions may be intellectual smoke screens. Once a Georgia Tech philosophy professor peppered me with questions, which I answered as best I could. Then I asked him, "If I could answer all your questions to your satisfaction, would you put your life in Jesus's hands?" His reply: "[Expletive] no!"

No one can completely answer every concern you may encounter, but here are short responses to the seven most commonly asked questions.

Evil and Suffering

The skeptic asks, "Why is there evil and suffering?"

Sigmund Freud called religion an illusion that humans invent to satisfy their security needs. To him, a benevolent, all-powerful God seemed incongruent with natural disasters and human evil.

God, though sovereign, gave people the freedom to follow him or to disobey him. This response does not answer all concerns (because he sometimes does intervene to thwart evil) but suggests that the problem of evil is not as great an intellectual obstacle to belief as some imagine.

Pain's emotional barrier to belief, however, remains formidable. Jesus understands suffering. He was scorned, beaten, and cruelly executed, carrying the guilt of our rebellion against God (Isa. 53:10–11).

When I see God, items on my long list of questions for him will include a painful and unwanted divorce, betrayal by trusted co-workers, and all sorts of disappointing human behavior and natural disasters. Yet in Jesus's life, death, and resurrection I have seen enough to trust him when he says, "In all things God works for the good of those who love him, who have been called according to his purpose" (Rom. 8:28).

Contradictions

The skeptic asks, "What about all the contradictions in the Bible?"

Ask your questioner for specific examples. Often people have none but rely on hearsay. If there is a specific example, consider these guidelines as you respond:

- Omission does not necessarily create contradiction. Luke, for example, writes of two angels at Jesus's tomb after the resurrection (24:1–4). Matthew mentions "an angel" (28:1–8). Is this a contradiction? If Matthew stated that only one angel was present, the accounts would be dissonant. As it stands, they can be harmonized.
- Differing accounts aren't necessarily contradictory. Matthew and Luke, for example, differ in their accounts of Jesus's birth. Luke records Joseph and Mary's starting in Nazareth, traveling to Bethlehem (Jesus's birthplace), and returning to Nazareth (Luke 1:26–2:40). Matthew starts with Jesus's birth in Bethlehem, relates the family's journey to Egypt to escape King Herod's rage, and recounts their travel to Nazareth after Herod's death (Matt. 1:18–2:23). The Gospels never claim to be exhaustive records. Biographers must be selective. The accounts seem complementary not contradictory.

Time and again, supposed biblical problems fade in light of logic, history, and archaeology. The Bible's track record under scrutiny argues for its trustworthiness.

Those Who Never Hear

The skeptic asks, "What about those who never hear of Jesus?"

God's perfect love and justice far exceed our own. Whatever he decides will be loving and fair.

A friend once told me that many asking this question seek a personal loophole, a way out, so they won't need to believe in Christ. C. S. Lewis in *Mere Christianity* writes, "If you are worried about the people outside [of Christianity], the most unreasonable thing you can do is to remain outside yourself."[1]

If Christianity is true, the most logical behavior for someone concerned about those without Jesus Christ's message would be to trust Christ and go tell them about him.

The Only Way

The skeptic asks, "How can Jesus be the only way to God?"

When I was in high school, a recent alumnus visited, saying he had found Jesus Christ at Harvard. I respected his character and tact and listened intently, but I could not stomach Jesus's claim: "I am the way and the truth and the life. No one comes to the Father except through me" (John 14:6).

Two years later, my spiritual and intellectual journey had changed my view. The logic that drew me (reluctantly) to his position involves three questions:

1. *If God exists, could there be only one way to reach him?* To be open-minded, I had to admit this possibility.
2. *Why consider Jesus as a candidate for that possible one way?* He claimed it. His plan of rescuing humans—"by grace . . . through faith . . . not by works" (Eph. 2:8–9)—was distinct from those requiring works, as many other religions do. These two kinds of systems were mutually exclusive. Both could be false or either could be true, but both could not be true.
3. *Was Jesus's plan true?* Historical evidence for his resurrection, fulfilled prophecy, and deity, and for the reliability of the New Testament convinced me I could trust his words.

A Crutch

The skeptic asks, "Isn't Christianity just a psychological crutch?"

Author and speaker, Bob Prall, my mentor, has often said, "If Christianity is a psychological crutch, then Jesus Christ came because there was an epidemic of broken legs."

Christianity claims to meet real human needs, such as those for forgiveness, love, identity, and self-acceptance. We might describe Jesus not as a crutch but as an iron lung, essential for life itself. Christian faith and its benefits can be described in psychological terms, but that does not negate its validity. Evidence supports Christianity's truthfulness, so we would expect it to work in individual lives, as millions attest.

A Leap of Faith

The skeptic asks, "Isn't believing in Christ just a blind leap of faith?"

We exercise faith every day. Few of us understand everything about electricity or aerodynamics, but we have evidence of their validity. Whenever we use electric lights or airplanes, we exercise faith—not blind faith but faith based on evidence. Christians act similarly. The evidence for Jesus is compelling, so we can trust him on the basis of the evidence.

Being Sincere

The skeptic asks, "Does it really matter what you believe as long as you're sincere?"

After discussing this, a respected psychologist told me, "I guess a person could be sincere in what he believed but be sincerely wrong." In the 1960s many women took the drug thalidomide, sincerely believing it would ease their pregnancies—never suspecting it could cause severe birth defects. Their belief was wrong.

Ultimately, faith is only as valid as its object. Jesus demonstrated by his life, death, and resurrection that he is a worthy object for faith.

Your questioners may be turned off because many Christians haven't acted like Jesus. Maybe they're angry at God because of personal illness, a broken relationship, a loved one's death, or personal pain.

Ask God for patience and love as you follow Peter's admonition: "But in your hearts set apart Christ as Lord. Always be prepared to give an answer to everyone who asks you to give the reason for the hope that you have. But do this with gentleness and respect" (1 Pet. 3:15).

39

Atheism

God Loves Atheists Too

Michael Landry

Three hungry ants in pursuit of food crawled up to a large chocolate cake wrapped in Saran Wrap. None of the ants had ever seen such an object, so each responded differently. One of the ants looked at the cake and concluded it was just one more inconvenient and unidentifiable obstacle to crawl over in his pursuit of sustenance (like the agnostic). The second ant was starving and wondered if this large object could be eaten. He tore off a piece of the Saran Wrap, tasted the cake, and concluded that he had found what he had been looking for (like the believer).

The third ant saw the first ant struggling to crawl over the cake and concluded, "How foolish to crawl over such a useless obstacle when you could simply walk by it. What a waste of time!" Then, seeing the second ant jubilantly celebrating, he said, "Some ants are so hungry that they hallucinate about the food they need. Doesn't he know that real food couldn't possibly look like that, much less be obtained so easily?" The third ant continued on in pursuit of something recognizable and predictable and would eventually settle for whatever he could understand and explain scientifically, even if it meant remaining hungry (like the atheist).

Unfortunately, an atheist, like the third ant, is likely to miss the very thing he needs and was created to pursue, because at first he cannot understand it completely. The question that needs to be answered is, How can I effectively communicate to someone who has already ruled out the existence of God and convince him that it would be reasonable and beneficial to reconsider the evidence?

Four Myths about Atheists

There are some preconceived notions people have about atheists. Many of these have made us reluctant to reach out to them.

1. *Atheists are more intelligent.* There is no need to be intimidated by an atheist. An atheist's ability to articulate her views is evidence of intelligence but doesn't mean she knows all the facts. We need to be equally prepared and able to articulate our faith and the evidence that led us to believe.
2. *Atheists are uncaring.* Atheists are often very generous and caring. I've known some who have donated funds for church medical mission trips because of their commitment to humanitarian causes. Please don't assume that atheists don't care about people. We will insult them and possibly erect another unnecessary barrier to reaching them if we make that assumption.
3. *Atheists are viciously anti-God.* Atheists are not all alike. Some are on a mission, but most of the atheists I've met are soft-spoken and lead an unassuming life. They are not all unified, teaming with the ACLU, and trying to remove the Ten Commandments from our government buildings or prayer from our public schools. An atheist is simply someone who cannot believe in God and doesn't want people *forcing* others to believe in him.
4. *Atheists are beyond help.* If a person dies without receiving Jesus Christ as his personal Savior, he will not have a second chance to reconsider. But as long as he is alive on this earth, there is still a possibility he will eventually see the truth, repent of his sin and unbelief, and receive God's gift of eternal life. Never give up.

   The former atheist C. S. Lewis surprised even himself when he finally and suddenly took that step of faith. He said, "I was going up Headington Hill on top of a bus . . . I became aware that I was holding something at bay, or shutting something out. . . . I could open the door or keep it shut. . . . The choice appeared to be momentous but it was strangely unemotional. . . . I chose to open it . . . I felt as if I were a man of snow at long last beginning to melt."[1]

A Strategy That Works

To reach atheists, we must stop thinking that someone else can reach them more effectively than we can. That kind of thinking may bring immediate relief but will also result in separating the atheist from the very one God has uniquely prepared to get through to him—*you.*

We are mandated to reach out to people (Matt. 28:19; 1 Cor. 9:22), but their response to us may not be what we hope or expect. It is important to never forget that we are not responsible for another's response but rather for the initiative we take and our obedience to the mandate. That's the reason our strategy must begin with prayer.

Pray about It

Begin by praying for a longsuffering concern for atheists and that your lifestyle would become a constant visual reminder of God's unconditional love toward them. Your authentic friendship, concern, and passion for God must be obvious and visible.

Then pray specifically for an atheist you know. The Bible says that unbelievers' eyes are blinded (2 Cor. 4:3–4) and their hearts are calloused (Rom. 1:28). Pray specifically for their eyes to be opened and their hearts to be softened.

Next, enlist prayer partners. Ask others to join you in praying for the atheist and for an opportunity to share Christ with him. I've found it helpful to ask people to pray for shorter periods of time (a week or less) and involve many more people over time.

Enlist the Right People for Help

Relationships are key components to reaching atheists. They may not believe in God, but they do believe in you and some other people. It is very important that you consistently and unapologetically live out the Christian life. Most atheists believe Christians are irrelevant, uneducated, naive, or inconsistent hypocrites. Strive to be transparent and consistent in your faith lifestyle (1 Pet. 3:15–17) and introduce them to others who are. Once that credibility is established, they will be intrigued and curious to find out why such a person would believe in God.

Expose the Atheist to God's Word

God's Word is alive (Heb. 4:12). Exposure to it always makes a difference. In fact the Bible says it this way, "So shall My word be that goes forth from My mouth; *it shall not return to Me void*, but it shall accomplish what I please, and it shall prosper *in the thing* for which I sent it" (Isa. 55:11 NKJV). Try challenging an atheist to read the New Testament and give you an honest review and evaluation. The atheist may reject the truth initially, but it will continue to work on her mind and heart thereafter.

As a former atheist, I still remember borrowing my sister's Bible and reading it so that I could argue the contents more effectively with other Christians. As I read the Gospels, I was forced to consider the facts about Jesus. The reading of Scripture informed me that the Christian life is about a personal relationship with God made possible through Jesus Christ. I began to rethink the whole issue. It eventually brought me to the edge of a decision personally, and I reluctantly took a step of faith. I've never been the same since.

Use Other Resources

There are so many resources that may prove helpful to reaching atheists. If he is a reader, then recommend books that deal with his questions. Some of my personal favorites are books by C. S. Lewis (*Mere Christianity*), Lee Strobel (*The Case for Christ*), Josh McDowell (*Evidence That Demands a Verdict* and *More Than a Carpenter*), and Henry Schaefer (*Science and Christianity: Conflict or Coherence*).

A Personal Word from a Former Atheist

I was a professing atheist in high school and went to college with an atheistic chip on my shoulder. Little did I know that more than two hundred high school students had been praying for me by name every day for more than three years. One of those students spent hours, on numerous occasions, debating the issues with me concerning the existence of God. He also had my respect because his lifestyle matched his beliefs about God.

It was in college that I borrowed a New Testament from my sister, so I could effectively debate the contents with those who were quick to use it in conversations. As I read the four Gospels, God used his Word to open my eyes to the misconceptions I held about the Christian life. I believed mistakenly that Christianity was simply a set of rules. Some of those rules I believed were beneficial to mankind, but I did not think it was necessary to believe in God to live by those rules. I still didn't know for sure about the existence of God, but I did take a chance privately and prayed something like this: "God, I'm not sure you are even there to hear me, but what I've just read about in this Bible seems to make sense. I am certainly one of those imperfect sinners that Jesus had to die for. If you really exist, I'd like to take you up on your offer and have a personal relationship with you. So I come on your terms. Now it's up to you to show me how real you are. This is Mike Landry, signing off. P.S. If you are not really there, then let's pretend this conversation never happened. But if you are, I'll be waiting."

That prayer of faith changed my life, and I have never been the same since. The prayers of Christians, the reading of Scripture, and the relationship of a caring and consistent Christian all contributed to bringing me to the point of decision.

Now it's your turn! Go now, while there's still time!

40

Buddhism

Making Sure the Gospel Is "Good News" to a Buddhist

Daniel Heimbach and Vic Carpenter

Buddhists regard the United States as a prime mission field, and the number of professing Buddhists in this country is growing rapidly due to surges in Asian immigration; endorsement of the religion by celebrities such as Tina Turner, Richard Gere, and Harrison Ford; and positive exposure in major movies such as *The Little Buddha*, *Seven Years in Tibet*, *Kundun*, and *The Last Samurai*. Buddhism is closely related to the New Age Movement and may be driving it to some extent. Certainly the influence of New Age thought in American life has led many to view Buddhism as an attractive alternative.

Historical Background

Buddhism was founded near present-day Nepal as a form of atheism that rejected ancient beliefs in a permanent, personal, creator God (Ishvara) who controlled the eternal destiny of human souls. Siddhartha Gautama rejected more ancient theistic beliefs because of the difficulty he had in reconciling the reality of suffering, judgment, and evil with the existence of a good and holy God. Buddhism is an impersonal religion of self-perfection, the end of which is death (extinction)—not life. The essential elements of the Buddhist belief system are summarized in the *Four Noble Truths*, the *Noble Eightfold Path*, and several additional key doctrines.

217

The *Four Noble Truths* affirm that (1) life is full of suffering (*dukkha*); (2) suffering is caused by craving (*samudaya*); (3) suffering will cease only when craving ceases (*nirodha*); and (4) this can be achieved by following the Noble Eightfold Path. This sacred *Eightfold Path* consists of right views, right aspiration, right speech, right conduct, right livelihood, right effort, right mindfulness, and right contemplation.

Other key doctrines include belief that nothing in life is permanent (*anicca*), that individual selves do not truly exist (*anata*), that all is determined by an impersonal law of moral causation (*karma*), that reincarnation is an endless cycle of continuous suffering, and that the goal of life is to break out of this cycle by finally extinguishing the flame of life and entering a permanent state of pure nonexistence (*nirvana*).

Bridges for Evangelizing Buddhists

Care must be taken to make sure the biblical gospel of Jesus Christ is truly perceived as "good news" to someone living within a Buddhist worldview. This can be done if the evangelist focuses on areas of personal need where the Buddhist belief system is weak. Some of these areas include the following:

- *Suffering.* Buddhists are deeply concerned with overcoming suffering but must deny that suffering is real. Christ faced the reality of suffering and overcame it by solving the problem of sin, which is the real source of suffering. Now those who trust in Christ can rise above suffering in this life because they have hope of a future life free from suffering. "We fix our eyes not on what is seen [suffering], but on what is unseen [eternal life free of suffering]. For what is seen [suffering] is temporary, but what is unseen [future good life with Christ] is eternal" (2 Cor. 4:18).
- *Meaningful self.* Buddhists must work to convince themselves that they have no personal significance, even though Buddhist men and women have the same needs and longings we all do. They must live and act as if individuals are unimportant, even though they all long to love and be loved, and all wish to be successful in their own personal endeavors. Jesus taught that each person has genuine significance. Each person is made in God's image with an immortal soul and an eternal destiny. Jesus demonstrated the value of people by loving us so much that he sacrificed his life to offer eternal good life to anyone who trusts him. "God demonstrates his own love for us in this: While we were still sinners, Christ died for us" (Rom. 5:8).
- *Future hope.* The hope of nirvana is no hope at all—only death and extinction. The hope of those who put their trust in Christ is eternal good life in "a new heaven and a new earth" (Rev. 21:1) in which God "will wipe every tear from their eyes. There will be no more death or mourning or crying

or pain, for the old order of things [suffering] has passed [will pass] away"
(v. 4).

- *Moral law.* Because karma, the Buddhist law of moral cause and effect,
  is completely rigid and impersonal, life for a Buddhist is very oppressive.
  Under karma there can be no appeal, no mercy, and no escape except through
  unceasing effort at self-perfection. Christians understand that the moral
  force governing the universe is a personal God who listens to those who
  pray, who has mercy on those who repent, and who, with love, personally
  controls for good the lives of those who follow Christ. "In all things God
  works for the good of those who love him" (Rom. 8:28).

- *Merit.* Buddhists constantly struggle to earn merit by doing good deeds,
  hoping to collect enough to break free from the life of suffering. They also
  believe that saints can transfer surplus merit to the undeserving. Jesus taught
  that no one can ever acquire enough merit on his own to earn everlasting
  freedom from suffering. Instead, Jesus Christ, who has unlimited merit (righteousness) by virtue of his sinless life, meritorious death, and resurrection,
  now offers his unlimited merit as a free gift to anyone who will become his
  disciple. "For it is by grace you have been saved, through faith—and this
  not from yourselves, it is the gift of God—not by works, so that no one can
  boast" (Eph. 2:8–9).

- *Desire.* Buddhists live a contradiction—they seek to overcome suffering by
  rooting out desire, but at the same time they cultivate desire for self-control,
  meritorious life, and nirvana. Christians are consistent—we seek to reject
  evil desires and cultivate good desires, according to the standard of Christ.
  "Flee the evil desires of youth, and pursue righteousness, faith, love and
  peace, along with those who call on the Lord out of a pure heart" (2 Tim.
  2:22).

Jesus and the Eightfold Path

Because the Buddhist thinks a good life consists of following the Eightfold
Path, the stages of the path can be used to introduce them to Christ as follows:

Right Views. Jesus is the way, the truth, and the life (John 14:6), and there is
  salvation in no one else (Acts 4:12).

Right Aspiration. Fights and quarrels come from selfish desires and wrong motives (James 4:1–3); right desires and motives honor God (1 Cor. 10:31).

Right Speech. A day of judgment is coming when God will hold men accountable for every careless word they have spoken (Matt. 12:36).

Right Conduct. The one who loves Jesus must obey him (John 14:23), and those
  who live by God's wisdom will produce good acts or fruit (James 3:17).

Right Livelihood. God will care for those who put him first (Matt. 6:31, 33), and all work must be done for God's approval (2 Tim. 2:15).

Right Effort. Like runners in a race, followers of Christ must throw off every hindrance, giving Christ their best efforts (Heb. 12:1–2).

Right Mindfulness. The sinful mind cannot submit to God's law (Rom. 8:7), and disciples of Christ must orient their minds as he did (Phil. 2:5).

Right Contemplation. The secret of true success, inner peace, self-control, and lasting salvation is submission to Jesus Christ as Savior and Lord and setting our heart and mind on things above where he now sits in glory waiting to bring the present order of sin and suffering to an end (Col. 3:1–4).

Witnessing to a Buddhist

When witnessing to a Buddhist, avoid terms such as *new birth, rebirth, regeneration,* or *born again* that could easily be confused with concepts of reincarnation. Use alternative phrases such as "endless freedom from suffering, guilt, and sin," "new power for living a holy life," "promise of eternal good life without suffering," or "gift of unlimited merit."

Seek to emphasize the uniqueness of Christ. Focus on the gospel message and do not get distracted by details of Buddhist doctrine. Use bridge concepts to connect with areas of felt need or special interest (see Bridges for Evangelizing Buddhists in this chapter) and be careful not to reduce Christian truth to a form of Buddhism. Buddhism has a history of accommodating other religions, so do not say, "Buddhism is good, but Christianity is easier." Try sharing your own testimony, especially your freedom from guilt, assurance of heaven (no more pain), and personal relationship with Christ.

Finally, you should always prepare for witnessing with a serious time of prayer. You will rarely, if ever, be effective witnessing to a Buddhist by relying merely on your natural abilities!

41

Confucianism

From A Ready Defense

Josh McDowell

Confucianism, a religion of optimistic humanism, has had a monumental impact on life, social structure, and political structure in China. The founding of the religion goes back to one man, known as Confucius, born a half-millennium before Christ.

The Life of Confucius

Although Confucius occupies a hallowed place in Chinese tradition, little is verifiable about his life. The best source available is *The Analects*, a collection of his sayings made by his followers. Long after his death, much biographical detail on his life surfaced, but most of this material is of questionable historical value. However, there are some basic facts that can be reasonably accepted to give an outline of his life.

Confucius was born Chiu King, the youngest of eleven children, about 550 BC in the principality of Lu, which is located in present-day Shantung. He was a contemporary of the Buddha (although they probably never met) and lived immediately before Socrates and Plato. Nothing is known for certain concerning his ancestors except the fact that his surroundings were humble. As he himself revealed: "When I was young, I was without rank and in humble circumstances."

His father died soon after his birth, leaving his upbringing to his mother. During his youth, Confucius participated in a variety of activities, including hunting and fishing; but, "On reaching the age of fifteen, I bent my mind to learning."

He held a minor government post as a collector of taxes before he reached the age of twenty. It was at this time that Confucius married. However, this marriage was short-lived, ending in divorce after producing a son and a daughter. Confucius became a teacher in his early twenties, and this proved to be his calling in life. His ability as a teacher became apparent and his fame spread rapidly, attracting a strong core of disciples who were drawn by his wisdom. He believed that society would not be changed unless he occupied a public office where he could put his theories into practice.

Confucius held minor posts until age fifty, when he became a high official in Lu. His moral reforms achieved immediate success, but he soon had a falling out with his superiors and subsequently resigned his post. Confucius spent the next thirteen years wandering from state to state, attempting to implement his political and social reforms. He devoted the last five years of his life to writing and editing what have become Confucian classics.

He died in Chufou, Shantung, in 479 BC, having established himself as the most important teacher in Chinese culture. His disciples referred to him as King Fu-tzu or Kung the Master, which has been latinized into Confucius.

The Sources of Confucianism

The five classics, as we have them today, have gone through much editing and alteration by Confucius's disciples, yet there is much in them that can be considered the work of Confucius. The five classics are:

The Book of Changes (I Ching)
The Book of Annals (Shu K'ing)
The Book of Poetry (Shih Ching)
The Book of Ceremonies (Li Chi)
The Annals of Spring and Autumn (Ch'un Ch'iu)

None of these works contains the unique teachings of Confucius, but they are rather an anthology of works he collected and from which he taught. Confucius's own teachings have come down to us from four books written by his disciples. They include:

The Analects
The Great Learning
The Doctrine of the Mean
The Book of Mencius

Confucianism is not a religion in the sense of man relating to the Almighty but is rather an ethical system, teaching man how to get along with his fellow-man, including moral conduct and the ordering of society. However, Confucius did make some comments on the supernatural, which give insight into how he viewed life, death, heaven, and so on. He once said, "Absorption in the study of the supernatural is most harmful."

When asked about the subject of death, he had this to say: "Chi-lu asked how the spirits of the dead and the gods should be served. The master said, 'You are not able to serve man. How can you serve the spirits?'

'May I ask you about death?'

'You do not understand even life. How can you understand death?'"

Although Confucianism deals solely with life here on earth rather than the afterlife, it does take into consideration mankind's ultimate concerns. The heavens and their doings are assumed to be real rather than imaginary. Since Confucianism gradually assumes control over all of one's life, being the presupposition from which all action is decided, it has necessarily permeated Chinese religious thought, belief, and practice as well.

Confucianism and Christianity

The ethical system taught by Confucius has much to commend it, for virtue is something to desire highly. However, the ethical philosophy Confucius espoused was one of self-effort, leaving no room or need for God.

Confucius taught that man can achieve everything by himself if he only follows the ways of the ancients, while Christianity teaches that man does not have the capacity to save himself but is in desperate need of a Savior.

Confucius also hinted that human nature is basically good. Later Confucian teachers developed this thought and it became a cardinal belief of Confucianism. The Bible, on the other hand, teaches that man is basically sinful and, when left to himself, is completely incapable of performing ultimate good. The teachings of the Bible about human nature and our need of a Savior are a stark contrast with the teachings of Confucianism.

> The heart is more deceitful than all else and is desperately sick; who can understand it?
>
> Jeremiah 17:9 NASB

> For all have sinned and fall short of the glory of God.
>
> Romans 3:23

> For by grace you have been saved through faith; and that not of yourselves, it is the gift of God; not as a result of works, so that no one may boast.
>
> Ephesians 2:8–9 NASB

He saved us, not on the basis of deeds which we have done in righteousness, but according to His mercy, by the washing of regeneration and renewing by the Holy Spirit.

Titus 3:5 NASB

Since Confucianism lacks any emphasis on the supernatural, it must be rejected as a religious system. Confucius taught an ethical philosophy that later evolved into a popular religion, though Confucius had no idea that this would happen and that his teachings would become the state religion in China. Nevertheless, Confucianism as a religious system is opposed to the teachings of Christianity and must be rejected summarily by Christians.

Reaching the Confucian

When trying to reach a Confucian for Christ, we must take into account the foundation that has already been laid in his thoughts. This person is generally going to believe he does not have a "sin problem" and that he will be all right as long as he does the right thing. Confucians may be noble human beings, but they have no cure for their sin and fail to recognize that they, just like all of humanity, need a Savior. The following are some helpful hints to keep in mind when sharing your faith with a Confucian:

- *Use the law of God (Ten Commandments).* The Bible teaches that the law is our tutor, which God uses to lead us to Christ. If it were not for the law, we would not realize we have a sin problem. The law shows people they are sinners in need of Christ.
- *Stress the holiness of God.* Understanding that we are sinners is much more powerful when we see ourselves before a holy God. If God cannot tolerate sin, and we are sinners, we have a problem.
- *Focus on Christ.* When the time is right, and you have shown the person in the Word of God his perfect standard and our failure to meet it, then reveal Christ. The death, burial, and resurrection will make more sense to someone who grasps her need for a sin substitute.
- *Be patient.* Do not be discouraged if the person does not come to Christ immediately. When someone has been raised and taught to believe a certain way, it may take a while for him to come out of his old beliefs.

42

Hinduism

Insights for an Effective Witness to Hindus

Natun Bhattacharya

Hinduism today is a global religion beyond the borders of India. While the majority of Hindus live in India and Nepal, there are immigrant Hindu communities spread all around the Western world, other Asian countries, and parts of Africa. According to some estimates, there are six to seven million Indians living outside India.[1] In the United States alone there are more than a million people of Hindu/Indian origin. Hinduism has influenced the popular culture of North America through the practice of Yoga, meditation, and other aspects of new spiritualities derived from Indian religious roots.

Hinduism is diverse and complex in its doctrine and practice.[2] The origin of Hinduism goes back to around 1500 BC.[3] Succeeding periods in the history of Hinduism went through many developments, often adding whole new schools of belief. Today Hinduism is more than religion. It is a way of life intricately blended with cultural values, traditions, and national identity.

Know the Hindu Religious Concepts

Despite all its complexity, Hinduism embraces the following common religious concepts:

- *Brahman*: the supreme spirit that is the all-pervading absolute reality or the impersonal force

225

- *Dharma*: religion or duty (roughly translated)
- *Atman*: one's self-being, a part of the universal self
- *Reincarnation*: *atman*, or self, being reborn into many lives
- *Karma*: the law that actions always have effects
- *Moksha*: salvation that ends all cycles of birth, merging one's self into the supreme universal self

These ancient religious concepts translate into everyday life for Hindus. Popular Hinduism has interpreted the key teachings and applied them to daily life. From birth to death, all stages of life are controlled by the demands of a religion that encompasses all of life.[4] There is no distinction between the religious and the secular. Worship of deities, rituals of pilgrimage, and the keeping of duties at various stages of life are observed in any given Hindu community. The demands of traditions are not questioned and are faithfully kept. Other than the priests and educated few, the masses cannot explain the volumes of scriptural contexts that shape the worldview of the Hindu.

Be Incarnational in Relationships

When a Christian wants to reach a Hindu for Christ, the best avenue for gaining an entry into his heart is taking time to live an incarnational lifestyle, following in Christ's footsteps. As you begin this kind of relationship, you do not really have to know a great deal about the religion of your Hindu friend, colleague, or neighbor. Just open your home and show that you genuinely care. As you progress in sincere friendship, your unconditional love for and interest in your Hindu friend will demonstrate the love of Christ beyond words. You need to be there as a friend available at tough times and good times. Be accessible when your Hindu friend drops in to talk, seek advice, or share her heart. It is such a relationship that will pave the way for an open dialogue.

Considering the hectic pace of life today, it takes sacrifice and resolve to pursue genuine friendships. However, the core of such a friendship is deeply embedded in the unique relationship orientation of Indian culture. Therefore, it is this kind of friendship that draws your Hindu friend and makes him feel at home. Authentic acceptance of your friend demonstrates Christ in you, thus opening the door for the Hindu to be interested in your faith.

Learn to Dialogue and Listen

Hinduism is a complex belief system that often seems contradictory to the Western linear and systematic way of thinking. There are apparent inconsistencies, such as belief in the ultimate reality or the impersonal force Brahman, along with the belief in the existence of gods and goddesses. Hindus will explain this apparent contradiction by saying deities are manifestations of one ultimate god—Brahman. One cannot describe precisely what a Hindu believes, given regional diversity, family, caste background, and age bracket. Hinduism is highly inclusive. You may meet a religious Hindu, an agnostic Hindu, or even an atheistic Hindu. Anyone born into a Hindu family is considered a Hindu. Being a Hindu is part of this person's cultural identity.

Asking questions (within the context of a relationship) about your Hindu friend's understanding of her religion will reveal to you where she stands in her faith. Sometimes a Hindu may have very little knowledge of formal and philosophical high religion. She may have grown up practicing traditional rituals—worship of deities and the celebration of popular festivals of Hinduism—yet be unable to articulate the teachings of Hinduism itself. In fact it has been my experience with a number of Hindus that, as they encounter questions on Hinduism from knowledgeable American friends, they begin to study seriously the classical Hindu teachings.

Once you have a basic understanding of how well versed a Hindu is on his religion, then you can individualize your witness to fit that person's situation. For example, a Hindu not thoroughly schooled in the tenets of Hinduism may find it difficult to follow your presentation based on your textbook knowledge of Hinduism. On the other hand, a Hindu thoroughly conversant with scholarly Hinduism may not engage in dialogue with you if she senses your grasp of Hinduism is too simplistic.

Above all, dialoguing with your Hindu friend concerning life's issues will open a door through which you can touch your friend at the point of his deepest-felt needs. Many Indian immigrants have crossed a huge cultural barrier to succeed in North America; often they continue to struggle to conform to the highly individualistic and task-driven North American way of life. They may live a double life—one at work where they must conform to Western norms and the other within the cocoon of their family and community. The cost of achievement has for many been the high price of marital conflict, struggle with their U.S.–born children, and a heavy burden of stress and isolation.

Understand the Hindu Worldview

The Hindu worldview is starkly different from the Christian and Western worldviews. Hindus believe this natural world is an illusion of the mind. They also believe in karma and reincarnation and that we are a part of the Brahman, or the divine. To them salvation, or *Moksha*, is to become merged into the ultimate reality, or Brahman, and freed from the cycle of rebirth and suffering.

Obviously they have a perspective of life uniquely their own. Hindus living in North America or elsewhere outside India may have been exposed to other worldviews. Yet their own worldview runs deep. When we present the gospel to the Hindus from our vantage point, we should not assume they will fully understand our frame of reference. Our message of salvation will be a lot more effective if we enter their world and speak in terms they can understand.

To illustrate this further, when we share the biblical view of who God is or what salvation is, we must have some understanding of what the terms *god* and *salvation* mean to a Hindu. If we are aware of their understanding of these theological concepts, then we will be able to consciously distinguish the biblical teaching from Hindu teaching. In addition, our worldview shapes our cultural values. The Hindu holds such values as loyalty and conformity to family and community and the importance of traditions. Often a Hindu is reluctant to become a Christian because of allegiance to these deeply rooted values. We need to acknowledge these concerns in our witnessing.

Address the Uniqueness of Christ

The most common Hindu objection to Christian faith is that Christ cannot be the only way to God. Thus his claim, "I am the way and the truth and the life. No one comes to the Father except through me" (John 14:6), is a challenge to a Hindu who is often so inclusive. Hinduism accepts many paths to salvation. A person can achieve liberation, or *Moksha*, through devotion to his personal deity, through good works, ritual, knowledge, and spiritual discipline.

At this point it is necessary for us to understand that the Hindu/Indian mind is not concerned about our kind of Western logical consistency or rationalism. No amount of argument on the historicity of Christianity and the validity of the Bible may open the Hindu heart. Rather, it is the work of the Holy Spirit to touch hearts. That said, our strategy in sharing Christ with our Hindu friends should be focused on telling the story of Christ's life, death, and resurrection, rather than on just selected texts. Hindu religion thrives on storytelling. It approaches spiritual knowledge in a holistic way. Encourage your friend to read the Gospels to discover the uniqueness of Christ for herself.

In your follow-up dialogues, reinforce Christ's story. The fact that you are exemplifying Christ in your relationship with your Hindu friends, listening to them, and sharing the life of Christ verbally is an eternal investment that will lead them to know Christ today or in the course of time.

43

Judaism

Five Simple Steps to Not Converting a Jew

Karen Covell

How do you talk to people who don't think they need Jesus? That is the story of my life. As a producer in the Hollywood entertainment industry, I work with Jewish people every day. Because the Christians fled from the film and television industry decades ago, some sharp Jewish businessmen, with the encouragement of their Jewish mothers, took over the media in Hollywood and are still the leading decision makers here today. I love these people. They are passionate, creative, shrewd business people whose directness is refreshing in an industry of vague creativity and unorthodox business practices. What you see is what you get. Of course, this attitude also, unfortunately, includes a disinterest in spiritual things.

Answers to Questions They Aren't Asking

Here's a truth often missed by Christians: Jewish people are God's chosen people, his own tribe. The problem is they don't believe they need Jesus. They're still waiting for their Messiah, and they're convinced Jesus isn't he. God loves his people and wants them to come to know him, and yet many of our Jewish friends and family members don't even believe in God, let alone Jesus. Many of God's chosen few are humanists, atheists, cult members, New Agers, or just spiritually empty, not unlike many of their ancestors.

229

As Christians, we know the Jewish people are in terrible danger without Christ, but they don't know it and don't seem very interested in finding out. Many have great lives, lots of money, successful businesses, well-educated children, and strong families. There seem to be no chinks in their armor, no missing pieces in their puzzle. What can we possibly offer them? Supernatural peace, for one thing, eternal life with God, and answers to the ultimate questions. But it's hard to answer questions no one's asking. So how do we reach them?

Who Jews Really Are

First of all, we need to understand who the Jews really are. Ten percent of America's population is Jewish. Most of them are proud to be Jewish, but they are divided even as a people, not agreeing among themselves as to who a Jew really is. Founder of Ariel Ministries, Dr. Arnold Fruchtenbaum, says, "Israeli law is very clear on who is not a Jew. It is totally unclear on who is a Jew."

Some are religious Jews, following the Scriptures to the letter of the law and living very conservative, holy, orthodox lives. Others are cultural Jews, commonly liberal, primarily committed to one another and to the Jewish community at large, very hip, and involved in political and social issues. But they have little, if any, spiritual beliefs. Jewish people are very aware of their heritage and the suffering of their people throughout history, but they don't know who their God really is, and most, of course, know nothing about the many detailed prophesies in their Scriptures pointing to Jesus. The cultural Jews I know have never read the Bible and know very little, if anything, about their Old Testament roots.

We must also understand that many Jews have been deeply hurt by Gentiles, all in the name of Jesus. My Jewish friend and former producing partner once told me her parents had sent her to parochial schools to give her the best education. However, some of the kids in her elementary school called her "Christ Killer" or "Jesus Killer" just because she was Jewish. Because of that negative influence, she wasn't open to hearing about my love for Jesus. I understood her hesitancy to embrace my faith as she revealed the complicated and delicate relationship between Christians and Jews. There are, indeed, many areas of misunderstanding and hurt from both Gentiles and Jews. But there are also ways to break through those obstacles, and it can start by Christians understanding Jews as a special group of people whom God loves very much.

Jews Don't Need to Be Converted

We have to change our belief that Jews need to be "converted" to Christianity. Jews will always be Jewish. Jesus was Jewish. We Gentiles are the ones who are converted when we become Christians, or followers of the Jewish Jesus. Our privilege is to reintroduce Jews to their God and let them know that Yeshua is indeed their long-awaited Messiah. Then we can tell them that the Christians are the ones who have been grafted into God's family. In fact Paul, a Jew, said, "I am not ashamed of the gospel, because it is the power of God for the salvation of everyone who believes: first for the Jew, then for the Gentile" (Rom. 1:16). We should be the ones who humbly accept Jesus as our Messiah, realizing that he came first for the Jews and then to us. What a difference that paradigm shift would make in talking to our Jewish friends and family members.

Jewish people who accept Jesus as their personal Savior (calling themselves Completed Jews, Messianic Jews, or Jewish believers) truly have the best of both worlds. They are one of God's original chosen people—and they live with Jesus! However, they often pay a great price to embrace this gift. Accepting Jesus comes with a sobering personal sacrifice to Jews, for most likely they will be shunned by their families, as betrayers, for denying their family bloodline and heritage. Also many Jewish believers I know feel as though they have fallen into a crack, not standing firmly with any group of people and not being fully understood by anyone.

Your Jewish Roots

We need to know our own Jewish roots by reading the Old and New Testaments and getting to know the Jewish law, traditions, prophecies, and even the holy days, such as Yom Kippur, Hanukkah, and Rosh Hashanah. God wants us to understand him and all that he has done with and through his people. "My people are destroyed from lack of knowledge" (Hosea 4:6).

Also we can ask our Jewish friends to tell us all they know about their Jewish family history and what it means to them. *Betrayed*, by Stan Telchin, is a powerful book about one family's personal Jewish heritage and their journey to Jesus[1]. It helps the reader understand the history of the Jews as it gives insight into the heart of a Jewish man. In this compelling true story, Telchin relays his trauma at hearing that his daughter, a college student, became a Completed Jew by believing in Jesus. He set out to prove her wrong and was slowly transformed as he studied the truths of Judaism and the life of his Messiah. My husband and I have given *Betrayed* as a gift to many Christians and to seeking Jewish friends to aid them in their own spiritual journeys.

Ask Questions

We must ask our Jewish friends questions that will cause them to think and come to their own conclusions. Traditionally, Jews like to discuss, question, and even argue issues of life, politics, and even faith. So begin by finding common ground. Then be affirming and go on to challenging and thought-provoking questions. For instance, start with, What do you think about God? Who do you think Jesus was? Have you ever read the Scriptures? Would you be willing to? Do you have a Bible? Would you like one? (If they say yes, get them a Bible.) What type of person do you think your Messiah will be? Did you know that the Old Testament is full of prophecies telling the Jews that their Messiah was coming?

A powerful question is to ask what they know about the sixty-six major prophecies in the Old and New Testaments that predict and explain the life and death of Yeshua (see the list at the end of this chapter). Of course, you must study these prophetic verses first so that you will "always be prepared to give an answer to everyone who asks you to give the reason for the hope that you have. But do this with gentleness and respect" (1 Pet. 3:15). It's not up to us to argue anyone into the kingdom or to convince someone of the truth of the gospel. All we have to do is bring up the topic and pray that the Holy Spirit will do the revealing, convicting, and convincing.

I'm always thrilled when I get the opportunity to discuss Jesus with my Jewish friends and/or work associates. I especially love telling them that Jesus was a Jew and that he came to Israel, to Jewish people (Matt. 15:24). Then he gave his life for them—his own people. We should thank the Jews for allowing us to come along for the ride, getting all that God gave them first, just because of his grace. When you look at it that way, it becomes exciting to talk to the Jewish people about their blessed and exciting heritage and their potentially glorious future.

Love and Pray!

Finally, if God has given you Jewish friends, co-workers, neighbors, or family members, love them. Let there be no division between you just because they are Jewish and you are Christian. Simply understand who they really are, remember not to try to "convert" them, study up on your Jewish roots from the whole Bible, and then ask questions and let them come to their own conclusions. It's a thrilling privilege to talk to your Jewish friends about Jesus, so don't freak out! Don't let fear stop you from passing on the Good News that God loves them so much that he already sent his Son, their Messiah, to them. And then pray, pray, pray! Pray for wisdom and the right words to say at the right time. Pray for other Christians to come into their lives. Pray for their hearts to be prepared for a divine appointment, and then be ready for God to use you in his miracle gift of salvation.

That the Scripture Might Be Fulfilled

Here are just eighteen of the sixty-six prophecies fulfilled by Jesus Christ:

1. The Messiah was to be born in

Bethlehem—prophesied in Micah 5:2; fulfilled in Matthew 2:1–6 and Luke 2:1–20.

2. The Messiah was to be born of a virgin—prophesied in Isaiah 7:14; fulfilled in Matthew 1:18–25 and Luke 1:26–38.

3. The Messiah was to be a prophet like Moses—prophesied in Deuteronomy 18:15, 18–19; fulfilled in John 7:40.

4. The Messiah was to enter Jerusalem in triumph—prophesied in Zechariah 9:9; fulfilled in Matthew 21:1–11 and John 12:12–16.

5. The Messiah was to be rejected by his own people—prophesied in Isaiah 53:1–3 and Psalm 118:22; fulfilled in Matthew 26:3–4; John 12:37–43; and Acts 4:1–12.

6. The Messiah was to be betrayed by one of his followers—prophesied in Psalm 41:9; fulfilled in Matthew 26:14–16, 47–50, and Luke 22:19–23.

7. The Messiah was to be tried and condemned—prophesied in Isaiah 53:8; fulfilled in Luke 23:1–25 and Matthew 27:1–2.

8. The Messiah was to be silent before his accusers—prophesied in Isaiah 53:7; fulfilled in Matthew 27:12–14; Mark 15:3–5; and Luke 23:8–10.

9. The Messiah was to be struck and spat on by his enemies—prophesied in Isaiah 50:6; fulfilled in Matthew 26:67; 27:30; and Mark 14:65.

10. The Messiah was to be mocked and insulted—prophesied in Psalm 22:7–8; fulfilled in Matthew 27:39–44 and Luke 23:11, 35.

11. The Messiah was to be put to death by crucifixion—prophesied in Psalm 22:14, 16–17; fulfilled in Matthew 27:31 and Mark 15:20, 25.

12. The Messiah was to suffer with criminals and pray for his enemies—prophesied in Isaiah 53:12; fulfilled in Matthew 27:38; Mark 15:27–28; and Luke 23:32–34.

13. The Messiah was to be given vinegar and gall—prophesied in Psalm 69:21; fulfilled in Matthew 27:34 and John 19:28–30.

14. Others were to cast lots for the Messiah's garments—prophesied in Psalm 22:18; fulfilled in Matthew 27:35 and John 19:23–24.

15. The Messiah's bones were not to be broken—prophesied in Exodus 12:46 and Psalm 34:20; fulfilled in John 19:31–36.

16. The Messiah was to die as a sacrifice for sin—prophesied in Isaiah 53:5–12; fulfilled in John 1:29; 11:49–52; Acts 10:43; and 13:38–39.

17. The Messiah was to be raised from the dead—prophesied in Psalm 16:10; fulfilled in Acts 2:22–32 and Matthew 28:1–10.

18. The Messiah is now at God's right hand—prophesied in Psalm 110:1; fulfilled in Mark 16:19 and Luke 24:50–51.

Did you know that in almost every synagogue, chapter 53 of Isaiah—the one chapter with more prophecies about Jesus than any other chapter in the Old Testament—is skipped over and not read? When we asked a Jewish leader why this was done, he said that there's no reason to read it because rabbis have never read it through the centuries. According to him, the content isn't the issue. The issue is the tradition: Since it has never been read before, there is certainly no reason to start now. We can challenge those who don't read it to consider why they would leave out that one chapter in the entire Old Testament, and we can ask them to read it. Then be sure to follow up and discuss what they thought about it. You can even copy those pages and give them to a Jewish friend to read. The challenge could be life-changing.

Did you know that the Old Testament was written hundreds of years before Jesus was born in Bethlehem? Portions of it were written thousands of years before. Yet all sections of it make predictions about the coming Messiah.

What are the odds that someone could correctly predict something about

you a thousand years before you were born? What if someone made sixty or more predictions about you? What are the odds they would all be correct? One mathematician figured that the odds of someone fulfilling just eight of the sixty major prophecies concerning the Messiah would be one in 100,000,000,000,000,000.

How big is that number? The odds are the same as if you covered the entire state of Texas with silver dollars stacked a foot high, printed on just one of the coins the phrase, "You've just won the Publisher's Clearinghouse Sweepstakes," and asked someone to ride a white horse haphazardly through the stack, lean over once at random, and pick up that one special coin. That's just for eight correct predictions. What would the odds be for sixty-six?

44

Islam

What Causes Muslims to Turn to Christ?

Abraham Sarker

For many Americans, questions, concerns, and misunderstandings surround the world's fastest-growing religion, Islam. In this chapter we'll look at some of the beliefs of Muslims, the adherents of Islam, and consider how to win them to Christ.

Muslims know that their eternal fate in heaven or hell is decided by Allah's will, so many Muslims strive fervently to do good deeds and gain passage to heaven, yet Islam provides no assurance of salvation, except through martyrdom in jihad (holy war).

Muslim Arguments

Believers in Islam consider their religion the final and best for all of mankind. Muslims also see it as their duty to take the whole world into the fold of Islam. They are taught about other religions and trained in how to debate the supremacy of Islam.

The Trinity

Muslims often attack the fact that the word *Trinity* does not appear in the Christian Bible. While they are correct that the word *Trinity* appears nowhere in Scripture, the doctrine of one God existing in three persons (Father, Son Jesus, and Holy Spirit) is amply supported by Scripture (see Matt. 28:18–19; John 14:16–17, 27; 17:21).

It's interesting that the Qur'an mentions the word *Trinity* but incorrectly describes this Christian belief as the Father, Mother Mary, and Son Jesus. Additionally, when Muslims hear the term *Son of God*, they think of a biological relationship instead of a unique spiritual communion. Ultimately, it will take the Holy Spirit to open their eyes to see this truth.

Muslim Arguments

Trinity

Mohammed   Muslims' Argument Cycle   Jesus

Bible

Jesus

Explaining the person and purpose of Jesus is critical to effectively sharing the gospel with Muslims. As the diagram below demonstrates, while Muslims acknowledge many wonderful characteristics about Jesus, such as his sinless life, performing of miracles, and even his role as Messiah, they deny the heart of his person and mission. Islam denies that he was the Son of God and unequivocally rejects the idea that he was ever crucified or raised from the dead.

We must recognize that Muslims misunderstand Jesus's attributes and the significant events of his life. Terms like *Messiah* and the *Word of God* have entirely different meanings to Muslims; Muslims do not know the same Jesus that you and I know.

Jesus
Muslim and Christian Views

Common Beliefs

Muslim View
Revered prophet

Not the
Son of God

Never crucified but
was taken to heaven

The Messiah for
the Jews only

Common:
Sinless

Virgin birth

Performed miracles

Word of God

Will return

Messiah

Christian View
Son of God
(He is God Incarnate)

Savior of the world

He was crucified
and resurrected

Part of the Trinity

Messiah for the
whole world

Bible

Muslims believe that Allah gave revelations to Moses, Jesus, and other prophets, but they contend that the Bible in existence today has been corrupted. Muslims further assert that Christians have misinterpreted portions of the Bible (particularly those that should foretell Mohammed's coming) and have left out whole sections of their Scripture.

Although Muslims will customarily refuse to recognize the validity of the Christian Bible, they will attempt to find evidence for the validity of their revered prophet within the Bible's pages.

Mohammed

Muslims believe resolutely that Mohammed is the last and best prophet ever sent by Allah. Consequently, they ask in frustration, "Why can't Christians accept Mohammed? We accept your prophet, Jesus; why can't you accept our prophet, Mohammed?"

Muslims assert that Christians should accept Mohammed as the final prophet because the Bible prophesied his coming. They believe that John 14:16–17, when Jesus states that a Counselor will come after him, indicates Mohammed's impending arrival.

Why can't Christians accept Mohammed's message or his role as a prophet of God? Although he was a strong leader in seventh-century Arabia and his influence as the founder of Islam has reached many parts of the globe, the answer to this question is simple: His message contradicts the message of the Bible.

What Christ Offers to Muslims

Although I didn't know it at the time, as a Muslim I longed for what Christ had to offer. Eventually I came to see that the Christian faith doesn't offer Muslims a good deal; in fact it offers a *great* deal! Consider the following four areas, key to the gospel of Jesus Christ, which met a deep void I felt in my life as a Muslim.

A Personal God

When I was a Muslim, I saw God as a distant, capricious judge who sent each individual either to heaven or to hell. His will was unknowable, and I had no personal connection with him.

My relationship to Allah was like a slave to his master. I performed my good deeds, hoping Allah would be pleased, yet I never knew if my good deeds would be enough. Allah of Islam seemed remote and inaccessible, yet deep within me I longed for a personal God.

In Christianity I found that I could have such a personal relationship with God through Jesus Christ. I could actually call God my Father (see Rom. 8:15

and 1 John 3:1)! Jesus lived among us and ultimately gave his life for us. He declared that his disciples would relate to him no longer as slaves to a master but as friends (see John 15:15).

A Loving God

The next great deal Christianity offers Muslims is the knowledge and experience that God loves us each unconditionally. In Islam Allah may love those who follow all the rules, but he doesn't love sinners.

I learned from the Bible that God loved me even when I was a sinner and that he sent his own Son to die in my place, so that I could spend eternity with him. Romans 8:38–39 brings me great comfort, for it assures me of God's steadfast love.

A Savior

As a Muslim I struggled to live a righteous life. I fulfilled all of my Islamic duties, and yet I, along with all other Muslims, could not say whether Allah would send me to heaven or hell when I died.

Quite simply, there is no assurance of salvation in Islam. As a Muslim, I lived in fear of never completing enough good works. Even if I amassed many more good deeds than bad ones, Allah might change his mind at the last moment and condemn me to hell.

What good news it is to know that Jesus died on the cross to pay for our sins so that we can have the assurance of salvation in Christ! A powerful biblical illustration of this amazing grace is when one of the thieves hanging beside Jesus on the cross cried out to Jesus, and the Savior replied, "Today you will be with me in paradise" (see Luke 23:42–43). This thief did not have the time to fulfill any Muslim duties, such as pray five times a day, fast in the month of Ramadan, or make a pilgrimage to Mecca. Yet Jesus, with his amazing grace, offered this repentant sinner eternal life.

The Holy Spirit

The Holy Spirit is a treasure and a gift too wonderful for words. There is no equivalent in Islam. When Jesus ascended into heaven, he left the Holy Spirit to guide and comfort the believers he left behind. When Mohammed died, however, he left behind only a book of laws, the Qur'an, and it offers little spiritual guidance or comfort, especially when compared to the guidance and comfort of the Holy Spirit. The Holy Spirit speaks to us through the Bible and remains with us and in us, supernaturally guiding and empowering us in every good work (see John 16:13; Acts 1:8; 2 Tim. 1:14; 1 John 3:24).

Practical Strategies for Sharing the Gospel

I believe that God led me, as a Muslim, to the cross of Jesus Christ because Christians were praying for me, showing me a godly lifestyle, loving me, and witnessing to me. These are critical to the salvation of other Muslims as well.

Your Prayer

Prayer is an essential tool in leading Muslims to Christ, for it is not we who draw them, but the Holy Spirit who draws them to the truth. We must also realize, however, that prayer for Muslims involves spiritual warfare (see Eph. 6:12).

Your Example

"Let your light shine before men, that they may see your good deeds and praise your Father in heaven" (Matt. 5:16). I cannot express how powerful to Muslims is the example of a Christian committed to serving God. Simply seeing the morality and joy of one called a follower of Jesus speaks volumes to Muslims.

Muslims often have a skewed perception of what a Christian is; they often associate Christianity with the ungodly things done by those claiming or assumed to be "Christian." We must live a godly lifestyle and share with our Muslim friends how our Western culture differs from what the Bible teaches about the way a Christian should live.

Your Love

Jesus gave us two central commands: to love God and to love our neighbors as ourselves (see Matt. 22:37–40). We must pray that God will give us a heart for Muslims like his own and that we will want to develop friendships with Muslims and eventually share with them the hope and joy found in a personal relationship with Jesus Christ. Muslims must see that our love is genuine and that it will continue to flow whether or not they choose to accept our faith.

Your Witness

As Francis of Assisi stated, "Preach the gospel at all times, and if necessary use words." Our lifestyle must present the message of the gospel before our words speak it aloud.

Share with your Muslim friend not only the message of the gospel and how he can find assurance of salvation in Christ, but also what God has done personally in your own life. While Muslims can try to discount what the Bible says, they cannot refute your own experience; and all people, deep down, hunger for the kind of hope, joy, and peace you have through a personal relationship with God in Christ.

A Few Dos and Don'ts

Beyond the four general suggestions above about how to share the gospel with a Muslim friend, consider a few practical dos and don'ts.

Dos

- *Develop friendships.* Muslims are hospitable people, and they will respond if you extend the same friendship to them. After you have developed a friendship, listen for and be sensitive to the spiritual and physical needs of your Muslim friends.
- *Respect your Muslim friends.* Respect Muslims as people and respect their religion. Try to see them as God sees them, as people he loves but who remain lost without the truth of Jesus Christ. Additionally, it is important not to stereotype all Muslims as terrorists. We must get to know them individually and value them as people.
- *Share your personal testimony.* Be prepared to describe what God has done in your life (1 Pet. 3:15). Muslims may try to attack Christian doctrine, but they cannot counter personal experience.
- *Be knowledgeable about Islam.* Christians must emphasize the unique elements of the gospel message. But in order to claim that Christianity offers the truth and the "best deal," one must become familiar with other faiths; otherwise no effectual comparison can be made.

Don'ts

- *Don't argue about Allah, the Trinity, or Jesus as the Son of God.* Don't refer to Allah as a false or pagan god. This will immediately bring a barrier in your witness. In the mind of a Muslim, the term *Allah* does not refer to an idol but to the Creator of heaven and earth. Instead of arguing about this term, acknowledge the truth that there is only one God (as Muslims would readily agree). Explain to your Muslim friend the nature of God, as you understand him. Communicate what God means to you.
- *Don't waste time arguing about the Trinity*, as your argument will rarely cause a Muslim to believe. The Trinity is a doctrine that requires faith to accept. Instead, pray for your Muslim friend to have the faith to believe, and focus your conversation on the person and purpose of Jesus.
- *Don't initially refer to Jesus as the Son of God.* This terminology brings an obstacle and confusion to many Muslims and can be explained later.
- *Don't attack Mohammed or Islam.* Don't attack your Muslim friend's belief in the prophet Mohammed or Islam. Respect her beliefs without compromising your own convictions.

- *Don't presume you know their beliefs.* Don't presume that you know what your Muslim friend believes. Not all Muslims follow orthodox Islam, and your Muslim friend may have a different understanding of his religion than other Muslims do. Ask your friend thought-provoking questions.
- *Don't forget to pray.* If we want to be effective in our witness to the Islamic world, we must first love Muslims. And to love Muslims, we must pray that God would plant his love for them in our hearts.

It is critical when ministering to a Muslim that you remain sensitive to the leading of the Holy Spirit. Allow him to guide you into (or deter you from) every word and action. Prayer is the key to preparing both your heart and the heart of Muslims for your witness.

A Final Challenge

Can Muslims accept Christ? My life is living proof that this is possible.

God has called us to reach out to our world with the message of his gospel, to let others know of the hope, joy, and peace to be found in a personal relationship with Jesus Christ.

How can you be a part of God's plan for Muslims? It is imperative that you pray, be a godly example, share Christlike love, and witness for Christ.

And what does Christ have to offer Muslims? Christ offers a *great* deal! While Allah of Islam is distant, the God of Christianity is a personal Father. While Allah shows conditional love, our God shows love unconditional and everlasting. While Islam offers hopelessness, Jesus, the living Savior, gives us hope. While Islam has a book without a guide, Christianity has a living Holy Spirit, guiding, comforting, and empowering every believer.

Will you share this message of hope?

45

New Age

Sharing the Truth

Bob Waldrep

When teaching about the New Age Movement, we often ask how many in the audience think that New Age beliefs are wrong. Whether the crowd is large or small, practically everyone agrees that they are against New Age teaching. But when we ask if someone can define what the New Age is, the response is always the same—silence. Unfortunately, our audiences are not isolated examples. Most Christians oppose New Age teaching and influence, but they often have no clear idea what it is.

This ignorance impedes intelligent and effective evangelism. It also makes us unable to recognize New Age influences, so that we fail to respond to its widespread encroachment into our culture, including our churches. Obviously, before we discuss witnessing to New Agers, we must first learn what the New Age Movement is.

First, the New Age is nothing new. It is a blending of several ancient religions and beliefs, including Hinduism, Buddhism, Taoism, paganism, occultism, and Gnosticism. However, these beliefs have also been blended with a liberal dose of Western materialism, which leads to a spirituality more palatable to Americans and other Westerners.

Because the New Age Movement is a synthesis of diverse beliefs, there is no central New Age church or similar organization, and not all New Agers share the same perspective. However, most do accept some, if not all, of the following ideas:

Monism: All is one.

Pantheism: All is God and God is all (sometimes expressed as, "All is part of the divine consciousness").

Enlightenment: True "salvation" comes through realizing our own divinity or oneness with the divine.

Reincarnation: After death, we are reborn as someone (or, in Hinduism, something) else.

Karma: We are rewarded and punished in our present life for the good and evil done in our past lives.

Maya: All is an illusion.

Relativism: There is no absolute truth (this belief allows New Agers to accept all religions as valid paths to the same ultimate spiritual reality).

Because all is one (monism) and all is divine (pantheism), New Agers conclude that everyone needs to be brought into awareness of his own divinity (enlightenment). Since there are many valid paths to reach this state (relativism), New Agers hold diverse beliefs about how enlightenment occurs. However, most New Agers believe that we learn the best path to our own enlightenment as we live multiple lives (reincarnation). Karma may hinder or help us along our path, depending on whether we are paying for the evil deeds of a previous life or reaping the benefit for good deeds. New Agers have differing beliefs about why reaching enlightenment is important, but they all believe that when enough people reach this state, it will bring about an ultimate good (world peace, for example).

Witnessing to New Agers

What is truth?

Pontius Pilate speaking to Jesus (John 18:38)

When Pilate asked Jesus his question, it may have been sincere or sarcastic, genuine or indifferent. We have no way of knowing. What we do know is that it is a great question and a good place to begin when witnessing to a New Ager.

Share the verse above with the New Ager, then say, "Pilate asked a great question. How would you have answered it?" Their response will reveal their worldview. Because New Agers believe in relativism (all religions are equally true), the New Ager may say, "You have your truth and I have mine" or "Truth is whatever I find it to be or want it to be."

Next, inform the New Ager that Pilate's question was a response to a statement from Jesus: "For this reason I was born, and for this I came into the world, to testify to the truth. Everyone on the side of truth listens to me" (v. 37). Then ask, "Based on what you know, how do you think Jesus would explain the truth he came to bear witness about?"

After hearing their response, state, "I believe we can learn what Jesus meant by looking at his own words in the Gospel record." It is important to point to Jesus when dealing with a New Ager because most of them respect Jesus as a great teacher or "way-shower," even if they don't hold any special reverence for the Bible or Christianity. You should point to the fact that Jesus ultimately defined truth as a person when he said, "I am the way and the truth and the life. No one comes to the Father except through me" (14:6). Now share passages from the Bible that clarify the message of Jesus, especially those in his own words.

The New Ager will probably raise objections. You cannot satisfy all of her objections, but there are some common ones you can answer. Remember to use logic and reason, and, most important, rely on the Holy Spirit, who must ultimately reveal truth to those who are alienated from God.

Responding to New Age Beliefs

The following are some commonly held New Age beliefs and the suggested responses that have proven to be effective.

- *There is no absolute truth; you have your truth and I have mine.* A common good response to this is, "Are you absolutely sure? Because your statement is itself an absolute truth claim." The fact is that we live in a world of absolutes—God made it that way. There are physical absolutes, moral absolutes, and spiritual absolutes.

- *All religions lead to the same place.* Point out that it is illogical to believe that all religions are valid paths to truth, since they present contradictory messages. Point out that this violates the rule of logic, the Law of Noncontradiction: "A" cannot equal "non-A." In other words, if the truth claims of two religions are contradictory, then we are left with only two possibilities: One is right and the other is wrong, or both are wrong; they cannot both be right (see John 14:6; Acts 4:12).

- *The physical world is illusion; only the spiritual realm of divine oneness is real.* Ask the person to give examples of how he is currently living his life according to this principle. Ask, "If a rock were coming toward your head, would you duck or would you simply stand still and let it hit you, since it is merely an illusion?" Try to give real-life illustrations like this to help him see that, in practice, people really don't live their lives as if there were no absolutes, as if truth were relative, and as if all were an illusion.

- *All is God.* Ask the person to define what he means by *God*. For the New Ager, God is an impersonal "it," a force. Ask how one relates to this impersonal force. Point out that an impersonal god leaves a person empty, just as talking to a wall would not be a meaningful conversation. What is the appeal of becoming joined to, or recognizing that we are part of, an impersonal force?

Then share the biblical view that there is only one God and that he is personal and relational (Deut. 6:4; Isa. 1:18; John 17:3); point out how much more fulfilling this is than the god offered by the New Age. This also gives you an opportunity to share your testimony about the meaningfulness of a personal relationship with God.

- *Reincarnation is true.* First, reincarnation is illogical. There are more humans on earth now than have lived in past centuries. Other life forms are also increasing in number overall, not decreasing. If reincarnation involves souls being born from a previous existence, where did all these additional souls come from? Reincarnation doesn't answer the question of life's origin; it only muddies the waters even more.

  Reincarnation stands in stark contrast to the biblical record of humanity's creation and final destination, as well as how many lives each person is given—one. Paul said that for the believer to be absent from the body is to be present with the Lord (2 Cor. 5:8), and the writer of Hebrews said, "It is appointed for men to die once and after this comes judgment" (Heb. 9:27 NASB). Jesus taught that a person has only one lifetime on which he will be judged (Matt. 25:31–46).

An important part of your witness to a New Ager is talking about our real problem, which is sin. Point out that even though sin is a real problem, God has provided a real solution—a true and complete solution—Jesus. Share the gospel using the presentation with which you are most comfortable. As you do, remember to pray that the Holy Spirit will open the New Ager's eyes to the real truth—Jesus.

46

The Occult

Reaching Pagans, Witches, and Spiritists

Bob Waldrep

Sharing one's faith with someone involved in the occult often seems an especially daunting task. The primary reason is that the great diversity of beliefs held by occultists leads to many misunderstandings and misconceptions, especially that occultists are "spooky," "scary," and generally "not like us."

The first steps in effectively witnessing to someone involved in occultism are to recognize the distinctions between different types of occultism and to overcome our misconceptions about it.

Three Types of Occultism

A common misconception Christians have about occultists is that all of them have the same or similar beliefs and practices. Nothing could be further from the truth. Within occultism there are many different groups with beliefs and practices distinct from and often opposed to the other groups. However, though there is great diversity within occultism, we can divide it into at least three categories.

Divination—seeking hidden knowledge (usually about the future) through psychic "readings" or other supernatural means, often accompanied by the use of various props. Such practices include astrology, palm reading, scrying (crystal balls and tea leaves), and Tarot cards.

Paganism (often called "neo-paganism")—a revival of ancient forms of worship. These include *animism* (belief that inanimate objects such as plants contain living spirits) and the worship of ancient deities, especially the all-encompassing Mother Goddess or Mother Earth (Gaia). Such groups and practices include *Wicca* or witchcraft (though some classify these as different groups) and *shamanism*.

Spiritism—involves the attempt to communicate with a spirit entity or deceased person through one's personal "powers" or the use of props. This category includes trance mediums, channeling, seances, Ouija Boards, and such well-known occultists as Edgar Cayce, John Edward, and James Van Praugh.

Overcoming Misconceptions

If we are to witness effectively to occultists, we must overcome our misconceptions about them and their beliefs.

Occult Not Cult

The terms *occult* and *cult* may sound similar, but they do not mean the same thing. Certainly some occult organizations may be defined as cults, but the terms should not be used interchangeably. Thus it is important to understand their proper usage.

The term *occult* is derived from the Latin word *occultus*, which means "secret, hidden, or concealed." Occultism is in its essence the study of "secret" or "hidden" things, typically related to the supernatural. When speaking of occultism from a Christian perspective, it refers to any attempt to gain supernatural knowledge or power apart from the true God of the Bible.

The term *cult* is frequently used to refer to pseudo-Christian groups—that is, groups that identify with Christianity but whose theology and practices are actually contrary to the essential doctrines of the Christian faith. (See chapter 47 for information on cults.) Occult organizations and individuals, however, seldom claim to be Christian and tend to distance themselves from Christian belief and practice.

Occultists Are Not Satanists

Christians frequently confuse occultists with Satanists. This is particularly offensive to individuals involved in occultism because most of them do not even believe Satan exists, much less worship him. Christians who claim occultists worship Satan invariably lose credibility with the occultists they are trying to reach. Wiccans are particularly insulted by this misconception.

While Christians recognize correctly that the belief systems of the various occult groups may be demonic in origin (1 Tim. 4:1), occultists do not accept this idea. Insisting that occultists are Satanists creates a barrier to evangelism efforts.

Their Appearance

Another common misunderstanding about occultists is that they are "different" from other people. Horror or fantasy movies and books have contributed significantly to the stereotypes about occultists—witches dress in black and wear pointed hats, for example. In reality, occultists may dress and act much like any other average person. They work at ordinary jobs, have families they love, and visit the same restaurants and shops that other regular folks visit.

It's their worldview that makes occultists different. In other words, they have completely different ideas about God, the world, the nature of man, sin, and the future of God's creation than do most other people. So occultists can't be recognized just by looking at their clothing or any other visible characteristic. We must look deeper and discover their beliefs regarding spiritual matters.

Their Views on the Bible

A final important point to consider when preparing to share with occultists is that typically they have little regard for the Bible and its claims.

The Bible is filled with admonitions to avoid occultism and the practices associated with it. To realize this, one need look only at the general warning in Deuteronomy 18:9–12. There are also many Bible passages that address specific practices and beliefs held by those who practice occultism today.

Astrology—Isaiah 47:13–14; Jeremiah 10:2; 27:9–10

Magic—Leviticus 20:27; 2 Kings 21:6; Isaiah 47:12; Micah 5:12; Acts 8:11–24; Galatians 5:19–21; Revelation 9:21; 21:8; 22:15

Fortune Telling—Leviticus 19:31; 1 Samuel 28; 2 Kings 21:6; 23:24; Isaiah 8:19; 19:3; 44:25; Jeremiah 14:14; 27:9–10; Ezekiel 13:3, 8; 21:21–23; Micah 5:12

Armed with such Bible passages, Christians might think they can dissuade occultists from their beliefs simply because God's Word says occultism is wrong. This is a common mistake. Occultists already know Christians disapprove of their beliefs, so Scripture's condemnation means little to them. After all, occultists usually reject the Bible anyway.

Of course, this does not mean that we should not use the Bible in our witnessing efforts or that we should not describe what the Bible says about a particular practice or belief. We should use it, because God's Word is powerful and sharper than a two-edged sword. However, we should be prepared to present our beliefs with reasonable arguments not merely in a series of verses.

Witnessing Tips

With these things in mind, here are some witnessing tips when sharing the gospel with an occultist:

- *We should remember that, while they are sinners like everyone else, occultists are not necessarily sinister or criminal individuals.* Most occultists are ordinary people just like us, dealing with the same problems and asking the same questions. The difference is they are getting their answers from a different source—a source that is taking them in the wrong direction. Before we ever begin to share the gospel with them, we must understand that they, like most of us, are seeking love, acceptance, and solutions to life's problems. It is our responsibility to share with them the ultimate answer to all of life's needs and questions—a personal relationship with Jesus. We must respond to the occultist, not with fear and hatred but by sharing Christ with respect and love (see Col. 4:6).

- *Once we have a proper motivation in witnessing to the occultist, we need to gain a basic understanding of their beliefs.* It is important to have a general understanding of the broad types of occultist groups so that we don't lump them all in the same category. In particular, we should not accuse them of being Satanists or of holding a belief they do not profess; this only lessens our credibility in their view.

- *We must be able to use the Bible to show why occultism is wrong, while keeping in mind that occultists generally disregard the Bible.* This means we need to be able to use other ways to show the weaknesses in occultism. Common sense, reason, and logic can show how some of their beliefs are inherently contradictory; scientific studies may be used to demonstrate that their claims about physical reality (such as those of astrology) are unreasonable or untrue. When the occultist rejects the truth of the Bible, seek some common ground on which to continue the discussion.

- *We* must *rely on the Holy Spirit.* Every witnessing experience is spiritual warfare, and this is especially true when sharing with occultists. Pray that the Holy Spirit will give the occultist discernment to see and escape the devil's snare.

- *Finally, and most important, we should always witness in a loving manner, regardless of the method we use.* One of the greatest evangelism tools that we have is love. Sadly, it is also the one that we most often fail to carry with us. Our misconceptions about occultists frequently lead us to perceive them as our enemies. But we must remember that we too were once enemies of God, helpless sinners, despising our Creator. Thus we should follow the example of Christ and reach out to *all* the lost, even those most vehement in their rejection of truth: "But God demonstrates his own love for us in this: While we were still sinners, Christ died for us" (Rom. 5:8).

47

Cults

Witnessing to a Cult Member

Floyd Schneider

W e've just discovered that our neighbors belong to a cult! How do we witness to them?"

This discovery could occur on any street any day of the week in today's world. The cults have grown explosively. They have redefined Christian terminology, added a trace of Bible knowledge, and been encouraged by the fact that many Christians are easily confused by their heresies.

True Christians must admit to themselves that they have been neglecting two foundational principles in their own personal evangelism. These are the need for diligent study of the Bible and the effectiveness of unconditional love.

Diligent Study

First, many believers seem to have lost the ability to defend rationally and intellectually the doctrines they hold to be true. Christians today have become too dependent on clergy to perform all the necessary chores of Christianity, and many Christians (or those who claim to be) go to church just to be entertained.

The most important item on the agenda, then, as we prepare to witness, is to *know the gospel first*. Believers need to take 2 Timothy 2:15 much more seriously: "Do your best to present yourself to God as one approved, a workman who does not need to be ashamed and *who correctly handles the word of truth*."

Believers need to know not only *what* they believe, but also *why* they believe as they do. It is a shame when a Christian has to run to the telephone to call an already overworked minister because the believer is confronted at his door by a couple of Jehovah's Witnesses or Mormons. A little consistent study of the Bible could give him all of the answers he needs and a tremendous sense of confidence in the Word and his ability to "refute those who oppose it" (Titus 1:9).

The story is told of the training program of the U.S. Treasury Department to teach their agents to detect counterfeit money. The new agents are required to memorize what real money looks like before they are allowed to come in contact with false money. After weeks of handling and studying real money, they have no problem identifying counterfeit money.

The principle is the same in dealing with a cult member. The better you know the Scriptures, or at least the basic message of the gospel, the more easily and quickly you will be able to identify and combat a counterfeit.

Unconditional Love

The second principle is the effectiveness of unconditional love. Our love needs to go out in two directions: toward other believers and toward cult members. We have seen supposedly strong Christians fall victim to a cult because the cult offered them love and acceptance, whereas they had no close friends in their own evangelical congregation. True Christianity is a balance of truth and love not just one or the other.

Cultists expect Christians to reject them. Many of the cults thrive on persecution. It feeds their ego to think that they are suffering for their faith. Most cultists believe that they have progressed beyond historic Christianity and have found the ultimate truth. This belief reveals itself in their attitude of superiority and resentment when someone tries to share the gospel with them. Often they are offended when a Christian tries to convert them. Usually cultists see the evangelical Christian as their enemy. They have transferred their antagonism for the gospel to the messengers of the gospel, and they believe that any person who disagrees with their views must be rejected.

The typical believer reacts to this antagonism by becoming defensive, instead of disarming the cultist by putting him or her at ease. Being friendly under fire is not easy, but it is necessary to break down the psychological conditioning of the cultist.

Establishing Common Ground

Having arrived at ground zero (teaching and love are back in their proper place), the Christian now needs some pointers on how to approach an actual situation.

The starting point is what Walter Martin in his book *The Kingdom of the Cults* calls "common ground."[1]

First, when you start a conversation with a cultist, you must insist that you both agree on the same final authority. In the case of the Christian, this must be the inspired Word of God, the Bible. Allow *only* the Bible to be used in the discussion and not the cultist's own literature. If this is not done, you will simply end up in an argument and possibly lose the opportunity of further discussions with your friend. To attract disillusioned Christians, many cults include some Scripture in their teachings. Therefore, you can insist that these Scriptures be the basis for your discussion. By so doing, you will be able to use them in biblical context and thus explain their true meaning.

Second, you (and only you) should open in prayer, in which *you preach the gospel* in your prayer for two or three minutes, quoting Scriptures on sin, the need for forgiveness, and the deity and work of Jesus Christ in salvation. Do not take the time to have a prayer meeting. Just get the Word of God into her mind through your prayer, for God says, "It will not return to me empty" (Isa. 55:11).

Third, knowing the doctrines of every cult would be advantageous but hardly feasible. It is helpful, however, if the believer knows the basis of all cult doctrine. All of the cults are dependent on good works and self-sacrifice to get into their heaven. All of them are based on a form of self-salvation that requires people to deliver themselves from sin through their own human effort with God's help.

The best defense against these false suppositions is a clear understanding of the biblical teaching of the person and work of Jesus Christ and his salvation. During the discussion, the Christian must *define* and *apply* the *historic* meaning of these terms to have an understandable conversation with a cultist. Otherwise, the Christian will always be frustrated that the cultist is saying the same words but meaning something entirely different!

A well-trained cultist can easily twist Scripture by redefining the terms, reading something into the text, or coming up with a unique interpretation of a "proof text." But the cultist can also be disarmed by the Scriptures.

The Burden of Proof

When your cultist friend comes up with a surprise interpretation of a verse, the burden of proof that he is right rests on him. You are not obligated to disprove every false view that comes along. You must hold the cultist responsible for proving that his view is right—on the basis of Scripture. Cultists have learned to intimidate Christians by insisting that their view is correct unless the Christian can disprove it.

In Matthew 24:4 Jesus said, "Watch out that no one deceives you." Almost always cultists will choose unclear verses in the Bible on which to base their doctrines. Just because you do not understand an unclear verse in the Bible does not mean that the cultist's view of that verse is correct. Ten different cults may each hold a view of a particular verse in the Bible, and they *all* could be wrong!

Point out to your cultist friend that a person who is seeking the truth should never base his doctrine on unclear verses because there is a much higher chance of coming up with the wrong interpretation (as evidenced by the multitude of cults!). Second Peter 3:16 might come in handy at this point. The burden of proof rests on the cultist not on the Christian.

This principle applies to so-called miracles as well. The Christian needs to give serious heed to the words of Jesus about these last days: "For false Christs and false prophets will appear and perform great signs and miracles to deceive even the elect—if that were possible" (Matt. 24:24).

When witnessing to a cult member, then, remember:

1. Know the basics of Christianity well.
2. Be friendly.
3. "Preach the gospel" by praying and including Scripture in your prayer.
4. Determine your final authority as "common ground."
5. Define the biblical terms, and insist that the cultist define his or her terms.
6. Use biblical terms as you and your friend have defined them.
7. Repeat steps 2 through 6 again and again.

48

Christendom

Why Church Membership Does Not Equal Salvation

Thom S. Rainer

His visit to my office was unexpected. Paul was seventy-five years old and a leader in our church. But Paul was about to share with me some shocking news.

I was serving as an interim pastor of the church, meaning I was the preacher for the church until they called a new senior pastor.

The church had multiple services, so I would often catch my breath between services in the vacated pastor's office. After the first worship service that Sunday morning, Paul asked if he could speak to me in the office. I invited him in.

Being an interim pastor is somewhat akin to being a grandparent. You shower the people with love and affection until they start acting up; then you turn them over to the new senior pastor.

I loved the members of this church, and though I would not want to admit favoritism to the rest of the congregation, Paul was one of my favorites. He simply had that sweet spirit and humble attitude that made you want to spend time with him. His words that Sunday morning were therefore totally unexpected.

"Paul," I said with a smile as we sat at a small table, "how can I help you?" He was nervous, and his response did not come immediately. I waited patiently until he gathered the strength to speak.

"I am not a Christian," he said with a quivering voice.

I was not certain that I heard him correctly. Paul had been baptized in the church some sixty years earlier. He was faithful in service and attendance. But before I asked him for clarification, he said it again: "I am not a Christian."

Paul explained to me how he had never fully grasped the gospel until a few weeks earlier. He shared how he finally understood the meaning of repentance. And he acknowledged that he had lived for the past six decades assuming that good works through service in the church would get him to heaven. But now he knew differently. Now he understood.

I had the privilege of clarifying the gospel to Paul. This time the words reflected a true change in his heart. This time he became a true follower of Christ. Two weeks later the church celebrated as a seventy-five-year-old man was baptized as a new believer in Christ.

The Problem of Unregenerate Church Members

Theologians often call unsaved members of churches "unregenerate members." The word "unregenerate" literally means "not born again." When the Rainer Group surveyed persons who had been members of churches prior to becoming Christians, we asked them why they were in a church as a non-believer.

The overwhelming number responded that they thought they *were* Christians. Yet later they would discover that they had been deluded, or they had deluded themselves.

We then asked them to share *why* they thought they had not become Christians as members. There were four common responses.

1. More than one-half of those we surveyed said they never heard a clear presentation of the gospel. Paul told me that he did not understand clearly the gospel until he heard the message several times in several sermons.
2. About four out of ten we surveyed indicated that they had confused other aspects of the church with salvation. For some, church membership held the same meaning as being a Christian. Others indicated that they thought "walking an aisle" or making a public statement of cognitive belief in Christ was a means of salvation.
3. Some viewed doing ministry in the church as sufficient to get them into heaven. In other words, they had a works concept of salvation, with the works taking place in the context of a local church.
4. About 10 percent of those we surveyed said that they joined the church originally *knowing* that they were not Christians. They were willing to be deceptive to gain the political or social capital that comes with being a member of a church.

How many members of churches are not Christians? The answer is elusive, but we made a modest attempt to answer the question.

The Number of Non-Christian Church Members

We must be careful not to presume omniscience in matters of eternity. Ultimately, we cannot know the eternal state of a person's soul. Christ did indicate that the fruit of a life could provide an indication of salvation (Matt. 7:15–20), but our sinful and imperfect nature does not allow us perfect discernment.

Thus, when we provide statistical evidence of regeneration, we do so with much caution. Our research is fallible and our discernment is far from perfect.

Our methodology was simple. We asked 315 church members two "diagnostic" questions. The first asked, "If you were to die today, do you know for certain that you would go to heaven?" The second question was asked only if they responded affirmatively to the first: "If God were to ask you why he should let you into heaven, what would you say?"

Our goal was to discern if these church members had a grasp of the gospel and to see if they had truly repented of sins and placed their faith in Christ. Again, we urge readers to view the results with caution and an awareness of the fallibility of such an approach.

Our researchers categorized the response of the church members into three groups. In the first group were those who clearly seemed not to have a grasp of the gospel. They had thus not made a true commitment to Christ. In the third group were those who seemed to grasp the gospel well and who had assurance that they had placed their faith in Christ. In between these two groups was a small number whom our researchers were unable to place in either of the other two groups. The results are shown in the following table:

Church members who *are not* Christians	31%
Church members who *may not be* Christians	14%
Church members who *are* Christians	55%

If our research approximates eternal realities, nearly one-half of all church members are not or may not be Christians.

The Church Responds

The results of the survey reveal that the issue of unregenerate church members is urgent and demands an immediate response from those who are true followers of Christ. There are at least four essential practices that must be a part of every church that wants to reach every member for Christ.

Clear Presentation of the Gospel

In many churches and in many personal evangelism encounters, the gospel has been diluted to meaninglessness. In our confused attempts not to offend the nonbeliever, issues such as repentance and conviction of sins have been replaced with false "gospels" of prosperity and self-esteem.

Many church members today are members without salvation, because they have not heard the clear and uncompromising message of the gospel. This misleading approach to Christianity must be replaced with a clear and unwavering message.

Decision Follow-Up

Do you remember Paul at the beginning of this chapter? Sixty years ago, during a public invitation at his church, he walked down the aisle and told the pastor that he wanted to join the church. Neither the pastor nor anyone else sought to discern if he really had placed his faith in Christ or if he understood the gospel. Paul would live the next six decades of his life uncertain and confused about his salvation but active in the church.

When public decisions for Christ are made, mature Christians who are willing to invest their lives in others must follow up. If Paul had had someone to mentor and disciple him, he would have discovered quickly that a decision for church membership is not the same as being saved.

Discernment in Personal Evangelism

Our research shows that only about 5 percent of Christians engage in personal evangelism on a consistent basis. Thus our first task is to encourage faithful obedience to the Great Commission. Christians must be urged to share their faith.

We also must exhort those who are sharing the gospel faithfully to show discernment when witnessing. Even if a person says he or she is a Christian and active church member, the person could be yet another unregenerate church member. As we develop relationships with others, we will begin to see evidence of their life in Christ, if indeed they are Christians. If we don't see the evidence, we should be sure to share Christ with the person.

Membership Classes

Our research also shows that the churches that require participation in membership classes have much higher rates of attendance and retention among their members. It is in these classes that a person can hear the gospel clearly and be confronted with the truth claims of Christ. Those who have made decisions thus become true disciples.

Members Who Are Christians

Paul continues to grow in maturity as a follower of Christ. He is now both a church member and, most important, a Christian. But he still wonders at times. He wonders why he never heard the gospel clearly presented in sermons over a sixty-year period. He wonders why no Christian ever shared with him an unambiguous gospel in that same period. He wonders how much more he could have done for the Savior if he had truly been a believer during the past six decades.

"Thom," he asked, "why are preachers and other Christians hesitant to share Christ without pulling punches? Why did I have to wait sixty years before I ever heard about repentance? Where are all the Christians? Why are they so quiet?"

Good questions, Paul. Very good questions.

Ordinary
People
by
Race

African American

God's Grace—Greater than Race

Dolphus Weary

Every believer needs to understand that our goal is to reach every person who is lost. We can't allow a culture of racial divide to cause us to pick and choose the person with whom we will share the gospel.

Look at the Great Commission. Jesus said, "All authority in heaven and on earth has been given to me. Therefore go and make disciples of all nations, baptizing them in the name of the Father and of the Son and of the Holy Spirit, and teaching them to obey everything I have commanded you. And surely I am with you always, to the very end of the age" (Matt. 28:18–20).

We tend to limit the meaning of *all nations* to foreign countries outside of the United States. But the United States is a multinational country. We need to come to grips with the fact that *all nations* means all people groups.

In this country we need to present the gospel message in a way that will reach all people groups. Evangelism must be intentional. It is a step-by-step process. Jesus gave every single one of us the Great Commission to carry out, so we should set our minds, our hearts, and our attention on reaching every single person with the gospel of Jesus Christ. Witnessing to people of a different race doesn't have to be awkward if we're willing to understand their culture and build a relationship with them.

Early on in high school, my basketball coach wanted me to learn how to shoot a layup with my left hand. Quickly I made a conscious decision that very seldom would I *need* to use my left hand. I would rather shoot with my right hand from both sides. Consequently I never learned how to shoot with my left hand. Now if I try to do it, it is so awkward because I never practiced.

Years ago the evangelical white church made a conscious decision that black people are not important to carrying out the Great Commission. Therefore the church leadership did not practice reaching out to win blacks to Christ and bring them into discipleship. We have created an environment where blacks don't feel the need to reach out to evangelize and disciple whites and whites don't feel the need to reach out to evangelize blacks.

Evangelism seems awkward if we keep asking questions like, "Can a white person lead a black person to Jesus?" or "Can a black person lead a white person to Jesus?" The answer is *absolutely*! We're not talking about the color of a person's skin; we're talking about the life-changing message of the gospel.

Beginning a Relationship with Someone of Another Race

You begin a relationship with someone of another race the same way you begin a relationship with someone of your own race. You must spend time getting to know the other person. It's not going to happen over one or two phone calls, one or two breakfasts. It's going to happen by going into the world of that person, going into his or her home. Time is important to building a relationship.

The place to begin is *vulnerability*. Learn how to open up. If folks from different races really want to communicate with each other, they've got to be honest and genuine. Often we are very shallow when we talk to a person of a different race, afraid of misunderstanding each other or using the wrong words. Once you develop a relationship, when there is a real friendship, you can say anything you want.

Building a relationship is an important vehicle for disseminating the gospel.

Revealing Jesus

We need to be careful not to reveal Jesus as a white Jesus or an American Jesus. Let people know Jesus is neither black nor white and Jesus is not American. His death on the cross was not for one group of people—it was for everybody. When he said, "It is finished," he meant that everybody can respond by faith in Jesus Christ by accepting him as Savior and Lord.

Tell people that Jesus accepts us right where we are. He doesn't ask us to clean up ourselves first. Sometimes people feel as though they don't measure up. Jesus just wants to know that we are willing to reach out and love him.

Barriers to Overcome

Reconciliation involves more than just getting whites and blacks to live and work side by side. It means accepting each other as human beings made in the image of God. It also involves an active concern for the well-being of each other.

Another way to break down barriers is to develop common meeting places. This has already happened through the public schools. But one place it hasn't happened very much is in the church. As a result, many of us are not around persons from other races and backgrounds enough to know what life is like for them.

There can be a denominational barrier because we sometimes push denomination more than we push Jesus. Another barrier is the political barrier. We push Jesus wrapped up in a Democratic platform or a Republican platform. When it comes to sharing Christ with others, we should stay away from politics.

We need to lift up the Bible and keep pointing people to Jesus. Our great message is that Jesus is still the answer. The core question is, "Have you personally released control of your life to Jesus Christ?"

Similarities

Regardless of race, ethnicity, or nationality, God has created each of us with the same heart and capacity for love. So the principle of evangelism is the same—to help people see that God has a plan for their lives. They need to know that sin separates us from God and keeps us from being everything he wants us to be. They need to know that when Jesus died on the cross, he didn't just die for white people or black people. Jesus died so that every single individual anywhere in the world could have access to the King of Kings and Lord of Lords.

There are periods of time—often for weeks and months at a time—that non-Christians do not see Christians come together. In fact our children go to Sunday school and church and never see adults, who proclaim how much they love the Lord, get together with other believers, especially across racial and denominational lines. The black young person and the white young person are both looking to see authentic Christianity.

We can achieve genuine reconciliation only through our obedience to the teachings of our Lord. The Christian community has the potential to do a mighty work for Christ, but we need to work together so our differences with each other do not get in the way of our common goals. A watching world sees and hears the message of Christ when the church demonstrates unity.

God took me, a black boy from a large single-parent family in rural Mississippi, who wanted to run away from this state, and led me to head up a ministry of reconciliation and unity in Mississippi. In my work with Mission Mississippi, God is causing me to ask, *Is the gospel strong enough to impact the historical problem of racism and cultural differences, especially in the body of Christ?* And the answer is clear: God's grace is greater than our races.

God is asking me, along with others, to be a bridge-builder within the Christian community. Jesus has commissioned all of us to share the gospel with the lost of every people group.

50

Asian

A Basic Approach to Reaching a Diverse People

Stanley K. Inouye

Asians in the United States are a complex mosaic of different languages, religions, and cultures. They include people who trace their ancestry to such countries as China, India, Japan, Korea, the Philippines, and Vietnam. They are U.S.–born citizens and recent immigrants. Some are Americanized and some are traditionally Asian. They are marrying non-Asians and having biracial-bicultural children, giving rise to a future generation of multiracial-multicultural grandchildren. Thus it is very dangerous to make broad sweeping generalizations about Asians and Asian Americans. And it is even riskier to suggest that there is a specific approach that is most effective in reaching them all.

However, some safe generalizations can be made that shape a sound and sensitive basic approach to personal evangelism that is effective with most Asians most of the time. This approach does not address the specific issues that are faced when dealing with someone from a specific religious background, language group, or Asian culture, but it does provide helpful general guidance. It is a relational approach based on an extremely broad and basic profile of people with Asian cultural backgrounds.

Cultural Profile

The following are observations that can be made about Asians in general.

265

- *Asians are highly relational and group-oriented.* They value harmony and are very sensitive to what others are thinking and feeling. Not raised to be rugged American individualists, they believe the needs of the group, especially the family, are more important than the needs of the individual. It should not be surprising then to hear some say that they would rather be in hell with their family than in heaven without them.

- *They tend to see their relationships with people and groups as permanent.* Once they belong, they always belong. Unlike people who freely join or leave groups, they carefully weigh the seemingly permanent consequences of entering new or leaving old relationships and groups. So it may take a long time before they make a decision to become a Christian, a decision that would change many relationships, especially those of family. For this reason an approach that seeks an immediate or quick decision may not work well with them.

- *They are concrete and contextual in the way they think and reason.* Not seeing truth as absolute no matter who says it, Asians believe truth is based on experience, their own or that of others they know and trust. They communicate truth through practical illustrations, real-life examples, and story. So seeking conversion by trying to convince them that the abstract plan of salvation is true based on airtight arguments or biblical authority may well miss the mark with them.

- *They are nonconfrontational.* Not believing honesty is the best policy if it offends, causes conflict, or otherwise jeopardizes relationships, they tend to be discreet and indirect in their communication. They avoid any topic of discussion of which they suspect others have a different perspective from their own. So if out of the blue someone shares the gospel and asks them to accept it, they feel awkward and are usually politely unresponsive.

- *They do not have a Judeo-Christian worldview.* They see the world through the eyes of Buddhism, Hinduism, Confucianism, Taoism, and other Asian religions and philosophies, which do not have the same basic concept of God as those from the West. Religion and culture are so closely tied in both the East and West that most people of Asian ancestry view becoming a Christian as not only a conversion of faith but also a conversion of culture. If they convert, they see themselves as becoming less, rather than more, of who they are, alienating themselves from family, nation, and culture. With little exposure to the Bible, Jesus, and Judeo-Christian beliefs, values, and practices, they cannot be expected to make a sound faith commitment to Christ in a short time.

Basic Evangelistic Approach

With a basic understanding of what they are like, it is now possible for us to imagine a sound and sensitive way to approach sharing Christ with people of Asian ancestry. We can begin by thinking about how we might get two people together who we know would want to become friends and build a permanent relationship of their own if they only had an opportunity to meet and become acquainted.

Applying this same relational process to evangelism, we can see it as a means of introducing one person (our Asian friend) to another (our Lord Jesus Christ), rather than a means of introducing a person to a new system of beliefs and values. We can look at it as taking place in three stages: *preparing* (for the introduction), *nurturing* (the relationship), and *encouraging* (increasing commitment). (*Note*: Because people of Asian ancestry are so group- and family-oriented, it is helpful to think of them not as isolated individuals but as members of whole networks, including others who should be considered in our outreach efforts.)

Stage One: Preparing

To prepare for the introduction, you must:

- *Pray.* Tell the Lord about your Asian or Asian American friend (in this case, let's call her Lisa). Share with him what you are learning about Lisa and how wonderful it will be if she becomes a part of his family. Tell other Christians, especially family members and close friends, the same things you have shared with God so they can pray with you and will want to participate with you in reaching out to her.
- *Tell Lisa great things about Jesus* and how he has transformed you and your relationships, especially the ways he has worked in your life and family. Tell Lisa good things about your Christian friends and relatives and stories of Christ's work in their lives.

Stage Two: Nurturing

To nurture the relationship, you should:

- *Arrange a time when you can do something both meaningful and fun together.* Look for an openness or, better yet, a desire in Lisa to meet Jesus and/or your Christian friends and relatives. Choose an activity that is informal and relational, like a barbecue or get-together at your home, and invite Lisa to join you. Saying a prayer of thanks over the meal and casually sharing God's work in your lives in her presence are enough of an introduction to Jesus at this time. This experience for Lisa with your friends and family should be the first of many.
- *Continue taking the initiative* to arrange times when you and your Christian friends and relatives can get together with Lisa until they feel comfortable enough to get together on their own. As natural opportunities arise, you and the other Christians should share about Jesus and your experiences with him. Over time, Lisa will ask questions about Jesus, about what he means

to you, and about the difference he makes in your lives. You can introduce her to the Bible as your primary source of insight and inspiration. You may even direct her to Christian resources, such as articles, books, videos, and films.

- *Begin inviting Lisa to gatherings that are explicitly Christian*, as talking about Jesus and spiritual things becomes increasingly a part of your times together. Bring her to a small group, Bible study, or church worship service or activity, beginning with the most informal and interpersonal and later moving to the more programmed and organizational. Encourage her to learn more about God on her own by studying the Bible, especially by learning about Jesus through the Gospels. Invite her to study the Bible with you or with others.

- *Invite Lisa to talk to Jesus in prayer*, either with you or on her own, when she has a fairly sound and basic understanding of who Jesus is. Invite her to voice her own prayers or pray silently when praying with you if she feels comfortable doing so.

Stage Three: Encouraging

The last stage is encouragement to be committed to Christ. You should:

- *Share with Lisa from time to time how you and others entrusted your lives to Jesus so he could begin transforming you from within.* At some point, if she expresses or otherwise demonstrates a desire to do likewise, an appropriate evangelistic sharing tool, such as the ones designed for Asian Americans by Iwa (see iwarock.org), might be helpful here. These tools present the gospel in a relational way and provide a sample prayer of commitment. If such a tool is not readily available, provide an example of what she might want to pray and ask her if it reflects her own thoughts and feelings toward God. If so, she can repeat it or express something like it on her own, aloud or silently. You can close with your own request for God's assurance in her life.

- *Support Lisa as she develops her own relationship with Christ.* Pray for her. Maintain personal contact, keeping apprised of how her relationship with the Lord is progressing. Introduce her to people, programs, and other resources that will help her grow in the specific areas of her life that God is addressing.

- *Help Lisa grow* in her relationship not only with God but with her family and friends. Help her reach out to them. Make sure other Christians embrace her, including those from your church. Or help her find her own support network.

- *Support Lisa if she has problems* progressing in her relationship with Christ, and be a bridge to God for her when she needs one.

The bottom line is: Introduce Asians to Jesus not to a belief system.

51

Hispanic

Luis Palau

When you think "Hispanics," what comes to mind? Here are a few things that you should know:

As a group, Hispanics are now the most influential minority group in America. Many are highly educated and successful. They serve with the President, in Congress, at the top of Fortune 500 companies, at the most elite universities and branches of the military, as judges and governors and mayors.

Like most ethnicities, Hispanics aren't a homogenous group. They represent more than two dozen countries and scores of cultures. Most value family highly and find ways to celebrate together throughout the year. Increasing numbers prefer not to be called Hispanic Americans. Instead, they see themselves as Americans who enjoy a rich Hispanic heritage. Many youth prefer to speak English rather than Spanish.

Many Hispanics in America are Christians or come from a Christian background. It's not hard to share the gospel of Jesus Christ with most Hispanics, because they believe the basic facts of the gospel. Many, however, haven't been invited to trust Jesus Christ alone for salvation. When invited, many say yes.

Hispanics represent one of the most important growing segments in churches across the nation, and Hispanic churches are springing up all over the country. Often established churches that support new Hispanic church plants see exciting results. Hispanics now serve as pastors of some of America's largest and fastest-growing churches. Many others serve as key lay leaders. An estimated 15 percent have the gift of evangelism. The more we can encourage these energetic, gifted men and women, the better!

In the Spanish-speaking world, the church is showing its evangelistic priority through missions. Argentina and other nations in Latin America have joined Asian nations, such as South Korea, Hong Kong, and Singapore, as missionary-sending nations. The division between missionary-sending and missionary-receiving nations has been obliterated. "From all nations to all nations" is happening.

My colleague James M. Williams, who directs our Latin American ministries, returned from El Salvador recently. A local church he visited was welcoming home a couple who is planting seeds of the gospel in an Arab country. In fact many Latin Americans are being sent to the Middle East.

Individuals, churches, and ministries that support Hispanic evangelists often reap an amazing harvest. Great hope and a sense of thrill grip the church in Latin America. Pastors are preaching the pure gospel without apology. Laypeople share their faith with authority.

A Love for Sharing the Gospel

Even the most humble Hispanics can make wonderful evangelists. During preparation for one of our evangelistic festivals, a very poor, shabbily dressed man attended the training classes we had for those who served in our temporary counseling offices. Generally, the better educated, socially established, and spiritually mature lay leaders of the local churches attend these classes. So it was unusual to see such a poor man participating in them. In addition, the man was illiterate. He was accompanied by a young nephew who read and wrote for him. Although the man attended every class, we didn't expect him to do much counseling. However, like many illiterate people, he had a fantastic memory and had learned much through the counseling classes.

Following one of the festival meetings, every available counselor was busy except the illiterate man. At that time a doctor walked in, requesting counsel. Most doctors are very sophisticated and fashionable, of course; this doctor was no exception. Before anyone could stop him, the shabbily dressed man took the doctor into a room for counseling.

When our counseling director learned of this, he was a bit concerned. He didn't know if the illiterate man would be able to communicate effectively with the sophisticated doctor. When the doctor came out of the counseling room, our counseling director asked if he could help him in any way.

"No, thank you," the doctor replied. "This fellow has helped me very much."

The next day the doctor returned for counseling with two other doctors. Our counseling director wanted to talk with him, but the doctor refused, asking for counsel with the illiterate man. By the end of the festival, that illiterate man had led four doctors and their wives to Jesus Christ!

Allowing God to Use You

God doesn't call every Christian to be an evangelist, but God has commanded each of us to evangelize. As a young man, though, I decided that I didn't have the gift of evangelism. It was obvious. No matter how zealously I preached, no one was coming to Christ. Nothing I did seemed to make a difference. I was inspired by the things I read and heard about Billy Graham's ministry, but I knew I didn't have whatever he had. I gave God a deadline: "If I don't see any converts through my preaching by the end of the year, I'm quitting." Oh, I would still be an active Christian, but I would resign myself to simply teaching other believers.

The end of the year came and went. No converts. My mind was made up. I was through with preaching. Now I was sure I didn't have the gift.

On Saturday morning about four days into the new year, the small church I attended held a home Bible study. I didn't feel like going, but I went anyway out of loyalty to the elders.

The fellow who was supposed to give the Bible study never showed up. So the man of the house said, "Luis, you are going to have to say something." I was completely unprepared.

I had been reading a book, however, by Dr. Graham titled *The Secret of Happiness*, which is based on the beatitudes. So I asked for a New Testament and read Matthew 5:1–12. Then I simply repeated whatever I remembered from Dr. Graham's book.

As I was commenting on the beatitude, "Blessed are the pure in heart, for they will see God," a lady suddenly stood up. She began to cry and said, "My heart is not pure. How can I see God? Somebody tell me how I can get a pure heart." How delightful it was to lead her to Jesus Christ!

I don't remember the woman's name, but I will never forget her words: "Somebody tell me how I can get a pure heart." Together we read in the Bible, "The blood of Jesus, his Son, purifies us from all sin" (1 John 1:7). Before the evening was over, that woman found peace with God and went home with a pure heart overflowing with joy.

When you win people to Jesus Christ, it's the greatest joy. Your graduation is exciting, your wedding day is exciting, your first baby is exciting, but the most thrilling thing you can ever do is win someone to Christ. And it's contagious. Once you do it, you don't want to stop.

I challenge you to pray: "Dear God, I want that experience. I want to know what it is to win someone to Jesus Christ." You can strengthen your vision for the lost by spending much time in prayer (especially for the unsaved), by acquainting yourself with the problems and concerns of others, and by recognizing the urgency of sharing the Good News.

Persuading others to follow Christ—that is our calling. May God grant us today a vision for the lost and the power to be effective communicators of the precious gospel of Jesus Christ.

Why be ashamed of the gospel? "It is the power of God for the salvation of *everyone* who believes" (Rom. 1:16). It changes lives here and now and for eternity!

52

Native American

Reaching North America's First Peoples

Jim Uttley Jr.

Native Americans are the most evangelized yet most unreached people group in North America. For more than five hundred years, missionaries, churches, and evangelists have been "evangelizing" the first peoples of this continent. However, today less than 3 percent of Native Americans would consider themselves evangelicals. This is a far cry from the nearly 20 percent of the U.S. population that consider themselves evangelicals.

What's gone wrong? What mistakes have been made, and how can we see more Native Americans come to know Jesus not only as the Creator but also as their Savior and Lord?

According to Richard Twiss, a Lakota from the Rosebud Reservation in South Dakota, Christianity has not effectively penetrated Native culture. He believes that this is partly due to the fact that, historically, non-Native Christians "have made little genuine effort to find value in Native Americans or their cultures. Rather, the Native cultures have been labeled and denounced part and parcel as pagan, often occultist and definitely sinful. Is there any wonder many Native people view Christianity as the White man's religion and blame Christians for the loss of their own culture and identity?"

Preparing to Evangelize Native Americans

Before we can evangelize any people, we must seek to understand their lives and culture, be sensitive to them as individuals, and have a genuine love for them. In attempting to evangelize Native Americans, we must take the following steps.

1. *Learn about First Nations people and their roots.* So much of what Christians in the mainstream know about Native Americans comes from an inaccurate Hollywood presentation—Tonto and the Lone Ranger, for example. The indigenous people of North America are perhaps the most misunderstood people on our continent.

   Those attempting to reach Native Americans often lump all Native peoples together as one group without realizing that there are more than five hundred tribal groups in the United States and Canada. While similar, each has its own distinct culture, language, and customs.

   Study the history of some of these tribes, especially the ones to whom you are attempting to witness. Learn something of their culture. Read Native American authors, such as Sherman Alexie, Vine Deloria, and Crying Wind. Get a feel for what life is like for the average Native American today.

2. *Realize that most Native Americans already have an awareness and respect for the Creator.* Traditional Native Americans are spiritual people. In other words, they don't compartmentalize their lives into spiritual and secular boxes. To them, everything in life is spiritual. This is why they attach sacredness to many things, including inanimate objects. Although Native Americans are very spiritual, the absence of Christ leaves a vacant hole in their hearts. As their spiritual journey brings them into an arena of openness to the gospel, this people group is usually eager to hear the message of the cross.

   Native Americans are open to promptings through dreams and acts of nature. Another way to put this is they see the Creator in all of life, as opposed to mainstream Christians who tend to see and hear God only when they're in a religious context, such as church on Sunday morning. Suggested reading: *One Church, Many Tribes* by Richard Twiss.[1]

3. *Ask God to give you an understanding and a heart to feel their pain.* Native Americans have suffered incredible abuses and trauma almost from the time the first Europeans came to this land, and religious people or religious institutions, such as the church, have had a hand in much of this abuse. For example, in Canada the government used churches to operate the infamous residential schools, which sought to educate thousands of Native children. However, hundreds suffered emotional, physical, and sexual abuse. Today's Native Americans are directly or indirectly affected by the abuse suffered by their parents and grandparents. Consider reading books like *The Grieving Indian* by Arthur H. and *Does the Owl Still Call Your Name?* by Bruce Brand. Read books dealing with the Battle of Wounded Knee, the residential school era, and the long, forced marches, such as the Trail of Tears.[2]

4. *Develop a relationship with Native Americans before seeking to witness.* Often Christians in the mainstream have tried to evangelize Native Americans with the attitude that "we've come to save you from your paganism and

to redeem your life." Native people are easily turned off by anyone who
approaches them with this kind of attitude.

5. *Come with an attitude of friendship and servanthood.* If you want to be effective in reaching indigenous people for Christ, you need to become their
friend. Don't come to preach but to listen. Learn to develop relationships
with people and be willing to serve, lending a helping hand.

6. *Use effective tools as resources in your witness.* There are a couple tools to
help in effectively communicating with Native people. *Indian Life* is an
evangelistic publication that presents the gospel in a culturally relevant
way.[3]

One of the most effective evangelistic tracts is "The Creator's Path,"
published by Indian Life Books. This is most effective in dealing with
traditional Native people.[4]

A Simple Way to Explain the Gospel

Choosing the Creator's path: The Creator created the world—the mountains,
trees, rivers, and seas. He created all the creatures on this fair land. The Creator
also created man and woman from the land and put them in charge to take care
of the Creator's work.

Man and woman were placed on the path of life. They were given the choice
of walking on the Creator's Path or going another way.

The people did not listen to the voice of their Creator. They chose to go their
own way and do what seemed right to them in their own spirits.

This caused the Creator much sadness. He loved his creation dearly and did
not want them to go their own way. He decided that there was only one way to
save man and woman from destroying themselves and all of his creation. He would
send his Son to become like them and live on the land.

The Creator sends his Son: The time came when the Creator's Son came down
to the earth and took on the form of a little baby. He came from a woman and
grew as a child. Soon he became a man—a young warrior. But this warrior was
different. He did not choose to fight. He came to bring peace and to teach.

Not everyone liked what the Creator's Son was saying. They did not want to
accept his message of forgiveness and salvation. Some of the people who followed
him wanted to make him their chief. Others wanted to kill him.

One day those who wanted to kill the Creator's Son became more powerful.
They were able to turn the hearts of their leaders against the Creator. They got
permission to have the Son put to death.

This Man had done nothing wrong, but they hung him on a tree and left him
there to die.

The Creator's Son's body was taken down from the tree and buried. But just
three days later, the grave was empty. He had come alive again. Later the Creator's

Son returned to the sky to be with his Father. Before he left the land, he told his followers that there would come a day when he would return and that they all would join him. This made them all very happy.

The Creator's book, the Bible, tells us that he created all things to worship him. It is his greatest desire that we have a personal relationship with him. Even though man chose to go his own way and run from the Creator, the Creator desires that man walk with him on the Path of Truth.

Through all time, people have tried to reach the Creator through other spirits, vision quests, living a moral life, religion, and through creation itself. The Creator's book gives us his plan for how to get on the Creator's Path to abundant living. Would you like to find that path?

Here's how to ask the Creator to become your Savior:

- Tell God that you want to accept his way to know true peace and joy.
- Tell him that you know that without his help, you understand that you will be separated from the Creator in life and in death.
- Accept Jesus as God's only provision to deal with your separation from him.
- Invite Jesus, God's Son, to take control of your life and place you in his care.
- Pray this prayer (or put it in your own words):

Dear Creator God,

I accept your way. I believe your Son Jesus died for my sins so I could become part of the family of God. Because you raised Jesus from the dead, I can experience "harmony of life" with your Son as my Shepherd. I'm sorry for my sins and turn from them. I ask you to take charge of my life. I offer this prayer to you through your Son, Jesus. Amen.

53

Recent Immigrants

God's Heart for the Immigrant

Renée Sanford

My heart for immigrants was molded when my parents decided to become sponsors for a Vietnamese family after the fall of Saigon.

The summer of 1975 I spent part of my birthday watching the airport tarmac, waiting for the arrival of a young couple who would spend the next six months living with our family and adjusting to their new life in the United States. What we didn't know beforehand is that the two guests would quickly become three—with the birth of their firstborn son two weeks after Man and Tin arrived. Then three became seven when Man's sister and husband and two children spent a month in our home after moving from another state to be closer to their family.

These first families that lived with us were strong believers—Tin was the son of a pastor—all fleeing the coming wave of persecution. We shared sweet fellowship even when their English was sparse.

Several years later, another Vietnamese family who had never heard of Jesus Christ came to stay in our home. We introduced them to our Christian Vietnamese friends and, before they left to settle in another state, they too had come to faith in Christ.

Not everyone can bring a whole family into their home to live. But each of us can have a heart and mind to bless the foreigners and the strangers that God has brought to our shores.

God Loves Immigrants

God's special heart for immigrants shows throughout Scripture. From the beginning, God commanded the Israelites to show special care to the "aliens"—those who came and lived among them as people separated from their country of origin. These were people who were in a position of not having the same rights and resources as they would have had in their own nation, and they were to be cared for in the same way as widows and orphans (Exod. 22:21; 23:9). God reminded the Israelites that they could remember how it felt to be aliens in Egypt and should show compassion—even love (Deut. 10:19). While they were never to adopt the false religion of the foreigners, God warned his people not to mistreat them (Jer. 7:5–7).

The early church found itself embracing many immigrants—starting with the day of Pentecost and continuing as Christians fled persecution and then left their own countries to advance the kingdom of God.

Ask God to Enlarge Your Heart

Even if you are not specifically involved in evangelism to immigrants, it's still important to have a heart for the foreigner. All of us have our comfort zones, but feeling comfortable is not the goal when it comes to reaching people for Jesus Christ. Some people just gravitate more naturally to people of other cultures, and some are specifically called to that ministry. But God desires each of us to love our neighbor—even our non-English-speaking neighbor—as ourselves.

Ask God to show you your prejudices and to change them. If you don't have an interest in people of other cultures, ask God to help you develop one. You don't have to produce it on your own; ask God to *give* you a heart for people of different races and cultures.

Many years ago my husband and I visited the Saudi Arabian exhibit at a World's Fair. Even before leaving the oppressive atmosphere of the exhibit, I determined that ministering to Muslims wasn't in my future. Let other people with different hearts reach out to these lost people I didn't want anything to do with them.

Within a year, however, God changed my prejudiced heart. My husband and I wanted to befriend international students, so one Friday evening we visited the international Christian coffeehouse at a nearby university. As soon as we walked in, a friend motioned us over to where he was sitting with a Muslim couple in traditional dress. We chatted and found that not only were Hamid and Fatima Muslim, they were Saudi Arabian!

Despite my former vow, we pursued what was obviously a divinely arranged appointment. Hamid and Fatima's relatives had rebuked them for not having any American friends. When they met us, they were thrilled to meet another couple with children. We began to spend time together as friends. That winter we took their family to the mountains to go inner tubing. One summer we spent a delightful day at the beach. We ate American meals together and enjoyed Fatima's wonderful Arabic cooking.

Through this friendship, we began to see them not simply as Muslims but as unique individuals. When we began to love them as people, our attitude toward other people like them changed too. God gave me a new heart for Muslims and taught me to ask him to continually cleanse my heart of prejudice.

As your heart expands, ask God to lead you to the people he desires you to befriend. I was more interested in meeting Jewish people. God led me to Muslim friends.

Will you ask the Lord to enlarge your heart toward immigrants and foreigners? Will you ask him to bring across your path the ones he desires for you to meet?

Immigrants in Your Community

To begin exploring how God would use you in reaching immigrants, start by asking a simple question that Mr. Rogers used to ask in song, "Who are the people in my neighborhood?" Start noticing people at the store. If you live in the city, take public transportation. You may start seeing—and hearing—people you hadn't noticed before. Read about local events in the newspaper. Whether it's the annual Polish Dinner or the Cinco de Mayo celebration, events such as these are clues to a strong ethnic community.

People come to this country from separate cultural experiences and are obviously not all the same. For this reason, it's best to specialize when ministering to immigrants. The U.S. Census Bureau reports that in 2004 thirty-three million foreign-born people lived in the United States. Think of all the possibilities!

Ask yourself, *Which ethnic group do I feel most drawn to? Which group does God seem to be bringing into my life?*

Learn about Other People

To learn about people from other countries, read books and articles on the subject. You could even host an exchange student. The important thing is to learn people's cultural values and look for ways to best communicate the gospel to them.

When working with immigrants, you will want to determine if individuals are more interested in hanging on to their cultural identity or quickly assimilating into America. The goal is to introduce them to "heavenly citizenship," but first you must understand the motives and desires that drive them. This will help you minister to them more effectively.

Be on the lookout for cultural differences that might be an obstacle—or a bridge—to sharing your faith. In our friendship with our Muslim friends, we were always careful to serve chicken or beef, since they are not allowed to eat pork. So we were a bit embarrassed when we were on a picnic and our young son wailed, "But I want a *ham* sandwich!" Hamid and Fatima were not offended—though that was the day we also learned that you never sit with your feet pointing toward people. Again, we didn't make any fatal mistakes, but we learned as quickly as we could how to keep from purposely offending our foreign-born friends.

Sometimes knowing a person's religious background can be an opportunity. Because I had read that Islam does value the holy Scriptures, I invited Fatima to do a study of the Qur'an that also involved learning from the Bible. I learned a lot about Islam as I read the Qur'an, and Fatima read from the Bible and asked questions that had never crossed her mind before.

Investigate Ministry Opportunities

If you don't see any immigrants in your immediate neighborhood, you can still find lots of opportunities to minister. Contact the public schools where you can volunteer to tutor new students or just be available to help with their adjustment. On my youngest son's first day of first grade, I noticed a little African girl who was on her own. Since I knew the teacher, I volunteered to help Ishma put away her backpack and settle into her desk.

Our older son began tutoring a Vietnamese boy from the neighborhood. Through that, we established a relationship with his mom and hope the little boy will come to church camp this summer.

Look for local ethnic churches and join them in their outreach efforts. Many times this involves simple support as they welcome friends and relatives to this country. Even if your church doesn't do ethnic outreach, you can be part of another church's ministry. One woman I know teaches English as a second language to students in a church in another part of her city. What gifts do you have that you could share with immigrants?

Involve Your Family

More than any service you could provide, a new immigrant is most blessed by your kindness and friendship. The lives of a loving, Christian family are a powerful witness to the Good News of Jesus Christ. A person can live in this country for a long time without ever stepping into the home of a believer. Invite your immigrant friend home for a meal, and accept his invitation to his home as well.

Children are a powerful bridge to relationships with other people—especially immigrant families. Hamid and Fatima chose to become our friends primarily because we had children. Parents of all nationalities care deeply for their children, and they respond when other people care for their children as well. Inviting children to special activities, programs, and summer camps is natural when they have spent time with your children in your home.

Best of all, your children will gain a perspective of God's love for all people. While you need to be sensitive to how much your family members want to be involved in immigrant evangelism, just spending time with people of other races and cultures will broaden their minds and hearts.

In what family activity could you easily incorporate an immigrant family? Choose a date for inviting someone to dinner who is new to your country and community. Teach your children how to befriend people from other countries, and encourage them to reach out to new classmates.

Share Your Culture and Faith

The felt need of many immigrants is to acclimate to the United States. Most people coming to this country are eager to adapt, and they are grateful for any way we can help them do that. But it's important to distinguish between sharing our culture and sharing our faith. This isn't easy because often we don't stop to think about the difference.

Remember the goal—heavenly citizenship is more important than American citizenship. Don't let your patriotism or lack thereof get in the way of your relationship. Even the most positive people may say things that offend you or that you think are off base. Remember, what they think about the United States is not as important as what they think of Jesus Christ.

On the other hand, typical American holidays can be great opportunities to share the true Christian message. When you celebrate Thanksgiving, Christmas, and Easter, tell the simple story behind each holiday and give a clear presentation of the Good News. It is helpful to differentiate between how the American culture celebrates a holiday and how Christians celebrate the same holiday from the heart. Much of this will be new to people from other countries that view all Americans as Christians.

Inviting a person to church can be like inviting her into yet another culture. It's probably not the most effective first step in evangelizing immigrants. If you do bring your immigrant friend to church with you, think of it as simply a "taste" to pique her curiosity and whet her appetite for a faith community. Make sure your church family knows how to welcome visitors who may not speak English very well, if at all.

As you open your eyes to the world around you, be prepared for God to enlarge your world and your heart through the people he brings into your life.

Let the adventure begin!

54

International Students

The World at Your Door

Tom Phillips

What do Kofi Annan, Secretary General of the United Nations, King Abdullah of Jordan, and Benazir Bhutto, former Prime Minister of Pakistan, all have in common? They all studied in American universities as international students.

There are more than seven hundred thousand international students studying in American universities. These students are typically the brightest and best from their countries, and often are future world leaders. They're interested in American culture, but most obtain their degrees and leave without ever seeing the inside of an American home. The U.S. church has a unique opportunity to influence the world's emerging generation without large financial investment, uprooting families, or substantial training.

International students don't need excitement or entertainment, but they do need to know people who are committed Christians, willing to share their faith in genuine ways while building authentic relationships. Christians don't have to develop a clever evangelistic presentation; we just need to love Jesus and have a desire to share his love in appropriate ways. It's incredible to realize that God has brought many people groups, even those from countries closed to the gospel, right here to our doorstep. I encourage you to take advantage of this opportunity.

Evangelism Built on Relationship

One primary difference between many international students and Westerners is the concept of relationship. While Americans value a nuclear family and individualism, many non-Westerners value the extended family and belonging to a social group. Americans are interested in competition, privacy, and entertainment, while non-Westerners view conversation as entertainment and enjoy socializing. These value differences make it easy to see why many international students feel lonely.

International students often tell a familiar story. They begin attending classes or move into their dormitory. While walking down the hall, they pass someone they've met. The international student says, "Hello." The American student says, "How's it going?" The international student responds, but the American student has passed and is already down the hall.

International students long for genuine relationships with someone they can talk with, do things with, participate in family life with, or just *be* with—someone who wants a relationship with them regardless of their spiritual interest.

Entertainment or Hospitality?

Often people feel the pressure that comes with traditional American entertaining, such as having a spotless house or cooking exceptional meals. However, entertainment is different from hospitality, and hospitality is what international students desire.

Imagine being where people know very little about your home country. You would like to pull out a map and show them where you grew up. You want to talk about the kind of food you like. You might even want to cook a typical meal from home. These are the same desires of international students.

Hospitality means including an international student in the regular rhythm and routine of your family. Do your kids play soccer? Take an international student to a game. Do you go hiking or picnicking? International students welcome the opportunity to go along, talk, and build a relationship. Remember that many non-Westerners value conversation more than entertainment. You can invite an international student friend to church, but don't insist that he come or base the future of your relationship on his decision.

Your Life as an Example

As you build a relationship with your international student friend, your beliefs and, more important, the way you live your life, will be a powerful testimony. It's not about outlining specific dos and don'ts. Rather, it's sharing the faith and trust you have in Jesus Christ as your Savior and living that out daily.

As your relationship grows, the student may ask questions about spiritual topics. You can also encourage talking about spiritual things by asking such appropriate questions as:

- Where do you consider yourself to be spiritually?
- What are some of the religious practices of your country? Does your family practice these? How about you?
- What do people in your country believe about God? Jesus Christ? The Bible? Do you also believe these things?
- What do you think are some of the main differences between your religion and Christianity?
- Would you like to learn more about God and our Christian culture?
- Do you have a Bible? Would you like one? I can get one for you in either English or in your language.

It's important not to force the discussion. Remember that we are to love international students regardless of whether they are interested in Christ. Our friendship must be unconditional.

Be Prepared

Some people are concerned about how they'll respond if a student *does* begin to ask questions about Christianity. It's important to "be prepared to give an answer to everyone who asks you to give the reason for the hope that you have" (1 Pet. 3:15). To effectively share the fundamentals of Christianity, you should be able to answer basic questions about Christian beliefs:

- What do Christians believe about God, the Bible, the meaning of life, mankind, sin, and so on?
- How does a person have a relationship with God?
- How do God and people communicate?
- Who is Christ? Why do you believe he rose from the dead?
- If Christianity is the only "way," what about my family and friends back home?
- How do we know God wants a personal relationship with us?

A good study Bible will help you prepare answers ahead of time. Another resource is *The Compact Guide to World Religions* by Dean C. Halverson.[1]

The verse in 1 Peter says that as we share our hope, we are to do so "with gentleness and respect."

Prayer and God's Word

We can accomplish nothing on our own, yet we often forget to rely on prayer and biblical wisdom. These are vital ingredients to a healthy, evangelistic relationship with an international student.

- Pray for the student daily. Ask others to pray for the student as well.
- Pray for unconditional love toward the student, using Christ as your example, and pray that you'll be consistent in following through with your commitment.
- Study Scripture—not just for teaching the student but also for your own spiritual growth. Your right relationship with God is the most powerful testimony to an international student who is much more focused on actions than on mere words.

Sharing Your Spiritual Journey

It's normal, in the course of any relationship, to tell our life story. For Christians, this includes our personal testimony. This can be one of the most nonoffensive tools for sharing our faith in Jesus Christ. As you share your own spiritual journey with an international student, she can learn from your experience, and it will open doors of conversation to further spiritual discussions. Take time to think about your story. You may want to write out your testimony, using the following questions as a guide:

- What was your life like before you became a Christian?
- What made you trust Christ for your salvation?
- How has your life changed?

Practice your testimony with a close friend and ask him to point out "church jargon" that would be meaningless to the student. Practice also helps you not wander with your storytelling.

Asking the Question and Following Through

Often believers build relationships, answer questions, and share their testimony without ever asking: "Would you like to pray to become a follower of Jesus Christ?" Since many students are from cultures where it's polite to always "agree," we want to be sensitive and not pushy. However, don't be afraid to ask.

Perhaps you've never prayed with anyone to accept Christ. It's very simple. You can ask the student if he wishes to pray alone, pray with you, or even pray after you. You can lead the student in a prayer to confess his sin and acknowledge a need for Jesus's salvation from that sin. If you don't get every word correct, God still knows the condition of your heart and the heart of the student.

The Great Commission says to "make disciples." If a student accepts Christ, continue your relationship through discipleship, Bible study, and prayer. Be consistent in following through to help the student grow spiritually. If the student never accepts Christ, continue to love the student and share the example of Christ through your life. You may be planting eternal seeds.

Getting Started

Getting involved with international students is easy. Begin by contacting an organization (such as International Students, Inc. at www.isionline.org) that ministers to international students. They may already have staff in your area looking for volunteers. Begin to pray now for the student that God will bring your way. Look for opportunities to learn more about countries and cultures around the world. Focus on deepening your own walk with God through Bible study, solidifying your understanding of Christianity's fundamentals, and developing your personal testimony. Take advantage of the opportunity to reach the world's leaders of tomorrow who are studying in America today. You can read more on this subject in *The World at Your Door* by Tom Phillips and Bob Norsworthy with Terry Whalin.[2]

Ordinary People by Life Situation

55

Abuse Victims

Believing the Right Things in the Wrong Ways

C. Richard Wells

The widespread devastating effects of family abuse have created what amounts to a hidden unreached people group. Victims of abuse exhibit distinctive patterns of behavior and need, and, therefore, they tend to hear the gospel with different ears. Like all other persons, abuse victims are sinners in need of a Savior, and the message of Jesus Christ is sufficient to save everyone, but abuse victims (almost all women) are often lonely, isolated, burdened by false guilt, and living on unrealistic hopes. Sharing the gospel with them calls for discernment, sensitivity, and personal investment. Victims of abuse are often longing for someone who cares, someone to count on, someone to offer real help. They are longing for Christ.

A Modern Plague

The statistics are overwhelming: Seven hundred thousand *reported* rapes every year; one in three women sexually abused in her lifetime; about one million incidents of domestic violence *reported* each year (75 percent may go unreported); almost 3.5 million cases of child abuse or neglect in 2003—up 27 percent from 1990; between 1976 and 1996, more than thirty thousand women murdered by husbands or boyfriends—30 percent of all female murder victims.

Modern medicine rid the world of epidemics that terrorized ancient man, but modern culture has its own plague—every bit as terrible. From "the cradle to the rocking chair, it seems abuse exists in some fashion,"[1] assuming many forms, attacking every age and class, and cleverly hiding itself from public view. The "abuse victims" category does not appear in demographic charts, but their experience sets them apart.

Take Jenny. She grew up with an alcoholic father who regularly abused her mother verbally and sometimes physically. Jenny covered for her parents, put on a bubbly facade, and, like many children of abusers, married young to get away—only to discover, too late, she had married a carbon copy of her father. (This pattern repeats itself over and over—as children from abusive families become abusers themselves or victims of new abuse.) Thankfully, Jenny found a way out of the cycle through Jesus Christ.

We shall return to her story, but we should pause here to ask a few pertinent questions. First, what do we mean by "abuse"? Second, who are the victims of abuse? Third, how do abuse victims "hear" the gospel? And fourth, what principles should guide us in sharing Christ with them?

Defining "Abuse"

While there is no single, generally accepted definition of "abuse," we can identify patterns of abusive relationships. According to Justice Department figures, spousal violence is overwhelmingly (92 percent) male to female. In child abuse, mothers outnumber fathers two to one (both parents are involved in almost one-fifth of the cases). Fathers, however, account for more physical (including sexual) abuse, mothers for neglect. Elder abuse is only slightly less common than child abuse and likewise involves both physical abuse and neglect, most often at the hands of sons. In half the cases, the abuser himself was an abused child.

Abuse assumes many forms. It can involve simple neglect (half of all child abuse) or emotional assaults, such as demeaning, ridiculing, blaming, or threatening, including threats of violence accompanied by gestures, intimidation, or close encounters like killing a pet or throwing a fist through the wall. Emotional abuse often accompanies or escalates into physical abuse, which can range from a shove to a beating to murder in the second degree. Almost by definition, sexual abuse is a mix of physical and emotional abuse—an act of (usually violent) physical harm that simultaneously (and often intentionally) humiliates and degrades.

Domestic violence, to take the most widespread example, follows an almost stereotypical three-phase pattern. First, tension builds. The woman "tries to control things by attempting to please her partner and keep his world calm."[2] Second, despite her best efforts, something provokes him, and he rapes or batters her. In the third phase, the perpetrator expresses remorse. He may lavish affection on his victim and often makes promises not to do it again.

Domestic violence also typically involves stressors, such as unemployment or financial problems that serve as catalysts. Abusive men are usually isolated socially, and abused women are often financially and/or emotionally dependent as well. In addition, ironically, both the abuser and abused often hold a high (if distorted) view of "traditional marriage," which, by discouraging divorce, can actually enable the abuser.

The Victims of Abuse

These patterns of relationships suggest that victims of abuse may exhibit characteristic behaviors as well. While there is no standard "victim" profile, an abused woman typically displays one or more of the following:

- *Distorted self-image.* She may believe that she is to blame or that she should be able to control the situation by doing the right thing.
- *Unrealistic hope.* Because her husband/partner expresses remorse and promises to change, the victim may continue to hold out hope that he will. Furthermore, the remorse often brings renewed affection, which fosters the woman's hope.
- *Isolation.* As with all suffering, an abusive relationship tends to isolate the victim. Many abusers are controllers, so women often find themselves gradually cut off from relational and support networks. Abused women almost always feel reluctant to share their "secret."
- *Guilt and shame.* In addition to assuming blame, the victim may feel guilty for failing to change her situation. She will often experience guilt over her feelings about her spouse/partner as well.

How Abuse Victims "Hear" the Gospel

Now, back to Jenny. As a little girl, she occasionally heard Bible stories, but she had never come to know Christ and had not attended church in years. Now, however, her marriage fueled a longing for something better.

As it happened, her job at a local manufacturing plant brought her into contact with three Christians. Harry was the most visible. He plastered the walls of his office with Bible verses. He talked about going to church and sometimes chided nonattenders—though good-naturedly. Evelyn, on the other hand, seldom mentioned her faith as such. She was a model employee, with a model marriage and model children. She grew up in a Christian family and taught Sunday school, just as her mother did before her.

Then there was Maxine. Maxine seemed to care. She would take time to listen, and she sympathized with Jenny, but she wouldn't hesitate to call her bluff. More than once Maxine offered to help, but she always stressed that only God could give

Jenny the help she needed most. Eventually Jenny accepted Maxine's invitation to church. And there, a few weeks later, she opened her heart to Christ.

Every person is unique, but Jenny's story highlights some common features in the way abuse victims "hear" the gospel. Most striking, perhaps, is *how* the experience of abuse drove Jenny to seek help. A truism of counseling holds that troubled persons do not seek help until they reach a crisis point. "Abuse" is crisis by definition, but, as we have seen, victims learn to cope with the crisis, hiding their secret in shame or wishful thinking. Paradoxically, they desperately want help and almost as desperately fear seeking help. Like Jenny, abuse victims are often just waiting for someone to come alongside.

For Jenny, that someone was Maxine. Why not Harry or Evelyn? Years later, Jenny would say that both of them seemed distant. Not that they were hypocritical, uncaring, or impersonal, but in her isolation Jenny doubted they could understand her situation, and even if they could, she doubted whether they would be willing to get involved in her mess. Like many victims, Jenny didn't want to burden them with her troubles.

But Maxine took the initiative. She could tell that things for Jenny were not right. Over time, Maxine drew out of Jenny the trouble in her heart (Prov. 20:5), without rejecting her when she began to talk about it. Maxine willingly offered to help, and for the first time she could remember, Jenny had someone she could count on.

Equally important, Jenny could count on Maxine to tell her the truth. From a gospel point of view, abuse victims believe all the right things in all the wrong ways. For example, they experience guilt, but it is almost always misplaced—for example, false guilt for not controlling the situation, without realizing that remaining in the relationship may be irresponsible. Victims often feel dependent—but on their spouse not on God. Or victims harbor hope—hope that things will get better despite contrary evidence, rather than hope in the God of hope (Rom. 15:13).

Maxine gently began to confront these distortions in Jenny's life, and gradually Jenny began to see her situation as it really was. Furthermore, Maxine refused to become a crutch for Jenny. Otherwise, Jenny might have simply switched her dependency from an abusive mate to a sympathetic friend, instead of to God.[3]

Some Principles for Sharing Christ

As noted earlier, every victim of abuse is unique. Still, just as we can discern patterns in abusive relationships and patterns in the behavior of victims, we can suggest some guidelines for bringing the gospel to bear in their lives.

- Since the overwhelming majority of abuse victims are women, the importance of women reaching abused women can hardly be overstated. Many victims feel uncomfortable even talking to a male about their secret. (Jealousy is often a major problem in abusive relationships, and talking with a man about the problem could make things much worse, at least in the abused woman's mind.) A man who encounters an abuse victim should enlist the involvement of his wife or other faithful women, not only for protection but to establish a caring relationship.

- More so than in most other cases, ministry with abuse victims blurs the distinction between "evangelism" and "counseling." Most abused women face major life issues. They often need help getting out of a dangerous situation and frequently lack financial and other resources to care for themselves and their children. No one can hope to share Christ meaningfully with them without the risk of involvement in their lives.

- Because many abused women have learned to hide their secret, or rationalize their situation, concerned Christians must educate themselves on signs of abuse, available resources, legal implications, and the like. A guide for asking diagnostic questions (appendix 1) and a checklist of early warning signs (appendix 2) are provided at the end of this chapter. Local agencies can provide additional helpful information.

- Just as Jenny came to Christ in the fellowship of a loving church, we must emphasize the value of a caring Christian family to nurture faith and discipleship. Many abuse victims, like Jenny, grew up in highly dysfunctional homes. They need Jesus Christ first of all, and, of course, they need to learn how to "do family," but they also *need a family*. In many cases, a warm, loving Christian community is the only real option.

Epilogue

Today Jenny is joyously married to a godly man. They have two boys and a baby girl. She plans to homeschool her children, and she works with kids at church. But her heart aches for women on the underside of life. She knows how they feel—the fear and the shame, the hopelessness, and the loneliness. And she knows how they long for someone to help.

Appendix 1: Are You an Abuse Victim?

Typical Somatic Symptoms and Complaints

- appetite disturbance—loss of appetite or overeating
- asthma
- chest, back, pelvic pain
- choking sensation
- chronic pain

- digestive problems
- fatigue
- gastrointestinal upset
- headaches
- hyperventilation

- injuries, bruises
- insomnia
- nightmares, often violent
- premature aging[4]

Typical Emotional Symptoms and Complaints

- agitation
- anxiety
- depression or symptoms of depression
- despair
- doubts of sanity, self-doubt
- drug or alcohol use or abuse, possibly overdose, other addictive behaviors
- dysphoria
- embarrassment
- evasiveness
- experiences the man as omnipotent
- extreme emotional reactivity
- fearfulness—feeling frightened or in constant state of terror
- feeling like abuse is deserved
- feeling out of control
- feeling worthless
- feelings of loss and grief
- frequent crying
- guilt
- homicidal thoughts

- hooked on hope
- hopelessness
- humiliation
- "if only" thoughts
- inability to relax
- isolation, feelings of being isolated
- jumpiness
- lack of energy
- learned helplessness
- loneliness
- low self-esteem
- nervousness
- often accompanied by male partner
- passiveness
- post-traumatic stress disorder (PTSD) symptoms
- powerlessness
- self-blaming
- shame
- shyness
- suicidal thoughts or attempts
- no warm memories[5]

Appendix 2: Early Warning Signs of Abuse

- The man dominates the woman verbally, criticizing and belittling her, throwing her off balance, or causing her to doubt her own worth and abilities.

- He makes all plans, neither inquiring about her desires nor gathering input from her.
- He alone sets the sexual pace, initiating all contacts and rejecting any of her sexual approaches.
- He makes most of the decisions about the future and announces them to her instead of including her in planning and decision making. He refuses to compromise or negotiate on major decisions.
- He is moody, making it difficult for her to predict what the next encounter with him will be like.
- He is chronically late without apology or remorse.
- He determines when they can discuss issues, if at all; he repeatedly justifies this control by claiming that he hates conflict.
- He is hostile toward others as well as her.
- His father was abusive to his wife.
- He demands control over his partner's contacts with friends and family and her finances.
- He publicly humiliates her, sometimes starting with put-down humor; rather than apologizing when she protests, he urges her to "get a thicker skin!" or "lighten up!"
- He slaps, pushes, or hits her.
- He exhibits rage, arrogance, pouting, or withdrawal if not given his way.
- He is suddenly cold or rejecting.
- His temper seems uncontrolled, and he manifests unprecipitated anger at others.
- He is highly critical of his partner.
- He makes comments meant to make the woman feel unsure of herself.
- He is verbally domineering.
- He flaunts his relationships with other women.[6]

56

Addicts

A Biblical Guide to Help Liberate Addicts

Brent Crowe

For the law of the Spirit of life in Christ Jesus has made me free from the law of sin and death.

Romans 8:2 NKJV

A few years ago I was asked to speak at an event in my hometown of Atlanta, Georgia. The purpose was to attract Atlanta's "harder crowd" by putting on a Christian rock festival where I would present the gospel.

As I walked to my car after the evening was over, I recognized Chris, an old high school friend of mine. After a two-second stare, he said, "Brent, I thought that was you up there." Seeing his pain, I asked him how he was doing and what he had been up to. He responded, "Everything's messed up; my life is a mess."

We went back to his apartment, and the longer our conversation went on, the more apparent it became that he had imprisoned himself with an addictive substance. He had built the walls so high around him that he couldn't see anything outside of his self-built prison. I explained to him how he could know God and, right then, at 4:00 in the morning, he could turn from the sin in his life and run into the arms of the Savior. His eyes filled with tears, and when I gave him the opportunity to pray a prayer of salvation, he immediately agreed to do so. We got on our knees around a large, black marble table and prayed a simple prayer.

Afterward I asked him how he felt, and he responded, "I feel new." He then began to chuckle and said, "You know, Brent, last night this black table was white with cocaine, and yet tonight I knelt at this same table and asked Christ to change my life." It was at that defining moment that Chris was transformed and began the process of being made into the image of Christ.

What can break the bond of a self-imprisoned addiction? Simply put, the gospel and only the gospel. Jesus did not go to the cross so that we could be in a constant state of "recovery." Nothing could be further from a biblical worldview. Christ died to rescue and redeem sinners and actually break down the walls of their prison. He died that the addict may be *recovered*.

In communicating the gospel to an addict, we are not discussing self-help or a twelve-step program. Individuals must be convinced of this fundamental truth: Only God can save me. The remainder of this chapter will focus on a plan to liberate those who feel powerless. Focus will be given to what all prisoners want and, to their surprise, what God wants for them—*freedom*. God desires for us to be free so that we may enjoy his Son and capture the moments of life to honor him. The following biblical model is based on the realization that when one is in Christ, he is in fact free.

Face the Facts—John 8:34

Many biblical counselors define addiction as "misplaced worship." It's the decision to idolize or have a love affair with an activity or an object. Worship will result in one of two things: Right worship will liberate us to be free in Christ, and wrong worship will enslave us in a form of perverted intimacy. We are all made for the purpose of worship and, as such, we *will* worship something. Perverted intimacy results when our worship is aimed at something other than God. The addict must understand that at the heart of his voluntary slavery is a worship problem. Freedom in Christ cannot be obtained from any other starting point than the conviction that worship and idolatry must be redirected.

Whole and Final Healing—Romans 8:2

The addict must believe that by the power of the gospel he can be freed from his addiction. The most prevalent theory on addiction is that it is a disease. This says to the addict, *This addiction is not my fault. I can't help it. I have a disease so it is beyond my control.*

Addicts claim to be a victim of this "disease" in the same way a person who has Parkinson's is a victim. This theory is perpetuated habitually by AA, the most renowned addictions support group. Step one of Alcoholics Anonymous states: "We admit we are powerless over alcohol," and each meeting begins with people introducing themselves as "an alcoholic." For all the good that AA does, this underlying core belief that alcoholics are victims flies directly in the face of Scripture.

The Bible says in 2 Corinthians 5:17: "If anyone is in Christ, he *is* a new creation; the old has gone, the new has come!" The addict must believe that something radical needs to take place in his life and that God can free him and can free him *completely*.

Sin, a Chronic Condition and a Conscious Choice—Romans 1:24–25

First, sin is the chronic condition of mankind—we all are afflicted by it. It is also a conscious choice, something we choose to do. An addict is a voluntary slave both *choosing to do* and at the same time in *bondage to* this life-dominating habit. Ignoring that sin is a conscious choice diminishes the idea of guilt and thus there is no need for forgiveness, as the sin was no one's fault to begin with. If this logic is carried through, then Jesus died in vain and there was no need for his sacrifice. The addict must recognize that his sin is a big problem that can be solved only by the great sacrifice of Jesus. It is not until the gravity of our sinful state and our sinful choices takes hold in our lives that we realize our desperate need for salvation.

The Biblical Worldview of the Nature of Humanity—Genesis 1:26–28

In witnessing to an addict, one must help her see a view of humanity through the grid of Scripture. "We are creatures of God made in the image of God. Humanity is to be understood as . . . a conscious purposeful act of God."[1] This means that while God knew humanity would choose to sin, he still chose to create us. Romans 3:10 says, "There is no one righteous, not even one," and is restated in verse 23: "For all have sinned and fall short of the glory of God."

The question then becomes, Why would God create humanity knowing we would sin? One word: grace. Humanity was created to enjoy God, and it is only in worship that true satisfaction and happiness can be found. Jonathan Edwards, a great pastor used of God to bring about a spiritual awakening in our country, said this of our purpose: "The enjoyment of God is the only happiness with which our souls can be satisfied."[2]

Repentance and Biblical Change—Matthew 5:29; Colossians 3:5

So now, how does change take place? Simply put, it happens through repentance. Oswald Chambers says, "Repentance is a gift of God."[3] Jim Berg, in his book *Changed into His Image,* says that biblical change requires mortification, meditation on Scripture and Christ, and manifestation of Christ.[4]

> *Mortification (Rom. 6:11).* This means that we are no longer subject to the addiction that has held us in bondage because we have turned from it and we are dead to it and are now alive in Christ. Repentance means that wherever we are in the journey of addiction, we turn to the cross. It is seeing the cross and immediately developing a hate for the sin that put Christ there. It is realizing that when Matthew 26:67 says the people "spit in his face and struck him with their fists. Others slapped him," it is really talking about me and my sin: With my sin, I spit in his face, and with my addiction, I slapped him.
>
> *Meditation on Scripture and Christ (Rom. 12:2).* The next step is to renew the mind and be transformed on a daily basis by the Word of God. A preface to an old Bible said this: "This Book reveals the mind of God, the state of man, the way of salvation, the doom of sinners, and the happiness of believers."
>
> *Manifestation of Christ (Eph. 4:24).* This signifies that we have now been transformed and are a child of God, a new creation. To manifest Christ means that we mirror the God within us rather than masquerade for the world around us.

Motivated by Forgiveness, Obey God—Romans 6:12–14

Christ rescued and redeemed us so that our hearts may be filled with an overwhelming gratitude and desire to worship him for what he has done and who he is. If a person comes to Christ but falls into a works-based system of pleasing God, then biblical change has not taken place. Christians are obedient and follow God out of a grateful heart not because of a list of dos and don'ts. The ability to follow God rests in his grace and the fact that he has forgiven us. If you are a Christian, living in a state of forgiveness, "sin shall not be your master, because you are not under law, but under grace" (v. 14).

H. Bonar, in *Longing for Heaven,* writes: "It is forgiveness that sets a man working for God. He does not work in order to be forgiven, but because he has been forgiven and the consciousness of his sin being pardoned makes him long more for its entire removal than ever he did before."[5]

Guidance—Galatians 6:1–2; James 5:19–20

Dr. Sam Williams, professor of biblical counseling at Southeastern Seminary, has written several practical steps to help a person begin his new life. A person witnessing to an addict should follow these guidelines to help him establish new boundaries for his life.

1. *Lifestyle assessment*: Help the addict change his daily life.
   - List specific destructive behaviors he is not to commit.
   - List "slippery slope" behaviors that lead to the above destructive behaviors (for example, no lingering looks at women).
   - Help him come up with suggestions for lifestyle changes (for example, limit Internet use).
2. *Accountability and prayer partners*: This needs to be done several times per week. It may also be helpful for the addict to have a prayer schedule and to schedule the prayer time when his temptation is strongest (for example, at night).
3. *Teaching spiritual disciplines*: Have him write out a plan on how he will maintain spiritual discipline. Be consistent in helping the addict stay on this plan.
4. *Developing "ways of escape"*: Construct walls and fences to minimize opportunities to backslide.
5. *Instruction and life-on-life discipleship*: Help teach him how to do spiritual battle and fight the good fight of faith and obedience. This should include practical biblical teaching on sanctification and on important concepts like putting off the old and putting on the new and renewing the mind. The addict must understand sin and sanctification.
6. *Replace idolatry with worship of the true God*: The addict must learn how to worship. Augustine said, "The root of all evil is wrongly directed desire." His desires and affections must be redirected.
7. *Loving others*: This would include confessing sin to others and seeking forgiveness, reconciliation, and restitution whenever possible.
8. *Dealing with deception*: Addictions and lies are bedfellows. Teach the addict about how serious and important honesty is (see Acts 5:1–11).
9. *Getting others involved in the plan for change*: This is the job for the church not for one person.
10. *Not getting discouraged with relapses*: They are all too common. Those who have successfully conquered addiction usually fail several times before they achieve victory.

In conclusion, to minister to addicts, you must have a passion for it. Sadly, it seems that the church does not want to dirty their hands with the most disgusting of sinners. Backs are turned, forgetting that at any given time, anyone could fall into addiction. Dr. Ed Welch, a leading biblical counselor and author, said it well when he stated, "The church should be full of grace; too often the church has used the Bible as a club rather than words of life."

One reason addicts may stay hidden behind the chemical curtain is because the church is seemingly apathetic and dry-eyed for the soul of an addict. Why is it that we wait until someone we care about falls into addiction before there are tears? As Christians, the compassion of Christ is not an option, and if we truly love him, we will care about the things he cares about and see people as he sees people—infinitely valuable. I pray the material before you will help you paint a picture of what the gospel of Jesus can do for those who are lost in the sin of addiction. We must help such people understand that they were not created for the prison in which they presently find themselves. They were meant to enjoy a personal relationship with Jesus. All of us must be encouraged not to stop short in the journey of life by allowing ourselves to be satisfied with earthly things. We can find our joy only in him.

C. S. Lewis writes, ". . . if we consider the unblushing promises of reward and the staggering nature of the rewards promised in the Gospels, it would seem that our Lord finds our desires not too strong, but too weak. We are half-hearted creatures, fooling about with sex and drink and ambition when infinite joy is offered. . . . We are far too easily pleased."[6]

Convicts

Fulfilling the Great Commission behind Bars

Mark Earley

I was in prison and you came to visit me.

Matthew 25:36

Remember those in prison as if you were their fellow prisoners.

Hebrews 13:3

My knees were killing me! I had been kneeling on the concrete floor in front of the jail cell for close to an hour. It was just before Christmas and a group of Prison Fellowship staff and local church volunteers were spending the day visiting women prisoners at a Virginia correctional center.

Ashley (not her real name), a young African American woman, was alone in a closed concrete cell with a small window at eye level and an opening for food passage at knee level. Speaking to her through the food opening, I could see that Ashley did not resemble the kind of person you might expect to find in prison. She did not look hardened, tired, bitter, or defeated. Instead, she was poised, articulate, and possessed a smile that radiated. Yet she was in prison for murder.

I asked her, "Where are you in your journey with God? If you were to die tonight, do you know for certain whether or not you would go to heaven?"

"I would not go to heaven," she said, suddenly shedding the smile that had been so bright when we had talked of her children. "With what I have done, I am too bad to go to heaven."

"Ashley," I asked, "can I share with you the Good News of Jesus?" She was more than eager. I knew the Holy Spirit was at work in her heart and she wanted God.

I shared with her the gospel of Jesus Christ, and I shared my own testimony of how I had tried to be good enough to get to God and his heaven, only to learn I needed a Savior. I read to her Ephesians 2:8–9 and inserted her name: "For it is by grace [Ashley] has been saved, through faith—and this not from [yourself], it is the gift of God—not by works so that [Ashley cannot] boast."

"Would you like to receive Jesus Christ as your Savior today?" I asked.

"Yes, I would," she said.

"Would you like to pray right now with me and confess your sin, repent, and ask Christ to save you and to fill you with his Holy Spirit?"

She was now sobbing as she turned to Christ as her Savior and Lord. She looked up and said, "I have not cried for a very, very long time."

I encouraged Ashley to begin reading the Gospel of John, to pray, to share her heart with God, and to join a Bible study in the prison. She said that she would.

This corridor of cold prison cells had been turned into a holy place with the visible working of God in Ashley's heart. I was rejoicing as I drew myself up off my aching knees and, with an ear of faith, could hear the angels rejoicing in heaven!

Lessons in Sharing Christ in Prison

Ashley was among my first, real-life evangelism experiences as the president of Prison Fellowship. But taking the gospel behind barbed wire and closed prison doors is something that our founder, Chuck Colson, and our volunteers have been doing on a regular basis for nearly thirty years. With Prison Fellowship seminars, Bible studies, and special evangelistic events going on in more than fifteen hundred correctional facilities every year, we have learned much about working within the American prison environment—now "home" to more than two million men and women.

We have come alongside several thousand hardworking prison chaplains, many of whom are unpaid. We have supported them and tried to lighten their burdens through sharing in the work. We do this because Jesus himself identifies strongly with the downtrodden behind bars: "Whatever you did for one of the least of these brothers of mine, you did for me" (Matt. 25:40).

Prison is intimidating—by design. The grimness of razor wire and concrete walls mirrors well the condition of the population. Prison degrades, humiliates, isolates, controls, and depresses all who enter. It harbors a real spiritual darkness. So before you even set foot in a prison to share the gospel, pray fervently.

That said, Jesus has told us to fear not, and the experience of Prison Fellowship staff and thousands of volunteers has borne out that prison can be one of the most exciting places to minister. Here are some principles that may help you in your pursuit of prison evangelism.

- *Prison ministry is not for the lone ranger.* You will experience both a sense of security and joy working as part of a team with other volunteers.
- *Always work with and through the prison chaplains.* Many have spent long hours and many years in the prison environment, and they have become skilled at separating those truly in search of God from those professing a "jailhouse conversion" that is not sincere. Chaplains know all the prison rules, and they know their warden. Respect the chaplains and abide by their suggestions and directions. There is so much to be done in ministering to the needs of men and women in prison, and the chaplains know they can't do it all themselves. Most will welcome sincere volunteers who are willing to come in and work with them and not against them.
- *While many prisoners may not seem very open to the gospel, most of them truly appreciate your coming to visit them.* Many have been abandoned by family and friends, and they hunger for caring human contact. They realize you are giving of your time freely to come into prison, and that means a lot to them.
- *At the same time, prisoners can quickly spot phoniness.* (They have played that game themselves, many times.) They will test you to see how "real" you are. Don't think you have to copy their particular style of talking or dramatize your own testimony to better identify with them. Never make promises you can't keep. Just be yourself. That will open up more doors.

Have an Open Ear

Before you share the gospel message, take time to listen—as Jesus often did. Your rapt attention is a great gift to give those whose sense of self-worth has been warped or crushed by prison and their own bad choices in life. Ask prisoners about their family, their hopes, their dreams. But never ask about their crimes, despite your curiosity. (You wouldn't want strangers asking about *your* worst sins, would you?) After a certain level of trust has been established, they might share this information with you.

There are several benefits to listening. It builds rapport. It gives you insight into the prisoners' lives. And—as nearly any prison ministry volunteer will tell you—it reveals that these men and women in prison are really a lot like you and me, despite the media's lopsided portrayal of prisoners. We have all made bad, self-serving choices in life that have hurt others and ourselves and have shown us our need for a Savior. We all have dreams for a better life for our loved ones and for us.

Building Trust

Prison evangelism often begins with leading a study of the Scriptures, because continued, relational contact builds trust—the hardest wall to get past in any prison. Those prisoners considered to be manipulators will drop out of the study if they are unable to control you. The sincere ones will be evident through their hunger to know Scripture. Pay attention to quiet individuals, often afraid to speak for fear of showing their ignorance of the Bible. Get to know them and reach out to them.

Be aware that many prisoners cannot read or write well. So never risk embarrassment by putting anyone on the spot to read a passage of Scripture aloud. Always ask for volunteers to read. You might consider using an easy-to-read version of the Bible and print out the text. You may also want to employ some fun, interactive teaching techniques, such as skits, role plays, or object lessons that reinforce an idea.

Be aware also of an informal but pervasive "prison code" that scorns and exploits signs of weakness. While many hurting men and women in prison may hunger for the love and forgiveness of Christ, they may risk pouring out their hearts and needs only in private, as did Ashley. Over time, your Bible study or chapel service may become a safe place for them to open up.

Abiding by the Rules

Always keep in mind that you are ministering in a *prison*, where the staff's ultimate concern is security. Be willing to put up with seemingly irrelevant forms or procedures to secure approval for your programs. Expect delays.

Respect all rules and restrictions, even if you don't fully understand the purpose. For example, do not bring anything into or out of the prison without advance approval of the staff. Check on any dress code restrictions and obey them.

For your own safety, don't give out your full name, home address, or telephone number to any prisoner. And don't get involved in any business transactions with prisoners. Be careful about physical contact inside prison. To a guard, a good Christian hug can look like a possible contraband transfer.

Training and Resources

Prison Fellowship has developed training for volunteers who wish to do prison ministry, and it is not necessary to be affiliated with Prison Fellowship to participate in the training. Some prisons now require all volunteers to take the free PF instruction before engaging in any type of in-prison ministry. Prison Fellowship gladly shares this information because we want to see effective prison evangelism, and it need not be our own. The basic course is offered several times a year in many communities near prisons. For information go to www.pfm.org.

Another resource is *Inside Journal*, Prison Fellowship's newspaper for prisoners, published eight times a year. *IJ* always includes a gospel presentation, as well as testimonies and information that can help prisoners survive prison, maintain family relationships, and improve their education. Volunteers in prison ministry are encouraged to distribute the newspaper free at facilities that will allow it. Another way to minister in prison is through our Pen Pal program. To learn more about Pen Pal or how to receive free copies of *IJ* for distribution, contact Prison Fellowship at 1-877-478-0100 or visit us online at www.prisonfellowship.org.

Prison ministry is a great undertaking, not just in the saving of souls but also for the health of the church. I believe many future leaders of the church will rise out of the prisons, much like Chuck Colson did in 1974. We would be happy to have others toiling in the harvest at our side, and we will gladly share what we have learned with you.

58

People Affected by Disability

Searching for Acceptance

Joni Eareckson Tada

Our heartbeat is to make the gospel accessible to people affected by disabilities and to help churches include people with disabilities. World Health Organization statistics tell us that more than 10 percent of a country's population includes people with disabilities (or now more commonly called people affected by disabilities). In the world there are 650 million disabled people. That means every community has someone with a disability. But often these disabled people are hidden away.

Because of the rejection that so many disabled people experience all through their life, they're often the most receptive to the Good News of the gospel. The gospel is about inclusion and acceptance. As we preach the message of acceptance and reconciliation of mankind to God through Jesus Christ, disabled people embrace it readily. They find God in their brokenness as they seek to make sense of the difficult situations in which their disability places them.

Any disabled person will say that it's people's attitudes that affect them the most. Society pushes disabled people to the margins and rejects them, because society likes to feel comfortable. Society likes beautiful people. As the church, we must model inclusion and pull them in. Look at the priority that Jesus gave to ministry with disabled people. We should look at our own ministry and the priority that we give them. Jesus gave us the pattern to follow when he told the story of the great banquet (Luke 14:12–14). Jesus is talking to the church. Reach out to disabled people. These people are indispensable. The body of Christ will never be complete until they are part of our congregations.

Practical Suggestions

Here are a few practical suggestions: If you encounter someone who is non-verbal, feel free to ask, "What is your sign for yes?" Then learn the sign for no. Once you learn the signs for yes and no, you can have a conversation with that individual just by phrasing your questions in such a way that they can be adequately answered with yes or no. If this person is so nonverbal that you cannot understand any speech at all, then break the alphabet up into parts and simply go through the alphabet. It's a great way to learn someone's name.

What about greeting someone with a disability? I often extend my hand. It's a gesture saying, "You're welcome to shake my hand," but a lot of people draw back. Other people go through physical gymnastics trying to intertwine their hands around mine in a classic handshake. Don't even worry about doing all of that. Do what you normally do with any person. If you usually shake hands, then reach out and shake an elbow or touch my wrist or squeeze my shoulder gently. Just bridge the distance.

If somebody is deaf and you do not know sign language, a smile communicates so much. Have good eye contact as well. Find a piece of paper and a pencil and jot down a few words of greeting. Then hand the pencil and paper to your deaf friend and let him respond to you.

Feel confident to share the gospel in simple terms with people who have mental impairments. Try to reach them through a medium they can understand. Love them into God's kingdom. God can give us a love like that.

To reach blind people for the Lord Jesus, provide the Bible in Braille or audio-tape. Invite them to your meetings so they can hear the gospel.

The grace of God is so wonderful that he can use a person in a wheelchair to help men and women walk with God; he can use deaf people so that the world can hear the gospel; he can use a blind person so that others may see.

The International Disability Center

For the 650 million people in the world with disabilities, hope is often hard to come by. The International Disability Center, scheduled to open in September of 2006, will enable Joni and Friends to serve as a beacon of hope and encouragement for the world's disabled population for generations to come.

With poverty, divorce, suicide, and unemployment ranking highest among the disabled, the need remains staggering. God has raised up Joni and Friends for such a purpose. Twenty-five years of ministry has yielded enormous impact, with thousands upon thousands of lives touched and changed. The need remains great.

The Center, located in Augora Hills, California, will also house The Christian Institute on Disability, offering a biblical response to critical issues that affect the disabled community (for example, bioethics, euthanasia, abortion). The Center will also develop disability curriculum, offer training, and provide internships, fellowships, and scholarships to students at Christian institutions of higher learning.

59

The Homeless

Sharing an Uplifting Message with the Downtrodden

Tony Cooper

Like other people groups, the homeless have their unique characteristics. Homelessness is a very complex issue with a number of major contributing factors: substance abuse, unemployment, underemployment, lack of affordable housing, lack of adequate transportation, health issues, divorce, death of a spouse or family member, mental health needs, self-esteem issues, economic pressures, and various other problems.

The great majority of those that find themselves homeless are homeless by chance not homeless by choice. Their plight was neither their intent nor their fault. Usually an overwhelming event over which they had no control touched their life. The majority of the homeless are basically no different from the average person except they are without a home, job, or close family.

Homelessness will eventually take its toll on an individual and will affect the total person physically, psychologically, and spiritually. That is the reason the remedy to homelessness has to have the ability to touch and reach the total person.

I believe homeless people are our modern-day outcasts, along with those who are HIV positive or who have AIDS. There are certainly many misperceptions and much misunderstanding regarding homelessness, which cause many to be prejudiced toward those struggling and suffering with homelessness. Many are apprehensive or even fearful when coming in contact with homeless people.

In my twenty years of working directly with the homeless, I've discovered there is no reason to be afraid or even apprehensive; there is a need for correct information and education. For example, the majority of the homeless are local people not transients. They come from our own communities and neighborhoods. The average age is approximately thirty-five, showing that people are becoming homeless at much younger ages than in the past. Approximately 30 percent are military veterans, men and women who have served our country. We are seeing more homeless families, primarily women and children. They make up the fastest growing population of new homeless. A large number of the homeless hold jobs. They are a part of the working poor. The homeless are us—men, women, and children who are hurting, suffering, and struggling with life's challenges.

So how do we minister to them? We share the gospel with them just as we do with anyone else. Romans 1:16 says "the gospel . . . is the power of God for the salvation of everyone who believes." In my opinion, not only is Luke 4:18 referring to Jesus's ministry and the work of the church, it is describing those struggling with homelessness. Jesus said he was anointed to "preach the gospel to the *poor*"; he was sent to "heal the *brokenhearted*, to preach deliverance to the *captives* and recovery of sight to the *blind*, to set at liberty those who are *oppressed*" (NKJV).

I realize God loves everybody and that salvation can reach any person who believes and receives. However, I believe Jesus went out of his way for the outcast, the destitute, and the untouchable. Some examples are the Samaritan woman at the well, the leper whom Jesus touched and healed, the man by the pool of Bethesda, the Gadarene demoniacs, and Zacchaeus. Jesus always had time and concern for the poor in spirit. If we are going to effectively share our faith and minister to the homeless, there are some things we need to understand.

Calling

As Christians we all are called by God to evangelize. The Great Commission tells us that. We do have a responsibility to communicate our faith and to let our light shine. However, to be effective I believe we need some divine direction toward homeless people. Even though in the beginning most of us will be naive and uneducated about how to deal with the homeless, we still need an internal motivation and sympathy for their situation and a strong desire to help them.

Compassion

Like Jesus, we must have compassion for hurting people. Compassion is similar to empathy. It causes us to hurt *with* people, not just feel sorry *for* them. Compassion will help us look beyond their faults and see their need. They need Jesus Christ in their lives just like everyone else.

Compassion is a by-product of agape love. This is God's love that causes us to have an unselfish concern for the welfare of another, to have unconditional positive regard for another.

But even agape love is at times tough love. Especially in ministering to the homeless, we should not be concerned about being unable to meet every need or answer every request. *No* is a good word when necessary. It doesn't mean "I don't care"; it means either "I can't" or "I'm not able to" or "that's not something I'm comfortable with."

Commitment

As Christians we should always be committed to whatever we do. Ministering to the homeless is no different. Commitment is necessary, especially when disappointment comes. Any time we deal with people, disappointment will follow. Sharing the gospel with the homeless can be exciting and challenging—exciting when you see people respond to the message and challenging because most homeless people do not immediately respond and some never do.

It has been said we are not called to be successful, just faithful. It is disappointing when people do not take advantage of the hope and help that God offers. When people reject the life-changing power of the gospel, we may become discouraged and disheartened. However, when they respond and a new life begins, all our disappointment and discouragement of the past changes to joy. Commitment gives birth to discipling, dedication, and determination. These are necessary ingredients of the Christian life and will benefit us as we share our faith.

Clear Communication

We must communicate the gospel message clearly and simply. This message is the same for all, whether they are down and out or up and out. The economic and social status of the hearer makes no difference. The ground is level at the foot of the cross. All of us need to accept Jesus Christ as our Lord and Savior by faith.

In sharing our faith with the homeless, we should not get sidetracked by their secondary needs. Yes, we must be concerned about their physical needs, and we should do what we can to address those. The best way to help them is to get involved with a ministry that is set up to minister to the homeless. Then we can direct the homeless or take them to a shelter that is capable of meeting their basic needs. However, we must always remember that their primary need is spiritual—help and hope that begins on the inside. The power of the gospel is the only thing that can transform a life. Second Corinthians 5:17 says, "If anyone is in Christ, he is a new creation; the old has gone, the new has come!"

Proper Understanding

In being a witness to the homeless, we must certainly be sincere, just not naive. We must understand that we cannot solve all of their problems or fix their hurts, but we can point them to an all-powerful God who is the Great Physician.

The homeless are survivors. They have had to adjust and at times be creative just to survive. Unfortunately, some have learned how to be manipulators, especially those that are struggling with substance abuse. Some have also learned that guilt can be used to motivate people to help. Also many homeless know that appealing to one's sense of compassion or sympathy works well. One example is the signs that say, "Will work for food." Most of these appeals are not genuine. Many have "hard luck" stories or believable reasons why they need money. For the majority, money is not what they really need. They need a changed life. I am not saying to always be suspicious, callous, or totally unbelieving. What I am saying is to be *cautious*—"Be as shrewd as snakes and as innocent as doves" (Matt. 10:16).

Maintaining emotional distance is a must as we minister to the homeless. Compassion is a must, but we can care for a person and be willing to help without assuming responsibility for him. I know this is hard to do, but it is necessary. This is similar to a counseling principle that says a counselor should not assume responsibility for the client or for how she responds to counseling.

We must continue to be patient and never give up on people. Many will not respond immediately. For some, a decision may take years, and others may never receive God's love. However, our responsibility is to continue to sow the seed because some will fall on good soil, and homeless people make up some of the good soil.

Remember, while Jesus was on earth as an adult, he referred to himself as being homeless. He says, "Foxes have holes and birds of the air have nests, but the Son of Man has no place to lay his head" (Luke 9:58). Also in Matthew 25:35–36, 40 he says, "I was hungry and you gave me something to eat, I was thirsty and you gave me something to drink, I was a stranger and you invited me in, I needed clothes and you clothed me. . . . Whatever you did for one of the least of these brothers of mine, you did for me."

When we share our faith with homeless people, it is imperative that we realize they are *people* that are temporarily without a home of their own. They are people who are hurting and struggling and desperately need to experience the love of God and the life-changing power of the gospel.

60

Millennials

*Confronting the Millennial Generation
and Extreme Sports Youth with the Gospel*

Paul Anderson

I believe it's going to take the clear, confrontational gospel to reach the hearts of youth in the millennial generation.[1]

Most of them have grown up in broken homes. We surveyed the junior high and high school skateboarders who come to our church, and close to three out of four have parents who are divorced. Ninety to ninety-five percent do not come from a Christian home.

These kids are being raised by television, videos, music, and MTV, which teach them all the wrong ideas about who God is and what morality, truth, and love are. The only representation of Christianity they see comes from watching the religion channel with people promising healing and forgiveness if the viewer sends in one hundred dollars. Millennials think it's a total joke.

They also hear Christians being bashed by the media for standing up for moral issues. Very few people have ever explained to them how awesome Jesus is.

The kids who come to Skatechurch, like many of the millennial generation, don't trust authority. They don't trust adults because many of their parents have not been trustworthy. More than one out of five girls in our culture has been sexually abused, often by a parent, relative, or "trusted" family friend.

Why am I motivated to preach the gospel to them? When I was a kid, my mom was an alcoholic who yelled at us every day. She yelled my dad out of the house.

One of the saddest days of my life was when I was twelve and I saw my dad drive away, never to live with us again.

I poured my life into skateboarding—the dress, the lingo, the tricks—so somebody would say, "Hey, you're cool." Skating, alcohol, vandalizing my neighbors' houses, stealing wood to build skateboard ramps—it all went together. My best friend, Clint Bidleman, and I became top freestyle competitors in San Luis Obispo, California.

For me to hear the gospel, the Lord had to bring people into my life who were obnoxious and bold. For instance, when I was almost seventeen, I went to a beach party to get drunk and heard the gospel from a preacher with a megaphone. "Jesus loves you guys," he shouted. My friends cranked up the volume on AC/DC's "Highway to Hell." I remember the contrast between the song and what he said, but I was afraid my friends would think I was a geek if I talked to him.

How can we reach the millennial generation and its extreme sports culture?

Be Bold

Some people think you should take the soft sell approach. Be their buddy first and earn the right to be heard. That's not in the Bible, that's Dale Carnegie—how to win friends and influence people. When you speak to people with boldness and confidence in the truth, they listen.

In the Bible the apostles were bold with people they had never met. Jesus was bold with people he'd never talked to, like the woman at the well. In thirty-seven seconds, if you go by the dialogue, he told her of eternal life and talked to her about her sin. The lady went away believing and began sharing her powerful testimony in her city (John 4:1–42).

We do Christianity a disservice when we are shy about proclaiming the gospel. These kids need to know now. They might go out this weekend and overdose on drugs or die in a car accident.

Be Authentic

This generation doesn't want a packaged three-step plan. They're looking for something that's real. They need to see the zeal for Christ that we have in our lives, because we fell in love with Jesus and can't help telling people about him. God has already put eternity in their hearts (Eccles. 3:11). They have by creation what Pascal called a God-shaped vacuum, which beyond the superficial, only God can fill.

We had a pastor's kid who had heard the gospel his whole life and was faking the Christian life, going to Bible study, but at the same time smoking pot with his high school friends. One day someone from Skatechurch broke off the gospel to him and he got it and gave his life to Christ. He ended up going to Bible college, receiving the highest score in the school on the Bible knowledge exam, teaching Bible study methods at the college, and later teaching biblical Hebrew at a local seminary.

These kids are zealous. The same zeal they have for skateboarding or being rebels or whatever else they're into is the zeal they can have when they receive Jesus Christ into their souls.

Care about Their Soul's Eternal Destiny

Do we really believe the following passage from Romans is true?

"WHOEVER WILL CALL ON THE NAME OF THE LORD WILL BE SAVED." How then will they call on Him in whom they have not believed? How will they believe in Him whom they have not heard? And how will they hear without a preacher? How will they preach unless they are sent? Just as it is written, "HOW BEAUTIFUL ARE THE FEET OF THOSE WHO BRING GOOD NEWS OF GOOD THINGS!"

However, they did not all heed the good news; for Isaiah says, "LORD, WHO HAS BELIEVED OUR REPORT?" So faith comes from hearing, and hearing by the word of Christ.

Romans 10:13–17 NASB

Do we believe in hell?

We live in temporal reality more than we live in eternity's scope. We don't believe life is transient. "Surely every man at his best is a mere breath. Surely every man walks about as a phantom" (Ps. 39:5–6 NASB). We think we are not supposed to tell Millennials about Christ because we might offend them. If we fear man more than we fear God, it may mean that some young person doesn't hear about eternal life.

Be a Friend of Sinners

It's the same as it was when Jesus Christ walked the earth. It will be the same three thousand years from now, if he doesn't come back sooner. You have to meet sinners where they are. Jesus was a friend of tax gatherers and sinners. He went to Zacchaeus's house. The apostle Paul didn't compromise the gospel; he related to people. He purposely made it a point to try to enter the world of their thoughts and lives so he could communicate the gospel.

There are two components that have to be present for evangelism to take place: The *gospel* needs to be *presented*, and the gospel needs to be presented *to unbelievers*. Without both it is not evangelism. Just hanging out with unbelievers is not evangelism and neither is preaching to the choir.

We don't have to compromise the gospel. Every one of us is engaged with nonbelievers in some way. It's often the natural web of relationships. I am a skateboarder, so it's just natural for me to proclaim the gospel to skaters.

When I came to Christ, I was a big-mouthed, skate-ramp-building skateboarder, and God used me to build ramps, skate with kids, and open my big mouth and preach.

Be Urgent

We should say, "Dude, this is the truth. You need this. You're going to hell without this." Something that happened in 1991 changed my perspective on the way I care about these kids and the way I speak to them.

One kid who came to Skatechurch just sat there and listened like a lot of kids do. Two weeks later, I read about him in the newspaper. He got high on drugs with a friend and tried to rob a house. The man who lived there found him inside and shot and killed him. I can't stop thinking about that kid—for well over a decade, 24 hours a day, 365 days a year—he's been in hell and he's never getting out. We must be urgent in our message that *today* is the day of salvation (2 Cor. 6:2).

Be Sure Everyone Has Heard

We sometimes have a faulty assumption that everyone's heard the gospel message so we just need to live it. While flying back from the Myrtle Beach Festival, I sat next to a thirteen-year-old on the airplane. I was reading my *Skateboard* magazine and noticed he was very interested in what I was doing, so I pulled out this little tract from my pocket, "Can You Do a 180°?" which speaks in skateboard terms about repentance.

I explained the gospel to Kyle and then asked, "Dude, have you ever heard that before?" He said, "No." He'd even been in a youth group and never heard it. I told him, "You can pray the prayer on the back of the tract if you truly want to turn from your sin. Do you want to do that, Kyle?"

Here was a thirteen-year-old kid in America who didn't know Jesus lived, died, and rose again on his behalf or that *he* could know him. Kyle accepted Christ as his Savior.

There's no promise that everyone will be saved. But the Bible does promise that the gospel is the power of God for the salvation of everyone who believes (Rom. 1:16). It is interesting to me that so many who are passionate to see God unleash his power on a sin-wrecked world are looking everywhere for the key. The Bible says the key is the gospel. God's power can be unleashed to save people through the spoken Word of God. This fact is seen in many New Testament letters (see Rom. 1:16–17; 10:17; 1 Cor. 1:21–24; Eph. 1:13; James 1:18; 1 Pet. 1:23).

There are still people out there who haven't heard the gospel. They need to know Jesus is awesome and that his story is good news for their lives.

61

The Affluent

Some Things Money Can't Buy

Scott Dawson

There is a certain awe surrounding people who have wealth. Power, prestige, and position seem to reside with a rich person. The Donald Trumps, the Bill Gateses, and the Oprah Winfreys of our day seem to have it all. Or do they? Wealth is a finicky asset. It can be here today and gone tomorrow.

According to *Forbes* magazine, which has listed the top 400 wealthiest Americans annually since 1982, "Only 58 individuals on that 1982 list have appeared on all subsequent rosters. Thirteen percent of the 1982 list came from just three families: 11 Hunts, 14 Rockefellers, and 28 DuPonts. In 2002 the list included only 1 Hunt, 3 Rockefellers, and 0 DuPonts."[1]

When we look into the life of a wealthy individual, we see the same search as we would see in the life of someone with little money—the search for *peace*. It is amazing that we can smash an atom and explore Mars, but we are not able to achieve personal peace. In a country that has been so blessed by wealth, we have not understood that money cannot buy peace. This is an important point to remember when dealing with a person of considerable wealth.

Why is it so hard to see wealthy people come to Christ? Jesus says it is harder for a rich person to go to heaven than for a camel to go through the eye of a needle (Matt. 19:23–24). This is a reference to a gate called "eye of a needle." The camel, with its weird shape and large load, could not maneuver through this entrance. Was Jesus referring to everyone with money? I don't think so. However, he does remind us that it is possible for wealth to consume an individual.

Difficulties in Reaching the Rich

Affluent people are one of the hardest segments of society to reach with the gospel. There are several reasons for this. Here are three:

- *Their wealth has allowed them to build natural barriers.* Having abundant resources in their grasp allows affluent people to escape, avoid, or ignore any confrontation or conversation they do not desire. A friend of mine who was sharing Christ with the CEO of a small company told me how hard it was to actually find the guy! Every time my friend would show up, the CEO would find some way of avoiding the conversation. My friend said he thought the CEO had someone on the payroll just to intercept any uncomfortable situations. The affluent can afford to use such interference for anything they want to avoid.

- *Most affluent individuals are like politicians.* They are used to everyone wanting something. For most Washington politicians each day is divided into fifteen-minute segments, during which they listen constantly to what people want from their office. I do not like to use absolute sentences, so I will say that it is *extremely unlikely* for a person to share Christ with an affluent individual without first developing a relationship. Without the relationship, the individual is always wondering what you want and why you are there.

- *Most affluent people have worked very hard for what is in their possession.* This is not to say wealthy people are stingy or selfish. However, their hard work does relate to great gain. From early on the wealthy person has worked long hours, schemed mega-deals, and used negotiation skills to get ahead. To this person's mindset, the gospel is completely foreign, because the gospel says we cannot work, pay, or achieve anything that is pleasing in God's eyes. Everyone is the same and what we have worked for so long has to be released into the hands of a God we cannot see. Can you imagine the difficulty in this proposition for the wealthy?

Witnessing Tips

For most of us, the only way to look for help is up, but a wealthy person can usually network, buy, or attain advice, help, or even friendship with his great resources. So how do we witness to him? Many wealthy individuals have come to Christ, and I have interviewed several. Some of the similarities in their path to Christ are amazing. Using the acronym *RICH*, standing for *Respect, Inspect, Connect,* and *Him,* I'll tell you what I have learned.

Respect

As we start the process of sharing Christ, the first thing to consider is to *respect* the *individual* not the position, possession, or power. Jesus teaches us to look at the person not the stuff. In each person's life there is a time when the wealth does not matter.

I sat with a gentleman, who is a believer, during his wife's surgery. He is a very wealthy man. He looked at me and said he realized that he could not write a check big enough to solve this situation and that only God could help him.

On her deathbed Jackie Kennedy Onassis asked her family to bring a minister in so she could die in peace. Everyone, rich or poor, needs a Savior. As you share Christ, remember to respect the person.

Inspect

When witnessing to a wealthy individual, you must *inspect* your motives. Consider this: Would you be just as passionate about sharing Christ with this individual if the wealth were not there? Remember, wealthy people are accustomed to everyone wanting something, and the book of James warns us against playing favorites with people because of their wealth. We must be ready to share Christ with everyone, not only those who can help us.

I had a wealthy person ask me why I had never asked him for money. We had known each other for several years, and I had probably won the right to ask for something for the ministry. I responded that as soon as I ask for money, I become another person who wants something from him. He was used to that. However, because of the lines that had never been crossed financially, a trust had developed spiritually.

Connect

We must *connect* with the person of wealth. What attracts this person to you? Here is a newsflash. It is not your charm, beauty, skill, or ambition; it is the love of God. If you have found yourself in a friendship with a wealthy person—or anyone else for that matter—please do not miss this exciting and crucial juncture of evangelism. God has granted you favor in this person's sight. God, who is sovereign, could have picked anyone to deliver his message and he decided on you. With this comes the responsibility of faithfulness. You are not responsible for whether the person receives Christ, but you must be faithful to deliver the message. When faithfulness is in your heart, you won't give up with a first "no" or an awkward moment in the conversation. Faithfulness is about understanding that your life has purpose in Christ.

Him

Finally, we must remember that life is all about *Him*. I struggled with this last letter, trying to find a word that fit. I looked through a dictionary and thesaurus, and finally it hit me—life is not about clever acronyms or alliterations; life is about Jesus Christ. Think about it, and it is glaringly obvious. Life is about knowing Christ!

Wealth is so terribly fragile. One wrong decision, one phone call or meeting, and it can all be gone. When Jesus and his disciples looked out at the crowd that was leaving them because of the "hard words" Jesus had taught, he looked at the disciples and asked if they were going to leave too. Peter responded, "To whom shall we go?" (John 6:68). Who else offers the peace, purpose, and love of Christ? Where else can your friend go to experience life? Nowhere. Life is about Christ.

During your next conversation, look at your friend and share your concern for her. Dismiss any selfish motivation and realize God has placed you there to be light. Above all else, realize that this person is searching for something wealth cannot buy, possessions cannot achieve, and estates cannot inherit! Give her Jesus!

62

The Poor

Seeking to Understand before Seeking to Be Understood

Monroe Free

Poverty is a great divider. Those who have resources and those who do not are typically divided geographically, socially, and even religiously. Most upper middle class and upper class people have to be intentional about knowing anyone who is poor. Thus most people in upper socioeconomic categories do not know anyone who lives in poverty. This leads to profound misunderstanding.

The feelings, perspectives, and experiences of people who are poor are different from those of the rest of society. What is it like to worry daily about how your needs will be met and whether you will be able to feed your child? How must it be to stand in line with tattered clothes, waiting for your food basket? What is it like to feel dependent always? How do these experiences shape you and your faith?

Jesus established the model for answering these questions. He came to us and found understanding through being present with us, seeking to experience life from our perspective. That fact draws us to him and gives credence to his words "I love you."

The most difficult task in ministry to the poor is establishing credibility. The poor have seen a lot of people attempt to do good, but their primary motivation was always meeting their own needs. Helping the poor caused these people to feel better, noble, spiritual, less guilty, or a part of a group. The poor have also seen and heard lots of folks who offered simple answers to complex questions. The poor are not impressed when we come to help until we prove ourselves to be more motivated by an understanding of the poor person's plight than by our own needs.

Many of the poor have learned to survive by reading people, and some can do it quite well. They often can sense when someone is insincere. It never helps to say, "I understand how you feel," because you do not. Asking open-ended questions and actively listening may help. Trying to understand, in a nonjudgmental way, what the poor person experiences, thinks, and feels is important. Being honest about the fact that you do not get it is good. Admitting that your life is different from theirs and that you do not face the same challenges is helpful. Sharing positive responses to the resiliency and courage of the poor person in an authentic way will be accepted.

Once after preaching in a chapel service at a rescue mission, I sat with a young man to talk for a few minutes. I was intentionally trying to evangelize on a personal level, after having done so from the pulpit. Relying on my best training, I asked if he believed God loved him. He responded, "I believe he pities me, but I don't believe he loves me."

My training had not prepared me to respond to those words, but they helped me understand why this man could not receive the most generous offering of the gospel. The problem was that I was in aggressive mode not incarnational mode. I said nothing. Later, as I reflected on that conversation with the homeless man, I wished that I had experienced it before I spoke to the crowd. I would have delivered a message that related to the misunderstanding of God and would not have tried to overcome their resistance to him.

Take Care of Them

Part of expressing an understanding of the poor is helping with their physical needs. When we feed folks who are hungry or shelter them when they have no home, we communicate that we understand what is important to them. When we deliver food to people and step around a hole in their floor to set down the groceries without offering a way to help repair the hole, we may lose credibility. Painting a house or repairing a roof, giving new clothes or school supplies, may put the recipients in a position to say, "These folks understand me."

Nothing establishes credibility like consistency. The gift of showing up regularly cannot be overemphasized. Relationships of trust develop around consistent care and concern. Going once with a fiery message or loads of charity does not have the effect of regular visits over time. The poor suspect anyone who helps sporadically but appreciate those who keep coming back.

Respect Them

The key to evangelizing the poor is having respect for them. The society we live in values people according to their socioeconomic status. Wealth is a sign of hard work, dedication, ingenuity, and, in some places, God's blessing. Often poverty is seen as a sign that these qualities are missing. The poor may begin to believe that themselves, perhaps because they have been told so in overt and covert ways.

Charlie was a poor, homeless, alcoholic man whom I found very intriguing. I helped him get into a treatment program. Then early one morning, I was informed that Charlie had left the program, so I went looking for him. When I found him and said, "Let's go back to the program and start again," he replied, "Preacher, why don't you leave me alone? I am nothing but a worthless ol' drunk." In that moment I realized that Charlie's problem was not that he drank too much, though he did. His problem was that his image of himself was "a worthless ol' drunk," and his behavior was just fulfilling that image.

I had the privilege of being a part of God's radical transformation of a homeless man named Cecil. I wondered what I had said or done that had made a difference in his relationship to God. He said this one day in a letter: "My life changed when I saw that you thought I was a man. When I saw that you thought I was a man, I began to believe that I was a man also."

Poor people need an identity change. Sometimes their self-image blocks their relationship with God. By our communication of respect, we may be a part of that old image cracking and a new one emerging. That may be the deciding factor in their acceptance of the grace Jesus offers, which leads to a radical new image. By our encouragement, kindness, presence, or teaching, we can suggest to them that what they believe about themselves may be wrong. When they look into our eyes and they see reflected back at them a person worthy of respect, then they may believe that, instead of a worthless drunk, they are a King's kid.

Beware . . .

Getting involved in evangelism to the poor the way I have suggested will cause you pain. When you hear their misery and see their struggles, it hurts. Disappointment and failure are parts of the process. Sometimes the fears and experiences of the poor cause issues from our past and present to come to the surface. People of higher socioeconomic categories have to step outside of their comfort zones and sometimes way outside of them. There will be uncomfortable moments, even embarrassing times. Some places where poor people live are dangerous. It takes courage to evangelize the poor.

A starting point in evangelizing the poor may be to work with an existing program and begin slowly. Serve a meal at a shelter and then sit at the table and get to know some of the people who are eating. Go with someone experienced, watch, and learn. Ask a program to help you find a young person with whom you can become a mentor. Start attending a church in a poor area of town. Tell the pastor that you want to learn and be a part of discipling the poor. Go to the poor and be with them where they are and listen until you have gained the credibility to be heard. Then speak with understanding. Look them in the eye, friend to friend, and watch God's radical transformation begin.

63

The Unemployed

Spiritual Counsel and Practical Advice

Luis Palau

Several years ago I was holding a series of meetings in Glasgow, Scotland, and the BBC challenged me about the local employment picture. "We have 24 percent unemployment here," they told me. "Probably a quarter of the people in your audience are unemployed. What do you say to them?"

"I never thought about it," I replied.

"Well, you'd better," they said, "because these people are desperate."

Their challenge forced me to consider what I would say to men and women driven to despair by unemployment. The following counsel comes from my own difficult time of unemployment.

Ideas for Dealing with Unemployment

Some of the following ideas for dealing with unemployment are practical and some are of a more spiritual nature. You probably won't want to impart them all in one encounter with an unemployed individual. Use your spiritual radar to find out what he or she is ready for. Slowly, over time, share the appropriate principles in response to your friend's needs.

Place Your Trust in God

Encourage your unemployed friends to call out to God. Don't be afraid to let them know that if they don't know Christ as their Savior, their situation is actually more desperate than they think! The Bible says, "All have sinned and fall short of the glory of God" (Rom. 3:23) and "The wages of sin is death." But don't stop with the bad news. Let them know the good news: "But the gift of God is eternal life in Christ Jesus our Lord" (6:23).

Invite your friends to trust God right away by inviting Jesus Christ into their heart. The apostle Peter tells us: "Salvation is found in no one else [except Jesus Christ], for there is no other name under heaven given to men by which we must be saved" (Acts 4:12).

Suggest the following prayer of commitment: "Lord, I come before you humbly, in the midst of my heartache and sorrow. Please forgive my sins. Thank you that Jesus died on the cross to cleanse my heart and rose again to give me new eternal life. Thank you that now I can enjoy the sure hope of heaven. Please lead me to a new job where I can tell others about you. I love you, Lord, and will live for you all the days of my life. Amen."

Try to Find God's Purpose for Joblessness

Urge unemployed individuals to accept their circumstances as from the hand of God. Notice I didn't say that they should *blame* God but that they should *accept their circumstances* as if they came from God. There's a big difference.

Tell them about Joseph. Chapters 37 through 50 of Genesis describe a dysfunctional family in which a deadly brew of jealousy, bitterness, and anger eventually bubble over into betrayal and almost murder. Joseph's brothers sell him into slavery, and for several years one calamity after another befalls him. He is falsely accused of rape and unjustly thrown into prison, where he languishes for a long time.

To outside observers, it had to appear that God had deserted Joseph, forgotten him, and discarded him. Yet in his own time the Lord used Joseph's terrible circumstances for a great purpose. At last, after God had elevated him to great power in the land of his captivity, Joseph understood this purpose. When his treacherous (and frightened) brothers returned to him years later, he told them, "You intended to harm me, but God intended it for good" (Gen. 50:20).

Let your friend know that a purpose lies behind everything that touches our lives, and our job is to find that purpose, if possible. If we're suddenly laid off, we can say, "I thought this was a great job, but God knows best. There must be a better thing for me to do than to work for this company. Now I have to find out what that is."

Spend Time Alone with God

Encourage your friends who are out of work to spend time alone with God. Give them a Bible, if they don't have one, and encourage them to read it. Suggest they start with the book of John. They can use a notebook to write down thoughts and questions and then return to you or another believer to discuss them. Encourage them to throw out all other books and set aside thirty minutes, an hour, or more to spend alone with God, keeping an open spirit to whatever he might reveal. Ask them to be open to the "new things" he may want to do in them.

Volunteer for a Service Organization

Suggest that the unemployed spend four hours a day volunteering with a worthy service organization or look for individuals in need to help. Who needs help around the house or in the garden to do a paint job or electrical repairs? Widows and the elderly can often use a helping hand. Tell your friends, "Don't stop working just because you're not being paid for it!"

Start a New Venture

Encourage unemployed individuals to spend another four hours a day looking for work or planning a new venture. Ask your friends who are out of work to do some honest self-evaluation. They should ask, *What retraining do I need? What am I good at? What do I enjoy? What resources do I have? What do people need? How can I meet those needs? To whom can I turn for some creative ideas?*

Plant and Grow

If they have a piece of land, however small, suggest they plant something, whether tomatoes or lettuce or potatoes or beans or whatever. If they don't have a piece of land, tell them to borrow one. Many people would be willing to let them use some land if they just say, "Look, I'm unemployed. I want to plant some vegetables. May I have a corner of your garden?"

In a little while they'll not only have something to eat, they'll also have the satisfaction that only farmers know.

Don't Even Think about Gambling or Barhopping

Instead of creatively investing their limited resources, many people blow them on gambling. Others go to the bar and sit there for hours, drowning their sorrows in alcohol and going home even poorer than when they left. Acknowledge to your friends that unemployment is no fun, but urge them not to make a difficult situation worse by wasting their limited resources on gambling, drinking, or carousing.

Help them out by suggesting alternatives. Invite them frequently to your home. Ask them to go along with you for hiking trips, picnics, football in the park, church activities . . . you get the picture.

A Word of Encouragement

Don't hesitate to recommend that your unemployed friends spend time with God and look for his purpose in their unemployment, even before they're saved.

When people are out of work, they are often more aware of their need for God and more willing to seek him than they would be otherwise. Time spent reading his Word and talking to him about their problems could be the first step toward a personal relationship with him.

Finally, remind your unemployed friends that though they are poor now, they don't have to stay in that condition. People may have abused or hurt them, but they don't have to remain victims. Let them know that this is an exciting opportunity to start not just a new career but a whole new life with Jesus Christ!

64

Outcasts

Reaching the Disenfranchised

Marty Trammell

What can we do to reach out to people who don't seem to fit in? If it is true that, in the past, books and magazines gave us the best insights into the hearts and minds of those with whom we shared Christ, it is perhaps just as true that today's blogs and chat rooms present the best picture of those outside the faith. These are the rooms where the "others" live, where the lost gather, where the lonely speak. This chapter describes how to share Christ with these people—fellow human beings we call the "disenfranchised."

Christ and the Disenfranchised

Christ's conversations with the disenfranchised startle us. Why the God-man with all the answers would wait to hear human questions and answers is provocative. But that's just what he does with the woman at the well. Though he knows immediately the answer to her need, he asks a question, listens, and waits for her to ask of him (John 4:7–9). Why? Perhaps it is because, in knowing all things, he understands that his listening heart will be partly responsible for her healing.

A *Reader's Digest* story tells of a little girl and a single mom who enter a toy store to buy a doll. As the little girl moves down the aisle, she asks her mother what each of the dolls can do. Some of the more expensive dolls walk, talk, sing, or eat. Finally, the little girl picks up a doll the young mother can afford. But when she asks what the doll can do, the mother notices there is no description on the box. Then an idea comes to her. She whispers to her daughter, "Honey, that doll listens." Although the little girl knew nothing about the cost of the other dolls, she chose the one that listened. This story reminds us that in some ways we never grow up, because we still choose people who listen. So do the disenfranchised. Listening is a simple but effective way to share Christ with the lost and lonely "others" in our world.

Becoming an E.A.R.

Most of us have seen these "others" on the talk shows, in the coffeehouses, and in the cubicles where we work. They are the abused, the gender-confused, the convicts, the divorced, and the friendless individuals. They stand out to us, because our culture has left them out. No one seems to hear them, see them, and certainly not touch them. Often these disenfranchised souls long for someone who will listen to their heart. Like the girl in the doll aisle, they are looking for a sign that reads: "This one listens."

It isn't easy to listen to those who have been left out. We must listen to them where they are—in a way that walks us out of our comfort zones—our coffeehouses, our cubicles, our homes. We can do this uncommon work by becoming "all ears." When we listen to people in a way they can understand, they will hear us.

Enter Their World

In his book *Caring Enough to Hear and Be Heard*, David Augsburger explains that for effective listening to take place, we need to learn how to enter the worlds where people live.[1] Entering their world will remove some of the communication barriers and help create an avenue for sharing the gospel. Sometimes entering their world means studying their interests. Attending an event with them, reading a book they recommend, or asking questions about their interests are practical ways to enter their world. Although there will certainly be some subjects and events we should avoid, rarely will these individuals invite us to attend events or read books they know will cause offense.

For example, in witnessing to disenfranchised individuals, I have often found it helpful to use plays from the modern theater. Dramas like *Waiting for Godot* by Samuel Beckett and *Six Characters in Search of an Author* by Luigi Pirandello present the hopelessness of life without God—a hopelessness these "others" know all too well. Like the pages of Ecclesiastes, these plays help us understand the disenfranchised thinker—those who feel the hopelessness of a world without God. Listening to their thoughts about the plays has made it easier for me to pray for them, to see past their habits, and to find bridges we could cross together toward the gospel. I haven't had great success with "praying the prayer" with these individuals, but in every case so far, they are moving closer to, not farther from, the truth.

Entering the worlds these people inhabit won't help us fully understand their hopelessness. It won't always bring them to Christ. But the least it will do is remind them that there is a God who listens, a God whose Good News is the news they need to hear.

Attend to the Meaning behind the Words

"You didn't listen to a thing I said!" How many times do words like these crush a conversation? How many times do they go unsaid and still affect a relationship? We all know what it feels like. When our words are left hanging in the air, we seldom feel like continuing to talk. The disenfranchised are no different. To them our evangelism must seem like a kind of verbal air hockey. Our words fly back and forth but seldom touch even the surface of their thoughts and feelings.

We find it hard to attend to the meaning behind their words, because, frankly, we're a bit put off or even offended by their meanings. But our insistence to speak only about the gospel with them crowds out their desire to connect with us in a solid relationship—one that, at a later date, might include the gospel.

The apostle Paul demonstrates listening for the meaning behind the words. When discussing theology with the philosophers on Mars Hill, Paul paid attention to their ideas. He noticed that they had inscribed "To an unknown God" on an altar there (Acts 17:23). Paul figured out that these philosophers had created the altar so they could avoid offending any remaining god their polytheism had left out. Paul used the altar and a phrase from one of their poets to explain that God is not "far from each one of us" (v. 27) and that "all people everywhere" need "to repent" (v. 30). Attending to the meaning behind their words can help us spot the altars and the phrases the disenfranchised use to convince themselves they do not need God.

Respond to Their Needs

A youth minister friend once told his youth group about the first time he kissed his wife. They were sitting beside a quiet stream when he asked, "Honey, can I kiss you?"

She was silent.

Although he considered the possibility that she didn't want to be kissed, he chose to believe she didn't hear him and asked again, "Honey, can I kiss you?"

Still, she didn't respond. Frustrated and wondering if he had already ruined his chances, he nonetheless was so persistent he asked again, only this time louder, "Honey, can I kiss you?"

She was silent. "Are you deaf?" he pleaded.

"Are you paralyzed?" she laughed.

The point is she wanted him simply to respond to the situation.

Only after we have *entered* a person's world and paid *attention* to the meaning behind their words can we *respond* in a way that ministers to them. (Then we are an E.A.R.) This is when sharing the gospel seems most effective. It is even the model we find crying from the pages of the New Testament. Jesus entered our world, attended to the meaning behind our words, and responded in a breathtaking way to our needs—especially our greatest need—salvation.

Although in the blogs and chat rooms we can learn much about the participants, unfortunately, once they stop writing, we can learn nothing more. The same principle applies to the disenfranchised around us. We must take advantage of the moment. Perhaps if we listen, we can hear them before they move on. Then they will know the only truly Good News: God's forgiveness welcomes them, the disenfranchised, into a family of friends.

Ordinary People by Gender or Sexual Orientation

65

Men

Reaching Men for Christ

Brian Peterson

More men than ever are seeking to connect with God and make sense of their lives—but they may never say so. How do we break through the hard shell?

As a young man in his teens and twenties, Josh was a six-foot, hotheaded, blond-haired maverick. His friends and family kept their distance from this "Tasmanian devil," as even the slightest offense would set Josh ablaze with rage. But all of that changed when he turned thirty. Josh discovered Buddha.

When Josh was a boy, he adopted the Christian beliefs of his family. He tells the story of his Christian roots—and then how everything changed when he announced he was homosexual. After that, what Josh remembers most is a steady stream of preaching from his mother and a comment from his sister that he would burn in hell. Tired of the strife, in 1999 he cut off most contact with his well-meaning family and found acceptance in a support group for students of Buddha.

In his new Buddhist faith, Josh says he no longer feels at odds with God, his rage is gone, and he no longer feels that his creator is distant from him—quite unlike he felt before. "Christianity taught me that God was closer when I behaved a certain way, and farther away when I didn't. I never felt I was good enough to be close to God." If Josh were your friend, what would you do?

Different Men, Same Roots

The true story of Josh's life may seem extreme, but most of us know men in very much the same boat. They may not be considering Buddhism or homosexuality as a lifestyle, but they are on a path of deception or distraction or ambivalence. And many feel quite happy on that path.

Even though some women struggle with these same problems, the numbers are quite different. According to a Barna survey of American adults, 75 percent of women say their faith is very important to them, while only 60 percent of men say the same. And the bottom line is that about 46 percent of women have accepted Christ for salvation, compared with 36 percent of men.

It's interesting, however, that just as many men as women say they are "searching for meaning and purpose in life" (48 and 49 percent, respectively). The stats suggest that men are looking for that deeper life, but it will take a major mind shift for them to seek solutions from a church, a group of Christians, or even from Jesus Christ himself.

The numbers also add up to an obvious conclusion: Reaching men for Christ won't be easy. Patrick Morley, author of *Man in the Mirror*, says it well: "Reaching men is a lot like playing basketball. Getting the job done amid arm-waving opposition is what the game is all about. The natural resistance we encounter in reaching men is part of the game."[1]

So if you and your church are having a hard time reaching men, know this: You're not alone. But giving up is not an option, and just one man turning to Christ can revolutionize an entire church and community. But before we look at how to lead a man to Christ, it's helpful to examine the plight of men in our culture today. What are their pressures, frustrations, and secret thoughts?

What's Bugging Men Today?

Here are some of the issues men are dealing with in the twenty-first century that often make them hard to reach.

- *Men are trapped in the rat race.* The twelve-hour workday shows no signs of slowing. Men are so wiped out by their work and family duties, they rarely have time to confront their spiritual needs. They are literally working themselves to spiritual and physical sickness and death.
- *Men are bored.* Boredom isn't necessarily cured by busyness. Men are bored by the endless list of things they are doing—things they never signed up for in life, things they must do to maintain a standard of living or preserve an image. Men are bored with their churches. They are overcome by the mundane, with no energy to break free.

- *Men are underchallenged to do the things they love.* On the job, men feel economic pressure to stay where they are, even if their dream would carry them to something entirely new. This can be especially true in some Christian settings where men are encouraged to be conservative and always play it safe. Rather than being challenged to live on the edge, to reach for their dreams, they are asked to have patience, to "wait until God speaks" before they make any major moves.
- *Men have lost touch with their masculine core.* Men have been feminized; they have forgotten (or have never known) the unique abilities and perspectives they have as men—and how desperately women and children need them. Men should feel free to act from their masculine nature.
- *Men are falling for the notion that their best years are over.* Our culture worships youth, and often men believe that young people have more value than older people. They sideline themselves from the game at age fifty—right when a synergism of their energy and experience is beginning.
- *Men are trying to be somebody other than themselves.* Too few men have felt the surge of confidence they can have by being themselves, rather than trying to be a copy of somebody else—or trying to live the macho image on today's billboards and commercials.

If the truth were known, nearly all men—including men of strong Christian faith—deal with one or more (or all!) of these issues at some time. And here's how all this connects with evangelism to men: We recognize our common needs and struggles, and we relate to men where they are. When we want to reveal the truth of Christ to other men, it often starts with a no-agenda friendship where trust is built as men talk about their common needs and seek solutions together.

Fortunately, a guy named Gary had somebody in his life who understood friendships, patience, and trust. It ultimately saved his life. Let's look at his story.

Case Study: The Rescue of Gary

From a distance, nobody would have expected problems in Gary's life. He seemed to be a confident and successful businessman and husband. In public he and his wife of eleven years seemed like the perfect match. It took only three years in a Fortune 500 company for Gary to prove his business acumen, and he was quickly promoted into management. Intoxicated by his work, the hours in the office extended later into the evenings, with more travel each month. On the business trips, Gary found himself relaxing more often with a drink, and an old habit of heavy drinking returned.

Being apart from his wife, and with his marriage clearly drifting, Gary still focused on his work. Then came the bomb. One day his wife announced she was no longer in love with him, and she asked for a divorce. She later told Gary about the other man. The pain was more than Gary could bear on his own. He continued drinking and then turned to drugs.

One evening, driving home after work, Gary was pondering what went wrong in his marriage, and he decided he wanted to share the whole story with Emilio, a next-door neighbor and longtime jogging buddy. Emilio had been praying for months for the right time to share his faith, but he had never felt the time was quite right with Gary. When Gary called, Emilio knew it was time. He suggested packing a lunch and hitting a running trail the next Saturday for some talk and exercise.

As they ran that day, Gary poured out his story to Emilio. Before the run was over, Emilio had told a similar story about his own life—and how God had broken through at just the right time. Gary was full of questions about Emilio's "relationship" with God, the claims of Christ, and the simplicity of salvation. Gary thought it over for a while, but within two weeks Emilio led him in a prayer to receive the gift of Christ.

It was too late to save Gary's marriage, but his newfound relationship with God helped him escape the drugs and alcohol. He found a church home and was gradually healing from the pain of his failed marriage as he rested in his salvation and focused on serving the needs of others. Out of his own experience, his own mistakes, Gary is now able to help others toward healing in their relationships.

The Power of a Shared Life

Gary and Emilio experienced the power of a shared life. It is this type of relationship that leads to success with men in evangelism. Respected men's leaders agree unanimously that building long-term relationships is the best way to lead a man to Christ.

When Jack Lewis, minister of education at Tulip Grove Baptist Church in Nashville, was asked why he thought his men's ministry was a success, he said, "We've tried to be a support group. We gather as men to pray for these guys." His church has a men's group of sixty to seventy active members, and they specialize in service evangelism, including disaster relief, monthly breakfasts, handyman's ministry, inner-city missions, feeding programs, and even golf tournaments to benefit ministry for men.

This type of hands-on service builds the trust that's necessary to reach men for Christ. As an example, Jack mentions a man who came to the church after getting a divorce and was fighting drugs and alcohol. The church heaped acceptance on him, and eventually he received Christ. Now he's a teacher and leader in the Sunday school and men's ministry. In fact he ended up leading his ex-wife and her new husband to Christ. "This is a service organization," says Jack, "and it works."

Lay leader Bill Rogers agrees. Even with men who are not yet believers, it seems they respond better if they can also be useful and give of themselves. "What has worked best for us," says Bill, "is when guys get out and work, things like a construction mission, where they take the skills they have and help someone else. There's nothing like working fourteen-hour days and sleeping on the floor of a church somewhere."

Bill, who has been serving at Woodmont Baptist Church in Florence, Alabama, for sixteen years, has watched his congregation double in size, now with fifteen hundred members. "Guys think they can never do evangelism," he says, but they almost always stand corrected when they let it happen naturally in the context of serving others.

Some men's leaders have been surprised how some men, even unbelievers, are much more likely to show up for a work project than a church meeting. Romy Manansala, Missions Division director for the Baptist Convention of New York, said this recently happened in his state when a church sent seventy-five volunteers to the Goodwill Games in Lake Placid. One man, an unbeliever, went to simply lend a hand, but after he had worked side by side with the others, he ended up praying to receive Christ into his life.

Ten Things Men Need

When it comes time to share your faith with a man, it pays to remember a few facts that are generally true about men and what they need. If you already have built the trusting relationship, this is the easier part.

1. *Men need respect.* "If we tell them they are wrong without explaining ourselves, they will feel disrespected," says Sean Taylor, strategist for Adult Mission Education for the North American Mission Board (NAMB). "We come in a position of equality, treating others as greater than ourselves."
2. *Men need space.* Don't expect a man to open up his life too fast, and try not to pry. When sharing your faith, do not push men too hard to make a decision. You don't go to the next step in a relationship until you are let in.
3. *Men need practical steps.* Men are physical by nature; they like to bring things into the physical world. Thus, if a spiritual truth is spoken, the next question from a man is, "What should I do?" "What does it mean practically?"
4. *Men need to process things in their minds first.* Men end up relating emotionally, but it's not the first step. Usually they will gravitate toward intellect and reason. You can also appeal to a man's sense of curiosity. Explore the questions and wonders and mysteries of life together. Don't pretend to be Mr. Know-it-all, but walk alongside your friend in his quest to discover God.
5. *Men need to ask questions.* "Many men have been traumatized by an evangelistic encounter," says Bill Rogers. "They want to know answers to questions

like, What about hypocrites? What about pain? Is Jesus the only way? You gotta take all those questions seriously."

6. *Men need to visualize.* They respond more to seeing than hearing. It comes naturally for most men to speak in word pictures or analogies. When a diagram is helpful to explain a concept, use it.

7. *Men need to see how Christlikeness is connected to excellence and success.* There's greatness at the core of every man, and Christ calls it forth. Show men that becoming a believer isn't just critical for getting to heaven; it's also critical for living on earth. Men want to know that they can become better at every role they have—husband, father, businessman, athlete, neighbor, friend.

8. *Men need to be heard.* It's hard enough to get a guy talking, so if he talks, try not to cut him off. Let him ramble if necessary. Listen to what he is saying. The longer he talks, the more he will drop his guard and speak freely.

9. *Men need to be treated like men.* In general, the church hasn't done much to affirm masculinity. Do you attend a feminized church? If your church is made up primarily of women, ask yourself some hard questions. Is your church somehow scaring off men? In some churches a male visitor might assume that getting a shot of estrogen would make him feel more at home.

10. *Men need a vision.* Guys need the energy that comes from pursuing something big. They need a sense of destiny and significance. Publisher Stephen Strang emphasized this in the March 2001 issue of *New Man* magazine: "Men need a vision and a purpose for their lives. Some would even say that lack of vision and the prevalence of problems like sexual addiction may be connected."[2] It could very well be that men feed their need for adventure with sexual diversions, and so fill the void that the lack of a healthy lifetime goal or vision creates.

Think about an unbelieving male friend that you know. Whether he's deceived, distracted, or just doesn't care about spiritual things, it will take more than a tract to draw him to Christ. We must win his trust, stick with him for the long haul, and treat him like a man.

Keys to Reaching Men

When it comes time to share your faith, keep these tips in mind:

1. *Meet him on his turf.* Don't make him come to a church building if he'd rather not, even if it means doing something *he* wants to do on a Sunday morning.

2. *Connect with the issues on his mind.* Is he worried about his teenage daughter? Concerned about his job? Listen to his concerns, remember them, and ask about them next time you meet, or send him a surprise email in the middle of the day, asking how things are going.

3. *Keep your evangelism simple.* Even the most simpleminded man can understand the salvation message. Trouble is, too many Christians don't know how to make a simple presentation of Christ without getting off track.

4. *Let down your guard first.* Talk about your own failures and weaknesses, and wait for him to feel the freedom to talk about his life. It may not happen right away, and that's fine.

5. *Forget the preaching.* A litany of Scripture is not usually what a man needs. When the chance comes, do it the natural way as Jesus did—making it simple, speaking his language, and waiting for the open door rather than kicking the door open.

6. *Speak in nonreligious terms.* Rather than asking the question, "Have you made Jesus your Savior and Lord?" start by saying, "Are you a man of faith? Do you believe in a God? How would you describe the God that you believe in?" Then, the door may easily open up to the validity of the Bible, the claims of Christ, and the very simple plan of salvation.

7. *Stay away from morbid introspection and endless self-analysis.* God doesn't nitpick us and doesn't expect us to do it to ourselves. He has a much more positive way to draw us naturally to a higher way of living. So when you share your faith, it's better to explore the grand wonders of being a believer: the sense of Christ's power and presence, eternal existence, and peace with God.

8. *Lighten up!* Laugh together, have fun, show your friend just how much fun living can be. Don't try to take the boy out of the man. With Christ as your champion and salvation your certainty, what other posture could be more fitting?

66

Women

Real Friendships and Our Jesus Stories

Martha Wagner

Sura lives a typical life of many women in Uganda. Her husband died of AIDS, and she has several children in her care. Cheryl is an executive for an international software company in Palo Alto, California. Both these women long to be loved, cherished, and valued by those around them. They desire to have a positive impact on their world. Women's circumstances vary greatly, given the culture and family in which they live, but in the deep places of our being, we are all very much alike.

Women are perfect creations of the living God and have the opportunity to return to their Creator through a relationship with Jesus Christ. It is imperative that we begin to offer this relationship in culturally appropriate ways, using methodology that speaks to the heartfelt needs of each woman.

Often today we lack answers to the most basic evangelistic question: How do we connect practically with the needs of ordinary women for the purpose of communicating God's love for them through Jesus Christ?

The Problem

In today's evangelical world, there are many excellent women Bible teachers; they are helping us grow in our faith in Christ. In contrast there are few women speakers or creative people who have a passion to tell the simple good news, clearly and plainly.

One of the strengths of our gender is relationships. Hence, we emphasize friendship evangelism, but do we truly practice this strategy? Because rejection by our peers is often a huge fear, we pass up opportunities to help our friends understand our belief in Jesus as Savior. We avoid jeopardizing our friendships. We are "friends" but not often *real* friends.

We may speak of church and being involved: "Jim and I were at Bible study last night. We have this great group." We avoid giving information about why our group is so significant. Are we really being friends to these people who are dying around us without Jesus? Are we a social club hoping the gospel travels via osmosis?

Let's not fool ourselves. Christian women are failing to evangelize unsaved women. One reason is that we do not cultivate friendships with the unchurched. We have many events for churchwomen. We still do things we did fifty years ago, such as cookie exchanges and mother-daughter teas. Do today's unchurched women see these events as meaningful or cross-cultural? If they attended, would they discover how to become a follower of Jesus or just a member of a Christian women's club?

In one case, as I was asked to close a women's brunch, there was an added request: "Please don't offend anyone." There is a subtle assumption that sharing the Good News will cause problems. I took a chance and shared how to follow Jesus. Seven women made faith decisions that day. It took only five minutes since the speaker had prepared them so well by telling the story of her relationship with Jesus and the victory she had experienced in her life—her Jesus story.

The Possibilities

We are made in the image of God and have a tremendous amount of innate creativity. It is time to utilize all that the Holy Spirit has given us. We need to become the women God intended. We are speakers, writers, vocalists, dancers, actors, visionaries, leaders, managers, and servants of our Creator.

Women are uniquely qualified to minister and to evangelize other women. Titus 2 states that older women are to help the younger in faith and belief (vv. 3–5). This is true in evangelism as well. We know the deep needs in one another's lives. It is time for women to have the courage to rise up and, using all available resources from the Holy Spirit, tell others about their need for faith in Jesus as Savior.

Every woman who believes in Jesus has tremendous potential to expand the kingdom of God. In Acts 2:17–18 Peter quotes the prophet Joel: "I will pour out my Spirit on all people. Your sons and *daughters* will prophesy. . . . Even on my servants, both men and *women*, I will pour out my Spirit in those days." Those days are now! Time is short and people are dying to hear about Jesus. What unique life message has God given to you?

Your Jesus Story

God has given you a life story for the purpose of showing others the victory Jesus has over sin and death. Your story may contain things that you do not want to remember and especially never speak about. However, many need to hear your victory story through your relationship with Jesus. Sharing your story can reap benefits for God's kingdom.

Giving Glory to God

Your story brings glory to God. You are a light on a hill; don't hide your light under a basket. Women are hurting. Physical, emotional, and sexual abuses are common problems. Does your story include any of these? Women long to be loved and cherished. Is Jesus in the process of showing you his great love? He can do the same for other women. Has Jesus done a work of healing in your life? Where would you be without him? Women are lonely and long for friendships. Did becoming a believer provide you with a new set of relationships?

Your personal story may be sad or traumatic. Jesus is capable of bringing to you and to others, through you, a great work of healing and refreshment. It is through Jesus that life can be new.

Building Community

Your story builds community. It is time for us, as Christian women, to step out from behind the facade called "perfect" and share with others who we really are. It takes courage, but when we are real, our friendships are deeper, more loving, and full of compassion for one another. We discover that we are like others. We are all people who have been damaged by the effects of sin and who need Jesus together.

Cindy had five sisters. She was thirteen when drugs became her strategy for survival. For fifteen years she lived through several damaging relationships and searched for spiritual truth. When a friend told her of Jesus, she followed him and found a new life. Jesus is still healing her, but she is a woman of victory. Cindy is a woman full of compassion, one who loves and is loved.

Evangelism

Your story is evangelism. Jesus prayed, "that all of them may be one, Father. . . . May they also be in us so that the world may believe that you have sent me" (John 17:21). Sharing our stories with unchurched friends gives them insight into the community of believers, a community that loves, believes, and cheers each other toward victory. People become hungry and long for the same experience. If we hide and look perfect, our stories never get told, and women cannot identify with us. We do not give them the greatest gift.

God's Greatest Gift

God's greatest gift to us is a relationship with himself made possible through the sacrifice of our Savior Jesus. Our gift to others is also relationship—our relationship with them that opens the way for them to have a relationship with Christ. Here are some important points to remember when reaching out to women.

- *Demonstrate sincere caring.* God sent Jesus to bring his creation back into relationship with him. He sends us to tell others about Jesus, so many can know of the saving hope, love, and compassion of God. We need to be real friends. As we offer relationship with the unchurched women in our lives, they discover relationship with and through Jesus. We are modeling what Jesus gave to us by giving it to them.

- *Utilize the church community.* What can we do to build relationships outside the walls of the church? Unchurched women must feel cared for enough to attend church. People must be met where they are. Discover their life-stage issues. These may include widowhood, divorce, singleness, and loneliness. In each life stage women are struggling with different issues. Young mothers need help parenting. Middle-aged women are dealing with letting their children grow up. The empty-nest women are hurting because the main focus of their lives has changed. Menopause is happening to many! We need help to know how to grow older gracefully.

  Groups that are formed to help meet these needs should be accessible to the unchurched. While these groups provide helpful and practical assistance for the various life stages in women's lives, they can also become entry points for women to hear our Jesus stories and have opportunity to follow him.

- *Create culturally relevant evangelistic opportunities.* I had prayed for years: "How can I effectively communicate the message of Jesus to the women in our culture?" Then, like a thunderbolt, the Holy Sprit gave me a vision for a play. It is funny and contemporary and it utilizes various entertainment media. God is using the play *Better than a Story* to communicate to women how to become followers of Jesus. The play examines the spiritual journeys of women and includes a clear presentation of the gospel. It is one idea from the Holy Spirit. Ask God for his creativity to shine through you.

- *Seek and follow God's direction.* Begin praying about how the Holy Spirit can use you to touch the lives of ordinary women with the Good News of Jesus. You will be surprised! Be prepared to be obedient, for he is worthy of all our efforts, however tiring and exhausting the idea may seem. The Holy Spirit gives us all we need to fulfill his mission.

As the women of the world look to Jesus for life's answers, their families, cities, and nations will be powerfully changed. Let us together go and make disciples of all nations, for he has given us all power and authority in heaven and on earth.

67

Singles

Needing a Savior

David Edwards

The one thing everyone has in common is that we have all been single at one time in our lives. Being single puts us in good company. As far as we know, God is still single and while he was on the earth, Jesus was single too.

Being single is neutral—neither good nor bad. Our lives are the final explanation of what we choose to believe and what we choose to do. Whether we marry or not is only one ingredient in the final explanation of ourselves. Christ stands at the critical crossroads, demanding a decision of each individual that will forever change the physical, mental, and spiritual description that will be the eternal explanation of us all.

Lose the Stereotypes

Not long after the groom carries the bride across the threshold of their home, another threshold is crossed; they both forget what it was like to be single. They look at their still single friends, and before long they begin to think of them with the same stereotypes that others tend to use:

Underachiever—"settled in" or no longer "driven."
Flawed—damaged goods, somehow incomplete.

Unhappy—not about anything in particular, but just unhappy about things in general. They have become crisis-driven.

In a state of sin—Contrary to what many angry preachers say, singleness is *not* a sin.

On the make—All single guys are "hawks," swooping in on the hunt, working the room, and leaving. All single women are "show ponies," advertising that they are on the take.

Social misfits—Not all singles have the people skills of the man living in the cemetery.

There are singles that these labels describe, but it benefits no one to use them. At the same time, there are successful singles that truly love being single. Regardless of the individual degree of success, all singles need to know Christ and the life he offers.

As long as singles are viewed as "abnormal" or "less than" by the evangelist, the message of Christ that is delivered comes to them packaged in an offensive wrapper or label, rather than open and ready for the taking. It is the responsibility of the evangelist to send a clear unwrapped message. He must remember that he is not speaking to caricatures; he is speaking to real people, and they deserve to be treated as such.

Liberate the Strategy of Hope

All singles must find Christ in the midst of their current situation, and God, working on our behalf, is capable of bringing good out of anything. Hope is found not by changing life's situation but by introducing the strategy of hope offered in Christ.

There are four main single-adult life situations:

1. *Never married*—By choice or circumstances, it doesn't matter. People are choosing to remain single longer, at times to pursue personal goals or improved self-discovery. We must communicate to these individuals that they are not *incomplete* without Christ, they are *lost* without Christ. The life Christ offers will give them the value and position they are seeking from the world.
2. *Divorced*—This is an increasing reality in our society. It's the responsibility of the evangelist not to rant about the evils of divorce but to admit that it happens and to offer hope in Christ. At issue is not whether divorce is right or wrong; the issue is the need of the divorced person for the unwavering love of God in Christ Jesus.
3. *Separated*—This can be one of the most uncomfortable places in life. If a couple is still legally married, neither is morally or legally free to pursue

another relationship. Loneliness can be the separated individual's constant companion. We must communicate that Christ identifies with separation. He put aside his heavenly nature and became one with humanity to bring salvation to us. He left the perfection of heaven for a flawed world. He endured the discomfort of loneliness so that we would never have to be truly alone.

4. *Widowed*—All too often, death terminates the life of both the one buried and the one trying to piece together what's left of life. The widowed single is particularly vulnerable, and many widowed singles are open to the loving relationship God offers through Christ. They ache for love down to their soul because they have lost someone whom they can never replace. The unconditional love of God meets them where they are and gives them life again.

Some singles are also single parents—plagued by feelings of fear, inadequacy, and betrayal. When these emotions are allowed to remain unchecked, hopelessness is the result. All single parents wrestle with the best way to handle their feelings. If they fail to respond properly, they run the risk of passing on their emotional immaturity to their children. Christ is the *One* who can introduce them to a new life that will provide them with the hope they crave.

Let the Scripture Speak

Transformation in the lives of singles doesn't originate from our stories and anecdotes, no matter how powerful they may be. The single adult is eternally made over when the truth of Scripture from the pages of the Bible is presented to him in a way that delivers truth to the neediest portions of his life. By retelling the stories of singles found in Scripture, the evangelist becomes more aware of the issues of singleness, and the accounts of these lives will deliver powerful truth that singles can readily understand.

Isaac. He lived at home with his parents until he was forty before he finally married. After he married Rebecca, they had two sons, Jacob and Esau, who became the fathers of two great nations.

Ruth. She didn't close herself off to the possibility for a future even after losing a spouse. She chose to live rather than to allow herself to slowly die of self-imposed pity.

Elijah. He was a man who lived his life fully for God. His life included travel and hardships, and, in the end, he passed on his anointing to another single man, Elisha.

Daniel. He was a man of integrity, intelligence, and leadership. He emerged from the ranks of slavery to serve in the king's court.

Joseph. He never lost his grip on the dream of God. In fact he interpreted the dreams of others in light of God's desire for mankind.

Mary Magdalene. From her sordid past, she was changed into a woman of extravagant worship.

Jesus. He is the ultimate example of a single life and the impact it can have on the world.

Lift Up the Strength of God

No matter how deep our hurts and overwhelming our fears, God wants to be our deliverer. He is our source of strength and will minister to us in every difficulty. This is the message we must convey to singles who struggle with painful life situations.

In Our Shattered Dreams

God brings possibility into hopeless circumstances. He is the life-giver and the freedom-bringer. Nowhere in Scripture does it say that God discounts the possibility for singles to experience complete and abundant life. Instead, the Bible says that God is aware of our needs and moves to meet these needs as we live in agreement with him. Matthew 6:33 (my paraphrase) says, "If you'll make *my* deal *your* deal, then I'll make sure your dreams are fulfilled."

In Our Seclusion

No one is so isolated that God does not see her, love her, and offer his forgiveness to her. Many singles feel segregated from society. Make certain that the only thing they feel from you is the focused attention of God, loving them and calling them to himself.

In Our Suffering

God is not the cause of our suffering. He fights against it. In the midst of pain, he is not our problem; he is our solution. He is not against us; he is for us. Only through the life and death of Christ on the cross are we able to adequately understand the role evil and suffering play in our lives.

Lead Them to a Spiritual Choice

The answer to life's problems does not lie in changing our circumstances. The answer lies in coming to grips with who Christ is and his involvement in our life.

All of life is impacted by the choices we make. This is especially true in our spiritual life. The goal is to lead singles to the place where they are lovingly confronted with the spiritual choice of what they will do with Christ.

By providing events where singles will gather and hear the claims of Christ, we are offering them opportunities to choose to follow him. There are a few important principles we must remember if events for singles are to accomplish the purpose for which they are planned. These events should demand our best efforts so that we create an environment that will facilitate their connectedness with God. Every event that is effective has the same three elements:

1. *It must be real.* It can't be anything contrived or silly, for example karaoke, reenactments of *Fear Factor*, and so on. Singles enjoy dinner and a movie, sporting events, and concerts. Today a popular activity is going to a coffeehouse where there is music, games, and sometimes a guest comedian.
2. *It must be relevant.* It has to address some kind of need in the single's life. There has to be some kind of payoff, such as making friends or feeling accepted by a group, for him to sacrifice other plans to come to your event.
3. *It must be relational.* There must always be the opportunity to form friendships with other single adults.

Communicating the truth of Christ to singles is not the most difficult task we will ever undertake, but it does require that we see them exactly as God sees them. First, they are in need of Christ, and then they are single. When the message we communicate follows this order, many single adults will be reached for Christ.

68

Homosexuals

Sharing the Gospel with Those We Don't Understand

Robert and Shay Roop

Christian psychiatrist John White, in his book *Eros Defiled*, writes that "a homosexual act is one designed to produce sexual pleasure between members of the same sex. A homosexual is a man or woman who engages in homosexual acts." This puts the emphasis on behavior rather than on people.

There are three types of homosexuals. Overt homosexuals engage in sexual acts, latent homosexuals have a same-sex attraction but do not act on that attraction, and circumstantial homosexuals engage temporarily in homosexual behavior because opposite sex partners are not available. Homosexuals are diverse, they come from all ages, professions, socioeconomic levels, and church denominations, and most often they do not fit the typical stereotype.[1]

The Causes of Homosexuality

There is no scientific proof of an identifiable cause of homosexuality. It may be that homosexuality is neither inherited nor the result of physiological abnormalities. For our purposes in evangelism, uncovering the cause of homosexuality should not be our focus. Jesus didn't ask the thief on the cross, "Why or how did you become a thief?" He read the man's heart and forgave him. As mortal evangelists, we are unable to read hearts, judge others, or understand many of our own behaviors. Jesus was clear when he said:

Do not judge, or you too will be judged.

Matthew 7:1

Why do you look at the speck of sawdust in your brother's eye and pay no attention to the plank in your own eye?

Luke 6:41

Be kind and compassionate to one another.

Ephesians 4:32

The Bible and Homosexuality

Fewer than thirteen passages in the Bible mention homosexuality, and it is clearly never approved, but neither is it singled out as being worse than other sins.[2] For example, in Romans 1 the passage condemns people who worship something other than God, but Paul makes no attempt to say here that *only* idolatrous homosexuality is wrong. Instead, he points out that when people don't care about God, he lets them get into all kinds of sinful situations, including overt homosexuality. Every time overt homosexuality is mentioned in the Bible, it is stated in a bad light. But what of latent or covert homosexuality?[3] To be tempted is not sin; it is dwelling on the temptation and engaging in sexual fantasy or lust that becomes sin. This is true with heterosexuals as well as homosexuals.

This is hard to understand if our interests lie in attraction to the opposite sex, but to be an effective witness to a homosexual, we must understand. For some, it's hard to reach out with Christian love to these individuals, but we are called to do just that. It is difficult to accept their perceptions, but we need to look past our own prejudice, as Jesus did when he ate with publicans and sinners (Mark 2:15). Sharing the gospel with homosexuals is complex, but we are called to be messengers of the Good News not judges of others' behavior.

Salvation for All

The picture of salvation is best seen in the crucifixion when the two thieves who hung on either side of Jesus addressed him. One appeared to mock the Savior, calling on him to save himself if he was truly the Son of God. The other, realizing the *truth* of who Jesus was, asked for forgiveness for his life of sin (Luke 23:32–43). This image is essentially a snapshot of all humanity. It was Jesus's presence that let each thief have the opportunity to see himself as needing his intervention. One acknowledged this truth, and the other was in denial, even though death was imminent.

Those who scoff at the concept of sin believe salvation is a dream of fools and that eternal life is an impossible fantasy. They see life as a quest for pleasure, wealth, and survival at any cost, elevating self above God. Then there are those that yearn for God's existence and, once hearing the message of salvation, immediately accept Christ as their Savior and begin applying biblical principles to their lives, based on the conviction of the Holy Spirit. The gospel must fall on all ears for the Great Commission to be fulfilled (Matt. 28:19–20).

Jesus replied only to the thief who asked for forgiveness. He said, "Today you will be with me in paradise" (Luke 23:43). He never spoke specifically of the man's life or required him to list his numerous sins. Jesus recognized the man's real desire for forgiveness and took away his sins, as well as the sins of the world, by his death.

Evangelism versus Counseling

Counseling is a relationship in which one individual seeks to help another person recognize, understand, gain insight into, and resolve his problems. But evangelism is simply telling the message of salvation and allowing the Holy Spirit to convict and bring insight to the person. Evangelism acts simply as a catalyst to awaken conscious awareness of the need for Christ. Too many times in witnessing, we attempt to be the Holy Spirit and do his job for him (John 16:8). The final exchange of eternal life for forgiveness of sin is done in the quietness of the cross between the Holy Spirit and the sinner.

Evangelism and the Homosexual

Jesus excludes no one, and the greatest need of a homosexual is acceptance. Typically homosexuals have experienced a life of feeling different, being separate and not included, and facing scorn and reproach. Their earliest memories may be voices perceived as saying, "You are not worthy of our love and friendship." Jesus's love does not give more value to some sinners than to others.

One of the worst things we can do when witnessing to a homosexual acquaintance is to shame her by suggesting that the sins of homosexuality are worse than other sins. Romans 2:4 says, "God's kindness leads you toward repentance." It would appear then that we are called to be ambassadors of God's kindness and love. When we approach a person with pride or arrogance, we are just the opposite. God wooed us with his kindness and grace. Why would he do less for the homosexual?

Before you attempt to evangelize gay people, you need to evaluate your beliefs and motives. If you have a fear of or disgust for homosexuals, or if you condemn them, you can do more harm for the kingdom of God than good. It is difficult to hide your true feelings, so the lack of genuine concern will come through. Jesus loved sinners and those who were tempted to sin. You may need to evaluate your feelings and beliefs before engaging in this awesome task and pray for the heart of God in this matter.

God holds Christians to a higher level of understanding than other people. He wants us to be the epitome of compassion, empathy, and humility. We are to point *to* the cross not *at* the person. We are to be unassuming and remove all prejudice, fear, and misconceptions from our minds. We need to appreciate that we are no more worthy to receive acceptance from God than the homosexual is.

When we feel called to share the gospel, it is not a license to attack or degrade people. Jesus said to the men who accused the woman caught in adultery, "If any one of you is without sin, let him be the first to throw a stone at her" (John 8:7). We need to be diligent to *pray* for the Holy Spirit's conviction of sin rather than accuse the sinner. Remember it was *Jesus* who said, "Go now and leave your life of sin" (v. 11).

Here are steps to take in witnessing to a homosexual:

1. Pray for wisdom and knowledge, as well as the mind of Christ, before sharing the gospel with homosexuals.
2. Evaluate your own beliefs, prejudices, motives, and attitudes before beginning this work.
3. Educate yourself about the variety of dimensions of homosexuality so as not to begin with stereotypical ideas born of ignorance.
4. Evangelize and share the effects that accepting Christ has had on your own life. Use Scripture, since it is "living and active. Sharper than any double-edged sword . . . it judges the thoughts and attitudes of the heart" (Heb. 4:12).
5. Be prepared for many questions, especially those dealing with the Bible and homosexuality. Try not to get defensive or take things personally.
6. Remember, you are the messenger not the message.
7. If you ask to pray with the individual before leaving, make sure it is a prayer of unconditional love, pointing to God's acceptance of all people. Jesus didn't clean us up before he accepted us. He came down and "while we were still sinners, Christ died for us" (Rom. 5:8).

To find greatness in God's kingdom, we must be servants to the world. We are to go beyond our own perceptions and see lost and hurting people through the eyes of God. We are commanded to share with *all* people the Good News, instead of picking and choosing who we think would be good candidates for salvation. As 1 Samuel 16:7 states, "The Lord does not see as man sees; for man looks at the outward appearance, but the Lord looks at the heart" (NKJV).

Lesbians

A Biblical and Personal Reflection

Brad Harper

The foundation for the Christian life is found in the two commands that Jesus said were the greatest: "Love the Lord your God with all your heart and with all your soul and with all your mind. . . . Love your neighbor as yourself" (Matt. 22:37, 39). Loving our neighbor is not only an act of obedience for the Christian, it is love for God that is a consequence of being loved by God. God's love is transformative, captivating our hearts and moving us toward Christlikeness.

Our response of love for Jesus Christ is no mere rational response to his work on our behalf. Instead, we are in the process of becoming "like him" as he transforms our hearts with his love. In the same way, love for our neighbors is the response of a heart transformed by the love of God.

In answer to the lawyer's question, "Who is my neighbor?" (Luke 10:29), Jesus told the parable of the good Samaritan. Jesus portrays as neighbors two persons separated by centuries of cultural animosity, divergent values, and different perceptions of God. Perhaps the divide between Jew and Samaritan is not too far off from the separation between homosexuals and heterosexuals today.

Homosexuals have spent most of their history in America as a rejected underclass, coming out in the past few decades only to find themselves in a pitched battle for social, civil, and now marital legitimacy. It's interesting that the Samaritan's mercy on his Jewish neighbor does not indicate a coming together of culture, values, or views of God. But his act is illustrative of what Jesus means when he says, "Love your neighbor."

Loving my homosexual neighbor is not merely a command issue, as if God forces us to act nicely toward "disgusting, not-quite-humans." Many evangelical Christians do not see much, if anything, in their homosexual neighbors worthy of their love and praise.

Evangelicals have referred to homosexuals as disgusting perverts who need to repent of their sin and receive Jesus, at which point they would automatically become heterosexual. They have referred to homosexuals in degrading ways, not realizing that there could be someone struggling with homosexuality sitting near them—in church.

I suggest that the biblical answer to the homosexual's lovability, the foundation for neighbor love, is the image of God. In Genesis 9:6 God tells Noah that murder is wrong because it sheds the blood of a being made in his image. And lest we think that God is talking only about obedient persons, we should note that God describes the post-flood human race as evil in every inclination of the heart (8:21).

God makes a clear differentiation between human life and the rest of creation. Humans are sacred, created by God to be in relationship with him and to respond consciously and freely to his direction. The text makes it clear that *every human being* carries this unique value to God, whether or not he is in obedient relationship with him. God's followers must respect and honor the supreme worth of all people.

Created in God's Image

As believers in Jesus Christ, we should see every aspect of God's creation as beautiful and worthy of praise, wherever we find it. If there is reason to praise God for the broken reflection of his nature in the church, then there is also reason to rejoice in the broken, but true, image of God reflected in our neighbors, Christian or non-Christian, gay or straight.

While my lesbian neighbors may not reflect the nature of God in their sexual union, there are many other ways in which they do. My lesbian neighbor, in spite of a damaged sexuality, is infinitely more capable of reflecting the glory of God than any other created thing is.

My neighbors are Sherry and Tara; Tara's sixteen-year-old daughter, Michelle; and their baby boy, Wyatt. Sherry and Tara are lesbian partners, a fact which we were aware of before they moved in two years ago.

My wife and I wondered how we could love our new neighbors. When they moved in, we engaged them in conversation, helped where we could, and treated them like we would anyone else. Over time we found that we enjoyed both talking and working together. For many months the subject of homosexuality never came up. We decided that we would talk about the issue if they wanted to, but that we would not raise it. I prayed that God would give me an opportunity to talk about Christ's love, and that they would bring that up too.

One day I was heading off for a run, and Sherry was out front working. She called to me and asked, "What exactly do you teach at the college?" I told her that I teach Christian theology. She smiled and said, "Oh, I love talking about theology because I'm still trying to find out exactly what my place is in this world." I had prayed for God to open a window, and he opened a garage door.

Sherry and I had a great conversation. She told me of some painful experiences with the church and with a number of individual Christians because of her sexual orientation. I sensed that she was searching for our response to her and Tara. I said, "Sherry, my worldview on homosexuality, the one I get from the Bible, is very different from yours. But the Jesus of the Bible, the one who loves me and gave his life for me, says that I can honor God by loving my neighbor. Sherry, we are so glad you are our neighbors. We want to be part of your lives and want you to be part of ours."

Sherry threw her arms in the air and yelled, "Yes!"

Since that day, we have been in each other's homes. We share food, tools, and yardwork. We have had several conversations about faith and sexuality. I believe they feel safe with us, as we do with them. As a believer in Jesus Christ, I pray that Sherry and Tara, who do not profess faith in Christ, will one day be confronted with both his magnificent love and his absolute lordship. I pray that they will receive his gift of forgiveness and surrender every aspect of their lives to him, including their sexuality.

Loving Our Neighbors

What does it mean for us to love our lesbian neighbors? We should simply love them as we would love anyone: Find needs and meet them, share our goods and homes, rejoice in the good things in their lives, share our stories of life and faith, and affirm God's love for them.

We should neither hide from the issue of homosexuality nor make it a point of the relationship. We should affirm the value of caring, sacrificial relationships. Can I affirm my lesbian neighbor's sexual relationship? No. But I can affirm self-sacrificing love between humans wherever it appears.

We must renounce and speak against all speech that degrades homosexuals as persons. In the church and in public we must reject all conversation that detracts from the fact that lesbians are persons created in God's image, persons he loves. While we must reject the idea that homosexual partnerships are marriages in the biblical sense, we must also be sensitive to social and legal benefits often kept from homosexuals. These are issues where compassion should lead us to address the problem—not by redefining marriage but by changing other laws.

In the case of lesbian neighbors who are non-Christians, we should focus on Jesus, not on homosexuality. The story of the woman caught in adultery in John 8 gives us a clear picture. What all sinners need most is to encounter Jesus, who comes with love and grace. Only after this encounter is sin addressed. The apostle Paul argues that it is the grace of God in Christ, coming without condemnation, which transforms our hearts to desire him and his ways (Romans 8).

In the case of lesbian neighbors who are professing Christians, the Bible does not allow sin to be swept under the rug. We must address the issue with professing Christian neighbors, but we need to do this thoughtfully and carefully, considering the distinction between the local church and individual Christians living in the public sphere. My personal responsibility is not to enforce church discipline. While I may not be able to share local church community with my Christian lesbian neighbor, I will still pray for and with her and welcome her into my home and life.

God's love for me in Christ is both a comforting and a fearful thing. It is, on the one hand, a love that brings a grace greater than all my sin; there is no peace that can match the peace of his even deeper and wider, all-forgiving love. On the other hand, his love is also a fierce love, one that refuses to allow me to make the rules for living a holy life that honors him.

It is this amazing love with which I must love my lesbian neighbor, accepting and rejoicing in her God-blessed personhood. I must also point her to Christ, who calls her to a biblical sexuality, designed by God to be expressed through sexual union and marriage, only between a woman and a man.

70

Discontents

How to Enjoy Being Who You Are

David Edwards

Everywhere I go, I find people who are bitter and unhappy with their life situation. I was speaking at a Thanksgiving banquet for unmarried adults. The church had hired a caterer to bring in a huge buffet. I was in line behind a rather large young woman who was angrily plopping food from the serving dishes onto her plate.

She lifted a large serving spoon of mashed potatoes, slapped them on her plate, and sighed, "Uhhh!" I put some spuds on my plate while she reached for the gravy ladle, lifted it, dunked it into her potatoes to make her own portable gravy lake, put the ladle back and groaned, "Geee!" She looked back at me, and we made brief eye contact. I passed on the gravy but watched her stack up three slices of ham and roast beef while mumbling to me over her shoulder, "Pft, another year come and gone, and I'm still single!"

I've never been known as the Etiquette King, so I said the first thing that popped into my head: "Yea, isn't God good!" After I realized what I had said, I decided I had enough food and left the line with just Jell-O and potatoes on my plate.

It seems wherever people are, they want to be somewhere else. If they're unmarried, they want to be married; if they make eight dollars an hour, they want to make fifteen. If they live at home with no expenses, they want an apartment on their own. Most of the people I meet can be characterized by one word, *discontented*. They have places they would rather be, things they would rather be doing, and people they would rather be doing those things with.

In this chapter, I want to give you some principles you can share with a celibate friend.

Searching for Contentment

I've discovered the reason people are so discontented is that they live with a very small and limited view of life. It's small and limited because it's centered and focused on themselves. Even many of the people who have "made it" by human and worldly standards are discontented because the entire focus of their lives is what they can achieve, how much they can accumulate, and how many people know their name.

Jesus said, "Seek first His kingdom and His righteousness, and all these things will be added to you" (Matt. 6:33 NASB). This verse has been the source of hope for many and the source of trouble for many more. It is my hope that this brief chapter will help you find the truth of this verse to be a hope and an encouragement.

Most people look for contentment in four areas: *emotions*, *things*, *people*, or *opportunities*. The unfortunate reality is that emotions are extremely difficult to manage, things fall apart and are outdated only days after we get them, people are completely unpredictable, and opportunities are more random than finding exactly what you are looking for by clicking the "I'm feeling lucky" Google search button.

If we are going to learn how to enjoy being who we are, we have to *locate our source of contentment*. Satisfaction will never be found in the way we feel, our possessions, our friends or family, or the prospects of our future. We must make the complex choice to live our lives in such a way that these things don't define the value of life for us. This is possible only when we look for our contentment in the life of Christ that God has placed within us.

Our contentment will be either *external*—derived from emotions, things, people, or opportunities—or *internal*—from our intimate connection with the life of Christ. External contentment is at best temporary. Internal contentment is eternal. When we look for satisfaction in the externals, we miss living life in the here and now. We miss out on the life that God has placed immediately in front of us. The result is intensified discontent.

Listening to the Call

Jesus promised contentment: "and all these things will be added to you." But the way to contentment is choosing to live life in a way that the externals don't determine our quality of life. Literally we have to exchange the natural for the unnatural. We have to relocate our source of contentment from feelings, possessions, people, and experiences to the life of Christ.

This relocation is not as difficult as we might imagine. God provides us with a homing signal. All we have to do is listen to the sacred call. This is the call of the life of Christ within us. It is the inside voice we hear telling us what God wants with us, from us, and for us. Regardless of our state in life, the sacred call signals us to order our lives in such a way that we gain an undistracted devotion to the Lord. An undistracted devotion means that we come alongside and stand with the Lord.

Jesus called this seeking first "his kingdom and his righteousness." It's impossible for us to do this if we're focused intently on the externals. His kingdom and righteousness come from the inside out not the outside in. We find them when we listen to his call and order our lives so that we can have undistracted devotion to him.

When we don't listen to the call, there are consequences that begin to show up. One consequence is that the relationships we have with others begin to erode. As a Christian our primary relationship is with Christ. This is the core around which all other relationships are built and maintained. When our primary relationship with Christ is not as it should be, neither are our relationships with other people. We are distracted from our focus on them.

If we don't listen to the call, we will also begin to make bad decisions. We get tired of waiting on Christ for things we want. We may begin to look for Mr. or Ms. Right, and if we can't find him or her, we'll settle for Mr. or Ms. Right Now. We will find ways to meet our own needs, and more often than not this means we make poor decisions.

Another consequence of not listening to the call is we begin to develop a distorted view of God. This skewed view tells us that God exists to meet our needs. And because he's doing such a lousy job of that, we're not going to submit our life to him. The deeper we move into these consequences, the more distant his call becomes. When we find ourselves in this place, we must plead with God: "Let me hear your call."

Our Choice

We don't have to wait until we experience the consequences of not listening to God's call. Before we even get to this point, we can choose to *live by the spirit of choice*. Choosing to live this way is choosing to believe that God is completely aware of our circumstances and conditions and that he is already positively responding to meet these needs, as we remain faithful.

God is aware of everything that touches our lives. He is even aware of the things that may touch our lives. God has never watched in horror as something unexpected happened to us. He has thought through every contingency and is ready for anything we might face. Already he is taking action to meet every future need. Depending on how we respond to the circumstances of life, he is prepared to give us appropriate help.

God never discounts our sexual desires or our longings for intimacy and physical connection. Instead, he asks us to bring these needs to him, fully believing that he knows what is best and is already actively working to provide for us.

The requirement is that we remain faithful. In other words we must trust him to fulfill our needs in his time. This means that we do not take matters into our own hands (yes, I mean exactly what I wrote) but leave them in his. This means that we make the best choices we can while listening to his sacred call. It means that we do these things while finding our contentment in the life of Christ not in the externals that surround us.

We will know when we're doing life the right way because we will be able honestly to say that regardless of our circumstances, we haven't lost hope. We haven't given up on God meeting our needs, and we continue to believe that he is aware of them and already actively working to meet them. We remain faithful to the hope we know to be true.

I can promise you that you'll never regret doing life God's way. I can't promise you that you'll never find yourself wanting to be somewhere you aren't, doing things you aren't doing, with people you'd really like to be with. But I can promise you the same things Jesus promised: "Seek first his kingdom and his righteousness, and all these things will be added to you."

If you know any celibates who are searching for meaning and fulfillment, show them that only God can fill the true void in their hearts.

Reaching a Celibate for Christ

My friend was a genuinely caring person whom I had known for a long time. When the subject of Christ came up, it was very natural for me to explain the idea of a relationship with my friend. However, when I look back on this experience now, I realize my mistake in sharing the gospel. My friend's understanding of *relationship* was very different from my understanding of the term.

It is often by accident that I find through conversation that a person is celibate. When I discover that someone is committed to celibacy, I try to find out the basis for his decision. Is his celibacy due to a personal conviction, a current situation, or the by-product of a relationship that has ended? True celibacy is a strong commitment for an individual to make and, therefore, an indication of the person's ability to dedicate his life to a cause.

We can share Christ with a celibate person on the basis of his being tempted in all things and yet was without sin (Heb. 4:15). Although this person may not have been in a sexual relationship, there is still a sin problem, as there is with everyone. Lust, greed, and pride are all sin in the eyes of God and, therefore, there is a need for Christ. Jesus was a celibate that gives a man or woman the perfect example of how to live.

Finally, celibacy can be the perfect state of absolute devotion to Christ. Revelation

14:4 says, "These are those who did not defile themselves with women, for they kept themselves pure. They follow the Lamb wherever he goes. They were purchased from among men and offered as firstfruits to God and the Lamb." Wherever the Lamb goes, those who are undefiled follow him. This beautiful picture of celibacy allows the individual to see the opportunity that is before her. It allows her to see the call of God as an even higher calling than that of celibacy.

In 1 Corinthians 7:8 Paul instructed, "Now to the unmarried and the widows I say: It is good for them to stay unmarried [celibate], as I am." Paul said this because he knew that if a person surrenders to God and commits to a celibate lifestyle, there are no ties that hinder his service to Christ. Jesus, Paul, and Mother Teresa are all pictures of celibate lives that were used to impact the world and further God's kingdom.

Stuart Walker

Notes

Chapter 3 Know the Difference

1. Victoria Rideout, Donal F. Roberts, and Ulla G. Foehr, comps., *Generation M: Media in the Lives of 8–18 Year-Olds,* (Menlo Park, CA, 2005).

2. Neil Postman, *Amusing Ourselves to Death: Public Discourse in the Age of Show Business* (New York: Penguin, 1985), 103.

3. Ibid., 118.

4. G. K. Chesterton, *Orthodoxy: The Romance of Faith* (New York: Dodd and Mead, 1908).

5. J. R. R. Tolkien, *The Lord of the Rings: The Two Towers* (Houghton Mifflin, 1994), 696.

6. C. S. Lewis, *Mere Christianity* (New York: Macmillan, 1976), 120.

Chapter 9 Everyday Illustrations

1. Mike Silva, *Would You Like Fries with That?* (Dallas: Word, 2005).

Chapter 13 When You Have the Answers

1. C. S. Lewis, *Mere Christianity* (New York: MacMillan, 1960), 40–41.

2. Clark H. Pinnock, *Set Forth Your Case* (New Jersey: Craig Press, 1967), 62.

3. J. T. Fisher, *A Few Buttons Missing* (Philadelphia: Lippincott, 1951), 273.

4. C. S. Lewis, *Miracles: A Preliminary Study* (New York: MacMillan, 1947), 113.

5. Philip Schaff, *The Person of Christ* (New York: American Tract Society, 1913), 97.

Chapter 14 When You Don't Have the Answers

1. Langdon Gilkey, *Naming the Whirlwind* (New York: Bobbs-Merrill, 1969), 181–82.

2. Paul Tournier, *To Understand Each Other* (Atlanta: John Knox, 1976), 8.

3. Ibid., 49.

4. George Seldes, comp., *The Great Quotations* (New York: Pocket Books, 1967), 816.

5. H. S. Vigeveno, *Is It Real?* (Glendale, CA.: Regal, 1971), 6.

6. John Warren Steen, *Conquering Inner Space* (Nashville: Broadman, 1964), 104–6.

Chapter 15 When to Raise New Questions

1. For more information on how to reach unchurched people, see Alvin L. Reid, *Radically Unchurched: Who They Are and How to Reach Them* (Grand Rapids: Kregel, 2002).

Chapter 16 Don't Be Afraid!

1. Stephen Olford, *The Secret of Soul Winning* (Chicago: Moody, 1963), 9–13.

Chapter 17 Spiritual Warfare

1. Samuel Wilson, "Evangelism and Spiritual Warfare," *Journal of the Academy for Evangelism in Theological Education* 10 (1994–95): 39.

2. Exclusivism is the belief that Jesus Christ is the *only* Savior, and explicit faith in him is necessary for

salvation. Pluralism asserts that there are many routes to God. Inclusivism affirms that Jesus is the only way to God, while denying the need for an explicit, personal faith response to him.

3. George Barna, *The Index of Leading Spiritual Indicators* (Dallas: Word, 1996), 72. See also Barna Research Online, 2000.

Chapter 20 Co-workers

1. E. M. Bounds, *Power through Prayer* (Chicago: Moody, 1979), 37.

Chapter 25 Senior Adults

1. D. James Kennedy, *Evangelism Explosion* (Wheaton: Tyndale House, 1996, 75–79.

2. Calvin Miller, *Walking with Saints* (Nashville: Thomas Nelson, 1995), 11–12.

Chapter 27 Youth

1. Jonathan Edwards, "Some Thoughts Concerning the Present Revival of Religion in New England," in *The Works of Jonathan Edwards*, ed. Sereno E. Dwight, vol. 1 (London: Banner of Truth Trust, 1834), 423.

2. George Barna, *Real Teens: A Contemporary Snapshot of Youth Culture* (Ventura, CA: Regal, 2001), 68.

Chapter 30 Athletics

1. Pat Williams, *Ahead of the Game* (Grand Rapids: Revell, 1999).

Chapter 35 Media

1. Speech given by Charles Colson at the National Press Club in Washington, D.C., on March 11, 1993; reprinted in "Crime, Morality, and the Media Ethics," *Christianity Today* (August 16, 1993), 29–32.

2. Cal Thomas, "Meet the Press," *Christian Herald* (September/October 1990), 18.

3. Ibid.

4. Luis Palau, *Calling America and the Nations to Christ* (Nashville: Thomas Nelson, 2005), 108.

Chapter 38 Agnosticism

1. C. S. Lewis, "The Case for Christianity" in *The Best of C. S. Lewis* (1947; reprint Grand Rapids: Baker, 1969), 449.

Chapter 39 Atheism

1. Armand M. Nicholi, *The Question of God* (New York: Free Press, 2002), 84–85.

Chapter 42 Hinduism

1. Paul G. Hiebert, *Missiological Issues in the Encounter with Emerging Hinduism in Missiology: An International Review* 28, no. 1 (2000).

2. Nirad C. Chaudhuri, *Hinduism: A Religion to Live By* (New York: Oxford University Press, 1979).

3. Gavin Flood, *An Introduction to Hinduism* (Cambridge: Cambridge University Press, 1999).

4. V. P. Kantikar and Owen Cole, *Hinduism: Contemporary Books* (Chicago: McGraw-Hill, 1995).

Chapter 43 Judaism

1. Stan Telchin, *Betrayed* (Grand Rapids: Chosen, 1982).

Chapter 47 Cults

1. Walter Martin, *The Kingdom of the Cults* (Minneapolis: Bethany, 1997).

Chapter 52 Native American

1. Richard Twiss, *One Church, Many Tribes* (Ventura, CA: Regal, 2000).

2. Arthur H., *The Grieving Indian* (Indian Life Ministries, 1988); Bruce Brand, *Does the Owl Still Call Your Name?* (Indian Life Ministries, 2000); Dee Brown, *Bury My Heart at Wounded Knee: An Indian History of the American West* (Owl Books, 2001); Gloria Jahoda, *Trail of Tears* (Wings, 1995); John Ehle, *Trail of Tears: The Rise and Fall of the Cherokee Nation* (Anchor, 1997).

3. For information on *Indian Life,* go to http://community.gospelcom.net.

4. For information on "The Creator's Path," go to http://ilm.gospelcom.net.

Chapter 54 International Students

1. Dean C. Halverson, *The Compact Guide to World Religions* (Minneapolis: Bethany, 1996).

2. Tom Phillips and Bob Norsworthy, with Terry Whalin, *The World at Your Door* (Minneapolis: Bethany, 1997).

Chapter 55 Abuse Victims

1. Grant L. Martin, *Counseling for Family Violence and Abuse*, vol. 6 of *Resources for Christian Counseling* (Dallas: Word, 1986), 15.

2. See Diane R. Garland, *Family Ministry: A Comprehensive Guide* (Downer's Grove, IL: InterVarsity, 1999), 594–97.

3. See the chapter "Unrepentant Recovery" in Gary and Carol Tharp Almy, *Addicted to Recovery* (Eugene, OR: Harvest House, 1994), 199–210.

4. Adapted from Susan Weitzman, *"Not to People Like Us": Hidden Abuse in Upscale Marriages* (New York: Basic Books, 2000), 233, 239.

5. Ibid.

6. Ibid.

Chapter 56 Addicts

1. Millard J. Erickson, *Introducing Christian Doctrine* (Grand Rapids: Baker, 1992).

2. Jonathan Edwards, *Christian Pilgrim: Collection of Sermons* (Nashville: Broadman and Holdman, 2004).

3. Oswald Chambers, *My Utmost for His Highest* (Uhrichsville, OH: Barbour, 1935), 255.

4. Jim Berg, *Changed into His Image* (Greenville, SC: BJU Press, 2000).

5. H. Bonar, *Longing for Heaven*.

6. C. S. Lewis, "The Weight of Glory," in *Transposition and Other Addresses* (1949; reprint, New York: Harper Collins, 1980), 21.

Chapter 60 Millennials

1. The millennial generation includes those born between 1977 and 1998.

Chapter 61 The Affluent

1. William P. Barrett, "The March of the 400," *Forbes*, (September 30, 2002), 80.

Chapter 64 Outcasts

1. David W. Augsburger, *Caring Enough to Hear and Be Heard* (Ventura, CA: Regal, 1982).

Chapter 65 Men

1. Patrick M. Morley, *The Man in the Mirror: Solving the Twenty-four Problems Men Face* (Brentwood, TN: Wolgemuth and Hyatt, 1989).

2. Stephen Strang, *New Man* (March 2001),

Chapter 68 Homosexuals

1. John White, *Eros Defiled* (Downers Grove, IL: InterVarsity, 1977), 121.

2. Genesis 19:1–11; Leviticus 18:22; 20:13; Deuteronomy 23:17; Judges 19:22–25; 1 Kings 14:24; 15:12; 22:46; 2 Kings 23:7; Romans 1:25–27; 1 Corinthians 6:9; 1 Timothy 1:9–10.

3. Gary Collins, *Christian Counseling: A Comprehensive Guide* (Waco, TX: Word, 1980), 318–19.

Recommended Reading

Allen, R. Earl. *Prayers That Changed History*. Nashville: Broadman, 1977.

Amsterdam 2000. *The Mission of an Evangelist*. Minneapolis: World Wide Publications, 2001.

Autrey, C. E. *Basic Evangelism*. Grand Rapids: Zondervan, 1970.

Barna, George. *Evangelism That Works: How to Reach Changing Generations with the Unchanging Gospel*. Ventura, CA: Regal, 1995.

Barnhouse, Donald Grey. *Words Fitly Spoken*. Wheaton: Tyndale House, 1969.

Bisagno, John. *How to Build an Evangelistic Church*. Nashville: Convention Press, 1971.

———. *The Power of Positive Evangelism: How to Hold a Revival*. Nashville: Broadman, 1968.

Boice, James Montgomery. *Christ's Call to Discipleship*. Chicago: Moody, 1986.

Bright, Bill. *Five Steps to Sharing Your Faith*. Orlando: New Life Publications, 1996.

Cahill, Mark. *One Thing You Can't Do in Heaven*. Atlanta: Genesis Group, 2002.

Caldwell, Max L. *Witness to Win*. Nashville: Convention Press, 1978.

Campbell, Regi. *About My Father's Business: Taking Your Faith to Work*. Sisters, OR: Multnomah, 2005.

Campolo, Tony, and Gordon Aeschliman. *Fifty Ways You Can Share Your Faith*. Downers Grove, IL: InterVarsity Press, 1992.

Cho, Paul Y. *More than Numbers*. Waco: Word, 1984.

Coleman, Robert E. *The Master Plan of Evangelism*. Grand Rapids: Revell, 1993.

———. *The Mind of the Master*. Old Tappan, NJ: Revell, 1977.

Comfort, Ray, with Kirk Cameron. *Revival's Golden Key*. Gainesville, FL: Bridge-Logos Publishers, 2002.

Covell, Jim and Karen, and Victorya Michaels Rogers. *How to Talk about Jesus without Freaking Out*. Sisters, OR: Multnomah, 2000.

———. *People Sharing Jesus*. Sisters, OR: Multnomah, 2000.

Decker, Ed. *Mormonism: What You Need to Know*. Eugene, OR: Harvest House, 1997.

Drummond, Lewis A. *The Word of the Cross: A Contemporary Theology of Evangelism*. Nashville: Broadman, 1992.

Drummond, Lewis A., and Paul Baxter. *How to Respond to a Skeptic*. Chicago: Moody, 1986.

Edwards, Gene. *How to Have a Soul Winning Church*. Tyler Soul Winning Publications, 1962.

Felter, David J. *Evangelism in Everyday Life*. Kansas City: Beacon Hill Press, 1998.

Hall, Mera Cannon. *Adults Learning to Witness*. Nashville: The Sunday School Board of the Southern Baptist Convention, 1962.

Havlik, John F. *The Evangelistic Church*. Nashville: Convention Press, 1976.

Hession, Roy. *The Way of the Cross*. Fort Washington, PA: Christian Literature Crusade, 1973.

Hybels, Bill, and Mark Mittelberg. *Becoming a Contagious Christian*. Grand Rapids: Zondervan, 1994.

James, Edgar C. *Day of the Lamb*. Wheaton: Victor, 1981.

Kennedy, D. James. *Evangelism Explosion*. Wheaton: Tyndale House, 1996.

Laurie, Greg. *How to Share Your Faith*. Wheaton: Tyndale House, 1999.

Little, Paul E. *Know Why You Believe*. Downers Grove, IL: InterVarsity, 1970.

Lovett, C. S. *Dealing with the Devil*. Baldwin Park, CA: Personal Christianity Chapel, 1979.

———. *Soul-Winning Made Easy*. Baldwin Park, CA: Personal Christianity Chapel, 1984.

Mann, A. Chester. *Moody Winner of Souls*. Grand Rapids: Zondervan, 1936.

McCallum, Dennis. *Christianity: The Faith That Makes Sense*. Wheaton: Tyndale House, 1992.

McCloskey, Mark. *Tell It Often—Tell It Well*. Grand Rapids: Revell, 1993.

McDowell, Josh. *More than a Carpenter*. Wheaton: Tyndale House, 1977.

Miles, Delos. *Introduction to Evangelism*. Nashville: Broadman, 1983.

Moore, Waylon B. *New Testament Follow-Up*. Grand Rapids: Eerdmans, 1963.

Nichols, Roger B. *Dare We Obey?* Cincinnati: Forward Movement Publications, 1968.

Nystrom, Carolyn. *Sharing Your Faith*. Grand Rapids: Zondervan, 1992.

Olford, Stephen F. *The Secret of Soul-Winning*. Chicago: Moody, 1963.

Owens, Daniel. *Sharing Christ When You Feel You Can't*. Wheaton: Crossway, 1997.

Packer, J. I. *Evangelism and the Sovereignty of God*. Downers Grove, IL: InterVarsity, 1991.

Palau, Luis. *The Only Hope for America*. Wheaton: Crossway, 1996.

Ponder, James A. *Motivating Laymen to Witness*. Nashville: Broadman, 1974.

Powell, Paul W. *Building an Evangelistic Church*. Dallas: Annuity Board of the Southern Baptist Convention, 1991.

Rainer, Thom S. *Surprising Insights from the Unchurched and Proven Ways to Reach Them*. Grand Rapids: Zondervan, 2001.

Rhodes, Ron. *Islam: What You Need to Know*. Eugene, OR: Harvest House, 2000.

———. *Jehovah's Witnesses: What You Need to Know*. Eugene, OR: Harvest House, 1997.

Rice, John R. *The Soul-Winner's Fire*. Wheaton: Sword of the Lord Publishers, 1941.

Robinson, Darrell W. *People Sharing Jesus*. Nashville: Thomas Nelson, 1995.

Robinson, John A. T. *Honest to God*. Philadelphia: Westminster Press, 1963.

Ryrie, Charles C. *The Final Countdown*. Wheaton: Victor, 1982.

Samuel, Leith. *Share Your Faith*. Grand Rapids: Baker, 1981.

Sanders, J. Oswald. *The Divine Art of Soul-Winning*. Chicago: Moody, 1950.

Sanderson, Leonard. *Personal Soul-Winning*. Nashville: Convention Press, 1958.

Schaeffer, Francis A. *The God Who Is There*. Downers Grove, IL: InterVarsity, 1968.

———. *True Spirituality*. Wheaton: Tyndale House, 1977.

Schuller, Robert H. *Reaching Out for New Life*. New York: Hawthorn, 1977.

Scroggie, W. Graham. *Is the Bible the Word of God?* Chicago: Moody, 1922.

Sproul, R. C. *Reason to Believe*. Grand Rapids: Zondervan, 1982.

Spurgeon, C. H. *Soul-Winner: How to Lead Sinners to the Savior*. 1963. Reprint, Grand Rapids: Eerdmans, 1995.

Stebbins, Tom. *Evangelism by the Book*. Camp Hill, PA: Christian Publications, 1991.

Stoner, Peter W. *Science Speaks*. Chicago: Moody, 1969.

Sweazey, George E. *Effective Evangelism: The Greatest Work in the World*. New York: Harper and Row, 1953.

Sweeting, George. *How to Witness Successfully.* Chicago: Moody, 1979.

Thompson, W. Oscar, Jr., with Carolyn Thompson. *Concentric Circles of Concern.* Nashville: Broadman, 1981.

Tozer, A. W. *That Incredible Christian.* Harrisburg, PA: Christian Publications, 1977.

Truett, George W. *A Quest for Souls.* New York: Harper, 1945.

Warren, Rick. *The Purpose-Driven Life.* Grand Rapids: Zondervan, 2002.

Washburn, A. V. *Outreach for the Unreached.* Nashville: Convention Press, 1960.

White, Perry E. *Office Christianity.* Nashville: Broadman, 1990.

Wiersbe, Warren W. *Sermons of the Century.* Grand Rapids: Baker, 2000.

Wilson, Bill. *The Best of Josh McDowell: A Ready Defense.* Nashville, Thomas Nelson, 1993.

Winter, Ralph D., and Steven C. Hawthorne. *Perspectives on the World Christian Movement.* Pasadena: William Carey Library, 1999.

Wood, Fred M. *Great Questions of the Bible.* Nashville: Broadman, 1977.

Worrell, George E. *How to Take the Worry out of Witnessing.* Nashville: Broadman, 1976.

Free Online Resources

Imagine a single place where a seeker could . . .

- Go to learn about the gospel of Jesus Christ
- Find answers to the hard questions about salvation he or she has never been able to get satisfactorily answered
- Review a database of testimonies to find how individuals with similar interests or backgrounds came to know Jesus Christ
- Find a comprehensive calendar of upcoming seminars, festivals, and crusades
- Participate in chats with guest experts who can answer tough questions

Imagine a single place where a *Christian* could . . .

- Go to learn how to witness in any given situation
- Find answers to almost any question a seeker may have about Jesus Christ
- Find practical advice and ideas on how to transition a conversation or situation from the secular to the spiritual
- Sign up to share his or her faith on a weekly basis and be provided the inspiration, tools, and support to hold him or her accountable
- Go to find the most current, comprehensive resource center for world evangelism
- Get all the resources his or her church needs to learn how to educate, equip, and inspire its membership to share their faith
- Create innovative incentives to challenge their membership to share their faith and have the results automatically tracked and reported
- Find a comprehensive calendar of upcoming conferences, festivals, crusades, and seminars on evangelism
- Personalize resources and customize them to his or her specific needs

There is such a place: **Sharingthefaith .com!**

This unique website's "Testimony Builder" will enable you to learn how to share your faith through an interactive online experience. Afterward, you will be able to email your testimony to friends and family, followed by a clear, winsome explanation of the gospel message and an opportunity for the recipient to trust Jesus Christ. Individuals who trust Christ and respond to your email will receive immediate follow-up care. Imagine the potential results!

Be sure to visit **Sharingthefaith.com** today!

Contributors

Lon Allison is the director of the Billy Graham Center and is an associate professor of evangelism at Wheaton College. You can learn more at www.wheaton.edu.

Paul Anderson, a skater since age eleven, grew up in the San Luis Obispo, California, skate culture in the late 1970s and early 80s. He trusted in Christ when he was seventeen. In 1987 he and his best friend, Clint Bidleman founded Skatechurch in the parking lot of Central Bible Church in Portland, Oregon. A building was completed and dedicated in 1996. Skatechurch's current eleven thousand square feet of indoor skating area include a mini-ramp and two street courses with multiple ledges, launches, quarter-pipes, banks, euro-gaps, and hand-rails. Approximately ten thousand skaters in the greater Portland area have heard the gospel through Skatechurch, and more than one thousand people have claimed Christ as Savior and Lord. You can learn more at www.skatechurch.net. For more information on Anderson's ministry, visit www.skatechurch.net or email info@skatechurch.net. Write him at 8815 NE Glisan Street, Portland OR 97220 or call 503-252-1424, ext. 181. He's available to speak at outreach events.

George Barna founded The Barna Group (formerly Barna Research Group) in 1984. The firm seeks to facilitate moral and spiritual transformation by providing primary research; musical, visual, and digital media; printed resources; leadership development for young people; and church enhancement. Barna has written more than three dozen books, including best sellers such as *Transforming Children into Spiritual Champions*, *The Frog in the Kettle*, and *The Power of Vision*. His biweekly research report is accessed by hundreds of thousands of people (www.barna.org), and he is a host and featured presenter on the CNN Satellite Network and on the VIPER Interactive Network. He lives with his wife and daughters in southern California.

Natun Bhattacharya grew up in a Hindu priest family. Through the witness of an Indian Christian worker, he came to understand the uniqueness of Christ's love and salvation. He holds a master of divinity degree from Northwest Baptist Seminary and a master of arts degree from the University of Northern Colorado. He conducts training seminars for missionaries and churches and has published articles on Hinduism and understanding worldviews.

Mark Cahill is a celebrated speaker who has shared the Lord with thousands of people at conferences, summer camps, retreats, schools, and Christian colleges. He is a graduate of Auburn University. His book, *One Thing You Can't Do in Heaven*, has more than 100,000 copies in print. For more information, check out www. markcahill.org.

Phil Callaway is an award-winning author and speaker, known for his humorous look at the Christian life. He is the best-selling author of a dozen books, including *Making Life Rich without Any Money*. Described as "Dave Barry with a message," Callaway is editor of Prairie Bible Institute's *Servant* magazine and a popular speaker at conferences, camps, and churches. His five-part video series *The Big Picture* is being viewed in eighty thousand churches. *Callaway* lives in Alberta, Canada, with his wife, Ramona, and their three teenagers. You can learn more at www.philcallaway.com.

Regi Campbell is a businessman and entrepreneur and the author of *About My Father's Business: Taking Your Faith to Work*. His company, Seedsower Investments, helps launch start-up companies with a technology emphasis. After beginning his career with AT&T, he became CEO of a small, early-stage company that became very successful, and he has since gone on to help launch nine other companies. Campbell has an MBA from the University of South Carolina. He serves on the board of High Tech Ministries and the Good Samaritan Health Center and has served as an elder with Andy Stanley at North Point Community Church, in Atlanta, one of America's largest churches. Campbell has been a "marketplace minister" for the last twenty years. He and his wife, Miriam, have two adult children and they live in Atlanta, Georgia. You can learn more at www.amfb.com.

Vic Carpenter is a Ph.D. candidate at Southeastern Baptist Theological Seminary. He has also served as a visiting lecturer at Wingate University Metro College.

Tony Cooper has been married to his wife, Dale, for thirty-six years. They have two adult sons, Tony and Ben. He is a U. S. Army veteran and an ordained minister, who had been involved in ministry for twenty-seven years. He received his bachelor's degree in Bible and theology from Toccoa Falls College in Georgia and his master's degree in counseling from Troy State University in Alabama. Cooper has been executive director of The Jimmie Hale Mission in Birmingham, Alabama, since August 1990. He serves on several boards and is involved in numerous organizations. You can learn more at www.jimmiehalemission.com.

Karen Covell is a mom and a television producer for shows such as *Headliners and Legends with Matt Lauer,* and *Changed Lives: Miracles of the Passion*. She is also an accomplished author and speaker, having spoken across America about witnessing, prayer, and Hollywood as a mission field, and she's the founding director of Hollywood Prayer Network. Covell, her husband Jim, and friend Victorya Rogers coauthored *How to Talk about Jesus without Freaking Out* and *The Day I Met God*. You can learn more at www.HollywoodPrayerNetwork .org.

Brent Crowe is the founder of URGENCY conferences and is an accomplished evangelist who has spoken across the nation and preached in many international crusades. He is also the dean of students for Student Leadership University and a spokesperson for Contagious Christianity, affiliated with the Willow Creek Association. Brent and his wife, Christina, reside in Wake Forest, North Carolina. He holds a BA from Bryan College, a MDiv in evangelism, and a MA in ethics from Southeastern Baptist Theological Seminary. You can learn more at www .brentcrowe.com.

Scott Dawson is the founder of the Scott Dawson Evangelistic Association, Inc. This ministry that began with simple testimonials and youth rallies has grown into an evangelistic association that reaches across age and denominational lines in an effort to offer a unifying message of hope—the Good News of Jesus Christ. Dawson is one of nine evangelists who make up the Next Generation Alliance, a strategic partnership with the Luis Palau Evangelistic Association. He lives in his hometown of Birmingham, Alabama, with his wife, Tarra, son, Hunter, and daughter, Hope. You can learn more at www.scottdawson.org.

Tarra Dawson, a stay-at-home mother of two children, actively supports her husband's ministry and is involved in the Scott Dawson Evangelistic Association. To learn more see www. scottdawson.org.

Lewis Drummond spent his life working in evangelism and church ministry—both as a student and as a practitioner. A close associate with Billy Graham, Drummond wrote twenty-one books, including *The Awakening That Must Come*, *Eight Keys to Biblical Revival*, and *The Spiritual Woman*, coauthored with his wife, Betty. Drummond also taught evangelism at the seminary level for many years and served as president of Southeastern Baptist Theological Seminary in Wake Forest before coming to Beeson Divinity School at Samford University, where he served as the first Billy Graham Professor of Evangelism and Church Growth. He ended his journey of lifelong ministry serving at the Billy Graham Training Center.

Jimmy Dusek served on staff at First Baptist Church in Orlando for more than twenty-two years. He is a native of Texas and a graduate of Baylor University and New Orleans Baptist Theological Seminary. He pastored in Alabama, Louisiana, Tennessee, and North Carolina before coming to Orlando and specializing in senior adults and pastoral care. He and his wife, Shirley, have two children and three grandchildren. The Duseks retired to Franklin, North Carolina, in 2004 and are serving local churches.

Mark Earley, president and CEO of Prison Fellowship USA, is a former missionary with The Navigators and former state senator and attorney general of Virginia. He oversees the national ministry founded by Charles Colson in 1976, which has since spread to 107 countries beyond the United States. PF works with thousands of churches and volunteers across the United States with a focus on fellowshipping with Jesus, visiting prisoners, and welcoming their children. Also contributing to this chapter were Ron Humphrey, Jeff Peck, and Becky Beane. You can learn more at www.pfm.org.

David Edwards travels full time speaking to all ages in a variety of settings. A gifted communicator, Edwards speaks from his heart about issues relevant to the Postmodern Generation, helping people discover the importance of a Christ-centered lifestyle. As a postmodern itinerant preacher, his mission is to reintroduce the truth of God's Word by meeting people where they are in life and bringing them one step closer in the process of knowing and becoming like Jesus Christ. Edwards has written twelve books, and you can find him at www.davetown.com.

Monroe Free is a principal in The Monroe Free Group, which offers nonprofit consulting and communication strategies. For twenty years he was involved in Rescue Mission Ministry. He served at Waterfront Rescue Mission in Pensacola, Florida, then as president and CEO of Knox Area Rescue Ministries in Knoxville, Tennessee. He has served as chairman of Knox County Coalition on the Homeless and Knox County Coalition on Family Violence and has served with many other local groups. Free is currently the chairman of the Southeastern Housing Foundation. His company works with several local and national ministries to the poor. You can learn more at www.monroefreegroup.com.

Timothy George is the founding Dean of Beeson Divinity School of Samford University and an executive editor of *Christianity Today*. He holds degrees from the University of Tennessee at Chattanooga (BA) and Harvard Divinity School (MDiv, ThD). A noted historian and theologian, George has written and edited numerous books, including *Theology of the Reformers*, *Baptist Theologians*, *John Calvin and the Church*, *The New American Commentary on Galatians*, and, most recently, *Is the Father of Jesus the God of Muhammad?* He also coauthored (with John Woodbridge), *The Mark of Jesus: Loving in a Way the World Can See*. He is a widely sought-after speaker on matters of Christian higher education, theological and biblical issues, and cultural trends. For more information you can go to www.beesondivinity.com.

Ted Haggard is the senior pastor of the eleven-thousand-member New Life Church. Haggard founded New Life Church in Colorado Springs in 1985; it is now the largest church in the state. He formed and serves as the president of both the Association of Life-Giving Churches, a network of local churches, and worldprayerteam.org, the only real-time global prayer network. Haggard is the author of several books, including the best-selling *Primary Purpose*. He and his wife, Gayle, live in Colorado Springs with their five children.

Colin Harbinson has been involved in the arts and missions in more than sixty nations. Widely known as the writer of *Toymaker and Son* and *Dayuma,* he also pioneered historic cultural exchanges through the arts, education, and business that significantly impacted the cause of Christ in Russia, Bulgaria, and China. Harbinson is currently dean of the arts at Belhaven College in Jackson, Mississippi, and the editor of *Creative Spirit,* an international journal on the arts and faith. You can learn more at www.belhaven.edu or www.colinharbinson.com.

Brad Harper grew up in the San Francisco Bay Area and remains a devoted '49ers fan. He committed his life to Christ at age five. He earned a doctor of philosophy in historical theology at St. Louis University and served for thirteen years as associate pastor and church planting pastor at two Evangelical Free churches in St. Louis. He now teaches theology at Multnomah Bible College in Portland, Oregon. Harper has published articles on the church's role in social ethics and on Roman Catholic/Evangelical dialogue. Brad and his wife, Robin, have been married since 1984 and have three children. For more information, visit www.multnomah.edu.

Daniel Heimbach was raised among Buddhists in Thailand and is author of "Buddhism" (an SBC interfaith witness belief bulletin). He has also written several books, including *True Sexual Morality: Recovering Biblical Standards for a Culture in Crisis.* Heimbach is professor of Christian ethics at Southeastern Baptist Theological Seminary in Wake Forest, North Carolina.

Jim Henry is senior pastor of First Baptist Church, Orlando, Florida. A native of Tennessee and a graduate of Georgetown College and New Orleans Baptist Theological Seminary, Jim has also pastored in Mississippi and Tennessee. His wife, Jeanette, is from Kentucky and a graduate of Belmont University. They have three children and five grandsons. For more information, go to fbcorlando.org.

Stanley K. Inouye is founding president of Iwa, an Asian American leadership and ministry development organization. Inouye has held national and international positions with Campus Crusade for Christ, directed the Asian American Christian Fellowship (AACF) of the Japanese Evangelical Missionary Society (JEMS), served nationwide as a consultant to churches, denominations, and ministry organizations, and has taught as an adjunct at Fuller Theological Seminary. He has spoken across the country and is a published author. You can learn more at www.iwarock.org.

Michael Landry is the senior pastor of the Sarasota Baptist Church in Sarasota, Florida. His strong evangelistic ministry emphasis stems from his unforgettable experience as a former atheist. He has also served churches in Georgia, Oklahoma, and Ohio and was the director of evangelism and church growth for ten years for more than six hundred Southern Baptist Churches in Ohio. He has been married for twenty-eight years to his wife, Cindy, and is the father of three children, Jason, Beth, and Michelle. You can learn more at www.sarasotabaptist.com.

Chuck Lawless serves as dean of the Billy Graham School of Missions, Evangelism, and Church Growth at the Southern Baptist Theological Seminary in Louisville, Kentucky, where he earned his Ph.D. Prior to joining the Graham School, he served as a senior pastor for fourteen years. He is the author of five books, including *Discipled Warriors: Growing Healthy Churches That Are Equipped for Spiritual Warfare.* He is founder of the Lawless Group, a church consulting firm. For more information go to www.lawlessgroup.com.

Josh Malone partners with local churches throughout the year to help them reach and disciple students and adults in their community. Malone blends vivid personal illustrations with uncompromised biblical truth to effectively reach unbelievers and equip believers. He speaks throughout the year at conferences, church events, student events, and school assemblies. Malone resides in Birmingham, Alabama, where he is a part of the Scott Dawson Evangelistic Association. To learn more visit www.scottdawson.org or www .joshmalone.com.

Rick Marshall served with the Billy Graham Evangelistic Association for twenty-three years. He was director of missions/crusades for Billy Graham and director of counseling and follow-up. Currently Marshall is serving various ministries via In Formation Consulting. He can be reached at rickm3birches@comcast.net.

Josh McDowell is an internationally known speaker and author or coauthor of more than ninety-five books. He is the champion of the Beyond Belief Campaign to equip parents and the church to ground their children and young people in why they believe and how to live out what they believe. For more information and to receive free resources, visit www.BeyondBelief. com.

Daniel Owens is the founder of Eternity Minded Ministries and has proclaimed the life-changing gospel of Jesus Christ to hundreds of thousands of people across America and in dozens of countries. Owens is the author of *Sharing Christ When You Feel You Can't*. He is a popular seminar presenter who has trained tens of thousands of Christians to build bridges to their unchurched world. For more information, visit www.eternityminded.org.

Luis Palau, author and Christian communicator, has shared the gospel with hundreds of millions through his worldwide ministry. His books and articles have been published in dozens of languages, and his radio broadcasts are heard daily on over 2,100 radio stations in 48 countries. Born in Argentina, Palau is a U.S. citizen who makes his home in Portland, Oregon. He and wife, Pat, have four sons and nine grandchildren. You can learn more at www.palau.org.

Patricia Palau has served, with her husband Luis, as a missionary-evangelist in Colombia and Mexico. She now ministers with the Luis Palau Evangelistic Association and has an active conference ministry of her own. You can learn more at www.palau.org.

Les and Leslie Parrott are a husband-and-wife team who share a passion for helping others build healthy relationships. In 1991 the Parrotts founded the Center for Relationship Development on the campus of Seattle Pacific University—a groundbreaking program dedicated to teaching the basics of good relationships. Each year they speak to more than one million people in the United States and abroad. Their books, in two dozen languages, have sold more than one million copies, including the bestselling and Gold-medallion winner *Saving Your Marriage before It Starts*. Find out more at www. realrelationships.com.

Roger Parrott is the president of Belhaven College in Jackson, Mississippi, serving twenty-five hundred students on three campuses. He earned his Ph.D. from the University of Maryland in higher education administration. Parrott is a third-generation college president and was one of America's youngest college presidents, first elected at age thirty-four. He serves on several boards and was chair of the 2004 Forum for World Evangelization hosted by the Lausanne Committee for World Evangelization. His wife, MaryLou, earned her Ph.D. in English. They have two home-schooled children. You can learn more at www.belhaven.edu.

Brian Peterson works with World Vision, a relief and humanitarian organization serving eighty million people in one hundred countries. He is a contributing writer and editor for several books and magazines and was also the founding editor of *New Man* magazine.

Tom Phillips was a crusade director with the Billy Graham Evangelistic Association for many years, directing crusades in several cities in the United States and globally. He has also served as the director of counseling and follow-up and played a key role in the development of current materials and programs. Phillips was president and CEO of International Students, Inc., based in Colorado Springs, Colorado, and then vice president of crusades and training for the Billy Graham Evangelistic Association and executive director of the Billy Graham Training Center in Asheville, North Carolina. Phillips is now serving with Pastor Mike MacIntosh at Horizon

Christian Fellowship in San Diego, California. You can learn more at www.horizonsd.org.

Thom S. Rainer is the President of Lifeway Resources of the Southern Baptist Convention in Nashville, Tennessee. He is the former founding dean of the Billy Graham School of Missions, Evangelism and Church Growth at the Southern Baptist Theological Seminary in Louisville, Kentucky. The author of fifteen books on the church and evangelism, his two most recent books are Gold Medallion finalists. www.RainerGroup.com

Sherman R. Reed is a retired Army Chaplain (Colonel), with thirty years of active and reserve service. He is a pastor and evangelist and president of Living Truth Ministries. Reed is a graduate of Purdue University, Nazarene Theological Seminary, and the U.S. Army Chaplains Command and General Staff College. He is an Army Reserve Ambassador for the Chief Army Reserve and lives in Lebanon, Tennessee. For more information, visit www.shermanreed.org.

Alvin L. Reid is professor of evangelism at Southeastern Baptist Theological Seminary. He has an extensive speaking ministry in more than forty states and several nations and has published extensively, including *Raising the Bar*, *Radically Unchurched*, *Light the Fire*, *Introduction to Evangelism*, *Firefall*, *Evangelism for a Changing World*, and *Revival*. His hobbies include pet snakes and playing the bass in the band One Way Up. Reid and his wife, Michelle, have two children, Josa and Hannah. Find out more at www.alvinreid.com.

Larry D. Robertson is the senior pastor of Hilldale Baptist Church in Clarksville, Tennessee, and former state evangelism specialist for the Tennessee Baptist Convention. He is married to Beth and they have two daughters, Morgan and Rebecca. He holds a doctor of philosophy degree in evangelism from New Orleans Baptist Theological Seminary. You can learn more at www.hilldale.org.

Tim Robnett has served as the international crusade director for Luis Palau Evangelistic Association for ten years and has spent four years

as the director of Next Generation Alliance, a partnership to encourage and equip the next generation of evangelists. In addition to his responsibilities with the Palau Association, he serves as associate professor of pastoral ministry and is the internship director at Multnomah Biblical Seminary in Portland, Oregon. Robnett and his wife, Sharon, live in Portland, near the international headquarters of the Palau Association. They have two children, Joel and Karen. Find out more at http://www.palau.org/nga.

Robert and Shay Roop are both licensed mental health counselors, and are Board Certified Sex Therapists. As husband and wife, they have worked in this field for more than twenty-five years and counseled adolescents, individuals, and couples. Dr. Shay Roop is the author of *For Women Only: God's Design for Female Sexuality and Intimacy*.

David Sanford serves as president of Sanford Communications, Inc., a company dedicated to developing life-changing Christian books, Bible-related products, magazine features, and online resources. Sanford and his wife, Renée, are authors of *How to Read Your Bible* and the four hundred pages of devotional application notes in the *Living Faith Bible*. He can be contacted at drsanford@earthlink.net.

Renée Sanford is a writer, editor, conference speaker, and mother of five children. She and her husband, David, live in Portland, Oregon, and head up Sanford Communications, Inc. Sanford is a graduate of Multnomah Bible College and is involved with missions and children's ministries at Spring Mountain Bible Church. She enjoys meeting people from all parts of the world, whether traveling overseas or living in an ethnically diverse urban neighborhood.

Abraham Sarker, author of *Understand My Muslim People*, was born and raised as a devout Muslim. While being trained as an Islamic leader, God miraculously opened his eyes and touched his heart with the gospel of Jesus Christ. Sarker holds a doctorate from Regent University and is an adjunct professor at Dallas Baptist University. He founded Gospel for Muslims Inc., a ministry dedicated to bringing hope to the millions of Muslims around the world. You can learn more at www.gospelformuslims.com and www. UnderstandMyMuslimPeople.com.

Floyd Schneider is the author of *Evangelism for the Fainthearted.* Teaching classes on evangelism, church growth, and missions, as well as international relations, and Islamic and European studies, Schneider chairs the Intercultural Studies Department at Emmaus Bible College in Dubuque, Iowa. He and his wife, Christine, served as missionaries in Austria for fifteen years, where they planted three independent Bible churches. Their current church plant is Riverside Bible Church in Dubuque. You can learn more at www.emmaus.edu.

Mike Silva is an internationally recognized evangelist. A former pastor, missionary, and national director of evangelism, Silva is an engaging speaker who has preached the gospel to hundreds of thousands of people around the world in crusades, conferences, festivals, and church services. He is the author of *Do You Want Fries with That?*, which gives 101 ideas for using everyday objects as gospel illustrations. For more information, visit the Mike Silva evangelism web site at www.mikesilva.org.

Steve Sjogren is founding pastor and launching pastor of Vineyard Community Church in Cincinnati. He has planted four churches (in Los Angeles, Oslo, Baltimore, and Cincinnati). Out of the Cincinnati church, around twenty more churches have been planted. The Cincinnati church has been dubbed the "Launching Pad" for its commitment to starting new works on a regular basis. Sjogren spends most of his time now coaching church planters, speaking at churches and conferences on servant evangelism and church leadership, and writing books and articles. He has written nine books—his most recent is *Irresistible Evangelism.* He lives with his wife, Janie, and their three children, Rebekah, Laura, and Jack, in West Chester, Ohio (on the north side of Cincinnati). You can learn more at www.stevesjogren.com.

Greg Stier is the founder and president of Dare 2 Share Ministries, International (D2S), based in Denver, Colorado. His goal is to train and equip one million Christian teens across America to share their faith with courage, clarity, and compassion. In 1988 Stier graduated from Colorado Christian University with a degree in youth ministry. He and his wife, Debbie, and their children, Jeremy and Kailey, live in Arvada, Colorado, and attend Grace Church. You can learn more at www.dare2share.org.

Jay Strack, nationally acclaimed speaker and author, is founder and president of Student Leadership University, an international nonprofit organization dedicated to equipping, empowering, and enabling students with leadership skills through unique, hands-on programs. In addition to his work with students, Strack has been called on to train and motivate more than fifteen million people in business, education, healthcare, ministry, government, nonprofit organizations, and the sports arena. He and his wife, Diane, reside in Orlando. You can learn more at www.studentleadership.net.

Joni Eareckson Tada is the founder and CEO of the Joni and Friends International Disability Center, an organization accelerating Christian ministry in the disability community. Since a diving accident in 1967 that left her a quadriplegic, Joni has worked as an advocate for disabled persons, authored thirty books, and become a highly sought after conference speaker. You can learn more at www.joniandfriends.org.

Marty Trammell teaches communication at Corban College in Oregon. He also helps pastor Valley Baptist of Perrydale. Trammell and his wife, Linda, have three sons who help them enjoy world missions, sports, and cross-country road trips. Visit www.corban.edu for more information.

Jim Uttley Jr., communications coordinator for Wiconi International, has been involved in Native American ministry since 1988. Uttley spent almost twenty-two years in Haiti as a missionary kid and later as a missionary with World Team and Crossworld before serving for thirteen years as an editor with Indian Life Ministries. He is a freelance writer and has written extensively on Haitian and Native American issues. He serves as a special correspondent for

Assist News Service. Uttley and his wife live in Winnipeg, Manitoba, Canada. They have three adult children and one grandson. You can learn more at www.wiconi.com.

Martha Wagner is founder and executive director of Hope Ministries International. Martha and her husband, Bill, live in Corvallis, Oregon. She received her master's degree in evangelism from Multnomah Biblical Seminary. Her passion is to reach women of all nations with the gospel. She has done this in African nations, India, and northern Europe. Creativity, initiative, and leadership are her strengths. Her latest endeavor is writing and producing a play communicating the gospel to women in the United States. You can learn more at www.betterthanastory.com.

Bob Waldrep is the President and Founder of the Crosswinds Foundation for Faith and Culture. Bob is the coauthor of *The Truth Behind the Secret* and a contributor to *The Popular Encyclopedia of Apologetics: Surveying the Evidence for the Truth of Christianity*. He scripted the documentary, *The Da Vinci Code Revealed*, and has appeared as an expert commentator for local, national, and international media. www.crosswindsfoundation.com

Herbert Walker attended Vanderbilt University and received his medical training from the University of Alabama at Birmingham. He and his wife, Marie, with their seven children, reside in Birmingham, where Walker oversees his thriving practice.

Rick Warren is the founding pastor of Saddleback Church in Lake Forest, California, one of America's largest and best-known churches. In addition, Warren is author of the *New York Times* best seller *The Purpose-Driven Life* and *The Purpose-Driven Church*, which was named one of the one hundred Christian books that changed the twentieth century. He is also founder of Pastors.com, a global Internet community for ministers.

Dolphus Weary, a husband and father of three, has served as executive director of Mission Mississippi, a racial reconciliation ministry, since 1998, after working for Mendenhall Ministries for nearly thirty years. Recently Weary was named president of the Mission Mississippi ministry that encourages unity in the body of Christ across racial and denominational lines. He is the author of *I Ain't Comin' Back*, which tells his story of growing up in Mississippi and learning to overcome the problems of racism, poverty, and injustice. Weary is a frequent speaker at various local and national conferences. For more information, visit www.missionmississippi.org.

C. Richard Wells has served as senior pastor of South Canyon Baptist Church in Rapid City, South Dakota, since 2003. He served on the founding faculty of Beeson Divinity School (Birmingham, Alabama) and for seven years as president of The Criswell College (Dallas, Texas) until his return to the pastorate. He holds doctoral degrees from Baylor University and the University of North Texas.

Pat Williams is senior vice president of the Orlando Magic, author of forty books, and one of America's top motivational, inspirational, and humorous speakers. He has spent forty-three years as a player and executive in professional baseball and basketball. He is also one of four sports executives in history to serve as general manager of four different franchises. Williams and his wife, Ruth, are the parents of nineteen children, including fourteen adopted from four foreign countries, ranging in age from nineteen to thirty-three. You can learn more at www.orlandomagic.com

Rusty Wright is an award-winning author, journalist, syndicated columnist, and international lecturer with Probe Ministries. He has spoken on six continents.

Jose Zayas is an international evangelist, author, and popular conference speaker. He serves as the teen evangelism director for Focus on the Family and is the founder of Jose Zayas Evangelism International. For more information, check out www.family.org or www.josezayas.org.

Scripture Index

Subject Index

absolutes, 178, 185, 243, 244

abuse, 289–95

accepting Christ as Savior, 77, 158–59, 262, 275, 312, 355

accepting others, 44–45, 174, 176, 184, 226, 249. *See also* love; respect

accountability, 165, 178, 373

addictions, 39, 64, 102, 294, 296–301, 324, 342

adults, 96, 149–51

African Americans, 261–64

agape love, 312

agnosticism, 209–12

alcohol, 87, 91, 301, 328. *See also* addictions

America, 174, 194, 266, 269, 280–82, 338

    evangelism models in, 45

    Jesus as not "American Jesus," 262

    Native Americans, 272–75

    and spiritual revival, 47–48, 153, 187

Amy Awards, 193–94

angels, 15, 55, 210

anger, 32, 100, 187, 327

animism, 247

apostles, the twelve, 49, 71, 76, 96, 315

arguing; argumentation, 45, 62, 92–93, 95, 232, 240, 252, 266

"armor of God," 105–7

arts, 33, 155, 163–67. *See also* entertainment

Asians, 265–68

astrology, 246–48

atheism, 95, 213–16

Augustine, St., 34, 300

authenticity, 62, 71, 136, 151–52, 170, 212, 215, 263, 304, 315–16

authority, public, 56, 181, 188–92

Baby Boomer generation, 149–52, 155

baptism, 39, 71, 148, 199, 204, 255, 261

Barna, George, 47–53, 134, 145, 154, 174, 338, 374

basic needs, 102–3

beauty, 27, 133, 307, 320

Berg, Jim, 298–99

Bible, 24, 67, 75–78, 105, 250

Bible study, 24, 75, 203, 268, 271, 284–85, 305

biblical worldview, 37–38, 165–66, 298, 359

birth of Jesus, 82–83, 157, 210, 233, 236

boldness in witnessing, 14, 44, 96, 99–103, 135, 137, 315

born again; new birth, 26, 146, 255

Buddhism, 217–20, 266

Builders generation, 145–48

business, 173–76. *See also* work

celibacy, 364–65

Chambers, Oswald, 187, 298

character, 37–39, 71. *See also* Christian life

children, 125, 150, 156–59. *See also* family

choice, 363–64

chosen people, 229, 231

Christendom, 254–58

Christian community, 48–49, 65, 92, 150, 165, 263–64, 293, 346–47

Christianity, 211. *See also* faith

    changing times and, 30–35

389